Instructional Media

*Fourth
Edition*

ROBERT HEINICH
Indiana University

MICHAEL MOLENDA
Indiana University

JAMES D. RUSSELL
Purdue University

Instructional
Media
and the
New Technologies of
Instruction

Macmillan Publishing Company
New York

Maxwell Macmillan Canada
Toronto

Maxwell Macmillan International
New York   Oxford   Singapore   Sydney

Editor: Robert B. Miller
Developmental Editor: Molly Kyle
Production Editors: Sharon Rudd, Mary Harlan
Art Coordinator: Peter A. Robison
Text Designer: Anne Flanagan
Cover Designer: Russ Maselli
Cover photo: Geoffrey Gove
Production Buyer: Pamela D. Bennett
Illustrations: Precision Graphics

This book was set in Clearface by Carlisle Communications, Ltd., and was printed and bound by Von Hoffman Press, Inc. The cover was printed by Von Hoffman Press, Inc.

Photo and illustration credits appear on pages 451–453.

Macmillan Publishing Company
866 Third Avenue
New York, New York 10022

Macmillan Publishing Company is part of the
Maxwell Communication Group of Companies.

Maxwell Macmillan Canada, Inc.
1200 Eglinton Avenue East, Suite 200
Don Mills, Ontario M3C 3N1

Library of Congress Cataloging-in-Publication Data

Heinich, Robert.
    Instructional media and the new technologies of instruction / Robert Heinich, Michael Molenda, James D. Russell.— 4th ed.
        p.   cm.
    Includes bibliographical references and index.
    ISBN: 0-02-353060-X
    1. Educational technology.   2. Audio-visual education.
I. Molenda, Michael.   II. Russell, James D.   III. Title.
LB1028.3.H45   1993
371.3′078 — dc20   92-28702
                                          CIP

Printing: 1   2   3   4   5   6   7   8   9   Year: 3   4   5   6   7

Preface

The years since the publication of the first edition of this text in 1982 have witnessed numerous innovations both in communications technology and methods used in education and training. The hardware innovations, being more visible, come to mind first, but changes in educational theory and practice have been of equal or greater importance. Consider, for example:

❑ the ascendancy of cognitive learning theory

❑ cooperative learning and discovery as new emphases in instructional practice

❑ burgeoning of distance education

❑ the restructuring movement in public education

❑ growth and change in corporate training

❑ expansion of professional opportunities in instructional technology

As we will see, technology is intimately related to all these changes.

Developments in Communications Technology

The computer revolution has arrived in education, spurred by the microcomputer's advantages of cost and ease of use. In the first edition, computer uses could easily be confined to one chapter. In the fourth edition, all of Chapter 8 and large parts of Chapters 7, 9, 10, 11, 13, and 14 are devoted to computer influences on education and training.

Digitization of information has extended beyond the computer to affect other media. Since the first edition the videodisc has moved from a minor position in home entertainment to a major role in interactive instructional systems. The compact disc (CD) was introduced in 1983 as a format for music recordings. It has now become commonplace as a storage device for digitized audio and video, for computer multimedia, and for print databases, as discussed in Chapters 8, 9, and 14.

Digitization, along with satellites and fiber optics, has vastly enhanced both wired and wireless communication. A chapter that in the first edition fit comfortably under the umbrella of "Television" now fairly bursts at the seams with audio, video, and computer conferencing along with a dozen other hybrids, under the title of "Telecommunication Systems."

The original chapter on "Multimedia Systems" mentioned the computer only as a *potential* control device for multi-image presentations. Today the computer is the *central* device for orchestrating interactive multimedia programs incorporating still and motion images with print, graphics, and sound.

In the first edition, the chapter on "Film" ended with this sentence: "It could well be that in the future, film will be a 'Flashback' in the chapter on video!" Chapter 7, now titled "Video and Film," explains why video has largely replaced film as a classroom presentation format.

The evolution of video is illustrated by the shrinkage of the portable video recorder from the bulky backpack plus camera of the early 1980s to the light, one-piece camcorder (and palmcorder) of the early 1990s.

Other technologies familiar in the early 1980s have gradually faded from the scene: the reel-to-reel tape recorder, 8mm film, some slide formats, and production tools such as the Kodak Visualmaker and mechanical lettering devices.

The Ascendancy of Cognitive Learning Theory

As we entered the 1980s the behaviorist perspective still dominated instructional technology. By the early 1990s the so-called cognitive revolution had propelled theories focused on mental states back to the fore. While Chapter 12, "Technologies of Instruction," retains the many solid contributions of behaviorism, it also features the technologies that have sprung from cognitive and social psychology roots. Educators' and trainers' concerns for higher-level mental skills and for the process skills associated with learning have given impetus to the cognitive movement.

The ability of computers to model aspects of human thinking ("artificial intelligence") has spurred the emergence of the field of cognitive science, which supports speculations about how learners process and use information. This research contributes another stream to the cognitive movement.

Another special interest of cognitivists is the problem-solving process. Technical developments that have made possible sophisticated computer programs that allow learner control in exploring large data bases—such as hypermedia—have given theorists the tools needed to demonstrate alternative instructional designs. These new influences of cognitivism show up in Chapters 1, 8, 9, 12, 13, and 14.

Cooperation and Discovery: New Emphases in Instruction

The decade since the first edition has seen a major shift in emphasis from independent, competitive learning toward cooperative learning. Field-based research on learners working together in a planned way has demonstrated the superior results of cooperative learning. Cooperative learning methods are highlighted in Chapters 1 and 12.

Since cognitive theories place so much emphasis on meaningful practice, the discovery method is back in vogue. Simulations and games—with and without computers—are being used to immerse learners in problem situations and to allow them a great deal of leeway in deciding how they will attain the learning objectives.

Burgeoning of Distance Education

Radio and television have been employed for educational purposes for as long as these media have existed. However, they were not really embraced by mainstream educators until the technology for high-quality two-way interaction was developed and the economic benefits were demonstrated. It was during the 1980s that these conditions came together. Schools, colleges, corporations, government agencies, and other organizations now depend on distance education systems to share specialized instructors and extend quality education to remote campuses or training centers. This movement, which was barely beginning at the time of the first edition, is now the dominant theme of Chapter 10, "Telecommunication Systems."

Restructuring of Public Education

The loss of confidence in the public schools accelerated throughout the 1980s and shows no sign of abating in the 1990s. The restructuring movement in its many forms is the response to the demand for change. Many educators, both within instructional technology and outside it, advocate the use of technology as a key element in restructuring. Chapter 14 discusses some of the impediments to institutional change, while Chapters 8, 9, 10, and 12 reveal the "hard" and "soft" technologies most likely to play central roles in restructuring.

Growth and Change in Corporate Training

During the past decade it has become increasingly obvious that a growing proportion of education is conducted outside the realm of schools and colleges. Corporate training is big business. And it has been transformed under the pressure of global competitiveness. No longer considered a fringe benefit or a "cost of doing business," the skill enhancement of employees is now seen as a critical component of a competitive strategy. Media, methods, and examples relevant to corporate training have become a larger concern throughout this book because more and more students in instructional media courses already work or anticipate working outside the realm of public schools.

Expansion of Professional Opportunities

Over the past decade nearly all teacher certification standards have come to require basic computer skills. In many jurisdictions it is possible to obtain additional certification to serve as an instructional computing specialist. Many school districts have created offices for computer coordination and have hired qualified specialists to staff

them. Some forward-looking districts expanded their existing instructional media departments to incorporate computing. Such an arrangement permits a closer coordination of computers with other media and with the full range of instructional issues.

Opportunities for instructional technology professionals have expanded in the private sector. As indicated in Chapter 1, corporate education relies on media much more than formal education does, and the systematic design of instruction is taken more seriously there as well. More and more companies seek training professionals who have strong backgrounds in media and instructional design. The changing scene of professional opportunities is covered in Chapter 14.

Keeping up with instructional media and the new technologies is somewhat frustrating. The field and its tools change so rapidly that one has to run just to stay in place. It is tempting to wish that the pace of change would slow down in the coming decade, but if it doesn't, no one will be surprised. That's what makes the field exciting and challenging.

Special Features

This edition maintains the special features introduced in the first three editions and adds one new feature. Adopting instructors indicate that these features aroused interest and contributed to better retention of media knowledge and skills among their students. The features are:

❑ **Outlines.** Each chapter begins with a broad outline of the contents, thus providing a quick advance organizer.

❑ **Objectives.** A detailed list of performance objectives precedes the text of each chapter.

❑ **Lexicon.** A short list of new or specialized vocabulary terms is introduced at the beginning of each chapter. This alerts readers to watch for these terms in the chapter, where they are discussed in context.

❑ **Close-Ups.** These serve as miniature case studies of media applications; some of the vignettes are drawn from business/industry settings.

❑ **Media Files.** Actual materials in different media formats are highlighted. The materials shown have been selected as *typical* of a given class, not as *exemplary*. No endorsement—nor even commercial availability—is implied.

❑ **How To . . .** Various media production and operation procedures are spelled out with clear, illustrated, step-by-step instructions. Each is boxed for easy reference.

❑ **Appraisal Checklists.** New checklists have been developed for appraising each media format. Users have permission to photocopy these lists for personal use. This makes it easy to preview materials systematically and to preserve the previews for later reference.

❑ **AV Showmanship.** This feature gives specific tips on delivering media presentations with flair and dramatic effect.

❑ **Flashbacks.** These are brief histories that lend a sense of perspective and often provide fascinating behind-the-scenes glimpses of historic developments.

❑ **Blueprints.** Each blueprint details how the ASSURE model applies to the use of specific instructional media. We believe these examples will enable students to apply the ASSURE model more readily in their own instructional planning.

❑ **The Cutting Edge.** This new feature appears at the end of Chapters 5, 6, and 7. Emerging media technologies are described with implications for potential use. Some of these innovations may not survive, others may be superceded, but all reflect the rapid pace of technological development.

Appendices

Appendix A contains suggested sources for the various types of materials discussed in the chapters. It has been thoroughly updated and revised for this edition. **Appendix B** has lists of sources of free and inexpensive materials. **Appendix C** deals with the issues of copyright law as they pertain to users of instructional media. Recent legal interpretations are discussed. Our point of view is that an informed approach to the spirit as well as the letter of the law can result in giving the instructor more "elbow room" than generally has been considered possible. The **Lexicon** terms and many other specialized terms are gathered into a revised **Glossary** at the end of the book.

For Instructors

If you are an instructor using this text, send your name and address to James D. Russell, School of Education, Purdue University, West Lafayette, IN 47907.

We offer the following services to instructors to assist them in putting together an outstanding course in instructional media.

❑ **Instructor's Guide.** Ask your Macmillan representative, or write to Macmillan directly, for a copy of this comprehensive guide. Additional content, suggestions for different ways to organize the course, test items for each chapter, and overhead transparency masters on perforated pages are features of the *Instructor's Guide*.

❑ **Telelecture.** We offer a free lecture by telephone to adopters of our text. Arrange the telelecture by calling any one of us in advance to be sure of availability. Some instructors use the telelecture as part of the study of Chapter 10. Others use it to discuss the future directions of the field or of the profession. Whatever your purpose, give one of us a call. Our phone numbers are in the *Instructor's Guide*.

❑ **Newsletter.** We keep in touch with our adopters by distributing a newsletter several times a year. The newsletter keeps instructors informed about developments and activities of interest. You'll receive it free of charge if you send your name and address to Jim Russell.

❑ **Workshops.** At the time the first edition was published, we realized that the annual convention of AECT did not provide a forum for teachers of media courses to exchange ideas and techniques. We decided to create such a forum by offering a preconvention workshop on methods of teaching a basic media course. We have conducted workshops at each AECT convention since 1982. These exchanges have been helpful both to the participants and to us. We have become better acquainted with the problems of teachers of media courses in a wide variety of institutions. The participants benefit not only from the activities of the workshops but also from the sharing of course outlines and materials through the network created by the workshop. We believe that their courses are better as a result of this experience.

We continue to welcome comments about the book. Please send suggestions to us so that we can keep future editions responsive to the demands of the times. Send the comments to Michael Molenda, Instructional Systems Technology, School of Education, Indiana University, Bloomington, IN 47405.

Robert Heinich
Michael Molenda
James D. Russell

Acknowledgments

Through each of the editions of this book we have been fortunate to have had guidance from the real experts—the people who teach the courses for which the book is designed. In preparing for this fourth edition we surveyed a sample of adopters to learn their opinions about what to add, emphasize, downplay, or delete. After the first drafts were written we then asked several more colleagues well respected in the field to critique them.

We here thank all those who gave their time and talent to help make this the most useful textbook it could be.

Jeannette Abi-Naber
Gonzaga University, Washington

Jacob Bapst
University of Rio Grande

Sandi Behrens
University of Pittsburgh

Ann D. Carson
Rosary College, Illinois

J. Gordon Coleman, Jr.
University of Alabama

Richard A. Cornell
University of South Florida

Dorothy Cox
Southern Illinois University

Don E. Descy
Mankato State University

Wallace Draper
Ball State University

Clifford Ehlinger
Mt. Mercy College

Gary Ferrington
University of Oregon

Richard C. Forcier
Western Oregon State College

Julie Furst-Bowe
University of Wisconsin—Stout

Jack Garber
University of Wisconsin—Eau Claire

Scott Grabinger
University of Colorado—Denver

David G. Gueulette
Northern Illinois University

Joseph Harriman
Mercer University

Norman Higgins
Arizona State University

Denis Hlynka
University of Manitoba

Edward A. Jensen
Brigham Young University

Pouri Kiami
Madonna College

Ronald L. Larson
Area Education Agency 6, Marshalltown, Iowa

Louise B. Lyons
University of Louisville

Mike Moore
Virginia Tech University

Roy Morgan
Indiana University

Gary R. Morrison
Memphis State University

Randall G. Nichols
University of Cincinnati

Amos C. Patterson
University of Toledo

Leonard F. Proctor
University of Saskatchewan

Tillman J. Ragan
University of Oklahoma

R. Douglas Ramsey
Heidelberg College

Landra L. Rezabek
University of Wyoming

Rhonda S. Robinson
Northern Illinois University

David Salisbury
Florida State University

Robert A. Senour
California State University, San Bernardino

James A. Shuff
Henderson State University

Sharon Smaldino
University of Northern Iowa

Don C. Smellie
Utah State University

Dennis K. Smeltzer
University of Missouri—St. Louis

Kathleen Stevens
Edinboro University of Pennsylvania

Rosemary S. Talab
Kansas State University

Robert F. Ward
Bridgewater State College

Barbara Watson
Eastern Michigan University

Forrest G. Wisely
Illinois State University

We especially thank those who contributed more directly by writing new material, looking up references, drawing illustrations, and taking photographs. Rick Provine, under the direction of Kristine Brancolini, Indiana University, carried out the bibliographic research for all the chapters and Appendices A and B, continuing the tradition of quality begun with the first edition. David Derkacy, freelance lensman of Bloomington, Indiana, was principally responsible for the many outstanding photographs new to this edition. Diane Jung-Gribble, Indiana University, lent her fine artistic talents to the new illustrations. Carl Stafford, Purdue University, provided content and comments on media-aware and media setups. Rosemary S. Talab, Kansas State University, brought us up to date on copyright issues and contributed significantly to the bibliography for Appendix C. Jeanne Brenneman, Sun Microsystems, gave careful analysis and critique of our discussion of computer applications. Don E. Descy, Mankato State University, went beyond editorial advice to provide new material, particularly on telecommunications. Dean Larson, Argonne National Laboratory, contributed to the sections dealing with safety issues. Ralph Pritchard, Macomb Intermediate Schools, Mt. Clemens, Michigan, updated us on applications of technology to special education. Alan Chute, AT&T, gave careful review and thoughtful comments to our discussions of telecommunications.

Others who provided specific material are cited in the text. The editorial, design, and production staffs at Macmillan rose to the challenge once again to find a way to surpass the accomplishments of the previous editions. It has meant a great deal to have them working side by side with us.

We are grateful to our colleagues from our own universities for their many and valued forms of support over the years.

Finally, we thank our families for all they do to make this undertaking possible.

Contents

Special Features

1

Media and Instruction

OUTLINE

Instruction and Learning

Media, Messages, and Methods

  Instructional Media

  Messages

  Methods

Instructional Communication

  Communication Models

  Field of Experience

  Feedback

  Transactional Nature of Communication

  The Concrete-Abstract Continuum

Psychological Bases of Learning

  Skinner and Reinforcement Theory

  Cognitive Psychology

  Behaviorist and Cognitive Approaches to Instruction

  The Social-Psychological Perspective

  An Eclectic Approach to Practice

  Technologies of Instruction

The Roles of Media in Instruction

  Instructor-Based Instruction

  Instructor-Independent Instruction

  Distance Education

  Special Education

Media in Education and Training

  Patterns of Media Use in Education

  Patterns of Media Use in Training

  Growth of Training Programs

Applying Research to Practice

  Media Comparison Studies

  Implications for Practice

Structure and Flexibility

Technology and Humanism

OBJECTIVES

After studying this chapter, you should be able to

1. Distinguish between instruction and learning.

2. Select and describe an instructional situation that lends itself to behaviorist principles of learning.

3. Select and describe an instructional situation that lends itself to cognitive principles of learning.

4. Explain schemata and describe how assimilation and accommodation affect schemata.

5. Describe technologies of instruction and cite an example.

6. Evaluate a recent learning experience in terms of the Shannon-Weaver communication model.

7. Apply the transactional nature of communication by analyzing audience reaction to a photograph of a controversial subject.

8. Explain the concrete-abstract continuum, indicating how it can be used to aid in the selection of media.

9. Relate Dale's Cone of Experience to the concrete-abstract continuum.

10. Define *medium* and name five basic categories of media.

11. Distinguish among message, method, and medium.

12. Discuss four roles of media in the instructional process, giving an example of media used in each role.

13. Compare the current uses of media in both education and training programs.

14. Identify five findings or implications from research on media.

15. Discuss your personal opinion of the relationship between humanism and instructional technology in the classroom.

LEXICON

instruction

learning

medium/media

method

cooperative learning

communication model

concrete-abstract continuum

iconic representation

digital representation

behaviorism

cognitivism

schema/schemata

assimilation

accommodation

technology

technology of instruction

The technical terms listed in this section are discussed in the book and are defined in the Glossary.

1

The Pervasiveness of Instructional Media

S ome call the present an age of media. The pervasiveness of mass media in our lives as forms of entertainment is obvious. Not so obvious, but nearly as pervasive, are the uses of media for learning. Consider these vignettes.

1. As he heads for work, a pharmaceutical salesman plugs into his car stereo the new cassette from the company sales training center. It introduces him to the distinctive features of Banvex, the new drug for respiratory infections.

2. In a quiet corner just off the shop floor at Regent Industries, Jean views a videocassette that shows the proper operation and safety features of the machine that she will be operating during her shift today. Jean "floats" among jobs as needed from day to day.

3. Flash cards are used by the therapist to teach word recognition to a mentally handicapped child at the rehabilitation center. The cards have a word on one side and a picture on the other; the "repeat" stack grows smaller as Tiffany masters each word.

4. The junior high school age Samaritan Club members are studying the meanings of the parables. They compete as teams during the after-school program at their local church. Matching the facts of the stories with the accepted interpretation is the purpose of the game.

5. Anne, a graduate student in veterinary medicine, uses an interactive video system in the university's learning center to practice responding to animal owners in stressful situations. The scenarios present situations Anne is likely to face in actual veterinary practice.

6. As she unobtrusively photographs housing conditions in the inner city, Stephanie, a high school senior, reflects upon what brought her here. She had volunteered to do a slide-tape report on urban problems for her social studies class.

7. A pair of fourth graders eagerly "boot" (start up) the "Exploratorium" disk on their classroom computer. They want to continue where they left off yesterday in a detective story. It challenges their logical reasoning skills in solving the mystery.

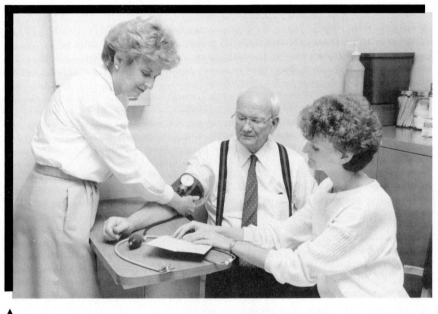

8. To learn how to take their blood pressure at home, Thelma and Harold listen to the nurse at the hospital as she guides the retired couple through a structured tutoring package. The nurse patiently answers any questions they have.

9. Dinner over, the Carter family settles into the family room to watch "This Old House." They are intrigued with the notion of buying and restoring an older house, and this television series provides them with valuable tips.

Here and now, in school and out, at home and at work, children and adults are enjoying the benefits of learning through media and the new technologies of instruction.

The goal of this book is to help put *you* into this picture.

INSTRUCTION AND LEARNING

Instruction is the arrangement of information and environment to facilitate learning. By environment we mean not only where instruction takes place but also the methods, media, and equipment needed to convey information and guide the learner's study. As implied in the preceding vignettes and as detailed later in this chapter, information and environment can be arranged on a continuum from very formal to very informal. The relationship between information and environment can change depending on the instructional goal. For example, in vignette number 6 on page 3, Stephanie must have a camera and seek out a location that will fulfill the requirements of the assignment. She will provide the information. In vignette number 5 (page 2), Anne goes to a learning center where she will find the equipment and the media necessary to complete her assignment. The information has been carefully prepared for her.

The arrangement of information and the environment is normally the responsibility of the instructor and the designers of media. The choice of the strategy of instruction determines the environment (the methods, media, equipment, and facilities) and how the information is assembled and used. As we discuss later, the method can range from teacher control to learner control. But we must remember that even with methods and media that encourage students to take control of learning, some guidance is inevitably built in. For example, the cooperative learning group in vignette number 4 on page 2 are deciding among themselves how to deal with the objectives of the program. On the other hand, instructor control can be direct even though incorporated into media, as in vignette number 2. By carefully examining the vignettes, you can see how the relationships among instructors, media, and students can vary from situation to situation.

Learning is the development of new knowledge, skills, or attitudes when the individual interacts with information and environment. Learning takes place all the time. We learn something just walking down the street and observing what goes on around us, or watching TV, or conversing with other people. But this type of incidental learning is not our major interest as education and training professionals. We are primarily concerned with the learning that takes place in response to our instructional efforts. How we design and arrange instruction has a great deal to do not only with what is learned but also with how the learner uses what is learned.

Learning psychologists have been studying how people learn for well over 100 years. While competing schools of thought explain learning differently, each has contributed valuable insights that are useful in the design of instruction.

Thus the instruction/learning process involves the selection, arrangement, and delivery of information in an appropriate environment and how the learner interacts with that information. In this chapter we first consider the methods, messages, and media used in instruction; second, we examine the communication process; and third, we consider the learning theories on which the design of instruction is based.

MEDIA, MESSAGES, AND METHODS

A *medium* is a channel of communication. Derived from the Latin word meaning "between," the term refers to anything that carries information between a source and a receiver. Examples of media are film, television, diagrams, printed materials, computers, and instructors. These are considered instructional media when they carry messages with an instructional purpose. The purpose of media is to facilitate communication.

Instructional Media

The various instructional media described in this book cover a wide range of types appropriate for learn-

Figure 1.1
Listeners with different cultural backgrounds may derive different meanings from the same message.

ers of all ages and backgrounds and for a wide variety of settings, formal and nonformal—from schools to colleges to businesses to homes, and places in between!

Nonprojected visuals such as photographs, diagrams, displays, models, and real objects are discussed in Chapter 4. In Chapter 5 projected media such as slides, filmstrips, and overhead transparencies are described. Chapter 6 deals with the uses of audio in instruction. Chapter 7 considers the moving image in video and in film. The computer's contribution to teaching and learning is the subject of Chapter 8. Combinations of media along with equipment that combines media are examined in Chapter 9. Various telecommunications systems and their uses in expanding learning opportunities are covered in Chapter 10. Chapter 12 describes a number of technologies of instruction and discusses their psychological foundations. Chapter 13 explores the interactive aspects as well as the educational uses of games and simulations.

Messages

In any instructional situation there is a message to be communicated. The message is usually subject-matter content, but it may be directions to the learners, questions about the content, feedback on the appropriateness of responses, or other information (see Figure 1.2).

Methods

Traditionally, instructional methods have been described as "presentation forms" such as lecture and discussion. In this text we will differentiate between instructional methods and instructional media. *Methods* are the procedures of instruction that are selected to help learners achieve the objectives or to internalize the content or message. *Media* (singular, *medium*) are carriers of information between a source and a receiver. Such vehicles are considered instructional media when they

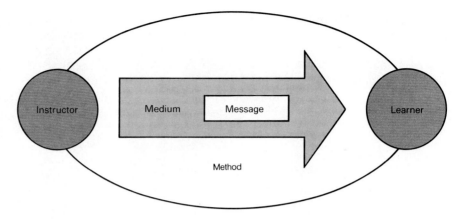

Figure 1.2
In the relationship between message and medium, the medium carries the message.

are used to carry messages intended to change behavior.

The ten methods described here are applicable to learners of all ages. They are presentation, demonstration, discussion, drill-and-practice, tutorial, cooperative learning, gaming, simulation, discovery, and problem solving. Virtually any of the media described later can be used to implement virtually any of these methods.

Presentation. In the presentation method a source tells, dramatizes, or otherwise disseminates information to learners. It is a one-way communication controlled by the source, with no immediate response from or interaction with the learners. The source may be a textbook, an audiotape, a videotape, a film, an instructor, and so forth. Reading a book, listening to an audiotape, viewing a film or videotape, and attending a lecture are examples of the presentation method.

For example, as part of your visit to a museum, you check out a cassette tape and player with private headphones. The audiotape and accompanying map guide you through the museum and present information about each of the exhibits and displays.

Demonstration. In this method of instruction the learner views a real or lifelike example of the skill or procedure to be learned (Figure 1.3). Demonstrations may be recorded and played back by means of media such as video or film. If two-way interaction or learner practice with feedback is desired, a live instructor or a tutor is needed.

The objective may be for the learner to imitate a physical performance, such as swinging a golf club or changing the oil in a car, or to adopt the attitudes or values exemplified by someone who serves as a model. In some cases the point is simply to illustrate how something works, such as the effect of heat on a copper strip. On-the-job training often takes the form of one-to-one demonstration, with the experienced worker showing the new one how to perform a procedure, such as operating a packaging machine. This arrangement allows questions and answers to correct any errors or misperceptions.

Discussion. As a method, discussion among students or among students and teacher can make a significant contribution throughout the instruction/learning process, whether in tutorials, small groups, or large groups. It is a useful way of assessing the knowledge, skills, and attitudes of a group of students before finalizing instructional objectives, particularly if it is a group the instructor has never seen before. In this context, discussion can help the

Figure 1.3
Demonstrations show a process to be learned or the way something works.

Figure 1.4
Tutorials are one of the most effective, but also one of the most expensive, instructional methods.

instructor establish the kind of rapport with and within the group that fosters collaborative and cooperative learning.

Discussion as a form of preparation for the presentation of media can be useful in guiding the attention of the audience during the presentation. Some media forms are more conducive to discussion *during* their use than others. For example, the overhead transparency lends itself to discussion techniques more easily than video.

Postpresentation discussions are essential to help answer any questions and to be sure that all students understand what the instructor intended. Discussion should be a major technique for evaluating the effectiveness of instruction, along with any written forms of evaluation. While useful with all age groups, adult learners particularly welcome the opportunity to participate in sharing experiences with other adults.

Drill-and-Practice. In drill-and-practice the learner is led through a series of practice exercises designed to increase fluency in a new skill or to refresh an existing one. Use of the method assumes that the learner

has previously received some instruction on the concept, principle, or procedure that is to be practiced. To be effective, the drill-and-practice exercises should include feedback to correct and remediate errors that the learner might make along the way.

Drill-and-practice is commonly used for such tasks as math facts, foreign language learning, and vocabulary building. Certain media formats and delivery systems lend themselves particularly well to student drill-and-practice exercises. For example, learning-laboratory instruction and programmed instruction are well suited to these purposes. Audiotapes can be used effectively for drill-and-practice in spelling, arithmetic, and language instruction.

Tutorial. A tutor—in the form of a person, computer, or special printed materials—presents the content, poses a question or problem, requests a learner response, analyzes the response, supplies appropriate feedback, and provides practice until the learner demonstrates a predetermined level of competency (see Figure 1.4). Tutoring is most often done on a one-to-one basis and is

frequently used to teach basic skills, such as reading and arithmetic.

Tutorial arrangements include instructor-to-learner (e.g., Socratic dialog), learner-to-learner, (e.g., tutoring or programmed tutoring), computer-to-learner (e.g., computer-assisted tutorial software), and print-to-learner (e.g., branching programmed instruction). These formats are discussed further in Chapter 12. The computer is especially well suited to play the role of tutor because of its ability to deliver speedily a complex menu of responses to different learner inputs.

Cooperative Learning. A growing body of research supports the claim that students learn from each other when they work on projects as a team.[1] Two or three students at a computer terminal learn more as they carry on discussions while working through the assigned problem. Some computer programs, such as the Macintosh *Aspects*, make it possible for several students to work interactively at separate com-

---

[1]   Robert E. Slavin, "Research on Cooperative Learning: Consensus and Controversy," *Educational Leadership* (December 1989–January 1990): 52–54.

puters. The "Science as a Process" laboratory-oriented program of the American Association for the Advancement of Science was built around cooperatively carried out experiments based on the knowledge that modern science relies on group effort.

Many educators have criticized the competitive atmosphere that dominates many classrooms in the public schools and higher education. They believe that pitting student against student in the attainment of grades is contrary to the societal requirements of on-the-job teamwork. Teacher and students often find themselves in an adversarial relationship in the cat-and-mouse game of test-taking and grading. Competition in the classroom also interferes with students learning from each other.

Critics of competitive learning urge instead an emphasis on *cooperative learning* as an instructional method. They argue that learners need to develop skills in working and learning together because their eventual workplaces will require teamwork. A common complaint of graduates about their schools is that they did not have experience working in teams.

Students can learn cooperatively not only through discussion of media presentations but also by producing media. For example, the design and production of a video or a slide set as a curriculum project presents an excellent opportunity for cooperative learning. The teacher should be a working partner with the students in a cooperative learning situation.

Some authorities make a distinction between cooperative and collaborative learning. When the teacher is working with students as a partner in learning, they use the term collaborative learning; they use the term cooperative learning when only students are working together.

Games. Gaming provides a playful environment in which the learners follow prescribed rules as they strive to attain a challenging goal. It is a highly motivating method, especially for tedious and repetitive content. The game may involve one learner (e.g., solitaire) or a group of learners (see Figure 1.5). Gaming often requires learners to use problem-solving skills or demonstrate mastery of specific content demanding a high degree of accuracy and efficiency (see Chapter 13).

A common type of instructional game is the business game. Participants form management teams to make decisions regarding a mythical corporation. The winning team is the one reaping the highest corporate profits.

Simulation. Using this method, the learner confronts a scaled-down approximation of a real-life situation. It allows realistic practice without the expense or risks otherwise involved. The simulation may involve participant dialog, manipulation of materials and equipment, or interaction with a computer (see Chapter 13).

Interpersonal skills and laboratory experiments in the physical sciences are popular subjects for simulations. In some simulations the learner manipulates mathematical models to determine the effect of changing certain variables, such as controlling a nuclear power plant. Role playing is another common example of the simulation method. In *Participative Decision Making,* preservice teachers learn about allocating school budgets. Students assume the roles of a teacher representing the union, a principal, a school board member, a member of the PTA, a taxpayer with no children in school, and a student representing the student council.

Discovery. The discovery method uses an inductive, or inquiry, approach to learning; it presents problems to be solved through trial and error (see Figure 1.6). The aim of the discovery method is to foster a deeper understanding of the content through involvement with it. The rule or procedure that the learner discovers may be derived from previous experience, based on information in reference books, or stored in a computer database.

Instructional media can help promote discovery or inquiry. For example, films may be used for discovery teaching in the physical sciences. Students view a film to observe the relationships represented in the visuals and then go on to discover the

Figure 1.5
Games require active involvement on the part of each player.

Figure 1.6
Discovery learning requires extra time but usually results in better retention.

principles that explain those relationships. For example, by viewing something as simple as a balloon being weighed before and after being filled with air, the student discovers that air has weight.

Problem Solving.

In this method the learner uses previously mastered skills to reach a resolution of a challenging problem. The learner must define the problem more clearly (perhaps state a hypothesis), examine data (possibly with the aid of a computer), and generate a solution. Through this process the learner can be expected to arrive at a higher level of understanding of the phenomenon under study.

One commonly used type of problem solving is the case study. For example, students in a business class are given information about a situation at a small manufacturing firm and are asked to design a solution to the problem of low production. One of the first decisions they make is to gather data on the situation and to determine whether the solution is training or, instead, changing the environment or attitudes of the workers.

In any instructional situation a variety of methods can and should be used. Most of these methods described here can be used to teach any content to any group of learners. However, some methods may be better for certain content or certain learners. Experience and trying the various methods with actual students will determine which method or combination of methods is most effective. Consider using a variety of methods to keep instruction interesting.

INSTRUCTIONAL COMMUNICATION

Instruction is the arrangement of information to produce learning. The transfer of information from a source to a destination is called communication. Because new learning usually depends on taking in new information, effective instruction cannot take place unless communication takes place. It is therefore helpful to know something about the communication process in order to use instructional media effectively.

Communication Models

One of the first models of the communication process was developed by Claude E. Shannon of the Bell Telephone Laboratories. Because of his background and job, Shannon was interested solely in the technical aspects of communication. However, Warren Weaver collaborated with Shannon to develop a broader application of this model to other communication problems.[2] The Shannon-Weaver model (see Figure 1.7) can be used to analyze instructional situations.

Many *communication models* have been designed, but the Shannon-Weaver model is especially useful because it allows us to identify and analyze the critical stages of instructional communication. In addition, Shannon breaks down information into "bits" and derives formulas for determining the number of bits in a message and how bits of information are handled under varying conditions of transmission, thereby laying the groundwork for the later digitizing of information that has become the foundation of modern information transfer.

The model works like this. A message, such as a description of the structure of the human heart, is selected by an information source. That message is then incorporated by the transmitter into a signal. The signal could be spoken words, a

---

2   Claude E. Shannon and Warren Weaver, *The Mathematical Theory of Communication* (Champaign, IL: University of Illinois Press, 1949), p. 7.

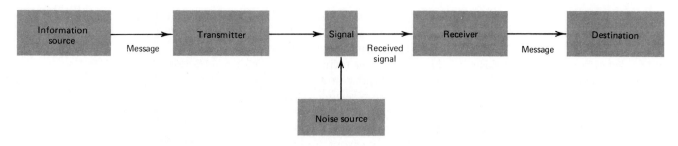

Figure 1.7
The Shannon-Weaver communication model

drawing on a chalkboard, or printed materials. The signal is then received by the receiver's ears or eyes and transformed into a message reaching the destination, for example, a student's mind. The model also applies in situations where the student selects the message. For example, when he or she goes to a media center to select material to study, the message is there waiting to be interpreted.

Acting on the signal as it is being transmitted are various distorting factors that Shannon called "noise." In a classroom, background sounds, glare on a chalkboard, and flickering lights are examples of noise.

It is important to keep in mind that meaning per se cannot be transmitted. What is actually transmitted are symbols of meaning, such as words and pictures. As authors of this book, for example, we cannot directly transfer to you the personal meanings we have built up in our own minds about instructional media. (We even have trouble doing this among ourselves!) We can only transmit verbal and graphic symbols from which you can evoke your own meanings. The most we can hope for is that our skills and knowledge will enable us to encode our messages in such a manner that your skills and knowledge can be used to decode and interpret them as we intended.

Field of Experience

One major purpose of instructional communication is to broaden and extend the field of experience of the learner. For instructional purposes,

however, the meaning of the message and how the message is interpreted are of paramount importance. The Schramm adaptation[3] of the Shannon model (see Figure 1.8) incorporates Shannon's concern with the technical aspects of communication, but its central concern is with communication, reception, and interpretation of meaningful symbols—processes that are at the heart of instruction.

As a classroom teacher, for example, you would prepare your students for an instructional video (e.g., through a preliminary discussion of the topic or an overview of its content) and you would design follow-up activities to reinforce and

---

[3] Wilbur Schramm, "Procedures and Effects of Mass Communication," in *Mass Media and Education,* ed. Nelson B. Henry (Chicago: University of Chicago Press, 1954), p. 116.

extend what has been learned from the video.

Ideally, material presented to, or selected by, a student should be sufficiently within his or her field of experience so that he or she can learn what needs to be learned, but enough outside the field of experience to challenge and extend that field. The boundary of the field of experience that is to be expanded by instruction is referred to by Vygotsky as the "zone of proximal development."[4] It is in this zone that messages go beyond communication into learning.

How far the instruction can extend beyond the student's field of experience before confusion sets in depends on many factors. Perhaps

---

[4] L. S. Vygotsky, *Mind in Society* (Cambridge, MA: Harvard University Press, 1978).

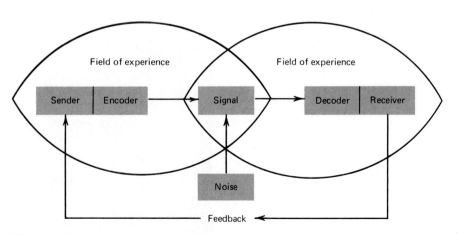

Figure 1.8
Schramm's adaptation of the Shannon-Weaver model emphasizes that only when the sender's and the receiver's fields of experience overlap is there communication.

the most important of these is the ability of the student. Able students can assume more of the responsibility for extending their own fields of experience than less able students. Slower students will need instructional content closer to their field of experience in order to be successful. Most retarded learners will require instruction that is almost entirely within their relatively limited field of experience. In Chapter 2, we will discuss how to determine "specific entry competencies," with particular attention to identifying the student's field of experience as he or she enters a lesson.

There will be times when the learning task (message) may not be within the field of experience of the *instructor*. When this occurs, both instructor and student seek to extend their respective fields of experience, and the instructor should not feel peculiar about being in this position. Some of the most effective learning takes place when instructor and student must seek answers together in a collaborative learning situation.

Feedback

Another very important distinction between video (or any other medium) as a communication medium and as an instructional medium involves feedback from the receiver (see Figure 1.9). We usually think of feedback in connection with tests, but many other techniques are available to indicate to the teacher how students are receiving instruction. Facial expressions, body language, discussion responses, student conferences, homework, and responses on short daily quizzes are all forms of feedback. Not only does feedback help us to ascertain whether instruction has been successful or unsuccessful, but it also tends to take the burden off the student and place it where it more appropriately belongs—on the sender of the message (the instructor). Instructors are frequently tempted to blame the student when instruction is not successful. The real problem may be that the instruction has not been designed or delivered appropriately.

You can use the communication models described here to analyze instructional problems. For example, if "noise" unduly interfered with your signal, you can repeat instruction under more favorable conditions. If you made an error in appraising your students' field of experience, you may need to identify a more appropriate entry level for your particular group. If the message was not encoded properly, you may need to identify more suitable materials, or you can adjust how you use the materials to produce more effective instruction.

Transactional Nature of Communication

Communication is an interpretive transaction between or among individuals. As noted previously, the sender of a message encodes it according to his or her skill and knowledge (field of experience), and the receiver decodes it according to his or her field of experience. In the feedback process, however, the receiver (student) does more than decode the message. He or she must also encode his or her interpretation of the signal for relay back to the sender (teacher), who, in turn, must decode it. In effect, receiver becomes sender and sender becomes receiver. And both interpret the message according to their fields of experience (see Figure 1.10).[5]

This is an extremely important point to keep in mind. You must decode your students' feedback signals according to *their* interpretation of instructional content, which may or may not be the same as yours, and which will very likely differ, at least in detail, from student

---

5   Schramm, "Procedures and Effects," p. 119.

Figure 1.9
In the classroom feedback from the learners informs the instructor of whether or not the point is being communicated.

Figure 1.10
A transactional model of communication shows the changing roles of sender and receiver.

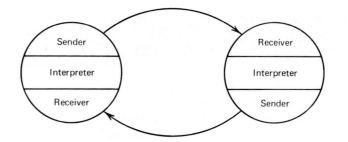

to student. For example, instructional information about the labor movement in the United States may be interpreted one way by the child of a business executive and another way by the child of a union member. Black students and white students may interpret a film on slavery quite differently. The limited sensory abilities of some handicapped students may lead them to interpret instructional content differently from non-handicapped children. Students raised in other countries will bring their cultural assumptions with them. For example, in the United States, the owl is often used as a symbol of wisdom, but in a region in Nigeria it is an omen of evil. In situations where students work together, differences between fields of experience can become part of the learning experience as students come to understand how their backgrounds influence their values. As an instructor, you must always be sensitive to the fact that student response to a communication signal is a product of student experience.

Feedback is particularly important when students are in learning situations that are not under the direct supervision of the teacher. The discussion of different interpretations of the material studied could be the most important part of the lesson.

The Concrete-Abstract Continuum

The psychologist Jerome Bruner, in developing his theory of instruction, proposes that the instruction should proceed from direct experience (enactive) to iconic representations of experience (such as pictures and films) to symbolic representation (such as words). He further states that the sequence in which a learner encounters materials has a direct effect on achieving mastery of the task.[6] Bruner points out that this applies to all learners, not just children. When a learning task is presented to adults who have no relevant experiences on which to draw, learning is facilitated when instruction follows a sequence from actual experience to iconic representations to symbolic or abstract representations.

As we will discuss later, an important first step in instruction is to determine the learner's current level of experience. Instructional media that incorporate concrete experiences help students integrate prior experiences and thus facilitate learning of abstract concepts. Many students have watched various aspects of the construction of a highway or a street. They have seen the machine that lays the asphalt down, they have seen graders at work, and they have seen a number of other stages of road building. However, they need to have all these experiences integrated into a generalized notion of what it means to build a highway. A video that can show all of these processes in relation to each other is an ideal way to integrate their various experiences into a meaningful abstraction.

Historically, improving the balance between concrete and abstract learning experiences was a key reason for using instructional media.

---

6 Jerome S. Bruner, *Toward a Theory of Instruction* (Cambridge, MA: Harvard University Press, 1966), p. 49.

However, current researchers question the distinctions between media made by earlier authors. The relationship between the concreteness and abstractness of various media and methods and their instructional effectiveness is not as clear-cut as we once believed. Most instructional materials use a combination of presentation forms that vary in their degree of realism or abstractness. For example, both motion media and filmstrips (still pictures) may be captioned or narrated (verbal symbols). In certain circumstances, line drawings (visual symbols) have been shown to be more effective than realistic photographs (still pictures). It now seems clear that learner response—the mental processing or overt practice conducted in response to the audiovisual stimuli—is as important as the nature of the instructional medium used. Regardless of the appeal of a method of presentation, the ultimate test is learner response and performance.

Decisions regarding trade-offs between the concreteness of a learning experience and time constraints have to be made continually by the instructor. In general, as you move up Dale's "Cone of Experience" (see "Flashback," p. 12) toward the more abstract media, more information can be compressed into a shorter period of time. It takes more time for students to engage in a direct purposeful experience, a contrived experience, or a dramatized experience than it does to present the same information in a motion picture, a recording, a series of visual symbols, or a series of verbal symbols. For example, a field trip can provide a learning experience relatively high in concreteness, but it

In one of the first textbooks written about the use of audiovisual materials in schools, Hoban, Hoban, and Zissman stated that the value of audiovisual materials is a function of their degree of realism. In developing this concept, the authors arranged various teaching methods in a hierarchy of greater and greater abstraction, beginning with what they referred to as "the total situation" and culminating with "words" at the top of the hierarchy.[a]

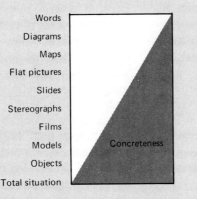

Words
Diagrams
Maps
Flat pictures
Slides
Stereographs
Films
Models
Objects
Total situation

Concreteness

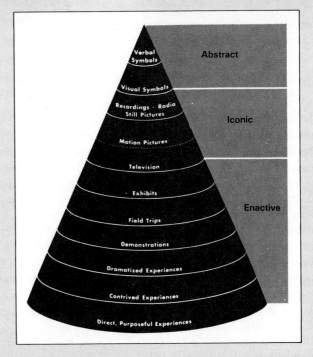

Dale's Cone of Experience. From *Audio-Visual Methods in Teaching,* Third Edition, by Edgar Dale. Copyright © 1969 by Holt, Rinehart and Winston, Inc., reprinted by permission of the publisher.

In 1946, Edgar Dale took the same construct and developed the "Cone of Experience."[b] In the Cone of Experience, we start with the learner as participant in the actual experience, then move to the learner as observer of the actual event, to the learner as observer of a mediated event (an event presented through some medium), and finally to the learner observing symbols that represent an event. Dale contended that learners could make profitable use of more abstract instructional activities to the extent that they had

built up a stock of more concrete experiences to give meaning to the more abstract representations of reality.

Psychologist Jerome Bruner, working from a different direction, devised a descriptive scheme for labelling instructional activities that parallels Dale's. As shown here, Bruner's concepts of enactive, iconic, and abstract learning can be superimposed on Dale's Cone. Bruner, though, emphasized the nature of the mental operations of the learner rather than the nature of the stimuli presented to the learner.[c]

[a] Charles F. Hoban, Sr., Charles F. Hoban, Jr., and Samuel B. Zissman, *Visualizing the Curriculum* (New York: Dryden, 1937), p. 39.

[b] Edgar Dale, *Audio-Visual Methods in Teaching,* 3rd ed. (New York: Holt, Rinehart and Winston, 1969), p. 108. Copyright 1946, 1954, © 1969 by Holt, Rinehart and Winston. Reprinted by permission of Holt, Rinehart and Winston, CBS College Publishing.

[c] Bruner, *Toward a Theory of Instruction,* p. 49.

also takes up a good deal of instructional time. A video depicting the same experiences as the field trip could be presented to the students in a much shorter period of time and with much less effort.

Similarly, a simulation (a contrived experience) such as the game *Ghetto* can help students relate to new situations and solve new problems, but such a simulation game does take more time than a more abstract learning experience such as watching a brief television documentary about ghetto life. In such cases, the instructor must decide whether the particular nature of the experience is worth the extra time it may take. As discussed later in this chapter, researchers have found that

training directors consider contrived experiences (role playing, simulations) well worth the time they take. They often use filmed or videotaped simulations which offer realism but take up less time than "live" simulations.

The instructor must also decide whether or not the learning experience is appropriate to the background experience of the students. The greatest amount of information can be presented in the least amount of time through printed or spoken words (the top of the concrete-abstract continuum and cone). But if the student does not have the requisite background experience and knowledge to handle these verbal symbols, the time saved in presentation will be time lost in learning. The instructor can only find out if the instructional method matches the learners' background by analyzing learner response. If students achieve what was expected of them, the instructional experiences were appropriate.

As Dale has pointed out, a model such as his Cone of Experience, although a simplification of complex relationships, is nonetheless a practical guide to analyzing the characteristics of instructional media and methods and how these media may be useful.

PSYCHOLOGICAL BASES OF LEARNING

Before the mid-1950s, three themes dominated research with media: (1) proving media can teach, (2) improving the effectiveness of media through evaluation techniques, and (3) developing better practices for using media in the classroom. While these studies made significant con-

tributions to our understanding of media design and use, they did not tell us much about how learning takes place and how learners process stimulus materials. In other words, these studies were in the realm of instructional communication theory and not learning theory.

During this same period of time, psychologists were developing learning theories that offered explanations of learning behavior, but these did not lead to guidelines for designing media.

Skinner and Reinforcement Theory

In the mid-1950s, the focus of learning research started to shift from stimulus design (communication) to learner response to stimuli. In the forefront of this movement was B. F. Skinner, a psychologist at Harvard University. Skinner was a *behaviorist* but with an important difference: he was interested in voluntary behavior, such as learning new skills, rather than reflexive behavior, as illustrated by Pavlov's famous salivating dog. He demonstrated that the behavior of an organism could be "shaped" by reinforcing, or rewarding, the desired responses to the environment. Skinner based his learning theory, known as reinforcement theory, on a series of experiments with pigeons, but he reasoned that the same pro-

cedures could be used with humans. The result was the emergence of programmed instruction, a technique of leading a learner through a series of instructional steps to a desired level of performance. Unlike earlier learning research, Skinner's work led directly to improved instructional design.

The response to his success was immediate and eventually pervasive. Psychologists, particularly educational psychologists, saw reinforcement theory and programmed instruction as a cure for many of the ills of education. One of the attractions of reinforcement theory was that it led very directly to a variety of instructional configurations: behavioral objectives, programmed instruction (see Figure 1.12), personalized systems of instruction, learning activity packages, and so on (see Chapter 12). Enthusiasts of programmed instruction called the process of specifying learning outcomes in terms of behavior and then devising the necessary steps to assure learner success in achieving those behaviors a "technology of instruction." Although programmed instruction per se has diminished in importance, the movement it spawned is alive and well in instructional development and other "systems" approaches to instruction, including computer-assisted instruction.

Figure 1.11
The instructor's skill in weaving audiovisual media into the lesson is the single most important determinant of successful learning from media.

Figure 1.12
Synchronized sound-slide
presentations can be coupled with
programmed instruction techniques for
effective individualized instruction.

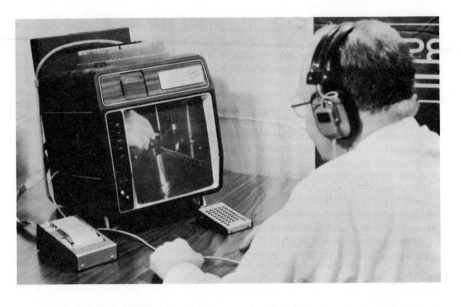

Cognitive Psychology

Behaviorists refuse to speculate on what goes on internally when learning takes place. They rely solely on observable behaviors. As a result, they are more comfortable explaining relatively simple learning tasks. Because of this posture behaviorism has limited application in designing instruction for higher-level skills. For example, behaviorists are reluctant to make inferences about how learners process information, even when doing so can be helpful in designing instruction that develops problem-solving ability.

Cognitive psychologists, on the other hand, are making their primary contribution to learning theory and instructional design by creating models of how information is received, processed, and manipulated by learners. This approach leads to a different way of looking at familiar learning patterns. For example, behaviorists simply state that practice strengthens the response to a stimulus. Cognitivists create a mental model of "short-term" and "long-term" memory. New information is stored in short-term memory where it is "rehearsed" until ready to be stored in long-term memory. If the information is not rehearsed, it fades from short-term memory. They go on to infer that learners then combine the information and skills

in long-term memory to develop "cognitive strategies," or skills for dealing with complex tasks. Cognitivists have a broader perception of independent learning than that held by behaviorists: students are less dependent on the guiding hand of the program designer and rely more on their own cognitive strategies in using available learning resources.

A close look at the work of the Swiss psychologist Jean Piaget will illustrate how a cognitive psychologist views the mental processes individuals use in responding to their environment. The three key concepts of mental development in Piaget's work are schemata, assimilation, and accommodation.[7]

Schemata. *Schemata* (singular *schema*) are the mental structures by which individuals organize their perceived environment. These adapt or change during mental development and learning. Schemata are used to identify, process, and store incoming information. They can be thought of as categories individuals use to classify specific information and experiences.

Very young children learn to distinguish between mother and father.

They soon separate dogs from cats and later become aware of different varieties of dogs. These differentiations based on experience lead to the development of schemata, or the ability to classify objects by their significant characteristics.

These cognitive structures change by the processes of assimilation and accommodation, which should be encouraged during instruction. Adult learners have a greater number of and more elaborate schemata than children.

Assimilation. *Assimilation* is the cognitive process by which a learner integrates new information and experiences into existing schemata.

Figure 1.13
Jean Piaget

---

7   Jean Piaget, *The Development of Thought: Elaboration of Cognitive Structures* (New York: Viking, 1977).

Piaget borrowed the term from biology where it refers to the process by which an organism eats food, digests it, and then assimilates or changes it into a usable form.

During learning, assimilation results from experiences. With new experiences, the schema expands in size but does not change its basic structure. Using the process of assimilation, the individual attempts to place new concepts into existing schemata.

These learning experiences can be real-life experiences. But rather than waiting for experiences to happen naturally, instructors cause experiences to happen through use of media and the new technologies of instruction.

Accommodation.   Because schemata change with experience, adult learners have a broader range of schemata than children. The process of modifying existing schemata or creating new ones is called *accommodation*.

When dealing with a new concept or experience, the learner attempts to assimilate it into existing schemata. When it does not fit, there are two possible responses: (1) the learner can create a new schema into which the new stimulus is placed, or (2) the existing schema can be modified so that the new stimulus will fit. Both of these processes are forms of accommodation.

Schemata evolve over time in response to many learning experiences. As instructors, we are responsible for providing, through appropriate instructional media, learning experiences that will result in the creation of new schemata as well as the modification of existing schemata.

Behaviorist and Cognitive Approaches to Instruction

While behaviorists stress external control over a learner's behavior, cognitivists stress internal, or learner, control over mental pro-

cesses. This difference in viewpoint influences how media are designed and used.

Behaviorists specify behavioral (performance) objectives, then limit instruction to whatever is necessary to master those objectives. When programmed instruction was introduced, material not directly related to the objectives was carefully screened out. Instructional design and media were highly structured. This approach has been very successful in teaching basic skills and knowledge.

Instructional designs based on cognitive psychology are looser in construction, allow students to employ their own cognitive strategies, and encourage interaction among students. Learning tasks that require problem solving, creative behavior, or cooperative activity lend themselves well to a cognitive instructional approach.

Unlike behaviorists, cognitivists do not limit their definition of learning to observable behavior. They believe that learners learn more than is expressed in immediate behaviors. They may at a later time use knowledge previously learned, but not previously expressed, in building their schemata.

The Social-Psychological Perspective

Social psychology is another well-established tradition in the study of instruction and learning. Social psychologists look at the effects of the social organization of the classroom on learning. What is the grouping structure of the classroom — independent study, small groups, or the class as a whole? What is the authority structure — how much control do students have over their own activities? And what is the reward structure — is cooperation or competition fostered?

In recent years, researchers such as Robert Slavin have taken the position that cooperative learning is both more effective and more socially beneficial than competitive

and individualistic learning.[8] He has developed a set of cooperative learning techniques that embody the principles of small-group collaboration, learner-controlled instruction, and rewards based on group achievement. These techniques are discussed more fully in Chapter 12.

An Eclectic Approach to Practice

Instructors and instructional designers need to develop an eclectic attitude toward competing schools of learning psychology. We are under no obligation to swear allegiance to a particular learning theory. We use what works. If we find that a particular learning situation is suited to a behaviorist approach, then we use behaviorist techniques. Conversely, if the situation seems to call for cognitive methods, that's what we use.

It follows that an eclectic approach is essential when selecting and designing media. Most educators support the cognitivists' emphasis on stimulus-rich materials, confident that students learn more, say, from a video, than may be expressed at the time. For example, a high school student may learn about the scientific method during a video of a chemistry experiment even though the objectives for the experiment do not list that topic; or a management trainee may learn a great deal about personality differences during a gaming exercise designed to teach an entirely different skill. On the other hand, there are situations, such as teaching basic knowledge (e.g., multiplication tables) or psychomotor skills (e.g., keyboarding), that call for the tighter control of behaviorist techniques.

Technologies of Instruction

As mentioned, the developers of programmed instruction called it a technology of instruction. They were referring to the process of analyzing

---

8   Robert E. Slavin, *Cooperative Learning: Theory, Research, and Practice* (Englewood Cliffs, NJ: Prentice-Hall, 1990).

instructional tasks, breaking them down into their subtasks, and then devising the steps necessary to bring the learner to a desired level of performance. In this book we have broadened the term technology of instruction to embrace a number of instructional arrangements that fit the criteria of technology as a process that leads to reliable results.

The principal definition of *technology* used in this book is "the systematic application of scientific or other organized knowledge to practical tasks."[9] Adapting this definition to instruction, we may define *instructional technology* as the application of our scientific knowledge about human learning to the practical tasks of teaching and learning. A technology of instruction, thus, is a particular, systematic arrangement of teaching/learning events designed to put our knowledge of learning into practice in a predictable, effective manner to attain specific learning objectives.

Over the years, many such arrangements have been devised, including programmed instruction (see Figure 1.14), computer-based instruction, audio-tutorial systems, modular instruction, simulations, and games. Some technologies of instruction incorporate audiovisual media, others do not. Some employ electronic or mechanical devices, but others, such as programmed texts and simulation games, may involve no such devices. (Specific technologies of instruction are discussed in detail in Chapter 12.) However, they all have one thing in common: they focus on the learner and on scientific principles of human learning.

THE ROLES OF MEDIA IN INSTRUCTION

Media can serve many roles in instruction. The instruction may be

The "teaching machine" was one of the first outgrowths of programmed instruction. The learner makes an overt response and checks the correctness of that response before proceeding to the next item.

dependent on the presence of a teacher, or instructor-based. Even in this situation, media may be heavily used by the teacher. On the other hand, the instruction may not require a teacher. Such instructor-independent instruction is often called "self-instruction" even though it is guided by whoever designed the media.

Instructor-Based Instruction

The most common use of media in an instructional situation is for supplemental support of the "live" instructor in the classroom (see Figure 1.15). Certainly properly designed instructional media can enhance and promote learning and support teacher-based instruction.

But their effectiveness depends on the instructor (as will be made clear in the chapters that follow).

Research has long indicated the importance of the instructor's role in effective use of instructional media. For example, early studies showed that when teachers introduced films, relating them to learning objectives, the amount of information students gained from films increased.[10] Later research confirmed and expanded on these original findings. Ausubel, for example, developed the concept of "advance organizers" as an aid to effective

9   John Kenneth Galbraith, *The New Industrial State* (Boston: Houghton Mifflin, 1967), p. 12.

10   Walter A. Wittich and J. G. Fowlkes, *Audio-visual Paths to Learning* (New York: Harper Brothers, 1946).

instruction.[11] An advance organizer may take the form of an overview of or an introduction to lesson content, a statement of principles contained in the information to be presented, a statement of learning objectives, and so on. Whatever the

form, it is intended to create a mind-set for reception of instruction.

Advance organizers can be effective instruments for ensuring that media play their proper role as supplemental supporters of instruction. Many commercially produced instructional materials today have built-in advance organizers, which may be used as is or adapted by the instructor.

Instructor-Independent Instruction

Media can also be used effectively in formal education situations where a teacher is not available or is working with other students (see Figure 1.16). Media are often "packaged" for this purpose: objectives are listed, guidance in achieving objectives is given, materials are assembled, and self-evaluation guidelines

---

[11] David Ausubel, *Educational Psychology* (New York: Holt, Rinehart and Winston, 1968).

Figure 1.15
Instructional media are most often used in the presence of a "live" teacher in the classroom.

Figure 1.16
Carefully designed media make independent learning effective.

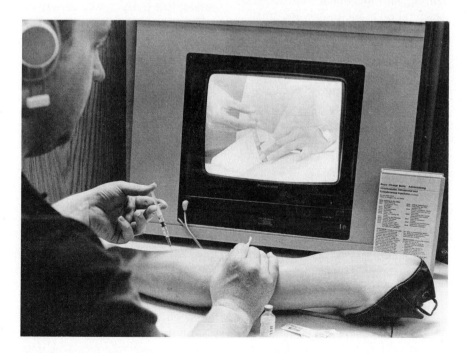

are provided. In informal educational settings, media such as videocassettes and computer courseware can be used by trainees at the work site or at home. In some instances an instructor may be available for consultation via telephone.

Cooperative learning is closely related to self-instruction. As students work together in groups or in collaboration with the teacher on learning projects, they take more responsibility for learning. Newer technologies such as hypermedia (see Chapter 9) encourage students to rely on their own cognitive strategies in learning. Cooperative learning with hypermedia can lead to stimulating interchanges among students as they go through and discuss their responses to the materials. Hypermedia programs that allow for user additions to nodes of information (or addition of new nodes) lend themselves particularly well to student reports of learning activities to fellow students as well as to the teacher. This can be a way of building in individual responsibility in group work.

The use of self-instructional materials allows teachers to spend more of their time diagnosing and correcting student problems, consulting with individual students, and teaching on a one-to-one and small-group basis.

How much time the teacher can spend on such activities will depend on the extent of the instructional role assigned to the media. Indeed, under certain circumstances, the entire instructional task can be left to the media. Experimental programs have demonstrated, for example, that an entire course in high school physics can be successfully taught through use of films and workbooks without direct classroom intervention by the teacher. Successful computer-based courses in calculus have been developed for use by able students whose high schools have no such course.

This is not to say, of course, that instructional technology can or should replace the teacher, but rather, that media can help teachers become creative managers of the learning experience rather than merely dispensers of information.

Distance Education

Distance education is a rapidly developing approach to instruction throughout the world. The approach has been widely used by business, industrial, and medical organizations. For many years doctors, veterinarians, pharmacists, engineers, and lawyers have used it to continue their professional education. These individuals are often too busy to interrupt their practice and participate in classroom-based education. Recently, academic institutions have been using distance education to reach a more diverse and geographically dispersed audience not accessible through traditional classroom instruction.

The distinguishing characteristic of distance education is the separation of the instructional team and student(s) during the learning process. As a consequence, the course content must be delivered by instructional media.

The media may be primarily print (books and paper-and-pencil tests), as in traditional correspondence courses. But today a wide variety of media are used. Audiocassettes, videotapes, videodiscs, computer courseware, and interactive videos can be sent to individual students. In addition, radio, broadcast television, telelectures (see Figure 1.17), and teleconferences are utilized for "live" distance education. The latter two delivery systems allow for interactive instruction between the instructor and the students.

Special Education

Media play an important role in the education of special students. Handicapped children in particular need special instructional treatment. Mentally retarded children need highly structured learning situations because their field of experience and ability to incorporate messages into

Figure 1.17
Students can learn effectively from instructors at a distance via a telecommunications distribution system.

Figure 1.18
The Kurzweil reading machine allows those with impaired sight to "read" printed material. The device scans the printed page, analyzes letter combinations through a computer, and speaks the words by means of a voice synthesizer.

mental constructs is limited (see Figure 1.8). They need to have much more of the message placed within the context of their field of experience in order to expand that field of experience. Students who have impaired hearing or impaired vision require different kinds of learning materials; more emphasis should be placed on audio for visually impaired students than for normally sighted individuals. Talking books, for example, are available for visually impaired students to use in special education programs and at home. Adjusting instruction for all of these groups requires a heavy reliance on media and materials and the appropriate selection of these materials to fit specific purposes.

Although severely handicapped students often attend special education classes, the trend today is to "mainstream" students whose disabilities do not preclude them from profiting from regular classroom activities. Instructional media specifically designed for such students (see Figure 1.18) or classroom adaptation of media to compensate for physical and mental disabilities can contribute enormously to effective instruction of handicapped students and can help prevent their unwarranted (albeit unintentional) neglect by the busy regular-classroom teacher.[12]

MEDIA IN EDUCATION AND TRAINING

Since the turn of the century, teachers have used various types of audio and visual aids to help them teach (see "Flashback," pp. 22–23). Recently, teachers have expanded their repertoire of materials and procedures to include the new technologies of instruction. The newer techniques include the use of microcomputers, compact discs, videodiscs, and satellite communications.

Patterns of Media Use in Education

A recent survey of equipment in the schools of Virginia reveals that computers are now the most numerous item of instructional equipment in elementary and secondary schools but also confirms continued reliance on traditional media (see Table 1.1). The most frequently inventoried piece of equipment after the computer is the audiocassette recorder/ player, followed by the record player, filmstrip projector, overhead projector, and TV receiver and monitor. We must keep in mind that equipment

Table 1.1

Inventory of selected equipment used in Virginia schools

Equipment	Classroom	Media Center	Other[a]	Total
Computers (for instruction)				49,094[b]
Audiocassette player	22,342	15,943	1,226	39,511
Record player	21,532	13,685	1,064	36,281
Filmstrip projector	13,438	12,212	705	26,355
Overhead projector	15,447	10,201	551	26,199
TV receiver/monitor	13,050	7,260	1,134	21,444
16mm projector	4,100	7,163	519	11,782
VHS recorder/player	1,650	3,997	409	6,056
Beta recorder/player	31	154	18	203
U-Matic recorder/ player	216	1,290	125	1,631
VHS video camera	155	1,180	163	1,498
Beta video camera	6	42	7	55
U-Matic video camera	18	226	23	267
VHS editing system	4	12	11	27
Beta editing system	2	11	2	15
U-Matic editing system	4	31	5	40
Slide projector	1,081	3,386	154	4,621
Videodisc player, level 1	25	32	13	70
Videodisc player, level 2	2	2	0	4
Videodisc player, level 3	9	11	2	22
Compact disc player	159	100	36	295
Teleconferencing equipment	122	23	255	400

Source: Adapted from David M. Moore, *Virginia Local Education Agency Technology Assessment,* Vol. 1 (Richmond, VA: Department of Education, 1988).

[a] Primarily auditoriums and special rooms

[b] From the 1989 computer survey reported in David M. Moore, *Virginia Local Education Agency Technology Assessment Project,* Vol. 2 (Richmond, VA: Department of Education, 1989). The location of the computers within each school was not part of the survey; many were located in computer laboratories.

lingers on in a setting even though use of the associated media formats may be declining. For example, phonograph records are being replaced by tapes and compact discs, but record players will remain in the schools until the records in their inventories wear out. We know that media centers are buying far more videos than 16mm prints, but film projectors still outnumber videocassette machines. The relatively rapid acceptance of computers dedicated

to instruction is encouraging, but the adoption of other new technologies, such as videodiscs, is slower than a perusal of the periodical literature would suggest. Although most educators would like to see newer technologies adopted at a faster pace, many acknowledge that the more traditional media still have a place in the school.

The Virginia State Department of Education has given distance education a big boost by providing each

---

12 *Using Technology* (Bloomington, IN: Agency for Instructional Technology, 1988). VHS, 29 minutes.

high school with a satellite down-link. While the primary purpose is to receive advanced placement courses distributed by the department, the high schools have the option of using the satellite dishes to receive other satellite signals for instruction.

Most teachers coming out of schools of education will have had considerable training in using the newer technologies. As their numbers increase, we can expect more pressure on school districts to increase their inventories of high-tech equipment with a consequent increase in use of newer technologies.

The growth of teleconferencing equipment is an indication of the schools' interest in distance education. Distance education networks such as TI-IN (see Chapter 10) should encourage the installation of satellite dishes and telecommunications systems for receiving and sending outreach programs.

Patterns of Media Use in Training

As one might expect, the media and methods preferred by training directors are often different from those used by educators. One of the major reasons for this is that the curricula of the schools are fairly uniform, whereas training programs are often industry specific. Formats of media that lend themselves to local production are preferred by training directors. For example, slides are used more frequently than filmstrips; in schools the reverse is true.

Another difference arises from the fact that training directors are dealing with adults rather than children and adolescents. Role playing, games, and simulations are used much more frequently in training programs, particularly with management, supervisory, and sales personnel (see Figure 1.19). These people's jobs require a great deal of interaction with people, and the types of training methods that develop relevant skills are given high priority. The trainees will have to call on those skills immediately after the

training session and are more likely to become impatient with methods more abstract than the situation demands.

According to the 1991 *Training* magazine survey, video-based instruction (see Figure 1.20) is used by more companies with more than 100 employees than any other medium.[13] Lecture, presumably sup-

---

[13] Chris Lee, "Who Gets Trained in What, 1991," *Training* (October, 1991): 47–59.

ported by overhead transparencies, is the next most frequently used instructional format. A full rundown of the various media and methods used in employee training is given in Figure 1.21. In interpreting the table remember that the survey reports the percentage of companies *using* the medium or method, *not* what percentage of training is *delivered* by the medium or method.

Note that for training traditional media are commonly used by more

Figure 1.19
Management trainees often participate in role-playing exercises to gain experience in dealing with people.

Figure 1.20
Because institutional training often requires materials custom-made for a specific setting, training videos are often produced on-site.

companies than some of the newer technologies. In recent years the percentage of companies using video has increased. The percentage of companies using games and simulations also has significantly increased. Surprisingly, the percentage of companies using teleconferencing (audio and video) and computer conferencing decreased in the past few years, perhaps due to less favorable economic conditions. These technologies will likely be relied on more heavily in the future. Note the difference between using computers in training and using computer-based training.

Interactive video is an expensive medium so it is not surprising that larger companies tend to use it more. Twenty-four percent of companies with more than 2,500 employees use interactive video. As the size of the organization decreases, the percentage of companies using it drops sharply.

Growth of Training Programs

Business, industrial, and financial institutions have today become major settings for instruction. The development of sophisticated instructional media and our growing knowledge of how to use these media for effective learning have opened up instructional options not only for students in formal educational institutions but also for learners outside such institutions. Today, virtually any institutional setting can become a classroom with the aid of, and sometimes even near-total dependence upon, instructional technology.

According to the *Training* survey, corporations spend over $43 billion a year on training programs. Eighty-seven percent of companies with more than 100 employees provide training in management skills and development; eighty-six percent provide technical skills and knowledge training. Remedial basic education is provided by thirty-seven percent. Many of the training programs and materials are designed and produced by outside suppliers. At over $43

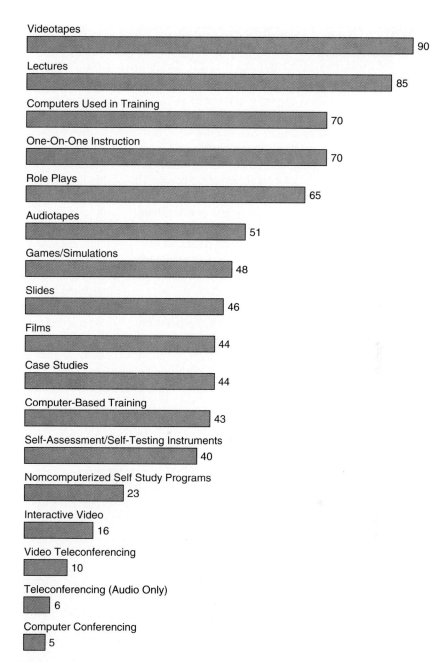

Figure 1.21

Instructional methods used for employee training (by percentage of organizations). Reprinted with permission from the October 1991 issue of *Training* Magazine. Copyright 1991, Lakewood Publications Inc., Minneapolis, MN, (612) 333-0471. All rights reserved.

billion, the training market is more attractive than the education market to many producers of instructional products.[14]

Many of the nation's labor unions operate extensive training programs for their members, and some even include funding for membership ed-

ucation in their contract negotiations. Hospitals and other social welfare institutions have developed educational facilities to help keep their personnel abreast of current techniques and professional practices. Libraries, museums, and community centers of all types are likely to be organized centers of out-of-school education; and, of course,

---

[14] Lee, "Who Gets Trained in What," 47–59.

Instructional media were originally referred to as "audiovisual aids." That phrase accurately describes their first role in elementary and secondary classrooms—that of serving as aids for the teacher. During the first decade of the twentieth century, school museums were created to house artifacts and exhibits for instructional purposes. The primary function of educational museums was to supplement and enrich the instructional programs of the school system. The first was the St. Louis Educational Museum, established in 1905. Horse-drawn wagons delivered instructional materials including charts, colored photographs, stereoscopic pictures, lantern slides, and maps to the schools.

Educational use of film began about the same time. Most films used for instructional purposes were theatrical, industrial, or government films. One of the early film projectors was developed by Bell and Howell in 1907. Like other media at the time, instructional films were considered aids to teaching rather than self-contained sequences of instruction.

During the first quarter of this century, the use of these materials was referred to as "visual instruction" or "visual education." Recorded sound on film was not available until the late twenties. Radio broadcasting developed during the same period, as sound recording and visual instruction quickly became audiovisual instruction.

The growth of instructional radio occurred primarily during the decade from 1925 to 1935. By the late 1930s radio education had begun its decline. Today it is easier to find a television set than a radio in most schools. Today school systems that operate their own radio stations typically do so to teach broadcasting skills and provide primarily entertainment programming.

During World War II, the use of media in American schools declined drastically because of the lack of equip-

ment and materials. However, a period of expansion was beginning in the industrial and military sectors. During this time, the United States government purchased 55,000 film projectors and produced 457 training films at a cost of over a billion dollars.[a]

Viewgraph, the name of the first company to produce overhead projectors, is the term that some military and industrial personnel still use to describe all overhead projection equipment. During the war, "viewgraphs" were developed by the navy for map briefings and instruction.[b] This early version of the overhead projector replaced the clumsy opaque projector because notes could be made directly on the material during use. Today the overhead is the most widely used piece of audiovisual equipment.

Following World War II there was a period of expansion in audiovisual instruction due in large part to its successful use during the war. At the same time, audiovisual research programs emerged with the hope of identifying principles of learning that could be used in the design of audiovisual materials. However, educational practices were not greatly affected by these research programs because many practitioners either ignored or were not aware of the findings.[c]

During the early 1950s many leaders in the audiovisual movement became interested in various theories or models of communication. These models focused on the communication process. The authors of these models indicated that during planning for instruction it was necessary to consider all of the elements of the communication process and not focus on just the medium, as many in the audiovisual field tended to do.

Instructional television experienced tremendous growth during the 1950s. In 1952 the Federal Communications Commission set aside 242 television channels for educational purposes. At the same time the Ford Foundation provided extensive funding for educational television. Credit and noncredit courses were offered on open- and closed-circuit television. Programs of wide educational and cultural interest have been offered on educational television stations. Today most educational television is offered via videotape, with the exception of the airing of news events as they take place. The television screen has begun to replace the movie screen for the viewing of prepared materials.

Programmed instruction can be traced to the work of psychologist B. F. Skinner in the mid-1950s. (See Chapter 12 for more details.) Whereas the other media we have been discussing are really presentation devices, programmed instruction utilizes principles of human learning and was the first of the new technologies of instruction. Skinner focused attention on a device called the "teaching machine." Later that device was replaced by books called "programmed texts." The programmed instruction movement reached its peak during the 1960s and paved the way for other technologies of instruction—audio-tutorial systems, personalized systems of instruction, and programmed tutoring in the 1970s. Computer-based instruction of the late 1970s and 1980s is based on the principles of learning used in programmed instruction.[d] Programmed instruction and other self-instructional approaches are fading from the formal education scene and are being replaced by computer-based instruction, which incorporates many of the same learning principles.

Textbooks are still the most commonly used instructional resource. Overhead projectors are readily available and are used as a presentation aid by many teachers. Commercially produced videocassettes are gradually replacing films as the most widely used form of projected media because of their relatively low cost and ease of use. Filmstrips and commercially prepared slides, along with audiotapes and printed study guides, are providing the basis for self-instruction in learning carrels and media centers. Today, media and technologies of instruction are providing direct educational experiences for students rather than being used just as teachers' aids.

[a] J. R. Olsen and V. B. Bass, "The Application of Performance Technology in the Military," *Performance and Instruction* 21, no. 6 (July–August 1982): 32–36.

[b] W. Wittich and C. Schuller, *Audio-Visual Materials: Their Nature and Use* (New York: Harper and Row, 1953), p. 351.

[c] Robert A. Reiser, "Instructional Technology: A History," in *Instructional Technology: Foundations,* ed. R. M. Gagne (Hillsdale, NJ: Lawrence Erlbaum, 1987), pp. 11–48.

[d] For a thorough discussion of the history of media, see Paul Saettler, *The Evolution of American Educational Technology* (Englewood, CO: Libraries Unlimited, 1990).

both national and local government agencies have contributed greatly to the trend toward instruction outside formal educational settings.

The implications of this growing phenomenon are clear. In view of the increasing diffusion of instruction in our society, formal educational institutions now must be viewed as just one among many settings for instruction. As more and more instruction moves outside the school setting, more and more reliance will be placed on instructional media to meet diverse learning objectives.

APPLYING RESEARCH TO PRACTICE

People who are just beginning study in the field of instructional media typically hold the misconception that it is a very young field, one in which formal research probably began around the 1950s or perhaps the 1960s. In fact, well-conceived psychological studies of learning from films were being conducted as early as 1919, when Lashley and Watson investigated the adaptation of World War I training films for civilian use.[15]

A large-scale study of the instructional uses of films in the Chicago public schools was reported by Freeman in 1924.[16] The Chicago school studies and the Lashley-Watson studies yielded considerable insight into the instructional potentials of film and arrived at surprisingly sophisticated conclusions about the role of media in the classroom. Many of their findings seem to have been rediscovered by researchers studying the "new medium" of each succeeding generation. In the following quotations from the Chicago school studies, try substituting the term

television, computer-assisted instruction, or *videodisc* wherever the term *film* or *visual media* is mentioned.

The relative effectiveness of verbal instruction as contrasted with the various forms of concrete or realistic material in *visual media* depends on the nature of the instruction to be given and the character of the learner's previous experience with objective materials.

The peculiar value of a *film* lies not in its generally stimulating effect, but in its ability to furnish a particular type of experience.

Films should be so designed as to furnish to the teacher otherwise inaccessible raw material for instruction but should leave the organization of the complete teaching unit largely to the teacher.

The teacher has been found superior to all *visual media* in gaining and sustaining attention.

Each of the so-called conventional forms of instruction that employ *visual media* has some advantage and some disadvantage, and there are circumstances under which each is the best form to use.[17]

A recent publication by the navy is a very practical translation of research into practice.[18] The translation is loose, based as much on reflective experience as on research, but the recommended procedures and techniques are helpful to the beginning practitioner. All aspects of training programs are touched on, not just the use of media.

A recent review of research by Kozma endorses the use of media in education.[19] The research reviewed suggests that the capabilities of a particular medium, in conjunction with methods that take advantage of

these capabilities, interact with and influence the ways learners represent and process information. The article reviews research on learning from print, print with pictures, television and video, and computer. It is particularly useful because the author includes intelligent use of the media in his assessment of their effectiveness in instruction. The practicing teacher can benefit directly from Kozma's analysis, which is more than one can say about many reviews of research.

Media Comparison Studies

These promising research beginnings were largely abandoned in favor of experimental designs in which one group of learners (the experimental group) is exposed to an audiovisual presentation of some sort while a similar group (the control group) receives more conventional instruction, often a lecture. All are given the same final test, the results of which are used to indicate the effectiveness of the experimental version. Sometimes two media forms are compared, for instance, film versus slide-tape. This type of study is known as a media comparison study.

Reviewers of media comparison studies regularly point out that a majority of the studies find "no statistically significant difference" in learning between the experimental treatment and the control treatment. Does this mean that audiovisual presentations are equivalent to lectures or that films are equivalent to slides-tapes in their impact on the audience?

Critics have pointed out a number of major faults in the very concept of media comparison studies that cast doubt on their utility as guides for making instructional decisions. First, the two media being compared were not always dramatically different in nature. In some cases the experimental medium being evaluated was nothing more than a filmed or videotaped lecture, to ensure that the two treatments had the same content and method,

15 K. S. Lashley and J. B. Watson, *A Psychological Study of Motion Pictures in Relation to Venereal Disease Campaigns* (Washington, DC: U.S. Interdepartmental Social Hygiene Board, 1922), p. 3.

16 Frank N. Freeman, *Visual Education* (Chicago: University of Chicago Press, 1924), p. 79.

17 Paul Saettler, "Design and Selection Factors," *Review of Educational Research* 38, no. 2 (April 1968): 116.

18 Navy Personnel Research and Development Center, *What Works: Summary of Research Findings with Implications for Navy Instruction and Learning* (Pensacola, FL: Direction of Chief of Naval Education and Training, 1988).

19 Robert B. Kozma, "Learning with Media," *Review of Educational Research* (Summer 1991): 179–211.

differing only in delivery system. The film or videotape chosen in the study may or may not have made use of color, motion, or other special visual possibilities of the medium. Furthermore, the test items used to measure achievement often were drawn largely from the verbal information in the soundtrack, not from the visual content. On the other side of the coin, the conventional instruction being evaluated varied greatly from study to study, consisting of whatever was considered to be the traditional method in a particular setting—a lecture, a lecture plus discussion, textbook reading, or any combination of these or other methods.

It's no wonder that the cumulative results of these media comparison studies are difficult to interpret. As one critic has put it, it is like trying to compare "can-of-worms A" with "can-of-worms B."

Unfortunately, the more successful the researchers were in controlling the conditions of the media treatment, the less it resembled what would be normal good practice in media use. For example, in order to control as many extraneous variables as possible, the media treatment ordinarily excluded such normal practices as introductory and follow-up discussion of the media presentation. What was needed to meet laboratory standards of purity bore little resemblance to what creative instructors do with either media-based or conventional instruction.

Analysis of the content treated in these studies reveals another problem—a bias toward cognitive objectives, as opposed to attitudinal, interpersonal, or motor skill objectives. Further, attainment of the objectives was usually measured by ordinary paper-and-pencil verbal tests. Thus, the experiments typically revolved around highly verbal content being measured by highly verbal instruments (often using college students as subjects—an unusually verbally adept sector of the general population). This may help explain why lecture and textbook treatments, being highly verbal, yielded comparable results to the media treatments.

Implications for Practice

For the practitioner, a major question arises: If the conclusion from a majority of studies is that there is no statistically significant difference in learning between the media-based and conventional instruction, does this mean that audiovisual presentations, say, are approximately equivalent to lectures in terms of instructional usefulness? Not necessarily. At most, it means that when certain audiovisual materials are used in the same way as a lecture is used for the same purposes as a lecture (e.g., verbal recall) with a random sample of learners—and all other conditions are held constant—outcomes measured by specific tests will be similar. The qualifications listed here, however, are assumptions that good instructors specifically reject in actual practice. They do not use audiovisual materials in the same way as print or lecture materials. They select media that suit particular objectives. Audiovisual presentations can be powerful, for example, in conveying a historical period's feel, in building empathy with others, or in showing a role model in action. They also integrate media with the methods (e.g., tutorial, drill-and-practice, discovery) that are best suited to stimulating the cognitive processes connected with achieving given objectives. Good instructors select media for those learners who can profit from them. And they evaluate effectiveness not just on the basis of immediate verbal recall but also on the basis of what impact the experience had on the imagination, feelings, and long-term comprehension of the learner.

From the media comparison studies, we can extract the following guidelines for media selection.

Select Materials Based on Their Specific Attributes.
An insight derived from the errors made in media comparison research is that one cannot generalize findings about one film to all films, or one video lesson to all video lessons. Each material has its own set of attributes. One videotape may make full use of the potential of the medium, featuring graphics, animation, drama, and so on, whereas another may be no more than a recording of a talking head. Each would have an entirely different impact on the imagination, feelings, and long-term comprehension of the viewer (despite the fact that each might yield the same score on an immediate posttest of verbal recall).

Materials must be examined in light of the specific objectives of the lesson and the specific needs and interests of learners. Does *this* film-strip supply the needed realistic pictures of everyday life in ancient Roman times? Does *this* computer-assisted instruction module provide practice in making the kinds of decisions that loan officers make? Does *this* videocassette show a close-up view of a proper weld? In short, what attributes are needed for proper communication of the idea involved, and does the specific material have those attributes?

Utilize Material for Maximum Impact.
If nothing else, research and practical experience have shown that much of the effectiveness of media depends on how they are integrated into the larger scheme. Wilbur Schramm, one of the most respected contemporary communication researchers, summarized it this way:

> Motivated students learn from any medium if it is competently used and adapted to their needs. Within its physical limits, any medium can perform any educational task. Whether a student learns more from one medium than from another is at least as likely to depend on *how* the medium is used as on *what* medium is used.[20]

---

[20] Wilbur Schramm, *Big Media, Little Media* (Beverly Hills, CA: Sage Publications, 1977), p. iv.

The user of the material can help increase the impact of any audiovisual material by applying these sound principles: select material with appropriate attributes, introduce it to learners by relating it to prior learning and indicating how it relates to today's objectives, present it under the best possible environmental conditions, elicit a response from viewers, review the content, and evaluate its impact.

The ASSURE model described in Chapter 2 was developed as a planning aid to help assure that media are used to their maximum advantage, not just as interchangeable substitutes for printed or oral messages. Contrary to the requirements of research, the requirements of practice demand that the conditions surrounding the use of the materials *not* be held constant. Indeed, one of the most important roles of media is to serve as a catalyst for change in the whole instructional environment. The effective use of media demands that instructors be better organized in advance, that they think through their objectives, that they alter the everyday classroom routine, and that they evaluate broadly to determine the impact of instruction on mental abilities, feelings, values, interpersonal skills, and motor skills.

STRUCTURE AND FLEXIBILITY

Research lends considerable support to the principle that the amount of time students spend on the instructional task is directly and positively related to achievement.[21] Media-directed instruction concentrates student time on task. For example, television teachers have frequently commented that their televised instruction is more concentrated and has fewer diversions than their classroom instruction. The learning

laboratory has the effect of increasing the time spent directly on task.

Students achieve more when instruction has some degree of structure, when they know what is expected of them, and when the instructional environment is arranged to facilitate achievement of instructional objectives.[22] For example, if inquiry skills are the goal of instruction, then the obligation of the teacher is to be sure the environment is arranged to facilitate the necessary gathering of data from which inferences can be made by the student. Both the kind and degree of structure vary with instructional objectives.

Structure gives students confidence because it reduces ambiguity about the objectives and purposes of learning. This is as true of adults in training programs as it is of students in schools and colleges. Acquisition of the skills necessary to do the job contributes more to a feeling of confidence than do motivational or inspirational sessions, concluded researchers at DCW Research Associates from a study of sales managers. Their findings "suggest that trainers concerned with motivational programs to enhance self-confidence in job performance might do well to look at task-oriented programs designed to assist individuals to get greater control of the elements of their jobs that tend to affect job performance."[23]

Structure, however, does not rule out flexibility. Even in a structured situation, accommodation should be made to individual needs and interests. Structured instruction need not be excessively task-oriented. Nor does it rule out exploration, creativity, and self-direction.[24]

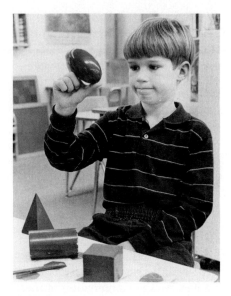

Figure 1.22
In Montessori schools carefully structured activities stimulate and channel children's curiosity.

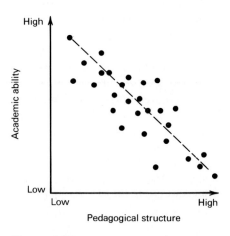

Figure 1.23
Learners with high academic ability tend to prefer less structure.

The correct blend of structure and flexibility to best meet your instructional objectives will depend on a variety of factors, including the subject matter under study and the learning characteristics of your students—that is, their age and general level of intelligence and their specific knowledge about and attitude toward the topic at hand.

Drill-and-practice exercises are likely to be more structured than, say, a discovery lesson in geography.

---

[21] N. L. Gage, *The Scientific Basis of the Art of Teaching* (New York: Teachers College Press, 1978), pp. 34–40.

[22] David L. Clark, Linda S. Lotto, and Martha M. McCarthy, "Factors Associated with Success in Urban Elementary Schools," *Phi Delta Kappan* (March 1980): 467–70. See also Gage, *Scientific Basis*, pp. 31–33.

[23] *Training* (October 1983): 16.

[24] Gage, *Scientific Basis*, p. 40.

We would also expect a mathematics lesson on fractions to be more structured than a social science lesson on contemporary urban problems.

In general, younger children respond well to, and indeed need, a high degree of lesson structure. The Montessori method for teaching very young children, for example, is highly structured, and its success depends on a carefully worked out sequence of instruction using specific materials (see Figure 1.22). Yet the uninformed visitor to a Montessori-type classroom might think the children are simply playing and having fun.

In general, lower-ability students prefer fairly well structured lessons, primarily because they do not have a high degree of confidence in their ability to work independently, or in their ability to pull together what are to them unrelated strands of subject matter. Higher-ability students respond well to a less structured approach because they have more confidence in their abilities (provided, of course, they are not students with high anxiety levels or ones who prefer structured situations for learning).

Motivation influences the tolerance students have for structured or flexible learning situations. Students who are highly motivated will be able to tolerate a very wide range of structure. Students with little motivation will do better in learning situations that guide them to specific instructional ends. If given too much flexibility or too much independence in a learning situation, students with relatively low motivation will tend to lose direction along the way and not arrive at the specific goals that were set in the learning situation, or they may abandon the pursuit of those goals completely during the course of instruction.

Keep in mind that by structure we mean the extent to which the management system leads the student step-by-step to the specific objectives set by the program. Structure has nothing to do with difficulty. In the case of students with low motivation, we are not suggesting that the material be difficult or present difficult problems, but that a structured learning situation can gently lead students toward instructional goals and instill a degree of confidence they would not pick up in a situation that was extremely flexible or that placed a great deal of the responsibility to learn on their shoulders.

The role of media in allowing flexibility in learning is clear: materials, print and audiovisual, are attractive alternatives to the routine of the lecture (see Figure 1.24). Materials that are relatively open-ended can be adapted to a variety of teaching/learning styles and situations. Self-instructional materials make possible such flexible arrangements as independent study and small-group work. Flexibility is enhanced when alternatives to "teacher talk" are available.

Whatever blend of structure and flexibility you choose, instructional media can help you achieve your goals. Media and media systems can be structured toward specific learning objectives, or they can easily be made open-ended and adapted to creative independent study and instructional flexibility.

TECHNOLOGY AND HUMANISM

More than a few observers of the educational scene have argued that the widespread use of instructional technology in the classroom must lead to treating students as if they too are machines rather than human beings—that is, that technology dehumanizes the teaching/learning process. It is, on the contrary, a major theme of this book

Figure 1.24
Audiovisual materials provide a springboard for small-group discussion—an alternative to the lecture and textbook.

Figure 1.25
Using lectures may or may not lead to humanistic ends. Are individual differences being addressed? Are students actively processing the information?

that, properly used, modern instructional media can individualize and thus humanize the teaching/learning process to a degree hitherto undreamed of. The danger of dehumanization lies not in the use of instructional media but in the way in which teachers perceive their students. If teachers perceive learners as machines, they will treat them as such, with or without the use of instructional media. If teachers perceive their students as human beings with rights, privileges, and motivations of their own, they will treat them as such, with or without the use of instructional media. In other words, it is not technology that tends to mechanize people but the uses to which people put technology.

One of our most thoughtful observers of life in the classroom is Philip Jackson of the University of Chicago. He found the quality of life in American classrooms somewhat impoverished, a condition that continues to concern contemporary observers. In his book *The Teacher and the Machine,* Jackson states that "the greatest intellectual challenge of our time is not how to design machines that behave more and more like humans, but rather, how to protect humans from being

treated more and more like machines."[25] He defines human mechanization as "the process by which people are treated mechanically; that is without giving thought to what is going on inside them." His illustrations of human mechanization in schools show how student attention, assignments, learning tasks, and discussion are mechanized with means as simple as the human voice and the teacher's right to turn students on and off.

Thus, the question is not so much what is used in the classroom as how are students treated. Put another way, what is important is not so much what a teacher teaches but how he or she teaches. For example, many teachers, particularly in English and social studies, may consider themselves "humanists," but in their teaching approach they may be anything but humanistic toward their students.

To reinforce this point, consider a case in which the introduction of machinery can make the instructional situation more humanistic. As research has indicated, students who

---
[25] Philip W. Jackson, *The Teacher and the Machine* (Pittsburgh, PA: University of Pittsburgh, 1968), p. 66.

have a high level of anxiety are prone to make mistakes and to learn less efficiently when under considerable pressure. Many teachers exert too much pressure on high-anxiety students, thereby making the instructional situation not only disagreeable but prone to error. Given the same sequence of instruction mediated through a machine that will continue only at the command of the student, the student can reduce the pressure simply by not responding. In other words, the machine awaits the command of the student to begin, whereas an overbearing teacher waits for no such command.

Contrary to what some educators believe, technology and humanism can work together or go their separate ways. Figure 1.27 suggests four basic mixes of technology and humanism. Here are some examples:

A. A college lecture with little or no interaction between professor and student

B. A course consisting of a required series of modules, each composed of performance objectives, materials to be used to complete objectives, and a self-evaluation test

Figure 1.26
Technology, in the form of audiovisual or print materials, can help free teachers for one-to-one interaction—doing what humans do best.

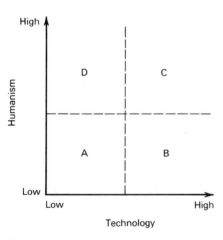

Figure 1.27
Technology and humanism are not opposite ends of a single scale, but two different variables, either of which can be high or low.

C. The same as B, except that students choose modules based on counseling sessions with an instructor and meet periodically to discuss the content of the modules

D. A group that meets on a regular basis to discuss common reading assignments

Figure 1.28
"I like educational toys. I like educational TV. I like educational reading material. It's education I don't like."

These examples are overly simplified and only illustrative, but they serve as a basis for analyzing the relationship between humanism and technology. They illustrate that training/instruction can be low in both humanism and technology, just as it can be high in both.

To reiterate, using instructional technology does not preclude a humane teaching/learning environment. On the contrary, instructional media can help provide a learning atmosphere in which students actively participate, as individual human beings, in the learning process. When instructional media are used properly and creatively in the classroom, it is the machines that are turned on and off at will, not the students.

REFERENCES

Print References

Adams, Dennis M. *Media and Literacy: Learning in an Electronic Age.* Springfield, IL: Thomas, 1989.

Adams, Dennis M., and Carlson, Helen. *Cooperative Learning and Educational Media: Collaborating with Technology and Each Other.* Englewood Cliffs, NJ: Educational Technology Publications, 1990.

Barnouw, Eric. *Tube of Plenty.* 3d ed. New York: Oxford University Press, 1990.

Chalk, Rosemary, ed. *Science, Technology, and Society: Emerging Relationships.* Papers from *Science,* 1949–1988. Washington, DC: American Association for the Advancement of Science, 1988.

Clark, Richard E., ed. "Instructional Technology and Media Research." *International Journal of Educational Research* 14, no. 6, (1990):485–579.

Costanzo, William V. "Media, Metaphors, and Models." *English Journal* (November, 1988):28–32.

Dijkstra, Sanne, et al., eds. *Research on Instruction: Design and Effects.* Englewood Cliffs, NJ: Educational Technology Publications, 1990.

Ellson, Douglas G. *Improving the Productivity of Teaching: 125 Exhibits.* Bloomington, IN: Phi Delta Kappa, 1986.

Fairweather, Peter. "Emerging Technologies or Different Paradigms?" *CALICO Journal* (June 1988):7–15.

Fiske, John. *Introduction to Communication Studies.* 2d ed. New York: Methuen, 1990.

Fleming, Malcolm L., and Hutton, Deane W. *Mental Imagery and Learning.* Englewood Cliffs, NJ: Educational Technology Publications, 1983.

Fox, G. T., and DeVault, M. V. "Technology and Humanism in the Classroom: Frontiers of Educational Practice." *Educational Technology* (October 1974):7–13.

Gagne, Robert M. *Instructional Technology: Foundations.* Hillsdale, NJ: Lawrence Erlbaum, 1987.

Gayeski, Diane M. "Why Information Technologies Fail." *Educational Technology* (February 1989):9–17.

Glaser, Robert. "The Reemergence of Learning Theory within Instructional Research." *American Psychologist* (January 1990):29–39.

Graves, Donna L. "A Selection of Valuable Audiovisual Materials to Promote Effective School Coping Skills." *Preventing School Failure* (Spring 1990):37–39.

Hatcher, Barbara, ed. *Learning Opportunities Beyond the School.* Wheaton, MD: Association for Childhood Education International, 1987.

Hoban, Charles F. "Educational Technology and Human Values." *AV Communication Review* (Fall 1977):221–42.

Johnston, Jerome. *Electronic Learning: From Audiotape to Videodisc.* White Plains, NY: Knowledge Industries, 1981.

Marsh, Patrick. *Messages That Work: A Guide to Communication.* Englewood Cliffs, NJ: Educational Technology Publications, 1983.

Melton, Reginald F. "The Changing Face of Educational Technology." *Educational Technology* (September 1990):26–31.

Osguthorpe, Russell T., and Zhou, Lian. "Instructional Science: What Is It and Where Did It Come From?" *Educational Technology* (June 1989):7–17.

Petrie, Joyce. *Mainstreaming in the Media Center.* Phoenix, AZ: Oryx Press, 1982.

Pettersson, Rune. *Visuals for Information.* Stockholm, Sweden: Esselte Forlag, 1988.

Proulx, R. "The Dialectics of Andragogy and Instructional Technology." *NSPI Journal* (July 1980):3–4.

Saettler, Paul. *The Evolution of American Educational Technology.* Englewood, CO: Libraries Unlimited, 1990.

Scaife, M. "Education, Information Technology and Cognitive Science." *Journal of Computer Assisted Learning* (June 1989):66–71.

Seels, Barbara. "The Instructional Design Movement in Instructional Technology." *Educational Technology* (May 1989):11–15.

Stakenis, Robert G., and Kaufman, Roger. *Technology in Education: Its Human Potential.* Fastback 163. Bloomington, IN: Phi Delta Kappa, 1981.

Thomas, James L., ed. *Nonprint in the Elementary Curriculum: Readings for Reference.* 2d ed. Littleton, CO: Libraries Unlimited, 1988.

Thompson, James P., and Jorgensen, Sally. "How Interactive is Instructional Technology." *Educational Technology* (February 1989):24–26.

Wadsworth, Barry J. *Piaget's Theory of Cognitive and Affective Development.* 4th ed. White Plains, NY: Longman, 1989.

Wedman, John F. "Increasing the Use of Instructional Media in the Schools." *Educational Technology* (October 1988):26–31.

Audiovisual References

Case Studies in Communication. Salenger Educational Media, 1982. 16mm film. 18 minutes.

The Child of the Future: How He Might Learn. Montreal: National Film Board of Canada, 1965. 16mm film. 60 minutes.

Communication Feedback. Rockville, MD: BNA Film, 1965. 16mm film. 21 minutes.

A Communication Model. Bloomington, IN: Indiana University Audio-Visual Center, 1967. 16mm film. 30 minutes.

Communication: The Name of the Game. Roundtable Film and Video, n.d. Videocassette. 28 minutes.

Communications. Calgary, Alberta: Access Network, 1989. Videocassette. 29 minutes.

Communications and Media. Learning Corporation of America, 1982. 16mm film or videocassette. 20 minutes.

Communications Primer. Classroom Film Distributor, 1954. 16mm film. 22 minutes.

Cultural Illiteracy. University Park, PA: Pennsylvania State University, 1988. Videocassette. 28 minutes.

Media for Presentations. Bloomington, IN: Indiana University Audio-Visual Center, 1978. 16mm film. 20 minutes.

Perception and Communication. Columbus: Ohio State University, 1967. 16mm film. 32 minutes.

This is Marshall McLuhan: The Medium Is the Massage. New York: McGraw-Hill, 1968. 16mm film. 53 minutes.

To Help Them Learn. Washington, D.C.: Association for Educational Communications and Technology, 1978. 16mm film. 21 minutes.

Understanding Educational Technology. Washington, D.C.: Association for Educational Communications and Technology, 1977. Sound filmstrip with cassette.

POSSIBLE PROJECTS

1–A. Read one of the books cited in the chapter or a book relating to a topic in the chapter and write or record on audiotape a report. The report should be approximately two and one-half double-spaced, typed pages or five minutes in length.

1–B. React to any of the topics or ideas presented in the chapter. Your reaction and comments may be written or recorded (approximately five double-spaced, typed pages or ten minutes in length).

1–C. Analyze an instructional situation (either real or hypothetical) and identify the elements of the communication process and their interrelationship.

1–D. Prepare a "position paper" (approximately five double-spaced typed pages) on a topic such as the role of humanism versus technology in education, or structure versus flexibility in teaching.

1–E. Describe an actual use of instructional media in an out-of-school setting based upon your experiences or readings.

2

Systematic Planning for the Use of Media

OUTLINE

OBJECTIVES

After studying this chapter, you should be able to

1. Describe six procedures (steps) in systematic planning for the use of media (the ASSURE model).

2. List two general characteristics of learners and two types of specific competencies that could affect media selection.

3. Describe learning style and include in your description four types of traits that affect it.

4. Discuss the rationale for stating objectives for instruction. Your discussion should include three purposes or uses of objectives.

5. Write objectives that include the audience, behavioral outcome, conditions (if appropriate), and degree of mastery.

6. Classify given objectives into cognitive, affective, motor skill, and interpersonal skills domains, and locate them within each domain.

7. Describe the basic procedures for selecting, modifying, and designing materials, and indicate when each procedure is appropriate.

8. Explain how learner characteristics affect the selection of media.

9. State two examples of situational constraints that affect the selection of media and methods.

10. Describe two ways of modifying materials without actually altering the original materials.

11. List and give examples of the five basic steps in utilizing instructional materials.

12. Identify general showmanship techniques in reference to planning, practice, and presentation.

13. Describe several methods for eliciting student response during and after using media.

14. Justify the need for requiring learner response when using media.

15. Compare and contrast the techniques for evaluating student achievement and the techniques for evaluating media and methods.

16. Choose techniques from this chapter to improve your use of media.

LEXICON

learning style

objective

criterion

cognitive domain

affective domain

motor skill domain

interpersonal domain

cognitive strategies

internalization

characterization

articulation

showmanship

covert/overt response

A Model to Help Assure Learning

A

Analyze Learners

The first step in planning is to identify the learners. Your learners may be students, trainees, or members of an organization such as a Sunday school, civic club, youth group, or fraternal organization. You must know your students to select the best medium to meet the objectives. The audience can be analyzed in terms of (1) general characteristics, (2) specific entry competencies—knowledge, skills, and attitudes about the topic, and (3) learning style.

S

State Objectives

The next step is to state the objectives as specifically as possible. The objectives may be derived from a course syllabus, stated in a textbook, taken from a curriculum guide, or developed by the instructor. They should be stated in terms of what the learner (audience) will be able to do (behavior) as a result of instruction. The conditions under which the student or trainee is going to perform and the degree of acceptable performance should be included.

S

Select Media and Materials

Once you have identified your audience and stated your objectives, you have established the beginning points (audience's present knowledge, skills, and attitudes) and ending points (objectives) of instruction. Your task now is to build a bridge between these two points. There are three options: (1) select available materials, (2) modify existing materials, or (3) design new materials.

THE ASSURE MODEL

All effective instruction requires careful planning. Teaching with instructional media is certainly no exception. This chapter examines how to plan systematically for the effective use of instructional media. We have constructed a procedural model to which we have given the acronym ASSURE, because it is intended to assure effective use of media in instruction.

The ASSURE model, a procedural guide for planning and conducting instruction that incorporates media, assumes that training or instruction really is required. For example, students must learn how to use the new laboratory microscopes, or assembly line workers must learn to handle safely the toxic materials they work with.

Unneeded or redundant instruction may be regarded as fairly unimportant in academic settings, but in business and industry training it is recognized as a major waste of time and money. Nevertheless, such instruction sometimes occurs, because

training is the most obvious solution to performance problems. For example, say the sales force of Amalgamated Houseware Industries is falling short of its target in sales of dustpans. So the marketing vice-president suggests that the training department develop a self-instructional motivational videocassette, "Dynamic Dustpan Sales Techniques." In reality, the salespeople may already know how to sell dustpans, but Amalgamated dustpans may be notoriously poorly engineered, or the whole market for

U   R   E

Utilize Media and Materials

Having either selected, modified, or designed your materials, you then must plan how the materials will be used. First, preview the materials and practice your presentation. Next, prepare the class and ready the necessary equipment and facilities. Then present the material using the showmanship techniques and suggestions described in this and later chapters of the text.

Require Learner Participation

Learners must practice what they are expected to learn and should be reinforced for the correct response. The first time they are expected to perform the behavior called for in the objectives should not be on the examination. Instead, there should be activities within the lesson that allow learners to respond and to receive feedback on the appropriateness of their response.

Evaluate and Revise

After instruction, it is necessary to evaluate its impact and effectiveness. To get the total picture, you must evaluate the entire instructional process. Did the learners meet the objectives? Did the media assist the trainees in reaching the objectives? Could all students use the materials properly?

Wherever there are discrepancies between what you intended and what you attained, you will want to revise the plan for the next attempt.

dustpans may be depressed, or higher commissions may be earned on other products in the Amalgamated line. If the cause of the problem is not a lack of knowledge, training will not solve the problem. A full-blown process of instructional development would begin with a needs assessment to determine whether instruction is truly required.

The ASSURE model focuses on planning surrounding the actual classroom use of media. It is less ambitious than models of instructional development, which are intended to guide the entire process of designing instructional systems. Such models include the processes of needs analysis, subject-matter analysis, product design, prototype tryout, system implementation, and the like. These larger-scale instructional development procedures typically involve teams of specialists and require major commitments of time and money. (Further information about instructional design can be found in the print references cited at the end of this chapter.) The AS-SURE model, on the other hand, is meant for use by the individual instructor in planning everyday classroom use of media.

ANALYZE LEARNERS

If instructional media are to be used effectively, there must be a match between the characteristics of the learner and the content of the lesson and its presentation. The first step in the ASSURE model, therefore, is analysis of your audience.

It is not feasible to analyze every psychological or educational trait of your audience. Several factors about your learners, however, are critical for making good media and method decisions. First, in the category of general characteristics are broad identifying descriptors such as age, grade level, job or position, and cultural or socioeconomic factors. General characteristics are factors that are not related to the content of the lesson. These factors help you determine the level of the lesson and select content, contexts, and examples that will be meaningful to the audience.

Under the heading of specific entry competencies you should think about knowledge and skills that the learners have or lack: prerequisite skills (Do learners have the knowledge base required to enter the lesson, such as the technical vocabulary?), target skills (Have learners already mastered some of the skills you are planning to teach?), and attitudes (Are there biases or misconceptions about the subject?).

A third factor, learning style, refers to the whole spectrum of psychological traits that affect how we perceive and respond to different stimuli, such as anxiety, aptitude, visual or auditory preference, and so on.

General Characteristics

Even a superficial analysis of learner characteristics can provide helpful leads in selecting instructional methods and media. For example, students with substandard reading skills may be reached more effectively with nonprint media. If you are dealing with a particular ethnic or cultural subgroup, you might want to give high priority to considerations of ethnic and cultural identity in selecting particular materials.

If learner apathy toward the subject matter is a particular problem, consider using a highly stimulating instructional approach, such as a dramatic videotape or a simulation game.

Learners entering a new conceptual area for the first time will need more direct, concrete kinds of experiences (e.g., field trips, role playing). The more advanced have a sufficient base for using audiovisual or even verbal materials.

Heterogeneous groups including learners varying widely in their conceptual sophistication or in their amount of firsthand experience with the topic can profit especially from an audiovisual experience such as a film or videotape. Such media presentations provide a common experiential base that can serve as an important point of reference for subsequent group discussion and individual study.

For instructors dealing with a familiar audience, analysis of general characteristics will be something of a given. At times, however, audience analysis may be more difficult. Perhaps your students are new to you, and you have had little time to observe and record their characteristics. Perhaps your learners are a more heterogeneous group than is ordinarily found in the classroom—business trainees, for example, or a civic club, a youth group, or a fraternal organization—thus making it more difficult to ascertain if all or even a majority of your learners are ready for the media and method of instruction you are considering. In such cases, academic and other records may be helpful, as well as direct questioning of and talking with learners and other group lead-

ers. Seasoned public speakers—those who regularly address unfamiliar audiences—make it a practice to arrive early and strike up a conversation with early arriving audience members. In this way they can pick up valuable clues about the types of people in the audience, their backgrounds, their expectations, and their mood.

Specific Entry Competencies

When you begin to plan any lesson, your opening assumption is that the learners lack the knowledge or skills you are about to teach and that they possess the knowledge or skills needed to understand and learn from the lesson. These assumptions are often mistaken. For example, a life insurance company used to routinely bring all its new sales associates back to the home office in Hartford, Connecticut, at the end of their first year for a course on setting sales priorities. Puzzled by the cool reaction of the agents, the trainer decided to give a pretest, which revealed that a majority of the trainees already knew perfectly well how to set sales priorities. The company shifted to a less expensive and more productive strategy of giving incentives to field representatives who sent in acceptable sales plans showing their priorities.

The second assumption—that learners have the prerequisite knowledge or skill to begin the lesson—can seldom be accepted ca-

Figure 2.1

A classic example of a presentation in search of an audience

sually in school settings. Teachers of mixed-ability classes routinely anticipate that some students will need remedial help before they are ready to begin a particular new unit of instruction. Furthermore, researchers studying the impact of different psychological traits on learning have reached the unexpected conclusion that a student's prior knowledge of a particular subject influences how and what he or she can learn more than does any psychological trait.[1] For example, students approaching a subject new to them learn best from structured presentations (even if they have a learning style that would otherwise indicate more open-ended, unstructured methods).

These realizations underline the importance of verifying assumptions about entry competencies through informal means, such as in-class questioning or out-of-class interviews, or more formal means, such as testing with standardized or teacher-made tests. Entry tests (Figure 2.2) are assessments, both formal and informal, that determine whether or not students possess the necessary prerequisites (entry skills). Prerequisites are competencies that

the learner must possess in order to benefit from the instruction but that you or the media are not going to teach. For example, you may be teaching an apprentice lathe operator to read blueprints and assume that he or she has the ability to make metric conversions—and hence not teach this. Such previously acquired skills, or prerequisites, should be assessed before instruction by giving an entry test.

Pretests are also given before instruction but are used to measure the content to be taught. If the learners have already mastered what you plan to teach, you are wasting your time and theirs by teaching it.

By analyzing what your audience already knows, you can select appropriate media and methods. For example, if you have a group diverging widely in entry competencies, consider self-instructional materials to allow for self-pacing and other aspects of individualization.

Learning Styles

Learning style refers to the cluster of psychological traits that determine how an individual perceives, interacts with, and responds emotionally to learning environments. According to Bonham, learning styles are "fixed patterns for viewing

the world. Their purpose is to select information to which the person will attend, to organize and integrate what is attended to, to moderate and control affective aspects of personality, and to adapt to situational constraints imposed by a task."[2]

It is clear that certain traits dramatically affect our ability to learn effectively from different media and methods. What is not so clear is which traits are most important. The variables discussed in the literature can be grouped under perceptual preferences, information-processing habits, motivational factors, and physiological factors.

Perceptual Preferences and Strengths. Learners may vary as to which sensory gateways they prefer using or are especially adept at using; the two are not necessarily synonymous, of course. The main choices are auditory, visual, tactile, and kinesthetic. Proponents of the importance of this variable claim that most students do not have a preference or strength for auditory reception, casting doubt on the widespread use of the lecture

[1] Walter Dick and Lou Carey, *The Systematic Design of Instruction,* 3d ed. (Glenview, IL: Scott, Foresman, 1990), p. 90.

[2] L. A. Bonham, "Learning Style Instruments: Let the Buyer Beware," *Lifelong Learning* (June 1988):12–16.

Figure 2.2
Entry tests help prevent the frustration students experience when asked to do work far above or below their ability level.

method. They find that slower learners tend to prefer tactile or kinesthetic experiences; sitting and listening are difficult for them. Dependence on the tactile and kinesthetic modalities decreases with maturity.

Information-Processing Habits.

This category includes a broad range of variables related to how individuals tend to approach the cognitive processing of information. Some of the contrasting traits include the following: analytical/global, focuser/nonfocuser, narrow/broad categorization, cognitive complexity/simplicity, reflective/impulsive, sharpener/leveler (regarding memory processes), and tolerant/intolerant of incongruity.

Gregorc's "style delineator" groups learners according to concrete versus abstract and random versus sequential styles; it yields four categories: concrete sequential, concrete random, abstract sequential, and abstract random.[3] Concrete sequential learners prefer direct, hands-on experiences presented in a logical order. They learn best with workbooks, programmed instruction, demonstration, and structured laboratory exercises. Concrete random learners lean toward a trial-and-error approach, quickly reaching conclusions from exploratory experiences. They prefer methods such as games, simulations, independent-study projects and discovery learning. Abstract sequential learners decode verbal and symbolic messages adeptly, especially when presented in logical sequence. Reading and listening to lectures are preferred methods. Abstract random learners are distinguished by their capacity to draw meaning from human-mediated presentations; they respond to the tone and style of the speaker as well as the message. They

do well with group discussion, lectures with question-and-answer periods, films, and television.

Motivational Factors.

A number of emotional factors have been found to influence what we pay attention to, how long we pay attention, how much effort we invest in learning, and how feelings may interfere with learning. Anxiety, locus of control (internal/external), degree of structure, achievement motivation, social motivation, cautiousness, and competitiveness are variables that are frequently cited as critical to the learning process.

"Anxiety," according to Tobias, "is one of the learner characteristics of major importance for instructional concerns."[4] Tobias describes how anxiety can interfere with cognitive processing before, during, and after learning. He also cites research demonstrating that motivational differences can dramatically affect the effort that students invest in a task and thereby affect learning outcomes.

Physiological Factors.

Factors related to sex differences, health, and environmental conditions are among the most obvious influences on the effectiveness of learning. First, it is well established that boys and girls tend to respond differently to various school experiences. For example, boys tend to be more competitive and aggressive than girls and consequently learn well with instructional games. Hunger and illness clearly impede learning. Temperature, noise, lighting, and time of day are everyday phenomena that affect our ability to concentrate and maintain attention. People have different preferences and tolerances regarding these factors.

Dunn has developed standardized instruments to measure the learning styles and environmental preferences

of adults which cover these physiological factors among others.[5] These instruments are among the best known and most widely used in school applications. Teachers who have prescribed individual learning programs based on analysis of these factors feel that they have practical value in improving academic achievement, attitude, and discipline.

The intent in using information about a student's learning style is to adapt instruction to take advantage of a particular style. Many students in a class may have the same or similar learning styles. Using learning styles in teaching can be compared to designing a house for a specific person. The components of houses are basically uniform—kitchen, living room, dining room, bedrooms, baths. However, they can be arranged in an unlimited number of configurations. Furthermore, there are many different styles of architecture, colors, textures, materials and so on. An architect skillfully selects and arranges all of these elements to meet the needs and preferences of an individual, couple, or family. In a similar manner a teacher chooses different instructional approaches to meet the needs of students with different learning styles.

STATE OBJECTIVES

The second step in the ASSURE model for using instructional media is to state the objectives of instruction. What learning goal is each learner expected to reach? More precisely, what new capability should the learner possess at the completion of instruction? Thus, an *objective* is a statement not of what the instructor plans to put into the lesson but of what the learner ought to get out of the lesson.

3   Anthony Gregorc, "Learning and Teaching Styles—Potent Forces behind Them," *Educational Leadership* (January 1979):234–36.

4   Sigmund Tobias, "Learner Characteristics," in *Instructional Technology: Foundations,* ed. Robert M. Gagne. (Hillsdale, NJ: Lawrence Erlbaum, 1987).

5   Kenneth Dunn, "Measuring the Productivity Preferences of Adults," *Student Learning Styles and Brain Behavior* (Reston, VA: National Association of Secondary School Principals, 1982).

Your statement of objectives should be as specific as possible. For example, "My students will improve their mathematical skills" is far too general to qualify as a specific lesson objective. It does, however, qualify as a goal, that is, a broad statement of purpose. Such a goal might serve as the umbrella for a number of specific objectives, such as "The second-grade students will be able to solve correctly any single-digit addition problem."

Why should you state instructional objectives? In the first place, you must know your objectives in order to make the correct selection of media and methods. Your objectives will, in a sense, dictate your choice of media and your sequence of learning activities. Knowing your objectives will also force you to create a learning environment in which the objectives can be reached. For example, if the objective of a unit of a driver's training course is "to be able to change a flat tire within fifteen minutes," the learning environment must include a car with a flat tire.

Another basic reason for stating your instructional objectives is to help assure proper evaluation. You won't know if your learners have achieved an objective unless you are absolutely sure what that objective is.

Without explicit objectives your students won't know what is expected of them. If objectives are clearly and specifically stated, learning and teaching become objective-oriented. Indeed, a statement of objectives may be viewed as a type of contract between teacher and learner: "Here is the objective. My responsibility as the instructor is to provide learning activities suitable for your attaining the objective. Your responsibility as the learner is to participate conscientiously in those learning activities."

The ABCDs of Well-Stated Objectives

A well-stated objective starts by naming the *audience* of learners for whom the objective is intended. It then specifies the *behavior* or capability to be learned and the *conditions* under which the capability will be observed. Finally, it specifies the *degree* to which the new skill must be mastered—the standard by which the capability can be judged. Writing useful objectives can be as easy as ABCD!

Audience. A major premise of systematic instruction is to focus on what the learner is doing, not on what the teacher is doing. Learning is most likely to take place when the learner is active, mentally processing an idea or physically practicing a skill. Because accomplishment of the objective depends on what the learner does, not what the teacher does, the objective begins by stating whose capability is going to be changed, for example, "ninth-grade algebra students" or "newly hired sales representatives." Of course, if you are repeating the objective in material written for student use, the informal "you" is preferable.

Behavior. The heart of the objective is the verb describing the new capability that the audience will have after instruction. This verb is most likely to communicate your intent clearly if it is stated as an observable behavior. What will the learner be able to *do* after completing instruction? Vague terms such as *know, understand,* and *appreciate* do not communicate your aim clearly. Better are *define, categorize,* and *demonstrate,* which denote observable performance. The Helpful Hundred list suggests some verbs that highlight performance.

THE HELPFUL HUNDRED
Suggested Behavioral Terms

Add	Defend	Kick	Reduce
Alphabetize	Define	Label	Remove
Analyze	Demonstrate	Locate	Revise
Apply	Derive	Make	Select
Arrange	Describe	Manipulate	Sketch
Assemble	Design	Match	Ski
Attend	Designate	Measure	Solve
Bisect	Diagram	Modify	Sort
Build	Distinguish	Multiply	Specify
Carve	Drill	Name	Square
Categorize	Estimate	Operate	State
Choose	Evaluate	Order	Subtract
Classify	Explain	Organize	Suggest
Color	Extrapolate	Outline	Swing
Compare	Fit	Pack	Tabulate
Complete	Generate	Paint	Throw
Compose	Graph	Plot	Time
Compute	Grasp (hold)	Position	Translate
Conduct	Grind	Predict	Type
Construct	Hit	Prepare	Underline
Contrast	Hold	Present	Verbalize
Convert	Identify	Produce	Verify
Correct	Illustrate	Pronounce	Weave
Cut	Indicate	Read	Weigh
Deduce	Install	Reconstruct	Write

Ideally, the behavior stated in the objective will reflect the real-world capability actually needed by the learner, not some artificial ability needed for successful performance on a test. As a surgical patient, would you want a surgeon who "is able to perform an appendectomy" or one who "is able to select the correct answers on a multiple-choice test on appendectomies"?

Conditions. A statement of objectives should include the conditions under which performance is to be observed. For example, may students use notes in describing the consequences of excessive use of alcohol? If the objective of a particular lesson is for students to be able to identify birds, will identification be made from color representations or black-and-white photographs? What tools or equipment will the student be allowed, or not be allowed, to use in demonstrating mastery of the objective? Thus, an objective might state, "Given a political map of Europe, you will be able to mark the major coal-producing areas." or "Without notes, textbook, or any library materials, you will be able to write a 300-word essay on the relationship of nutrition to learning."

Degree. The final requirement of a well-stated objective is to indicate the standard, or *criterion,* by which acceptable performance will be judged. What degree of accuracy or proficiency must the learner display? Whether the criteria are stated in qualitative or quantitative terms, they should be based on some real-world requirement: How well must the machinist be able to operate a lathe in order to be a productive employee?

Time and accuracy are meaningful dimensions in many objectives. How quickly must the observable behavior be performed? For example, should students be able to solve five quadratic equations in five minutes or ten minutes? How accurate must

a measurement be—to the nearest whole number or within one-sixteenth of an inch or plus or minus 1 mm?

Quantitative criteria for judging acceptable performance may sometimes be difficult to define. How, for example, can an English instructor state quantitative criteria for writing an essay or short story? The English instructor might stipulate that the student's work will be scored for development of theme, characterization, originality, or the like. A model story might be used as an example.

The important consideration in appraising your objectives is whether the intent of the objectives, regardless of their format, is com-

municated to the user. If your objectives meet all the criteria in the "Appraisal Checklist" (page 43) but still do not communicate accurately your intentions to your colleagues and students, they are inadequate. The final judgment on any objectives must be determined by their usefulness to you and your learners.

Classification of Objectives

Classifying objectives is much more than an academic exercise for educational psychologists. It has practical value because the selection of instructional methods and media depends on the types of objectives be-

---

Check Yourself: Behaviors

Are the following statements written in behavioral (performance) terms? (Complete and then check your answers below.)

Yes   No

_____ _____ 1. The labor negotiations trainee will grasp the true significance of the Taft-Hartley Act.

_____ _____ 2. The carpentry vocational trainees will learn the common tools in the woodworking shop.

_____ _____ 3. The first-year medical student will be able to name all the bones in the hand.

_____ _____ 4. The high school debate club member will include ten supporting facts in a written paragraph on "The Value of National Health Insurance."

_____ _____ 5. The junior high school student will list on the chalkboard three major causes of the American Civil War.

_____ _____ 6. The kindergarten student will return art supplies to the storage area after using them.

_____ _____ 7. The high school sophomore will show a favorable regard for volleyball by joining an intramural volleyball team.

_____ _____ 8. The Anthropology 101 student will develop a sense of the cultural unity of humankind.

_____ _____ 9. By the end of their orientation, new employees will appreciate the importance of productivity within the corporation.

_____ _____ 10. The elementary school student will demonstrate a desire for a clean environment by voluntarily picking up litter in the classroom and on the playground.

Answers

1. No 2. No 3. Yes 4. Yes 5. Yes 6. Yes 7. Yes 8. No 9. No 10. Yes

ing pursued, and so does the choice of evaluation instruments.

An objective may be classified according to the primary type of learning outcome at which it is aimed. Although there is a range of opinion on the best way to describe and organize types of learning, three categories, or domains, of learning are widely accepted: cognitive skills, affective skills, and motor skills. To these we add a fourth, interpersonal skills, because of their importance in training and instructional methods involving teamwork.

In the *cognitive domain* learning involves an array of intellectual capabilities that may be classified either as verbal/visual information or intellectual skills. Verbal/visual skills require the learner to provide a specific response to relatively specific stimuli. They usually involve memorization or recall of facts. Intellectual skills, on the other hand, require thinking activity and the manipulation of information.

The *affective domain* involves feelings and values. Affective objectives may range from stimulating interest in a school subject to encouraging healthy social attitudes to adopting a set of ethical standards.

In the *motor skill domain* learning involves athletic, manual, and other such physical skills. Motor skill objectives include capabilities ranging from simple mechanical operations to those entailing sophisticated neuromuscular coordination and strategy, as in competitive sports.

Learning in the *interpersonal domain* involves interaction among people. Interpersonal skills are people-centered skills that require the ability to relate effectively with others. Examples include teamwork, counseling techniques, administrative skills, salesmanship, discussion, and customer relations.

The Cognitive Domain

The original classification scheme for the cognitive domain proposed

Check Yourself: Conditions

Do the following statements include an acceptable statement of condition? (Complete and then check your answers below.)

Yes   No

1. Given a political outline map of South America, the sixth-grade student will be able to name eleven of the thirteen countries.

2. After completing the beginner's course, the young stamp collector will be able to distinguish a "plate block" from a "first-day cover."

3. Without the aid of a calculator or any reference materials, the student of statistics will be able to calculate the chi-square value for a given set of data.

4. The management trainee in the labor negotiations course will be able to categorize correctly examples of different types of strikes (e.g., wildcat strike, sit-down strike, sympathy strike).

5. The naval officer candidate will be able to determine if an actual submarine is in "diving trim" when provided with data on its weight and volume.

6. The primary school student will be able to construct a sundial using the illustrated instructions in the science workbook.

7. The Red Cross lifesaving badge trainee will be able to rescue swimmers who show signs of distress.

8. A college student enrolled in the music appreciation class will recognize the pattern typical of the romantic symphony in Beethoven recordings played in class.

9. Given two water-filled goblets and a spoon, the science education teacher-trainee will be able to demonstrate the principle of sympathetic vibration.

10. The speech therapist will be able to classify speech defects into one of the five main types of speech problems (e.g., aphasia).

Answers:

1. Yes 2. No 3. Yes 4. No 5. Yes 6. Yes 7. No 8. Yes 9. Yes 10. No

by Bloom envisioned a rather orderly progression from simple to complex mental abilities, as follows:

1. *Knowledge.* Recalling specifics, remembering, defining, recognizing, repeating. Example: "You will recite from memory the poem *Paul Revere's Ride* by Longfellow."

2. *Comprehension.* Translating, interpreting, paraphrasing, summa-

rizing, extrapolating. Example: "You will describe in your own words the story of *Paul Revere's Ride.*"

3. *Application.* Using ideas and information. Example: "You will relate events in *Paul Revere's Ride* to modern communication techniques during a time of war."

4. *Creation.* Breaking down an example or system into its components; combining components to

Check Yourself: Degree

Do the following statements include a properly stated degree or criterion of acceptable performance? (Complete and then check your answers below.)

Yes   No

_____ _____   1. On a questionnaire at the end of the course, each management trainee will write at least two favorable comments about the course.

_____ _____   2. The machine shop trainee will be able to operate properly the Model 63-9 metal lathe.

_____ _____   3. In a controlled situation without access to any references, the college student of romantic poetry will be able to write an essay on the three major themes in Shelley's poetry.

_____ _____   4. During a nature hike, the youth camper will be able to identify correctly at least three different geological formations.

_____ _____   5. The basketball squad member will be able to sink 75 percent of her free throws in a single practice session.

_____ _____   6. The vocational education student in basic electricity will operate a potentiometer to determine the resistance of resistors.

_____ _____   7. In a ballet practice session, each new dance company member will display proper form.

_____ _____   8. While being observed without his or her knowledge, the high school chemistry student will demonstrate awareness of all the safety precautions listed on the chart in the laboratory.

_____ _____   9. The football team member will be able to name correctly the formations illustrated by each of twelve diagrams.

_____ _____   10. Given a list of authors, the junior high school student will match the names of each with titles of their works.

Answers:

1. Yes   2. No   3. No   4. Yes   5. Yes   6. No   7. No   8. Yes   9. Yes   10. Yes

create a new product. Example: "You will compose an original poem using the rhyme scheme and imagery of *Paul Revere's Ride*."[6]

The many examples of each of the classifications suggested by Bloom make them particularly useful in relating objectives to desired types of performance. The examples cover a wide range of subject matter.

Many instructional designers, however, prefer a different set of categories proposed by Gagne et al. which emphasizes the distinction between verbal/visual information, intellectual skills, and cognitive strategies.[7] The last category helps relate learning styles to instructional methods and goes beyond Bloom's classification.

1. *Verbal/visual information.* Factual knowledge stored verbally or visually in memory. It consists of single images, facts, labels, memorized sequences, and organized information. Examples: "to recall that Mackenzie King served as prime minister of Canada three times between 1921 and 1948," "to recite the first paragraph of John F. Kennedy's inaugural address." This category also includes the somewhat higher-level skill of comprehending—understanding the meaning of a fact. Example: "to summarize in your own words the contributions of President Kennedy to the civil rights movement."

2. *Intellectual skills.* The ability to use symbols to organize and manipulate the environment. The two most basic forms of symbols, words and numbers, allow us to read, write, and compute. The following abilities underlie the continuum of capabilities that form the intellectual skill category:

   a. *Discrimination.* To distinguish between two different stimuli, that is, to see the difference between physically similar objects. Example: "to distinguish between a turboprop and a turbofan jet engine."

   b. *Concept learning.* Classifying things or ideas into categories on the basis of some shared attributes. Example: "to identify a bat as a mammal."

   c. *Rule using.* Applying principles to a variety of situations. Using mathematical equations or following the rules of grammar to construct sentences in a foreign language are rule-using capabilities.

3. *Cognitive strategies.* The internal control processes that govern the learner's ability to visualize, think about, and solve problems. The sophistication of our cognitive strategies determines how

6 Adapted from Benjamin S. Bloom, ed., *Taxonomy of Educational Objectives, Handbook I: Cognitive Domain* (White Plains, NY: Longman, 1984).

7 Robert Gagne, Leslie Briggs, and Walter Wager, *Principles of Instructional Design,* 3d ed. (New York: Holt, Rinehart and Winston, 1988).

❑ APPRAISAL CHECKLIST
Objectives

	Included	Missing
Audience		
Specifies the learner(s) for whom the objective is intended	❑	❑
Behavior (action verb)		
Describes the capability expected of the learner following instruction ❑ stated as a learner performance ❑ stated as observable behavior ❑ describes a real-world skill (versus mere test performance)	❑	❑
Conditions (materials and/or environment)		
Describes the conditions under which the performance is to be demonstrated ❑ equipment, tools, aids, or references the learner may or may not use ❑ special environmental conditions in which the learner has to perform	❑	❑
Degree (criterion)		
States, where applicable, the standard for acceptable performance ❑ time limit ❑ range of accuracy ❑ proportion of correct responses required ❑ qualitative standards	❑	❑

creatively, fluently, or critically we will be able to think. Example: "to resolve logical contradictions by questioning the assumptions behind each."

The Affective Domain

The affective domain is organized according to degree of *internalization*, or the extent to which an attitude or value has become part of the individual:

1. *Receiving.* Being aware of and willing to pay attention to a stimulus (listen or look). Example: "The student will sit attentively while the teacher reads Longfellow's *Paul Revere's Ride.*"

Figure 2.3
The fruits of a lesson aimed at some poorly specified affective objectives
PEANUTS reprinted by permission of UFS, Inc.

2. *Responding.* Actively participating, reacting in some way. Example: "The student will ask questions relating to *Paul Revere's Ride.*"

3. *Valuing.* Voluntarily displaying an attitude, showing an interest. Example: "The student will ask to read another story or poem about Paul Revere."

4. *Characterization.* Demonstrating an internally consistent value system, developing a characteristic life-style based upon a value or value system. Example: "The student will devote a percentage of his or her free time to studying American history."[8]

The Motor Skill Domain

The motor skill domain may be seen as a progression in the degree of coordination required:

1. *Imitation.* Repeating the action shown. Example: "After viewing the film on the backhand tennis swing, you will demonstrate the swing with reasonable accuracy."

2. *Manipulation.* Performing independently. Example: "Following a practice period, you will demonstrate the backhand tennis swing, scoring seven of the ten points on the performance checklist."

3. *Precision.* Performing with accuracy. Example: "You will demonstrate an acceptable backhand tennis swing, returning successfully at least 75 percent of practice serves to the backhand."

4. *Articulation.* Performing unconsciously, efficiently, and harmoniously, incorporating coordination of skills. Example: "During a tennis match, you will execute the backhand stroke effectively against your opponent, returning nine out of ten of all types of shots hit to the backhand side."[9]

The Interpersonal Domain

Interpersonal skills can be classified into six categories:

1. *Seeking/giving information.* Asking for/offering facts, opinions, or clarification from/to another individual or individuals. Example: "You will ask your supervisor about the meaning of a new work rule."

2. *Proposing.* Putting forward a new concept, suggestion, or course of action. Example: "You will make a job enrichment suggestion to your supervisor."

3. *Building and supporting.* Extending, developing, enhancing another person, his or her proposal, or concepts. Example: "In a departmental meeting you will suggest an amendment to someone's motion."

4. *Shutting out/bringing in.* Excluding/involving another group member from/into a conversation or discussion. Example: "In a departmental meeting you will ask a quiet member to give his or her ideas."

5. *Disagreeing.* Providing a conscious, direct declaration of difference of opinion, or criticism of another person's concepts. Example: "During a lunchroom discussion you will defend a new work rule against a colleague's attack."

6. *Summarizing.* Restating in a compact form the content of previous discussions or considerations. Example: "Before giving

[8] Adapted from David R. Krathwohl et al., *Taxonomy of Educational Objectives, Handbook II: Affective Domain* (White Plains, NY: Longman, 1964).

[9] Adapted from the published works of E. Simpson (University of Illinois) and R. H. Dave (National Institute of Education, New Delhi, India).

Figure 2.4
In a group of handicapped learners there may be as many different standards for each objective as there are individuals.

your comments in a departmental meeting you will summarize the arguments that have been presented."[10]

Objectives and Individual Differences

Objectives in any of the domains just discussed may, of course, be adapted to the abilities of individual learners (see Figure 2.4). The stated philosophy of most schools and colleges is to help students fulfill their full potential. In a physical education class with students of mixed ability, for instance, the midsemester goal might be for all students to be able to complete a run of 100 meters outdoors, but the time standards might vary. For some, twelve seconds might be attainable; for many others, sixteen seconds; and for some, twenty might be realistic. For a physically handicapped student, it might be a major victory to move ten meters in one minute.

Objectives are not intended to limit what a student learns. They are intended only to provide a minimum level of expected achievement. Serendipitous or incidental learning should be expected to occur (and be encouraged) as students progress toward an objective. Each learner has a different field of experience (as discussed in Chapter 1), and each has different characteristics (as discussed earlier in this chapter). Because of such individual differences, incidental learning takes different forms with different students. Class discussions and other kinds of student involvement in the instructional situation, therefore, should rarely be rigidly limited to a specific objective. Student involvement should allow for incidental learning to be shared and reinforced. Indeed, in order to foster incidental learning

and provide for individual differences, it is sometimes advisable to have students specify some of their own objectives.

In nonacademic organizations, such as the military or industry, the philosophy behind the training program may be quite different. Here the purpose is to operate the organization as efficiently as possible, and individuals are trained for roles in the organization. Objectives are written to reflect the actual demands of specific jobs, individuals are trained or selected for those jobs based on their ability to meet the standards stated in the objectives.

---

[10] Adapted from Neil Rackham and Terry Morgan, *Behaviour Analysis in Training* (London: McGraw-Hill, 1977).

Check Yourself: Domains

Classify the following objectives into the appropriate domain: C = cognitive, A = affective, M = motor skill, or I = interpersonal skills. (Complete and then check your answers below.)

_____ **1.** Given the necessary supplies, the student nurse will administer an injection following the procedures listed on page 66 of the textbook.

_____ **2.** The sales trainee will demonstrate how to sell a hot tub. The trainee will role-play with another member of the class and include an opening, middle, and closing of the sale as demonstrated by the instructor.

_____ **3.** The fourth grader will list from memory the names of the Great Lakes.

_____ **4.** Home-owners will recycle at least 50 percent of the trash generated in their household.

_____ **5.** The manager will discipline employees who are late to work in a firm and consistent manner.

_____ **6.** The high school algebra student will choose to prepare a report on a mathematician such as George Boole. The report will describe the individual's contribution to the study of mathematics.

_____ **7.** The elementary teacher will be able to plan a unit of instruction following the ASSURE model.

_____ **8.** The diabetic adult will follow the dietary restrictions suggested by the doctor.

_____ **9.** The pitcher for the girl's softball team should be able to throw a softball through the middle of an automobile tire from 46 feet with 80 percent accuracy.

_____ **10.** The college speech student will name the seven parts of a speech as presented in the textbook.

Answers:

1. Motor	2. Interpersonal	3. Cognitive	4. Affective	5. Interpersonal
6. Affective	7. Cognitive	8. Affective	9. Motor	10. Cognitive

SELECT MEDIA AND MATERIALS

A systematic plan for using media certainly demands that the media be selected systematically in the first place. The selection process will be presented here in two stages: (1) choosing an appropriate media format and (2) selecting, modifying, or designing specific materials within that format.

Choosing a Media Format

Choosing a media format can be a very complex task considering the

Robert F. Mager

Ralph Tyler, a professor at Ohio State University, is generally considered to be the father of performance objectives as we know them today. Tyler's original interest was in test-item construction. His main contribution was to point out the importance of constructing test items based on behaviorally stated objectives that could be determined by analyzing the curriculum content.[a]

However, it was those in the programmed instruction movement, particularly Robert Mager, who popularized the use of objectives by educators. Mager was a research scientist at Fort Bliss, Texas, working on a study to compare an experimental version of a course with an ongoing army course. He drafted the objectives for the course and insisted that they be signed by the proper authorities before instruction began. Later, while employed by Varian Associates in Palo Alto, California, he was involved in designing a one-day session on programmed instruction for school administrators. In order to teach them to discriminate between properly written and poorly written programmed instruction, Mager decided to write a branching program with a variety of instructional errors:

> But what topic to write on? I couldn't think of one. I stared at the typewriter, counted the leaves on the tree outside the window, and checked my fingernails. Nothing. Finally, while thinking about the nature of the target population (audience), I had a flash! I'll fix you, I said to myself. I'll write about a topic that will get you so emotionally aroused that you won't be able to see programming from the subject matter. And I began to type out a dogmatic (error-filled) branching program called "How to Write Objectives." In addition to such pedagogical niceties as branching the reader to pages that didn't exist, I berated them on the wrong answer pages with comments such as "How can you sit there and SAY a thing like that. You're lying and you know it." And "Now look here! I don't want to have any trouble with you. So read the little gem: 'How do YOU know? Have you ever tried seriously to specify exact objectives for an academic course? Or are you upset simply because what is being suggested sounds like work?' "[b]

Mager's initial program on writing objectives was duplicated, and it generated a great deal of discussion and provided practice in spotting good and bad characteristics in an instructional program. In Mager's words, "The day was a huge success."[c]

Later Mager learned that at least two professors at local colleges were using his error-laden practice program as a text in their education courses, so he modified the original program and published *Preparing Objectives for Programmed Instruction* in 1961.[d] He and others quickly realized that his objectives could be applied to much more than just programmed learning, so the following year the book was rereleased with the title *Preparing Instructional Objectives.*[e] The book is a classic in the field of education; now in its revised second edition, it has sold over two million copies. As Mager says, "If you're not sure where you're going, you're liable to end up someplace else—and not even know it."

---

[a] Ralph Tyler, "The Construction of Examinations in Botany and Zoology," *Service Studies in Higher Education,* Bureau of Educational Research Monograph, no. 15 (Columbus: Ohio State University, 1932).

[b] Robert F. Mager, "Why I Wrote . . ." *NSPI Journal* (October 1976):4.

[c] Mager, "Why I Wrote":4.

[d] Robert F. Mager, *Preparing Objectives for Programmed Instruction* (Palo Alto, CA: Fearon, 1961).

[e] See references at end of this chapter.

vast array of media available, the variety of learners, and the many objectives to be pursued. Over the years many different formulas have been proposed for simplifying the task. They are referred to as media selection models, and they usually take the form of flowcharts or checklists.

Within most media selection models the instructional situation or setting (e.g., large-group, small-group, or self-instruction), learner variables (e.g., reader, nonreader, or auditory preference), and the nature of the objective (e.g., cognitive, affective, motor skill, or interpersonal) must be considered against the presentational capabilities of each of the media formats (e.g., presenting still visuals, motion visuals, printed words, or spoken words). Some models also take into consideration the capability of each format to give feedback to the learner.

The limitation of such media selection models is their emphasis on simplicity. Reducing the process to a short checklist may lead one to ignore some possibly important considerations.

Our approach in this book is to give you the tools to construct your own schema for selecting appropriate media formats. We accept the desirability of comparing the demands of the setting, learner characteristics, and objectives against the attributes of the various media formats. But only you can decide how to weight these considerations: what options you have in terms of setting, which learner characteristics are most critical, and what elements of your objectives are most important in your own situation. You will need to balance simplicity and comprehensiveness in any schema you decide to employ.

Obtaining Specific Materials

Having decided what media format suits your immediate instructional objective, you face the problem of finding specific materials to convey the lesson. This is certainly one of the most important problems that instructors face, given the research finding that on the average 90 to 95 percent of instructional class time is spent on activities based on the use of instructional materials.[11]

Obtaining appropriate materials will generally involve one of three alternatives: (1) selecting available materials, (2) modifying existing materials, or (3) designing new materials. Obviously, if materials are already available that will allow your students to meet your objectives, these materials should be used to save both time and money. When the media and materials available do not match your objectives or are not suitable for your audience, an alternate approach is to modify the materials. If this is not feasible, the final alternative is to design your own materials. Even though this is a more expensive and time-consuming process, it does allow you to prepare materials to serve your audience precisely and meet your objectives.

Selecting Available Materials

The majority of instructional materials used by teachers and trainers are "off the shelf," that is, ready-made and available from school, district, or company collections or other easily accessible sources. How do you go about making an appropriate choice from available materials?

Survey of Sources. Your first step might be to survey some of the published media reference guides to get a general idea of what is available. Unfortunately, no single comprehensive guide exists to all audiovisual materials available in all media formats in all subjects; you may have to consult several sources.

One of the more comprehensive sources is a set of indexes published

Figure 2.5
"A–V Online" compact disc. The complete NICEM indexes are on a single compact disc.

by NICEM (National Information Center for Educational Media). The NICEM indexes are arranged according to media format, such as slides, filmstrips, overhead transparencies, and 16mm films. In addition, there are several indexes devoted to specific topics, cutting across multiple media formats, such as environmental studies, health and safety, psychology, and vocational/technical education. These indexes do not include evaluations. A CD-ROM version of these indexes is available under the title "A-V Online" (Figure 2.5).

There also is a separate databank for information and materials on special education: NICSEM (National Information Center for Special Education Materials). NICSEM publications provide information on the content of materials and their applicability to specific handicapping conditions. This information is intended to help in preparing individualized education plans for handicapped learners. (See Appendix A for details about NICEM and NICSEM.)

If you are working in elementary or secondary education, you might consult several additional sources that cover a broad range of media

---

[11] P. Kenneth Komoski, "How Can the Evaluation of Instructional Materials Help Improve Classroom Instruction Received by Handicapped Learners?" in *Educating All Handicapped Children*, ed. R. Heinich (Englewood Cliffs, NJ: Educational Technology Publications, 1979), pp. 189–91.

CLOSE-UP

Consumer Testing of Educational Products

P. Kenneth Komoski

As the Consumers Union provides objective evaluative information about household products to general consumers, the Educational Products Information Exchange (EPIE) Institute provides educational hardware and software evaluations to the education and training communities.

The EPIE Institute is a nonprofit agency that has been in operation since 1967. Its purpose is to "gather and disseminate descriptive and analytical information—along with empirical information on performance and effects on learners—about instructional materials, equipment, and systems." P. Kenneth Komoski has been executive director of EPIE since its founding.

EPIE accepts no advertising or commercial sponsorship of any kind. All income is derived from subscriptions, contract services from state and local education agencies, and grants. Its newsletter *EPIEgram* covers a wide range of topics from textbooks to computer technology and is published nine times a year. It is published in affiliation with Sterling Harbor Press. EPIE also offers the following evaluation services of use to teachers and school systems.

The Education Software Selector (*TESS*) is a comprehensive database of educational software at every level from preschool to college. Over the years *TESS* has been available in a variety of formats.

Eight major integrated instruction systems (or integrated learning systems) are evaluated in *The EPIE Report on Computer-Based Integrated Systems*. The report draws on extensive research by experts in software evaluation and curriculum.

EPIE's Curriculum Analysis Services for Education (CASE) provides a school with a means of analyzing, designing, and aligning its stated curriculum outcomes, its textbooks, and other instructional resources. A school's testing program can be compared to state and national tests and curriculum priorities. The service provides grade-by-grade printed reports that are useful for understanding and improving a school's curriculum and instructional program.

To learn more about the institute and its services, contact EPIE Institute, 103-3 W. Montauk Highway, Hampton Bays, NY 11946.

---

formats such as *Core Media Collection for Elementary Schools* and *Core Media Collection for Secondary Schools*. These books recommend specific audiovisual titles as core materials for elementary and secondary school library collections.

For general and adult audiences, a major reference source is the *Reference List of Audiovisual Materials Produced by the United States Government*. It describes all the training and educational materials produced by the armed forces and other government agencies that are available for general purchase. (See Appendix A for further details on all the reference sources discussed here.)

Beyond the sources just described, there are also more specialized guides and indexes that are limited to specific media formats or specific subjects. These are too many and too diverse to list here, but some are mentioned in the individual chapters dealing with different media formats, and others are gathered under the heading of "Specialized Information Sources" in Appendix A. Also, see Appendix B for sources of free and inexpensive materials.

Selection Criteria.   The actual decision about whether to use a particular piece of instructional mate-

rial depends on several factors. Among the major questions to ask are the following:

❏ Do the objectives of the material match my own?

❏ Do my learners have the required entry capabilities (reading ability and vocabulary level are often important)?

❏ Is the information accurate and up to date?

❏ Is the presentation likely to arouse and maintain interest?

❏ Does it promote the active involvement of learners?

❏ Is the technical quality acceptable?

❏ Has the producer provided evidence of effectiveness, such as results of field tests?

❏ Is it free from objectionable bias?

Over the years scholars have debated over what criteria should be applied in selecting materials. Studies have been conducted to try to quantify and validate various criteria. The net result is an understanding that different criteria are suitable for different situations. For example, a remedial reading teacher might decide to use a particular filmstrip primarily because its vocabulary level is just right, regardless of any other qualities. On the other hand, an elementary school teacher with a class that is very diverse ethnically might sort through materials to find those with a special sensitivity to racial and ethnic issues.

Other selection criteria vary with different media formats. Film and video materials, for example, raise the issue of the pace of presentation, whereas this would not be relevant for overhead transparencies. In examining computer-assisted instruction courseware, one would look for relevant practice and remedial feedback, but these would not be expected in a filmstrip. To account for these differences this book provides a separate "Appraisal Checklist" for each media format. You will notice that certain criteria appear consistently in each checklist (they are all listed after the table of contents). These are the criteria that we feel have the securest basis in research and real-life experience. The "Appraisal Checklists" have been provided to give you a systematic procedure for judging the qualities of specific materials. But it's up to you to decide which criteria are most important to you in your own instructional setting.

The Instructor's Personal File.

Every instructor should develop a file of media references and appraisals for personal use. The notes on these cards need not be extremely detailed. You are primarily interested in recording the instructional strengths and weaknesses of a specific film, software program, workbook, or other media you have used. Figure 2.6 illustrates a format that is relatively simple and will fit on a 4-by-6-inch card. Under "synopsis," you can note the basic content of the item. Under "utilization pointers and problems," you might note information about vocabulary used in the material, lack or inclusion of opportunities for student response, timeliness of the content, inclusion of sensitive topics, and so on.

Modifying Available Materials

If you cannot locate entirely suitable materials and media off the shelf, you might be able to modify what is available. This can be both challenging and creative. In terms of time and cost, it is a more efficient procedure than designing your own materials, although the type and extent of necessary modification will, of course, vary.

Perhaps the only visual available showing a piece of equipment being used in a junior high woodworking class is from a repair manual and contains too much detail and complex terminology. A possible solution to the problem would be to use the picture but modify the caption and simplify or omit some of the labels.

In a business or industry orientation program for new employees, you may be using a slide set developed by corporate headquarters. Where possible and appropriate, you can replace existing slides with slides showing local facilities and local personnel.

Or perhaps there is just one film available that shows a needed visual sequence, but the audio portion of the film is inappropriate because it is at too high or too low a conceptual level or discusses inappropriate points. In such a case, a simple solution would be to show the film with the sound turned off and provide the narration yourself. Another modification technique, which many instructors overlook, is to show just a portion of a film, stop the projector, discuss what has been presented, then continue with another short segment followed by additional discussion (see Figure 2.7). A similar approach may be used for sound filmstrips with audiotape. You can rerecord the narration and use the appropriate vocabulary level for your audience—and even change the emphasis of the visual material. If a transcript of the original narration is available, you probably will want to refer to it as you compose your own narration.

Title: _____ Format: _____

Length: _____ Source: _____ Technical data: _____

Synopsis:

Utilization pointers and problems:

Figure 2.6
File cards in your personal media file provide an informal record of the usefulness of particular materials.

Figure 2.7
The most basic way of modifying material such as a film or video program is to show segments of the program interspersed with group discussion.

Modification also can be made in the audio portion of foreign language materials (or English language materials used in a bilingual classroom). Narrations can be changed from one language to another or from a more advanced rendition of a foreign language to a simpler one.

Videocassette recorders now provide teachers with the opportunity to modify television programs that previously were available only as shown on the air. With video playback units available in most schools, many producers now distribute programs having educational potential in videotape format. Programs may also be recorded off the air for replay on playback units.[12] Procedures and practices for modification of videotape are much the same as for film. Videocassette recorders also, of course, give the teacher much more flexibility in using television programs for instructional purposes. Programs can be shown at whatever time best suits the instructional situation and to whatever student

group or groups can profit most from viewing them.

One frequently modified media format is a set of slides with an audiotape. If the visuals are appropriate but the language is not, it is possible to change the language. It is also possible to change the emphasis of the narration. For example, an original audiotape might emphasize oceans as part of an ecosystem, whereas the teacher may want to use the slides to show various types of fish found in oceans. By rewriting the narration, the teacher could adapt the material to his or her purpose while using the same slides. Redoing the tape can also change the level of the presentation. A slide-tape presentation produced to introduce a new product could have three different audiotapes. One tape could be directed toward the customer, another could be prepared for the sales staff, and the third for the service personnel.

Instructional games can be readily modified to meet particular instructional needs. It is possible to use a given game format and change the rules of play in order to increase or decrease the level of sophistication. Many instructional games require the players to answer ques-

tions. It is relatively easy for the teacher to prepare a new set of questions at a different level of difficulty or even on a new topic.

If you try out modified materials while they are still in more or less rough form, you can then make further modifications in response to student reaction until your materials meet your exact needs.

A word of caution about modifying commercially produced materials (and, indeed, about using commercial products in general): be sure your handling and use of such materials does not violate copyright laws and restrictions. If in doubt, check with your school administrator or legal advisor. (Copyright laws and guidelines are discussed in Appendix C.)

Designing New Materials

It is easier and less costly to use available materials, with or without modification, than to start from scratch. There is seldom justification for reinventing the wheel. However, there may be times when your only recourse is to design your own materials. As is the case with selecting from available materials, certain basic considerations must be taken

---

[12] Broadcast materials vary in their recording restrictions. See Appendix C for general guidelines; consult a media specialist regarding specific programs.

into account when designing new materials:

- *Objectives.* What do you want your students to learn?
- *Audience.* What are the characteristics of your learners? Do they have the prerequisite knowledge and skills to use or learn from the materials?
- *Cost.* Is sufficient money available in your budget to meet the cost of supplies (film, audiotapes, etc.) you will need to prepare the materials?
- *Technical expertise.* Do you have the necessary expertise to design and produce the kind of materials you wish to use? If not, will the necessary technical assistance be available to you? Try to keep your design within the range of your own capabilities. Don't waste time and money trying to produce slick professional materials when simple inexpensive products will get the job done.
- *Equipment.* Do you have available the necessary equipment to produce or use the materials you intend to design?
- *Facilities.* If your design calls for use of special facilities for preparation or use of your materials, are such facilities available?

- *Time.* Can you afford to spend whatever time may be necessary to design and produce the kind of materials you have in mind?

UTILIZE MEDIA AND MATERIALS

The next step in the ASSURE model is the one that all the other steps lead up to and away from: the presentation itself. To get maximum learning impact from your presentation, you must follow certain procedures which have been identified in formal research stretching back to U.S. military training in World War II and the practical experience of several generations of teachers: preview the materials, practice the presentation, prepare the environment, prepare the audience, and present.

Preview the Materials

No instructional materials should be used blind. During the selection process you should have determined that the materials are appropriate for your audience and objectives. Published reviews, reports of field tests, distributors' blurbs, and colleagues' appraisals all add evidence. However, the prudent instructor will insist on previewing the materials (Figure 2.8). Only a detailed knowl-

edge of the contents can enable you to wrap the lesson around the audiovisual material properly.

For example, an industrial trainer ordered a videotape on fraction-to-decimal conversions. The information describing the videotape indicated that the content was exactly what many of the company employees needed. The videotape arrived ten days before the presentation, but the trainer did not take time to preview it. When the videotape was shown, it met with giggles and laughs; although the content was appropriate, the videotape was addressed to an elementary school audience. The adults were understandably distracted by the level of the narration and the examples used.

In other cases, sensitive content may need to be eliminated or at least discussed prior to showing the materials to prevent student embarrassment or upset. In one case, an elementary teacher and her young students were horrified to find that an unpreviewed and ostensibly unobjectionable film on Canada's fur seals contained a sequence showing baby seals being cold-bloodedly clubbed to death by hunters.

Practice the Presentation

After previewing the materials, you should practice your portion of the presentation (Figure 2.9). It is advisable to go through the presentation at least once well in advance and then to review your notes immediately before the presentation. However, do not overpractice, or the presentation will sound canned.

Some presenters prefer to practice before a mirror; others like to have a colleague or friend provide feedback. Media can be used to provide a replay of your practice. An audiotape recording will let you hear what you said and how you said it. If you are concerned about how you look, how you handle manipulable objects, or whether or not you have any distracting mannerisms, you should use a video recording. The

Figure 2.8
Preview the material.

camera and recorder can be set up in the rear of the room to capture your presentation.

The newness of the material, the importance of the presentation, and the amount of time available will determine how many times you practice and the type of "mirror" you use—a real mirror, a friend, an audiotape recorder, or a videotape recorder. The importance of practice cannot be overstated. Don't just walk through it in your mind; actually stand up and perform as you will in front of your group.

Prepare the Environment

Wherever the presentation is to take place—classroom, auditorium, meeting room, or whatever—the facilities will have to be put in order. Certain factors are taken for granted for any instructional situation—comfortable seating, adequate ventilation, climate control, suitable lighting, and the like. Many media require a darkened room, a convenient power supply, and access to light switches. At the least the instructor should check that the equipment is in working

order and should arrange the facilities so that all the audience can see and hear properly (see Figure 2.10). More specific information on audiovisual set-ups can be found in Chapter 11.

Prepare the Audience

Research on learning tells us very clearly that what is learned from a presentation depends highly on how the learners are prepared for the presentation. In everyday life we notice that entertainers are obsessed

Figure 2.9
Practice the presentation.

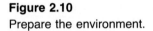

Figure 2.10
Prepare the environment.

Figure 2.11
Prepare the audience.

Figure 2.12
Present the material.

with having the audience properly warmed up. Preparing the audience (Figure 2.11) is just as important when you are giving a presentation with media.

A proper warm-up, from an instructional point of view, generally consists of an introduction giving a broad overview of the content of the presentation, a rationale telling how it relates to the topic being studied, a motivating statement which creates a need to know by telling how the learner will profit from paying attention, and cues directing attention to specific aspects of the presentation. Several of these functions—directing attention, arousing motivation, providing a rationale—may be served simply by informing the viewers of your specific objectives.

In certain cases, other steps will be called for. For example, unfamiliar vocabulary may need to be introduced, or special visual effects, such as time-lapse photography, may need explanation. Other preparation steps relevant to particular media will be discussed in later chapters.

Present the Material

This is what you've been preparing for, so you will want to make the most of it. Our term for this is *showmanship*. Just as an actor or actress must control the attention of an audience, so must an instructor be able to direct attention in the classroom (Figure 2.12). The later chapters on individual media describe showmanship techniques relevant to each specific media format. General showmanship tips for all types of presentations are given on pages 54–56.

REQUIRE LEARNER PARTICIPATION

The fifth step in the ASSURE model is to provide opportunities for learners to practice the capability being taught. Educators have long realized that active participation in the learning process enhances learning.

In the early 1900s John Dewey urged reorganization of the curriculum and instruction to make student participation a central part of the process. Later, behavioral psychologists such as B. F. Skinner demonstrated that instruction providing for constant reinforcement of desired behaviors is more effective than instruction in which responses are not reinforced.

More recently, cognitive theories of learning, which focus on internal mental processes, have also supported the principle that effective learning demands active manipulation of information by learners. Gagne has concluded that there are several necessary conditions for effective learning of each type of objective; the one condition that pertains to all objectives is practice of the desired skill.[13]

The implication for designers and instructors is clear. The most effective learning situations are those that require learners to perform activities that build toward the objective. The form of the participation may include repetitive drill of new spelling or vocabulary words, solving math problems on a worksheet, rehearsal of a basketball play, or creating an original product such as a term paper. Responses may be *overt* (outwardly observable) or *covert* (internal, not observable). An example of an overt performance is manipulating task cards illustrating the stages of mitosis. A covert performance is silent repetition of phrases heard on a French language tape.

Some media formats lend themselves to participation more than others, at least on the surface. For example, student response to projected still pictures is easier to manage than response to a motion picture. Learners can read or elaborate on captions in filmstrips, discuss what is on the screen, or refer to other materials while the image is

held on the screen. (Substitution of sound filmstrips for silent ones tends to weaken this advantage.) However, learners can also participate in and respond to the showing of a film. For example, May and Lumsdaine demonstrated that overt responses (vocalized verbal responses) during a film improved learning. The same authors cited research demonstrating that psychomotor skills are learned better if practiced while the skills are being performed in a film.[14] Overt written responses during the showing of a film (or any other fixed-pace medium) have been shown to facilitate learning, unless the responses are so involved that students are prevented from watching the film.

Immediate confirmation of a correct response is particularly important when working with students of lower-than-average abilities (see Figure 2.13). For such students, evidence of immediate success can be a strong motivating force for further learning.

Discussions, short quizzes, and application exercises can provide opportunities for response and reinforcement during instruction. Follow-up activities can provide further opportunities. Teacher guides and manuals written to accompany instructional materials often suggest techniques and activities for eliciting and reinforcing student response.

Research on the internationally renowned television series "Sesame Street" and "Electric Company" demonstrates impressively the importance of following up a media presentation with practice activities. Research on "Sesame Street" showed that frequent viewers not only learned the specific skills presented but also had higher scores on a test of verbal IQ and more positive attitudes about school. Johnston pointed out, though, that "parental encouragement and supplementary

---

[13] Robert M. Gagne, *The Conditions of Learning,* 4th ed. (New York: Holt, Rinehart and Winston, 1985).

[14] Mark A. May and A. A. Lumsdaine, *Learning from Films* (New Haven, CT: Yale University Press, 1958).

Planning

An effective presentation begins with careful and thorough planning.

1. *Analyze your audience.* What are their needs, values, backgrounds, knowledge levels, and misconceptions?

2. *Specify your objectives.* What do you hope to accomplish? How much time do you have to present? Limit your objectives and content to the time available.

3. *Specify benefits and rationale for the audience.* Why is the presentation important for the audience? If you can not answer this question, perhaps you should not give the presentation.

4. *Identify the key points to cover.* Brainstorm the main ideas. Put them on note cards or stick-on notes. Most presentations will have from five to nine main points.

5. *Identify the subpoints and supporting details.* Again use note cards or stick-on notes. Try to limit yourself to 5 to 9 subpoints for each main point.

6. *Organize the entire presentation into a logical and sequential order.* One organizing strategy is this:

Preview/Overview	—Tell them what you are going to tell them.
Present	—Tell them.
Review	—Tell them what you told them.

Practice

1. Use key word notes, not a script. Print key words on index cards. Never read from a script; written language is different from spoken language.

2. Mentally run through the presentation to review each idea in sequence.

3. Do a stand-up rehearsal of your presentation. Try to practice in the room where you will be presenting or one similar to it.

4. Give a simulated presentation, idea for idea (not word for word) using all visual aids and props.

5. Practice answers to questions you anticipate from the audience.

6. Videotape (or audiotape) yourself or have a colleague sit in on your rehearsal and give you feedback.

Placement of Equipment and Materials

1. Check your equipment setup in advance of your presentation. Change the arrangement, if necessary, to meet your needs. When the equipment is in place, make sure everything operates properly.

2. For films, slides, and video projection, place the screen front and center. (See Figure A).

3. Place the overhead projector screen or flip chart at a 45-degree angle and near the corner of the room. Place overhead screen to your right if you are right-handed. Place flipchart to your left if you are right-handed. Each should be reversed if you are left-handed. (See Figure B.)

4. Position objects being studied in the front and center. Remove them when they are no longer being studied. (See Figure C.)

Anxiety

1. Nervousness and excitement are normal before and during a presentation. Some anxiety and concern is important for an enthusiastic and dynamic presentation.

2. Proper planning and preparation should reduce your anxiety.

3. Harness your nervous energy and use it positively with body movement, supporting gestures, and projecting your voice.

4. Breathe slowly and deeply. Your cardiovascular system will slow and ease the symptoms of anxiety.

Delivery Stance

1. Stand up when presenting. When you stand, you and your message command more attention. (See Figure D.)

2. Stand facing the audience. Place your feet 10 to 12 inches apart and distribute your weight equally on both feet. Your knees should be unlocked, hands out of pockets with arms at your side. Facing the audience full-front is the strongest position. Three-quarters full-front is weaker; profile is weaker yet. Weakest is the one-quarter view, with the back nearly turned toward the audience. The use of chalkboards or charts will push you toward the weak position unless you consciously avoid it. (See Figures E, F, G and H.)

3. Stand to one side of lectern (if you must use one). Stepping to the side or in front of it places you on more personal terms with the audience. It allows you to be seen and to be more natural.

4. Move while you speak. Speakers who stand in one spot and never gesture experience tension. Move and gesture, but don't overdo it. (See Figure I.)

Voice

1. Use a natural, conversational style. Relate to your audience in a direct and personal manner.

Figure A
In this example the screen, because of its placement in the center, has dominance over the presenter.

Figure B
Here the presenter, situated at the front center, has more dominant placement.

Figure C
Here the presenter is in a moderately strong location, but the display table, at the front center, takes precedence.

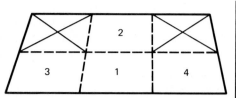

Figure D
The front of the classroom, the "stage," can be divided into six sections. The front three areas are generally stronger than the back, and the center is stronger than either side. The left side (as seen by the audience) is stronger than the right.

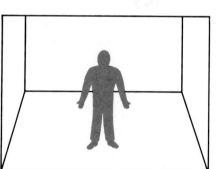

Figure E
The full-front body position is the strongest one.

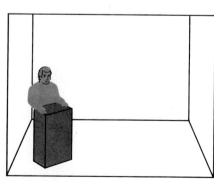

Figure F
Three-quarters full front is the second strongest position.

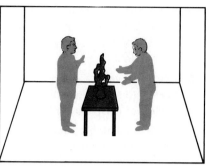

Figure G
Standing in profile, these figures are in a rather weak body position.

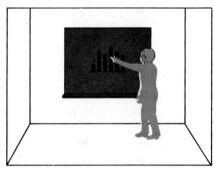

Figure H
A one-quarter view is the weakest body position.

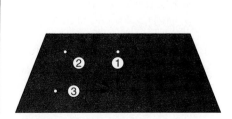

Figure I
The three stage movements shown here give the greatest emphasis to the presenter (in the order indicated by the numbers).

2. Don't read your presentation. Don't read from your overheads or handouts. If part of your presentation is just information transfer, give the audience a copy and let them read it.

3. Use vocal variety. A monotone is usually caused by anxiety (rehearsal should help this). Relax with upper and lower body movements.

4. Use a comfortable pace. When you are anxious, your rate of speaking usually increases. Relax and speak in a conversational tone.

5. Speak up so you can be heard in the back of your audience. If you speak up, your rate will slow down—solving two problems! Ask people in back row if your volume is appropriate.

6. A pause (silence) after a key point is an excellent way to emphasize it. The more important the idea, the more important it is for you to pause and let the words sink in before going on to the next idea.

Eye Contact

1. Don't speak until you have established eye contact with your audience. Eye contact will make your presentation similar to a one-on-one conversation.

2. An excellent way to keep your audience's attention is to look eye-to-eye at each person for at least three seconds. Don't quickly scan the audience or look at the back wall, screen, or notes for long periods of time.

3. Maintain eye contact with your audience. If you must write something on a flip chart, overhead, or chalkboard, stop talking while you write.

Gestures

1. Use natural gestures. Learn to gesture in front of an audience exactly as you would if you were having an animated conversation with a friend.

2. Don't put your hands in your pockets. Don't clasp your hands behind your back. Don't wring your hands nervously. Don't play with a pen or other object.

Humor

1. Use humor only if you are comfortable with it.

2. Use humor throughout the presentation, not necessarily just at the beginning.

3. Humor is a double-edged sword and can be dangerous. Make fun of yourself, not your audience. Do not tell sexist or ethnic jokes.

Visuals

1. Help to attract and hold audience's interest. People like to see key words, diagrams, and drawings.

2. Reinforce and clarify verbal concepts. A picture *is* worth a 1,000 words!

3. Make key points memorable and help the listener remember your message. Most people remember visuals longer than they remember words and numbers.

4. Visuals lose their effectiveness if overused. A guideline is to use about one visual per minute.

5. In designing visuals:

   Use headlines only

   Eliminate unnecessary words

   Write large so words can be read from the back row

   Use drawings and diagrams whenever possible

   Limit to 36 words per visual (6 lines of 6 words each)

6. After using visuals, redirect audience's attention back to you:

   Shut off overhead projector when there is a lengthy explanation and there is no need for the audience to see the transparency. Don't turn the machine off and on so frequently that it becomes distracting (thirty seconds is a guideline).

   Turn a flip-chart page to a blank one when you are finished referring to it. If the flip-chart pages have been prepared in advance, leave blank pages between each prepared sheet so the next prepared page will not show through.

   Erase any writing on the chalkboard or whiteboard when it is no longer needed.

   Break up slide presentations by inserting a black or translucent slide at points where an explanation is needed or where questions will be asked or answered.

   Show or demonstrate an object by revealing it when needed and covering it when no longer in use. Otherwise your audience will look at the object and be distracted from your presentation. Avoid passing an object around the audience. Instead, walk around the audience and show the object to everyone briefly and make it available at the end of the presentation.

Murphy's Law

1. Disasters happen. Be prepared for them. Some can be planned for, some can't.

2. Disasters become catastrophic only to the degree that you react to them. If you fall apart, it is a disaster. If you take it in stride, it may be just a minor problem.

3. Don't apologize for mistakes or what you didn't do or should have done. If you don't draw attention to them, many people won't even notice them.

Evaluation

1. Immediately following your presentation, evaluate it.

2. Write down any ideas for revisions that would improve it.

Figure 2.13
Audiovisual media can provide both
practice and feedback.

materials were essential to achieving
the effects observed."[15] In the case
of "Electric Company," children with
low reading ability who watched the
programs in school under teacher
supervision showed significant reading improvement. Johnston concluded that "learning definitely did
occur when viewing was insured,
and when teachers supplied additional learning materials and helped
the children to rehearse the material
presented on television."

EVALUATE AND REVISE

The final component of our ASSURE
model for effective learning is evaluation. The most frequently used type
of evaluation is the paper-and-pencil
test; the most frequently claimed
purpose of evaluation is to measure
student achievement. There are,
however, many purposes of evaluation. Three that we will discuss here
are evaluation of learner achievement, evaluation of media and
methods, and evaluation of the instructional process.

Evaluation of Learner Achievement

The ultimate question in the instructional process is whether or not
the students have learned what they

15 Jerome Johnston, *Electronic Learning:
    From Audiotape to Videodisc* (Hillsdale,
    NJ: Lawrence Erlbaum, 1987).

were supposed to learn. Can they
display the capabilities specified in
the original statement of objectives?
The first step in answering this
question was taken back near the
beginning of the ASSURE process,
when you formulated your objectives, including in that statement of
objectives a criterion of acceptable
performance. You now want to assess whether the learner's skill
meets that criterion.

The method of evaluating
achievement depends on the nature
of the objective. Some objectives call
for relatively simple cognitive skills;
for example, recalling Ohm's law,
distinguishing adjectives from ad-
verbs, describing a company's absence policy, or summarizing the
principles of the Declaration of Independence. Objectives such as these
lend themselves to conventional
written tests or oral examinations.
Other objectives may call for
process-type behaviors (for example,
conducting an orchestra, performing
a forward roll on a balance beam,
operating a metal lathe, or solving
quadratic equations), the creation of
products (a sculpture, a written
composition, a window display, or an
account ledger), or exhibiting attitudes (tolerating divergent political
opinions, appreciating expressionist
painting, observing safety procedures while on the assembly line, or
contributing money to community
charities).

The evaluation procedures should
correspond to the objectives stated
earlier in the ASSURE model. For
example, assume the objective is
"Given a diagram of the human tra-
chea, the student nurse will explain
a bronchocele, describing cause and
treatment." A possible test item
would be "What is a bronchocele?
Describe the cause and treatment in
your answer."

In broadcaster training the objective might be "Given the pertinent
information, facts, and figures, the
student will write a twenty-second
and a thirty-second broadcast news
story using correct broadcast style."
The evaluation could be "Using the
information provided, compose a
twenty-second radio news story using the correct broadcast style."

For military training an objective
could be "With the aid of a topographic map, the officer will call for
field artillery fire using the four essential items of information in prescribed military sequence." The written test could ask "How would you
call for artillery fire upon point X
on the accompanying topographic
map?"

Capabilities of the process, product, or attitude type could be assessed to some extent by means of
written or oral tests. But test results
would be indirect and weak evidence
of how well the learner has mastered the objectives. More direct and
stronger evidence would be provided

Figure 2.14
A performance-type skill should be judged by observation.

Performance Checklist: Driving Skills

Name_____ Class_____

Check yes or no with an X in the appropriate column.

Did the student	**Yes**	**No**
1. Fasten seat belt before starting car?	_____	_____
2. Use the nine o'clock and three o'clock hand position on steering wheel?	_____	_____
3. Drive with the flow of traffic yet stay within the speed limit?	_____	_____
4. Come to full and complete stops at stop signs?	_____	_____
5. Keep at least a two-second interval behind the vehicle ahead?	_____	_____
6. Stay in the proper driving lane—not cross center line?	_____	_____
7. Obey all traffic signs and signals?	_____	_____
8. Negotiate all turns properly (according to driving manual)?	_____	_____
9. Avoid excessive conversation with passengers?	_____	_____
10. Display courtesy to other drivers?	_____	_____

Instructor's name _____ Date _____

by observing the behavior in action. This implies setting up a situation in which the learner can demonstrate the new skill and the instructor can observe and judge it (see Figure 2.14).

In the case of process skills, a performance checklist can be an effective, objective way of recording your observations, as shown with the checklist for driving skills. Other types of activities that can be properly evaluated through performance checklists are sales techniques, telephone-answering skills, and face-to-face customer relations. During the instructional process these types of activities may need to be evaluated in a simulated situation, with other learners, or with the instructor role playing the customer or client.

Attitudes are admittedly difficult to evaluate. For some attitudinal objectives, long-term observation may be required to determine if the goal has really been attained. In day-to-day instruction we usually have to rely on what we can observe here and now, however limited that may be. A commonly used technique for

Attitude Scale: Biology

Each of the statements below expresses a feeling toward biology. Please rate each statement on the extent to which you agree. For each, you may (A) strongly agree, (B) agree, (C) be undecided, (D) disagree, or (E) strongly disagree.

A	B	C	D	E
Strongly Agree	Agree	Undecided	Disagree	Strongly Disagree

_____ 1. Biology is very interesting to me.

_____ 2. I don't like biology, and it scares me to have to take it.

_____ 3. I am always under a terrible strain in a biology class.

_____ 4. Biology is fascinating and fun.

_____ 5. Learning biology makes me feel secure, and at the same time it is stimulating.

_____ 6. Biology makes me feel uncomfortable, restless, irritable, and impatient.

_____ 7. In general, I have a good feeling toward biology.

_____ 8. When I hear the word *biology,* I have a feeling of dislike.

_____ 9. I approach biology with a feeling of hesitation.

_____ 10. I really like biology.

_____ 11. I have always enjoyed studying biology in school.

_____ 12. It makes me nervous to even think about doing a biology experiment.

_____ 13. I feel at ease in biology and like it very much.

_____ 14. I feel a definite positive response to biology; it's enjoyable.

Product Rating Checklist: Welding

Name_____ Date_____

Rate the welded product by checking the appropriate boxes. Add comments if you wish.

Base metal(s)_____ Filler metal(s)_____

Profile	Excellent	Very Good	Good	Fair	Poor	Workmanship	Excellent	Very Good	Good	Fair	Poor
Convexity	❑	❑	❑	❑	❑	Uniform appearance	❑	❑	❑	❑	❑
(¹⁄₃₂-inch maximum)						Arc strikes	❑	❑	❑	❑	❑
Fusion on toe	❑	❑	❑	❑	❑	Bead width	❑	❑	❑	❑	❑
Overlap	❑	❑	❑	❑	❑	Bead start	❑	❑	❑	❑	❑
Amount of fill	❑	❑	❑	❑	❑	Bead tie-in	❑	❑	❑	❑	❑
						Bead termination	❑	❑	❑	❑	❑
Overall Evaluation:						Penetration	❑	❑	❑	❑	❑
						Amount of spatter	❑	❑	❑	❑	❑

Evaluator Comments:

---

making attitudes more visible is the attitude scale, an example of which is shown regarding biology. A number of other suggestions for attitude measurement can be found in Robert Mager's *Developing Attitude Toward Learning.*[16]

For product skills, a product rating checklist can guide your evaluation of critical subskills and make qualitative judgments more objective, as in the accompanying example regarding welding. Other types of products that lend themselves to evaluation by a rating scale include pastry from a bakery, compositions in an English course, and computer programs.

Evaluation of Media and Methods

Evaluation also includes assessment of instructional media and methods. Were your instructional materials effective? Could they be improved? Were they cost-effective in terms of student achievement? Did your presentation take more time than it was really worth? Particularly after

Figure 2.15
The ability to create a product should be evaluated by the quality of the product itself.

---

[16] See references at end of this chapter.

first use, instructional materials need to be evaluated to determine if future use, with or without modification, is warranted. The results of your evaluation should be entered on a form in your personal media file. Did the media assist the students in meeting the objectives? Were they effective in arousing student interest? Did they provide meaningful student participation?

Class discussions, individual interviews, and observation of student behavior should be used to evaluate instructional media and methods (Figure 2.16). Failure to attain objectives is, of course, a clear indication that something is wrong with the instruction. But analyzing student reaction to your instructional methods can be helpful in more subtle ways. Student-teacher discussion may indicate that your audience would have preferred independent study to your choice of group presentation. Or perhaps viewers didn't like your selection of overhead transparencies and feel they would have learned more if a film had been shown. Your students may let you know, subtly or not so subtly, that your own performance left something to be desired.

You may solicit learner input on the effectiveness of specific media such as a film or videotape. You may design your own form or use one similar to the "Module Appraisal Form" shown here.

Figure 2.16
Analysis of student reactions to lessons is an integral part of the instructional process.

Module Appraisal Form

User _____   Date_____

	Clear					Unclear	
1. The objectives of this module were	7	6	5	4	3	2	1

	Very Interesting					Dull	
2. The learning activities were	7	6	5	4	3	2	1

	Adequate					Inadequate	
3. The scope (coverage) was	7	6	5	4	3	2	1

	Difficult					Easy	
4. The module was	7	6	5	4	3	2	1

	Excellent					Poor	
5. Overall, I consider this module	7	6	5	4	3	2	1

Evaluation of the Instructional Process

Although ultimate evaluation must await completion of the instructional unit, evaluation is an ongoing process. Evaluations are made before, during, and after instruction; for example, before instruction, learner characteristics are measured to ensure that there is a fit between existing student skills and the methods and materials you intend to use. In addition, materials should be appraised prior to use. During instruction, evaluation may take the form of student practice of a desired skill, or it may consist of a short quiz or self-evaluation. Evaluation during instruction usually has a diagnostic purpose; that is, it is designed to detect and correct learning/teaching problems and difficulties in the instructional process which may interfere with attainment of objectives.

Evaluation is not the end of instruction. It is the starting point of the next and continuing cycle in our systematic ASSURE model for effective use of instructional media.

Revision

The final step of the instructional cycle is to sit back and look at the results of your evaluation data gathering. Where are there discrepancies between what you intended to happen and what did happen? Did stu-

dent achievement fall short on one or more of the objectives? How did students react to your instructional methods and media? Are you satisfied with the value of the materials you selected? If your evaluation data indicate shortcomings in any of these areas, now is the time to go back to the faulty part of the plan and revise it. The model works, but only if you constantly use it to upgrade the quality of your instruction.

REFERENCES

Print References

Media Utilization

Amend, Robert H., and Schrader, Michael A. *Media for Business.* White Plains, NY: Knowledge Industry Publications, 1991.

Bloom, Benjamin S., et al. *Taxonomy of Educational Objectives, Book 1: Cognitive Domain.* White Plains, NY: Longman, 1984.

Burbank, Lucille, and Pett, Dennis. "Designing Printed Instructional Materials." *Performance and Instruction* (October 1986): 5–9.

Cooper, Colleen R., and Anderson, William A. "How to Increase Classroom Participation." *Instructional Innovator* (January 1984):49–52.

DeBello, Thomas C. "Comparison of Eleven Major Learning Styles Models: Variables, Appropriate Populations, Validity of Instrumentation, and the Research Behind Them." *Reading,*

Writing, and Learning Disabilities (1990):203–222.

Dunn, Rita; Beaudry, Jeffrey S.; and Klavas, Angela. "Survey of Research on Learning Styles." *Educational Leadership* 46 (March 1989):50–58.

Fortune, Jim C., and Hutson, Barbara A. "Does Your Program Work? Strategies for Measuring Change." *Educational Technology* (April 1983):38–41.

Frederick, Peter J. "The Lively Lecture—8 Variations." *College Teaching* (Spring 1986):43–50.

Gagne, Robert M. *Instructional Technology: Foundations.* (Hillside, NJ: Lawrence Erlbaum, 1987.

Gronland, Norman E. *How to Write and Use Instructional Objectives.* 4th ed. New York: Macmillan, 1991.

Krathwohl, David R. *Taxonomy of Educational Objectives, Handbook 2: Affective Domain.* White Plains, NY: Longman, 1964.

Lanese, Lorena D. "Applying Principles of Learning to Adult Training Programs." *Educational Technology* (March 1983):15–17.

Mager, Robert F. *Developing Attitude Toward Learning.* 2nd ed. Belmont, CA: David S. Lake, 1984.

_____. *Goal Analysis.* 2d ed. Belmont, CA: David S. Lake, 1984.

_____. *Making Instruction Work.* Belmont, CA: David S. Lake, 1984.

_____. *Measuring Instructional Results.* 2d ed. Belmont, CA: David S. Lake, 1984.

_____. *Preparing Instructional Objectives.* Rev. 2d ed. Belmont, CA: David S. Lake, 1984.

Mager, Robert F., and Pipe, Peter. *Analyzing Performance Problems.* 2nd ed. Belmont, CA: David S. Lake, 1984.

Martinetz, Charles F. "A Checklist for Course Evaluation." *Performance and Instruction* (June–July 1986):12–19.

Moller, Leslie. "Planning Programs for Distant Learners Using the ASSURE Model." *Tech Trends* 36, no. 1 (1991):55–57.

Reiser, Robert A., and Gagne, Robert M. *Selecting Media for Instruction.* Englewood Cliffs, NJ: Educational Technology Publications, 1983.

Reynolds, A., and Anderson, R. H. *Selecting and Developing Media for Instruction.* 3d ed. New York: Van Nostrand Reinhold, 1992.

Romiszowski, A. J. *The Selection and Use of Instructional Media.* 2d ed. New York: Nichols, 1988.

Select Student Instructional Materials. 2d ed. Columbus, OH: National Center for Research in Vocational Education, 1988.

Thompson, James G., and Jorgensen, Sally. "How Interactive is Instructional Technology? Alternative Models for Looking at Interactions between Learners and Media." *Educational Technology* (February 1989):24–26.

Tremblay, Roger, and LeBlanc, Raymond. "Developing Teaching Materials for a Multidimensional Curriculum." *Canadian Modern Language Review* (October 1990):132–58.

Presentation Skills

Arredondo, Lani. *How to Present Like a Pro.* New York: McGraw-Hill, 1991.

Kenney Michael. *Presenting Yourself: A Kodak How-to Book.* New York: Wiley, 1982.

LeRoux, P. *Selling to a Group: Presentation Strategies.* New York: Harper and Row, 1984.

Mager, E. W. *Classroom Presentation Skills Workshop.* Carefree, AZ: Mager Associates, 1985.

Mandel S. *Effective Presentation Skills: A Practical Guide for Better Speaking.* Los Altos, CA: Crisp Publications, 1987.

Pett, Dennis. "Effective Presentations." *NSPI Journal* (April 1980):11–14.

Instructional Design

Briggs, Leslie J.; Gustafson, Kent L.; and Tillman, Murray H., eds. *Instructional Design: Principles and Applications.* 2d ed. Englewood Cliffs, NJ: Educational Technology Publications, 1991.

Clark, Ruth Colvin, et al. "Training Content Experts to Design Instruction." *Performance and Instruction* (September 1983):10–15.

Cranton, Patricia. *Planning Instruction for Adult Learners.* Toronto: Wall and Thompson, 1989.

Dick, Walter, and Carey, Lou. *The Systematic Design of Instruction.* 3d ed. New York: Scott Foresman, 1990.

Gagne, Robert M., et al. *Principles of Instructional Design.* 3d ed. New York: Holt, Rinehart and Winston, 1987.

Kemp, Jerrold E. *The Instructional Design Process.* New York: Harper and Row, 1985.

Nadler, Leonard. *Designing Training Programs. The Critical Events Model.* Reading, MA: Addison-Wesley, 1982.

Romiszowski, A. J. *Designing Instructional Systems.* New York: Nichols, 1984.

_____. *Developing Auto-Instructional Materials.* New York: Nichols, 1987.

_____. *Producing Instructional Systems.* New York: Nichols, 1986.

West, Charles K.; Farmer, James A.; and Wolff, Phillip M. *Instructional Design: Implications from Cognitive Science.* Englewood Cliffs, NJ: Prentice-Hall, 1991.

Audiovisual References

Can We Please Have That the Right Way Round? Northbrook, IL: Video Arts, n.d. 16mm film or videocassette. 22 minutes.

How to Make a Presentation. Calgary, Alberta: Access Network, 1988. Videocassette. 30 minutes.

Individualizing Instruction. Beacon Films, 1983. Videocassette. 27 minutes.

Making Your Case. Northbrook, IL: Video Arts, n.d. 16mm film or videocassette. 25 minutes.

Measuring Instructional Effectiveness. Herndon, VA: Industrial Training Corp., n.d. Videocassette. 30 minutes.

Media Utilization. Norwood MA: Beacon Films, 1983. Videocassette. 29 minutes.

Non-Verbal Communication. Santa Monica, CA: Salenger Educational Media, 1982. 16mm film. 17 minutes.

Novel Techniques for Evaluating Media. Boulder, CO: University of Colorado, 1982. Audiocassette.

Patterns for Instruction. Beverly Hills, CA: Roundtable Films, 1981. Videocassette and leader's guide. 21 minutes.

Principles for Learning and Instruction. Norwood, MA: Beacon Films, 1983. Videocassette. 29 minutes.

Teaching and Testing for Results. Columbia, SC: Educational Program Service, 1983. Videocassette. 30 minutes.

Teaching to Objectives, Parts 1 and 2. Columbia, SC: Educational Program Service, 1983. Videocassettes. 30 minutes each.

POSSIBLE PROJECTS

2–A. Plan a presentation using the procedures described in this chapter. Your description must include

1. Description of learners
    a. General characteristics
    b. Specific competencies: knowledge, skills, and attitudes
    c. Learning style
2. Objectives for the presentation
3. Description of how you selected, modified, or designed instructional materials
4. Procedures for the use of the materials
5. Plans for learner involvement and reinforcement
6. Evaluation procedures

2–B. Classify a set of at least five objectives into the cognitive, affective, motor skill, or interpersonal domain.

2–C. Write at least five objectives for a lesson you might actually teach; cover as many domains and categories as possible.

2–D. Select a chapter from a textbook of interest to you and derive a set of at least five objectives that you feel are intended by the author.

2–E. Select a lesson you might teach, such as a chapter from a textbook, and develop a set of evaluation instruments (not necessarily all paper-and-pencil test items).

2–F. Compare all of the Appraisal Checklists in this book. Compile a list of the different rating criteria that appear in all of the "Appraisal Checklists" (except the one for objectives).

3

Visual Design

OUTLINE

OBJECTIVES

After studying this chapter, you should be able to

1. Describe the function of a visual in the communication process.

2. Discuss the relationship between the degree of realism in a visual and the amount of learning from it.

3. Describe the relationship between people's preferences for visuals and the amount of learning from these preferred visuals.

4. Discuss briefly the effect of developmental age and cultural background on learning from visuals.

5. Identify three techniques for learning from making visuals.

6. Define *visual literacy.*

7. List three important findings of eye movement research and explain how they can be used in designing effective visuals.

8. Describe three categories of visuals and identify how each type should be used with adult learners.

9. Identify uses of the elements of art and principles of design in examples of visuals.

10. State guidelines for legibility and color contrast in adding lettering to a visual.

11. Discuss four duplicating methods, including the relative costs, advantages, and limitations of each method.

12. Explain the basic principles of photography, including the elements of light, subject, camera, and film.

13. Describe the function(s) of the following camera parts: aperture, shutter, view finder, focus, and film advance.

14. Discuss and apply the rules for effective composition when taking photographs.

LEXICON

referent

iconic

decoding

encoding

visual literacy

arrangement

rule of thirds

balance

shutter

viewfinder

composition

THE USE OF VISUALS

We are a visual society, one that has experienced the increasing production and distribution of visual messages in recent years. Television comes immediately to mind, but images are all around us. New technologies of printing and reproduction have also contributed to the flood of visual messages in books, periodicals, and newspapers as never before. We are bombarded with visual messages on billboards and posters (Figure 3.1). Advertising of all kinds has become increasingly visual. Product instructions are becoming less verbal and more illustrative. Highway signs (especially international driving signs) are almost totally visual. Even T-shirt makers have gotten into the act!

From an instructional point of view, we know that most people are visually oriented. They learn about 10 percent from listening, but over 80 percent from what they see. More importantly, they remember only about 20 percent of what they hear, but over 50 percent of what they see and hear.

Because so much learning takes place through visuals the design and use of visuals in instruction is extremely important. Most of the media discussed in this text—overhead transparencies, slides, films, television, and even computer software—have a visual component.

This chapter describes the characteristics of instructionally effective visuals, the concept of visual literacy, how people look at visuals, and how to design and use visuals effectively. In addition, there are sections on photography, creating layouts of printed materials, cartooning, sketching, drawing, making bulletin board displays, and designing computer screens.

A major synthesis of research studies comparing visual-based lessons (e.g., photographs, overhead transparencies, and video) with conventional instruction pointed to the overall superiority of the visual treatment.[1] However, the degree of superiority was found to depend on the subject matter and on the utilization practices of the teacher.

THE FUNCTIONS OF VISUALS

The primary function of a visual as a communication device is to serve as a more concrete *referent* to meaning than the spoken or written word. Words are arbitrary symbols. They don't look or sound (usually) like the thing they represent. Visuals, however, are *iconic* (see Dale's Cone of Experience on page 12). They normally resemble the thing they represent. As such, they serve as concrete clues to meaning. It is a general principle of human communication that the likelihood of successful communication is increased

---

[1] Peter A. Cohen, Barbara J. Ebeling, and James A. Kulik, "A Meta-Analysis of Outcome Studies of Visual-Based Instruction," *Educational Communications and Technology Journal* (Spring 1981):26–36.

when concrete referents are present. When the thing being discussed is not at hand, the next best referent is a visual representation of it.

Visuals can also motivate learners by increasing their interest in a text or presentation. They attract attention, sustain attention, and generate emotion. Reiteration is another important function of visuals. They can underscore the information in printed material or verbal narration by presenting it in a different form. Visuals can simplify information that is difficult to understand and remember. Charts and diagrams, especially those that make analogies to familiar concepts, can make it easier to store and retrieve such information. They can also serve an organizational function by illustrating the relationships among elements or concepts being studied.

REALISM IN VISUALS

One fundamental difference among visuals is their degree of realism. No media form, of course, is totally re-

Figure 3.1
Visuals surround us in our everyday lives.

Figure 3.2
An illustration of the frailties of verbal communication

Figure 3.3
The graphic symbol, cartoon, line drawing, and photograph represent a continuum of realism in visuals.

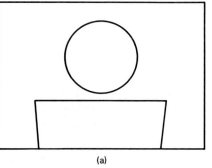
(a)

(b)

(c)

(d)

alistic. The real object or event will always have aspects that cannot be captured pictorially, even in a three-dimensional color motion picture. The various visual media can, however, be arranged from highly abstract to relatively realistic, as shown in Figure 3.3.

One might be inclined to conclude that effective communication is always best served by the most realistic visual available. After all, the more realistic a visual is, the closer it is to the original. This, however, is not necessarily so. There is ample research to show that un-

der certain circumstances realism can actually interfere with the communication and learning process. For example, the ability to sort out the relevant from the irrelevant in a pictorial representation grows with age and experience. So, for younger children and for older learners who are encountering an idea for the first time, the wealth of detail found in a realistic visual may increase the likelihood that the learner will be distracted by irrelevant elements of the visual.

As Dwyer notes in his review of visual research, "The arbitrary addi-

tion of stimuli in visuals makes it difficult for learners to identify the essential learning cues from among the more realistic background stimuli."[2] Dwyer concludes that rather than being a simple yes-or-no issue, the amount of realism desired has a curvilinear relationship to learning. That is, either too much or too little realism may affect achievement adversely (Figure 3.4).

---

[2] Francis M. Dwyer, *Strategies for Improving Visual Learning* (State College, PA: Learning Services, 1978), p. 33.

Figure 3.4
Visuals tend to become less useful in instruction as they approach the extremes of very abstract or very realistic.

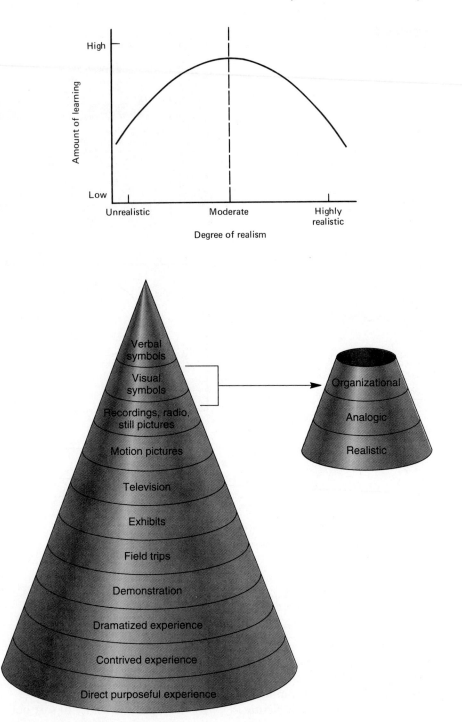

Figure 3.5
Categories of visuals

TYPES OF VISUALS

Visuals can be classified into three categories: realistic, analogic, and organizational (Figure 3.5).[3] Realistic visuals are those that show the actual object or subject under study.

They vary in detail and degree of realism. For example, a color photograph of an airplane is a realistic visual (Figure 3.6).

Analogic visuals convey a concept or topic by showing something else and implying a similarity. Teaching about electricity flow by showing water flowing in series and parallel pipes is an example of using analogic visuals. An analogy for white

blood cells fighting off infection might be an army attacking a stronghold. This type of visual helps the learner interpret new information in light of prior knowledge and thereby facilitates learning (see Figure 3.7).

Organizational visuals are visuals such as flowcharts, graphs, maps, schematics, and classification charts. (See Chapter 4 for details on types

---

[3] H. A. Houghton and D. M. Willows, eds. *The Psychology of Illustration,* Vol. 2 (New York: Springer Verlag, 1987).

Figure 3.6
A realistic visual

Figure 3.7
The solar system is often used as a visual analogy to explain the composition of an atom.

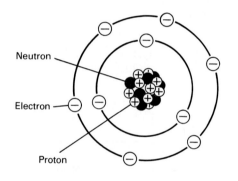

Neutron

Electron

Proton

Figure 3.8
This chart, representing a later section of the chapter, presents textual material in a format that makes the organization clear.

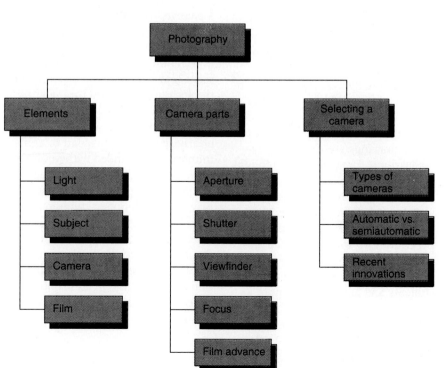

Photography

Elements

Camera parts

Selecting a camera

Light

Subject

Camera

Film

Aperture

Shutter

Viewfinder

Focus

Film advance

Types of cameras

Automatic vs. semiautomatic

Recent innovations

of charts and graphs.) These graphic organizers can show relationships among the main points or concepts in textual material. This type of visual helps communicate the organization of the content (see Figure 3.8).

VISUAL PREFERENCES OF LEARNERS

Teachers have to make appropriate choices between effective illustrations and preferred illustrations. People do not necessarily learn best from the kinds of pictures they prefer. For example, research on picture preferences indicates that children in upper elementary school tend to

1. Prefer color to black and white.
2. Choose photographs over drawings.
3. Choose realism in form and color.
4. Prefer simple over complex illustrations (younger children).
5. Prefer complex over simple illustrations (older children).[4]

Most learners prefer colored visuals over black-and-white visuals. However, there is no significant difference in the amount of learning except where color is related to the content to be learned. For example, when workers must learn to assemble electrical components with different colored wires, the presence of color is essential. Photographs are preferred over line drawings by most learners, even though in many situations drawings are more effective for learning. Drawings can highlight the important details. Even though many learners prefer very realistic visuals over abstract representations, teachers must strike a balance between the two to achieve their instructional purposes. Young learners prefer simple visuals, whereas older students and adults prefer more

complex visuals. Nevertheless, simpler visuals are usually more effective, whatever the age group.

USING VISUALS IN INSTRUCTION

Students can learn from visuals in two ways. First, they must be able to "read" visuals accurately, understand the elements of visuals, and interpret them. This skill is referred to as *decoding*. Second, they should be able to create visuals as a tool to communicate effectively with others and be able to express themselves through visuals. This skill is called *encoding*. The development of both decoding and encoding skills requires practice.

Decoding: Interpreting Visuals

Seeing a visual does not automatically ensure learning from it. Learners must be guided toward correct decoding of visuals. How a learner decodes a visual is affected by many variables.

Prior to the age of twelve, children tend to interpret visuals section by section rather than as a whole. In reporting what they see in a picture, they are likely to single out specific elements within the scene. Students who are older, however, tend to summarize the whole scene and report a conclusion about the meaning of the picture. Hence, abstract symbols or a series of still pictures whose relationship is not clearly spelled out may fail to communicate as intended with younger viewers (see Figure 3.9). On the other hand, highly realistic visuals may distract younger children. However, Dwyer notes, "As a child gets older, he becomes more capable of attending selectively to those features of an instructional presentation that have the greatest potential for enhancing his learning of desired information."[5]

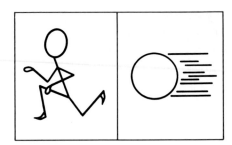

Figure 3.9
An active posture, as in the drawing on the left, communicates movement more reliably than arbitrary graphic conventions such as speed lines, as in the drawing on the right.

In teaching, we must keep in mind that decoding visuals may be affected by the viewer's cultural background. Different cultural groups may perceive visual materials in different ways. In a sense, this variable might be subsumed under prior learning experience, as discussed in Chapter 2. But these differences are more difficult to appraise. Cultural background has a strong influence on learning experience. For example, let's say your instruction includes visuals depicting scenes typical of the home life and street life of inner-city children. It is almost certain that students who live in such an area will decode these visuals differently than will students whose cultural (and socioeconomic) backgrounds do not include first-hand knowledge of inner-city living. Similarly, scenes depicting life in the Old West might be interpreted quite differently by an American Indian child than they would be by a black, white, or Mexican-American child.

The symbolic connotations of color and color preference may also be culturally based. Individuals from different cultures vary widely in their perception of the color spectrum. Westerners tend to see red, orange, yellow, green, blue, and violet as more or less distinct and equidistant points along a spectrum. But this kind of color perception is by no means universal. Even less universal are the symbolic values given to various colors. Black, for exam-

[4] Barbara Myatt and Juliet Mason Carter, "Picture Preferences of Children and Young Adults," *Educational Communication and Technology Journal* (Spring 1979):47.

[5] Dwyer, *Strategies for Improving Visual Learning*, p. 229.

Figure 3.10
The cultural biases of a communicator, although unspoken, may be perceived vividly by viewers having a different cultural background.

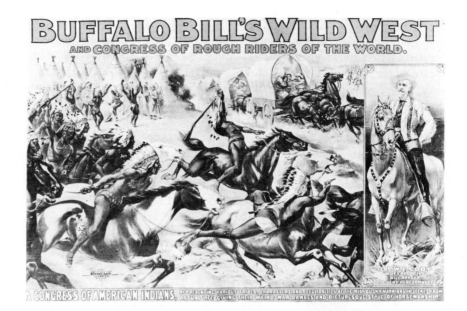

Figure 3.11
Symbolic images may be interpreted differently depending on cultural background.

ple, is generally accepted in Western countries as the color of mourning. In some Eastern countries, however, the color of mourning is white.

Although you cannot eliminate all misconceptions in decoding arising out of differences in cultural background, you should always be cautious about using visuals that may, without prior explanation, cause confusion for some of your students.

Encoding: Creating Visuals

One of the best ways to develop encoding skills is to encourage students to present their message through a pictorial medium. Most

MEDIA FILE
Story-Sequencing Card Sets

Beginning or remedial readers can improve comprehension and logic skills by arranging story cards in proper sequence. Each set of cards tells a story in comic strip form. Clues to proper sequence are given in the pictures and text on each card. Shape and size of the cards give additional hints. Five different sets are available, each emphasizing a particular comprehension skill: sequencing, cause and effect, main ideas, drawing conclusions, and predicting outcomes.

Source: Educational Insights

older students have access to a camera. They should be encouraged to present reports to the class by means of carefully selected sets of slides. The 35mm slide is also a medium for students to use to develop their aesthetic talents. Portable videotape equipment is also an excellent way of giving students the opportunity to present ideas and events pictorially.

One skill nearly always included in visual education curricula is that of sequencing. Reading specialists

have long known that the ability to sequence, that is, to arrange ideas in logical order, is an extremely important factor in verbal literacy, especially in the ability to communicate in writing.

Children who have grown up constantly exposed to movies and television may expect the visuals they encounter in school to be similarly packaged and sequenced. They may need practice in arranging visuals into logical sequence as this is a learned skill, like the verbal se-

quencing in reading and writing. For this reason, many visual education programs, especially for primary school children, emphasize creative activities that call for arranging and making visuals.

THE CONCEPT OF VISUAL LITERACY

Prior to the mid-1960s, the concept of literacy was applied almost exclusively to the ability to read and write. Then we began to hear of a

CLOSE-UP

Visual Literacy Education

Visual literacy education programs have been developed all over the United States and in many other countries to introduce students to the concepts and skills related to interpreting visuals and communicating visually. These programs are designed for children from preschool through high school and encompass both the encoding and the decoding of visual information in all media. Visual literacy has now become well accepted as an important aspect of the curriculum at all levels of education.

One such program in the Minneapolis Public Schools involves students in many viewing skills activities and media production projects with the aim of developing critical viewing and thinking skills. Students examine all media with a focus on how elements such as color, camera angle, and pacing can affect the impact of visual messages. "Visual Education," the district's curriculum guide, encourages teachers to consider visual learning styles, and the importance of visuals in developing creativity and critical thinking skills. In many media centers around the district, students create poster campaigns, design new products and advertising, examine their television viewing habits, and analyze commercial messages. They produce videos using camcorders and design projects in audio, photography, and other media.

In programs like this all over the country, teachers are encouraged to think visually and to focus students' attention on the visual aspects of textbooks and storybooks while reading. Since visuals inundate today's students, their ability to read, understand, create, and analyze the persuasiveness of visuals has become even more important. Media production, computer design, and critical thinking skills can all enhance a student's ability to work and succeed in an increasingly visual world.

Elementary teachers have discovered the appeal of visual activities such as tangrams, visual searches, and three-dimensional shapes. Sequencing, patterning, visual analogies, visual perception, visual attributes, and categorization are all concepts that are enhanced by visual teaching materials, such as Venn diagrams, pentominoes, hidden pictures, drawings, memory games, and video clips. Students work alone or together on visual learning activities and develop communication, organization and reporting skills in the process.

Source: Rhonda S. Robinson, Northern Illinois University

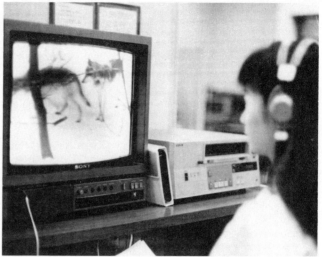

Figure 3.14
Viewing and interpreting visuals (decoding) represents just one aspect of visual literacy.

Figure 3.12
Reading in print literacy parallels interpreting (decoding) in visual literacy.

Figure 3.15
Learning to interpret visuals without learning to create them is like learning to read but not learning to write.

Figure 3.13
Writing in print literacy parallels creating (encoding) in visual literacy.

different kind of literacy, visual literacy. This new concept of literacy was based on the realization that specific skills are needed to "read" and "write" visual messages, just as they are needed to read and write printed ones.

Visual literacy is the learned ability to interpret visual messages accurately and to create such messages. Thus, interpretation and creation in visual literacy may be said to parallel reading and writing in print literacy.

Visual literacy has also become a movement within the field of education. The movement now has its own professional association, the International Visual Literacy Association, with its own periodicals. (For information, write to Educational

One day in the late 1640s in Massachusetts, Cotton Mather, ever zealous to make Puritan New England the cultural center of the New World, noted in his journal his disappointment that a certain "incomparable Moravian" was not, after all, to become an American by accepting the presidency of Harvard College:

> That brave old man, Johannes Amos Comenius, the fame of whose worth has been trumpeted as far as more than three languages could carry it, was indeed agreed . . . to come over to New England, and illuminate their Colledge and Country, in the quality of a President, which was now become vacant. But the solicitation of the Swedish Ambassador diverting him another way, that incomparable Moravian became not an American.

Who was this Johannes Amos Comenius? Why had his fame as an educator spread all the way from Europe to Mather's Massachusetts Bay Colony?

Comenius was born in 1592 in Moravia (now part of Czechoslovakia). He was a clergyman of the United Brethren, an evangelical Protestant reform sect known popularly today as the Moravian church. At the time of his consideration for the presidency of Harvard, he was living in exile in Sweden. Indeed, the religious persecutions of the Thirty Years War and its aftermath had forced Comenius to live most of his life away from his native Moravia.

Despite this and the deprivations of war, Comenius achieved fame throughout Europe as an educational reformer and writer of innovative textbooks and other educational works. His *Janua Linguarum Reserata* (*The Gate of Language Unlocked*) was a Latin language textbook that taught a basic vocabulary of 8,000 carefully selected words and the principal points of Latin grammar. The instructional strategy of the *Janua* consisted of Latin sentences about a variety of topics, forming a kind of encyclopedia of basic human knowledge of that time. Comenius also argued that the teaching of languages should be divided into stages parallel to four human developmental stages. For this insight Piaget acknowledged Comenius as a forerunner of genetic psychology.[a] The *Janua* became one of the great pedagogical best-sellers of all time, and it influenced, wittingly or unwittingly, virtually all later scholars of language instruction.

Comenius was, in addition, one of the earliest and certainly the most renowned champions of what we call visual literacy and visual education. The last fourteen years of his life were spent in Amsterdam. It was from his haven there that Comenius oversaw the publication in 1657 in Nuremberg of the work for which he is today best known and on

IOHAN ~ AMOS COMENIVS, MORAVVS. A° ÆTAT 50: 1642
Crols sculpsit

which he had been working for years: *Orbis Sensualium Pictus* (*The Visible World Pictured*).

Orbis Sensualium Pictus was the first illustrated textbook specifically designed for use by children in an instructional setting. (It was not the first children's picture book. The English printer Caxton, for example, had produced an illustrated edition of Aesop's *Fables* as early as 1484.) The design and illustrations of Comenius's text were expressly intended to enhance learning. The 150 woodcut drawings were learning and teaching devices, not mere decorations. The text embodied application of educational theories espoused by the author over a period of forty years. It is interesting to note, for example, that Comenius chose Aristotle's observation *Nihil est in intellectu, quod non prius fuit in sensu* ("There is nothing in the mind which was not first in the senses") to adorn his title page. The primacy of this principle has been supported increasingly by modern psychological research.

---

[a] Jean Piaget, *J. A. Comenius: Pages Choisies* (Paris: UNESCO, 1957).

Orbis Sensualium Pictus is truly remarkable for having incorporated, more than 300 years ago, so many educational concepts that seem thoroughly modern. Underlying Comenius's use of visuals was a theory of perception based on the idea that we learn through our senses and that this learning imprints a mental image which leads to understanding. A real object is preferable for this process, but visuals may be used in the learning environment as substitutes for the real thing.

The design and illustrations of *Orbis Sensualium Pictus*, the author tells us in his preface, were intended "to entice witty children to it, that they may not conceit a torment to be in the school, but dainty fare. For it is apparent, that children (even from their infancy almost) are delighted with pictures, and willingly please their eyes with these sights." His pedagogical aim was that children "may be furnished with the knowledge of the prime things that are in the world, by sport and merry pastime."

The idea that learning should be a "merry pastime" rather than a burdensome chore is startlingly modern. Indeed, centuries were to pass before this basic educational philosophy became what it is today—the common wisdom. Aptly called "that incomparable Moravian" in his own time, Johannes Amos Comenius may still be called so in ours.

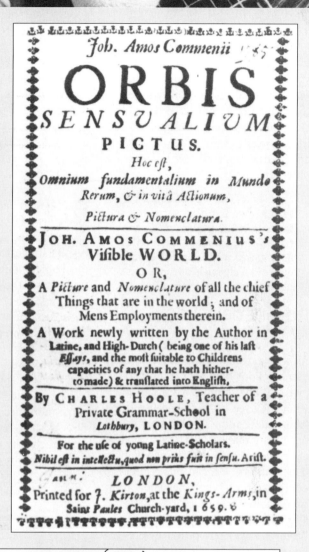

Joh. Amos Commenii

ORBIS
SENSUALIUM
PICTUS.

Hoc est,
Omnium fundamentalium in Mundo Rerum, & in vitâ Actionum, Pictura & Nomenclatura.

JOH. AMOS COMENIUS's
Visible WORLD.
OR,
A Picture and Nomenclature of all the chief Things that are in the world; and of Mens Employments therein.

A Work newly written by the Author in Latine, and High-Dutch (being one of his last Essays, and the most suitable to Childrens capacities of any that he hath hitherto made) & translated into English,

By CHARLES HOOLE, Teacher of a Private Grammar-School in Lothbury, LONDON.

For the use of young Latine-Scholars.
Nihil est in intellectu, quod non priùs fuit in sensu. Arist.

LONDON,
Printed for J. Kirton, at the Kings-Arms, in Saint Paules Church-yard, 1 6 5 9.

---

(104)

LI.

Piscatio.

[illustration]

Fishing.

(105)

The Fisher-man 1. catcheth fish, either on the shoar, with an Hook, 2. which hangeth by a line from the angling-rod, and on which the bait sticketh; or with a Cleek-Net, 3. which hanging on a Pole, 4. is put into the water; or in a Boat, 5. with a Trammel-Net 6. or with a Weel, 7. which is laid in the water by Night.

Piscator 1. captat pisces, sive, in littore, Hamo, 2. qui ab *arundine* filo pendet, & cui inhæret *Esca*; sive *Fundâ*, 3. quæ pendens *Perticâ*, 4. aquæ immittitur; sive, in *Cymbâ*, 5. *Reti*, 6. sive *Nassâ*, 7. quæ per Noctem demergitur.

Technologies Resource Center, Virginia Tech, Blacksburg, VA 24061-0232.)

The importance of visual literacy in today's society cannot be overstressed. Teachers of young children have a special responsibility to see that students do not leave their classrooms visually illiterate. Visual literacy can even be thought of as an essential survival skill. As one observer puts it:

> There is no easy way to develop visual literacy, but it is as vital to our teaching of the modern media as reading and writing was to print. It may, indeed, be the crucial component of all channels of communication now and in the future.[6]

HOW PEOPLE LOOK AT VISUALS

All instructors ought to be concerned about how people look at pictorial and graphic materials and what they see in them because these factors determine what people get out of the materials. There are basically two ways to determine what people notice. We can make inferences based on what they show they have learned from pictorial materials. This approach is favored by behaviorists who rely primarily on learner responses. Or we can determine the pattern of eye movements as they look at the same pictorial material. This approach is frequently used by researchers in stimulus design.

Recent eye movement research has concentrated on how learners shift attention from print to pictures in illustrated text material. For example, one study examined how good and poor fourth grade readers used text and pictures to learn about the characteristics of unfamiliar animals.[7] While including pictures improved retention by all learners, good readers tended to study the pictures prior to reading and rarely afterward, but poor readers frequently moved back and forth between text and pictures. This evidence supports arguments that illustrations should be next to the text they portray. Close placement would not get in the way of good readers and would significantly help poor readers. Another study used eye movements to determine precisely how different students use diagrams to understand the workings of a mechanical system.[8] The results suggest that people with low mechanical ability need diagrams to understand the text while people with high mechanical ability can construct the mechanical system primarily from prior knowledge and the text.

If the ways in which people view and interpret pictures and graphics can be guided, then people will learn more because attention will be directed to relevant content and not misdirected by irrelevant cues.

Research on the eye movements of people looking at still photographs indicates that viewers tend to look first at the upper-left-hand portion of a picture. The edges of the picture area in Figure 3.16 have been divided into thirds. The percentage at each intersection represents the frequency with which people first look at that part of the picture area. If upper and lower percentages are combined, we see that observers tend to look first at the left-hand side of a picture two out of three times.

This information is relevant not only to decisions about where you should place important content in a picture area but also to expectations about how people will interpret certain graphic representations.

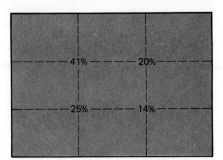

Figure 3.16
Research in the United States indicates a tendency for viewers to begin reading a picture in the upper left.

When designing visuals, we can take advantage of this research by placing at least the start of our main message where the eye first strikes the area. The research does not imply that all important information should be located in the upper-left area or even in the left half of a picture. But it does indicate that if the message is required (by the nature of the content) to be in the lower right, the eye of the observer will have to be led there. This can be achieved by using such pictorial elements as color, composition, and texture. The important point is that the tendency of people not to look first in the lower right must be compensated for if the message is located there.

Another important finding demonstrates the importance of movement. When the picture on the screen is static, viewers tune out after a while. When the image is changed by introducing motion or changing the picture, viewers tune in again. Changes in the image help keep students' attention on the visual.

VISUALS AND ADULT LEARNING

We often think that pictures are for use with young children. However, visuals can play an important part in adult learning as well. Dwyer and his associates have conducted over 100 studies involving several thou-

6   Donis A. Dondis, *A Primer of Visual Literacy* (Cambridge, MA: MIT Press, 1973).

7   R. Rusted and V. Coltheart, "The Effect of Pictures on the Retention of Novel Words and Prose Passages," *Journal of Experimental Child Psychology* 28 (1979):516–24.

8   M. Hegarty and M. A. Just, "Understanding Machines from Text and Diagrams," in *Knowledge Acquisition from Text and Pictures,* ed. H. Mandl and J. Levin (Amsterdam: Elsevier, 1989), pp. 171–94.

Figure 3.17
Visuals generally enhance adult learning.

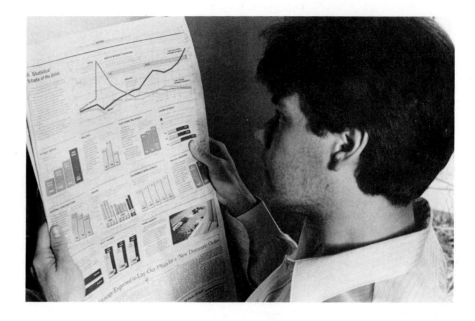

sand adult learners since 1965.[9] In their research they have found that pictures generally facilitate adult learning (Figure 3.17). Adults who read a verbal passage supplemented with visuals remember more than adults who read only the passage.

Researchers have found that adult learners may also benefit from drawing their own pictures. A number of studies have been conducted to investigate the effects of training learners to generate their own graphic organizers for textual material. Typically, the learners have been asked to draw the organization of the content or material. In one study some adults were given the text, others read and were given a graphic organizer, and others read and generated their own graphic organizer.[10] In this case the latter group learned the most. Findings from such research suggest that a graphic organizer may not be very helpful unless the learners generate it themselves or manipulate it in some way.

Visuals can facilitate problem-solving activities. When given a word problem in math, learners should be encouraged to draw the situation before trying to solve the problem. By allowing the learner to picture the problem, visuals facilitate understanding of the situation presented.

Flowcharts improve the learner's speed in performing procedures and reduce the number of errors made. Flowcharts can also improve the comprehension of directions when compared with directions given in a verbal format.

DESIGNING VISUALS

Well-designed visuals—charts, posters, graphics for slides or television, bulletin board displays, and the like—not only promote learning of the subject matter but also provide aesthetic models for students' own creative growth.

When you are creating visuals, the important elements of art and principles of design are best considered by starting with a preliminary sketch of the intended visual. At this stage little attention is paid to rendering the artistic details, but careful consideration is given to choosing the right words and images,

arranging them for best effect, selecting a lettering style, and choosing colors.

The elements of art include line, shape, texture, and color. Lines may be straight, curved, jagged, or broken. They attract and direct attention. Shape refers to a two-dimensional form and may be either specific or general. Texture may be rough, smooth, fuzzy, slick, and so on. Color can greatly enhance the ability of your visual to attract attention and to communicate.

The principles of design relate to arrangement, balance, and unity. Arrangement describes the pattern of the elements in the visual. Balance may be formal (symmetrical) or informal (asymmetrical). Visuals should not be out of balance. Unity describes related or repeated themes, colors, shapes, and types or direction of lines in the visual. The visual should represent a single idea.

Line

The line is a one-dimensional structural device that attracts attention by moving the eye around or to a specific area. Lines suggest action, direction, and movement. Lines can also divide or tie things together, and can be used as a structure on which to build. Here are some ways

---

[9] Dwyer, *Strategies for Improving Visual Learning.*

[10] D. A. Norman and D. E. Rumelhart, *Explorations in Cognition* (San Francisco: Freeman, 1975).

Figure 3.18
Horizontal lines suggest tranquility.

Figure 3.19
Vertical lines attract our attention against a horizontal background.

Figure 3.20
Diagonal lines imply movement and action.

in which lines are commonly used (see Figures 3.18, 3.19, and 3.20):

❏ Horizontal lines give a feeling of stability and rest.

❏ Vertical lines imply strength; they draw the eye upward.

❏ Diagonal lines strongly imply movement, action, and dynamism. Crossed diagonals give a sense of conflict. Curved lines also give a feeling of motion. These factors help explain the popularity of rounded patterns and S and Z patterns as basic arrangements for visuals.

Shape

A line closed upon itself becomes a shape. Shapes are two-dimensional and can form the outline of objects. Shapes can work together to create a meaningful whole. Some shapes communicate just from their silhouette without any internal detail (e.g., an apple, a cross, or a heart). Other shapes can be classified as geometric or amorphous.

Texture

Most visuals are two-dimensional, including lines and shapes. However, a third dimension of form can be added with the use of texture or actual materials (see Figure 3.21). Texture is a characteristic of three-dimensional objects and materials. It can convey a clearer idea of the subject to the viewer by suggesting the sense of touch. Texture can be used to give emphasis, provide separation, or enhance unity. For example, cotton can be used to represent clouds. Real objects such as book jackets can add interest and dimension to a bulletin board. Company products can be incorporated into a display. Components of equipment can be shown with drawings and lettering for emphasis.

Color

Appropriate color choices can not only enhance and enrich your visual

Figure 3.21
The textures in this display add interest and information.

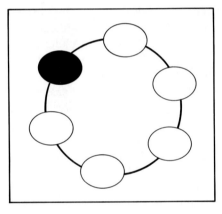

Figure 3.22
Contrast attracts attention, as illustrated by the color contrast in this visual.

designs but also suggest moods and indicate movement. Color commands attention and adds visual impact (see Figure 3.22). Some of the other functions of colors in a visual are (1) to heighten the realism of the image by depicting actual colors, (2) to point out similarities and differences, (3) to highlight important information and details, and (4) to create a particular emotional response.

Artists have long appreciated that blue, green, and violet are perceived

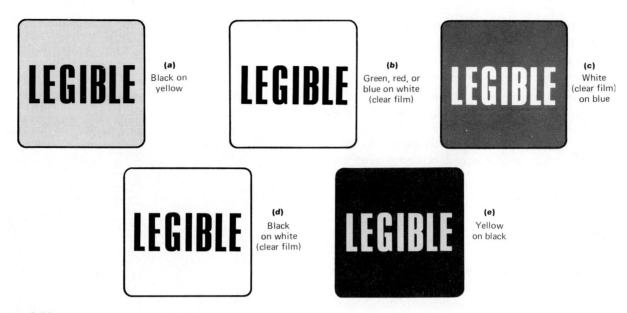

Figure 3.23
Suggested color choices for visuals. Most legible is black on yellow (example a) and so on in descending order of legibility.

as "cool colors," whereas red and orange are considered "warm colors." It is now understood that a physiological basis for this perception exists, the manner in which colors are focused in the human eye. Warmer colors appear to approach the viewer while cooler colors seem to recede. You can capitalize on this tendency by highlighting important cues in red and orange, thus helping them leap toward the viewer. Color also influences legibility (see Figure 3.23).

Color choice is a very personal thing. Dare to invent your own color combinations. You can also use contrast to emphasize points, create a mood, or provide visual interest. Because color can have such a strong impact, use it where it is important. Do not overuse it or it will lose its effect.

The results of several research studies have been summarized by Bergeron.[11] Among his findings is

Figure 3.24

that learners recall longer what they see in red. Use red for material you want your learners to remember. On the other hand, blue elements receive less of the learner's attention. Use blue for less important components of a visual. People tend to look at yellow objects first. You can use yellow to highlight important parts or key words in a visual.

Arrangement

The visual and verbal elements of the layout should be arranged in a pattern that captures the viewer's attention and directs it toward the important details or concepts. Line, space, and form are the primary elements you will manipulate. The *arrangement* should be clear enough

[11] Roland Bergeron, "The Use of Colors to Enhance Training Communications," *Performance and Instruction* (August 1990):34–37.

HOW TO . . .
Design Printed Materials

When preparing printed instructional materials such as handouts, worksheets, and study guides, there are a number of factors to consider. They include headings, writing style, page layout, type style/mechanics, visuals, and highlighting. Here are a number of principles to guide the design of printed materials.

Headings

❑ Label all text so readers can locate the information they need.

❑ Provide headings to allow learners to skim for an overview and to retrieve information later.

❑ Use headings to show the organization of the content (e.g., start each new page with a main heading).

❑ Use side heads (e.g., words in left margin) to call attention to important concepts.

❑ Use different type style for headings.

Writing Style

❑ State the main idea or theme at the beginning of text.

❑ Put topic sentences at beginning of each paragraph.

❑ Use simple sentences and writing style.

❑ Use active voice where possible.

❑ Include technical terms with definitions so they won't be misconstrued or misspelled.

Page Layout

❑ Provide ample white space (use wide margins and uncrowded format) to facilitate reading, note taking, and location of information for review.

❑ Use unjustified right margins (justification adds to expense and production time with no effect on reading rate or comprehension).

❑ Increase the space between lines in a note-taking handout to increase the amount of information noted.

❑ Be clear and consistent in page layout (use the same type of text in the same typeface, size, and layout from page to page).

Type Style/Mechanics

❑ Choose typeface styles with simple designs (such as gothic or roman sans serif) for headings.

❑ If material is typed, use a space and a half between lines for ease of reading.

❑ Avoid breaking words (hyphenating) at the end of lines.

❑ Limit the number of words per line to approximately the learner's age, for preteenagers.

Raising Capable Young People

Visuals

❑ Keep visuals simple (avoid too much realism in visuals).

❑ Direct attention to visuals through questions and activities.

❑ Place visuals as near the related text as possible.

❑ Use larger visuals if more detail is required.

Highlighting

Highlighting techniques for printed materials include color, size of type, italics, and boldfacing.

❑ Highlight important ideas, thus limiting the demands on the learner to locate key points and ideas.

❑ Do not use capitals for highlighting because they are difficult to read within text (capitals are okay for short headings).

❑ Avoid author-provided underlining because it has little or no effect on retention of content (underlining can be used to highlight negatives, e.g., *not* and *except*).

Sources: James Hartley, *Designing Instructional Text*, 2nd ed. (New York: Nichols, 1987). Also David H. Jonassen, ed., *The Technology of Text: Principles of Structuring, Designing, and Displaying Text* (Englewood Cliffs, NJ: Educational Technology Publications, vol. 1, 1982, and vol. 2, 1985).

to attract and focus attention quickly. A regular geometric shape (e.g., oval, rectangle, triangle) provides a convenient framework to build on because its pattern is predictable to most viewers (Figure 3.25). Arrangements that approximate certain letters of the alphabet have the same virtue. The letters C, O, S, Z, L, T, and U are frequently used as underlying patterns in display layouts (see Figures 3.26 and 3.27). Of course, the words used in the layout, as well as the pictures, form part of the arrangement.

Besides using a basic underlying shape, one other principle should guide your arrangement: the *rule of thirds*. Elements arranged along any of the one-third dividing lines take on importance and liveliness, and can even suggest movement. The most dominant and dynamic position is at any of the intersections of the one-third dividing lines (especially the upper-left intersection).

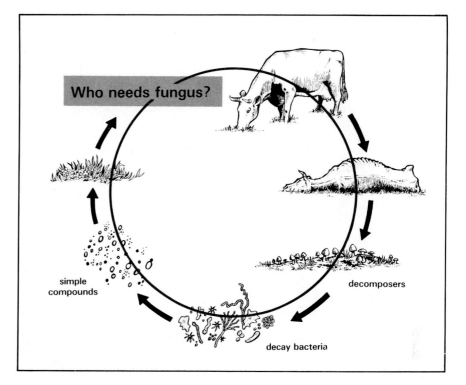

Figure 3.25
Arrangement should follow an overall pattern such as the letter O shown here. The arrows are important.

Figure 3.26
A Z arrangement provides flow and leads the viewer's eye from top to bottom. A pathway or arrows are necessary for the Z pattern to work. Note the change in size of circles from smaller to larger in the foreground.

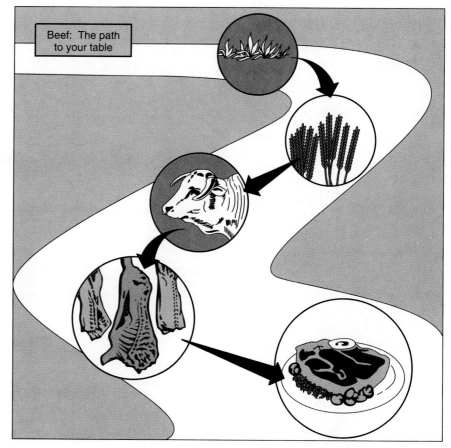

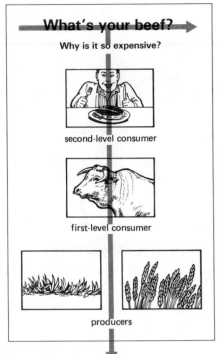

Figure 3.27
A T pattern provides stability and
formal balance.

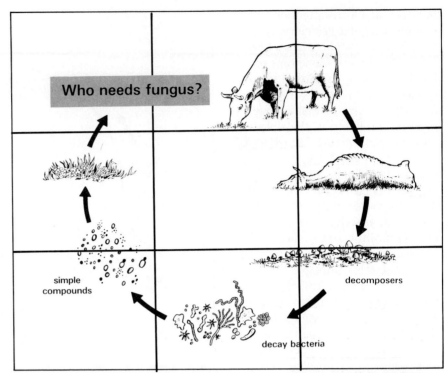

Figure 3.28
The "rule of thirds" suggests that the most important elements in a visual
should be placed near the intersections of lines dividing the visual into thirds.

The most stable and least interesting point on the grid is dead center. Items placed in the corners or at the edges tend to create an unbalanced, uncomfortable feeling.

Balance

A psychological sense of equilibrium, or *balance*, is achieved when the "weight" of the elements in a display is equally distributed on each side of an axis, either horizontally, vertically, or both. When the design is repeated on both sides, the balance is symmetrical, or formal.

In most cases, though, for visuals that will catch the eye and serve an informational purpose you should aim to achieve an asymmetrical, or informal, balance. Here, there is rough equivalence of weight, but different elements are used on each side (e.g., one large open square on one side, three small dark circles on the other). Informal balance is pre-

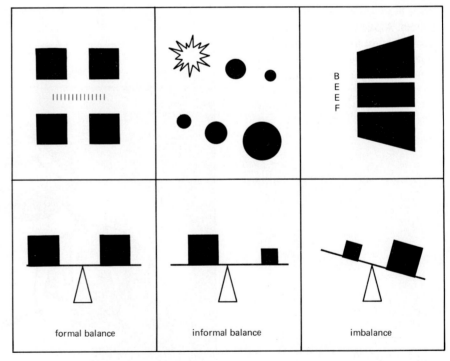

Figure 3.29
Three types of balance are illustrated by the visuals in the top row and depicted
by analogy in the bottom row.

ferred because it is more dynamic and more interesting (see Figure 3.29). Arrangements such as the C, S, Z, and the like are frequently used as frameworks for asymmetrical layouts.

Imbalance—using a distinctly disproportionate weight distribution—ordinarily should be avoided as it tends to be jarring.

Unity

Unity is the relationship among the elements of a visual that allows them to function together. It concerns not only the verbal content but also the visual presentation.

Unity is achieved by using related or repeated themes, colors, shapes, and types or directions of lines. A mistake frequently made is to crowd too much into one space. Eliminate every element that is not essential to the communication of your idea (see Figure 3.30). Present only one idea at a time!

Interaction

Some particularly effective visuals allow the learner to interact with the visual or manipulate materials on the visual. Answer cards to math facts can be moved into the correct position by the student. The teacher or learners can move dials on a weather display to indicate the forecast for the day or the actual weather outside the classroom.

Figure 3.30
Visuals should present a single idea for effective communication, as shown by this billboard.

Figure 3.31
Design professionals carefully select and arrange design elements to communicate a specific message.

In a manufacturing plant the visual display may be modified each day to indicate the number of accident-free hours worked by the employees. Workers may also be asked to manipulate materials on a display in the break room.

The R of the ASSURE model applies to all forms of media. Viewers can be asked to respond to visual displays by actually getting involved with them. The interaction should be for the purpose of increasing learning or enhancing awareness.

We have introduced some general design principles. Design is around you all the time. Professional designers are paid well to design newspaper ads, billboards, magazines, and commercial displays. Use their compositions as ideas for the layout of your own visuals, but be aware that not all things in print have been professionally designed; therefore some designs may not be effective for their intended audience. Learn to observe carefully and remember what you have seen. Sharpen your senses, and then make practical applications of the good designs you find.

LETTERING VISUALS

Most visuals incorporate some type of lettering. The style of the lettering should be consistent and should harmonize with the other elements of the visual. For straightforward informational or instructional purposes a plain, not decorative lettering style is recommended. The gothic or roman sans serif (without serifs) style is most readable. Equally important, these alphabets are easily reproducible by hand lettering (see Figure 3.32).

For best legibility, use lowercase letters, adding capitals only where normally required. Short headlines may be written in all capitals, but phrases of more than three words and full sentences should follow the rule of lowercase lettering.

The color of the lettering should contrast with the background color both for the sake of simple legibility and for the sake of emphasis in cases where you want to call particular attention to the verbal message. Legibility depends mainly on contrast between the lettering color and the background color.

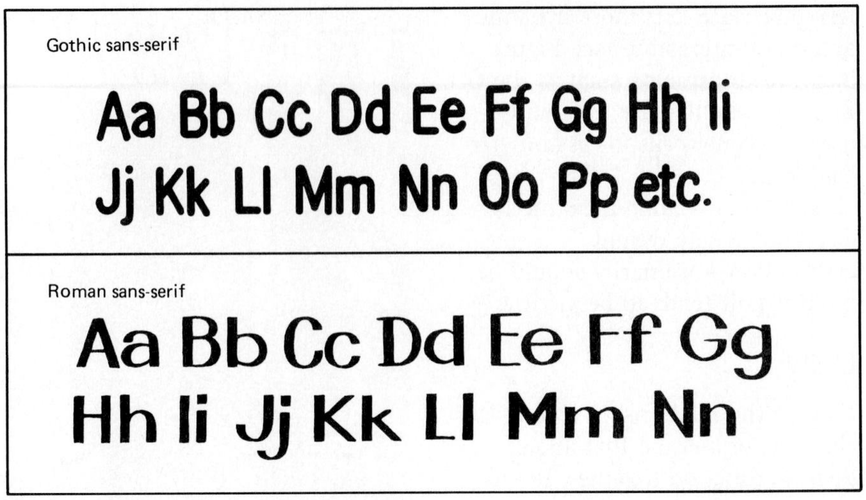

Figure 3.32
These types of lettering are most readable for titles and simple captions.

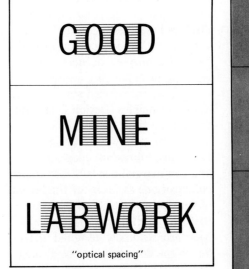

Gothic sans-serif

Aa Bb Cc Dd Ee Ff Gg Hh Ii
Jj Kk Ll Mm Nn Oo Pp etc.

Roman sans-serif

Aa Bb Cc Dd Ee Ff Gg
Hh Ii Jj Kk Ll Mm Nn

Figure 3.33
Minimum heights of lowercase letters for visibility at increasing distances for bold typefaces

Height of lowercase letters

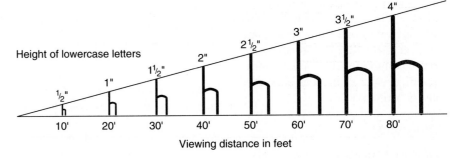

Viewing distance in feet

Size of Lettering

Displays such as bulletin boards and posters are often meant to be viewed by people situated thirty, forty, or more feet away. In these cases the size of the lettering is crucial for legibility. A common rule of thumb is to make lowercase letters one-half inch high for each ten feet of viewer distance. This means, for example, that to be legible to a student seated in the last seat of a thirty-foot-long classroom the lettering would have to be at least one and one-half inches in height. Figure 3.33 illustrates these minimum specifications for lettering height.

Spacing of Lettering

The distance between the letters of the individual words must be judged by experience rather than on a mechanical basis. This is because some

GOOD

MINE

LABWORK

"optical spacing"

Figure 3.34
Irregular combinations of letters require estimating equal amounts of white space between each pair of letters. The technique is called "optical spacing."

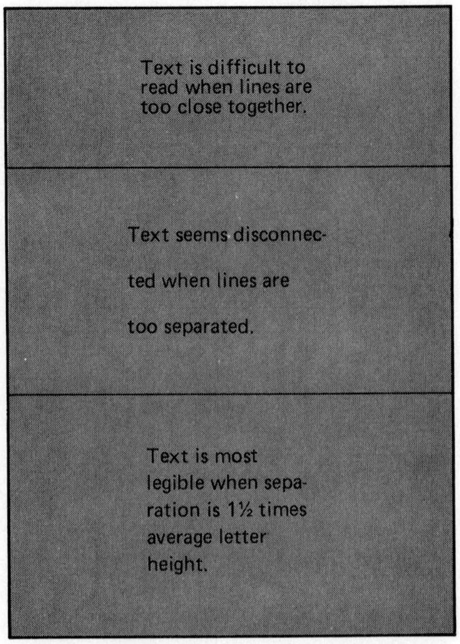

Text is difficult to read when lines are too close together.

Text seems disconnec-

ted when lines are

too separated.

Text is most legible when separation is 1½ times average letter height.

Figure 3.35
Various text separations illustrate the appropriate vertical spacing between lines.

HOW TO . . .
Design Visuals

Information/Instructional Purposes

❑ Use visuals whenever possible to illustrate ideas.

❑ Present a single concept in each visual.

❑ Break down complex visuals into simpler ones or build them up step-by-step.

❑ Minimize text on each visual; maximum of six words per line and six lines per visual.

Graphic/Picture Elements

❑ Use visuals that are not too abstract or too realistic.

❑ Use scale or common object to indicate size of unfamiliar objects.

❑ Eliminate distracting backgrounds.

❑ If feeling of depth is important, use another object to create the foreground.

❑ Use the "rule of thirds."

❑ Avoid splitting visual exactly in half with a horizontal line.

❑ Use graphs to present data.

❑ Use bold (thick), plain typefaces.

Text/Lettering Elements

❑ Avoid using many different typefaces (styles of letters) on the same visual.

❑ Use italics, boldface, underlining, or color for emphasis.

❑ Use lowercase lettering, adding capitals only when normally required.

❑ Center title at top of visual.

❑ Use short, concise, meaningful, descriptive titles that contain key words.

❑ Spacing between lines should be $1\frac{1}{2}$ times word height.

Color

❑ Use brightest and lightest color to focus attention on important elements.

❑ Use lettering and visuals that contrast with background color.

❑ Use consistent background colors in a series of visuals.

❑ Limit the number of colors on a visual.

Layout

❑ Make visuals as simple as possible; avoid excessive detail.

❑ Make sure your visual appears balanced.

❑ Use a horizontal format for overhead transparencies and slides.

❑ Make visual legible; if audience can't read it, don't use it.

❑ Use pleasing layout (balanced, orderly, left-justified).

Source: Adapted from "Principles of Visual Design," presentation by Carl Stafford and James Russell at the National Society for Performance and Instruction annual conference in Toronto, Ontario, March 30, 1990.

---

letters (e.g., capital A, I, K, and W) are quite irregular in shape compared to the rectangular letters (e.g., capital H, M, N, and S) and circular letters (e.g., capital C, G, O, and Q). When the rectangular letters or circular letters are combined with each other at equal spacing, there are rather regular patterns of white space between letters. But when irregular letters are combined with others in this way, the patterns of white space can be very uneven. The only way to overcome this potentially distracting unevenness is to space all your letters by "optical spacing," that is, by what *appears* even to the eye (see Figure 3.34).

The vertical spacing between lines of printed material is also important for legibility. If the lines are too close together, they will tend to blur together at a distance; if they are too far apart, they will seem disjointed, not part of the same unit. For a happy medium, the vertical space between the lines should be slightly less than the average height of the lowercase letters. To achieve this, use a ruler to draw lines lightly on your blank layout. Separate baselines by about one-and-one-half times the height of the lowercase letters. Lettering on these lines will then result in text with the correct spacing (see Figure 3.35).

❏ APPRAISAL CHECKLIST
Visuals

Title _____ Format _____

Producer _____ Date _____

Audience/Grade Level _____

Objectives (stated or implied)

Brief Description

Rating	High		Medium		Low	Comments
Information and Instructional Purposes: visualized, single concept, simple, minimum text	❏	❏	❏	❏	❏	
Graphic and Picture Elements: appropriate realism, size indicated, background, foreground, rule of thirds	❏	❏	❏	❏	❏	
Text/Lettering Elements: bold, few typefaces, lowercase, title centered at top, key words, spacing	❏	❏	❏	❏	❏	
Color: focuses attention, contrast, consistent, limited number	❏	❏	❏	❏	❏	
Layout: simple, balanced, horizontal, legible, pleasing	❏	❏	❏	❏	❏	

Strong Points

Weak Points

Reviewer _____

Position _____

Recommended Action _____ Date _____

_____

HOW TO . . .
Sketch

Faces

Use an oval and add a minimum of lines to indicate features and expressions.

1. Start with a circle or oval.
2. Add ears in the middle on each side.
3. Draw a nose between the ears.
4. Place the eyes near the top of the nose.
5. Draw the mouth halfway between the nose and chin.
6. Add hair and other features.

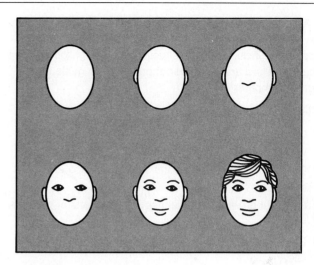

Body

Begin with stick figures, which can show action. With practice, add detail to your characters.

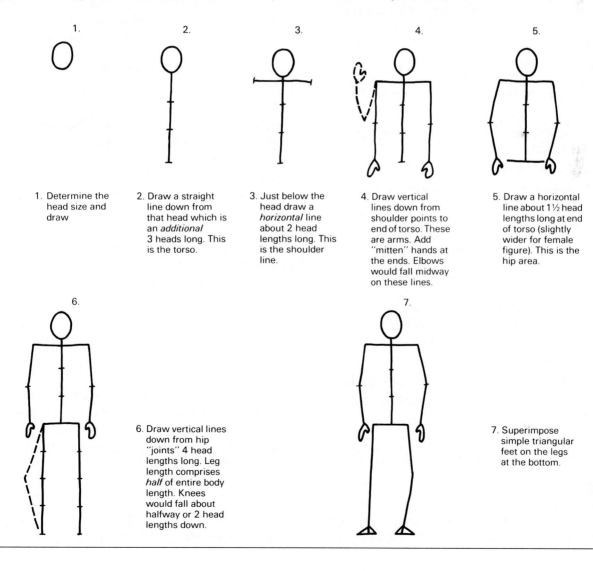

1. Determine the head size and draw

2. Draw a straight line down from that head which is an *additional* 3 heads long. This is the torso.

3. Just below the head draw a *horizontal* line about 2 head lengths long. This is the shoulder line.

4. Draw vertical lines down from shoulder points to end of torso. These are arms. Add "mitten" hands at the ends. Elbows would fall midway on these lines.

5. Draw a horizontal line about 1½ head lengths long at end of torso (slightly wider for female figure). This is the hip area.

6. Draw vertical lines down from hip "joints" 4 head lengths long. Leg length comprises *half* of entire body length. Knees would fall about halfway or 2 head lengths down.

7. Superimpose simple triangular feet on the legs at the bottom.

When preparing instructional materials for use on computer screens, there are a number of factors to consider. They include titles, instructions, text, highlighting, and graphics. Here are a number of principles to guide the design of computer screens.

Titles

❑ Use short, concise, meaningful titles; avoid unnecessary words.

❑ Center titles at the top of the screen or place at the left margin.

❑ Spell out all words; do not use abbreviations or contractions.

❑ Describe the purpose or content of the screen in the title.

❑ Limit the title to not more than three lines.

❑ Place at least one blank line between the title and the text.

❑ Put title in boldface letters.

Instructions

❑ Use short sentences (not more than seven words).

❑ Provide step-by-step instructions.

❑ State instructions in a positive manner, except for serious warnings and cautions.

❑ State instructions in the active voice.

❑ Use clear wording in instructions; avoid highly technical terms or abbreviations.

Text

❑ Write in simple, uncluttered, and clear sentences.

❑ Use both upper- and lowercase letters to enhance readability.

❑ Use single screens under learner control for advancing (i.e., do not advance screens automatically).

❑ Provide double space within paragraphs.

❑ Put a period at the end of each sentence.

❑ Include only one paragraph per screen when possible.

❑ Use left justification (margins that are aligned) only.

❑ Break the lines of text at natural phrasing points (especially for poor readers).

❑ Avoid splitting words at the end of a line.

Highlighting

Highlighting techniques draw attention to words, text, or graphics and include color, size of type, underlining, boxes, asterisks, intensity, blinking or flashing elements (which may be the strongest attention getter), inverse images, and a cursor for pointing.

❑ Use italics, if possible, to emphasize text without decreasing readability.

❑ Leave an extra space before and after any word displayed in reverse video (inverse text).

❑ Use blinking or flashing only for very important messages, then return to normal or alternative highlighting after getting the learner's attention.

❑ Avoid using blinking or flashing in two locations on the same screen.

❑ Avoid "hot" colors such as pink and magenta, because they appear to pulsate.

❑ Use sound, if available, to signify that user action is needed.

❑ Limit the use of highlighting; overuse may let design techniques upstage the content.

Graphics

❑ Avoid excessive detail or realism.

❑ Break down complex graphics into simpler parts.

❑ Present graphics simultaneously with corresponding text.

❑ Use color to focus attention on important components.

❑ Limit the number of colors on the screen at any one time (no more than four).

❑ Use effective combinations of color (avoid red and green, blue and yellow, green and blue, and red and blue).

❑ Use color as a redundant cue (should be effective on monochrome screen, too).

Sources: Wilbert O. Galitz, *Handbook of Screen Format Design,* 2d ed. (Wellesley Hills, MA: QED Information Sciences, 1985). Also Jesse M. Heines, *Screen Design Strategies for Computer-Assisted Instruction* (Bedford, MA: Digital Press, 1984).

HOW TO . . .
Enlarge Visuals

One especially handy application of opaque and overhead projectors is to enlarge visuals for classroom display. You can make your own enlargement of any original picture that you want to display on the chalkboard, poster, or as part of a bulletin board.

❑ **Using Opaque.** Place printed material to be copied in the projector.

❑ **Using Overhead.** Using an overhead pen, trace the figure on a clear sheet of acetate, and place on projector.

Then, in either case,

❑ Dim the lights.

❑ Tape a sheet of paper or cardboard to a wall or tack it to a bulletin board.

❑ Direct the projected image onto the surface where you want to draw the image (paper, cardboard, or chalkboard).

❑ Adjust the distance of the projector from the wall to enlarge (or reduce) the image to the size desired. Move the projector farther back to enlarge (or closer to reduce).

❑ Trace over the projected image in whatever detail you wish.

Your students will be impressed with your "artistic ability," and maybe you will be too.

Types of Lettering

A wide variety of lettering techniques for visuals exist. The simplest is freehand lettering with markers and felt-tip pens, which come in an array of colors and sizes.

Letters can be cut from construction paper or other materials. Precut letters are also available in stationery and office supply stores. The letters are easy to use, because most come with an adhesive backing; however, they are rather expensive.

Many media centers and graphic production units in business and industry now use mechanical lettering devices such as the Kroy 88 (though desktop publishing is slowly taking its place). The style and size of the letters are determined by the interchangeable large plastic wheels. The letters are "printed" on strips of clear plastic or colored film. Once the backing has been removed, the letters will adhere to most surfaces. Desktop publishing systems are also frequently used to prepare lettering in various styles and sizes. The lettering ranges from a fraction of an inch in height for overhead transparencies to over a foot high for banners.

DRAWING, SKETCHING, AND CARTOONING

As described in Chapter 4, drawings, sketches, and cartoons are nonprojected visuals that can greatly enhance learning. There are many sources of these in magazines, textbooks, and advertisements. One often overlooked source is *you*. You don't have to be an artist to draw.

There are some basic guidelines and many how-to books that can help you communicate effectively using these graphic media.

With a little practice, you may be surprised by how well you can draw. Simple drawings can enhance chalkboard presentations, class handouts, bulletin boards, and overhead transparencies. For ideas on getting started, see "How To . . . Sketch" on page 87 and the references at the end of this chapter.

INSTRUCTOR-DUPLICATED MATERIALS

On occasion you may want to distribute your own printed materials to students. These materials may be handouts, viewing notes for videotapes, outlines for presentations,

Table 3.1
Summary of duplicating processes

Method	Principle	Materials and Approximate Cost	Evaluation
Spirit (for example, Ditto brand spirit duplicator)	Carbon impression on master transferred to paper with alcohol	Master: $0.08 Paper: $3.00/ream	Master easily prepared; operation simple; good for up to 150 copies in multicolor
Stencil (mimeograph)	Ink passes through openings in waxlike stencil and is picked up by paper in contact with stencil	Stencil: $0.30 Paper: $3.00/ream	Care needed in making master; machine more complex than spirit; each color requires separate operation; quality slightly better than spirit; cleanup takes time
Electrostatic (for example, Xerox brand plain paper copier)	Negatively charged ink powder is on a positively charged metal plate, from which it is transferred to paper by electrostatic attraction	Copy: $0.02–$0.05 Machine costs vary	Can copy anything; fair to good quality; machine cost high; operation simple after adjustments
Offset printing	Ink adheres to image on plate; transferred to blanket and then to paper	Master: $0.40–$0.70 Copies: $1.00/100	Inexpensive plates and preparation of plates of some types; quality excellent; operation requires technician; clean-up time lengthy

THE FAR SIDE   By GARY LARSON

© 1986 Universal Press Syndicate

"Oh, lovely—just the hundredth time you've managed to cut everyone's head off."

Figure 3.36

study guides for mediated materials, or tests. With the availability of graphics and text programs for personal computers, desk-top publishing has become a reality. With word processing you can write, edit, and check your spelling at the computer. Graphics can be added from clip art or from your own sketches.

Once your materials have been completed, they need to be duplicated. There are several duplication processes. Schools tend to use spirit duplication, mimeograph machines, and some photocopying, whereas businesses rely heavily on photocopying and offset printing. The characteristics and approximate costs of each of these processes are described in Table 3.1.

PHOTOGRAPHY FOR INSTRUCTION

Elements of Photography

All cameras, regardless of their size, shape, or type, operate on the same basic principles. There are four elements required for photography: light, a subject, a camera, and film. Light (sunlight or flash) is reflected from the subject and passes through the lens to form an invisible image on the film called an exposure. Let's look at the four elements in more detail.

Light. Light may be from natural sources (i.e., sunlight) or from artificial sources (light bulbs or camera flash units). The film must be exposed to the proper amount of light. Too little exposure and the picture will be dark; too much and the picture will be too light.

Subject. The subject should be interesting and imaginative. The subject should be "composed," or framed, in the picture properly. (See "How To . . . Compose Better Pictures" on pages 92–93.)

Camera. The camera is a light-tight box with a lens to collect the light from the subject and to focus the light on the film. The amount of light getting into the camera is controlled by the lens opening and the shutter speed.

Film. Film is a light-sensitive material that records the image. The image becomes visible after it is processed by chemicals. With Polaroid film, the chemicals are part of the film package.

Parts of a Camera

Cameras have many parts, but the most important parts common to all cameras are the aperture, the shutter, the viewfinder, the focus, and the film advance (see Figure 3.37).

Aperture. This is the lens opening that regulates the amount of light that enters the camera. On some cameras the size of the opening is fixed; on other cameras there are two or three possible settings for the aperture. On many cameras, however, the size of the lens opening is adjustable over a broad range.

Shutter. The *shutter* controls the length of time that light enters the camera and reaches the film. Again, there is only one shutter speed on simple cameras but several on more complex cameras. The shutter speed refers to the period of time that light is allowed to enter the camera. On the shutter speed control knob the speed is usually given as a whole

number such as 250, 125, or 30. However, these numbers refer to fractions of a second (i.e., 1/250 of a second, 1/125 of a second, and 1/30 of a second). The higher the number, the shorter the time that the shutter is open. The very fast shutter speeds (with the shutter open only a very short period of time) allow you to photograph rapidly moving objects, such as race cars.

Viewfinder. The *viewfinder* allows you to see what the film will "see" when the shutter is opened. In many cameras the viewfinder is near the top of the camera and you look parallel to the lens opening. Consequently, you may not see exactly what will appear in the photograph. Except at very close range, the discrepancy is negligible. With a single-lens reflex camera, a movable mirror allows you to view directly through the lens. The mirror is moved out of the way when a photograph is taken.

Focus. This is the setting of the lens that determines the sharpness of the image. Inexpensive cameras often cannot be focused and have just one setting which is usually good for objects from five feet to infinity. Other cameras have a full range of focus from three feet to infinity. The focus may be determined by a distance scale (to the subject) and is indicated in feet and/or meters. Other cameras have a range finder with a double image or a split image.

Film Advance. This device moves the exposed image and positions unexposed film in place for the next photograph. In older cameras it was possible to get a double exposure if the film was not advanced by the photographer. Most of today's cameras will not allow you to push the shutter release until the film hasbeen advanced. The typical film-advance mechanism is a lever mounted on the upper-right-hand side of the camera. Some cameras

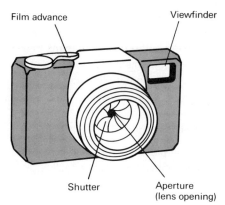

Figure 3.37
Components of a typical camera

Figure 3.38
A 35mm viewfinder camera with many programmable features and auto-focus

have an attachment for rapid advance, which allows you to take many pictures in a few seconds. This feature is not necessary for most educational applications. Many of the newer cameras have automatic film advance along with automatic focus.

Selecting a Camera

The type of camera you choose depends on the kinds of pictures you find useful for instruction. If you do not take extreme close-ups and do not have use for telephoto and other special lenses, then you may prefer a range-finder camera for portability, reliability, and simplicity (Figure 3.38). The quality of the image

Taking better pictures means making the subject most prominent and composing the elements of the picture.

SUBJECT

How you place your subject in the frame is critical in taking effective pictures.

❑ Zero in on your real subject. Cut out the unnecessary elements in a picture, even if it's yourself.

❑ Scale indications are important, particularly if the object being photographed is not common.

❑ Eliminate distracting backgrounds that may also cause poor exposure (e.g., make sure blinds or draperies are closed if you are shooting toward them).

❑ If you are photographing a moving object, put more space in front of the object than in back of it.

❑ Be cautious about possible distortion when taking dramatic angle shots. When taking pictures of a building, get as high as you can to reduce the angle of a shot. This is where a telephoto lens comes in handy.

❑ If a feeling of depth is important, place an object in the foreground, but not so that it is distracting.

COMPOSITION

In addition to the preceding comments, the following will help you frame your pictures for a more pleasing appearance and instructional clarity.

❑ Use the "rule of thirds." Divide a picture area in thirds both vertically and horizontally. The center of interest should be near one of the intersections of the lines.

- ❏ Avoid splitting a picture exactly in half with a horizontal line. It is tempting to do so in photos that include the horizon.

- ❏ When taking a scenery shot or one of a building, framing the scene with something in the foreground, such as the branches of a tree, often improves the picture in terms of interest and perspective.

- ❏ Learn to control depth of field, the region of sharp focus in front of and behind your subject. Shallow depth can often make a subject more dramatic. On the other hand, extreme depth can make scenery more striking. Depth of field can be controlled by varying the distance between you and your subject, the lens used, and the f/stop selected.

You will notice your photographs steadily improving as you master the composition of your subject.

taken with a moderately priced range-finder camera is very good.

If, however, you need to take extreme close-ups, have a use for a variety of lenses (wide angle, telephoto), and do a lot of copying, then a single-lens reflex (SLR) camera is what you want. Although it is bulkier and more difficult to use, the SLR is more flexible than a range-finder camera (Figure 3.39).

Both types of cameras are available in models with automatic and semiautomatic exposure controls. Before the incorporation of photocells and microprocessors into cameras, even amateur photographers had to know the relationship between film speed, lens opening (f/stop), and shutter speed. Today's picture taker need learn only a few simple steps from the instruction manual to achieve a proper exposure on the film. Sometimes unusual lighting situations call for modifications of camera-determined settings. A little experience with the camera will guide such modifications. Relieved of the necessity to determine exposure, the photographer can concentrate on composing the picture (see Figure 3.40).

New cameras are packed with computer technology. These "point-and-shoot" cameras have automatic loading, film-speed setting, exposure, focus, flash, and winding.

New developments in photography include digital cameras. Rather than using chemicals to preserve the visuals on film, these cameras store full-color images in a digital format. A charge-coupled device (see page 154) in the back of the camera converts light energy to digital data. Since there is no film, there is no waiting for processing and developing. Images can be viewed immediately on a monitor. The digital image can be transmitted over telephone lines or downloaded to a computer. This type of photography is especially useful for desktop publishing and presentations. If a color photograph is desired, a printer can convert the digital data to a full-color print. While there is a gap in

Figure 3.39
A 35mm SLR camera, programmable and fully manual with auto or manual focus

Figure 3.40
Automatic features allow the amateur photographer to concentrate on composing the desired picture.

quality between digital images and photographic prints, that gap is narrowing.

Most instructors in education and training use slides far more often than they do prints. Unless you can

afford the luxury of two cameras—and don't mind carrying them around—you will probably be better off keeping slide film in your camera. If you find later that you need prints, very satisfactory ones can

ANALYZE LEARNERS

General Characteristics

The high school students are in their first-year Spanish course. They attend the only high school in a small town in the southeastern United States. Consequently, the class members represent diverse socioeconomic backgrounds. Their grade levels range from freshman to senior, and their ages from fourteen to eighteen. The grade point averages go from a D average to an A average. The class members are highly motivated because the course is an elective. None of the students have physical or emotional handicaps.

Entry Competencies

Some of the students have learned common Spanish words and phrases on their own. In the course the teacher has taught about 100 words, so all the students have a limited reading and speaking vocabulary.

The students have a very positive attitude toward learning to read and to speak Spanish. Some hope to travel in Spanish-speaking countries. The teacher usually takes a small group of students to Mexico during the spring break. Others plan to take a second course in Spanish while still in high school. A few plan to continue their study of Spanish in college.

STATE OBJECTIVES

The objectives for the Spanish vocabulary lesson are as follows:

1. Given an example of or the English word for a common color, the first-year Spanish student will pronounce correctly and write correctly the name of that color 90 percent of the time.

2. Given a visual showing or the English word for a common object, the first-year Spanish student will pronounce correctly and write correctly the name of that object 90 percent of the time.

SELECT, MODIFY, OR DESIGN MATERIALS

In looking for materials to teach Spanish words for colors and objects, the teacher was unable to find anything other than the textbook. Realizing that the students learned from practice and interaction, the teacher wanted to incorporate these into the lesson. Upon further consideration, the teacher realized that none of the materials could be modified to adequately meet the objectives of the lesson and the characteristics of the students, so the teacher decided to design an original bulletin board.

The bulletin board was titled "Los Colores de Objetos." The teacher selected visuals of a dozen colorful objects (e.g., a green chair, a red box, a blue boat, and a brown horse) and mounted the pictures on the bulletin board. Next to each visual were its color and name in Spanish. These were covered by a large index card with a question mark on it.

UTILIZE THE MATERIALS

The materials were actually used by the students and not the teacher. The teacher distributed worksheets with the numbers one through twelve and a place to write the color and name of the object.

Individually or in small groups the students were to look at the visuals, write the Spanish words on the worksheet, then lift the flap (index card) to reveal the correct color and name in Spanish.

REQUIRE LEARNER PARTICIPATION

The teacher designed interaction into the bulletin board. The students were to construct their Spanish words and then check their answers under the flaps. They were immediately given feedback as to the correctness of their responses.

An additional form of interaction resulted from the students' talking while at the bulletin board—challenging each other to get the correct answers, speaking the words in Spanish, and correcting each other's written and spoken answers. The result was a dynamic, interactive learning session.

EVALUATE

The teacher evaluated the effectiveness of the bulletin board by watching the students' responses to it and listening to their positive comments about it. In addition, the students were given a weekly quiz each Friday covering the words that had been on the bulletin board that week. The bulletin board provided self-evaluation for the students as they learned while practicing the words for that week.

be made from slides. If very large photographs are required (eight by ten inches or larger), laser technology can make prints of remarkable quality from slides. However, if you prefer using print film, slides can be made from your color negatives at many camera shops.

Having chosen a camera and type of film, you will find guidelines for taking instructionally useful photos in the "How To" feature on pages 92–93.

For hints on planning a slide or slide-tape presentation, see "How To . . . Develop a Sound-Slide Presentation" on pages 254 in Chapter 9. Further technical information on photography and suggestions for working with student photography can be found in the audiovisual references at the end of this chapter.

APPLICATION OF THE ASSURE MODEL TO VISUALS

After having analyzed the audience and content as described in Chapter 2, you must state your objectives. If the objective indicates the need for visuals in instruction, you next select, modify, or design visuals to meet this need. The "Appraisal Checklist: Visuals" on page 86 can be very helpful in the selection process. If you need to modify the visuals selected, the sections of this chapter on lettering visuals and drawing, sketching, and cartooning should be good references. These same sections are valuable if you need to design your own visuals for instruction. In addition, refer to the section on designing visuals. If the visual will be part of a bulletin board, the "How To . . . Develop a Bulletin Board Display" (page 121) contains some guidelines.

Following the selection, modification, or design of visuals, you will want to utilize them properly. The section of this chapter beginning on page 70, "Using Visuals in Instruction," has guidelines on how to assist learners in decoding (reading) and encoding (making) visuals. In the next two chapters on nonprojected and projected visuals there are several "Showmanship" sections which provide suggestions for the use of visuals.

When selecting, modifying, or designing visuals as well as deciding how you plan to use them, you should consider how you will require learner response from the visuals. As discussed, one of the sets of principles to be considered in designing visuals is interaction (page 83). Interaction provides for learner response and increased learning. Finally, the instruction involving visuals must be evaluated in terms of student learning and overall effectiveness, as discussed in Chapter 2. If you follow the ASSURE model in your use of visuals, your chances of successful instruction are increased.

REFERENCES

Print References

Adams, Dennis M., and Hamm, Mary E. *Media and Literacy: Learning in an Electronic Age.* Springfield, IL: Charles Thomas, 1989.

Balan, Phyllis, "Improving Instructional Print Materials through Text Design." *Performance and Instruction* (August 1989):13–18.

Bloomer, Carolyn M. *Design Principles.* 2d ed. Blue Ridge Summit, PA: Tab Books, 1989.

Braden, Roberts, and Hortin, John A. "Identifying the Theoretical Foundations of Visual Literacy." *Journal of Visual Verbal Languaging* 2, no. 2 (1983):37–42, 58–66.

Braden, Roberts, ed. *About Visuals: Research, Teaching and Applications.* Blacksburg, VA: Virginia Tech, 1989.

Cassidy, Jack. "Using Graphic Organizers to Develop Critical Thinking." *Gifted-Child Today* (November–December 1989):34–36.

Cassidy, Michael, and Knowlton, James Q. "Visual Literacy: A Failed Metaphor?" *Educational Communications and Technology* (Summer 1983):68–90.

Curtiss, D. *Introduction to Visual Literacy: A Guide to the Visual Arts and Communication.* Mountain View, CA: Mayfield Publishing, 1989.

Doelker, Christian. "Audio-Video Language—Verbal and Visual Codes." *Educational Media International* (March 1980):3–4.

Donoho, Grace. "Measures of Audiovisual Production Activities with Students." *Drexel Library Quarterly* (Spring 1985):91–104.

Do You See What I Mean? Learning through Charts, Graphs, Maps, and Diagrams. Dickson, Australia: Curriculum Development Centre, 1980.

Dwyer, Francis M., ed. *Enhancing Visualized Instruction.* State College, PA: Learning Services, 1987.

Fleming, Malcolm. "Characteristics of Effective Instructional Presentation: What We Know and What We Need to Know." *Educational Technology* (July 1981):33–38.

Gropper, George L. *Text Display: Analysis and Systematic Design.* Englewood Cliffs, NJ: Educational Technology Publication, 1991.

Hortin, John A. "A Need for a Theory of Visual Literacy." *Reading Improvement* (Winter 1982):257–67.

_____. "Instructional Design and Visualization." *Performance and Instruction* (September 1983):20–21.

_____. "Research for Teachers on Visual Thinking to Solve Verbal Problems." *Journal of Educational Technology Systems* (1984–1985):299–303.

_____. "Visual Literacy and Visual Thinking." In *Australian Society of Educational Technology National Yearbook, 1981,* ed. L. J. Ausburn. Hawthorn, Australia: ASET, 1982.

Kemp, Jerrold E., and Smellie, Don C. *Planning, Producing, and Using Instructional Media.* 6th ed. New York: Harper Collins, 1989.

Lloyd-Kolkin, Donna, and Tyner, Kathleen R. *Media and You, an Elementary Media Literacy Curriculum.* Englewood Cliffs, NJ: Educational Technology Publications, 1991.

Matkowski, B. S. *Steps to Effective Business Graphics.* San Diego, CA: Hewlett-Packard Company, 1983.

McKim, Robert. *Experience in Visual Thinking.* 2d ed. Monterey, CA: Brooks/Cole, 1980.

Pattison, Polly. *Publication Design and Printing Basics for Cooperative Edu-*

cation Professionals. Kalamazoo, MI: Cooperative Education Marketing, 1990.

Pettersson, Rune. Visuals for Information: Research and Practice. Englewood Cliffs, NJ: Educational Technology Publications, 1989.

Pictures of Ideas: Learning through Visual Comparison and Analogy. Dickson, Australia: Curriculum Development Centre, 1980.

Postman, Neil. Conscientious Objections: Stirring Up Trouble about Language, Technology and Education. New York: Knopf, 1990.

Simonson, Michael R., and Volkner, Roger P. Media Planning and Production. Columbus: Merrill, 1984.

Sless, David. Learning and Visual Communications. New York: Wiley, 1981.

Thomas, James L. Nonprint Production for Students, Teachers, and Media Specialists: A Step-by-Step Guide. 2d ed. Littleton, CO: Libraries Unlimited, 1988.

Tufte, E. R. The Visual Display of Quantative Information. Cheshire, CT: Graphics Press, 1983.

————. Envisioning Information. Cheshire CT: Graphics Press, 1990.

Visual Education, An Interdisciplinary Approach for Students K–12 Using Visuals of All Kinds. Minneapolis, MN: Minneapolis Public Schools, 1987.

Walker, David A. Understanding Pictures: A Study in the Design of Appropriate Visual Materials for Education in Developing Countries. Amherst, MA: University of Massachusetts Center for International Education, 1980.

What a Picture! Learning from Photographs. Dickson, Australia: Curriculum Development Centre, 1981.

Zelanzy, G. Choosing and Using Charts. New York: Visual Communication Consultant, 1972.

Periodicals

Journal of Visual Literacy, International Visual Literacy Association.

Strategies, quarterly newsletter for K–12 teachers of media and literacy.

The Visual Literacy Review, International Visual Literacy Association.

Audiovisual References

Art Elements: An Introduction. Santa Monica, CA: BFA Educational Media, 1981. 16mm film. 18 minutes.

Audiovisual Production Techniques. Indiana University Audio-Visual Center, 1982. Sound-slide series (6 series). Series titles: "Designing Visuals That Communicate" (4 sets); "Fundamentals of Photography" (3 sets); "Lettering for Instructional Materials" (5 sets); "Visuals for Projection" (3 sets); "Audio Principles" (3 sets); "Duplication" (2 sets); and "Electricity and the Media Specialist" (1 set).

Basic Lettering for Audiovisual Materials. Iowa City, IA: University of Iowa, 1985. VHS Videocassette. 6 minutes.

Bring Your Message into Focus. Eastman Kodak Co., 1982. Kit (dissolve-slide program). 20 minutes.

Copystand Photography. Iowa City, IA: University of Iowa, 1990. VHS Videocassette. 9 minutes.

Elements of Design. Bloomington, IN: Agency for Instructional Technology, 1988. Videocassette, 15 minutes.

Experiencing Design. Burbank, CA: Encore Visual Education, 1975. Four sound filmstrips. 58 frames.

How Does a Picture Mean? Washington, D.C.: Association for Educational Communications and Technology, 1967. Filmstrip. 76 frames.

How to Take Better Pictures. Media Tree, 1982. Slide set with audiocassette.

Learning to See and Understand: Developing Visual Literacy. White Plains, NY: Center for Humanities, 1973. Sound-slide set. 160 slides. 42 minutes.

Making Sense Visually. Washington, D.C.: Association for Educational Communications and Technology, 1969. Sound filmstrip. 76 frames.

Oh, C. Y. Introduction to the Preparation of Instructional Materials. 32 slide-tape sets, textbook, and student manual. Edmonton, Canada: Avent Media, 1980.

Photography: How It Works. Rochester, NY: Eastman Kodak Co., 1979. 16mm film. 12 minutes.

Principles of Picture Design. Bloomington, IN: Agency for Instructional Technology, 1988. Videocassette. 15 minutes.

The Simple Camera. Washington, D.C.: Association for Educational Communications and Technology. 12 filmstrips.

Spirit Duplicator. Iowa City, IA: University of Iowa, 1985. VHS Videocassette. 6 minutes.

Taking Better Pictures. Athens, GA: University of Georgia, 1984. Videocassette series.

A Visual Fable. Washington, D.C.: Association for Educational Communications and Technology, 1973. Sound filmstrip, with record or cassette. 18 minutes.

POSSIBLE PROJECTS

3–A. Locate an example of each type of visual: organizational, analogic, and realistic.

3–B. Design some instructional activities to improve the visual literacy skills of learners you now work with or might in the future. Your description of the lesson should include the materials (or a description of the materials), the role and activities of the students, and the role of the instructor.

3–C. Select a series of photographs from your own collection and criticize them in terms of composition.

3–D. Select a visual or a display and appraise it in terms of intended audience, objectives, arrangement, balance, and color.

3–E. Design a rough layout of a display related to your interests. Appraise it in terms of arrangement, balance, and color.

4

Nonprojected Visuals

OUTLINE

OBJECTIVES

After studying this chapter, you should be able to

1. Discuss the uses of models and real objects for instruction.

2. Discuss five purposes of and the procedures for conducting a field trip.

3. List five attributes (advantages or limitations) of nonprojected still pictures.

4. Describe at least three classroom applications of still pictures.

5. Identify five criteria for selecting still pictures and apply the "Appraisal Checklist: Still Pictures" to actual materials.

6. Define *graphic material* and describe three types of graphics.

7. Describe five applications for graphic materials in your teaching.

8. Apply the "Appraisal Checklist: Graphic Materials" to actual materials.

9. Demonstrate at least three techniques (showmanship tips) to enhance the use of still pictures and graphics with a group.

10. Identify two methods of preserving nonprojected visuals and state three reasons for doing so.

11. Compare the advantages and limitations of rubber cement mounting with those of dry mounting.

12. Describe five surfaces or devices for displaying visuals.

13. Demonstrate at least three techniques (showmanship tips) for improving your utilization of chalkboards and multipurpose boards.

14. State a major advantage that cloth boards and magnetic boards have over chalkboards.

15. Demonstrate five techniques (showmanship tips) to enhance the use of flip charts.

16. Discuss three purposes for exhibits and dioramas.

LEXICON

study print

graphics

bar graph

line graph

circle graph

pictorial graph

dry mounting

lamination

multipurpose board

copy board

flip chart

exhibit

diorama

Many of the instructional materials discussed in this chapter are so common that instructors are inclined to underestimate their pedagogical value. Materials don't have to be exotic or expensive to be useful. Small can indeed be beautiful, and inexpensive can be effective! In fact, in some situations—for instance, with lack of electricity, isolation, a low budget, or small class size—these simpler materials may be the only media available (Figure 4.1).

Even though the focus in this chapter is on nonprojected visuals, the discussion includes some topics that technically might not be classified as visuals. These include real objects, models, field trips, and the devices used to display visuals: chalkboards, cloth boards, magnetic boards, and flip charts.

REAL OBJECTS

Real objects, such as coins, tools, artifacts, plants, and animals, are some of the most accessible, intriguing, and involving materials in educational use (Figure 4.2). The gerbils that draw a crowd in the kindergarten, the terrarium that introduces

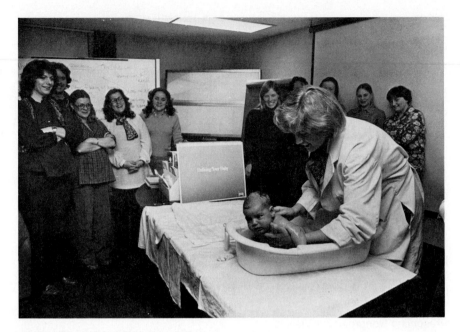

Figure 4.2
There is no substitute for the real thing when learning some tasks.

middle schoolers to the concept of ecology, the collection of Revolutionary era coins, the frogs dissected in the college biology laboratory, the real baby being bathed in the parenting class—these are just a few examples of the potential of real objects to elucidate the obscure and stimulate the imagination.

These concrete objects are the instructional aids most closely associated with the experiences at the bottom of Dale's cone of experience: direct purposeful experiences (see Chapter 1). As such, they are ideal media for introducing learners to a new subject. Used as part of concept learning, they give meaning to otherwise merely abstract words.

Real objects may be used as is or modified to enhance instruction. Examples of modification include

❑ Cutaways. Devices such as machines with one side cut away to allow close observation of the inner workings (Figure 4.3).

❑ Specimens. Actual plants, animals, or parts thereof preserved for convenient inspection.

❑ Exhibits. Collections of artifacts, often of a scientific or historical

nature, brought together with printed information to illustrate a point (Figure 4.4).

Besides their obvious virtues as a means of presenting information, raising questions, and providing hands-on learning experiences, real objects can also play a valuable role in the evaluation phase of instruction. They can be displayed in a central location. Learners can identify them, classify them, describe their functioning, discuss their utility, or compare and contrast them. Such a testing situation emphasizes the real-world application of the topic of

Figure 4.1
Nonprojected visuals are the most widely used media in many isolated, rural areas around the world.

Figure 4.3
A cutaway of a machine reveals its hidden components.

study, aids transfer of training, and helps transcend the merely verbal level of learning.

MODELS

Models are three-dimensional representations of a real thing. A model may be larger, smaller, or the same size as the object it represents. It may be complete in detail or simplified for instructional purposes. Indeed, models can provide learning experiences that real things cannot provide (see Figure 4.5). Important details can, for example, be accented with color. Some models can be disassembled to provide interior views not possible with the real thing.

Models of almost anything, from airplanes to zebras can be purchased for classroom use. A wide variety of plastic model kits are also available for assembly by you or your students. Assembly itself can be instructional. Classroom construction of plastic model kits appeals to children of all ages (and, indeed, to adults) and can stimulate inquiry and discovery. Assembly activities help sharpen both cognitive and psychomotor skills.

Mock-ups, which are simplified representations of complex devices or processes, are prevalent in industrial training. By highlighting essen-

Figure 4.4
Cultural artifacts come to life when presented in a well-designed exhibit.

Figure 4.5
An anatomical model, being three-dimensional, is a more concrete referent than a photograph, drawing, or even a motion picture.

AV SHOWMANSHIP

Real Objects and Models

❑ Familiarize yourself with the object or model before using it in classroom instruction.

❑ Practice your presentation. If your object or model is a working one, be sure you know how it works and what might go wrong.

❑ Be sure your audience does not get the wrong impression of the size, shape, or color of the real object if the model differs from it in these respects.

❑ Whenever feasible, encourage your students to handle and manipulate the objects and model under study.

❑ Store objects out of sight when they are not being used for instruction. Left standing around, they are likely to take students' attention away from other classroom activities.

tial elements and eliminating distracting details, mock-ups clarify the complex. They are sometimes constructed as working models to illustrate the basic operations of a real device (see Figure 4.6). This situation allows individuals or small groups to manipulate the mock-up at their own convenience, working with the subject matter until they comprehend it. A mock-up of a microcomputer might have the internal components spread out on a large board with the components labeled and the circuit diagrams printed on the board. The most sophisticated type of mock-up, the simulator, is discussed in Chap-

ter 13. A simulator is a device, such as a flight simulator, which allows learners to experience the important aspects of a real-life process without the risks.

Models and real objects are the recommended media when realism is essential for learning—with concepts that involve three dimensions; tasks that require identification by size, shape, or color; and hands-on or laboratory practice.

When considering students' learning styles, teachers often give models and real objects a high priority. Most learners, including adults, when given a choice express a preference for hands-on experiences

rather than passive listening. "Please touch" is a most welcome invitation.

FIELD TRIPS

The field trip, an excursion outside the classroom to study real processes, people, and objects, often grows out of students' need for firsthand experience. It makes it possible for students to encounter phenomena that cannot be brought into the classroom for observation and study (Figure 4.7). Field trips may include a trip of a few minutes into the school yard to observe a tree, a trek across the street to see construction work, or a longer trip of several days

Figure 4.6
A mock-up of an engine electrical system provides the trainee with a full-scale working model in which only distracting details have been deleted.

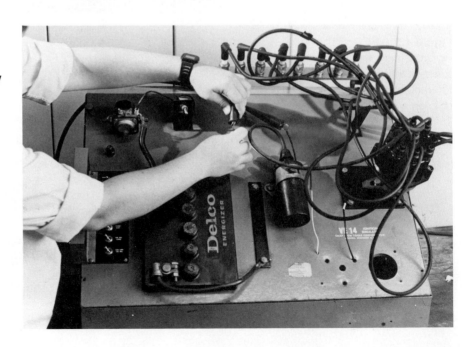

to tour historical locations. Popular field-trip sites include zoos, museums, public buildings, and parks.

Real-life experiences such as field trips are particularly valuable for learners who have a kinesthetic perceptual strength, that is, a preference for bodily involvement. This preference is very common among young children, of course. As they grow older, they tend to develop a stronger ability to learn from other sensory channels—seeing and listening. But even adults enjoy and profit from field experiences. In fact, Dunn found that 70 percent of the adults studied preferred learning from real-life experiences versus 5 percent

from reading and 26 percent from seeing or reading.[1]

For a field trip to be justified, it should grow out of and be directly related to the regular course of study. Objectives should be developed for the field trip. There should be lead-in as well as follow-up activities. The lead-in prepares the students for the field trip; the follow-up helps them get the most from the field trip.

---

[1] Kenneth J. Dunn, "Measuring the Productivity Preferences of Adults," in *Student Learning Styles and Brain Behavior* (Reston, VA: National Association of Secondary School Principals, 1982).

Figure 4.7
Field trips provide students with opportunities for firsthand observation.

HOW TO . . .
Conduct a Field Trip

Planning

1. Have a clear picture of the purpose and objectives of the trip.
2. Have a clear overview of the content of the trip. Preview the trip yourself.
3. Make arrangements with the school principal, the host, and other teachers (if they are involved). Secure consent of the parents for students to make the trip.
4. Arrange transportation.
5. Provide sufficient supervision. Emphasize appropriate dress. Set up safety precautions and ground rules.

Preparing

1. Clarify the purpose of the trip with the entire group. Build interest in the trip through preparatory activities such as

    Class discussion

    Stories

    Reports

    Films

    Teacher-student planning

2. Give explicit directions to students regarding

    What to look for

    Questions to ask

    Information to be gathered

Notes to be made

Individual or group assignments

Conducting

1. Arrive promptly at the field-trip site.
2. Encourage students to observe carefully and to ask questions.
3. Obtain available materials that can be used later.
4. Account for all students before starting the return trip.

Follow-up

1. Conduct follow-up of the field trip with

    A discussion of how the trip related to the purpose

    Reports

    Projects

    Demonstrations

    Creative writing

    Independent individual research

    Exhibits of pictures, maps, charts, graphs, drawings, etc.

2. Write a thank-you letter to the host, guides, parent chaperons, drivers, and others who were instrumental in conducting the field trip. Notes written by the class or a student committee are most appreciated.

A field trip can serve many pedagogical purposes:

❏ Provide enrichment of factual information read in textbooks and make words on the printed page more meaningful

❏ Improve attitudes, expand understanding, and increase skills

❏ Provide firsthand experiences with objects, places, situations, and human relationships that cannot be provided in the classroom

❏ Sharpen awareness of the students' environment

❏ Expose students to careers that they might want to pursue

❏ Blend the classroom, the immediate community, and the larger world into a more meaningful whole

The evaluation, or follow-up, is an equally vital aspect of a field trip. If the purpose for making the trip is to get additional factual information, the evaluation will be more formal. If the objectives are the formation of attitudes and appreciation, follow-up activities might include discussion, role playing, or creative art projects. Whatever form it takes, the follow-up activity should be used to assess the success of the trip. Both the content covered and possible ways to improve future trips should be addressed. (See "How To . . . Conduct a Field Trip" on page 103.)

STILL PICTURES

Still pictures are photographic (or photographlike) representations of people, places, and things. The still pictures most commonly used in instruction are photographs, postcards, illustrations from books, periodicals, catalogs, and so on, and *study prints,* oversized illustrations commercially prepared to accompany specific instructional units (see Figures 4.8 and 4.9).

Advantages

Nonprojected still pictures can translate abstract ideas into a more

Figure 4.8
Nonprojected visuals include models, photographs, maps, and charts.

Figure 4.9
The smaller flash cards show details of the larger picture.

realistic format. They allow instruction to move down from the level of verbal symbols in Dale's cone of experience to a more concrete level.

Still pictures are readily available in books (including textbooks), magazines, newspapers, catalogs, and calendars. In addition, you can purchase large study prints for use with groups of students from educational

supply companies, or you can obtain them from your media center or library.

Still pictures are easy to use because they do not require any equipment. They are relatively inexpensive. Many can be obtained at little or no cost. Still pictures can be used in many ways at all levels of instruction and in all disciplines.

❑ APPRAISAL CHECKLIST
Still Pictures

Title (or content of picture) _____

Series Title (if applicable) _____

Source _____ **Date** _____ **Cost** _____

Subject area _____

Intended audience _____

Objectives (stated or implied)

Brief Description

Entry Capabilities Required

❑ Prior subject-matter knowledge/vocabulary

❑ Reading ability

❑ Other:

Rating	High		Medium		Low	Comments
Relevance to objectives	❑	❑	❑	❑	❑	
Authenticity/accuracy of picture	❑	❑	❑	❑	❑	
Clarity (uncluttered by irrelevant distracting elements)	❑	❑	❑	❑	❑	
Composition	❑	❑	❑	❑	❑	
Timeliness; avoids out-of-date elements, such as dress	❑	❑	❑	❑	❑	
Clarity of scale (familiar objects imply size of unfamiliar)	❑	❑	❑	❑	❑	
Legibility for classroom use	❑	❑	❑	❑	❑	
Technical quality (durability)	❑	❑	❑	❑	❑	

Strong Points

Weak Points

Reviewer _____

Position _____

Recommended Action _____ Date _____

_____

CLOSE-UP

Using Still Pictures

S till pictures can be used by students of all ages. This student examines examples of endangered species as part of a class project. The teacher assigns an endangered animal to a small group of students. Each small group cooperates and prepares a brief oral report to share with the class. During the presentation visuals of the assigned species are shown to the class. Following each group's presentation the teacher facilitates a discussion and summarizes key points. The still pictures are then displayed on a bulletin board along with other visuals of endangered species.

Study prints are used by a fifth grade teacher to show examples of pollution. The teacher works with the students in small groups. While some of the students are working on other activities in the classroom and in the media center, the teacher gathers ten to twelve students around him to discuss the study prints. His objective is for the students to be able to describe the common causes of pollution. The students are shown the study prints and then are asked to describe what procedures they would recommend for improving the environment.

Limitations

Some photographs are simply too small for use before a group. It is possible to enlarge any picture photographically, but that can be an expensive process. The opaque projector (described in Chapter 5) can be used to project an enlarged image before a group.

Still pictures are two-dimensional. The lack of three-dimensionality in a picture can be compensated for by providing a group of pictures showing the same object or scene from several different angles or positions. Also, a series of sequential still pictures can suggest motion (see Figure 4.10).

Applications

Photographs may be used in a variety of ways. Teacher-made or student-made photographs may be used to illustrate and to help teach specific lesson topics. Photographs of local architecture, for example, can illustrate a unit on architectural styles. (In this case, the students' skill in "reading" a visual could be reinforced by the instructor's pointing out that merely looking at the buildings in our environment is not the same as really "seeing" them.) Photographs taken on field trips can be valuable sources of information for classroom follow-up activities.

Students can and should understand that textbook pictures are not decorations, but are intended to be study aids and should be used as such. Students should be encouraged to give attention to them. Skill in decoding textbook pictures may also be included in instructional objectives to motivate the learners to use them for study purposes. The quality and quantity of illustrations are, of course, important factors in textbook choice. (See "Appraisal Checklist: Still Pictures," p. 105). Pictures from newspapers and periodicals may be used in similar ways.

Photographic study prints—enlargements printed in a durable form for individual use—also have many applications in the instructional setting. They are especially helpful in the study of processes—the production of iron or paper, for example, or the operation of the internal combustion engine. They are also very useful in teaching the social sciences. In geography they may help illustrate relationships between people and their environment that, because of space limitations, could not easily be depicted in textbook pictures.

All types of nonprojected still pictures may be used in testing and evaluation. They are particularly helpful with objectives requiring identification of people, places, or things.

Figure 4.10
A series of still pictures can approximate the impression of a motion picture sequence.

Nonprojected still pictures may also be used to stimulate creative expression such as telling or writing stories or composing poetry.

GRAPHIC MATERIALS

Our second major category of nonprojected visuals is graphic materials, often referred to simply as graphics. *Graphics* are nonphotographic, two-dimensional materials designed specifically to communicate a message to the viewer. They often include verbal as well as symbolic visual cues.

As a group, graphics demand special caution in use by instructors. Because the images are visually symbolic rather than fully representational, they leave more room for viewers to misinterpret the intended meaning. (This phenomenon was discussed in Chapter 3.) For example, research on newspaper readers' interpretations of editorial cartoons indicates that a large proportion of viewers may draw conclusions that are the opposite of what the artist intended. Psychologists find that people tend to project their own hopes, fears, and preconceptions onto images or verbal messages that are ambiguous. This is the basis of

the Rorschach or "inkblot" diagnostic test. The younger or less visually literate the audience, the more guidance the instructor will have to provide to ensure that the intended message is conveyed.

Here we will explore five types of graphics commonly found in the classroom situation: drawings (including sketches and diagrams), charts, graphs, posters, and cartoons.

Drawings

Drawings, sketches, and diagrams employ the graphic arrangement of lines to represent persons, places, things, and concepts. Drawings are, in general, more finished and representational than sketches, which are likely to lack detail. Stick figure compositions, for example, would be sketches. Diagrams are usually intended to show relationships or to

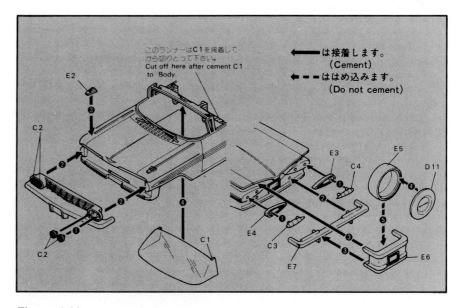

Figure 4.11
The use of visual symbols reduces drastically the need for words in this multilingual diagram for assembling a plastic scale model of an automobile.

TYPES OF CHARTS

Organization charts show the structure or chain of command in an organization such as a company, corporation, civic group, or government department. Usually they deal with the interrelationship of personnel or departments.

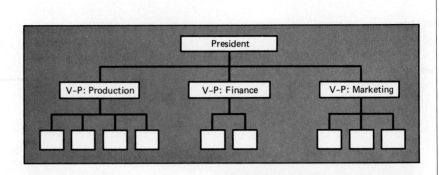

Classification charts are similar to organization charts but are used chiefly to classify or categorize objects, events, or species. A common type of classification chart is one showing the taxonomy of animals and plants according to natural characteristics. Dale's cone of experience classifies media from concrete to abstract.

Time lines illustrate chronological relationships between events. They are most often used to show historical events in sequence or the relationship of famous people and these events. Pictures or drawings can be added to the time line to illustrate important concepts. Time lines are very helpful for summarizing a series of events.

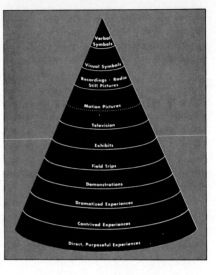

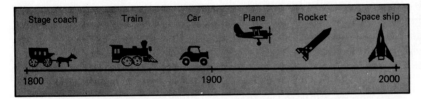

Tabular charts, or tables, contain numerical information, or data. They are also convenient for showing time information when the data are presented in columns, as in timetables for railroads and airlines.

Flowcharts, or process charts, show a sequence, a procedure, or, as the name implies, the flow of a process. Flowcharts are usually drawn horizontally and show how different activities, ingredients, or procedures merge into a whole.

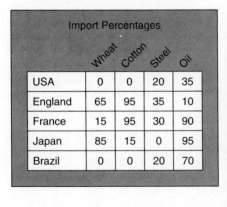

Import Percentages

	Wheat	Cotton	Steel	Oil
USA	0	0	20	35
England	65	95	35	10
France	15	95	30	90
Japan	85	15	0	95
Brazil	0	0	20	70

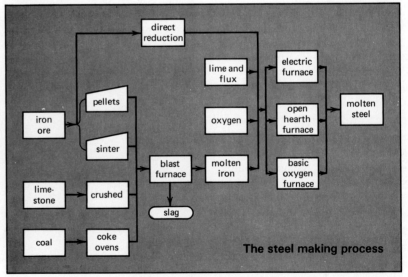

The steel making process

Figure 4.12

A line graph can make a table of data much easier to interpret.

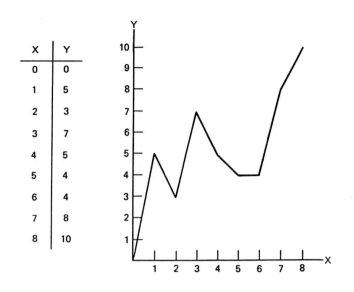

X	Y
0	0
1	5
2	3
3	7
4	5
5	4
6	4
7	8
8	10

help explain processes, such as how something works or how it is constructed (Figure 4.11).

Drawings can be used in the same manner as to photographic still pictures. Drawings are readily found in textbooks and other classroom materials. They can be used in all phases of instruction, from introduction of the topic through evaluation. Because they are likely to be less detailed and more to the instructional point than photographic materials, they are easily understood by students of all ages.

Teacher-made drawings can be very effective teaching and learning devices. They can be drawn on the chalkboard (or some other appropriate surface) to coincide with specific aspects of the instructional unit. They can also be used as substitutes for or adjuncts to still pictures. For example, stick figures can be quickly and easily drawn to show motion in an otherwise static representation.

Charts

Charts are graphic representations of abstract relationships such as chronologies, quantities, and hierarchies. They appear frequently in textbooks and training manuals as tables and flowcharts. They are also published as wall charts for group viewing in the form of organization charts, classification charts (e.g.,

the periodic table), and time lines (see "Types of Charts," p. 108).

A chart should have a clear, well-defined instructional purpose. In general (especially for younger students), it should express only one major concept or configuration of concepts. If you are developing your own charts, be sure they contain the minimum of visual and verbal information needed for understanding. A cluttered chart is a confusing chart. If you have a lot of information to convey, develop a series of simple charts rather than a single complex one. In other words, keep it simple.

A well-designed chart should communicate its message primarily through the visual channel. The verbal material should supplement the visual, not the reverse.

Graphs

Graphs provide a visual representation of numerical data. They also illustrate relationships among units of the data and trends in the data. Many tabular charts can be converted into graphs, as shown in Figure 4.12.

Data can be interpreted more quickly in graph form than in tabular form. Graphs are also more visually interesting. There are four major types of graphs: *bar, pictorial, circle,* and *line* (see p. 110). The type you choose to use will depend

largely on the complexity of the information you wish to present and the graph-interpretation skills of your audience. Numerous computer software programs can generate graphs. You enter the data, select the type of graph desired, and the computer does the rest. Some programs even provide output in a variety of colors.

Posters

Posters incorporate visual combinations of images, lines, color, and words and are intended to catch and hold the viewer's attention at least long enough to communicate a brief message, usually a persuasive one. To be effective, posters must be colorful and dynamic. They must grab attention and communicate their message quickly. One drawback in using posters is that their message is quickly blunted by familiarity. Consequently, they should not be left on display for too long. Commercial billboards are an example of posters on a very large scale.

Posters can be used effectively in numerous learning situations. They can stimulate interest in a new topic, a special class, or a school event. They may be employed for motivation—luring students to a school meeting or to the media center, for example, or encouraging them to read more. In industrial

TYPES OF GRAPHS

Bar graphs are easy to read and can be used with elementary age students. The height of the bar is the measure of the quantity being represented. The width of all bars should be the same to avoid confusion. A single bar can be divided to show parts of a whole. It is best to limit the quantities being compared to eight or less; otherwise the graph becomes cluttered and confusing. The bar graph, a one-scale graph, is particularly appropriate for comparing similar items at different times or different items at the same time; for example, the height of one plant over time or the heights of several students at any given time. The bar graph shows variation in only one dimension.

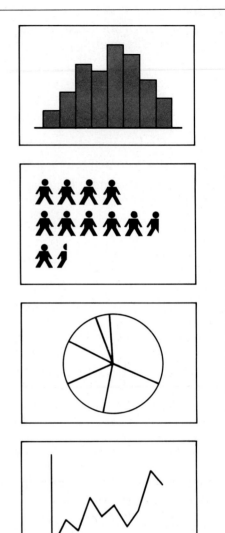

Pictorial graphs are an alternate form of the bar graph in which numerical units are represented by a simple drawing. Pictorial graphs are visually interesting and appeal to a wide audience, especially young students. However, they are slightly more difficult to read than bar graphs. Since pictorial symbols are used to represent a specific quantity, partial symbols are used to depict fractional quantities. To help avoid confusion in such cases, print values below or to the right of each line of figures.

Circle (or pie) graphs are relatively easy to interpret. In this type of graph, a circle or "pie" is divided into segments, each representing a part or percentage of the whole. One typical use of the circle graph is to depict tax-dollar allocations. The combined segments of a circle graph should, of course, equal 100 percent. Areas of special interest can be highlighted by illustrating a piece of pie separately from the whole.

Line graphs are the most precise and complex of all graphs. Line graphs are based on two scales at right angles. Each point has a value on the vertical scale and a value on the horizontal scale. Lines (or curves) are drawn to connect the points. Line graphs show variations in two dimensions, or how two or more factors change over time. For example, a graph can show the relation between pressure and temperature when the volume of a gas is held constant. Because line graphs are precise, they are very useful in plotting trends. They can also help simplify a mass of complex information.

AV SHOWMANSHIP

Still Pictures and Graphics

❑ Use large visuals that everyone can see simultaneously. (If visuals are not large enough for all to see, use one of the projection techniques described in Chapter 5.)

❑ Use simple materials.

❑ Cover irrelevant material in visuals with plain paper.

❑ Hold visuals steady when showing them to a group by resting them against a desk or table or putting them on an easel.

❑ Limit the number of pictures used in a given period of time. It is better to use a few visuals well than to overwhelm your audience with an abundance of underexplained visuals.

❑ Use just one picture at a time except for purposes of comparison. Lay one picture flat before going on to the next.

❑ Keep your audience's attention and help them learn from a visual by asking direct questions about it.

❑ Teach your audience to interpret visuals (see Chapter 3).

❑ Display questions pertaining to each visual alongside it. Cover the answers with flaps of paper. Have each student immediately check his or her own response for accuracy.

❑ Provide written or verbal cues to highlight important information contained in the visuals.

❑ APPRAISAL CHECKLIST
Graphic Materials

Title (or content of graphic) _____

Series Title (if applicable) _____

Source _____

Date _____ **Cost** _____

Subject Area _____

Intended Audience _____

Format

❑ Drawing

❑ Chart

❑ Graph

❑ Poster

❑ Cartoon

Objectives (stated or implied):

Brief Description

Entry Capabilities Required

❑ Prior subject-matter knowledge/vocabulary
❑ Reading ability
❑ Mathematical ability
❑ Other

Rating	High		Medium		Low	Comments
Relevance to objectives	❑	❑	❑	❑	❑	
Accuracy of information	❑	❑	❑	❑	❑	
Likely to arouse/maintain interest	❑	❑	❑	❑	❑	
Likely to be comprehended clearly	❑	❑	❑	❑	❑	
Technical quality	❑	❑	❑	❑	❑	
Legibility for use (size and clarity)	❑	❑	❑	❑	❑	
Simplicity (clear, unified design)	❑	❑	❑	❑	❑	
Appropriate use of color	❑	❑	❑	❑	❑	
Appropriateness of accompanying verbal information	❑	❑	❑	❑	❑	
Provisions for discussion	❑	❑	❑	❑	❑	

Strong Points

Weak Points

Reviewer _____

Position _____

Recommended Action _____ Date _____

education courses, science laboratories, and other situations where danger may be involved, posters can be used to remind people of safety tips (see Figure 4.13). Posters can also be used to promote good health practices such as not using drugs. An effective teaching and learning technique is to have students design posters as part of a class project, during fire prevention week or dental health month, for example.

Posters may be obtained from a variety of sources. Commercial poster companies publish catalogs containing pictures of their wares. Other companies and advertising organizations have posters available without cost to teachers for use in their classrooms. Some common

sources of posters are airlines, travel agencies, and government departments and agencies. Movie posters and political posters are also available. Stores and supermarkets are often willing to give posters (and other display materials) to teachers when they are no longer needed.

You can make your own posters with colored markers, computer printouts, and devices that print poster-sized pages. If you draw your own posters follow the visual design guidelines in Chapter 3 and refer to "How to . . . Sketch" (page 87) and "How to . . . Enlarge Visuals" (page 89) for helpful suggestions to enhance your posters. Computer-generated posters and banners can be made by taping together standard-size printer paper. Software, such as "Print Shop," can facilitate poster design and production.

Newer devices, such as Poster-Printer by Varitronics (Figure 4.14), can convert 8½-by-11-inch originals into 23-by-33-inch posters. The originals can be hand-drawn visuals, computer output, overhead transparency masters, or the like. The machines use high-speed electronics and a thermal printing process, which means no ink, toner, or ribbons. The process takes about a minute. The paper comes in a variety of colors (white, pink, yellow, or blue) and several print colors are available (black, red, blue, or orange). In addition to posters these machines can be used to generate prepared flip-chart pages and signs.

Cartoons

Cartoons, line drawings that are rough caricatures of real people and events, are perhaps the most popular and familiar graphic format. They appear in a wide variety of print media—newspapers, periodicals, textbooks—and range from comic strips intended primarily to entertain to drawings intended to make important social or political comments. Humor and satire are mainstays of the cartoonist's skill.

Rivero/Clarín/Buenos Aires

Figure 4.15
Political cartoons can be used to trigger discussion of current events.

Cartoons are easily and quickly read and appeal to children and adults alike. The best of them contain wisdom as well as wit. They can often be used by the teacher to make or reinforce a point of instruction. Appreciation and interpretation, however, may depend on the experience and sophistication of the viewer. Research studies consistently have found that people tend to project their own feelings and prejudices onto editorial cartoons. For example, a politician shown slinging mud at his opponent might be seen by supporters as a hero punishing the "wicked." Further, because they usually refer to contemporary figures or deal with current issues and events, editorial cartoons quickly become dated. Today's immediately recognized caricature can become tomorrow's nonentity. Be sure the cartoons you use for instructional purposes are within the experiential and intellectual range of your students.

PRESERVING NONPROJECTED VISUALS

One drawback in using nonprojected visuals in the classroom is that they are easily soiled or otherwise damaged as they are passed from student to student. Repeated display, storage, and retrieval can also add to wear and tear. Mounting and laminating are the two most effective preserva-

Figure 4.13
Posters combine visuals and words to quickly communicate an important message.

Figure 4.14
The PosterPrinter converts a notebook-size original into a poster that is eight times larger.

tion techniques, and they can contribute to the instructional effectiveness of nonprojected visuals.

Mounting

Mount nonprojected visuals on construction paper, cardboard, or other such materials for durability. The color of the mounting material should not draw attention away from the visual. It is generally a good idea to use pastel or neutral tones rather than brilliant or primary colors. Using one of the minor colors in the visual as the color for the mounting can enhance harmony. The total effect of your mounting should be neat and pleasing to the eye. Borders, for example, should be evenly cut, with side borders of equal width and the bottom border slightly wider than the top.

A variety of glues, cements, and pastes are available for mounting purposes. When used according to directions, almost all of them are effective. Some white glues, however, are likely to cause wrinkles in the picture when the adhesive dries, especially if used full strength. If you run into this problem, dilute the glue; for example, use four parts Elmer's glue to one part of water. Cover the entire back of the visual evenly with the adhesive before placing it on the mounting board. If excess adhesive seeps out around the edges, wipe it off with a damp cloth or sponge.

Figure 4.16
Glue sticks are convenient and effective for doing paste-ups and mounting small objects.

Glue sticks, marketed under names such as Stix-A-Lot and Pritt, may be used in place of liquid glues (Figure 4.16). They have the advantage of not running out around the edges of the material. Rubber cement can eventually damage and discolor photographs. Glue sticks are less likely to do this.

Rubber Cement Mounting. One of the most commonly used adhesives for mounting purposes is rubber cement. It is designed specifically for use with paper products. It is easy to use and less messy than many other liquid glues. Excess cement can easily be wiped away, and it is inexpensive. Rubber cement does, however, have two disadvantages. When the container is left uncovered for any length of time, the adhesive tends to dry out and thicken. Periodic doses of thinner (available commercially) may be necessary to keep the cement serviceable. A second disadvantage is that the adhesive quality of rubber cement tends to diminish over a period of time. Constant exposure to dry air may eventually cause it to lose its grip. This disadvantage can be compensated for with special precautions as noted for permanent rubber cement mountings (see page 114). However, even these mountings will not last indefinitely.

Dry Mounting. *Dry mounting* employs a specially prepared paper impregnated with heat-sensitive adhesive. The paper is available in sheets and rolls and is marketed under such names as Fusion-4000 and MT-5. The dry-mounting tissue bonds the backing material to the back of the visual. A dry-mount press is used to supply the heat and pressure necessary to activate the tissue's adhesive. The process is rapid and clean and results in permanent high-quality mounting. (See the "How to . . . Dry Mount Pictures" on page 115.)

One disadvantage of dry mounting is that it is relatively expensive.

However, it is possible to dry mount visuals without a dry-mount press by using an ordinary household iron. Set the iron on "silk" or "rayon." *Do not use steam.* The tip of the household iron can be used in place of the special tacking iron.

Laminating

Lamination provides visuals with protection from wear and tear by covering them with a clear plastic or plasticlike surface. Lamination helps to protect visuals against tears, scratches, and sticky fingers. Soiled surfaces can be wiped clean with a damp cloth.

Lamination also allows you to write on your visuals with a grease pencil or water-soluble ink for instructional purposes. The writing can be easily erased later with a damp cloth or sponge. A teacher of mathematics, for example, might write percentage figures on a laminated illustration of a pizza or a pie to help teach the concept of fractions. You can also have students write on laminated materials. When the lesson is completed, the markings can be erased and the material is ready for further teaching. Classroom materials other than nonprojected visuals (e.g., workbook pages) can also be laminated to add extra durability and to allow for erasable writing by teacher and students.

Clear plastic sheets with adhesive backing (such as Con-Tact shelf paper) are available for laminating purposes. Remove the backing cover to expose the adhesive and carefully press the clear plastic sheet on the visual. Any portions of the plastic sheet that extend beyond the edges of the visual can be cut off or doubled back for additional protection.

Laminating can be done with a dry-mount press (see page 116). Rolls of laminating film for use with a dry-mount press are available from commercial sources. Or a laminating machine can be used (Figure 4.17). These machines use two rolls of laminating film and cover

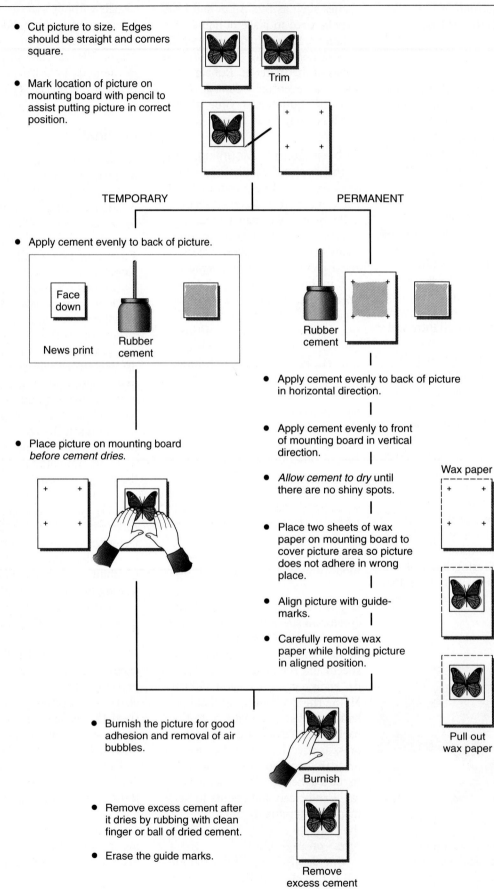

- Cut picture to size. Edges should be straight and corners square.

- Mark location of picture on mounting board with pencil to assist putting picture in correct position.

Trim

TEMPORARY

PERMANENT

- Apply cement evenly to back of picture.

Face down

News print

Rubber cement

Rubber cement

- Apply cement evenly to back of picture in horizontal direction.

- Apply cement evenly to front of mounting board in vertical direction.

- *Allow cement to dry* until there are no shiny spots.

- Place two sheets of wax paper on mounting board to cover picture area so picture does not adhere in wrong place.

- Align picture with guide-marks.

- Carefully remove wax paper while holding picture in aligned position.

- Place picture on mounting board *before cement dries.*

Wax paper

Pull out wax paper

- Burnish the picture for good adhesion and removal of air bubbles.

Burnish

- Remove excess cement after it dries by rubbing with clean finger or ball of dried cement.

- Erase the guide marks.

Remove excess cement

HOW TO . . .
Dry Mount Pictures

1. Dry the mounting board and picture before trimming picture by placing them in dry-mount press for about one minute at 225°F. Close press, but *do not lock.*

2. Place a sheet (either side up) of dry-mounting tissue over the *back* of the *untrimmed* picture, with sheet beyond the edges.

3. Attach the tissue to the back center of the picture with tip of a tacking iron set on "medium."

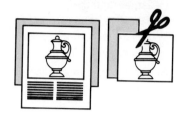

4. Turn picture and tissue over and trim both simultaneously to desired size. (A paper cutter works best, but a razor knife and metal straightedge or scissors may be used.)

5. Place the picture and dry-mounting tissue on the mounting board and align in proper position.

6. Tack the tissue to the mounting board *at two opposite corners.*

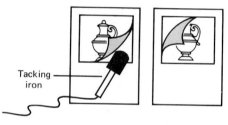

Tacking iron

7. Cover mounting board and picture with clean paper on both sides.

8. Place in dry-mount press preheated to 225°F for about one minute.

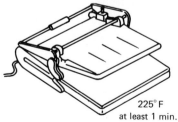

225° F
at least 1 min.

9. Remove from dry-mount press and allow the materials to cool. (Placing the cooling materials under a metal weight will help prevent curling.)

HOW TO . . .
Laminate Pictures with a Dry-Mount Press

1. The dry-mount press should be heated to 225°F. If you live in an area with high humidity, you may get better results if you preheat the visual (to remove excess moisture) in the press for about one minute. Close the press but do not lock it.

2. Cover the picture to be laminated with a piece of laminating film slightly larger than the picture. The inside of the roll (dull side) contains the heat-sensitive adhesive and should be toward the visual. Press the film onto the picture with your hands. Static electricity should cause the film to stay in place.

3. Put the picture and laminating film in a cover of clean paper to protect the visual and to prevent the adhesive from getting onto the surfaces of the dry-mount press.

4. Insert the material in the press for one minute. Remove it; if the adhesion is not complete, put it back into the press for another minute. It may be helpful to put a magazine or a ¼-inch stack of paper on top of the picture to increase the pressure and improve adhesion between the picture and the laminating film.

Figure 4.17
Both sides of a visual can be laminated simultaneously with a laminating machine.

both sides of the visual simultaneously. The visuals are fed into the machine which provides the appropriate heat and pressure. The excess film can than be trimmed from around the visual with sissors or a paper cutter.

Filing and Storing

You will find it handy to have a system for filing, storing, and retrieving your nonprojected visuals. The nature of the filing system that you use will depend on the number of

nonprojected visuals in your collection and how you intend to use them. The simplest filing system usually involves grouping them according to the teaching units in which they are used. Elementary teachers often categorize them by

Figure 4.18
Large-format mounted visuals can be stored conveniently in an artist's portfolio.

subject or curriculum area (e.g., math, science, language arts, social studies) and then subdivide them by topic (e.g., seasons, other countries, jobs, addition, subtraction, place value, telling time). Some instructors, especially those who teach just one subject, set up their filing system according to the chapters in their textbook, the topics they cover, or objectives. Teachers who use just a few visuals sometimes file them with their other teaching materials for each lesson.

Many teachers store their pictures in file folders or large mailing envelopes. If the pictures are slightly larger than the mailing envelope, you can slit the envelope on two adjacent sides to make a pocket. If the pictures are considerably larger than the 9-by-11-inch file folders or the envelopes you have available, you can use artists' portfolios, which are available in various sizes up to 36 by 48 inches (Figure 4.18).

In addition to a workable filing system and proper-size storage containers, you should have a clean, out-of-the-way place to store your visuals when they are not in use. The storage location can range from elaborate built-in drawers or filing cabinets to simple cardboard storage cartons. There is no problem in us-

ing cardboard cartons to store files of pictures and other visuals if you have a clean and dry location for the cartons.

DISPLAY SURFACES

If you are going to use nonprojected visuals, such as photographs, drawings, charts, graphs, or posters, you need a way to display them. Nonprojected visuals may be displayed in the classroom in a wide variety of ways, ranging from simply holding up a single visual in your hand to constructing elaborate exhibits for permanent display. Classroom surfaces commonly used for display of nonprojected visuals include chalkboards, multipurpose boards, pegboards, bulletin boards, cloth boards, and magnetic boards. Flip charts may also be used for display of visuals. Exhibits, a display format incorporating a variety of materials such as real objects and models along with visuals, are also common. How you display your visuals will depend on a number of factors, including the nature of your audience, the nature of your visuals, the instructional setting, your lesson

objectives, and, of course, the availability of the various display surfaces.

Chalkboards

The most common display surface in the classroom is, of course, the chalkboard (Figure 4.19). Once called blackboards, they, like chalk, now come in a variety of colors. Although the chalkboard is most commonly used as a medium of verbal communication, it can be used as a surface upon which to draw visuals (or pictures can be fastened to the molding above the chalkboard, taped to the board with masking tape, or placed in the chalk tray) to help illustrate instructional units and support verbal communication. Graphics, such as sketches and diagrams or charts and graphs, may be drawn on the chalkboard for display to the class.

A chalkboard is such a commonplace classroom item that instructors often neglect to give it the attention and respect it deserves as an instructional device. Using a chalkboard effectively requires conscious effort.

Figure 4.19
The chalkboard is universally recognized as a flexible and economical display surface.

❑ Put extensive drawing or writing on the board before class. Taking too much time to write or draw creates restlessness and may lead to discipline problems.

❑ Organize in advance *what* you plan to write on the board and *where* you plan to write it.

❑ Cover material such as a test or extensive lesson materials with wrapping paper, newspaper, or a pull-down map until you are ready to use it.

❑ Eye contact with students is important! Face the class when you are talking. Do not talk to the board. Do not turn your back to the class any more than absolutely necessary.

❑ Vary your presentation techniques. Do not overuse or rely entirely on the board. Use handouts, the overhead projector, flip charts, and other media during instruction when appropriate.

❑ Print neatly rather than using script. For a 32-foot-long classroom, the letters should be 2 to 2½ inches high and the lines forming the letters should be ¼-inch thick.

❑ Check the visibility of board from several positions around the room to be sure there is no glare on the surface. In case of glare, move the board (if portable) or pull the window shades.

❑ If your printing normally runs uphill or downhill, use water-soluble felt-tip pen markings as temporary guidelines for straighter printing. The guidelines will not be wiped off by a chalk eraser but may be washed off when no longer needed.

❑ Hold the chalk or marker at an angle so that it does not make scratching or squeaking noises.

❑ Use color for emphasis, but don't overuse color. Two or three different colors work best.

❑ Move around so you do not block what you have written on the board. Do not stand in front of what you have written.

❑ Use drawing aids such as rulers, stencils, and templates (patterns) to save time and improve the quality of your drawings.

❑ For frequently drawn shapes, use a template cut from wood or heavy cardboard. A dresser drawer knob or empty thread spool mounted on the template makes it easier to hold in position while tracing around it.

❑ Outline your drawings with barely visible lines before class and then fill them in with bold lines in front of the class. Your audience will think you are an artist!

Multipurpose Boards

Some classrooms are equipped with *multipurpose boards* (Figure 4.20) instead of chalkboards. These are also called white boards or marker boards. As the name implies, they can be used for more than one purpose. Their smooth white plastic surface requires a special erasable marker rather than chalk. Do *not* use permanent felt-tip markers such as "Marks-A-Lot" or "El Marko." These markers may permanently damage the surface.

The white surface is also suitable for projection of films, slides, and overhead transparencies. Materials cut from thin plastic, such as figures and letters, will adhere to the surface when rubbed in place. Some of these boards have a steel backing and can be used as a magnetic board for display of visuals.

In addition to their variety of uses, these multipurpose boards have the advantage of being able to display bright, colorful lines. At least eight different colors of markers are currently available. They are dustless so there is no chalkdust to get on your clothes. These boards are preferred for use around computers since chalkdust can harm computers and diskettes.

A multipurpose board will provide many years of use if cared for properly. The board should be completely erased after each use. It can be erased like a chalkboard using a felt eraser. Do not let the marks remain on the board overnight. The longer the marks remain on the board, the more difficult they are to erase. Old marks may be erased by tracing over them with a black erasable marker and erasing immediately.

For general cleaning, simply wipe the board clean with a soft, damp cloth. If further cleaning is necessary, use a mild spray cleaner, such as "Sparkleen." You can also apply a soapy detergent solution and rub briskly with a soft, clean cloth. Always rinse thoroughly with clean water and dry with a soft towel after cleaning.

The special erasable markers require some special care. They have a solvent base that dries quickly. This is the key to their erasability. The markers should be kept tightly capped and should be stored in a horizontal position with the cap tight when not in use to prevent them from drying out. If a cap is accidentally left off, the tip will go dry. When this happens, it *may* be possible to restore its usability. Cap the marker, turn it upside down, and shake vigorously up and down for twenty seconds. Leaving this marker stored overnight with the tip end down may also help.

Copy Boards

A high-tech variation of the multi-purpose board is the copy board, or electronic whiteboard (Figure 4.21). This device makes reduced-size paper copies of what is written on the board. It looks like a smaller multipurpose board but actually contains five screens or frames that can be scrolled forward and backward. You can prepare content beforehand on any or all of the five surfaces. During your presentation they can be revealed one at a time and new information added as desired. You can move the writing surface forward or backward to the desired frame quickly and easily.

You can write on the copy board using any erasable marker. If you make a mistake, erase your error as you would on any multipurpose board.

The special feature of the copy board is that four of the five frames can be copied in about ten seconds. The fifth frame is for manual use only. You can make as many copies of each frame as you like by pushing

Figure 4.20
Multipurpose boards are replacing chalkboards in business and industrial training classrooms and in some educational institutions.

Figure 4.21
Diagrams and words written on a copy board can be reproduced on paper with the push of a button.

the appropriate button. All material is copied in black and white using thermal sensitive paper. It is possible to copy one, two, or four frames together on a single 8½-by-11-inch sheet of paper.

By copying the information almost instantaneously, you are free to erase the board and continue to teach without losing valuable time or ideas. You can make copies for yourself or for everyone at the session to avoid extensive note taking. Everyone gets the same copy of what was presented, so there are no omissions or errors (except in what you did or did not put on the board).

The copy board is especially valuable for brainstorming sessions and for summarizing group discussions. The copies are particularly helpful for students who miss class. Complex drawings can be included without having students hand copy them. Notes can be taken into the field, laboratory, or assembly plant for immediate use.

Due to the high cost of current models, the copy board is not commonly found in school settings.

Pegboards

Another popular display surface is the pegboard (Figure 4.22). It is particularly useful for displaying heavy objects, three-dimensional materials, and visuals.

Pegboards are made of tempered masonite with ⅛-inch holes drilled

1 inch apart. Pegboard material is usually ⅛-inch thick and comes in 4-by-8-foot sheets which can be cut to any size. Special metal hooks and holders can be inserted into the pegboard to hold books, papers, and other objects. A variety of these special hooks are available in most hardware stores. Golf tees can also be inserted into the holes for holding lightweight materials such as posters and visuals mounted on cardboard. For a background effect, the entire pegboard surface can be covered with cloth or colored paper.

Golf tees or the special hooks can then be inserted through the cloth or paper.

Bulletin Boards

The name *bulletin board* implies an area in which bulletins—brief news announcements of urgent interest—are posted for public notice. This may have been the original purpose of bulletin boards, but it does not describe the most general use of these display spaces. Physically, a bulletin board is a surface of vari-

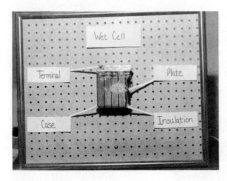

Figure 4.22
Pegboards are especially useful for displaying heavy objects.

Figure 4.23
Bulletin boards, long a standard in elementary classrooms, are now used increasingly in higher education and corporate settings.

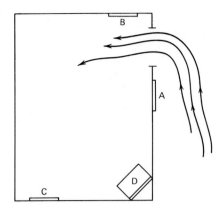

Figure 4.24
The location of a display depends on its intended use. High-traffic locations (such as A and B) are most suitable for motivational messages and short announcements. Quiet corners (such as C) and individual learning centers (such as D) are appropriate for displays to be studied in some detail.

able size and shape made of a material that holds pins, thumbtacks, and other sharp fasteners without damage to the board. In practice, bulletin board displays tend to serve three broad purposes: (1) decorative, (2) motivational, or (3) instructional.

The decorative bulletin board is probably the most common, certainly in schools. Its function would

seem to be to lend visual stimulation to the environment.

Displaying student work exemplifies the motivational use of bulletin boards. The public recognition offered by such displays can play an important role in the life of the classroom. It fosters pride in achievement, reinforcing students' efforts to do a good job. It is also a relatively effortless display for the teacher to put together.

The third broad purpose of bulletin boards is instructional, complementing the educational or training objectives of the formal curriculum. Rather than merely presenting static informational messages, displays can be designed to actively invite participation. Such displays ask questions and give viewers some means of manipulating parts of the display to verify their answers, such as flaps, pockets, dials, or movable parts.

Another form of learner participation is to take part in the actual construction of the display. For example, to introduce a unit on animals an elementary teacher might ask each student to bring in a picture of a favorite animal. The students would then make a bulletin board incorporating all the pictures. Or a geometry teacher might divide

Checklist for Instructor-Prepared Bulletin Boards

❑ Emphatic—conveys message quickly and clearly

❑ Attractive—color and arrangement catch and hold interest

❑ Balanced—formal or informal

❑ Unified—repeated shapes or colors, or use of borders hold display together visually

❑ Interactive—involves the viewer

❑ Legible—lettering and visuals can be read across the room

❑ Lettered properly—spelled correctly, plain typeface, use of lowercase except where capitals needed

❑ Correlated with lesson objectives

❑ Durable—well constructed physically, items securely attached

❑ Neat

For more specific guidelines on visual design see Chapter 3.

HOW TO . . .
Develop a Bulletin Board Display

1. *Decide upon an objective.* Limit the display to one topic or objective. Presenting more than one main idea usually results in confusion on the part of the viewers.

2. *Generate a theme and incorporate it into a headline.* It is a challenge to work out a catchy theme that will entice the viewer into further examination of the display. Wording should be simple, couched in the viewer's language, and visually integrated into the arrangement of the display.

3. *Work out a rough layout.* Guidelines for literate visuals are discussed in Chapter 3. The blueprint you develop here should reflect those guidelines.

4. *Gather the materials.* Obtain or make the illustrations, photographs, or other visual materials. Select a background material, such as cloth, wrapping paper, aluminum foil, colored construction paper, or shelf paper. Lines on the display can be made from ribbon, yarn, string, wire, or paper strips. Lettering may be freehand, drawn using a lettering guide, pressed on with dry-transfer type, or cut from construction paper; preformed plastic and ceramic letters are also available.

5. *Put up the display.* Setting up the display should be easy if all the preceding steps have been carried out. Step back and appraise it from a technical standpoint, and observe student reactions to evaluate its instructional effectiveness

her class into five groups and assign each group a different geometric shape. As each shape is studied, the appropriate group would construct a bulletin board on that shape. Or a discussion leader in a book club might prepare a portable bulletin board to stimulate discussion of the book everyone has read for the monthly meeting.

Bulletin boards need not always be attached permanently to the wall. Portable boards may be set on an easel for temporary display. Beware of having too many bulletin boards, though. Too many competing visual displays in one place can lessen their individual impact.

Figure 4.25
The placement of a display should vary according to the average height of the intended viewers. A useful rule of thumb is to align the middle of the display with the viewer's eye level.

Cloth Boards

Cloth boards are constructed of cloth stretched over a sturdy backing material such as plywood, Masonite, or heavy cardboard (Figure 4.26). The cloth used for the board may be of various types, including flannel, felt, or hook-and-loop material.

Flannel is inexpensive and readily available. Pieces of flannel stick together when gentle pressure is applied. Visuals cut from flannel can be drawn on with felt-tip markers and put on the flannel board. You can also back still pictures and graphics with flannel. Coarse sandpaper sticks to flannel and can also be used to back visuals for attachment to the board. Pipe cleaners, available in a variety of colors, and fuzzy yarns stick to the flannel and can be used for drawing lines and letters. Felt, slightly more expensive than flannel, has the same properties. With flannel and felt, durability of adhesion is less than might be desired, so slant the board slightly to help prevent materials from slipping or falling off.

The most expensive cloth board is made from hook-and-loop materials (such as Velcro). The hook-and-loop board has a fine but fuzzy surface composed of tiny, strong nylon

Figure 4.26
Cloth boards are often used to involve students in storytelling.

HOW TO...
Make a Cloth Board

The base of the cloth board can be a piece of plywood, particle board, or heavy cardboard of whatever size you desire. Tan or gray materials make a good background. Cut the cloth material several inches larger than the board. Stretch the cloth tightly over the edges of the board and fasten it with small nails, thumbtacks, staples, or tape. Covering the face of the board with white glue (Elmer's glue) before covering it will help the cloth to adhere to the board. Do not put the glue on too heavily, or it will soak through the cloth and appear unsightly, even though it dries clear.

A two-sided cloth board can be made by sewing two pieces of cloth together in the form of a bag. Two different colors of cloth can be used to give you a choice of backgrounds. The wood base or heavy cardboard is then inserted into the bag and the open end sewn or pinned in place. Pinning it in place allows you to remove the cloth in order to clean it.

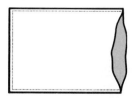

Make a bag by sewing three sides of the cloth.

Turn it inside out and insert a stiff backing

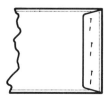

Pin the open end in place.

loops. The material used for backing visuals and other items to be attached to the board has a coarse, hooklike texture. When pressed together, the two surfaces stick firmly. The hooklike material can be purchased in rolls or strips. One great advantage of the hook-and-loop board is that it can support large and heavy visuals, even entire books and three-dimensional objects. One square inch of the cloth can support up to ten pounds of properly backed visual material.

Cloth boards are particularly useful for instruction requiring that visuals be easily moved around to illustrate a process or sequence. They can also be easily removed from the board.

Teachers of reading and other creative activities often use the cloth board to illustrate stories, poems, and other reading materials. Visuals depicting characters and scenes in a story, for example, can be placed on the board and moved around as the story unfolds. Creativity may be further encouraged by allowing the

children to manipulate cloth-board materials. Shy children may particularly profit from this kind of activity. It encourages them to speak through the visual representations of story characters as they move the illustrations on the board.

Be sure you have proper storage space for your cloth board and cloth-board visuals when not in use. Proper storage will help keep them clean and prevent them from being bent or torn. If possible, store your materials on a flat surface rather than stacking them up against a wall. If you use sandpaper backing on your visuals, put paper between them during storage, as sandpaper can scratch the surface of visuals.

Magnetic Boards

Magnetic boards serve much the same purpose as cloth boards, but their adhesiveness is due to magnetism. Visuals are backed with magnets and then placed on the metal surface of the board. Magnetic

boards, magnets, and flexible strips of magnetic materials for use in backing are available commercially. Plastic lettering with magnetic backing is available from supply stores and can be used for captioning visuals.

Any metal surface in the classroom that a magnet is attracted to can serve as a magnetic board. For example, some chalkboards are backed with steel and will thus attract magnet-backed visuals. Chalk can be used on such chalkboards for captioning or to depict lines of association between visuals. Steel cabinets and metal walls and doors can also be used as magnetic boards.

You can make your own magnetic board from a thin sheet of galvanized iron, a cookie sheet, a lap tray, or any similar thin sheet of metal. Paint the sheets in the color of your choice with paint designed for use on metal surfaces or cover with Con-Tact paper. Unpainted surfaces are likely to be unattractive and cause glare. Another alternative is to fasten steel screening to a nonmetal surface, such as plywood, and cover it with a piece of cloth.

The major advantage of magnetic boards is that maneuvering visuals is easier and quicker than with cloth boards. For example, magnetic boards are often used by physical education instructors to demonstrate rapid changes in player positions. Magnetic boards also have greater adhesive quality. Visuals displayed on a magnetic board are not likely to slip or fall. They move only when you want to move them.

Flip Charts

A *flip chart* refers to a pad of large-size paper fastened together at the top and mounted to an easel. The individual sheets each hold a limited verbal/visual message and can be arranged for sequential presentation to a small group. The messages can be written extemporaneously while the presenter is talking or can be prepared in advance and revealed one at a time. Poster makers, such as PosterPrinter, can be used to pro-

duce flip-chart pages (see page 112). Commercially produced materials are also available in this format; they are especially prevalent in reading and science instruction and military training. Preprepared visual sequences are especially useful for instruction involving sequential steps in a process. The diagrams or words can serve as cues, reminding the presenter of the next point in the presentation.

The most common use of flip charts, though, is for the extempo-

Figure 4.27
Magnetic boards allow quick manipulation of materials.

Figure 4.28
Flip charts are standard equipment in most business and industry training rooms.

AV SHOWMANSHIP

Flip Charts

❏ Position the flip chart at an angle so everyone can see it. Place the flip chart in the right front corner (as you face the audience) if you are right-handed, the left front corner if you are left-handed.

❏ Be sure the easel is properly assembled and the pages are securely fastened so the flip chart will not fall apart during your presentation.

❏ Prepare lettering and visuals in advance or outline their shape using a light blue pencil and then trace them during your presentation.

❏ For group-generated responses, draw lettering guidelines with a blue pencil.

❏ Keep lettering and visuals simple but large enough for everyone to see.

❏ Outline lettering and visuals lightly in pencil before presentation; then go over them with the marker during presentation.

❏ Use more than one color, but not more than four.

❏ Use broad-tip marking pens that provide contrast but will not bleed through to the next sheet.

❏ Print rather than using cursive writing.

❏ Keep words short or use well-understood abbreviations.

❏ Include simple drawings, symbols, and charts.

❏ Talk to the audience, not to the flip chart.

❏ Avoid blocking the audience's view of the flip chart.

❏ Be sure your materials are in proper sequence.

❏ Have a blank sheet exposed when not referring to the flip chart.

❏ Reveal pages only when you are ready to discuss them, not before.

❏ Put summary points on the last sheet rather than paging back as you make your summary.

---

raneous drawing of key illustrations and key words to supplement a stand-up presentation (see Figure 4.28). The flip chart is an extremely versatile, convenient, and inexpensive media format. It requires no electrical power, has no moving parts to wear out, can be used in a wide range of lighting conditions, is portable, and requires only a marking pen as peripheral equipment. Next to the chalkboard it is the most user-friendly audiovisual tool. But don't let the flip chart's simplicity fool you. Using it professionally takes some practice (see above).

Audience members, too, seem to regard the flip chart in friendly terms. It seems casual and comfortable, a pleasing change of pace in an increasingly high-technology world. It is an exceptionally valuable aid to any group discussion process. Ideas contributed by group members can be recorded in a way visible to all participants. Comments and corrections can be made and the results can be preserved. Finished sheets

can be torn off the pad and taped to walls or windows for later reference. Flip charts are available in a variety of sizes for large-group use, and others, often referred to as travel easels, are designed for portability.

Exhibits

Exhibits are displays of various objects and visuals designed to form an integrated whole for instructional purposes (Figure 4.29). Any of the visuals discussed in this chapter, including models and real objects, can be included in an exhibit, and any of the display surfaces discussed can contribute to an exhibit. Exhibits can generally be used for the same instructional purposes and in the same ways as their individual components are used.

Exhibit locations are readily available in most classrooms. Simple exhibits can be set up on a table, shelf, or desk. More complex exhibits may require considerable floor

space and special constructions (a booth, for example).

There are two types of exhibits—displays and dioramas. A display is a collection of materials, while a diorama shows a three-dimensional scene.

Displays. A display is an array of objects, visuals, and printed materials (e.g., labels and descriptions). Most displays include descriptive information about the objects or visuals shown. Instructional displays are used in the classroom (Figure 4.30), in museums, and in many other settings.

Student assembly of a display can be a motivating learning experience, and it can both foster retention of subject matter and sharpen visual skills. For a lesson in transportation, one sixth grade teacher had each student bring in a replica of a vehicle. Some students made their own vehicles from construction paper. Others brought in toys from home or contributed vehicles assembled from hobby kits (e.g., boats, cars,

Figure 4.29
A complex exhibit such as this one at the Lowell, Massachusetts, National Historical Park, brings together real objects, still pictures, and other visuals with verbal information.

Figure 4.30
This simple teacher-made display consists of related artifacts arranged for easy observation by students.

trucks, trains, space ships). The teacher placed tables and other classroom furniture along a wall to provide the children with a shelf on which to arrange their three-dimensional visuals. On the wall above this display surface, the teacher placed a long sheet of paper containing a time line. The time line illustrated forms of transportation from early time (humans and beasts), through the present (trains, cars, planes), and on into the future (space vehicles from *Star Wars* and *Star Trek*). The display was a great success.

Dioramas. *Dioramas* are static displays consisting of a three-dimensional foreground and a flat background to create a realistic scene (see Figure 4.31). The foreground is usually a landscape of some sort with models of people, animals, vehicles, equipment, or buildings. The naturalistic background may be a photograph, drawing, or painting. The diorama is usually contained within a box, with the sides of the box providing addi-

tional backdrop. The rear corners or the entire back may be rounded to provide an illusion of depth, and lights can be added for a special effect.

Dioramas are usually designed to reproduce reality of the past or present or depict future events. Examples in museums are often life-size, whereas those used in classrooms are usually on a smaller scale. In industry, dioramas can be constructed to show company products in use.

Teachers may construct dioramas to illustrate their lessons or to introduce major topics. Students can be asked to design their own dioramas as a follow-up activity to instruction. Scenes from history, particularly battles, are often portrayed with model figures. Animals can be shown in their natural habitats for a biology class. Scenes including towns and landscapes from various parts of the world make stimulating dioramas for geography instruction. Prehistoric landscapes and geologic formations are also popular topics for dioramas.

APPLICATION OF THE ASSURE MODEL TO NONPROJECTED VISUALS

The ASSURE model discussed in Chapter 2 applies to nonprojected visuals as well as to all other media. However, because of the diversity of formats and countless uses of nonprojected visuals, it is difficult to provide a concise set of principles and procedures for them.

First, you must analyze your audience. Find out what they already know about the topic and what types of visuals or materials they prefer. Then state your objectives in terms of what you want your audience to be able to do after viewing the presentation of visuals, real objects, models, or exhibits.

When selecting, modifying, or designing visuals, you should decide on visuals or materials that will best communicate your instructional message under the conditions in which you will be using them. Keep them simple! Be certain that all titles, lettering, figures, and the visuals themselves are large enough to

Figure 4.31
Dioramas can depict current scenes, historical events, or future possibilities.

ANALYZE LEARNERS

General Characteristics

The assembly line workers at the Reliable Furnace Company manufacture small gas furnaces. They range in age from eighteen to sixty-eight and include both males and females. All are high school graduates, but most have low reading abilities (the average is ninth grade, with a range from sixth to fourteenth).

Because of attrition and shifts of workers to different jobs on the assembly line, a burner-box assembler needs to be trained about once each week. The assembler's job requires manual dexterity and mobility. Because various colored wires are soldered to different locations, the trainee cannot be color blind.

Entry Competencies

The chief requirements are the ability to follow assembly instructions (which may be committed to memory after several weeks on the job) and to solder. Because soldering is required for other jobs within the company and is a skill many of the workers already know, it will not be taught as part of the lesson. A separate module on soldering techniques is available for those who need it.

Employees who have worked for the company less than four months are highly motivated to be successful and want to please the supervisor. This is especially true of the younger workers (less than twenty-five years old). The more mature individuals and those with more than a year's seniority generally just want to get by with as little effort as possible.

STATE OBJECTIVES

Upon completion of the burner-box assembly unit, the worker will be able to

1. Assemble the burner box for a small gas furnace according to company specifications within seven minutes when given the necessary components and appropriate tools.
   Subobjectives include
   a. Solder the control wires onto the correct terminals with a solder joint that will conduct current and withstand a five-pound pull.
   b. Position the top and side panels on the base and attach with metal screws. Panels must be in proper position and all screws must be firmly seated.

There are several other subobjectives as well as this affective objective.

2. Wear safety goggles and work gloves during the entire assembly process. (The workers know they should do this, but don't always do so.)

SELECT, MODIFY, OR DESIGN MATERIAL

After checking through catalogs of industrial training materials and talking with training directors from other furnace-manufacturing firms, Jan Smith, the training coordinator, concluded that there were no off-the-shelf materials suitable for use or for modification. Consequently, she decided to develop a set of drawings and photographs to be incorporated into a small (9-by-12-inch) flip chart for use by the trainee. Because of the need for hands-on practice and training (approximately one worker per week), a self-instructional unit will be developed incorporating actual burner components, the flip chart, and an audiotape. Humor will be used to enhance motivation for those employees who are not motivated.

UTILIZE THE MATERIALS

The trainee will be allowed to use the materials and practice the assembly as many times as necessary in the training room. A trainer will be available to answer questions and to evaluate the completed burner boxes.

REQUIRE LEARNER PARTICIPATION

When the trainer is satisfied that the task has been mastered, an experienced employee will provide additional on-the-job training (OJT) at the assembly line. The experienced worker will demonstrate the task under actual working conditions with the assembly line running. Then the trainee will take over, with the experienced worker providing guidance and encouragement until the trainee is competent and confident.

EVALUATE

The trainee and the training will be evaluated based on a number of factors. The number of defective or inoperative burner boxes identified by quality control or during installation is one criterion. Periodically the line supervisor will observe the workers for safety procedures (gloves and goggles) and assembly sequence. Accident and injury reports will also be sent to the training department.

Figure 4.32

be seen from the intended viewing distance.

Many techniques for using non-projected visuals are included in the showmanship tips in this chapter. Plan your presentation or display carefully. Start from where the audience is (as determined from your audience analysis). Organize the presentation in a logical sequence.

Build learner activity and response into the use of the visuals or display. Involve the viewers as much as possible. Repetition and emphasis will help your audience remember key points. Watch them to see if they are following the presentation. Use questions and dialogue to keep them interested and to provide opportunities for learner response.

Finally, as recommended in the ASSURE model, evaluate your visuals and associated presentation. Through formal and informal evaluation, determine if most of your audience was able to meet your objectives. Determine which parts of the presentation were most and least favorably received. Solicit feedback from your audience, and then make the necessary revisions.

REFERENCES

Print References

Nonprojected Visuals

Alesandrini, K. L. "Pictures and Adult Learning." *Instructional Science* (May 1984):63–77.

Brandt, Richard C. *Flip Charts: How to Draw Them and How to Use Them.* San Diego, CA: University Associates, 1986.

Bullough, Robert. *Creating Instructional Materials.* 3d ed. Columbus: Merrill, 1988.

Center for Vocational Education. *Prepare Teacher-Made Instructional Materials.* Athens, GA: American Association for Vocational Instructional Materials, 1987.

————. *Present Information with Models, Real Objects, and Flannel Boards.* Athens, GA: American Association for Vocational Instructional Materials, 1977.

Coplan, Kate. *Poster Ideas and Bulletin Board Techniques for Libraries and Schools.* 2d ed. New York: Oceana Publications, 1981.

Do You See What I Mean? Learning through Charts, Graphs, Maps, and Diagrams. Dickson, Australia: Curriculum Development Centre, 1980.

Hollister, Bernard C. "Using Picture Books in the Classroom." *Media and Methods* (January 1977):22–25.

Holub, Brenda, and Bennett, Clifford T. "Using Political Cartoons to Teach Junior/Middle School U.S. History." *Social Studies* (September–October 1988):214–16.

Hynes, Michael C. "Selection Criteria." *Arithmetic Teacher* (February 1986):11–13.

Jones, Colin. "Cartoons in the Classroom." *Visual Education* (November 1976):21–22.

Kemp, Jerrold E., and Smellie, Don C. *Planning, Producing, and Using Instructional Media.* 6th ed. New York: Harper Collins, 1989.

Kohn, Rita. *Experiencing Displays.* Metuchen, NJ: Scarecrow Press, 1982.

Krulek, Stephen, and Welderman, Ann M. "The Chalkboard—More than Just for Chalk." *Audiovisual Instruction* (September 1976):41.

Marino, George. "A Do-It-Yourself 3-D Graph." *Mathematics Teacher* (May 1977):428–29.

Meilach, Dona Z. *Dynamics of Presentation Graphics.* Homewood, IL: Dow Jones–Irwin, 1986.

Morlan, John E., and Espinosa, Leonard J. *Preparation of Inexpensive Teaching Materials.* 3d ed. Belmont, CA: David S. Lake, 1988.

Satterthwait, Les. *Graphics: Skills, Media and Materials.* 3d ed. Dubuque, IA: Kendall-Hunt, 1988.

Scheer, Janet K. "Manipulatives Make Math Meaningful for Middle Schoolers." *Childhood Education* (November–December 1985):115–21.

Smith, Judson. "Choosing and Using Easels, Display Boards, and Visual Control Systems." *Training* (May 1979):51, 52–53.

Sumey, Violet, and Wade, Saundra. *Library Displays.* Minneapolis, MN: T. S. Denison, 1982.

Trimblay, Roger. "Using Magazine Pictures in the Second-Language Classroom." *Canadian Modern Language Review* (October 1978):82–86.

Waller, Robert H. W. "Four Aspects of Graphic Communication: An Introduction to This Issue." *Instructional Science* (September 1979):213–22.

Wildman, Diane. "Researching with Pictures." *English Journal* (March 1990):55–58.

Bulletin Boards

Alisin, Mary Lou. "Bulletin Board Stand-outs." *Early Years* (September 1977):66–69.

Burke, K., and Kranhold, J. *The Big Fearon Bulletin Board Book.* Carthage, IL: Fearon Teacher Aids, 1978.

Bush, Katherine P., et al. "Bulletin Boards, Displays, and Special Events." *Book Report* (January–February 1989):9–15, 17–23, 26.

Center for Vocational Education. *Prepare Bulletin Boards and Exhibits.* Athens, GA: American Association for Vocational Instructional Materials, 1977.

Cummins, Glenda J., and Lombardi, Thomas P. "Bulletin Board Learning Center Makes Spelling Fun." *Teaching Exceptional Children* (Winter 1989):33–35.

Flores, Anthony. *Instant Bulletin Boards.* (Carthage, IL: Fearon Teacher Aids, 1983).

"Hands-on Bulletin Boards." *Instructor* (January 1984):34–37.

Kincheloe, Joe L. "No More Turkey-Lurkeys!" *Instructor Innovator* (September 1982):24–25.

Prizzi, Elaine, and Hoffman, Jeanne. *Interactive Bulletin Boards.* Carthage, IL: Fearon Teaching Aids, 1984.

Soltow, Willow. "Quick and Easy Bulletin Boards." *Children and Animals* (February–March 1988):18–20.

Audiovisual References

Display and Presentation Boards. Chicago: International Film Bureau, 1971. 16mm film or videocassette. 15 minutes.

Dry Mounting Audiovisual Materials. Iowa City, IA: University of Iowa, 1985. VHS videocassette. 7 minutes.

Dry Mounting with Heat Press. Salt Lake City, UT: Media Systems, Inc., 1975. Filmstrip or slides. 40 frames.

Heat Laminating. Salt Lake City, UT: Media Systems, Inc., 1975. Filmstrip or slides. 40 frames.

Laminating Audiovisual Materials. Iowa City, IA: University of Iowa, 1985. VHS videocassette. 7 minutes.

Lettering: A Creative Approach to Basics. Stamford, CT: Educational Di- mensions Group, 1978. 2 sound film-strips with audiocassettes.

Production Techniques for Instructional Graphic Materials. Columbus, OH: Charles E. Merrill, 1977. 27 filmstrips in basic series, 12 filmstrips in advanced series, 18 audiocassettes.

Tables and Graphs. Weekly Reader Film-strips. Guidance Associates, 1981. 4 filmstrips with audiocassettes. Grades 3–6.

Three-Dimensional Displays. Burbank, CA: Encore Visual Education, 1975. 4 sound filmstrips with audiocassettes.

Suppliers of Materials and Equipment

Bulletin Boards, Cloth Boards, Magnetic Boards, and Multipurpose Boards

Bangor Cork Co., Inc.
William and D Streets
Pen Argyl, PA 18072–0125

Charles Mayer Studios, Inc.
168 East Market Street
Akron, OH 44308

Ghent Manufacturing, Inc.
P.O. Box 355
Lebanon, OH 45036

Graphics, Mounting, Laminating, and Lettering

Dick Blick
Box 1267
Galesburg, IL 61401

Chartpak
One River Road
Leeds, MA 01053

Seal, Inc.
550 Spring Street
Nangatuck, CT 06770–9985

Visualon
9000 Sweet Valley Drive
Cleveland, OH 44125

Realia and Models

Edmund Scientific
101 East Gloucester Pike
Barrington, NJ 08007

Hubbard
P.O. Box 104
Northbrook, IL 60065

Summit Learning
P.O. Box 493
Fort Collins, CO 80522

POSSIBLE PROJECTS

4–A. Select three pictures at least 5 by 7 inches and mount one with temporary rubber cement, one with permanent rubber cement, and a third with dry-mount tissue.

4–B. Select several pictures that are approximately 8½-by-11 inches and laminate them.

4–C. Select a set of still pictures you might use in your teaching. Then appraise them using the "Appraisal Checklist: Still Pictures." Turn in the pictures and appraisal forms.

4–D. Plan a lesson in which you use a set of still pictures. Within this lesson show evidence that you have followed the utilization principles suggested. Submit pictures with lesson.

4–E. Devise for your subject field one graph (line, bar, circle, pictorial) and one chart (organization, classification, time line, tabular chart, flow chart). Each of these should be prepared on a separate sheet. Evaluation will be based on the "Appraisal Checklist: Graphic Materials."

4–F. Make a list of ten possible posters students could make to depict aspects of your teaching area. Prepare one yourself to serve as a model or motivational device. The poster should be at least 12 by 14 inches.

4–G. Review Chapter 3 or examine books on bulletin board displays. Prepare rough layouts for two displays pertinent to your subject area. Construct one of these.

4–H. Obtain an example of a real object or model that you could use for instruction. Submit the object or model and a description of how you would use it, including an objective.

4–I. Prepare a cloth board, magnetic board, flip chart, or exhibit. Submit the material, a description of the intended audience, the objectives, how it will be used, and how it will be evaluated.

5

Projected
Visuals

OUTLINE

OBJECTIVES

After studying this chapter, you should be able to

1. Define *projected visuals.*

2. Describe the characteristics and operation of overhead transparency projection systems including three advantages and three limitations.

3. Discuss two applications of the overhead in your teaching field.

4. Describe three utilization techniques for enhancing your use of the overhead projector.

5. Describe the following techniques for overhead transparency projection: write-on, thermal film method, electrostatic method, and spirit duplication.

6. Describe three design guidelines that can enhance the effectiveness of overhead transparencies in instructional situations.

7. Describe the characteristics of slides including three advantages and three limitations.

8. Synthesize an instructional situation in which you might use a series of locally produced slides.

9. Describe how to copy visuals with a single-lens reflex camera.

10. Demonstrate the correct technique for thumb spotting slides.

11. Describe two utilization techniques for enhancing your use of slides.

12. Describe the characteristics of filmstrips, including three advantages and limitations.

13. Synthesize an instructional situation in which you might use a commercially produced filmstrip.

14. Describe two utilization techniques for enhancing your use of filmstrips.

15. Describe the characteristics and operation of opaque projection systems, including two advantages and three limitations.

16. Discuss two applications of opaque projection in your teaching field.

17. Describe three utilization techniques for enhancing the effectiveness of opaque projection in instructional situations.

18. Describe new technical developments in photography.

LEXICON

projected visuals

overhead projection

fresnel lens

transparency

thermal film

electrostatic copying (xerography)

spirit duplication

slide

filmstrip

opaque projection

charge-coupled device

Because an illuminated screen in a darkened room tends to rivet the attention of viewers, projected visuals have long been popular as a medium of instruction as well as entertainment. The lighted screen is a silent shout—a shout likely to be heard and heeded even by the most reluctant learners.

It is not too fanciful to conjecture that some of this attraction is due to the aura of magic that seems to surround such presentations. The room lights are dimmed; the viewers grow quiet in expectation; a switch is thrown and (presto!) a large, bright image appears on the screen. You have their attention. They are ready to receive your message. Exploit this readiness by selecting materials that will maintain the viewers' attention and by using them in a way that involves viewers actively in the learning process.

Projected visuals refer to media formats in which still images are enlarged and displayed on a screen. Such projection is usually achieved by passing a strong light through transparent film (overhead transparencies, slides, and filmstrips), magnifying the image through a series of lenses, and casting this image onto a reflective surface. Opaque projection is also included in this category. In opaque projection, light is cast onto an opaque image (one that does not allow light to pass through), such as a magazine picture or printed page. The light is reflected from the material onto mirrors, which transmit the reflection through a series of lenses onto a screen.

The focus of this chapter is on the characteristics and applications of overhead projection, slides, filmstrips, and opaque projection—the most widely accepted means of using projected visuals in education and training settings.

OVERHEAD PROJECTION

Because of its many virtues, the *overhead projection* system has advanced rapidly in the past several

decades to become the most widely used audiovisual device in North American classrooms and training sites.

The typical overhead projector is a very simple device (Figure 5.1). Basically, it is a box with a large aperture or "stage" on the top surface. Light from a powerful lamp inside the box is condensed by a special type of lens, known as a *fresnel lens,* and passes through a transparency (approximately 8 by 10 inches) placed on the stage. A lens-and-mirror system mounted on a bracket above the box turns the light beam 90 degrees and projects the image back over the shoulder of the presenter.

Because of the widespread familiarity of overhead projection, the general term *transparency* has taken on, in the instructional setting, the specific meaning of the large-format 8-by-10-inch film used with the overhead projector. Transparencies may be composed of photographic

film, clear acetate, or any of a number of other transparent materials capable of being imprinted with an image by means of chemical or heat processes.

Transparencies may be used individually or may be made into a series of images consisting of a base visual with one or more overlays attached to the base with hinges. Complex topics can be explained step-by-step by flipping on a series of overlays one at a time that add additional features to a diagram (see Figure 5.2).

Advantages

The overhead projection system has a number of unique features that give it the tremendous versatility for which it is acclaimed by so many instructors.

Its bright lamp and efficient optical system generate so much light on the screen that the overhead can be used in normal room lighting.

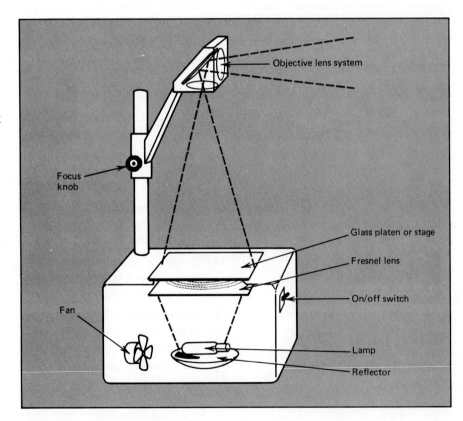

Figure 5.1
Overhead projector, cutaway view

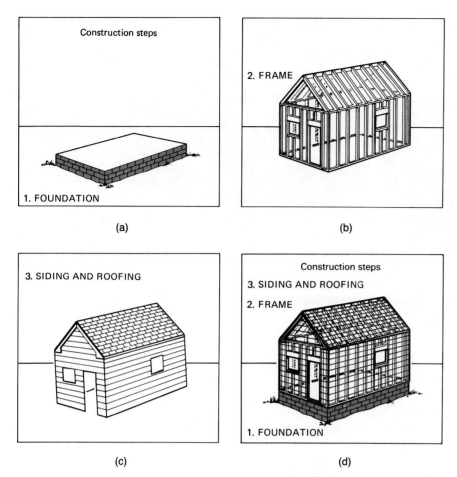

Figure 5.2
By means of overlays, complex visuals can be built up step-by-step.

Figure 5.3
With the overhead projector, the presenter maintains eye contact with viewers.

The projector is operated from the front of the room with the presenter facing the audience, allowing direct eye contact to be maintained (Figure 5.3).

Most overhead projectors are lightweight and easily portable. All are simple to operate.

A variety of materials can be projected, including cutout silhouettes, small opaque objects, and many types of transparencies.

Projected materials can be manipulated by the presenter. You can point to important items, highlight them with colored pens, add details during the lesson (notes, diagrams, etc.) by marking on the transparency with a marking pen, or cover part of the message and progressively reveal information. As noted previously, complex visuals can be presented in a series of overlays.

Commercially produced transparencies are available covering a broad range of curriculum areas. A major directory of commercially available overhead transparencies is published by the National Information Center for Educational Media (NICEM)— *Index to Educational Overhead Transparencies.* (See Appendix A for details and other sources.)

Instructors can easily prepare their own transparencies (several common methods of production are explained later in this chapter).

Information that might otherwise have to be placed on a chalkboard during a class session (lesson outlines, for example) may be prepared in advance for presentation at the proper time. Research indicates that retention of main points improves significantly when visual outlines are presented.

The use of overhead transparencies also has positive effects on attitude in business meetings. In a study by the Wharton Applied Research Center, candidates for master's degrees in business administration participated in a business simulation that included group meetings to decide whether or not to introduce a new product. The findings showed that

❑ More individuals decided to act on the recommendations of presenters who used overheads than on the recommendations of presenters who did not.

❑ Presenters who used overheads were perceived as better prepared, more professional, more persuasive, more credible, and more interesting.

❑ Groups in which presenters used overheads were more likely to reach consensus on their decisions than groups where no overheads were employed (Figure 5.4).[1]

---

[1] *A Study of the Effects of the Use of Overhead Transparencies on Business Meetings* (Philadelphia: Wharton Applied Research Center, The Wharton School, University of Pennsylvania, 1981).

Figure 5.4
In business meetings projected images help focus attention, channel discussion, and facilitate reaching a consensus.

MEDIA FILE   *The ABCs of Drafting*
Overhead Transparencies

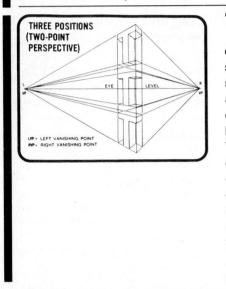

This set of overhead transparencies covers an entire course in drafting. Although designed for grades six through eight, it has been used successfully in high school. One of the advantages of overhead transparencies is that the basic illustrations can be adapted to different age levels. The set consists of thirty-six well-drawn illustrations on sturdy transparency material. The instructor's guide comes complete with reproductions of all the transparencies and step-by-step instructions for their most effective use.

Source: DCA Educational Products Inc.

Another study suggests that teachers who use the overhead projector tend to be more organized than teachers who rely on notes or printed outlines. Students in this study participated more frequently in discussions in the classes where the overhead was used.[2]

Limitations

The effectiveness of overhead projection presentations is heavily dependent on the presenter. The overhead projector cannot be programmed to display visual sequences by itself, nor is an audio accompaniment provided.

The overhead system does not lend itself to independent study. The projection system is designed for large-group presentation. Of course, an individual student could look at a transparency by holding it up to the light or laying it on a light table; but because captions or audio tracks are not a part of this format, the material would ordinarily not be self-instructional.

Printed materials and other non-transparent items, such as magazine

---

MEDIA FILE   *Automotive Technology: Engine Systems*
Overhead Transparencies

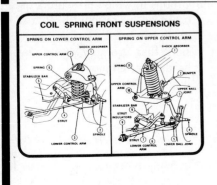

This is a comprehensive set of sixty transparencies designed for a high school or vocational school course in automotive repair. Many of the transparencies have overlays. The instructor's guide has descriptions of each transparency. The descriptions give the order in which the overlays are to be used. The transparencies are printed on sturdy plastic.

Source: DCA Educational Products Inc.

2   James Cabeceiras, "Observed Differences in Teacher Verbal Behavior When Using and Not Using the Overhead Projector," *AV Communication Review* (Fall 1972):271–80.

illustrations, cannot be projected immediately, as is possible with the opaque projector. To use the overhead system such materials have to be made into transparencies by means of some production process.

Distortion of images is more prevalent with the overhead than with other projection systems. The projector is commonly placed at desktop level to facilitate the instructor's writing on transparencies. The screen, on the other hand, needs to be placed on a higher level for unobstructed audience sight lines. This discrepancy in levels causes a distortion referred to as the "keystone effect." (This problem and its solution are discussed in Chapter 11.)

Applications

As indicated by its ubiquitous presence in the classroom, the overhead system has a myriad of group-instruction applications, too numerous to list here.

One indication of the breadth of applications is the fact that commercial distributors of transparencies have made available materials for virtually all curriculum areas, from kindergarten through college level and in business and industry. These materials range from single, simple transparencies to elaborate sets replete with multiple overlays, masking devices, and other teaching aids. Transparent plastic devices such as clocks, engines, and the like are available. These can be manipulated by the instructor to demonstrate how the parts interact as they are displayed on the screen.

Projection of Computer Displays. Anyone who has ever sought to demonstrate use of a computer program to a group has needed to display an image larger than the monitor screen. A video projector serves the purpose but is very expensive. A much less expen-

Figure 5.5
Devices are available that permit computer output to be projected from the stage of the overhead projector.

Figure 5.6
Most overhead projector users like to draw directly on the transparency, in this case to add significant details to a previously prepared visual.

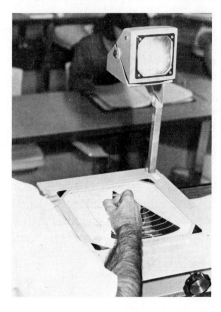

sive solution is a liquid-crystal display screen that fits on the stage of an overhead projector (Figure 5.5). The screen is plugged into the output of the computer, and whatever appears on the computer monitor is also projected by the overhead so that all may easily follow the demonstration (see Chapter 8).

Creating Overhead Transparencies

As previously noted, one of the major advantages of the overhead system is that instructors—and students—can easily prepare their

own transparencies. Beginning with simple hand drawing on clear acetate sheets, numerous other methods of preparing transparencies have evolved over the years. We will look closely at only the processes most commonly used at the classroom production level—direct drawing, thermal film process, and electrostatic film process (xerography).

Direct Drawing Method. The most obvious way of quickly preparing a transparency is simply to draw directly on a transparent sheet with some sort of marking pen (Figure 5.6). Clear acetate of five to ten mils (.005–.010 inches) thickness is recommended. Other types of plastic can be used, even household food wrap and dry-cleaning bags. Although some of these alternatives may be a great deal cheaper than the thicker acetate, some of them also impose limitations in terms of durability, ease of handling, and ability to accept different inks (i.e., disintegrating completely under alcohol-based inks). If available, blue-tinted acetate is preferred because it reduces the glare of the projected image.

Although the glass platen or stage of the overhead projector generally measures about 10 by 10 inches, your drawing and lettering should be restricted to a rectangular "message area" of about 7½ by 9½ inches. This fits the dimensions of acetate sheets, which are commonly cut into rectangles of 8 by 10 inches or 8½ by 11 inches.

Some overhead projectors come equipped with a pair of roller attachments made to carry long rolls of plastic that can be advanced or reversed by a small hand crank. This assures a steady supply of transparency material for extemporaneous use. It also allows a series of images to be prepared in advance in proper sequence. Such rolls can be saved for later reuse.

In addition to the transparency, you will need a writing instrument. Felt-tip marking pens are the handiest for this purpose. They come in two general types—water-soluble and permanent ink. Within these two types a wide variety of pens are available. Not all are suitable for overhead transparencies. Here are some important cautions to keep in mind:

❏ Markers with water-soluble ink generally will not adhere well to acetate; the ink tends to bead up and disappear as the water evaporates. A label stating "for overhead marking" means it will adhere to acetate and project in color. Such special pens can be erased readily with a damp cloth. This allows you to reuse the acetate sheet, a considerable advantage in view of the escalating cost of acetate, which is a petroleum product.

❏ Virtually all the permanent-ink felt-tip pens will adhere to acetate, but only those labeled "for overhead marking" are sure to project in color. Otherwise, the ink itself may be opaque and project only in black.

❏ Permanent inks really are permanent. They can be removed only with special plastic erasers (Figure 5.7).

Less frequently used but very serviceable are wax-based pencils, often referred to as grease pencils. Unless otherwise marked, they will project black. The great advantage of wax-based pencils is that they can be erased from acetate with any soft, dry cloth.

Finally, there are some specially treated ("frosted") acetate sheets made to be typed on directly or written on with a pencil. However, the frosting reduces the amount of light transmitted through the film, thereby decreasing legibility. In addition, typewritten letters are usually too small to be readable by the whole group. If a larger typeface is available (such as Primary or IBM's Orator), typing on frosted sheets may be acceptable if you do not have access to a thermal-process machine (see next section). If an enlarging photocopy machine is available, a standard typeface can be enlarged and then made into a thermal film transparency. Frosted sheets should be used only as a last resort.

Thermal Film Process. In the *thermal film* process infrared light passes through a specially treated acetate film onto a prepared master underneath. The artwork and lettering on the master are done with a heat-absorbing material such as India ink, ordinary lead pencil, or another substance containing carbon. An image is "burned into" the film wherever it contacts such carbonaceous markings.

Depending on the film used, a number of different color patterns are possible. The most common pattern is color or black print on a clear or pastel background, analogous to positive film. Clear or colored lines can also be put on a black background, analogous to negative film.

Another option is the use of printed, commercially prepared transparency masters. Thermal film producers and other audiovisual publishers offer a broad range of printed masters with many thousands of individual titles covering virtually all curriculum areas. Some publishers offer sets of masters specifically correlated with the leading textbooks in language arts, reading, math, social studies, and science.

To use commercially prepared thermal masters, simply remove one from the book or folder in which it is packaged, lay the thermal film on it with the notch in the upper-right corner, and run both through the copier. Commercial masters may, of course, be altered by the instructor

Figure 5.7
Plastic erasers will remove permanent ink, at least that of the same manufacturer.

HOW TO . . .
Make Thermal Transparencies

1. Prepare the master. Any ordinary white paper may be used. Draw the artwork by hand or paste illustrations from other sources (magazine illustrations, photocopies, etc.) onto the master. Lettering, added by hand, by mechanical lettering guide, or by paste-up of existing lettering, must consist of a carbonaceous substance. An alternative is to create the visual by using any type of materials and then electrostatically copying it and using the copy as the master. (Note that some electrostatic copies work better than others. Experiment with what is available to you.)

2. Place a sheet of thermal acetate over the master. Most brands of acetate have a notch in one corner of the film to ensure that it is put on correctly. The notch should always be placed at the upper-right-hand corner of the master.

3. Feed the two sets into a thermal copy machine, using the dial setting recommended by the manufacturer. Transfer of the image to the acetate requires only a few seconds. Then separate the two sheets. The film is ready for projection! The master is not affected in the production process and may be reused to make additional copies of the transparency.

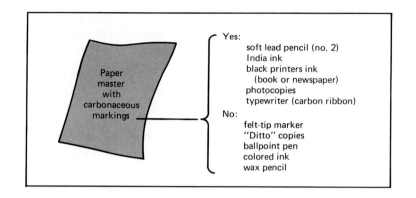

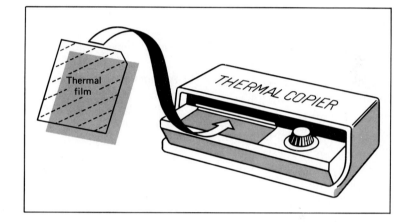

to better suit the needs of a particular audience.

Electrostatic Film Process (Xerography).
The rapidly evolving technology of xerography provides another method of producing transparencies. All plain paper copying machines that operate by the electrostatic process can now be used to prepare black-and-white transparencies. Some models, such as the Xerox 6500, can produce high-quality full-color transparencies

from originals on paper or from slides, but these costly machines are not widely available. Many commercial copying services can make full-color transparencies from your original at a reasonable price.

Similar to the thermal process, *electrostatic copying* requires a paper master and specially treated film. In this case the film is electrically charged and light sensitive (rather than heat sensitive). The steps just outlined for thermal film are essentially the same as those

needed to produce an electrostatic film transparency. However, because the xerographic process responds to darkness of the image rather than carbon content, it is not necessary to confine the artwork to carbonaceous images. Any substance that yields a good opaque mark can be used.

Spirit-Duplication Process.
If you are already planning to make a spirit-duplicator master (often referred to by the brand name, Ditto),

it is just one simple extra step to make a transparency from that master.

After you have prepared a regular master by *spirit duplication* and mounted it on the duplicating machine, feed in a sheet of frosted acetate with the etched side up. If greater permanence is desired, the resulting transparency can be sprayed with a clear-plastic spray, such as Krylon, which will remove the matte effect and protect the ink image from smearing.

An advantage of this process is that it allows you to use a master you may have prepared for another purpose to produce a transparency. Your students may then refer to their own copies of the visual while you project an image of it. A disadvantage is that the process requires some special materials—the frosted acetate and plastic spray.

Computer-Generated Masters.

Software packages that can combine graphics with varying sizes of print are available for most computers on the market. The printed masters produced by such programs can be used to make the overhead transparencies. If a laser printer is available, professional-quality masters can be made very easily. Computers are so commonplace in schools and offices that production of high-quality overhead masters by software programs will likely render obsolete some of the other methods mentioned in this section.

Overheads from Slides.
Several companies manufacture equipment that can make high-quality, full-color transparencies directly from 35mm slides. The transparencies produced have all the color, clarity, and definition of the original. The machines are too expensive for schools and small companies to acquire. However, many print and photocopy shops have the equipment, so when an important presentation requires top quality, the

HOW TO . . .
Design Overhead Transparencies

Whatever production process you choose for preparing your transparencies, keep in mind these design guidelines based on research and practical experience:

❑ *Horizontal format* covers projected viewing area best. Screens are frequently rectangular and better fit the horizontal format. On a square screen, the audience has difficulty seeing the bottom fourth of a vertical format transparency.

❑ *Visual ideas* should be used for overheads. Diagrams, graphs, and charts should be incorporated. If not, consider using chalkboard or print to convey verbal information.

❑ A *single concept* should be expressed in simple, uncluttered visuals. Presenting more than one concept can be confusing.

❑ *Minimum verbiage* should be included, with not more than six words per line and six or fewer lines per transparency.

❑ *Key words* help the audience remember each point. These are usually most effective as "headlines" at the top of the visual.

❑ *Legibility* is important. One quick way to check it is to lay the transparency on the floor over a white piece of paper. If you can read it from a standing position, your audience should be able to read it when projected. Use letters at least ³⁄₁₆-inch high.

❑ *Overlays* can explain complex ideas by adding information sequentially to the base transparency.

transparencies can be made at a reasonable cost.

We are seeing the emergence of "imaging" shops in response to the

capabilities of the new technologies of image creation. Photographic production shops, as well as photocopy stores, are acquiring the computer and printing equipment to make prints, slides, and transparencies with the software now available. A recent software development allows a shop of this kind to go directly from digital information, both text and images, to full-color printing press plates. The combination of all these capabilities can make your local photocopy store a one-stop text and imaging center.

SLIDES

The term *slide* refers to a small-format photographic transparency individually mounted for one-at-a-time projection.

The size of slides most frequently encountered in educational use is 2 by 2 inches (5 by 5 centimeters) measured by the outer dimensions of the slide mount. When 35mm and other popular types of slide film are sent out to be processed, they are usually returned mounted in 2 by 2-inch mounts. The actual dimensions of the image itself will vary with the type of film (Figure 5.8) and camera.

Advantages

Because slides can be arranged and rearranged into many different sequences, they are more flexible than filmstrips or other fixed sequence materials.

As photographic equipment is continually refined and simplified, more and more amateurs are able to produce their own slides. Automatic exposure controls, easy focusing, and high-speed color film have contributed to this trend. High-quality color slides can be taken by any amateur photographer.

The assembly of slide programs is facilitated by today's automatic projectors (Figure 5.9), which hold sets of slides in trays and feed them into place in sequence. Most automatic projectors also offer the convenience of remote control advancing of slides, allowing the presenter to remain at the front of the room or off to one side while advancing the slides via a push-button unit connected by wire to the projector. Wireless remote control is also available. Certain models can be preset to advance automatically. This feature allows continuous showing in exhibits, display cases, and other automated situations.

General availability and ease of handling make it relatively easy to build up permanent collections of slides for specific instructional purposes. Instructors may collect and store their own collections, or the slides may be compiled and kept in a learning resource center. Such collections enable users to assemble presentations partially or wholly from existing pictures, thus reducing the expense required for new production.

Slides can be integrated into individualized instruction programs. Although slides have been developed primarily as a large-group medium, recent hardware innovations have

AV SHOWMANSHIP

Overhead

In addition to the general utilization practices, here are some hints specifically related to overhead projection:

❑ Use the same size frame for all your transparencies. Then you can tape a guide on the projector platform so that each image projects onto the same screen area.

❑ Start by projecting an outline to show learners what will be presented.

❑ Avoid diminishing the possible impact of overhead projection by using the projector as a doodle pad. For random notes or verbal cues, use the chalkboard.

❑ Shift the audience's attention back to you by switching off the projector when you have finished referring to a particular transparency.

❑ Plan ways to add meaningful details to the transparency during projection; this infuses an element of spontaneity. If the basic transparency is a valuable one which will be reused, cover it with a blank acetate before drawing.

❑ Place your notes (key words) on the frame of the transparency. Do not try to read from a prepared script.

❑ Use dual projectors to retain the overall outline while covering secondary issues on a second projector. Dual projection is also helpful in difficult-to-read presentations.

❑ Point to specific portions using a pencil as a pointer. Lay the pencil directly on the transparency, because any elevation will put the pencil out of focus and any slight hand movement will be greatly exaggerated on the screen. Avoid pointing to the screen.

❑ Reveal information one line at a time to control pace and audience attention by placing a sheet of paper under the transparency.

❑ Mask unwanted portions by covering them with a sheet of paper or using cardboard windows to reveal one section at a time.

❑ Overlay new information in steps. Build up a complex idea by superimposing transparencies one at a time. Up to four overlays can be used successfully.

made slides feasible for small-group and independent study as well (Figure 5.10). However, the complex nature of these new mechanisms makes them relatively expensive. Thus, slide-tape viewers for individual use are more likely to be found in learning resource centers than in classrooms.

Figure 5.8
Common slide formats

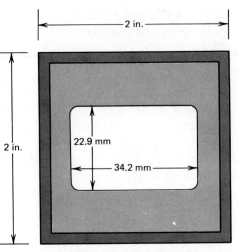

35-mm film, "the standard"

Limitations

Because slides, unlike filmstrips, come as individual units, they can easily become disorganized. Even when they are stored in trays, if the locking ring is loosened, the slides can come spilling out.

Slide mounts come in cardboard, plastic, and glass of varying thicknesses. This lack of standardization can lead to jamming of slides in the slide-changing mechanism: cardboard becomes dog-eared and the frayed edges get caught in the mechanism; plastic mounts swell or warp in the heat of the lamp; glass mounts thicker than the aperture chamber fail to drop into showing position.

Slides that are not enclosed in glass covers can accumulate dust and fingerprints. Careless storage or handling can easily lead to permanent damage.

Directing the viewer's attention to a particular spot on the screen has always been a problem with slides, as well as filmstrips. Some instructors use narrow-beam flashlights but these generally are not bright enough to stand out. Now several companies manufacture pointers based on laser technology. Because the beam is a very bright red, laser pointers enable an instructor to direct the audience's attention to any place on the screen.

A final limitation of slides is their cost in comparison to filmstrips. The cost per frame of a commercially produced slide set may be two to three times the cost per frame of a filmstrip of equal length.

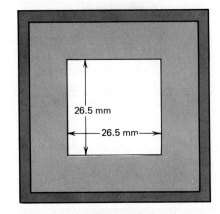

35 mm
"half-frame" film

Type 126 film
"Instamatic"

MEDIA FILE: *The Mexican-Texans to 1865*
Slide-Cassette Set

A number of states (and provinces in Canada) sponsor the production of a variety of educational materials for use in schools. Texas certainly is in the forefront of this movement. One of the more prolific agencies is the Institute of Texan Culture in San Antonio. Among the many audiovisual materials it has produced is this slide set. The early history of Texas as part of Mexico is told through biographies of outstanding Mexican-Texans and the roles they played in events leading up to the Texas revolution. During the time Texas was a republic, Mexican-Texans continued to make history.

Source: Institute of Texan Culture

Figure 5.9
The Ektagraphic III is Kodak's latest updating of the Carousel line of slide projectors.

Applications

Like other forms of projected visuals, slides may be used at all grade levels and for instruction in all curriculum areas. Many high-quality slides are available commercially, individually, and in sets. In general, the fine arts, geography, and the sciences are especially well represented with commercially distributed slides.

The following examples give some idea of the types of slide materials available through commercial channels. A major directory of commercially available slides is published by the National Information Center for Educational Media (NICEM)—*Index to Educational Slides.* (See Appendix A for details and other sources.)

Local Production of Slides

A major advantage of slides as an instructional device is the ease with which they can be produced by instructors as well as students. Modern cameras are so simple to operate that even the most amateur of photographers can expect usable results. As with all locally produced materials, instructor- and student-made slides are likely to have an immediacy and a specificity lacking in commercially produced instructional materials. Further, such locally produced efforts gain credibility by depicting local people and conditions.

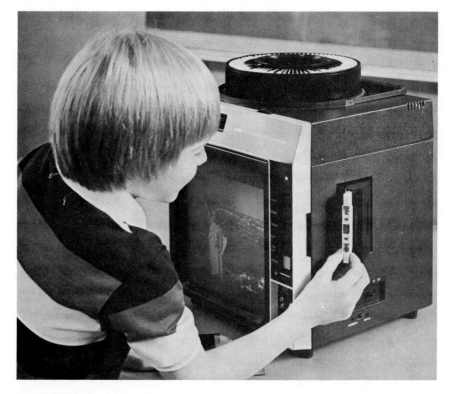

Figure 5.10
The slide-tape format has been adapted for individual viewers.

MEDIA FILE *Folklore Under the Big Top*
Slide-Cassette Program

The state humanities councils, funded by the states and the National Endowment for the Humanities, sponsor and produce audiovisual programs for use by schools and the general public. The Indiana Humanities Council has been particularly active in producing videos and slide-cassette sets of cultural and historical value to Hoosiers. Rochester, Indiana, was the home base and winter quarters for the Cole Brothers Circus from 1935 to 1940. Photographs from the period and interviews with people who remember those years help recreate the sights and sounds of the circus for those who never experienced the Big Top in an open field.

Source: Indiana Humanities Council

HOW TO . . .
"Thumb Spot" Slides

There are eight possible ways a slide can be placed in a projector. Seven of them are wrong (e.g., upside-down, backwards, sideways). To avoid all seven mistakes a standardized procedure is recommended for placing a reminder spot on the slide.

❑ First, your slides should be arranged and numbered in the order in which they are to be shown.

❑ Then take each slide and hold it the way it is supposed to be seen on the screen, that is, right-side up with the lettering running left to right, just as it would be read. If the slide lacks lettering or other orienting information, hold it so that the emulsion side (the duller side) is toward the screen.

❑ Then simply place a spot (or number) on the bottom left-hand corner.

❑ This spot is referred to as a "thumb spot" because when the slide is turned upside down to be placed in the projector, your thumb will grip the slide at the point of the thumb spot, as shown.

❑ Before all the slides are put in the tray in proper order, some users like to run a felt-tip pen across the tops of the slide mounts in a diagonal line. This way if some slides later get out of order, they can be replaced just by following the line.

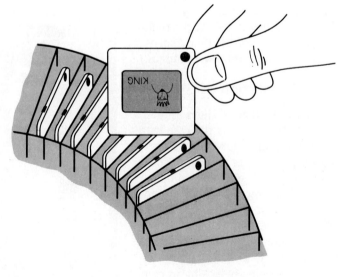

144

CLOSE-UP

National History Day

Each Spring, middle, junior high, and high school students gather in each state to present their research on the year's chosen theme. They present their material in a variety of formats: stage performances, videos, exhibits, slide shows, and computer programs. The research these students do is often worthy of graduate students. The state winners in each category go on to Washington, D.C., for the final competition. The photo shows two junior high students getting ready to show their slide presentation on Susan B. Anthony. A five-page report on National History Day by Marilyn Page, "Active Learning in Secondary Schools: Educational Media and Technology," is available from ERIC (ED323987). The report stresses the value of cooperative learning.

Figure 5.11
Teacher photographing court house for a slide set on local landmarks

Among the myriad possibilities, here are some typical subjects for slide presentations:

❏ Providing a tour for new employees of a local business without walking through the plant

❏ Making a visual history of your community, school, or organization

❏ Demonstrating local operating and sales procedures for real estate agents

❏ Documenting student activities, products of student work, and community problems (e.g., crime and pollution)

❏ Presenting a preoperative explanation of a surgical procedure tailored to a specific surgeon's patients

❏ Showing people at work in various jobs, for career awareness

❏ Illustrating the uses of a company's products throughout the world

❏ Teaching a step-by-step process with close-ups of each operation

❏ Simulating a field trip

❏ Promoting public understanding of your school or organization

Copying Visuals with a Single-Lens Reflex Camera

Many single-lens reflex cameras now have a combination zoom and macro lens. A macro lens permits taking photos at close range. This combina-

HOW TO . . .
Copy Visuals with a Single-Lens Reflex Camera

❑ **The Camera.** The single-lens reflex camera is the best type to use for making copies of flat materials and small objects. What you see in the viewfinder is what you get on the film, unlike with range-finder cameras where the closer you get to the subject, the greater the difference between what you see and what gets on the film. Focusing is much more accurate with an SLR. When the image is sharp in the viewfinder, it will be sharp on the film. The interchangeable-lens feature adds considerably to the range of copying capability.

❑ **The Lens.** The normal lens on a 35mm camera can focus as close as 1.5 to 2 feet. This corresponds to a picture area about 6 by 9 inches, and will take care of most of your copying needs. However, if you need to copy a smaller area, you will have to modify the lens arrangement. The less expensive solution is to use supplementary lenses. These come in steps of magnification expressed as +1, +2, +3. When you buy them, take your camera to your local camera store to make sure the lens set matches your camera lens. The more expensive solution is to buy a macro lens. This lens replaces the normal camera lens. Macro lenses come in a variety of configurations, so consult your local camera store or media specialist to find the best arrangement for your needs.

❑ **Exposure.** Virtually every camera sold today has automatic exposure control. Because a single-lens reflex camera monitors the light as it comes through the lens, any modifications of exposure made necessary by the use of other lenses or filters will be taken care of automatically. Many cameras permit you to increase or decrease the exposure. This feature can be quite useful in compensating for material that is too light or too dark, or in increasing or decreasing contrast. If your camera has this feature, practice with it until you learn how to use it judiciously.

❑ **Using a Tripod.** While copying with a hand-held camera is possible, the best results are achieved by mounting the camera on a stable platform such as a tripod. If you are copying flat material, it can be fastened to an

A macro lens and close-up supplementary lenses

outside wall about the height of the camera on the tripod. Then the camera and tripod are positioned the appropriate distance from the material, the lens focused, and the exposure made. The material is best mounted in open shade. However, if the material has low contrast, you may need to mount it on a sunlit wall, but be sure you are not getting undesirable reflections or bright spots. A handy way of eliminating glare is to use a polarizing filter. Consult your local camera store for the proper size for your camera and helpful hints on how to use it. A polarizing filter is especially useful in eliminating glare when photographing something beneath a water surface and in darkening the sky for dramatic effects, but it also has a tendency to flatten outdoor scenes, for example, by eliminating the reflections from sunlit leaves.

❑ **Tabletop Photography.** The camera mounted on a tripod is a handy way to photograph small objects: coins, flowers, insects, etc. The object can be placed on a coffee table in a well-lighted area and the tripod and camera oriented so that the object is well displayed. The

---

tion permits reproduction of flat visual materials, such as maps, charts, illustrations, and the like, and small three-dimensional objects without the need for specialized photographic skills. The automatic exposure feature takes the guesswork out of setting shutter speed and lens opening. The flexibility of the lens eliminates the need for supplementary lenses for all but the smallest of objects and visual materials.

The material to be copied can be pinned to a wall or placed on a horizontal surface and photographed.

The camera should be put on a tripod so you can more carefully control image location and camera movement (Figure 5.12). If a tripod is not available, the copy can be made outdoors using a hand-held camera loaded with fast film. Media centers usually have a copy stand. If

comments about supplementary and macro lenses apply here too. Don't use a wide-angle lens because the image will be distorted; the part of the object closest to the lens will be out of proportion to the rest of the object

❑ **Using a Copy Stand.** If you do a lot of copying, you will want to look into using a copy stand. Your media center may have one that you can use. At a minimum, a copy stand has a flat bed where the material is placed and a vertical post on which the camera is mounted. From there, copy stands become more elaborate and may include an adjustable platen to hold the material flat and adjustable floodlights attached to the base. After the material to be copied is placed on the base, the camera is moved up and down and the material adjusted until the viewfinder shows the image you want. If supplemental lighting is necessary, use the polarizing filter to take care of any glare that might result. A copy stand is best used for flat materials. Three-dimensional objects are

better photographed on a table using a tripod-mounted camera because you can choose the angle and lighting that shows the object to its best advantage.

❑ **Lettering.** If you want to add lettering to the material being photographed, remember to keep the letters in proportion. If the area being copied is fairly large, the letters must be large also. If the area is small, the letters must be small because they will be enlarged when the slide is enlarged. Judge the size of the lettering in proportion to the material by studying what you see in the viewfinder.

❑ **Copying Slides.** Copying slides requires a special piece of equipment. It looks like a miniature copy stand. But the slide to be copied is lighted from beneath. The camera, mounted on the vertical post, can be adjusted to copy all or part of the slide. This is a useful but expensive piece of equipment. Your media center may have one. Otherwise, for the few times you may need to copy slides, a commercial shop is the simplest way to go.

Using a tripod for tabletop photography

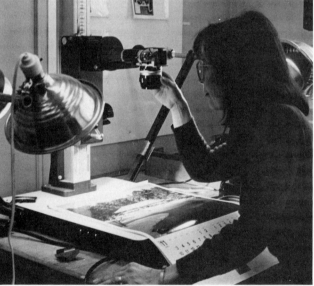

Using a copy stand to photograph flat materials

so, the camera is best mounted on it for carefully controlled copying. (See "How To . . . Copy Visuals with a Single-Lens Reflex Camera.")

Computer-Generated Slides.
Computer programs that can generate complex graphic displays are now commonplace (Figure 5.13). Recently, however, special systems have been developed that allow you to construct a graphic on the monitor screen and then have a 2-by-2-inch slide made of the display. Slides made this way are superior in resolution and color quality to the im-

age on the monitor. In fact, computer-generated slides have better resolution than high-definition television. The software has made slide production so easy that training programs in business and industry have increased the use of this medium dramatically in the last few

Figure 5.12
High-quality copies of visuals can be made using a single-lens reflex camera mounted on a tripod.

years. Slides are an inexpensive way to tailor training to local needs.

These special programs and associated equipment are too expensive for individual purchase, but audiovisual production centers in many colleges and universities and in industry have made computer-generated slide services available to their staffs. Many custom audiovisual production shops make computer-generated slides from graphics submitted by customers who do not want to acquire the necessary program and equipment to produce their own.

Polaroid Instant Slides. Polaroid makes a device that produces slides from 8½-by-11-inch documents or illustrations. Simply place the illustration in the copier, push the button, and a minute later out comes the slide. If you want better quality and you are not in a hurry, Polaroid 35mm Presentation Chrome film can be used. It requires the same processing as Ektachrome. The Polaroid system is expensive and is limited in the size of the material that can be copied, but its convenience and reliability make it attractive.

Polaroid Slides from Video. Polaroid also has a device that makes photographic prints or slides of any image from a videocassette recorder, video camera, videodisc player, or computer graphic workstation. Polaroid calls this device a Freeze Frame Video Image Recorder, or Freeze Frame for short. The Freeze Frame device plugs directly into the equipment generating the video image. Polaroid also makes an adapter for a 35mm camera that

makes instant slides from any exposure made.

FILMSTRIPS

A *filmstrip* is a roll of 35mm transparent film containing a series of related still pictures intended for showing one at a time. Various filmstrip formats have evolved since the advent of the filmstrip over a half century ago. The most widely used format today is the single-frame filmstrip (Figure 5.14). Note that in the single-frame format the images are printed perpendicular to the length of the film, whereas in the slide format the images are parallel to the length of the film. Commercially produced filmstrips typically contain about twenty to sixty images, or frames, and are stored rolled up in small plastic canisters.

Until the 1960s most filmstrips were silent; that is, there was no audio accompaniment. Narrative information was printed at the bottom of each frame. Since that time there has been a growing trend toward having recorded sound tracks accompany the filmstrip. Initially the narration, music, sound effects, and so on were recorded on phonograph records and were played on record

Figure 5.13
Software programs make it easy to generate slides and overhead transparencies on the computer. The image shown on the monitor does not reflect the high resolution of the completed slide.

AV SHOWMANSHIP

Slides

In addition to the general guidelines for audiovisual utilization discussed in Chapter 2, here are several specific practices that can add professionalism to your slide presentations:

❑ Use a remote control advance device; this will allow you to stand at the side of the room. From this position you can keep an eye on the slides while maintaining some eye contact with the audience.

❑ Make certain your slides are in sequential order and right-side up. Disarrangement can be an embarrassment to you and an annoyance to your audience. See "How To . . . 'Thumb Spot' Slides" (page 144) for a foolproof method of marking slides.

❑ Employ visual variety. Mix the types of slides, using verbal title slides to help break the presentation into segments.

❑ Prepare a way to light up your script after the room lights are dimmed; a penlight or flashlight will serve this purpose.

❑ Limit your discussion of each slide. Even a minute of narration can seem long to your audience unless there is a complex visual to be examined at the same time.

❑ Plan and rehearse your narration to accompany the slides if it is not already recorded on tape.

❑ If there is a "talky" section in the middle of your presentation, put a gray or black slide on rather than holding an irrelevant slide on the screen. (Gray slides can be produced locally or purchased from commercial sources. They let through enough light to allow the presenter to be seen, avoiding total darkening of the room.)

❑ Consider adding a musical accompaniment to your live or recorded narration. This can help to establish the desired mood and keep your audience attentive. But do not have music playing in the background when providing narration.

❑ Begin and end with a black slide. A white flash on the screen at the beginning and end is irritating to the eye and appears amateurish.

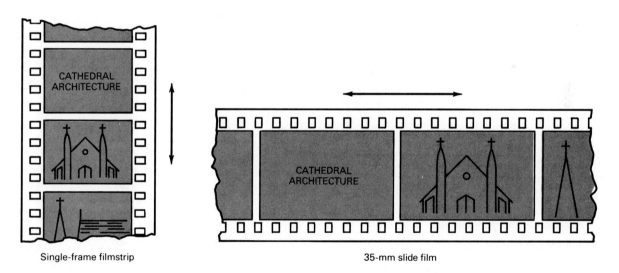

Single-frame filmstrip   35-mm slide film

Figure 5.14
Comparison of the single-frame filmstrip and the 35mm slide format

players either separate from the projector or built into it. Currently, audiocassette tapes are the standard means for giving sound filmstrips their "voice" (Figure 5.15). The sound track is not recorded on the filmstrip itself; rather, it comes on a separate cassette tape which is played on a regular cassette recorder or on one built into the filmstrip projector unit. (Figure 5.16).

For most sound filmstrips, the record or tape contains, besides the sound track, a second track carrying inaudible signals that automatically trigger the projector to advance to the next frame. Depending on the capability of the projector, users generally have a choice of manually advancing the filmstrip according to audible beeps or setting the projector to run automatically according to the inaudible synchronization pulses.

Figure 5.15
Filmstrip sets synchronized with
audiocassettes are a popular format.

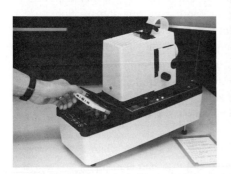

Figure 5.16
A sound-filmstrip projector that uses
audiocassettes to advance the frames
automatically.

Advantages

The filmstrip has gained considerable popularity because of its compactness, ease of handling, and relatively low cost. A filmstrip of sixty frames will fit comfortably in the palm of your hand and weighs only a few ounces. It is inserted easily into a simple projector. A commercially distributed filmstrip costs substantially less per frame than a set of slides or overhead transparencies purchased from a commercial source.

The sequential order of the frames can often be a teaching and learning advantage. A chronological or step-by-step process can be presented in order without fear of having any of the pictures out of sequence or upside down, as can sometimes happen with slides.

In contrast to audio and motion media, the pace of viewing filmstrips can be controlled by the user. This

MEDIA FILE: *Profiles of Black Americans*
Filmstrip-Cassette Set

The first filmstrip in this set is devoted to black political leaders, including former Supreme Court Justice Thurgood Marshall, shown at the left. The second refers to black leaders in the professions, the third to blacks in the performing arts, and the last to blacks in sports. Part of SVE's Basic Skill Boosters series, the guide includes the complete script of the narrative for each filmstrip and helpful suggestions for using the series in class. Reading comprehension exercises offer additional information about the contributions of blacks and skill building in vocabulary and reading.

Source: Society for Visual Education

MEDIA FILE: *Canada: Portrait of a Nation*
Filmstrip-Cassette Set

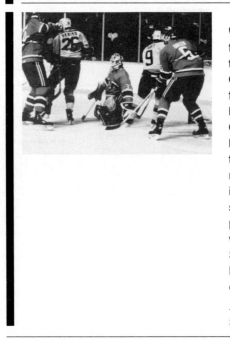

Junior high students in the United States (the audience for this filmstrip-cassette set) may not know that hockey is the national sport of Canada. After experiencing these five filmstrips and audiocassettes, they will learn this and many other facts about Canada and its peoples. They will learn how the people of Canada earn their living by tapping the country's rich natural resources as well as working in today's high-tech industries. The set also focuses on the environmental problems Canada faces, some of which are shared with the United States. The social and political gains being made by Native Americans are described.

Source: Society for Visual Education

capability is especially relevant for independent study but is also important for teacher-controlled group showings. A slow, deliberate examination of each frame might be suitable for the body of a lesson, whereas a quick runthrough might suffice for purposes of preview and review. Not only the pace but also the level of instruction can be controlled. Particularly with silent filmstrips, the vocabulary or level of narration supplied by the presenter can be adapted to audience abilities.

Filmstrips lend themselves well to independent study. Many types of tabletop viewers are made especially for individual or small-group use. Young children have no difficulty loading the light, compact filmstrips into these viewers. The fixed sequence of the frames structures the learner's progress through the material. The captions or recorded narration add a verbal component to the visuals, creating a convenient self-contained learning package. And because the user controls the rate of presentation, the filmstrip allows self-pacing when used for independent study.

Limitations

Having the frames permanently fixed in a certain sequence has disadvantages as well as advantages. The main drawback is that it is not possible to alter the sequence of pictures without destroying the filmstrip. Backtracking to an earlier picture or skipping over frames is cumbersome.

Because the filmstrip is pulled through the projector by means of toothed sprocket wheels, there is the constant possibility of tearing the sprocket holes or damaging the filmstrip. Improper threading or rough use can cause tears which are very difficult for you to repair, although, if you have a 35mm splicing block, not impossible. (In cases where damage to the sprocket holes is extensive, the frames can be cut apart and mounted individually to be used as slides.)

Applications

Because they are simply packaged and easy to handle, filmstrips are well suited to independent study (Figure 5.17). They are popular items in study carrels and media centers. Students enjoy using filmstrips on their own to help prepare research reports to their classmates.

MEDIA FILE: *California: The Golden State*
Filmstrip Set

This set of four filmstrips for intermediate grades comes with some uncommon features. Each filmstrip begins with a set of learning objectives, and each contains vocabulary frames to alert teachers and students to key words. A set of twenty-four "skill sheets" provides written exercises that reinforce the content of the filmstrips. The four filmstrips are titled (1) California's Geography; (2) California's Early History through the Gold Rush; (3) California: Statehood and After; and (4) California: Diversity, Challenge, and Change.

Source: Society for Visual Education

MEDIA FILE: *Native Americans*
Sound-Filmstrip Sets

These two sets, a total of eight filmstrips, present an overview of the history of the original human residents of North America and provide closer looks at outstanding figures in Native American history. For example, one of the filmstrips is devoted to Sequoyah, who is credited with being the only person in history ever to create an entirely new written language. Early in the nineteenth century he devised a system of symbols representing all the sounds of the Cherokee language. Sacajawea is also profiled. The relationship between Native Americans and the U.S. government over the years is treated in detail. The original artwork is creative and attractive. Upper elementary students will find these filmstrips appealing.

Source: Nystrom

The major difference in application between slides and filmstrips is that slides lend themselves to teacher-made presentations, whereas filmstrips are better suited to mass production and distribution. Further, slide sets tend to be used in a more open-ended fashion than filmstrips. Today filmstrips are usually packaged as self-contained kits; that is, the narration to accompany the pictures is provided either in the form of captions on the filmstrip or as a recorded sound track on cassette. Other teacher support materials may be integrated into the kit.

As with the other sorts of projected visuals discussed in this chapter, filmstrips find appropriate applications in a wide variety of subjects and grade levels. Their broad appeal is attested to by the constantly growing volume of commercial materials available. Tens of thousands of titles are already in distribution. Indeed, it would be difficult to identify an audiovisual medium offering a larger number of titles in distribution.

MEDIA FILE: *The Magnificent Dinosaurs*
Filmstrip-Cassette Set

This series includes four filmstrips and audiocassettes. In addition to providing a great deal of accurate information on how dinosaurs lived, died, and were sometimes fossilized, the work of paleontologists at Dinosaur National Monument, Utah, is featured. They are shown chipping away the sandstone in which the dinosaurs were buried, examining fossils, and reconstructing the ancient beasts.

Source: United Learning

Figure 5.17
The tabletop sound-filmstrip viewer can serve an individual or a small group, and it can be viewed in a fully lighted room.

MEDIA FILE: *News Maps of the World*
Filmstrips

This set of silent, captioned filmstrips consists of one filmstrip on the Eastern Hemisphere and one on the Western Hemisphere. The captions are designed to be used as springboards for discussion by students and teachers. As the title of the set indicates, the emphasis is on current events, with some historical background provided. The maps are important in placing events in their geographical context. The schools are frequently criticized for not teaching enough geography; this set will help teachers respond to that criticism.

Source: Knowledge Unlimited

Filmstrip

The general utilization guidelines for audiovisuals discussed in Chapter 2 apply comprehensively to filmstrip use. There are several additional points, though, that pertain especially to filmstrips:

❑ Do not feel compelled to run the filmstrip all the way through without stopping. You can do this as a kind of overview and then go back and reshow it, pausing for discussion at key frames.

❑ Encourage participation by asking relevant questions during the presentation. You may want to ask the students to read any captions. This is a particularly good reading activity for elementary students.

❑ Use filmstrips to test visually the mastery of visual concepts. You can, for instance, project individual frames without the caption or sound track and asking students to make an identification or discrimination.

A small sample of the range of filmstrips on the market is illustrated in the "Media Files" on pages 150–52. A major directory of commercially available filmstrips is published by the National Information Center for Educational Media (NICEM)—*Index to 35-mm Filmstrips*. (See Appendix A for details and other sources.)

An innovation introduced in 1984 may foreshadow a future role for the filmstrip as an element in interactive video programs. The Society for Visual Education (SVE), a major commercial distributor of filmstrips, produced a single videodisc incorporating more than 30,000 still pictures. The videodisc player is connected to a microcomputer containing a computer-assisted instruction program. The computer program presents verbal instruction *and* controls the videodisc player, calling up particular pictures onto the display screen as needed. The entire videodisc—all 30,000 images—can be scanned in less than five seconds and the desired frame inserted in the lesson. While interactive video (see Chapter 7) is usually thought of as combining moving images (television) with computer interaction, in many learning situations only still pictures are needed. The SVE system could

Figure 5.18
Opaque projector, cutaway view

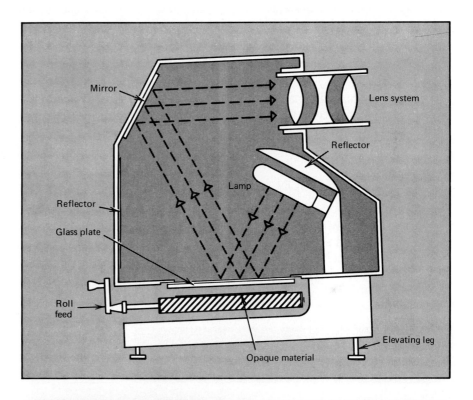

Figure 5.19
The opaque projector can be used to magnify small objects as well as print materials and pictures.

THE CUTTING EDGE

Magnetic and Digital Photography

S everal camera companies have announced all-electronic cameras. The light entering the camera is focused not onto film but onto a *charge-coupled device* which converts the colors of the original scene into electrical impulses. These are then stored on a tape as magnetic charges to be displayed on a TV screen or processed into photographic prints. (The charge-coupled device is also used in camcorders, as explained in Chapter 7, p. 190.)

This system depends on an analog process because the image is recorded magnetically. Many experts, however, expect a totally digitized system to eventually take over the magnetic system. In this system, the charge-coupled device would convert colors into a digital code stored in some form. One of the obstacles facing the companies working to develop a digitized system is meeting the standard of high-definition television (HDTV). In order to secure the highest quality for display, the technology must be compatible with HDTV.

Storage devices are increasing in capacity and coming down in cost. Charge-coupled devices are improving dramatically, with a whole new generation likely to emerge for HDTV use. By the year 2000, the cameras we will be using may look like what we are using now, but the insides will be unrecognizable by the photographer of today.

---

suit these situations, eliminating television production costs and recycling vast libraries of existing pictures.

OPAQUE PROJECTION

Opaque projection is a method of enlarging and displaying nontransparent material on a screen. A very bright light is reflected from the material to be displayed rather than passed through it. The opaque projector was among the first audiovisual devices to come into widespread use and is still used because of its unique ability to project a magnified image of two-dimensional materials and some three-dimensional objects.

The opaque projector works by directing a very strong incandescent light (typically about 1,000 watts) down onto the material. This light is reflected upward to strike a mirror, which aims the light beam through a series of lenses onto a screen (Figures 5.18 and 5.19).

The process of reflected, or indirect, projection is optically less efficient than the direct projection process used for showing slides, filmstrips, and overhead transparencies. Consequently, the image on the screen is dimmer, and more complete room darkening is required. Still, opaque projection makes such a wide range of visual materials available for group viewing that it

---

AV SHOWMANSHIP

Opaque Projection

I n addition to the general principles of audiovisual utilization discussed in Chapter 2, there are several special techniques that apply particularly to opaque projection.

❑ Because the opaque projector requires near-total room darkening, be prepared to operate in the dark. A student should be stationed at the light switch to help you avoid tripping over students, cords, and other obstacles in getting to and from the projector in the dark. Although the projector does spill quite a bit of light around its sides, you may need to use a flashlight to follow any prepared notes or script.

❑ Most opaque projectors are equipped with a built-in optical pointer, a bright arrow that can be aimed at any point on the screen. Experiment ahead of time so that you will be able to aim the pointer effectively during the presentation. It can be used to focus viewers' attention to particular words on a printed page, details of an art work, and so on.

❑ For some purposes (especially in teaching elementary school language arts) it is useful to arrange pictures on a long strip or roll of paper. In this way you can put a series of illustrations into a fixed sequence to tell a story or show steps in a process. This simulates the action of a filmstrip.

❑ The opaque projector will accept a wide range of picture sizes. When you are setting up the projector, be sure to use the largest of your illustrations to fill the screen area. If you use a smaller picture, the bigger one will extend beyond the edges of the screen when you get to it. This will force you to stop in the middle of the presentation (and thus distract your audience) to adjust for the big picture.

☐ **APPRAISAL CHECKLIST**
   Projected Visuals

Title _____

Format

Series Title (if applicable) _____
☐ Overhead transparency

Source _____
☐ Slide

Length _____ frames _____ minutes (sound track)
☐ Sound/slide

Date _____ **Cost** _____
☐ Filmstrip

Subject Area _____
☐ Sound filmstrip

Intended Audience _____

Objectives (stated or implied)

Brief Description

Entry Capabilities Required

☐ Prior subject-matter knowledge/vocabulary

☐ Reading ability

☐ Mathematical ability

☐ Other:

Rating	High		Medium		Low	Comments
Relevance to objectives	☐	☐	☐	☐	☐	
Accuracy of information	☐	☐	☐	☐	☐	
Likely to arouse/maintain interest	☐	☐	☐	☐	☐	
Likely to be comprehended clearly	☐	☐	☐	☐	☐	
Technical quality	☐	☐	☐	☐	☐	
Promotes participation/involvement	☐	☐	☐	☐	☐	
Evidence of effectiveness (e.g., field-test results)	☐	☐	☐	☐	☐	
Free from objectionable bias	☐	☐	☐	☐	☐	
Provisions for discussion/follow-up	☐	☐	☐	☐	☐	

Strong Points

Weak Points

Reviewer _____

Position _____

Recommended Action _____ Date _____

Context. Company sales have been on a plateau for three years and the general sales manager has devised a strategy to expand existing markets and open new ones. His goal is to convince management and the marketing division to adopt the new marketing strategy.

ANALYZE LEARNERS

General Characteristics

The audience consists of the chief executive officer (CEO), the marketing vice president, the financial vice president, and three regional sales managers. The financial vice president joined the company two years ago, but the others have been with the company at least ten years. The financial vice president believes a sharp increase in profits would firmly secure her job. The marketing members of the audience feel somewhat threatened by the implication that their efforts have been ineffective and are apprehensive about the difficulties involved in restructuring the sales force. The CEO is concerned about a board of directors disgruntled over stagnant sales. He wants to be convinced but not at the expense of creating a hostile sales group.

Entry Competencies

Each member of the audience has successful business experience but in different areas. The financial vice president appraises all company activities strictly by the balance sheet. The marketing vice president wants to show an interest in overall company performance but looks at proposals from the point of view of the marketing division. The regional sales managers believe they have developed loyal and effective sales forces. All have demonstrated the ability to grasp quickly the ramifications of new ideas.

STATE OBJECTIVES

1. The CEO will endorse the proposal by agreeing to present it to the board of directors.

2. The financial vice president will estimate the impact of the proposal on the profit margin of the company.

3. The marketing vice president will demonstrate support by suggesting a plan to restructure the sales apparatus.

4. The regional sales managers will indicate how the sales representatives can benefit from an expanded market.

5. The marketing vice president and the regional sales managers will agree to meet with the general sales manager to develop an implementation strategy including a training program for sales representatives.

SELECT MEDIA AND MATERIALS

The general sales manager is well aware that he has a tough audience to convince. A well-organized and illustrated presentation is a must. An equally important consideration is the need to maintain constant interaction with the audience during the presentation. He consults with the company training director on the media to be used. She suggests overhead transparencies as the heart of the presentation with a flip chart available for spontaneous notes and reactions. Together they go to a local graphics design shop to work out the sketches for the transparencies based on his notes. The graphics are designed using computer software and, when approved, the transparencies are generated. Several color photographs are part of the presentation and they are made into transparencies using the color copying machine in the graphics shop.

UTILIZE MATERIALS

The general sales manager has selected a meeting room best suited for overhead projection and has prepared for the meeting by arranging for pads, pencils, and beverages. He reviews past accomplishments of the company, paying particular attention to the important contributions of the people in the room. He stresses how the company has responded successfully to similar challenges in the past. He then starts to unfold his plan, inviting comments as he goes along. He notes comments to be discussed more fully on the flip chart.

REQUIRE LEARNER PARTICIPATION

By inviting comments, he draws the audience into being collaborators rather than spectators. As he answers questions indicating misgivings, the audience gradually begins adding to his presentation. The presentation ends up more like a conference than a sales pitch. Instead of thinking about the plan later, they are talking about it now. The CEO enthusiastically asks the general sales manager to present the proposal to the board. The financial vice president volunteers to work up the sales projections into a financial statement. The marketing personnel set a time and place to put together an implementation strategy.

EVALUATE AND REVISE

The objectives have been achieved, but now the general sales manager must adapt the presentation to a new audience, the board of directors. He particularly reviews the questions and comments of the CEO as guides to the approach to use with the board. He also wants to work closely with the financial vice president on the presentation of the fiscal projections of the marketing strategy.

He is eager to talk to his former associates on the sales force to prepare himself better for the meeting with the marketing vice president and the regional sales managers.

should not be overlooked as a teaching tool.

Advantages

Opaque projection allows on-the-spot projection of readily available classroom materials, such as maps, newspapers, and illustrations from books and magazines.

It permits group viewing and discussion of student work, such as drawings, student compositions, solutions to math problems, and the like.

Three-dimensional objects, especially relatively flat ones such as coins, plant leaves, and insect specimens can be magnified for close-up inspection.

Limitations

The relative dimness of the reflected image demands nearly complete room darkening if the visual is to be clear enough for instructional purposes. Areas that cannot be sufficiently darkened are unsuitable for opaque projection.

The opaque projector is bulky, heavy, and cumbersome to move.

The high-wattage lamp generates a lot of heat, making parts of the projector unsafe to touch. The heat may also damage the materials being projected if they are exposed too long to the projector's light. If metal objects are being projected, they may rapidly become too hot to handle.

Applications

The opaque projector is useful for many small groups or classroom-size groups (up to about twenty) that need to view printed or visual material together. Applications may be found in all curriculum areas at all grade levels. Here are just a few typical examples:

All subjects. Group critique of student work and review of test items

Art. Group discussion of reproductions of paintings and archi-

tectural details; study of advertising layouts

Business. Group work on business and accounting forms, organization charts, sales territory maps, parts of a product, and the like

Home economics. Group viewing of sewing patterns, textiles, recipes, close-up views of fabrics and weaving styles; and so forth

Industry. Projection of blueprints for group study; description of assembly line flow with production diagrams

Language arts. Group critique of student compositions, picture books, or reference books

Medical. Group study of anatomical drawings; discussion of diabetic diets and food exchange charts

Military. Review of maps and official documents; illustration of flight plans

Music. Group reading of musical scores

Religious education. Bible story illustrations; group examination of religious documents

Science. Magnification of specimens; group study of geologic maps, tables of random numbers, and the like

Social studies. Map study; viewing of artifacts from other cultures, postcards, and atlas illustrations

One especially handy application of the opaque projector is for copying or adapting illustrations for classroom display. You can make your own enlargement of any original picture that you might want to display on the chalkboard or as part of a bulletin board. The procedure is easy. Place the material to be copied in the projector and dim the room lights. Adjust the projector to enlarge (or reduce) the image to the size you want, and direct the projected image onto the surface on which you are working. Then trace over the projected image in whatever detail you wish. Every line of

the original can be reproduced, or just the outlines for a more stylized effect. Your students will be impressed with your "artistic ability," and maybe you will be too.

SELECTION CRITERIA FOR PROJECTED VISUALS

In this chapter we have attempted to survey broadly the many similarities and differences among several major formats of projected visuals—overhead projection, slides, filmstrips, and opaque projection. You might have noticed that the differences are mainly small technical differences that lead to trade-offs in cost, portability, flexibility, and so on. Basically, projected visuals look very much alike on the screen. For the viewer there is, in most cases, no significant difference among these formats in terms of learning impact. So it is appropriate that the chapter close by emphasizing the commonalities among the various types of projected visuals. The "Appraisal Checklist: Projected Visuals" (page 155) is designed to apply equally to the various formats.

REFERENCES

Print References

Barman, C. "Some Ways to Improve Your Overhead Projection Transparencies." *American Biology Teacher* (March 1982): 191–92.

Beasley, Augie E. "Audio-Visual Production: Making Your Own." *Book Report* (September–October 1988):10–25.

Beatty, LaMond F. *Filmstrips.* Englewood Cliffs, NJ: Educational Technology Publications, 1981.

Berry, Vern. "Review of 'Fast' Methods for Producing 2x2in. Slides." *Journal of Chemical Education* (July 1990):577–82.

Bodner, George M. "Instructional Media: Resisting Technological Overkill—35-mm Slides as an Alternative to Videotape/Videodisk." *Journal of College Science Teaching* (February 1985):360–63.

Bohning, G. "Storytelling Using Overhead Visuals." *Reading Teacher* (March 1984):677–78.

Burton, D. "Slide Art." *School Arts* (February 1984):23–26.

Clark, Jean N. "Filmstrips: Versatility and Visual Impact." *Media and Methods* (January–February 1988):20–21.

Crowe, Kathy M. "Effective Use of Slides for Bibliographic Information." *Research Strategies* (Fall 1989):175–79.

DeChenne, J. "Effective Utilization of Overhead Projectors." *Media and Methods* (January 1982):6–7.

Gersmehl, Philip J. "One Commandment and Ten Suggestions: Teaching the Video Generation with Slides." *Journal of Geography* (January–February 1985):15–19.

Green, Lee. *501 Ways to Use the Overhead Projector.* Littleton, CO: Libraries Unlimited, 1982.

Hess, Darrel. *Audio-Visual Techniques Handbook.* Washington, D.C.: National Council of Returned Peace Corps Volunteers, 1988.

Hoy, Frank. "Electronic Camera Provides Instant Images on TV Screen." *Journalism Educator* (Spring 1989):30–34.

Keefe, Jeanne M. "The Image as Document: Descriptive Programs at Rensselaer." *Library Trends* (Spring 1990):659–81.

Kemp, Jerrold E., and Smellie, Don C. *Planning, Producing, and Using Instructional Media.* 6th ed. New York: Harper Collins, 1989.

Kiss, Marilyn. "From Peru to Pamplona: Integrating Slides into the Lesson Plan." *Hispania* (May 1989):422–25.

Kueter, Roger A., and Miller, Janeen. *Slides.* Englewood Cliffs, NJ: Educational Technology Publications, 1981.

Lefever, Margaret. "A Mother Lode of Images for Teaching History." *Social Education* (May 1987):265.

McBride, Dennis. *How to Make Visual Presentations.* New York: Art Direction Book Company, 1982.

Meilach, Dona Z. "Overhead Projectors Take on New Dimensions." *Audio Visual Communications* (August 1990):32–36.

Pett, Dennis W. "Design of the Audio Track for Instructional Slide Sets and Filmstrips." *Performance and Instruction* (October 1989):1–4.

Pettersson, Rune. *Visuals for Information: Research and Practice.* Englewood Cliffs, NJ: Educational Technology Publications, 1989.

Pope, Carol, and Kutiper, Karen. "Instructional Materials: Finding the 'Story in Each of Us' through Instructional Media." *English Journal* (March 1988):76–77.

Radcliffe, Beverly. "Using the Overhead Projector for Homework Correction." *Foreign Language Annals* (April 1984):119–21.

Raines, Claire. *Visual Aids in Business.* Los Altos, CA: Crisp Publications, 1989.

Sheard, B. V. "They Love to Read Aloud from Filmstrips." *Teacher* (May 1973):66ff.

Van Vliet, Lucille W. "Tackling Production Techniques: The Opaque, It's Great." *School Library Media Activities* (April 1986):36–37.

Waggener, Joseph. "Important Media Classics: Filmstrips, Tape Recorders, and Record Players." *Media and Methods* (January–February 1989):16, 18–19, 66–67.

Warner, Linda A. "Consider Your Camera." *Science and Children* (April 1985):20–22.

White, Gene. "From Magic Lanterns to Microcomputers: The Evolution of the Visual Aid in the English Classroom." *English Journal* (March 1984):59–62.

Wildman, Diane. "Researching with Pictures." *English Journal* (March 1990):55–58.

Winters, Harold A. "Some Unconventional Uses of the Overhead Projector in Teaching Geography." *Journal of Geography* (November 1976):467–69.

Audiovisual References

"Color Lift" Transparencies. Salt Lake City, UT: Media Systems, 1975. Filmstrip or slides. 40 frames, captioned.

Effective Projection, Photography for Audiovisual Production, and *The Impact of Visuals in the Speechmaking Process.* Eastman Kodak, 1982. 3 filmstrips with audiocassettes.

"I like the Overhead Projector Because . . ." Washington, D.C.: National Audiovisual Center, 1977. Filmstrip with audiocassette. 12 minutes.

Thermofax (covers making thermal transparencies). Iowa City, IA: Audiovisual Center, University of Iowa, 1986. Videotape.

Use of the Overhead Projector and How to Make Do-It-Yourself Transparencies. Swan Pencil Co., n.d. 80 slides with cassette. 18 minutes.

The following ½-inch VHS videocassettes are available from Audiovisual Center Marketing, C215 Seashore Hall, University of Iowa, Iowa City, IA 52242.

Sound Filmstrip Projector. 1983. 7 minutes.

Overhead Projector. 1983. 7 minutes.

Opaque Projector. 1983. 7 minutes.

35mm Slide Projector. 1983. 7 minutes.

POSSIBLE PROJECTS

5–A.   Take a series of slides for use in your teaching. Describe your objectives, the intended audience, and how the slides will be used.

5–B.   Design a lesson around a commercially available filmstrip. Describe your objectives, the intended audience, how the filmstrip will be used, and how the lesson will be evaluated. (If possible, submit the filmstrip with the project.)

5–C.   Prepare transparencies using both the write-on and thermal methods.

5–D.   Prepare a set of visuals for use with an opaque projector.

5–E.   Preview a set of slides or a filmstrip. Complete an appraisal sheet (from the text or one of your own design) on the materials.

5–F.   Examine two of the selection sources for slides, filmstrips, or overheads and report on the kinds of materials you believe would be appropriate for your teaching situation.

6

Audio Media

OUTLINE

OBJECTIVES

After studying this chapter, you should be able to

1. Distinguish between hearing and listening.

2. Identify four areas of breakdown in audio communication and specify the causes of such breakdowns.

3. Describe four techniques for improving listening skills.

4. Discuss ten attributes of audio media, including five advantages and five limitations.

5. Describe four types of audio media most often used for instruction. Include in your description the distinguishing characteristics and limitations.

6. Identify two important instructional characteristics of compact discs.

7. Describe one possible use of audio media in your teaching field. Include the subject area, the audience, objective(s), role of the student, and the evaluation techniques to be used.

8. Identify five criteria for appraising and selecting audio materials.

9. Discuss the techniques for making your own audiotapes, including guidelines for the recorder controls, the acoustics, microphone placement, tape content, and audio presentation.

10. Describe how to edit audiotapes.

11. Describe two procedures for duplicating audiotapes.

12. Identify the advantages of rate-controlled audio playback.

13. Select the best audio format for a given instructional situation and justify the selection of that format, stating advantages and disadvantages.

LEXICON

hearing

listening

open reel tape

cassette

compact disc

digital recording

audio card

oral history

acoustics

rate-controlled playback

If you were asked which learning activities consume the major portion of a student's classroom time, would you say reading instructional materials, answering questions, reciting what one has learned, or taking tests? Actually, typical elementary and secondary students spend about 50 percent of their school time just listening. College students are likely to spend nearly 90 percent of their time in class listening to lectures and seminar discussions. The importance, then, of audio media in the classroom should not be underestimated. By audio media we mean the various means of recording and transmitting the human voice and other sounds for instructional purposes. The audio devices most commonly found in the classroom are the phonograph or record player, the cassette tape recorder, and the audio card reader.

Before going on to discuss these audio formats in particular and audio media in general, let's examine the hearing/listening process itself, as it pertains to the communication of ideas and information and to the development of listening skills.

THE HEARING/LISTENING PROCESS

Hearing and listening are not the same thing, although they are, of course, interrelated. At the risk of some oversimplification, we might say that hearing is a physiological process, whereas listening is a psychological process.

Physiologically, *hearing* is a process in which sound waves entering the outer ear are transmitted to the eardrum, converted into mechanical vibrations in the middle ear, and changed in the inner ear into nerve impulses that travel to the brain.

The psychological process of *listening* begins with someone's awareness of and attention to sounds or speech patterns, proceeds through identification and recognition of specific auditory signals, and ends in comprehension.

The hearing/listening process is also a communication/learning process. As with visual communication and learning, a message is encoded by a sender and decoded by a receiver. The quality of the encoded message is affected by the ability of the sender to express the message clearly and logically. The quality of the decoded message is affected by the ability of the receiver to comprehend the message.

The efficiency of communication is also affected by the hearing/listening process as the message passes from sender to receiver. The message can be affected by physical problems such as impaired hearing mechanisms. It also can be affected by auditory fatigue. The brain has a remarkable capacity for filtering out sounds it doesn't want or need to hear. We have all had the experience of tuning out a boring conversationalist or gradually losing cognizance of noises (the ticking of a clock, traffic outside a window, etc.) that seemed obtrusive when we first encountered them. Nevertheless, in the classroom extraneous noise can cause auditory fatigue and make communication difficult. A monotonous tone or a droning voice can

Figure 6.1
Elementary and secondary students spend about half of their in-school time listening to others.

also reduce communication efficiency by contributing to auditory fatigue.

The message can also be affected by the receiver's listening skills or lack of them. The receiver must be able to direct and sustain concentration on a given series of sounds (the message). He or she must have the skill to think ahead as the message is being received (we think faster than we hear, just as we think faster than we read or write) and use this time differential to organize and internalize the information so that it can be comprehended.

Figure 6.2
At the college level about 90 percent of class time is spent listening.

Figure 6.3
In the hearing/listening process impediments at each step act like filters, reducing the perceived meaning to a small fraction of the intended meaning.

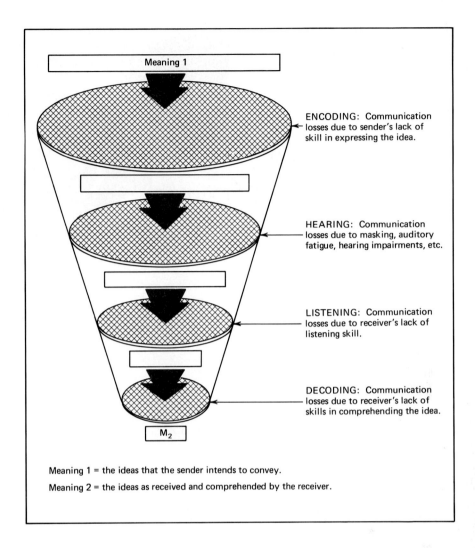

Meaning 1

ENCODING: Communication losses due to sender's lack of skill in expressing the idea.

HEARING: Communication losses due to masking, auditory fatigue, hearing impairments, etc.

LISTENING: Communication losses due to receiver's lack of listening skill.

DECODING: Communication losses due to receiver's lack of skills in comprehending the idea.

M₂

Meaning 1 = the ideas that the sender intends to convey.

Meaning 2 = the ideas as received and comprehended by the receiver.

Breakdowns in audio communications, then, can occur at any point in the process: encoding, hearing, listening, or decoding, as illustrated in Figure 6.3. Proper encoding of the message depends on the sender's skill in organizing and presenting it. For example, the vocabulary level of the message must be within the vocabulary range of the receiver. And, of course, the message itself must be presented in such a way that it is within the receiver's experiential range. The transmission process can be affected if the sender speaks too loudly or too softly or if the receiver has hearing difficulties or auditory fatigue. Communication can be reduced by the listener's lack of attentiveness or lack of skill in auditory analysis. Finally, communication can break down because the receiver lacks the experiential background to internalize, and thus comprehend, the message.

DEVELOPING LISTENING SKILLS

Until recently, much attention in formal education was given to reading and writing, a little to speaking, and essentially none to listening. Now, however, listening is recognized as a skill that, like all skills, can be improved with practice (Figure 6.4).

Hearing is the foundation of listening. Therefore, you should first determine that all of your students can hear normally. Most school systems regularly request the services of speech and hearing therapists who administer audiometric hearing tests that provide the data you need. There are also standardized tests that measure students' listening abilities. These tests are often administered by the school district, so you should check to see if listening test scores are available.

There are a number of techniques the teacher can use to improve student listening abilities:

1. *Directed listening.* Before orally presenting a story or lesson, give the students some objectives or questions to guide their listening. Start with short passages and one or two objectives. Then gradually increase the length of the passage and the number and

Figure 6.4
Listening skills are being taught at all educational levels and form a major component of many management development programs.

complexity level of the objectives or questions.

2. *Following directions.* Give the students directions individually or as a group on audiotape and ask them to follow these instructions. You can evaluate students' ability to follow the audio instructions by examining worksheets or products of the activity. When giving directions orally, the "say it only once" rule should be observed so that a value is placed on both the teacher's and students' time and the incentive to listen is reinforced.

3. *Listening for main ideas, details, or inferences.* Keeping the age level of the students in mind, you can present an oral passage and ask the students to listen for the main idea and then write it down. A similar technique can be used with details and inferences to be drawn from the passage.

4. *Using context in listening.* Younger students can learn to distinguish meanings in an auditory context by listening to sentences with words missing and then supplying the appropriate words.

5. *Analyzing the structure of a presentation.* The students can be

asked to outline (analyze and organize) an oral presentation. The teacher can then determine how well they were able to discern the main ideas and to identify the subtopics.

6. *Distinguishing between relevant and irrelevant information.* After listening to an oral presentation of information, the student can be asked to identify the main idea and then rate (from most to least relevant) all other ideas that are presented. A simpler technique for elementary students is to have them identify irrelevant words in sentences or irrelevant sentences in paragraphs.

CHARACTERISTICS OF AUDIO MEDIA

Advantages

Audio media have many desirable attributes. First and foremost, they tend to be inexpensive forms of instruction. In the case of audiotape, once the tapes and equipment have been purchased, there is no additional cost because the tape can be erased after use and a new message recorded.

Audio materials are readily available and very simple to use. They

can be adapted easily to any vocabulary level and can be used for group or individual instruction.

Students who cannot read can learn from audio media. For young nonreading students, audio can provide early language experiences.

Audio can present stimulating verbal messages more dramatically than print can. With a little imagination on the part of the teacher, audio can be very versatile.

Audiocassette recorders are very portable and can even be used "in the field" with battery power. Cassette recorders are ideal for home study. Many students already have their own cassette machines. Audiotapes are easily duplicated in whatever quantities are needed.

Limitations

As with all media, audio instructional devices have limitations. Audio tends to fix the sequence of a presentation even though it is possible to rewind the tape and hear a recorded segment again or advance the tape to an upcoming portion.

Without someone standing over them or speaking with them face to face, some students do not pay attention to the presentation. They may hear the presentation but not listen to and comprehend it.

The initial expense of playback and recording equipment may be a problem. Development of audio materials by the instructor is time-consuming. Determining the appropriate pace for presenting information can be difficult if your listeners have a wide range of listening skills and experiential backgrounds.

Storage and retrieval of audiotapes and phonograph records can also cause problems.

AUDIO FORMATS

Let's examine the comparative strengths and weaknesses of the audio formats most often used for instructional purposes—cassette tape, phonograph records, compact discs, and audio cards (Figure 6.5). The differences in these media are summarized in Table 6.1.

Audiotapes

The major advantage of magnetic audiotape over discs is that you can record your own tapes easily and economically, and when the material becomes outdated or no longer useful, you can erase the magnetic signal on the tape and reuse it. Tapes are not as easily damaged as discs, and they are easily stored. Unlike discs, broken tapes can be repaired.

Of course, there are some limitations to magnetic tape recordings. In the recording process background noises or a mechanical hum may sometimes be recorded along with the intended material. Even a relatively low-level noise can ruin an otherwise good recording. The fact that audiotapes can be erased easily can pose a problem as well. Just as you can quickly and easily erase tapes you no longer need, you can accidentally and just as quickly erase tapes you want to save. It is difficult to locate a specific segment on an audiotape. Counters on the recorder assist retrieval, but they are not very accurate.

When magnetic tape recording was first introduced to the public in 1946, the tape was mounted on open reels, similar to 16mm film. The tape had to be threaded through the tape recorder and the free end of the tape secured to an empty take-up reel. This is why this tape format is often referred to as reel-to-reel. The now familiar cassette was introduced at the Berlin Radio Show in 1963. Within a few years the convenience, flexibility, and portability of the new format made *open reel tapes* obsolete for playback in classroom and training site. However, they are still used for producing the master recordings from which records, cassettes, and compact discs are made.

The cassette tape is in essence a self-contained reel-to-reel system with the two reels permanently installed in a rugged plastic case, or *cassette* (Figure 6.6). The ⅛-inch-wide tape is permanently fastened to each of the reels. Cassette tapes are identified according to the amount of recording time they contain. For example, a C-60 cassette can record sixty minutes of sound using both sides (that is, thirty minutes on each side). A C-90 can record forty-five minutes on each side. Cassettes are available in C-15, C-30, C-60, C-90, and C-120 lengths, and other lengths can be specially ordered. The size of the plastic cassette containing the tape is the same in all cases, and all can be played on any cassette machine.

The microcassette, as the name suggests, is a smaller version of the standard audiocassette. Because the smaller size makes it convenient to carry around, the microcassette is most frequently used to record ideas, comments, and dictation when away from office, classroom, or home.

The cassette is durable; it is virtually immune to shock and abrasion. It is the easiest of the tape formats to use because it requires no manual threading. It can be snapped into and out of a recorder in seconds. It is not necessary to rewind

the tape before removing it from the machine. Accidental erasures can be avoided by breaking out the small plastic tabs on the edge of the cassette.

Storage is also convenient. A cassette collection can be stored in about one-third the space required for open reel tapes with the same amount of program material on them.

With all of these positive attributes you might wonder if there are any drawbacks. Unfortunately, longer cassette tapes, particularly

Figure 6.5
A wealth of recorded material is available in the common audio formats: cassettes, compact discs, and phonograph records.

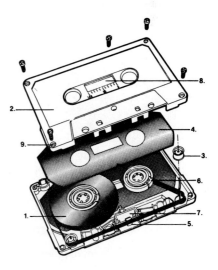

Figure 6.6
Exploded view of an audiocassette: (1) ⅛-inch tape, (2) styrene housing, (3) idler rollers, (4) lubricated liner, (5) pressure pad, (6) hub and clip, (7) metal shield, (8) clear index window, (9) screw (or other closure).

Table 6.1
Common audio formats

		Speeds	Advantages	Limitations	Uses
Cassette audiotape	Size: 2½ by 4 by ½ in. Tape ⅛ in. wide	1⅞ ips[1]	Very portable (small and light) Durable Easy to use (no threading) Can prevent accidental erasing Requires little storage space	Tape sometimes sticks or tangles Noise and hiss Poor fidelity with inexpensive players Broken tapes not easy to repair Difficult to edit	Listening "in the field" using battery power Student-made recordings Extended discussions Individual listening
Microcassette	Size: 1⁵⁄₁₆ by 1³⁄₃₂ by ²¹⁄₆₄ in. Tape ⅛ in. wide	¹⁵⁄₁₆ ips	Very compact Portable	Not compatible with other cassettes Poor fidelity	Dictation by business executives Amateur recording Recording field notes
Phonograph record (disc recording)	 Diameters: 7, 10, 12 in.	78 rpm[2] 45 rpm 33⅓ rpm 16⅔ rpm	Excellent frequency response Compatibility of records and phonographs Selection easily cued Wide variety of selections Inexpensive	Impractical to prepare locally Easily scratched Can warp Requires much storage space	Music Long narrations Classroom listening Historical speeches Drama, poetry
Compact disc	Size: 4.72 in. 	Variable high speed	Very durable High fidelity No background noise Random search of data	Playback only Expensive	Music Drama Data storage
Audio card	3½ by 9 in. or 5½ by 11 in. ¼ in. magnetic stripe	2¼ ips 1⅛ ips	Sound with visual Student can record response and compare with original Designed for individual use Participation; involvement	Most cards less than 8 seconds Time-consuming to prepare	Vocabulary building Concept learning Associating sounds with visuals Technical vocabulary

[1] ips = inches per second

[2] rpm = revolutions per minute

C-120s, sometimes become stuck or tangled in the recorder due to the thinness of the tape. If this happens, and unless the content on the tape is one of a kind and of considerable value to you, you are best advised to throw the tape away. If it sticks or gets tangled in the machine once, it is likely to do so again. If a cassette tape breaks, its small size and difficult access make it much more difficult to splice than the open reel tape. However, there are special cassette splicers that make the job easier. The frequency response and overall quality (fidelity) of cassette playback units are not as good as those of reel-to-reel machines or record players because of the small speakers in most portable cassette playback units. However, for most instructional uses the quality is more than adequate.

A major directory of commercially available audiotapes is published by the National Information Center for Educational Media (NICEM)—*Index to Educational Audio Tapes.* (See Appendix A for details and other sources.)

Phonograph Records

Until recently, the phonograph record was the most popular format for playing recorded audio content at home and at school. But now many producers of popular and classical music are phasing out records in favor of audiocassettes and compact discs. Consequently, the long-playing record (LP) is rapidly disappearing from the shelves of music stores.

The phonograph record, however, is still active in the education market because of attributes that make it attractive as an instructional format. Selections are separated by "bands," thereby making cuing of segments easier. The location or band of each segment of the recording is usually indicated on the label of the record and on its sleeve or dustcover. Because phonograph records are stamped from a master

in a fairly high-speed process, they are relatively inexpensive.

Despite all the advantages of phonograph records, they are not without serious limitations from an instructional point of view. The greatest drawback is that you cannot economically prepare your own records. Also, a record is easily damaged if someone drops the stylus (needle) on the disc or otherwise scratches the surface. Excess heat and improper storage may cause the disc to warp and make it difficult, if not impossible, to play. Storage can pose another problem in that records take up more space than cassette tapes with the same amount of information recorded on them.

All types of sounds—the spoken word, the sound of a hurricane, the mating call of the yellow-billed cuckoo, Beethoven's Ninth Symphony—are recorded on phonograph records. A major directory of commercially available records is published by the National Information Center for Educational Media (NICEM)—*Index to Educational Records.* (See Appendix A for details and other sources.)

Compact Discs

Someone once commented that the more sophisticated technology becomes, the more it seems like magic. That certainly is true of an audio format that was introduced in 1983, the *compact disc* (CD). Physically, the compact disc looks like a small, silver phonograph record without grooves. The digital code is in the form of tiny pits in clear plastic, protected by a thin covering of an acrylic resin (see "Close-Up: How a Compact Disc Works" on p. 168). The disc is only 12 centimeters (4.72 inches) in diameter. This small disc, rotating much faster than a phonograph record, stores an incredible amount of information. Some CDs contain as much as seventy-five minutes of music.

The technology of the CD makes it an attractive addition to education and training programs. Teachers can

quickly locate selections on the disc and even program them to play in any desired sequence. Information can be selectively retrieved by trainees or programmed by the trainer. A major advantage of the CD is its resistance to damage. There are no grooves to scratch or tape to tangle and tear. Stains can be washed off, and ordinary scratches do not affect playback of the recording.

Compact disc technology has been accepted rapidly for use in the home. But the cost of a CD—almost twice that of a record or cassette—plus the need for a CD player will slow its acceptance in the education market. However, when prices eventually come down, the CD's advantages, especially its resistance to damage, will make it a standard format for using audio in education.

When compact discs were introduced to the high fidelity market in 1983, many audio enthusiasts put pressure on equipment manufacturers to market digital tape recorders. Finally, the first digital cassette tape recorders became available in the fall of 1987. These machines make it possible for anyone to make a *digital recording.* The digital tape recorder is expensive. Although attractive to the home market, the machine will be accepted slowly in education and training because of the cost.

Audio Cards

Another widely used audio instructional format is the *audio card* (Figure 6.7). An audio card is approximately the size of a business envelope. It contains a strip of magnetic recording tape near the bottom edge. The audio card is essentially a flash card with sound. The card is inserted into a slot on a machine, such as the Audiotronics Tutorette, and a transport mechanism moves the card through the slot. Up to fifteen seconds of sound can be played through the speaker (or headset for individual use). The audio card is used in a dual-track system that allows the student to

How a Compact Disc Works

Until the compact disc was developed, all retail audio recordings were analog recordings; that is, they retained the essential wave form of the sound, whether as grooves in a phonograph record or as patterns of magnetized particles on audiotape. CDs are made using digital recording. Analog information, whether in the form of music, speech, or print, is transformed into a series of 1s and 0s, the same mathematical code used in computers. A powerful laser burns a microscopic pit into the plastic master for each 1 in the digital code. A blank space corresponds to 0. The laser moves in an ever-widening spiral from the center of the master to the edge, leaving on the disc hundreds of thousands of binary bits (1s and 0s). As a low-power laser beam in the playback unit picks up the pattern of pits and blank spaces, the beam is reflected back into the laser mechanism, and the digital code is transformed back into the original analog sound. The laser mechanism does not come in direct physical contact with the CD and can move independently of the disc, unlike the stylus in a record groove or a tape head. This means that the laser beam can scan the CD and quickly locate desired information. In other words, the CD can be programmed so the user can quickly access any part of the disc. CD players for the home can indicate what track is playing, the sequence in which tracks will be played, how many more tracks are on the disc, and remaining playing time. Another characteristic of digital recording is the complete absence of background noise.

The compact disc, shown one-half actual size, is a three-layer sandwich. The digital code in the form of pits is on the top side of a clear, tough plastic very much like Plexiglas. A reflective coating of aluminum, or sometimes silver, is placed on top of the pitted plastic surface. A protective coating of an acrylic resin is applied on the top of the reflective surface. Label information is printed on top of the resin. This arrangement protects the program information from both the top and bottom surfaces of the disc. The laser beam reads the code through the clear plastic and is reflected back by the aluminum (or silver) layer. The manufacturing process must be carried out in an environment completely free of dust because of the almost microscopic size of the pits.

Unlike an LP, the recording on a CD begins near the center and ends at the outer rim. Also unlike an LP, the CD does not rotate at a constant speed. The speed varies from 500 rpm at the innermost track to 200 rpm at the outer edge.

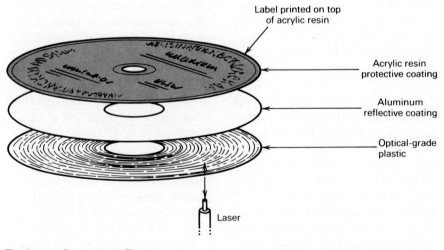

Label printed on top of acrylic resin

Acrylic resin protective coating

Aluminum reflective coating

Optical-grade plastic

Laser

The layers of a compact disc

Figure 6.7
The audio-card reader allows individual or small-group practice of skills that can be broken down into small steps. At 2¼ ips, about a dozen words can be recorded on a ten-inch card.

THE CUTTING EDGE

The Digital Compact Cassette and Mini-Disc

When compact discs were introduced to the high fidelity market in 1983, many audio enthusiasts put pressure on equipment manufacturers to market digital tape recorders. The introduction of digital tape recorders was delayed, however, until the audio industry developed the Serial Copy M Copy Management System (SCMS) to prevent multigenerational copying from CDs. While the digital tape recorder makes it possible for anyone to make an original digital recording and make one copy of a compact disc with perfect fidelity, it is a technology not likely to be adopted by the general consumer market. A digital tape recorder and the blank tapes are expensive. But perhaps more important is its incompatibility with the standard audiocassette system. Producers of recorded music are reluctant to put money into a format that very few consumers will acquire.

Acting on these limitations, Philips, the giant Dutch company that created both the audiocassette and the compact disc, developed what it calls the digital compact cassette (DCC). Philips unveiled the system to the public in January 1991. The DCC format will allow digital-quality taping at a price comparable to cassette decks. Standard audiocassettes will be playable on the DCC.

The DCC has some features that add to its flexibility and convenience. Its auto-reverse feature works in both record and playback modes. Like a videocassette, the DCC cassette has a metal cover that protects the tape when not in use and slides back when inserted in the machine.

The DCC has two sets of heads: one set for digital recording and playback and one set for analog playback. The digital compact cassette is much more likely to catch on than the digital tape recorder. However, because of cost and current capital investment in standard cassette recorders, the education and training markets will no doubt lag behind the home consumer market.

CDs have been eagerly accepted by consumers as a preferred audio format, but for audiophiles on the go (walking, jogging, or driving) they have two serious drawbacks: size of the playback equipment and skips due to sudden vibration. Now Sony has demonstrated a mini-disc (MD) that solves both problems. The MD stores up to seventy-four minutes of audio but is only two and a half inches in diameter. The playback unit can be smaller than a cassette player. That solves the size problem. Skipping is compensated for in two ways: the playback head repositions itself after a bump, and a memory chip holds up to three seconds of sound that might have been lost.

The reduction in size of the disc with no loss of playing time is accomplished by a magneto-optical technique that Sony introduced a few years ago for high-volume computer data storage. The disc is coated with a thin magnetic layer. A laser momentarily heats a tiny spot to 400°F and a magnetic head records the signal in the heated spot. In playback, an optical pickup reads both the polarity and the intensity of the light reflected from the spots. These are then reassembled into the original audio.

The bad news is that you will have to buy another piece of equipment. So its back to your friendly stereo dealer! And you can put that CD of Beethoven's Ninth on the shelf, on top of the cassette that's on top of the stereo LP that's on the top of the mono LP that's on top of the 78 (if you're old enough). Technology marches on!

HOW TO . . .
Record Your Own Audiotapes

A major advantage of audiotapes is the ease with which they can be prepared by teachers and learners. All that is needed is a blank audiotape, a tape recorder, and a bit of know-how. If your organization does not have a recording studio, here are some fast and easy techniques for preparing your own tapes. The results may not be of true professional quality, but most instructors have found products made in this way to be useful and effective.

Physical Environment

Record in an area that is as free as possible from noise and sound reverberations. A small room such as an office is preferable to a normal-size classroom. Sparsely furnished rooms with plaster walls and ceilings and bare cement or tile floors are likely to be excessively "live," causing distracting sound reverberations that will interfere with the fidelity of the recording. Such areas can, of course, be improved by installing acoustic tiles and carpeting. The recording setup should be at least six feet from the chalkboard, windows, or hard walls. You may have to make do with temporary improvements to improve quality, for example, throw rugs or even heavy blankets or sheets of cardboard on the floor. Fabric-covered movable screens and drawn window shades may help.

Tape Recorder

❑ Expensive equipment is not necessary.

❑ Familiarize yourself with the operation of the particular tape recorder you intend to use.

❑ Advance the tape beyond the leader before recording. You cannot record on the clear plastic, nonmagnetic leader of the tape (about ten seconds).

❑ Record an excerpt of about a minute and play it back to check volume and tone. Nothing is more frustrating than to record ten or fifteen minutes of a tape only to find that the microphone was not plugged into the recorder. A practice run will avoid most of these types of problems.

❑ If an error is made while recording, stop the tape recorder, reverse to a segment of tape containing a natural pause, engage the record mode, and continue recording.

❑ Refer to the instruction manual. Determine the proper recording level (volume) and tone. Many newer recorders have an automatic volume control making adjustment on the machine unnecessary.

Microphone

❑ Place the microphone on a floor or table stand away from hard surfaces such as chalkboards, windows, or bare walls. If a stand is not available, place on a hand towel or other soft cloth. Because many tape recorders generate unwanted clicking, whirring, and humming noises, keep the microphone as far away from the recorder as possible.

❑ Place the microphone to achieve maximum pickup of desired sounds and minimal pickup of extraneous ones. Place the microphone so it will pick up all the voices. Avoid handing the microphone from one person to another. If necessary, move people instead, before recording.

❑ Maintain a constant distance from the microphone. As a rule of thumb, your mouth should be about a foot from the microphone. If you are much closer, p's and b's will tend to "pop" and other breathy sounds may become annoying.

❑ Speak over the top of the microphone, not directly into it.

---

record his or her own response on the card and then play it back for comparison with the prerecorded response. If the student's response is incorrect, it can be erased and rerecorded correctly by simply running the audio card through the machine again while depressing the record lever. Both the student's and the prerecorded response can be replayed as often as desired by just flipping a lever. The prerecorded message is protected from erasure by a switch on the back of the machine. The teacher can use the switch to change the prerecorded message.

APPLICATIONS OF AUDIO MEDIA

The uses of audio media are limited only by the imagination of teachers and students. They can be used in all phases of instruction from introduction of a topic to evaluation of student learning. Perhaps the most rapidly growing general use of audio media today is in the area of self-paced instruction and in "mastery learning." The slower student can go back and repeat segments of instruction as often as necessary because the recorder-playback machine is a very patient tutor. The accelerated

Tape Content

❑ Introduce the subject of the audiotape at the beginning of the recording. For example, "This is Computer Science 101, Lesson 12, on computer languages. . . ." Identifying the tape is particularly important if it is to be used for individual instruction.

❑ Explore the subject with the students, don't just tell them about it. A lecture on tape is deadly!

❑ Involve your listener(s) in meaningful learning activities whenever appropriate for your objectives. You might, for example, supply a study guide or worksheet for students to use along with the tape (see Figure 6.9, p. 176). Include ample space for students to take notes while listening to the tape. Instruct listeners to look at a diagram, specimen, table, or photograph; to use equipment; or to record data—so they don't simply sit and listen. Simple and direct activities are more effective than complex, involved ones.

❑ Keep the tape short even if it is to be used by adult learners. Fifteen to twenty-five minutes is a good guideline for adults. Make it even shorter for younger students.

❑ Provide variety throughout the tape by using appropriate sounds, music, short dialogues, and voices of experts in your field. These provide variation and add realism to the study, but should be used functionally.

❑ Repetition by the tape narrator is usually unnecessary. Repetition can be achieved by having the student replay appropriate tape segments.

Audio Presentation Techniques

❑ Use informal notes rather than a complete script. Reading from a script may sound very boring. If you feel you must work with a more formal script, remember that preparing a good script requires special writing and reading skills.

❑ Use index cards for notes rather than handling large sheets of paper near the microphone. If your students will be using a study guide while listening to the tape, make your notes on the study guide and use it while making the recording.

❑ Use a conversational tone. Talk as you would normally talk to a friend. Explore the subject with the student, don't lecture at them.

Vary your tone of voice frequently.

Speak cheerfully and enthusiastically.

Enunciate clearly.

Speak rapidly (most people can listen faster than the average person talks).

Minimize "uh's" and other distracting speech habits.

❑ Direct the student's attention to what you will discuss *before* discussing it. Tell the student what to look for. For example, if the diagram is on page 4, then tell the listener, "Look at the diagram on page 4. There you will see . . ." The same technique is necessary if you are using slides in conjunction with the audiotape. "As you see in Slide 6, the process starts in the upper right-hand corner and proceeds . . ."

❑ Provide a brief musical interlude (approximately ten seconds) as a signal for the student to turn off the tape recorder and perform any activities or exercises. The student can then return to the tape, hear the music again, and know that nothing has been missed.

❑ Include a tone or other nonvocal signal to indicate when to advance slides rather than continually repeating "Change to the next slide." Electronic tone devices are available for this purpose, a door chime can be used, or a simple technique for producing your own signal is to tap a pen or spoon on a half-full drinking glass.

---

student can skip ahead or increase the pace of his or her instruction.

Prerecorded audio materials are available in a wide variety of subjects. For music classes, records and tapes can be used to introduce new material or to provide musical accompaniment. The sounds of various musical instruments can be presented individually or in combinations. In preschool and primary grades, tapes and records can be used for developing rhythm, telling stories, playing games, and acting out stories or songs. In social studies, the tape recorder can bring the voices of persons who have made history into the classroom. The sounds of current events can also be presented.

One special application of prerecorded audio media is "talking books" for blind or visually impaired students. A Talking Books Program has been set up by the American Printing House for the Blind to make as much material as possible available to the visually impaired. At present over 135,000 book titles are available, along with recordings of over 200 current periodicals. The service is a cooperative effort of the Library of Congress and fifty-three regional libraries in the United States. Audiocassettes are the standard format, but new books are fre-

The technology of recorded sound has gone through several transformations since Edison recited "Mary had a little lamb" into the horn of the first phonograph and to his own astonishment heard his voice played back to him. That was in 1877.

Because Edison kept detailed notes on his pursuit of an idea and wrote comments on his method of inquiry, the invention of the phonograph affords us a rare insight into how a resourceful and imaginative technologist works. The ability to put seemingly unrelated events together to generate new knowledge and new devices is an important hallmark of both scientists and technologists. Edison once gave this advice to aspiring inventors: "When you are experimenting and come across anything you don't thoroughly understand, don't rest until you run it down; it may be the very thing you are looking for or it may be something far more important."

Early in 1877 Edison had invented a carbon transmitter for Bell's telephone, so transmission of sound was on his mind. At the same time, he was trying to expand the usefulness of the telegraph. He was working on a device that could imprint on paper tape the Morse code coming over a telegraph line and then reproduce the message at any desired speed. A steel spring pressed against the paper helped keep the tape in a straight line. Edison noticed that when the tape was running at a high speed, the dots and dashes hitting the spring gave off a noise that Edison described as a "light musical, rhythmic sound, resembling human talk heard indistinctly." During his work on the carbon transmitter, Edison, who was already hard of hearing, attached a needle to the diaphragm of the telephone receiver in order to judge the loudness of the sound. By holding his finger lightly to the needle, loudness could be judged by the strength of the vibration.

Recalling this experience, and applying it to his interest in transmission of sound and his work with the telegraph, Edison set about to determine if the needle vibrations could be impressed on a suitable material. After experimenting with a number of materials, Edison, for reasons unknown, decided to use tinfoil wrapped around a cylinder as his recording medium with two needle-diaphragm units, one for recording and one for playback. In December 1877 he applied for a patent.

Edison's vision of the potential of sound recording was amazingly prescient, but the first commercial exploitation of the invention was a novelty. The Edison Speaking Phonograph Company, formed on January 24, 1878, and not under Edison's control, charged admission to demonstrations of the machine during which members of the audience were invited to come up to the stage to record their voices. But the novelty wore off, and Edison's attention was diverted to the challenge of electric lighting.

Alexander Graham Bell built a laboratory in Washington, D.C., to work on improving the phonograph. His work led to an improved cylinder which made the device useful for business dictation. Bell's efforts also made possible the first "juke box." Machines were manufactured that would play a recording when the customer dropped a nickel in the slot. But this novelty also wore off.

The next major advance was made in 1887 by a German immigrant, Emile Berliner, when he developed the idea of a stylus engraving lateral grooves as it moved across a disc coated with a pliant but firm material. The flat disc had a greater potential to be mass-produced than did the cylinder. When he hit on the idea of making a metal master that could stamp out duplicates, the flat disc became the accepted format.

But recordings were still acoustic. Horns, not microphones, were used to gather and direct the sound waves that drove the recording diaphragm and needle. Playback was the same only in reverse. Quality was still poor and volume limited. Electricity, already employed in the telephone, was the answer. In 1920 two British inventors, Lionel Guest and H. R. Merriman, successfully recorded a ceremony in Westminster Abbey by transmitting the signals from their electric microphone over phone lines to their laboratory. A few years later, the vacuum tube amplifier made possible an all-electronic system. From then until the end of World War II, slow, steady improvements in recording technology made the 78-rpm record, in ten- and twelve-inch sizes, the standard. However, only four minutes of sound could be accommodated on each side of the disc. Then the long-playing record and magnetic tape recording shook up the record industry.

In June 1948 Peter Goldmark of Columbia Records demonstrated the long-playing record (LP) that was destined to drive 78-rpm records from the home market. The record that he demonstrated contained twenty-three minutes of music on each side. Subsequent improvements increased the time to thirty or thirty-two minutes per side. The public responded positively and quickly to the new format. But magnetic tape recording would have an even more dramatic effect.

Until 1946 all recordings were made by cutting grooves in a disc surfaced with soft but firm material from which a metal master was made. This was a cumbersome, delicate process that was troublesome in the lab and infuriating on location. There were simply too many opportunities for Murphy's law to operate. Magnetic recording came along just at the right time to become the standard for making the recordings from which masters could be cut later under ideal conditions.

Magnetic recording was the direct cause of the proliferation of record companies that occurred after 1947. A relatively small investment in high-quality equipment enabled a small company to make tapes that could be marketed directly or sold to established record companies for distribution. For example, Caedmon Records was started by two young women who hired an engineer with the necessary equipment and set out to record authors reading from their works. Their first prize was Dylan Thomas, the Welsh poet, and from that beginning they built the largest catalog of recorded literature in the industry.

The idea of recording sounds magnetically has been around since 1899 when a Danish inventor recorded sound on paper tape impregnated with iron oxide and also on magnetizable wire. However, the absence of electronic amplification stymied development. Other inventors experimented with magnetic recording, particularly in Germany, where a magnetic recorder for dictation was marketed in 1937. During World War II, British and American intelligence detected evidence that the Germans were using recordings of superior quality. Their suspicions were confirmed when, on September 11, 1944, the Allies captured Radio Luxembourg and found in the station a magnetic recorder that played fourteen-inch reels of tape at thirty inches per second with remarkable fidelity. Within a short period of time American companies, capitalizing on the German developments, were marketing magnetic tape and recorders that could record and play back with unprecedented quality. Wire recorders also became available, but wire was not as reliable or as convenient a recording medium.

The idea of stereo recording also had been around for a long time, but there was no marketable medium until magnetic tape recordings were made available to the public. In 1955 stereo recordings on magnetic tape were marketed but on reel-to-reel tape, a format that the general public did not find congenial. Then in 1957 cutting a stereo groove in a master disc was perfected, and stereo discs soon flooded the market. LPs were the standard format for stereo until 1970, when advances in audiocassette technology, including the Dolby method of suppressing background noise, challenged the LP. Now both the LP and cassette are facing formidable competition from the compact disc (CD).

In slightly more than 100 years recorded sound has progressed from the barely audible voice of Edison etched in an impermanent groove on tinfoil to the ability to record a Mahler symphony with astounding clarity and richness on an almost indestructible compact disc.

Source: This feature is based primarily on Roland Gelatt, *The Fabulous Phonograph, 1877–1977* (New York: Collier Books, 1977). The two Edison quotes are from that book.

quently first distributed on 8-inch flexible records which require special players.

Audiotapes can easily be prepared by teachers for specific instructional purposes. (See "How To . . . Record Your Own Audiotapes," pp. 170–71, and Chapter 11.) For example, in industrial arts, audiotapes can describe the steps in operating a machine or making a product. Recordings of class presentations by the teacher can be used for student makeup and review. One of the most common uses of audio materials is for drill work. For example, the student can practice spelling vocabulary words recorded by the teacher on tape, take dictation or type from a prerecorded tape, or pronounce foreign language vocabulary.

History can come alive when students get involved in an *oral history* project. This entails recording interviews with living witnesses of the recent or more distant past.

Tape recorders can be used to record information gleaned from a field trip. Upon returning to the classroom, the students can play back the tape for discussion and review. Many museums, observatories, and other public exhibit areas now

---

Checklist for Instructor-Prepared Audiotapes

❑ Minimum extraneous background noise

❑ Constant volume level

❑ Voice quality and clarity

❑ Clarity of expression

❑ Conversational tone

❑ Listener involvement

❑ Coordination with worksheet or study guide, if used

❑ Content clear

❑ Duration not too long

MEDIA FILE: *Thinking about Drinking*
Six Cassettes

Teenage abuse of alcohol continues to be a major concern. This series of twelve half-hour programs, originally broadcast on the Public Broadcasting System (PBS), deals in an engrossing manner with many aspects of the problem. A few of the titles are: *Media Images of Alcohol, The Lady Drinks, Driving under the Influence,* and *The Latino Perspective.* By using case histories of well-known national figures, such as Betty Ford, and dramatizations the programs avoid a deadly lecture format. More than 150 interviews with experts in the field enliven the tapes. The programs are intended for faculty as well as for students and parents. Teachers can contribute significantly to reducing drinking problems among students; the tapes tell them how.

Source: SounDocumentaries

MEDIA FILE: *A Kid's Eye View of the Environment*
CD/Cassette

Michael Mish based this series of songs on his many visits to schools in southern California to talk to children about the environment. He found them to be more aware and concerned about environmental problems than he expected. He took the topics they were most concerned about, for example, recycling, water and air pollution, and the greenhouse effect, and put them into music. The songs are engaging, with choruses that children can sing along with. The messages should get primary age children talking about making this a safer, cleaner world.

Source: Mish Mash Music

supply visitors with prerecorded messages about various items on display, which may (with permission) be rerecorded for playback in the classroom.

Students can also record themselves reciting, presenting a speech, performing music, and so on. They can then listen to the tape in private or have the performance critiqued by the teacher or other students. Initial efforts can be kept for comparison with later performances and for reinforcement of learning. Many small-group projects can include recorded reports that can be presented to the rest of the class. Individual students can prepare oral book reports and term papers on tape for presentation to the class as a whole or one student at a time. One high school literature teacher maintains a file of taped book reports that students listen to before selecting books for their own reading. It is also possible for the students and teacher to bring interviews with local people or recordings of discussions of local events and concerns into the classroom.

An often overlooked use of audio materials is for evaluating student attainment of lesson objectives. For example, test questions may be prerecorded for members of the class to use individually. Students may be asked to identify sounds in a recording (e.g., to name the solo instrument being played in a particular musical movement or to identify the composer of a particular piece of music). Students in social studies classes could be asked to identify the historical person most likely to have made excerpted passages from famous speeches, or they could be asked to identify the time period of excerpted passages based on their content. Testing and evaluating in the audio mode is especially appropriate when teaching and learning have also been in that particular mode.

MEDIA FILE: *The Professional Guide to Career Success*
Cassette Tape and Workbook

Whether you're entering the job market for the first time or seeking to move up from where you are, help in making your job search more effective is always welcome. This new cassette-workbook program enables job seekers to identify and take advantage of the unadvertised job market, where 80 to 85 percent of all job openings exist; ensures that a new job is economically and professionally rewarding; and enhances their job security in today's uncertain market. The package, consisting of six audio cassette tapes integrated with a workbook, lays out a step-by-step search strategy.

Source: Information Management Institute

MEDIA FILE: *A Jug Band Peter and the Wolf*
Record/Cassette

Here is a fun version of Prokofiev's classic *Peter and the Wolf* arranged for a band of folk instruments (and a few standard instruments played in folk style). The instruments include fiddle, mandolin, guitar, banjo, kazoo, whistle, mouth harp, jug, washtub bass, and clarinet. The accompanying booklet has an explanation of how the music was transcribed to retain the spirit of the original. Though the instruments are different, the story line is the same. This is not recommended as a replacement of the original but should be used as an interesting adaptation. Dave Van Ronk, a folksinger, does the narration. On the second side Van Ronk sings a group of folk songs that should appeal to children.

Source: Alacazam!

Figure 6.8

In the language laboratory, audio- and videotapes allow modeling of proper speech, student response, corrective feedback, and evaluation of mastery.

Audiotapes have long been used in foreign language instruction (Figure 6.8). A recent study in Canada compared first-year undergraduate French students taught by text and a similar group taught by audio. Both groups did equally well on written tests, but the group taught by audio performed better on oral tests.[1]

CASSETTE: THE CONSTANT COMPANION

A few years ago, the American Psychological Association surveyed a sample of its membership to determine their preferred medium for continuing professional development. The cassette won handily, beating out traditional standbys such as newsletters, workshops, and conferences. Like print, the cassette can go wherever the individual goes, and players are as common as tele-

---

[1] Linda R. Jackson and Richard Nice, "Language Texts or Language Tapes: Relationship between Input and Instruction and Translation Performance among First Year Undergraduates in French," *Canadian Modern Language Review* (May 1988):715–25.

Objective 3:
Compute Depreciation Using the Straight-Line Method.

Straight-Line Method Summarized

Formula: $\dfrac{\text{Cost of the Asset} - \text{Estimated Salvage Value}}{\text{Number of Accounting Periods in Productive Life}}$

Application: $\dfrac{\$1{,}250 \text{ Cost} - \$250 \text{ Salvage}}{5 \text{ Years of Productive Life}} = $ $200 to be depreciated each year

· ·

TURN OFF TAPE AND COMPLETE ACTIVITY NO. 4.

· ·

Activity 4

A machine costs $2,600 and was estimated to have a four-year service life and a $200 salvage value. Calculate the yearly depreciation using the straight-line method.

Answer:_____

· ·

TURN ON TAPE AND COMPLETE ACTIVITY
NO. 5 WHILE LISTENING

· ·

Activity 5

Advantages of the units-of-production method are

1. _____

2. _____

3. _____

4. _____

Disadvantages of the units-of-production method are

1. _____

2. _____

Figure 6.9

Sample page from a study guide to accompany an audio lesson in accounting

phones, more so when one considers that there are more cassette players than phones in cars.

American corporations are using cassettes most often as extensions of sales training and for personnel development. An executive of the Gillette Corporation estimates that the company's sales representatives in rural areas spend the equivalent of eighteen to twenty-five weeks a year in their cars. During that time, they can be receiving product information, sales leads, and customer information.

Many companies and individuals have found cassette tapes extremely useful for personnel development. Usually the tapes are closely integrated with workbooks for two reasons: (1) requiring the user to go back and forth from tape to workbook helps to sustain attention, and (2) overt response strengthens learning (R in the ASSURE model). Perhaps the most commonly used cassette programs are the ones that develop basic skills: reading improvement, writing skills development, listening skills. Motivational programs are also popular.

Some companies have exploited the dramatic capabilities of the audio medium in management training programs dealing with conflict resolution and stress management. The low price of cassettes compared to video or a series of seminars plays an important part in the decision to use audiotape.

Sponsors of conferences and conventions frequently offer cassette recordings of sessions, thereby making important information more widely available. For example, the Association for Educational Communications and Technology, through a commercial company, makes cassettes of sessions available before the close of the convention as well as by mail.

Driving, walking, and jogging are primarily responsible for the rapidly increasing number of literary works on cassettes. Many have found that those long drives, two-mile hikes,

and five-mile jogs lend themselves to catching up on the bestsellers they don't have time to read. A directory of producers and distributors of books on tape is listed at the end of the chapter (see Hoffman entry under "Print References)."

MEDIA FILE: *Classic Children's Tales*

Jackie Torrence has received many plaudits for her storytelling skills, including four American Library Association awards. She has appeared on numerous national TV and radio programs and the cover of *Parade* magazine. This recording was made in response to many requests for her to do classic children's tales, such as "Little Red Hen," "Three Billy Goats Gruff," and "Goldilocks and the Three Bears." Her warmth and sensitivity come through the recording; if you close your eyes, you can see her gestures and facial expressions. Storytelling as a folk art is alive and well, and Jackie Torrence is one of its leading exponents.

Source: The Rounder Records Group

SELECTING AUDIO MATERIALS

In selecting audio materials to use in your instruction, first determine what materials are available locally. If appropriate materials are not

---

HOW TO . . .
Prevent Accidental Erasure of Cassette Tapes

Cassette tapes provide protection against accidental erasure. At the rear corners of each cassette are small tabs which can be broken out. The tab on the left controls the top side of the tape (side A). The tab on the right controls the bottom side (side B). No machine will record a new sound on a side of a tape for which the appropriate tab has been broken out.

If you want to reuse the tape, carefully place some cellophane tape over the hole where the tab was removed. The tape can then be used for a new recording. Most prerecorded tapes come with both tabs already removed to prevent accidental erasure.

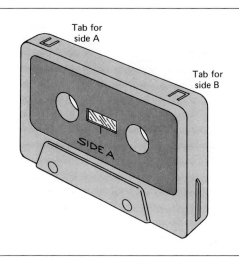

Tab for side A

Tab for side B

SIDE A

Prerecorded Audio Cards (Vocabulary Practice). In an elementary classroom, the teacher uses a set of audio cards for vocabulary building. They are used on an individual basis with children who are having difficulty grasping the meaning of words because they cannot attach the appropriate spoken word to the printed form of the word or to the object it represents. The audio cards provide simultaneous visual and auditory stimuli designed to increase a child's spoken vocabulary. The teacher shows the student how to use the machine and the cards, then lets the child work alone. Later, the teacher uses the same cards without the machine, holding them up one at a time and asking the child to say the word.

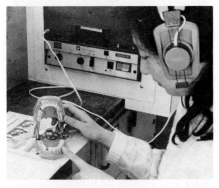

Teacher-Prepared Audiotapes (Direct Instruction). In a vocational-technical school, dental laboratory technology students are instructed on the procedures for constructing prosthetic devices such as partial plates and bridges by listening to an audiotape prepared by their instructor. To be efficient and effective in their work, these students must have both hands free and their eyes must be on their work, not on a textbook or manual. Audiotapes allow the students to move at their own pace, and the instructor is free to circulate around the laboratory and discuss each student's work individually.

Teacher-Prepared Audiotapes (Shorthand Practice). In a high school business education class, the students practice taking dictation by listening to audiotapes prepared by the teacher and other individuals in the school, such as the principal, guidance counselor, or industrial arts instructor. The variety of voices on the tapes allows the students to practice dealing with different voices, different accents, and a variety of dictation speeds. The business teacher categorizes the tapes according to difficulty of transcription and word speed. The students begin with the easy tapes and then move to more difficult ones. The teacher is also experimenting with a variable-speed tape recorder, which will allow her to present the same tape to the students at a variety of speeds. Individually, the students use the variable-speed recorder to determine how fast they can take dictation and still maintain accuracy.

Prerecorded Audiocassette (Sales Information). The sales representative of a manufacturing company pops a cassette into the sound system of the car and, after a few seconds, a popular tune fills the air. The song fades away as the voice of the marketing manager comes in: "What's new at Marflap Manufacturing is a vastly improved system for. . . ." Another song follows the information about the new system and, after that, more news about Marflap products. The cassette makes the automobile a learning environment, thereby making use of otherwise wasted time.

Teacher-Prepared Audiotapes (Listening Skills). A teacher of ninth grade students with learning difficulties (but average intelligence) provides instruction on how to listen to lectures, speeches, and other oral presentations. The students practice their listening skills with tapes of recorded stories, poetry, and instructions. Commercially available tapes of speeches and narration are also used. After the students have practiced their listening skills under teacher direction, they are evaluated using a tape they have not heard before. The students listen to the five-minute tape without taking notes and then are given a series of questions dealing with important content from the passage.

Student-Prepared Audiotapes (Gathering Oral History). One of the most exciting projects in a twelfth grade social studies class is the oral history project. The students interview local senior citizens regarding the history of their community. Only one student interviews each senior citizen, but the interviewing task is rotated among the students, and the entire class assists in determining which questions should be asked. In preparation for this project, the students study both national and local history. All the tapes prepared during the interviews are kept in the school media center. Excerpts are duplicated and edited into programs for use with other social studies classes and for broadcast by the local radio station. This audiotape project serves the dual purpose of informing students and local residents about local history and collecting and preserving information that might otherwise be lost.

Student-Prepared Audiotapes (Oral Book Report). The tape recorder can be used for presenting book reports. Students may record their book reports during study time in the media center or at home. The reports are evaluated by the teacher, and the best ones are kept on file in the media center. Other students are encouraged to listen to them before selecting books to read. Since the reports are limited to three minutes, the students are required to extract the main ideas from the book and to organize their thoughts carefully. During the taping, they practice their speaking skills. They are encouraged to make the report as exciting as possible in order to get other students to read the book.

Student-Prepared Audiotapes (Self-Evaluation). As part of a sales training program in a large insurance company, trainees learn sales presentation principles through taped examples and associated programmed booklets. They are then asked to prepare a series of their own sales presentations for different types of clients and for selling different types of insurance. The trainees outline their presentations, practice, and then record them on audiotape. For example, they role-play making a presentation on group health insurance to the board of directors of a large corporation. After the simulated presentation they listen to the recording and evaluate their performance using a checklist provided in the teaching materials. If they are not satisfied with their performance, they can redo the tape. Since no instructor is present, the inexperienced salesperson is not embarrassed by mistakes made during a training period. Later the instructor will listen to and critique the tape for the individual trainee. The final step in the training program is a live presentation, with the other trainees role-playing the clients.

available, refer to the various directories of audio materials (see Appendix A). Materials both commercially and locally produced that seem appropriate should be previewed before introducing them to your students. The "Appraisal Checklist: Audio Materials" can serve as a model for the sort of form you can use to guide your selection decisions.

DUPLICATING AND EDITING AUDIOTAPES

It is a relatively simple procedure to duplicate (or "dub") an audiotape. You can duplicate your tapes by one of three methods: the acoustic method, the electronic method, or the high-speed duplicator method.

The acoustic method (see Figure 6.10) does not require any special equipment, just two recorders (cassette, reel-to-reel, or one of each).

One recorder plays the original tape, and the sound is transferred via a microphone to a blank tape on the other recorder. The drawback of this method is that fidelity is reduced as the sound travels through the air to the microphone, and the open microphone may pick up unwanted noise from the environment.

The electronic method avoids this problem (see Figure 6.11). The signal travels from the original tape to the dubbing recorder via an inexpensive patch cord. The cord is attached to the output of the first machine and the "line" or auxiliary input of the second. It picks up the signals of the original tape and transfers them electronically to the duplicating tape.

If a dual-well cassette recorder, which holds two cassettes, is available, tapes can be copied very easily. Many of these machines can copy a tape at double normal speed, cutting duplicating time in half, but check the copy for speed accuracy. Inexpensive dual-well equipment is not noted for its precision; a full-size dual-well tape deck is much more reliable.

The high-speed duplicator method requires a special machine. Master playback machines have a series of up to ten "slave units," each of which can record a copy of the original tape at sixteen times its normal speed.

Multiple copies of a thirty-minute cassette tape can be duplicated in about one minute. Since the master and slave units are connected by a patch cord, fidelity is likely to be very good, and there is no danger of picking up background noise.

You may wish to edit your audiotapes, either to remove errors and imperfections or to adapt a tape to a

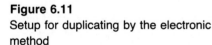

Figure 6.10
Setup for duplicating by the acoustic method

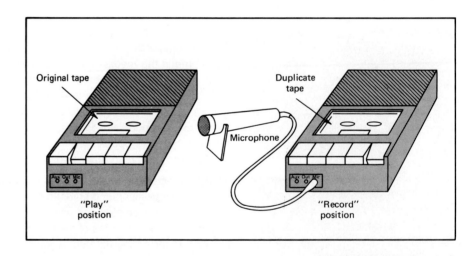

Figure 6.11
Setup for duplicating by the electronic method

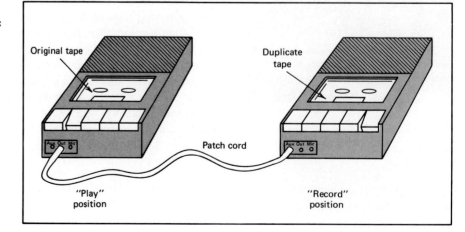

specific learning situation. Set up two recorders as described for tape duplication and then record just the portion of the original tape that you want on the second tape.

The dual-well cassette recorder or deck facilitates editing. Selected parts of the original can be assembled easily by using the copying feature of these machines.

RATE-CONTROLLED AUDIO PLAYBACK

An important but little-known piece of audio equipment is a cassette tape deck that can play back recorded speech either at a faster or slower rate than the rate at which it was recorded, but with no loss of voice quality or intelligibility.

Before this technological breakthrough, playing a tape back at a higher speed resulted in high-pitched distortion, as if the speaker were a chattering chipmunk. Slowing down the playback resulted in a low-pitched, unintelligible garble.

The pedagogical significance of this rate-controlled playback lies in the fact that although the average person speaks at 100 to 150 words per minute, most of us can comprehend spoken information at the rate of 250 to 300 words per minute. Research has shown that most students learn as quickly and retain as much when spoken instruction is speeded up. The visually impaired, in particular, can benefit by having the option to listen to words almost as fast as a sighted person can read them.

On the other hand, slowing down recorded instruction also has instructional advantages, especially in working with slow learners or in special education situations and in foreign language instruction. It is also useful in ordinary circumstances for emphasizing a specific instructional point or for explaining a particularly difficult one.

Early speech compressors were costly and their technology was not very refined. The machines could

---

MEDIA FILE: *The Johnstown Flood of 1889*
Cassette

This is storytelling at its finest, serving the interests of education. Syd Lieberman, storyteller par excellence, was invited to Johnstown, Pennsylvania, to help commemorate the 100th anniversary of the great flood. During his research on the flood, he decided to emphasize the human aspects of the catastrophe. For example, in this recording he contrasts the carefree celebration on Memorial Day (May 30 in those days) with the cataclysmic collapse of the dam the next day. By concentrating on what happened to individual members of selected families, he personalizes the vast destruction of the flood, thereby transforming a historic event into an engrossing narrative. Social studies students will find this cassette an exciting way to study history, and may find they want to research other historic events and present them as stories. If so, they should read Syd Lieberman's article, "Breathing Life into History," in the Spring 1990 issue of *Storytelling* magazine (pp. 8–11).

Source: Syd Lieberman

---

only be set at certain fixed speeds, such as 200 words per minute. The entire recording had to be made and played back at this rate.

Newer compressors provide for variable speed rates. Recorders can now be equipped with rate-control devices that, using a tape recorded at normal speaking speed, are capable of providing variable rates of speech at the discretion of the listener, from half the normal speed to two and a half times normal speed. Changing the rate during playback allows the listener to listen at his or her own pace, skimming over familiar material at a high rate, slowing down for material that may require more time for comprehension.

Research has shown that learning time can be cut (as much as 50 per-

cent and an average of 32 percent) and comprehension increased (as much as 9.3 percent and an average of 4.2 percent) by using compressed and variable-speed audiotapes.[2] One reason that comprehension increases with accelerated listening rate may be that the listener is forced to increase his or her concentration on the material and is also freed from the distractions that often accompany normal speech, such as pauses, throat clearing, and other extraneous sounds. A slow, monotonous speaking rate also allows listeners' minds to wander.

---

[2] See Olsen (1979) and Short (1978) under "References."

❑ **APPRAISAL CHECKLIST**
Audio Materials

Title _____

	Format	Speed
Series title (if applicable) _____	❑ Cassette	____ ips
Source _____	❑ Open reel	
Date _____ Cost _____ Length _____ Minutes _____	❑ Record	____ rpm
Subject Area _____	❑ Compact disc	

Intended Audience _____

Objectives (stated or implied)

Brief Description

Entry Capabilities Required

❑ Prior subject-matter knowledge/vocabulary

❑ Reading ability

❑ Mathematical ability

❑ Other:

Rating	High		Medium		Low	Comments
Relevance to objectives	❑	❑	❑	❑	❑	
Accuracy of information	❑	❑	❑	❑	❑	
Likely to arouse/maintain interest	❑	❑	❑	❑	❑	
Technical quality	❑	❑	❑	❑	❑	
Promotes participation/involvement	❑	❑	❑	❑	❑	
Evidence of effectiveness (e.g., field-test results)	❑	❑	❑	❑	❑	
Free from objectionable bias	❑	❑	❑	❑	❑	
Pacing appropriate for audience	❑	❑	❑	❑	❑	
Clarity of organization	❑	❑	❑	❑	❑	
Appropriate vocabulary level	❑	❑	❑	❑	❑	

Strong Points

Weak Points

Reviewer _____

Position _____

Recommended Action _____ Date _____

BLUEPRINT

An Author Reads Her Short Story

Context. This is a class in contemporary American literature in a community college in the Pacific Northwest. The instructor has decided on Eudora Welty to represent southern fiction. She has chosen her short story "Why I Live at the P.O." and plans to include a recording of Miss Welty reading the story.

ANALYZE LEARNERS

General Characteristics

All of the students are taking the class because they plan to transfer to a four-year institution. Most are recent high school graduates, but a number of the women in the class are using the community college to resume educations interrupted by marriage and children. Reading abilities range from grades eight to fourteen.

Entry Competencies

The students are fairly well motivated but the instructor has discovered that they have little familiarity with contemporary literature. Most can locate Mississippi on a map, but very few of the students have been to the deep South so the Mississippi accent of Miss Welty may be difficult for them to understand. Because the story deals with family squabbles, the instructor is counting on the experiences of the older women in the class to give an important dimension to the class discussions.

STATE OBJECTIVES

After listening to the recording, the students will be able to

1. State the main theme of the story.
2. Discuss the motivations of the main characters.
3. Identify the relationships among the main characters.
4. Restate the Southern idioms in the story in their own language.
5. Compare the behaviors of the characters to how people they know would behave in the same situation.

SELECT MEDIA AND MATERIALS

The instructor selected "Why I Live at the P.O." because she knew about the recording by the author. She believes that hearing as well as reading the short story will help the slower readers. She knows that Miss Welty is an amateur photographer and that a book of her photographs of people and scenes in her native Jackson, Mississippi, has been published. After securing permission from the publisher, the instructor asks the media center to make a series of slides from selected photographs from her copy of the book to give the students the flavor of the environment of the story.

The instructor asks the southern wife of a faculty member to read the narration she has written to accompany the set of slides. This will give the students some practice listening to a southern accent before hearing Miss Welty.

UTILIZE MATERIALS

The classroom is acoustically suitable for hearing the tape, but the instructor realizes that a playback unit with better speakers than those on her portable machine will be necessary. She arranges with the media center to obtain a good playback unit. She has also requested a slide projector and screen and has arranged the slides in the tray.

The reading assignment included material on the influence of the South on southern writers. On the day before the oral reading, the instructor handed out a sheet listing colloquialisms from the story with explanations.

On the day of the reading, the instructor introduces the woman who will read the narration for the slides and proceeds to present the slide set. The slide presentation elicits a number of questions about life in the South. The instructor then introduces the recording, closing with the warning that contrary to what they may have heard about languorous Southern speech, Eudora Welty speaks very rapidly.

REQUIRE LEARNER PARTICIPATION

The students are encouraged to ask questions during and following the slide presentation. They take notes during the reading of the short story. After the recording, the class engages in a discussion of the short story. The older women in the class give their insights into the problems of family relations.

The instructor asks for sayings and expressions the students know that are comparable to those from the South.

As a culminating exercise, the students are asked to write a short essay comparing the characters in the story to people they know.

EVALUATE AND REVISE

From the discussions in class, the instructor determines that the recording added to the understanding of the theme and the motivations of the characters. On the basis of the response to the slide presentation, the instructor decides to use the technique in other units of the course.

The essays demonstrate that the students gave a good deal of thought to the way behavior patterns are influenced by where people live.

A brief multiple-choice test on the people in the story is used to determine how well the students understood the interactions among the characters.

Research also indicates that variable-speed audiotapes can be very effective in increasing reading speed. One junior high school teacher prepared variable-speed tapes of printed material for his students to listen to as they read the material. The students' reading rates gradually increased with increases in their listening rates. The ear, it seems, helps train the eye.

REFERENCES

Print References

Alley, Douglas. "Radio Tapes: A Resource for English Teachers." *English Journal* (October 1979):40–41.

Bloodgood, Janet W. "The First Draft on Tape (In the Classroom)." *Reading Teacher* (November 1989):188.

Bradtmueller, Weldon G. "Auditory Perception as an Aid to Learning in the Content Areas." *Journal of the Association for the Study of Perception* (Spring 1979):27–29.

Brown, Cynthia S. *Like It Was: A Complete Guide to Writing Oral History.* New York: Teachers and Writers Collaborative, 1988.

Christenson, Peter G. "Children's Use of Audio Media." *Communication Research* (July 1985):327–43.

Conte, Richard, and Humphreys, Rita. "Repeated Readings Using Audiotaped Material Enhances Oral Reading with Children with Reading Difficulties." *Journal of Communication Disorders* (February 1989):114–18.

DeMuth, James E. "Audio Cassettes as a Means of Professional Continuing Education of Pharmacists." *Adult Education* (Summer 1979):242–51.

Feldman, Leonard. "Mighty Mini." *Audio* (August 1991):26, 28.

Forster, Patricia, and Doyle, Beverly A. "Teaching Listening Skills to Students with Attention Deficit Disorders." *Teaching Exceptional Children* (Winter 1989):20–22.

Gibbons, Jane. "Young Children's Recall and Reconstruction of Audio and Audiovisual Narratives." *Child Development* (August 1986):1014–23.

Harnishfeger, L. *Basic Practice in Listening.* Denver, CO: Love Publishing, 1990.

Hartley, James. "Using Principles of Text Design to Improve the Effectiveness of Audiotapes." *British Journal of Educational Technology* (January 1988):4–16.

Hoffman, Preston J. *An Evaluative Directory of Producers and Distributors of Unabridged Books on Cassette Tape.* Urbana, IL: Graduate School of Library and Information Science, 1988.

James, Charles J. "Are You Listening: The Practical Components of Listening Comprehension." *Foreign Language Annals* (April 1984):129–33.

Jarnow, Jill. *All Ears: How to Choose and Use Recorded Music for Children.* New York: Penguin Books, 1991.

Kaplan, Jane P. "The Role of the Active Listener." *French Review* (February 1988):369–76.

Larsen, S., and Jorgensen, N. "Talking Books for Preschool Children." *Journal of Visual Impairment and Blindness* (February 1989):118–19.

McAlpine, Lynn. "Teacher as Reader: Oral Feedback on ESL Student Writing." *TESL Canada Journal* (November 1989):62–67.

Moody, Kate. "Audio Tapes and Books: Perfect Partners." *School Library Journal* (February 1989):27–29.

Olsen, Linda. "Technology Humanized—The Rate Controlled Tape Recorder." *Media and Methods* (January 1979):67.

Postlethwait, S. N. "Audio Technology: Audio Tape for Programming Instruction." *Educational Broadcasting* (July–August 1976):17–19.

Rickelman, Robert J., and Henk, William A. "Children's Literature and Audio-Visual Technologies." *Reading Teacher* (May 1990):682–84.

Shapiro, Edward S., and McCurdy, Barry L. "Effects of a Taped-Words Treatment on Reading Proficiency." *Exceptional Children* (January 1989):321–25.

Short, Sarah H. "The Use of Rate Controlled Speech to Save Time and Increase Learning in Self-Paced Instruction." *NSPI Journal* (May 1978):13–14.

Sommers, Jeffrey. "The Effects of Tape-Recorded Commentary on Student Revision: A Case Study." *Journal of Teaching Writing* (Fall–Winter 1989):49–75.

Ullom-Morse, Ann, et al. "The Use and Acceptance of Compressed Speech by Nursing Students." *NALLD Journal* (Winter 1979):20–27.

Waggener, Joseph. "Important Media Classics: Filmstrips, Tape Recorders, and Record Players." *Media and Methods* (January–February 1989):16, 18–19, 66–67.

Wieder, Alan. "Oral History in the Classroom: An Exploratory Essay." *Social Studies* (March–April 1984):71–74.

Zimmerman, William. *How to Tape Instant Oral Biographies.* New York: Guarionex Press, 1982.

Audiovisual References

Basic Audio. Alexandria, VA: Smith-Mattingly Productions, 1979. Videocassette. 30 minutes.

How Audio Recordings Are Made. Pleasantville, NY: Educational Audio-Visual, 1988. Videocassette. 32 minutes.

Learning about Sound. Chicago: Encyclopedia Britannica Educational Corporation, 1975. 16mm film. 17 minutes.

Sound Recording and Reproduction. Salt Lake City, UT: Media Systems, Inc., 1978. 6 filmstrips with audiocassettes.

Tape Recorders. Salt Lake City, UT: Media Systems, Inc., 1978. Filmstrip with audiocassette.

Tips on Tapes for Teachers. Boulder, CO: National Center for Audio Tapes, 1972. Audiocassette.

Utilizing the Tape Recorder in Teaching. Salt Lake City, UT: Media Systems, Inc., 1975. 2 filmstrips with audiocassette.

The following ½-inch VHS videocassettes are available from Audiovisual Center Marketing, C215 Seashore Hall, University of Iowa, Iowa City, IA 52242.

Portable Audio Cassette Recorder. 1983. 7 minutes.

Sharp Audiocassette Recorder. 1989. 14 minutes.

Audio Made Easy. 1989. 10 minutes.

POSSIBLE PROJECTS

6–A.   Prepare an audiotape including your voice and some music. It will be evaluated using the criteria in the "Checklist for Instructor-Prepared Audiotapes" (p. 174). Include a description of how the tape will be used, along with its objective(s).

6–B. Obtain any commercially prepared audio materials and appraise them using a given set of criteria, such as "Appraisal Checklist: Audio Materials," or using your own criteria.

6–C. Do a short oral history of your school or organization by interviewing people associated with it for a long time. Edit your interviews into a five-minute presentation.

6–D. Prepare an outline for a short oral presentation. Deliver your presentation as if you were addressing the intended audience and record it. Critique your presentation for style as well as content. Revise and present again.

6–E. Practice editing by deliberately recording a paragraph from a news report or a literary work with the sentences out of order. Put the paragraph back in proper sequence by editing the recorded tape.

6–F. Develop a brief audio-tutorial lesson. Choose a basic skill, such as spelling or arithmetic, or prepare a performance aid (e.g., how to make out a bank check or how to fill out an application form). Design the lesson with paper and pencil first, then record the tape. Try the lesson out on your fellow students.

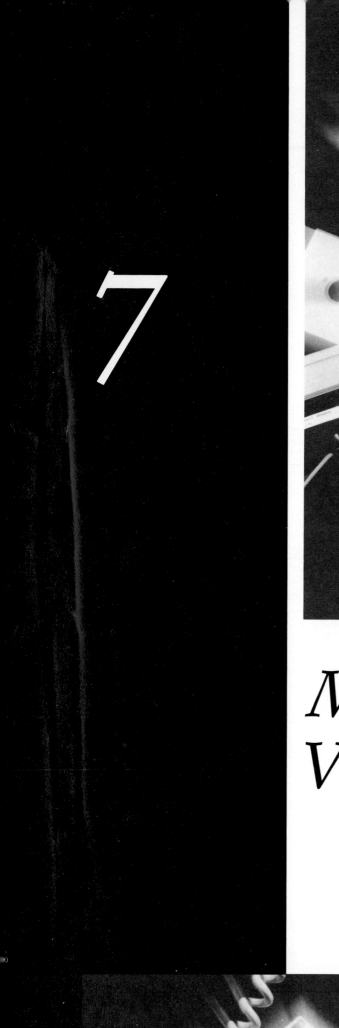

7

Motion Media: Video and Film

OUTLINE

The Moving Image: Video and Film

Video Defined

Video Formats

Film Defined

Film Formats

Differences Between Video and Film

Special Attributes of Motion Media

Manipulation of Space

Alteration of Time

Compression of Time: Time Lapse

Expansion of Time: Slow Motion

Animation

Documentaries as Social Commentaries

Sponsored Videos and Films

Using Motion Media

Understanding Motion Media Conventions

Advantages of Motion Media

Limitations of Motion Media

Adoption of Video in Education

Instructional Video Use in Corporations

Selecting Videos and Films

Teaching with Motion Media

Local Video Design and Production

OBJECTIVES

After studying this chapter, you should be able to

1. Define *video* and *film.*

2. Describe how video and film create an illusion of motion.

3. Identify the video formats in most common use.

4. Describe the special capabilities of videodiscs compared to videocassettes.

5. Explain how high-definition television will improve video quality.

6. Contrast video and film on technical and pedagogical grounds.

7. Explain why video is supplanting film as the motion media format of choice in instruction and training.

8. Name at least two attributes of motion media.

9. Distinguish between time lapse and slow motion.

10. Define *documentary* and explain how a specific documentary fits the definition.

11. Identify two motion media conventions that must be learned.

12. Name at least five advantages of videos and films as instructional resources.

13. Select a film or video that engages the values of the audience (e.g., on abortion or AIDS) and design a lesson plan around it.

14. Explain at least three limitations of videos and films as instructional resources.

15. Characterize the status of video in educational institutions.

16. Describe the utilization patterns of video in corporate training programs.

17. Outline the process of selecting a video or film for classroom use.

18. List at least five criteria that are important in the appraisal of videos and films.

19. Make at least four concrete suggestions for improving classroom utilization of videos and films.

20. Diagram the setup for a single-camera video production.

LEXICON

motion media

video

frame

persistence of vision

charge-coupled device

dichroic mirror

videodisc

film

optical sound track

time lapse

slow motion

animation

documentary

motion media conventions

zoom lens

THE MOVING IMAGE: VIDEO AND FILM

The instructional applications of video and film will be examined side by side in this chapter. We use the term *motion media* to include both. Historically, these media had different origins. Film, the earlier of the two, originated in the chemical process of photography, whereas video is based on the electronic technology of television. The recording of moving images has progressed from film (chemical process) to videotape (electronic and magnetic process) to tapes and discs made through the process of digitizing. However, all these formats are currently used to store and display moving images which are normally accompanied by sound. As we will see, the formats differ considerably in cost, convenience, and flexibility.

This chapter considers how the recorded moving image is displayed and manipulated by the teacher or learner. Chapter 10 deals with the many ways in which video and audio signals are transmitted to the learning site and the instructional implications of those delivery systems.

Video Defined

The primary meaning of *video* is the display of pictures on a television-type screen (the Latin word *video* literally means "I see"). Any media format that employs a cathode-ray screen to present the picture portion of the message can be referred to as video. Thus, we have videocassettes, videodiscs, interactive video, video games, and so on.

The phosphorescent images of video are composed of dots of varying intensity on the screen. Every thirtieth of a second 525 lines of dots are "sprayed" onto the back of the cathode-ray screen, creating one full screen, or *frame*. The rapid succession of frames is perceived as a moving image because of an optical phenomenon called *persistence of vision*: the eye and brain retain an image cast upon the retina of the eye for a fraction of a second after that image is removed from view. If a second image is presented before the trace of the previous image fades, the images blend together, creating the illusion of continuous motion (see "Close-up: How a Video Camera Works," p. 190).

The sound that accompanies the video image is recorded magnetically on videotape and digitally on videodisc, as on audiotape and compact discs, respectively (see Chapter 6).

Originally video was synonymous with broadcast television, but the concept has expanded dramatically in recent years with the proliferation of new technologies that are connected to television sets such as home computers, videocassette recorders, video games, electronic banking, specialized cable TV services, and many other hybrids that are still emerging. These new services continue to multiply because it tends to be cheaper and more efficient to transmit information electronically than to transport information, goods, or people physically.

Video Formats

Video versions of the moving image are recorded on magnetic tape and digital disc, each packaged in forms that vary in size, shape, speed, and the playback mechanism they use. The most common video formats are summarized in Table 7.1.

Videotape. The VHS ½-inch format is the preferred medium for commercial distribution of moving images (Figure 7.1). Virtually all of us have rented a VHS version of a movie, and most of us have recorded a TV program on VHS for later or repeated viewing. Time-shifting the TV schedule has become a major sport in American homes. VHS is also the current preferred format for amateur and nonstudio production of recorded moving images in education. Amateur video production is so prevalent that a network TV pro-

Figure 7.1
The ½-inch videocassette format

Figure 7.2
Comparison of U-matic, VHS, and 8mm cassettes

gram, "America's Funniest Home Videos," can be sustained by it.

Within the past decade, VHS has replaced 16mm film as the format of choice for distribution of educational "films." The VHS version is considerably cheaper than the 16mm version and has been so universally accepted that some companies are offering their recent productions only in VHS.

Training programs in business and industry still show a slight preference for the larger ¾-inch cassette format, called U-matic, for production purposes, but the trend is to the ½-inch VHS format (see Figure 7.2). For distribution of video the VHS format is the overwhelming choice.

A relatively new format is 8mm videotape. The smaller size makes for a more compact video recorder (camera). This format is being widely accepted by the amateur videographer for recording family events and other occasions of personal interest. However, the size advantage may not be significant enough to replace VHS in the education and training markets.

Table 7.1
Common video formats

Formats	Speeds	Advantages	Limitations
Videodisc Diameter: 12 inches	30 min. per side	Flexible storage capacity: can hold 54,000 images, still or motion, or audio Fast random access to specific frames Highly durable; no wear with use Inexpensive when mass produced	Not for local production Originals expensive to produce Limited acceptance in education so far, so software is limited
Videocassette (U-matic) Tape width: ¾ inch	3.75 ips (10–60 min.)	Self-contained and self-threading Compatible with all other U-Matics Superior video quality	Found more in corporate training and TV news field recording, not as common in education
Videocassette VHS Tape width: ¾ inch	Beta = 1.57 ips VHS = 1.31 ips (30–180 min at standard speed)	Self-contained and self-threading More compact than open reel or U-Matic All VHS compatible with each other; same for Beta Abundant software available Easy local production	Video quality lower; not broadcast quality Two competitive standards; VHS ten times more popular than Beta Quality deteriorates with use
Videocassette (8 mm) Tape width: 8 mm (about ¼ inch)	(60–120 min)	Most compact format Full compatibility among all makes and models Easy local production	Video quality lower Limited acceptance in education so far; little software available

CLOSE-UP

How a Video Camera Works

Light enters a video camera through the lens. In a portable camera (camcorder), the light is focused onto a light-sensitive electronic assembly called a *charge-coupled device* (CCD) which changes the wavelengths into electrical charges. A filter connected to the CCD separates the charges by color. These video signals are amplified and sent to the recording mechanism in the camera. The audio is picked up by a microphone attached to the camera (or by a detached mike) and recorded on one edge of the videotape.

Before the development of the CCD, the video camera had to house three tubes, one for each primary color. A system of *dichroic mirrors* sent each color to its respective tube. This made the camera so bulky that the signals had to be sent to a separate videotape recorder. The CCD made it possible to include the recording mechanism in the camera, thus creating the portable units so much in favor for nonstudio videotaping. Because of its superior quality, the dichroic mirror system is still preferred for studio production.

The recorded videotape can be played back through the camera itself or through a videotape player. A video signal is so complex that the videotape speed must be much greater than that for an audio recording. This is achieved

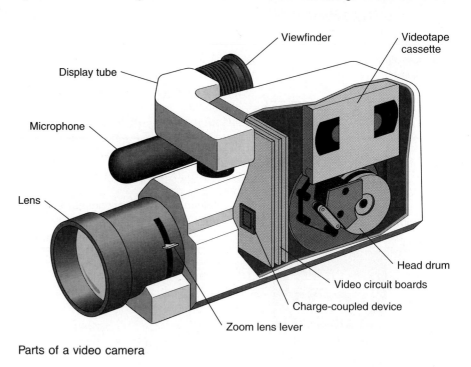

Parts of a video camera

Videodisc. The original and most common type of *videodisc* resembles a silver, shiny phonograph record (Figure 7.3). Images and sound are digitally recorded in the same manner as the compact disc (see page 168). This videodisc can hold up to thirty minutes of motion video images or up to 54,000 still images, or a mix of both motion and still images. As with the CD, the videodisc can be indexed for rapid location of any part of the program material. However, the indexing must be incorporated into the disc during production; it cannot be added by the user. When a videodisc playback unit is connected to a computer, the information of the disc can become an integral part of a computer-assisted instructional program. The computer program makes use of the index on the disc.

Laser disc images are sharper

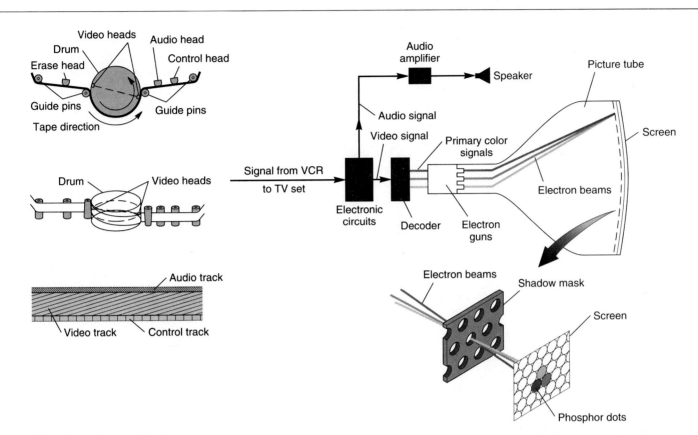

Video recording and display

by rotating the record/playback head, called the drum, at high speed while the tape moves across it in a helical path. The video signal occupies the greater part of the tape while the edges carry the audio and the signals that frame the image on the screen.

The magnetic signals on the tape are converted to electrical impulses that are decoded into the primary colors: blue, red, and green. These signals are amplified and projected onto the screen by an electronic gun. The screen surface is covered with more than 300,000 phosphor dots arranged in groups of three for the three colors. A metal perforated mask behind the screen keeps each electron beam in line with its own color dots and away from interfering with the other colors. The electronic gun scans the picture tube thirty times a second. Persistence of vision converts these scans into a moving image.

than those from a videotape. Video-disc images have a horizontal resolution of 350 lines, compared to only 240 lines for a videocassette. When high-definition television (HDTV) arrives, the images will be at least equal in quality to 16mm film. In contrast to film, videodisc images will not deteriorate in quality with repeated use. Film is notorious for fading and changing color over time and with frequent showings. The audio quality of videodisc is significantly better than that of film or videotape.

Videodiscs are becoming an increasingly popular method of displaying movies. In the case of a film

Flip the pages of the text from here to page 209. If you flip them fast enough, the still pictures will appear to move, approximating a half second of screen action.

classic, critical analysis of the film and its production background are often included, as noted in the Media File on *Citizen Kane* (p. 203). A few educational film companies are releasing some of their titles on videodisc, but educators have been slow to purchase them. The playback equipment for videodiscs is nowhere near as common as videotape player/recorders. One reason for this is that videodiscs cannot be recorded on and, therefore, videodisc equipment can only play back, not record. Pioneer Electronic Corporation has introduced a machine that can record moving images, but the price and limited recording time (thirty-two minutes) make acquisition by

Figure 7.3
A videodisc and player

Figure 7.4
"I think it's an old VCR."

schools and training programs unlikely.

Compact Disc.   As of now, CDs are not used solely for recording and displaying moving images. Moving images on CDs normally include verbal and still image information in computer-controlled programs (see Chapter 8).

High-Definition Television (HDTV).

The quality of the video image is determined primarily by the number of lines that are projected on to the front surface of the tube. The greater the number of lines, the sharper the image and the more accurate the rendition of color. At present, the standard used in North America is 525 lines scanned on the tube thirty times every second. Several systems have been proposed that would double the number of lines. When a new system is adopted, projected video in particular will be improved dramatically. But the new standard will also sharply increase the cost of video recording and reproduction. Historically, the cost of new technology drops when it is widely adopted. Whether the increased quality will justify the higher cost of HDTV can only be determined by time.

Film Defined

Film refers to the celluloid material on which a series of still images are chemically imprinted. This series of transparent images, when projected at twenty-four images (or frames) per second, is perceived by humans as a moving image. As with video, the illusion of motion is caused by persistence of vision.

In order to avoid the appearance of an incomprehensible blur on the screen, the film projector has a shutter that shuts out the light while the mechanism is actually moving the film from one frame to the next. Ironically, we don't see the actual movement of the film, but our brain creates an illusion of

movement from a series of still images projected on the screen.

The sound that accompanies a film is contained in a sound track that runs along one edge of the film (Figure 7.5). The most common type of sound track, the *optical sound track,* is actually a photographic image of sound recorded on the film as varying shades of dark and light (Figure 7.6).

Film Formats

Motion picture film comes in various widths and image sizes. For films shown in theaters 35mm film is most commonly used. For instructional films and other types of films made to be shown in schools, 16mm film is the most common format.

A decade ago, the most common motion-media format for school productions and for "home movies" was 8mm film. "Super-8" was the preferred format because it has a larger picture area than the original 8mm film. However, the lower cost and greater convenience of the ½-inch and 8mm videotape formats have made 8mm film obsolete. Many people with 8mm films of personal value have had the images transferred to videotape.

Differences Between Video and Film

Because media research[1] indicates that displays having the same basic features—motion, color, and sound—have the same basic effects on cognitive, affective, and motor learning, you might conclude that for pedagogical and practical purposes they are essentially equivalent. Not so. Both videotape and videodisc are pedagogically more flexible than

────────────

[1]   Gene L. Wilkinson, *Media in Instruction: 60 Years of Research* (Washington, DC: Association for Educational Communication and Technology, 1980).

CLOSE-UP

Why a Movie Moves

Because the camera photographs a scene as a series of separate, discrete images, motion picture film consists of a sequence of slightly different still pictures called frames. When these frames are projected on a screen at a certain speed (at least twelve, usually twenty-four, frames per second), the images appear to be in continuous motion.

Each still picture (frame) is held stationary at the film aperture (1) (on left of diagram). While it is stationary, the shutter (2) is open, permitting the light from the projection lamp to pass through the image, go through a focusing lens system (3), and display the picture on the screen. Then the shutter closes and a device like a claw (4) engages the sprocket holes and pulls the film down so that the next frame is in position, as shown on the right side of the diagram. The claw withdraws, the shutter opens, and the next picture is projected on the screen.

Although the film moves past the aperture intermittently, the top sprocket wheel (5) pulls the film into the projector at a steady twenty-four frames per second (sound speed), and the bottom sprocket wheel (6) pulls the film out of the projector at the same steady rate of speed. If no slack were put into the film at the upper and lower loops (7 and 8), the film would be torn apart. These two loops compensate for the two different motions the film must have. Because sound cannot be accurately recorded or reproduced on a film that is not moving smoothly, the intermittent movement of the film must be smoothed out by the bottom sprocket and an idler system before the film reaches the sound drum.

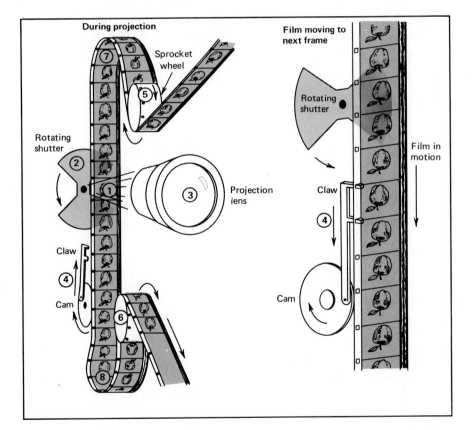

From Wyman, Raymond, *Mediaware Selection, Operation, and Maintenance,* 2nd. ed. Copyright © 1969, 1970. Wm. C. Brown, Dubuque, Iowa. Reprinted by permission.

Figure 7.5
In the 16mm optical sound system, the sound accompanying a specific image is recorded on the film 26 frames ahead of the frame containing that image. The proper setting of the lower loop of the film on the projector is critical for keeping the image and sound synchronized.

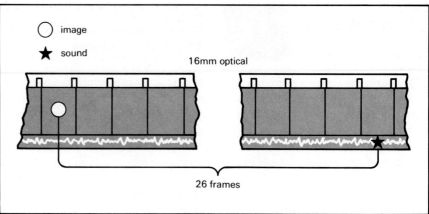

Figure 7.6
In playing back an optical sound track, the light from the exciter lamp passes through the sound track, picking up the "image" of that recorded sound. This image is then focused on a photoelectric cell. These very weak signals are amplified and then converted back into sound waves by the speaker.

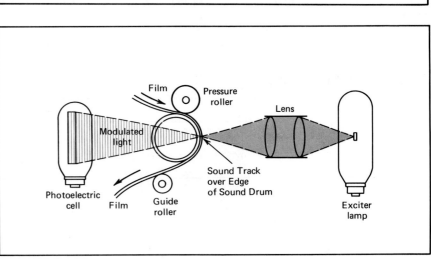

film. Both video formats have fast-forward and reverse search capabilities, while film does not. Video formats, particularly videodisc, can be indexed, making it possible to locate specific sections of a program. Certain special effects, such as slow motion, can be obtained during the video presentation, whereas slow motion must be built into film in the production stage. VCRs can be remotely controlled, meaning that the instructor (or operator) does not have to stay close to the machine. Because of the ease of operating the equipment, video lends itself to individual study much more readily than film. All of this means that video can be incorporated more easily than film into a variety of pedagogical methods.

A VCR and TV set are easier than films for the instructor to use. Many people learn how to operate a VCR while growing up. On the other hand, not many people, even as adults, know how to operate the more complex film projector and set up the screen. With video, the operator does not have to worry about focusing the image or making sure the screen is oriented properly with the projector. In addition, the film image on the screen is more easily degraded by ambient light.

But if the video image has to be projected, the operational advantages of video are reduced. Adjusting the video image to the screen can be as, if not more, time-consuming than adjusting the film image.

A video copy of a title is much less expensive than its film counterpart and costs less to maintain. Replacement of damaged film footage is a major maintenance item. Video and film centers have found that purchasing, handling, storing, distributing, and maintaining video is a great deal easier on the budget (and personnel) than film. As for equipment, the combination of video player and monitor costs less than a 16mm film projector.

There is no question that the projected image of a new film print is still superior in color saturation, range of contrast, and definition to that of video, although the newer video projectors are closing the image gap. (High-definition TV may even be better than 16mm film.) However, the vast majority of instructors will gladly trade off the superior film image for the pedagogical and operational advantages of video, much to the chagrin of die-hard film enthusiasts.

In the first edition of this book, we mentioned that some future edition would include a "Flashback" on film in the chapter on video. It could appear as soon as the next edition.

SPECIAL ATTRIBUTES OF MOTION MEDIA

Because most of us are inclined to think of video and film as media designed primarily to produce a realistic image of the world around us, we tend to forget that a basic attribute of the moving image (whether recorded photographically on film or electronically on videotape) is its ability to manipulate temporal and spatial perspectives. Manipulation of time and space not only serves dramatic and creative ends; it also has important implications for instruction.

Manipulation of Space

Motion medias permit us to view phenomena in microcosm and macrocosm, that is, at extremely close range or from a vast distance. Charles and Ray Eames made a film called *Powers of Ten* that within a few minutes takes us from a close-in observation of a man lying on a beach to views of the man as observed from distances expressed as increasing powers of ten until he disappears from sight. Perspective then changes quickly in the reverse direction and the film ends with a microscopic view of the man's skin. A similar effect can be seen in a National Film Board of Canada film *Cosmic Zoom* (Figure 7.7). This film starts with a microscopic examination of the skin of a man in a rowboat and then moves farther and farther away until we lose track of him entirely and, from some vantage point far from earth, see only

Figure 7.7
From *Cosmic Zoom*

MEDIA FILE: *AIDS: Questions with Answers*
Video

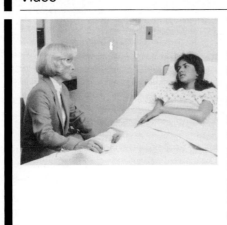

This video on the controversial and crucial topic of AIDS was made for use in grades 9 through 12. Group interviews with teenagers helped the authors discover the concerns, attitudes toward, and misconceptions teenagers have about AIDS. Questions about symptoms, acquisition, prevention, and testing are answered in the video. Scenarios that describe potentially harmful as well as non-harmful situations make this video realistic and interesting.

Source: Meridian Education Corporation

---

the world of which he is a part. Both films are extremely effective examples of how motion media can manipulate spatial perspective.

Multi-image presentations are often manipulations of space. For example, the film *A Place to Stand* persuades the viewer that Ontario, Canada, is a great place to live by showing exciting scenes from different parts of the province in split-image format. As many as six different images are on the screen at one time. The viewer gets the impression of being instantly transported around the province.

Alteration of Time

Motion media permit us to move through space in what might be called altered time. The *Cosmic Zoom* film shows movement through space in continuous time and far faster than we could possibly move in reality. But we can also take out pieces of time, so to speak, as we move through space. For example, we are all familiar with the type of film sequence in which two automobiles approach each other at high speed and the film suddenly cuts to a scene showing the wreckage of both cars. Time has been taken out of that sequence, but we accept the fact that the two cars did come to-

gether in real continuous time. In other words, film convinces us that we have witnessed an event even when we have not seen it in its entirety. This is an important convention for educational as well as entertainment films. For example, it would take an impossibly long time for students to actually witness a highway being constructed, but a carefully edited film of the different activities that go into building a highway can recreate the essentials of such an event in a few minutes.

Compression of Time: Time Lapse

Motion media can compress the time that it takes for an event to occur. We have all seen moving images of flowers slowly opening before our eyes. Simple arithmetic indicates that if a process normally takes four hours and we want to be able to see that process in one minute on the screen, then a single picture must be taken of that process every ten seconds. When shown at normal speed, the process will

FLASHBACK

Mr. Edison's Dream

Thomas A. Edison, whose work in developing the kinetograph (a camera that used film rolls) and the kinetoscope (a peep-show device) contributed greatly to the development of motion pictures, had high hopes for the instructional value of this popular medium.

As depicted in the cartoon from the *Chicago Tribune* of 1923, he fully expected the motion picture to revolutionize education, give new life to curriculum content, and provide students with new motivation for learning.

We all know that the history of the motion picture took a turn quite different from that anticipated by Edison. "Movies" were quickly and eagerly adopted as an entertainment medium, but in education the acceptance of film as a useful medium has been glacially slow. Part of the problem was technical. The standard size for film quickly became set at 35mm, which meant that equipment for projection was bulky and expensive. Also, the film base that was used for many years, cellulose nitrate, was extremely flammable, and many state regulations required a film to be projected only from an enclosed booth and by a licensed projectionist. Thus, films were too expensive for schools to use for other than special occasions. There was also resistance on the part of the educational establishment to acknowledge the educational value of this "frivolous" new invention. Its very success as an entertainment medium automatically made it suspect as an educational tool.

The first extensive use of film as an educational medium occurred during World War I, outside the classroom, when psychologists working with the U.S. Army produced a series of training films on venereal disease.

After World War I, several prestigious organizations combined forces to produce a series of American history films that became known as the *Yale Chronicles of America Photoplays.* This series of films was the subject of extensive research and documented for the first time the effectiveness of films in direct instruction, even though the

Thomas A. Edison

films were considerably handicapped because they were made in the silent era.

When sound on film finally did become a reality, many educators resisted its use in educational films. They felt that by putting a sound track on a film the producer was imposing external standards on every class in the country. They insisted that teachers should be free to narrate films according to principles and practices prescribed locally. Teacher narration of films, however, was favored by theorists and administrators but not by practitioners. (Anyone who has ever attempted to narrate a film knows what a difficult task it can be.) Some administrators also resisted the use of sound films in the classroom because this newer technology made existing inventories of silent-film projectors and silent films obsolete.

World War II gave an even greater impetus to the educational use of films. In a crash program to train Americans in the skills necessary to produce weapons, the Office of Education engaged in an extensive program of film production under the leadership of Floyde Brooker. Most of the films produced by the Office of Education were technical.

The armed forces also produced films during this period for training purposes, and their research indicated that films (and other audiovisual media) contributed significantly to the success of their training programs.

The success of instructional technology, including film, in achieving war-related instructional objectives created sentiment among educators and laypeople alike for more widespread use of this technology in the nation's schools.

The late 1950s witnessed the introduction of 8mm film into education. Cartridged, looped 8mm films quickly acquired the label "single-concept films" because they concentrated on presenting a single event or process for study. Because 8mm cartridges were easily inserted in their projectors and the projectors were small, portable, and simple to use, they lent themselves particularly well to individual and small-group study and to incorporation in programs of individualized instruction. However, mechanical problems with the projectors and the vulnerability of the film itself discouraged use.

In the meantime, as sales of 16mm educational films increased, commercial publishers were encouraged to produce film "packages." Along with the individual film for a

Floyde Brooker directing one of the World War II training films for the U.S. Office of Education

specific learning objective, companies began to market series of films to be incorporated as major components of various courses. This trend led in the late 1950s to the introduction of complete courses on film. Encyclopædia Britannica Films, for example, produced a complete course in high school physics, consisting of 162 half-hour films in color.

Television soon became the primary source of most filmed courses used in the instructional setting, and with the rise of videotape technology, television itself, both educational and commercial, became a major force in the growing use of recorded moving images for instructional purposes.

Mr. Edison's dream of the immediate and overwhelming impact of the film on education may have been a little fuzzy around the edges—as dreams sometimes are—but it was not, after all, so far off the mark. It took a quarter century longer than the Wizard of Menlo Park had anticipated for the film to become an important factor in education and another quarter century for it to reach a state of instructional prominence. His dream did come true, in its own time and in its more realistic way—as dreams sometimes do.

Figure 7.8
In time lapse, a slow event is condensed into a short screen time by allowing several seconds to elapse between shooting each frame of film.

Figure 7.9
In slow motion, a fast event is expanded into a longer screen time by shooting at a speed greater than twenty-four frames per second.

Figure 7.10
Animation in video and film is easy to produce with the aid of computer-generated images.

take just one minute. This technique, known as *time lapse,* has important instructional uses. For example, the process of a chrysalis turning into a butterfly is too slow for easy classroom observation. However, through time-lapse cinematography, the butterfly can emerge from the chrysalis in a matter of minutes on the screen (Figure 7.8). (Renowned British composer Sir Michael Tippett attributes the inspiration for his fourth symphony to seeing a time-lapse film of the growth of a single cell into a baby—an interesting instance of one medium triggering creativity in another.)

Expansion of Time: Slow Motion

Time can also be expanded in motion media through a technique called *slow motion.* Some events occur too fast to be seen by the naked eye. By photographing such events at extremely high speeds and then projecting the image at normal speed, we can observe what is happening (see Figure 7.9). A chameleon catches an insect too rapidly for the naked eye to observe. High-speed cinematography can slow down the motion so that the process can be observed.

Motor skill tasks are often better analyzed if photographed at higher-than-normal speeds and studied at normal speed. Many training programs can be improved by this type of task analysis.

Animation

Time and space can also be manipulated by animation. *Animation* is a technique in which the filmmaker gives motion to otherwise inanimate objects. If such an object is photographed, then moved a very short distance and photographed on one frame of film, moved again, then photographed again, and so on, the object when projected will look as though it has been continuously moving through space. (Flipping pages 191–213 of this chapter back-

wards at the bottom corner illustrates this effect.) There are various and more or less sophisticated techniques for achieving animation, but basically animation is made up of a series of photographs of small displacements in space of objects or images. Animation, however, can even be achieved without the use of a camera. As popularized by Canadian filmmaker Norman McLaren, images can be drawn directly on film, which, when projected sequentially, will give the illusion of movement.

With the continuing evolution of computer programs that can manipulate visual images adroitly, we are experiencing a rediscovery of the art of animation through the video display format (Figure 7.10). Computer-generated animation sequences are being used more and more in instructional video programs to depict complex or rapid processes in simplified form.

DOCUMENTARIES AS SOCIAL COMMENTARIES

The documentary as a special genre of film and television has a long history of use as social commentary, or for education in the broader sense of the term. The *documentary* attempts to depict essentially true stories about real-life situations and people. Through the work of filmmakers such as Robert Flaherty in the United States and John Grierson in England, the documentary has also acquired a reputation for artistic merit.

Grierson defined the documentary as "a creative treatment of actuality." He believed that the documentary should be a point of view, that it should be a vehicle for presenting and interpreting "human problems and their solutions in the spheres of economics, culture, and human relations." Thus, Grierson, Flaherty, and other like-minded filmmakers inaugurated the concept of the documentary as a socially significant film form rather than merely a vehi-

Figure 7.11
Although not a true ethnographic film, *Nanook of the North,* made in 1922, portrayed the impact of modernization on Eskimo life.

Figure 7.12
The plight of the homeless today is vividly explored in *Lost Angeles: The Story of Tent City.*

cle for presentation of newsreel footage and travelogue material.

Flaherty's early film on the Eskimos of Hudson Bay, *Nanook of the North,* is generally credited with generating worldwide recognition of the documentary as a distinct film genre. By the late 1930s many countries had inaugurated documentary film units or were commissioning documentaries from independent producers. In the United States important and classic documentaries were produced both by government film units (e.g., *The River, Power and the Land*) and by independent film units (e.g., *The City, Valleytown, And So They Live*). In Great Britain, government units produced documentary classics such as *Night Mail* and *Song of Ceylon.* In Spain renowned feature film director Luis Buñuel made the striking film *Las Hurdes* (released in the United States as *Land without Bread*). In Belgium Henri Storck directed what is regarded by many as the classic

film on slums and slum clearance, *Les Maisons de la Misére* (1937). In the Soviet Union the work of Dziga Vertov culminated in the technical and conceptual tour de force *Man with a Movie Camera* (1929). In Germany, two controversial but classic films by Leni Riefenstahl, *Triumph of the Will* (a film of the Nazi Party Congress of 1934) and *Olympia* (the 1936 Olympic games in Berlin), were prominent among a number of powerful documentaries.

Newsreels were a standard part of commercial movie programs in the 1930s and 1940s. Presented before the showing of the feature film, newsreels were little more than illustrated headlines depicting current news in segmented and superficial form. *The March of Time* series (1934) took a different approach—a documentary approach. For an average length of eighteen minutes, *The March of Time* examined one topic in moderate depth and often with a point of view. Today, many of *The March of Times* films are still valuable as historical perspectives of critical events and issues. For example, the *March of Time* film *Palestine,* made before the state of Israel was formed, gives students an opportunity to examine a current issue from a unique historical point of view.

During World War II the documentary was widely used by all combatants in training programs and for propaganda purposes. More than a few propaganda documentaries, however, also had lasting artistic and historical merit—John Huston's *Let There Be Light,* for example, and Humphrey Jennings's *The Silent Village* and *Diary for Timothy.*

Today television has become the prime influence on the continuing development of documentaries. The commercial networks (broadcast and cable) and the Public Broadcasting System regularly produce significant

documentaries. Programs such as "60 Minutes" and "20/20" examine important topical issues. Special programs, such as "The Second Russian Revolution," present in-depth analyses of recent events and issues. The miniseries "The Civil War" is an example of a documentary presentation of a critical period in American history. Programs such as "Nova" and the National Geographic specials offer outstanding documentaries in science, culture, and nature. Virtually all television documentaries are available for purchase as videos. Independent video- and filmmakers are increasingly looking to public television as a primary market (The PBS series "Spirit of Place" was designed to showcase independent productions.) When this happens, the secondary market becomes public libraries, schools, regional centers, and four-year institutions.

Sponsored Videos and Films

Private companies, associations, and government agencies sponsor motion media for a variety of reasons. Private companies may make them to promote their products or to enhance their public image. Associations and government agencies sponsor videos and films to promote causes, such as better health habits, conservation of natural resources, or proper use of park and recreation areas. Many of these sponsored films make worthwhile instructional materials (see Figure 7.15). They also have the considerable advantage of being free.

A certain amount of caution, however, is called for in using sponsored films for instructional purposes. Some private-company films may be too flagrantly self-serving. Or they may deal with products not very suitable for certain instructional settings; for example, the making of alcoholic beverages or cigarettes. Some association and government films may contain a sizable dose of propaganda or special pleading for pet causes along with their content. Ralph Nader's Center for the Study of Responsive Law has

---

MEDIA FILE: *A More Perfect Union*
Videodiscs

This series of eight videodiscs is an outstanding example of the flexibility that can be built into the videodisc format. The programs come with a 100-page master index with study guides for each segment, which the teacher can access quickly at appropriate moments. The study guide and index make the series ideal for independent study. The subject of the series is the United States Constitution viewed as a living and constantly evolving document, from debates during the Constitutional Convention to landmark Supreme Court decisions.

Source: Encyclopaedia Britannica Educational Corporation

MEDIA FILE: *Samsara: Death and Rebirth in Cambodia*
Video/Film

Samsara, from Sanskrit, means perpetual repetition of birth through the present to the future. This winner of the prestigious John Grierson Award at the 1990 American Film and Video Festival documents the lives of the Cambodian people long troubled by war, and brings a humanistic perspective to a country in deep political turmoil. The film focuses on the Cambodians' struggle to reconstruct their shattered society in a climate of war and with limited resources. Ancient prophecy, Buddhist teachings, folklore, and dreams help us understand the Cambodians' world view which guides their lives.

Source: Film Distribution Center

---

issued a report highly critical of instructional materials distributed free by industry.[2] It claims that many sponsored materials subtly influence the curriculum in socially undesirable ways. Certainly you must preview sponsored films.

Properly selected, many sponsored films can be valuable additions to classroom instruction. Modern Talking Picture Service is one of the major distributors of sponsored films. The best single source of information on sponsored films is the *Educator's Guide to Free Films and Videos*. Details on this and similar

---

2   Sheila Harty, *Hucksters in the Classroom: A Review of Industry Propaganda in the Schools* (Washington, DC: Center for Study of Responsive Law, 1980).

Figure 7.13
From the widely acclaimed series, *The Civil War,* presented on the Public Broadcasting System

Figure 7.14
The tragedy of teenage suicide is treated sensitively in *Empty Chairs.*

Figure 7.15
Images of Einstein, distributed by IBM, is a sponsored film, the content of which is unrelated to the sponsor.

free and inexpensive sources are given in Appendix B.

USING MOTION MEDIA
Understanding Motion Media Conventions

The devices and techniques used in making motion media to manipulate time and space are for most of us readily accepted conventions. We understand that the athlete whose jump is stopped in midair is not actually frozen in space, that the flashback is not an actual reversal of our normal time continuum, that the light bulb does not really disintegrate slowly enough for us to see that it implodes rather than explodes. Teachers, however, must keep in mind that the ability to make sense out of *motion media conventions* is an acquired skill. When do children learn to handle flashbacks, dissolves, jump cuts, and so on? Unfortunately, we know very little about when and how children learn to make sense of filmic manipulation of reality, and much research on the matter remains to be done.

Some insight into the kind of difficulties students may encounter can be gleaned from the experiences of filmmakers involved with adults unfamiliar with standard film conventions. After World War II, film crews from the United States were sent to various parts of the world to make instructional films designed to help people better their skills in farming, housing, sanitation, and so forth. One crew member working in rural Iran noted that in the United States filmmakers could have a man walk out a door in lower Manhattan and immediately pick him up in another shot at Times Square. In Iran this technique was not possible. Viewers in rural Iran, however, because they were at that time unfamiliar with the conventions of time-space manipulations, could not accept this filmic view of reality. They wanted to see the man making the journey to Times Square.

John Wilson, another American film producer of the period, commented:

> We found that the film is, as produced in the West, a very highly conventionalized piece of symbolism, although it looks very real. For instance, we found that if you were telling a story about two men to an African audience and one had finished his business and he went off the edge of the screen, they wanted to know what happened to him; they didn't accept that this was just the end of him and that he was of no more interest to the story. . . . We had to follow him along a street until he took a natural turn. . . . It was quite understandable that he could disappear around the turn. The action had to follow a natural course of events.[3]

The film is not, of course, alone among media in its reliance on accepted conventions for interpretation and appreciation. Flashback techniques are regularly used in literature and usually accepted by readers. The theatrical convention of the aside is readily accepted by playgoers. The following anecdote about Picasso illustrates how a new artistic

---

3   Joan Rosengren Forsdale and Louis Forsdale, "Film Literacy," *The Teachers College Record* (May 1966):612.

convention may seem to the uninitiated to be merely a distortion of reality rather than, as intended, a particular and valid view of reality. It also illustrates how a convention (in this case a convention of photography) can become so readily accepted and commonplace that we are amusingly surprised at being reminded it exists.

Picasso showed an American soldier through his villa one day, and on completion of the tour the young man felt compelled to confess that he didn't dig Picasso's weird way of painting, because nothing on the canvas looked the way it really is. Picasso turned the conversation to more acceptable matters by asking the soldier if he had a girl back in the States. The boy proudly pulled out a wallet photograph. As Picasso handed it back, he said "She's an attractive girl, but isn't she awfully small?"[4]

A great deal can be learned about different cultures through their approach to producing motion media. After Navajo Indians were shown how to operate a camera and editing equipment, they were asked to come back with finished films. Their view of space and time was quite different from that of the Anglo university crew who had trained them. For example, the Navajos used fewer close-ups, placing more emphasis on the place of the individual in the land, and past, present, and future were not as clearly defined.[5] On the basis of this experiment, and others like it, we know that cultural values shape the way people look at their world.

Advantages of Motion Media

The special attributes just detailed suggest some of the ways that film

---

[4] Forsdale and Forsdale, "Film Literacy,"
    609.

[5] Sol Worth and John Adair, *Through Navajo Eyes: An Exploration in Film, Communication and Anthropology* (Bloomington, IN: Indiana University Press, 1972).

MEDIA FILE: *Two Dollars and a Dream*
Video/Film

Madame C. J. Walker, the child of slaves freed by the Civil War, became America's first self-made millionairess. She made her fortune by parlaying a homemade beauty formula into a line of skin and hair-care products that she marketed nationwide. She and her daughter lived on a grand scale in Harlem. Through the use of rare film footage and stills, this program offers a view of the social, economic, and political history of African-Americans from 1867 to the 1930s.

Source: Filmakers Library, Inc.

MEDIA FILE: *The Second Russian Revolution*
Videocassettes

Originally produced by the Discovery Channel and the British Broadcasting Company, this series of six videocassettes tells the incredible story of the breakup of the Soviet Union. Members of the then-ruling Politburo speak, in surprisingly candid interviews, about the power struggle within the Kremlin that led to the ouster of Gorbachev and the declarations of independence by the Russian and other republics. The interviews were conducted during the Spring and Summer of 1990 when *glasnost* (ironically, a Gorbachev initiative) was at its height. Boris Yeltsin, President of the Russian Republic, and Eduard Shevardnadze, former Foreign Minister of the USSR, are two of the more than 100 key participants who were interviewed. This is an outstanding example of how education benefits from the documentary efforts of television.

Source: Coronet/MTI Film and Video

and video lend themselves to educational applications. Some of their other instructional advantages are as follows.

Motion. Moving images have an obvious advantage over other visual media in portraying concepts in which motion is essential to mastery (such as tying knots or operating a potter's wheel).

Processes. Operations, such as assembly line steps or science experiments, in which sequential movement is critical can be shown more effectively by means of motion media.

Safe observation. Visual recordings allow learners to observe phenomena that might be dangerous to view directly, such as an eclipse of the sun, a volcanic eruption, or warfare.

Skill learning. Research indicates that mastery of physical skills requires repeated observation and practice. Through recorded media a performance can be viewed over and over again for emulation.

Dramatization. Dramatic recreations can bring historical events and personalities to life. In business or industry training they allow us to observe and analyze human relations problems.

Affective learning. Because of their great potential for emotional impact, films can be useful in shaping personal and social attitudes. Documentary and propaganda films have often been found to have a measurable impact on audience attitudes.

Problem solving. Open-ended dramatizations are frequently used to present unresolved confrontations, leaving it to the viewers to discuss various ways of dealing with the problem.

Cultural understanding. We can develop a gut-level appreciation for other cultures by seeing film and video depictions of everyday life in other societies. The whole

MEDIA FILE   *Citizen Kane*
Videodisc

The Criterion Collection is a set of videodiscs aimed at students of film appreciation. Each contains not only the original commercial film but also, on a separate track, other supplementary material. In this case the film is Orson Welles's masterpiece about the rise and fall of a newspaper magnate. It is supplemented with a visual essay by Bob Carringer with over 100 photos and the original theatrical trailer.

Source: Voyager Company

MEDIA FILE   *Family Gathering*
Video/Film

Although the film opens with the internment of Masuo Yasui and his wife Shidzuyo, and the separation of their family five days after the bombing of Pearl Harbor, *Family Gathering* is as much about the use of family archival material (home movies, photographs, letters), archival newsreels, and interviews in reconstructing the history of the Yasui family in the United States as it is about the effects of World War II on the Japanese community on the west coast. In 1911 Masuo Yasui emigrated to the United States, finally settling in Oregon, where he and his wife were farming when the war began. Forty years after their internment, their granddaughter, Lise Yasui, gathered the material and conducted the interviews that tell the history of her family. The film is also a fascinating study in how the visual record shapes the history we remember and reconstruct.

Source: New Day Films

genre of ethnographic films can serve this purpose; some examples of feature-length ethnographic films are *The Hunters, The Tribe that Hides from Man, The Nuer,* and *River of Sand.*

Establishing commonality. By viewing films or video programs together, a disparate group of people can build up a common base of experience to discuss an issue effectively.

Limitations of Motion Media

As with all other instructional media, there are limitations to the instructional applications of film and video. Here are some of the more obvious limitations.

Fixed pace. Although film projectors can be stopped for discussion during a film, this is not usually done in group showings. And even though the videocassette player has more flexibility than the film projector, the temptation is to let the video play uninterrupted. Because the program runs at a fixed pace, some viewers may fall behind while others are waiting impatiently for the next point. Not everyone's mind runs at 24 (or 30) frames per second.

Still phenomena. Although film and video are advantageous for concepts that involve motion, they may be unsuitable for other topics where detailed study of a single visual is involved, for example, a map, a wiring diagram, or an organization chart.

Misinterpretation. Documentaries and dramatizations often present a complex or sophisticated treatment of an issue. A scene intended as satire might be taken literally by a young or naive viewer. The thoughts of a main character may be interpreted as the attitudes and values of the filmmaker. For example, the film *Phoebe* uses a stream-of-consciousness approach as Phoebe fantasizes about what the reactions of her parents and her

---

MEDIA FILE *The City of Gold*
Video/Film

Winner of many awards and an Oscar nominee, this film classic (now available in video) tells the story of Dawson City in the Klondike, scene of the greatest gold rush in history. The film begins with footage of present-day Dawson City, then moves to a fascinating series of still photos taken during the gold rush, and returns to the present. A provocative narration describes life in the gold camp and raises questions about what the men who rushed to the Klondike were seeking. The music adds greatly to the atmosphere of the film.

Source: National Film Board of Canada

MEDIA FILE *Alexander, Who Used to Be Rich Last Sunday*
Video/Film

Alexander's grandparents give him and his two brothers $5 each with the usual caution about spending money wisely. However, a "rich" Alexander fritters away his money on whimsical purchases, including gobs of bubble gum, a half-melted candle, and a one-eyed teddy bear. About the time he realizes he needs to save money, he no longer has any. He tries unsuccessfully to start a toy rental service and searches pay phone coin-return boxes for change. His only hope is an early return of his grandparents. An excellent video for getting primary age children to discuss how to handle "big" money.

Source: AIMS Media

---

boyfriend will be to her announcement that she is pregnant. Some students (and parents) have misinterpreted the speculations of a troubled mind as being the attitude of the filmmaker toward all the characters in the story.

Cost. Film has become an expensive medium, both the software and the hardware. The video version of a title is generally about two-thirds of the cost of the film version, and the combination of a video player and video monitor costs less than a film projector. These are the major reasons why institutions are willing to write off their considerable capital investment in films and projectors and adopt videocassettes as the format of choice for moving images. But videocassettes are still too expensive for schools and training programs to purchase in quantity, and the cost of equipment limits the number available in schools.

Logistics. Due to the cost per unit, videos and films are acquired, stored, and distributed by central agencies in school districts, regional centers, universities, training centers, and public libraries. Collections in individual schools are normally very small. Training programs usually have to rent videos and films from a distributor or from corporate headquarters. This means videos and films have to be ordered well in advance of their intended use. Arrangements have to be made so that the correct title arrives at the right place at the right time and that the proper equipment is available and in good condition. The complexity of these arrangements discourages many instructors.

Adoption of Video in Education

In 1980 a survey of school district, county, and regional media programs reported very few videos compared to films in their collections of motion media.[6] At that time film was the overwhelming choice when new titles were added to collections. Even though many producers of educational programs made available contracts permitting copying of film and video titles onto videotape, few districts entered into such agree-

---

[6] Doris R. Brodeur and Robert Heinich, "Third Annual Survey of the Circulation of Nonprint Educational Media in the Public Schools, 1979–80," in *Educational Media Yearbook 1982,* ed. J. W. Brown (Littleton, CO: Libraries Unlimited, 1982).

MEDIA FILE *The Red Balloon*
Film

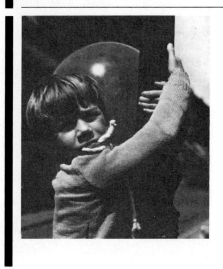

Perhaps the most popular children's film ever made, this Academy Award winner was voted the best of all films awarded Blue Ribbons during the first ten years of the American Film Festival (1958–68). A fantasy, the nonnarrated film tells the story of a boy whose faithful balloon follows him to school and church and through the streets of Paris. A street gang chases the boy and his balloon in order to destroy it. At the end, all the balloons of Paris converge to carry the boy off to a fantasy land of peace.

Source: Janus Classic Collection/Films Inc.

MEDIA FILE *A Case of Working Smarter, Not Harder*
Film

Training films can be competitive at film festivals as well as effective instructionally. This award-winning film demonstrates that good managers have the ability to focus on long-range goals as well as on immediate objectives. A case study, the subject of the film is a manager who changes from an overworked, compulsive problem solver to an effective, productive innovator. The system he develops draws attention from the public as well as the business community. Research has established that a film is more effective when the target audience can project itself into the roles portrayed on the screen. This film exemplifies that quality.

Source: CRM Films

---

ments. The vast majority of the limited number of videos that were distributed by educational agencies were locally produced; these were often travelogues made by teachers on vacation.

Today video has far surpassed film as the format of choice for presentation of motion media in educational institutions, primarily because of its

ease of use, lower cost per copy, and lower cost of equipment (Figures 7.16 and 7.17). Furthermore, film is more easily damaged than videotape

Figure 7.16
Television is frequently the original source of documentaries subsequently available to schools on videotape.

and replacement film footage is very expensive. Replacing a damaged videotape in its entirety is frequently cheaper than replacing damaged film footage. For all of these reasons, video has become universally adopted in education.

During the past decade, Quality Education Data, a research organization based in Denver, Colorado, has been tracking the growth of video and microcomputers in the public schools. After noting the phenomenal growth of VCRs in the schools, they conclude:

Figure 7.17
Video projectors are getting smaller and their projected images are getting closer to the quality of 16mm.

Video usage may be the strongest new element in instruction in the 90's. While micro usage is strong and growing, the level of expertise required to instruct with micros is quite high. VCRs, on the other hand, are a consumer product with which teachers are familiar. The use of sophisticated visual techniques, of master teachers on video, of programs time-shifted so that students can watch during regular class periods, the possible future use of interactive video in the classroom—all of these factors make the future look bright for educational video usage.[7]

As the report points out, video fits more comfortably into the group mode of instruction favored by teachers, in contrast with the computer tutorial approach.

Instructional Video Use in Corporations

Training programs in business and industry turned from film to video

---

[7] Jeanne Hayes, ed. *Microcomputer and VCR Usage in Schools* (Denver, CO: Quality Education Data, 1988), p. 78.

much earlier than educational institutions. Video now is so widely accepted that it is the most frequently used training medium by businesses that have more than fifty employees. In addition to the advantages already cited, production of video is much easier to handle in-house. With internal production all phases of production can be managed internally at fairly low cost, whereas only the largest companies can afford in-house film production. While educational institutions have relatively similar curriculum needs and therefore can rely primarily on commercially produced materials, training and communication needs for the most part are situation specific, making in-house production a necessity.

In addition to the demands of customization there is the factor of rapid change. Increasing competition and technological change dictate an instructional medium that can turn out updated and modified programs rapidly.

Corporate use of video therefore contrasts sharply with school use in terms of the amount of locally produced material that is used. Most large corporate users maintain professional-quality production studios and facilities for in-the-field location shooting. There are, of course, a good number of corporate skills that are generic in nature such as supervisory skills, management of meetings, and stress management. These lend themselves to off-the-shelf, or commercially produced, media.

According to a study conducted in 1990, the utilization of video in training and communication programs is quite varied. When business organizations were asked to identify the purposes for which they made videos, their responses broke down into the following categories and percentages (of total video production)[8]:

Training (38%). We would expect video to be used most frequently in training employees at all corporate levels. Thus it is somewhat

---

[8] Fred Cohn, "Corporate Video '90," *Corporate Video Decisions* (July 1990):25–30.

surprising that this percentage of total video production isn't higher. Many organizations are willing to invest in video for

- ❏ Orientation of new employees
- ❏ Training in job-related skills
- ❏ Development of interpersonal abilities for management
- ❏ Introduction of new products, policies, or markets
- ❏ Customer training
- ❏ Standardization of training among dispersed offices

Sales and marketing presentations (20%). Is there anyone who hasn't seen a video sales pitch in a supermarket or a mall? This is the most visible use of video in marketing products and services, but other uses abound, from demonstrations to retail customers to presentations of new products by manufacturers to their retail outlets (see Figure 7.18).

Employee information (16%). Videos in this category keep employees informed about the well-being of the company, new products, employee benefits, and so on.

Community involvement (12%). Demonstrating corporate responsibility to the community and environment is the purpose of production in this category. For example, a mining company might produce a video on restoring pit mines to a natural state.

Shareholder presentations (3%). Videos of company achievements are frequently produced for showing at stockholders' annual meetings. Some companies make available video interviews with company CEOs and other executives for viewing at home by individual stockholders.

Other (12%). The major entry here is videotaping of product performance for internal study. No doubt a small part of this use is for entertainment at company affairs (e.g., a company version of "America's Funniest Home Videos").

Portability and ease of use are advantages in all the above uses of video. For example, a life insurance company can send a video to its sales representatives for them to study at home. And each representative can take the video to a potential client's home knowing a VCR will probably be available. In the case of recording product improvements, employees can study immediately product performance rather than having to wait for film processing.

Figure 7.18
Unlike 16mm film, video can easily be used by the amateur. Here a travel agent is practicing a presentation.

Selecting Videos and Films

Locating Video Materials.

Program guides and directories can help keep you abreast of available materials in your areas of interest and guide you toward selection of materials best suited to your particular teaching needs. The most comprehensive listing of current educational video recordings is NICEM's *Film and Video Finder.* Other broad catalogs are *Videolog* and *Video*

Source Book. (These and other more specialized catalogs are described in Appendix A.)

Locating Films.

Given the high cost of 16mm films as well as the impracticality of local production, an individual school or small organization is unlikely to have its own film collection. So most instructors must acquire films on loan from an outside agency such as the school district, state library, or rental library. A basic resource for you, then, is a collection of catalogs of those rental agencies you are most likely to turn to for films. To be more thorough in your search you will want *The Educational Film/ Video Locator,* a comprehensive listing of the films that are available in various college and university rental collections. If you are just beginning your search, you should consult the *Film and Video Finder,* the most comprehensive listing of currently

---

AV SHOWMANSHIP

Video and Film

First, here are some generic tips that apply equally to the enhancement of video or film presentations:

❑ Check lighting, seating, and volume control to be sure that everyone can see and hear the presentation.

❑ Get students mentally prepared by briefly reviewing previous related study and evoking questions about today's topic.

❑ List on the chalkboard the main points to be covered in the presentation.

❑ Preview any new vocabulary.

❑ Most important, get involved in the program yourself. Watch attentively and respond when the presenter asks for a response. Be a good role model. Highlight major points by adding them to the chalkboard during the lesson.

❑ Support the presentation with meaningful follow-up activities.

Second, here are showmanship tips that apply specifically to film showings:

❑ Many classrooms have a wall-mounted screen in the front of the room. In some classrooms, unfortunately, the door is near the front of the room and often has a large window in it or a window area beside it. If light from the hall interferes with the brightness of the projected image, you may have to cover part or all of the window area with poster board or butcher paper. If this is not possible, move the projector closer to the screen to get a brighter picture. Remember that a smaller, brighter image is better than a larger, dimmer one.

❑ You should always set the focus and note the correct sound level before the class assembles; then turn the volume knob back down to zero and run the film back to the beginning. Some films have focus and sound-level adjustment footage before the start of the film. If so, you can properly set focus and sound before you reach the beginning of the film.

❑ It is *not* good showmanship to project the leader (the strip of film with the number countdown on it). The first image the audience should see is the title or opening scene of the film.

❑ When ready, start the projector, turn on the lamp, and turn the volume knob to the predetermined level (this is particularly important when the film has no introductory music). Fine adjust the focus and sound after you start the projector.

❑ Most projectors must run a few seconds before the sound system stabilizes. Therefore, if you stop the film to discuss a particular sequence, the viewers may miss a few seconds of narration or dialogue when you start the projector. If you do this, turn the volume knob down, back up the film a few feet, start the projector, turn on the lamp, and then turn up the sound.

❑ When the film is over, turn off the lamp, turn down the sound, and stop the projector. Run the rest of the film footage through after class. Rewind the film if you are going to show it again. If you are not showing it again, and if you used the same size reel the film came on, you need not rewind the film. The agency you got it from will rewind the film during routine inspection. Before putting the film back in the container, fasten down the end of the film with a piece of tape. The film normally arrives with the film held down with tape. Peel it off and stick it on the projection cart so that you can use it later to hold the end down. The film is better protected when this is done.

THE CUTTING EDGE

Desktop Editing of Video

Standard video editing equipment is very expensive. Recent developments in chip technology, however, make it possible to edit videotape, and even create special effects, by simply installing a special circuit board called a "card" in a personal computer.

One card, developed by NewTek for the Amiga computer, allows the addition of special effects such as dissolves, wipes, and fades to live or recorded video. The card also makes it possible to superimpose images from different video sources, including its own character generator for titles and captions. Even color characteristics can be manipulated by the card.

Several cards are available that can rearrange segments of a videotape. With these cards the operator can select specific parts of various tapes, store them, and then rearrange them in the desired sequence. If the new arrangement is not effective, you can just re-edit.

It is not an exaggeration to say that the right combination of cards makes it possible to do studio production without the studio. Corporate training programs with their situation-specific needs are already exploring the possibilities. Education institutions will be able to produce instructional video for local curriculum needs such as community study in the primary grades. Schools and colleges could buy footage from several companies and repurpose the footage to make their own instructional videos. Student-produced videos will become more common and much more sophisticated. These cards could revolutionize the production of motion media in education and in corporate settings.

---

available films; it provides listings by subject. (Other more specialized film catalogs are mentioned in Appendix A.)

Appraising Videos and Films.

After you have located some potentially useful films or videos, you will want to preview them and appraise them. Some schools and organizations have standard appraisal forms

Figure 7.19
Private as well as public schools pool their resources to build video and film collections. Shown is Carolyn Fisher with part of the video collection she oversees for the Independent Schools Multi-Media Center, New York City.

ready to use. Some of these are meticulously detailed, covering every possible factor; others are much more perfunctory. A good appraisal form is one that is brief enough not to be intimidating but complete enough to help individuals choose materials that may be useful not only for now but for future applications. It should also stand as a public record that can be used to justify the purchase or rental of specific titles. The "Appraisal Checklist: Video and Film" (page 214) includes the most commonly used criteria, particularly those that research indicates really do make a difference. You may wish to use it as is or adapt it to your particular needs.

Teaching with Motion Media

The next step after selecting your materials is to put them into actual use in the classroom.

Preview. Films and videocassettes should be previewed for appraisal and selection, but they should also be checked after they arrive in the classroom. Avoid potential embarrassment by making sure that the film on the reel is the one that you ordered and that it contains the subject matter and treatment that you expected.

Prepare the Environment.
Before students can learn from any media presentation, they first have to be able to see it and hear it! Provide proper lighting, seating, and volume control. These elements are described in detail in Chapter 11.

Prepare the Audience. Research in educational psychology as well as the practical experiences of thousands of teachers in all sorts of settings demonstrate that learning is greatly enhanced when learners are prepared for the coming activity.

To start the warm-up before the video/film lesson, review previous related study. Help students see how today's lesson fits into the total picture. Create a need to know. Stimulate curiosity by asking questions, and evoke questions the students would like to have answered on the subject.

Clarify the objectives of the lesson. Mention specific things to look for in the presentation. It helps to list such cues on the chalkboard or on a handout so that students can

From *Movement in Classical Dance,* Indiana University Audio-Visual Center.

refer to them as the lesson proceeds (and during the follow-up activities). If large amounts of new information are being presented, give students some advance organizers, or memory hooks on which they can hang the new ideas. Be sure to preview any new vocabulary as needed.

Present the Material.

A well-designed video/film presentation will call for frequent student participation. By responding yourself, you provide an example the students will follow. Learners are quick to detect and act according to your attitude toward the material. Many studies have indicated that the instructor's attitude—often conveyed nonverbally—significantly affects students' learning from media.

Situate yourself so that you can observe learner reactions. Watch for clues indicating difficulties or boredom. Note individual reactions for possible use in the follow-up discussion. Deal with individual discipline problems as quickly and unobtrusively as possible.

Require Learner Participation.

If active participation was not explicitly built into the video/film program it is all the more important to stimulate response after the presentation. The ability to generalize new knowledge and transfer it to real-life situations depends on learner practice under a variety of conditions. The possibilities for follow-up activities are virtually limitless. A few of the common techniques are

❑ *Discussion.* Question-and-answer sessions, buzz groups, panel discussions, debates
❑ *Dramatization.* Role playing, skits, oral presentations

Figure 7.20
Preview the material.

Figure 7.21
Prepare the environment.

Figure 7.22
Prepare the audience.

Figure 7.23
Present the material.

Figure 7.24
Postviewing discussion is an integral part of the total lesson, especially when using affectively oriented video and film materials.

Figure 7.25
Video recording in the field is made easier and more flexible with modern camcorders.

Figure 7.26
The camcorder quickly makes any classroom into a micro-teaching site.

❑ *Projects.* Experiments, reports, exhibits, models, demonstrations, drawings, story-writing, bulletin boards, media productions

Evaluate. Assessment of student learning can be carried out informally by observing performance during the follow-up activities. Individual projects can be good indicators of successful learning. In many cases, though, more formal testing serves a valuable purpose. First, tests that are followed by feedback of correct answers can provide an efficient review and summary of the main points of the lesson. Second, objective tests can help pinpoint gaps that need to be followed up in the classroom, and they can identify individuals who need remedial help. In this way, the instructor can complement the media component by catering to individual differences in ways the media cannot.

Local Video Design and Production

A feature that separates video from many of the other audiovisual media is that the instructor is not limited to off-the-shelf materials but can with reasonable ease prepare custom materials to fit local needs.[9] Do-it-yourself television has become commonplace since the popularization of the battery-operated portable video recording systems. This technological advance has liberated video production from the confines of the engineer-dominated studio. More recently, the development of the camcorder (camera and recorder built into a single book-size unit) has increased the ease and portability of ½-inch recording (Figure 7.25). It allows video production to be taken into the field, wherever that might be: the science laboratory, the classroom, the counseling office, the athletic field, the factory assembly line, the hospital, the neighborhood, even the home (Figure 7.26). Equally important, the simplicity of the system has made it feasible for nonprofessionals, instructors, and students alike, to create their own video materials.

Locally produced video can be used for virtually any of the purposes described earlier in relation to

---

[9] A helpful, well-illustrated guide for the beginning video producer is Mendel Sherman, *Videographing the Pictorial Sequence* (Washington, DC: Association for Educational Communications and Technology, 1991).

still pictures, audio, and film; but its unique capability is to capture sight and sound for immediate playback. So this medium would fit best with activities that are enhanced by immediate feedback: group dynamics sessions, athletic practice, skills training, and interpersonal techniques.

Other applications that emphasize the local aspect of local video production are

❑ Dramatization of student stories, songs, and poems

❑ Student documentaries of school or neighborhood issues

❑ Preservation of local folklore

❑ Demonstrations of science experiments and safety drills

❑ Replays of field trips for in-class follow-up

❑ Career information on local businesses

Of course, many organizations have more elaborate facilities than simple single-camera field units. But closed-circuit TV studios and the like are the domain of the media specialist or engineer. Our focus is on the typical sort of system that instructors might expect to be using by themselves.

COMPONENTS OF THE SINGLE-CAMERA SYSTEM

Camera

The heart of the portable video camera is the pickup tube, which is basically a vacuum tube that converts light rays into electronic signals that are transmitted through a cable to the video recorder. The camera may be a viewfinder type. The viewfinder camera is so named because it has built into it a small TV set that allows the operator to monitor the image being received by the pickup tube. Even small hand-held cameras typically contain built-in viewfinders with one-inch screens. The nonviewfinder camera costs several hundred dollars less since it lacks the built-in monitor. It may be used as a fixed camera, however, and it can be used for other local production purposes if it is hooked up to a separate monitor, allowing the operator to aim and focus the camera according to the image shown in the monitor.

Microphone

Hand-held cameras usually come with a microphone built into the front of the camera. This microphone has automatic level control, a feature that automatically adjusts the volume to keep the sound at an audible level. The camera, so to speak, "hears" as well as "sees." The problem is that these microphones amplify all sounds within their range, including shuffling feet, coughing, street noises, and equipment noise, along with the sounds that are wanted. You may, therefore, want to bypass the built-in microphone by plugging in a separate microphone better suited to your particular purpose.

A video camera and separate video recorder for a small studio setup

In selecting a microphone, remember that television is more than pictures. Indeed, the audio track usually carries more critical information than the visual. (If you doubt this, try watching your favorite TV show with the sound turned off.) So the selection and handling of the microphone are of vital importance. The best advice is to think of your portable video system as an audio recorder plus a video recorder, and to make the same careful preparations as you would for an audio recording session.

The lavalier, or neck mike, is a good choice when a single speaker is being recorded. It can be clipped to a tie or dress, hung around the neck, or even hidden under light clothing. A desk stand may be used to hold a microphone for a speaker or several discussants seated at a table. The microphone might be unidirectional or omnidirectional, depending on the number and seating arrangements of the speakers. For situations in which there is unwanted background noise or the speaker is moving, a highly directional microphone should be used, usually held by hand and pointed toward the sound source.

Monitor/Receiver

The final major component of the single-camera video tape recorder (VTR) system is the monitor/receiver, the device on which the recording is played back. The name is derived from the dual capabilities these units usually possess. Television signals may be sent through cables in the form of a video signal, as in a closed-circuit TV studio. A monitor is a TV set built to pick up video signals; a receiver is a TV set built to pick up radio frequencies. A monitor/receiver is a unit especially adapted to receive both. The flick of a switch allows it to go from off-air pickup to playback of a VTR connected to it by cable.

Recording Setup for the Single-Camera System

Here are some tips for arranging and using equipment for single-camera VTR recording.

1. The monitor/receiver and recorder are set on a sturdy mobile cart. This allows easy movement of the equipment around the room. The cart can be swiveled around so that the monitor/receiver faces the camera operator (to allow monitoring when a nonviewfinder camera is being used). In most cases it is advisable to turn the monitor/receiver away from on-camera performers to avoid distracting them during recording. It can easily be swiveled back for later instant replay viewing.

2. The camera is mounted on a sturdy, wheeled tripod, maximizing mobility and stable support.

3. The camera is outfitted with a zoom lens, an expensive option, but one that adds great flexibility to the system. The *zoom lens,* having a variable focal length, can be adjusted to provide a wide-angle view, a medium view, or a close-up view with just a twist of the wrist. You should, however, resist the impulse to zoom in and out during a shot unless there is very good reason for doing so.

4. The camera and mobile cart are placed close to the wall. This arrangement helps reduce the likelihood of passersby tripping over the profusion of cables that connect all the components to each other and to the power source.

5. The camera is aimed away from the window (or other bright light source). Cameras used in this sys-

A generalized setup for single-camera recording

tem usually are equipped with automatic light-level control enabling them to adjust automatically to the brightest light striking the lens. If there is a window in back of your subject, the camera will adjust to that light, thus throwing your subject into shadowy darkness. An important caution when recording outdoors: one of the greatest hazards to the pickup tube in your camera is exposure to direct sunlight. Aiming at the sun can cause its image to be burned into the pickup tube, possibly causing irreparable damage.

6. The subjects are well lighted. If natural light is insufficient, you may supplement it with incandescent or fluorescent lighting in the room. Today's pickup tubes oper-

ate well with a normal level of artificial light.

7. The camera is positioned so that the faces of all subjects can be seen. A common mistake in taping a classroom scene is to place the camera at the back of the room. This provides a nice full-face view of the teacher, but makes reaction shots of the students nearly impossible to see. Placement of the camera at the side of the classroom is a reasonable compromise when recording classroom interaction.

8. A desk-stand microphone is used. This allows pickup of the voices of all subjects, while reducing the pickup of unwanted background noises.

❑ **APPRAISAL CHECKLIST**
Video and Film

Title _____

Series Title (if applicable) _____

Source _____

Date _____ **Cost** _____ **Length** _____

Subject Area _____

Intended Audience _____

Objectives (stated or implied)

Brief Description

Entry Capabilities Required

❑ Prior subject-matter knowledge/vocabulary

❑ Reading ability

❑ Mathematical ability

❑ Other:

Format

❑ 16mm film

❑ ¾ videocassette

❑ ½-inch VHS videocassette

❑ ½-inch Beta videocassette

❑ Videodisc

Rating	High		Medium		Low	Comments
Relevance to objectives	❑	❑	❑	❑	❑	
Accuracy of information	❑	❑	❑	❑	❑	
Likely to arouse/maintain interest	❑	❑	❑	❑	❑	
Technical quality	❑	❑	❑	❑	❑	
Promotes participation/involvement	❑	❑	❑	❑	❑	
Evidence of effectiveness (e.g., field-test results)	❑	❑	❑	❑	❑	
Free from objectionable bias	❑	❑	❑	❑	❑	
Pacing appropriate for audience	❑	❑	❑	❑	❑	
Use of cognitive learning aids (e.g., overview, cues, summary)	❑	❑	❑	❑	❑	

Strong Points

Weak Points

Reviewer _____

Position _____

Recommended Action _____ **Date** _____

ANALYZE LEARNERS

General Characteristics

The class is a self-contained one with twenty-nine fifth graders (sixteen girls, thirteen boys) in an urban elementary school. The average age is ten years; the average reading level is fourth grade.

The class has an ethnic and racial mixture typical of an urban setting. Seventeen come from single-parent families.

The students are lower middle class in socioeconomic status. Motivation is usually a challenge with this class.

Entry Competencies

Regarding today's topic, the Panama Canal, awareness is low. In yesterday's discussion of Central America only Nicaragua and El Salvador were mentioned without prompting. There is an old barge canal on the north side of town, so many students were able to identify canals as human-built waterways but were vague about their purposes.

STATE OBJECTIVES

The fifth grade social studies students will be able to

1. Locate the Panama Canal on a wall map of North and South America.

2. Explain the main advantage of the Panama Canal as a shortcut between the Atlantic and Pacific oceans.

3. Visually recognize a canal, distinguishing it from other waterways.

4. Discuss the Panama Canal's historic importance, citing at least its commercial and military advantages and the achievement of overcoming the obstacles to its construction.

5. Demonstrate that they value the cooperative effort represented by the building of the Panama Canal by participating actively in a group project.

SELECT MEDIA AND MATERIALS

The teacher surveys the *Film and Video Finder* under the topic "Panama Canal" and finds four titles that look promising. Two of these are in the school district film library. After previewing both, she selects one because the content and vocabulary come closest to the level of her class. She notes that the political description of Panama is no longer accurate, so she prepares some comments to correct it.

UTILIZE MATERIALS

Because motivating interest is predictably difficult, she begins to stimulate students' curiosity by rolling down the wall map of North and South America and asking how a traveler in the days before airplanes and automobiles might get from New York to San Francisco. What if you were a merchant who wanted to ship tools and work clothes to the miners of the gold rush in Alaska in 1898? What if you were an admiral needing to move his fleet rapidly from the Atlantic to the Pacific?

Having identified the problem, the teacher states that the film is going to show the solution developed early in the twentieth century. She lists several key questions on the overhead projector.

After reviewing the questions by having students take turns reading them, she asks them to look for the answers to these questions while viewing the film. She then shows the film.

REQUIRE LEARNER PARTICIPATION

After showing the film, the teacher divides the students into groups of three to discuss the questions. Each group elects a recorder who will write the answers agreed to by the group.

After a few minutes of discussion the teacher brings the whole class back together in a large group and calls on two or three recorders to give their answers to question 1, with the whole class reacting to these. This process is repeated for the rest of the questions.

The teacher concludes by going back to question 3, focusing on how the builders of the canal succeeded because of their systematic plan and determination to overcome all obstacles. If we were going to construct a display to tell the story of the Panama Canal, what steps would we have to carry out? What ideas would we put into our display? With questions such as these the teacher builds interest in constructing a display, works out a time line, and organizes the students into groups to carry out the assignment.

EVALUATE AND REVISE

The teacher collects the recorders' written notes and checks to see how accurately the questions were answered. She makes note of test items keyed to the objectives to be included on the written test at the end of this unit. As students work on the display project, she will be able to check the accuracy of the information being put into the display and, regarding the affective objective(s), she will circulate among the work groups to assess the enthusiasm exhibited in their work.

REFERENCES

Print References

Adams, Dennis. "Visual Environments: Simple Video Production Techniques." *School Arts* (December 1989):14–16.

_____ . "A Low Cost Production Model for Small Format Video Production." *TechTrends* (January 1988):17–20.

Arwady, Joseph W. "The Oral Introduction to the Instructional Film: A Closer Look." *Educational Technology* (July 1980):18–22.

Bragg, Richelle Rae, and McWilliams, Micki. "Cultural Exchange: A Video Pen Pal Program." *Journal of Geography* (July–August 1989):150–51.

Cartwright, Steve R. *Secrets of Successful Video Training*. White Plains, NY: Knowledge Industry Publications, 1990.

Cassidy, J. M. "Lights, Camera, Animation!" *School Arts* (February 1984):36–38.

Choat, Ernest, and Griffin, Harry. "Modular Video with Children Aged 3 to 11." *British Journal of Educational Technology* (May 1988):123–30.

Compesi, Ronald J. *Small Format Television Production*. Boston: Allyn and Bacon, 1990.

Considine, David M. "The Video Boom's Impact on Social Studies: Implications, Applications, and Resources." *Social Studies* (November–December 1989):229–34.

Davis, Shawn. "The Eyes Have It." *Gallaudet Today* 18, no. 4, (1988):30–31.

DeLuca, Stuart M. *Instructional Video*. Boston: Focal Press, 1991.

Gaffney, Maureen, and Laybourne, Gerry Bond. *What to Do When the Lights Go On: A Comprehensive Guide to 16mm Films and Related Activities*. Phoenix, AZ: Oryx Press, 1981.

Gayeski, Diane M. *Corporate and Instructional Video*. 2nd ed. Englewood Cliffs, NJ: Prentice-Hall, 1991.

Goss, Jeanne. "Bibliography of Resources for Media Centers." *Sightlines* (Summer 1990):29–32.

Griffin, C. W. "Teaching Shakespeare on Video." *English Journal* (November 1989):40–43.

Hedley, Carolyn N. "What's New in Software? Videocassettes for Parenting." *Journal of Reading, Writing, and Learning Disabilities International* 5, no. 4 (1989):363–68.

Hughes, Mary Anne. "Communicating with Video." *School Library Media Activities* (March 1988):25–27.

Jones, Emily S., and Dratfield, Leo. "40 Years of Memorable Films." *Sightlines* (Fall–Winter 1983–84):15–17.

Kelly, Maureen E., and Hauser, Doreen A. "Time-Saving Training with Videos." *Vocational Education Journal* (May 1990):30–31.

McDonald, Bruce, and Orsini, Leslie. *Basic Language Skills Through Films: An Instructional Program for Secondary School Students*. Littleton, CO: Libraries Unlimited, 1983.

Marsh, Cythia. "Some Observations on the Use of Video in the Teaching of Modern Foreign Languages." *British Journal of Language Teaching* (Spring 1989):13–17.

Melamed, Lanie. "Sleuthing Media Truths: Becoming Media Literate." *History and Social Science Teacher* (Summer 1989):189–93.

Pelletier, Raymond J. "Prompting Spontaneity by Means of the Video Camera in the Beginning Foreign Language Class." *Foreign Language Annals* (May 1990):227–33.

Regina, Theresa E. "Composing Skills and Television." *English Journal* (November 1988):50–52.

Rickelman, Robert J., and Henk, William A. "Children's Literature and Audio/Visual Technologies." *Reading Teacher* (May 1990):682–84.

Rockman, Saul. "If Not Now, When? The Rationale for Technology in the History/Social Science Classroom." *Social Studies Review* (Spring 1986):30–34.

Sherman, Mendel. *Videographing the Pictorial Sequence*. Washington, DC: Association for Educational Communications and Technology, 1991.

Smith, Barry. "How to Use Video in Training." *Journal of European Industrial Training* 12, no. 7 (1988):2–67.

Smith, Jean. "Teaching Research Skills Using Video: An Undergraduate Library Approach." *RSR/Reference Services Review* 16, no. 2 (1988):109–14.

Squires, Nancy, and Inlander, Robin. "A Freireian-Inspired Video Curriculum for At-Risk High School Students." *English Journal* (February 1990):49–56.

Thompson, Nancy G. "Media and Mind: Imaging as an Active Process." *English Journal* (November 1988):47–49.

Tibbs, Pat. "Video Creation for Junior High Language Arts." *Journal of Reading* (March 1989):558–59.

Turner, Doris. "The Art Teacher's New Tool: The Video Camcorder." *School Arts* (December 1989):27–28.

Urban, Marty. "Video Biographies: Reading, Researching, and Recording." *English Journal* (December 1989):58–59.

Vick, Nancy H. "Freedom to View: Coping with Censorship." *Sightlines* (Spring 1981):5–6.

Watson, Robert. *Film and Television in Education: An Aesthetic Approach to the Moving Image*. New York: Falmer Press, 1990.

Audiovisual References

Basic Film Terms: A Visual Dictionary. Santa Monica, CA: Pyramid Films, 1970. 16mm or videocassette. 15 minutes.

Basic Television Terms: A Video Dictionary. Santa Monica, CA: Pyramid Films, 1977. 16mm or videocassette. 17 minutes.

Camera Techniques for Video. Great Falls, MT: Video International Publishers, 1980. Videocassette. 30 minutes.

Claymation. Santa Monica, CA: Pyramid Films, 1980. 16mm or videocassette. 20 minutes.

The Eye Hears and the Ear Sees. Montreal, Canada: National Film Board of Canada, 1970. 16mm or videocassette. 59 minutes.

Forty-Eight Hours: Lights, Camera, War—The Making of the Film "Glory." New York: Carousel Films, 1988. 16mm or videocassette. 43 minutes.

Frame by Frame: The Art of Animation. Santa Monica, CA: Pyramid Films, 1973. 16mm or videocassette. 13 minutes.

Learning with Film and Video. Los Angeles, CA: Churchill Films, 1988. 16mm or videocassette. 20 minutes.

Making "Do the Right Thing." New York: Icarus Films, 1989. 16mm or videocassette. 58 minutes.

Professor Bunruckle's Guide to Pixilation. Van Nuys, CA: AIMS Media, 1988. 16mm or videocassette. 16 minutes.

Video Encyclopedia of the Twentieth Century. New York: CEL Educational Resources, 1986. 75 videocassettes or 38 videodiscs; index; and four-volume reference set.

Videotape-Disc-Or . . . Columbia, SC: Educational Program Service, 1983. Videocassette. 30 minutes.

Visual Effects: Wizardry on Film. Los Angeles, CA: Churchill Films, 1988. 16mm or videocassette. 29 minutes.

All of the following ½-inch VHS videocassettes are available from Audiovisual Center Marketing, C215 Seashore Hall, University of Iowa, Iowa City, IA 52242.

Single Camera VCR System. 1983. 7 minutes.

16mm Projector. 1983. 7 minutes.

Romancing the Eiki: The Story of a Slotloading Projector. 1988. 11 minutes.

Pre-production Planning for Video. 1990. 10 minutes.

Scriptwriting: Filling the Empty Page. 1990. 16 minutes.

Recording the Video Image. 1990. 18 minutes.

Videotape Editing. 1990. 8 minutes.

Operating the Camcorder. 1990. 8 minutes.

POSSIBLE PROJECTS

7–A. Preview a film and appraise it using a form such as the "Appraisal Checklist: Video and Film" found in this chapter.

7–B. Observe a eacher using a film or video program in a classroom situation and critique the teacher's practices.

7–C. Use one or more of the selection aids described in Appendix A to compile a list of films or video programs available on a topic of interest to you.

7–D. Plan a lesson in a subject area of your choice in which you will incorporate the use of a film or video program. Follow the outline shown in the "Blueprint" in this chapter.

7–E. Preview one of the documentary films described in this chapter. Prepare a review, either written (about 700 words) or recorded on audiotape (approximately five minutes long). Briefly summarize the content of the film and describe your reaction to it.

8

Computers

OUTLINE

Computers and Individualized Instruction

Background on Computers in Education and Training

Advantages of Computers

Limitations of Computers

Roles of Computers in Education and Training

    The Computer as an Object of Instruction

    The Computer as a Tool for Instruction

    Computer-Assisted Instruction

    Computer-Managed Instruction

    Computer Networks

    Computer-Generated Instructional Materials

    Computer-Based Instructional Design

    Integrated Learning Systems

    Computers in the Media Center

Computer Software

    Selecting Software

    Using Computers in the Classroom

Computer Hardware

    Basic Computer Components

    Selecting Hardware

OBJECTIVES

After studying this chapter, you should be able to

1. Describe the development of computer technology and its applications to instruction over the past four decades.

2. Discuss five advantages and five limitations of computers.

3. Generate examples of the use of the computer (a) as an object of instruction and (b) as a tool during instruction.

4. Distinguish between computer-assisted instruction (CAI) and computer-managed instruction (CMI).

5. Compare and contrast the six methods of computer-assisted instruction in terms of the role of the teacher, the role of the computer, and the role of the learner, including a specific example of courseware in each mode.

6. Generate examples of the use of the computer for computer-managed instruction to (a) provide computer-based testing, (b) prescribe media, materials, and activities, and (c) keep records.

7. Discuss two applications of computer networks for instruction including two advantages and two limitations of computer networks.

8. Describe two applications, two advantages, and two limitations of integrated learning systems.

9. Explain how computers can assist in generation of instructional materials, instructional design, and media centers.

10. Outline the process (steps) and materials needed for selecting computer-based materials.

11. Apply the "Appraisal Checklist" to a sample CAI program.

12. Identify and briefly describe the five common components of a computer system, given a generalized schematic diagram.

13. Describe four computer storage formats including the physical characteristics and storage capacity of each.

14. Suggest five criteria besides cost that might be important considerations in purchasing a computer for instructional purposes.

LEXICON

computer-assisted instruction (CAI)

computer-managed instruction (CMI)

computer literacy

microprocessor

database

computer network

integrated learning system (ILS)

software

courseware

hardware

ROM (Read Only Memory)

RAM (Random Access Memory)

CD-ROM (Compact Disc—Read Only Memory)

The computer with its virtually instantaneous response to student input, its extensive capacity to store and manipulate information, and its unmatched ability to serve many individual students simultaneously is widely used in instruction. The computer has the ability to control and manage a wide variety of media and learning material—films, filmstrips, video, slides, audiotapes, and printed information. The computer can also record, analyze, and react to student responses that are typed on a keyboard or indicated with a mouse. Some display screens react to the touch of a student's finger.

There are two types of computer-based instruction: *computer-assisted instruction (CAI)* and *computer-managed instruction (CMI)*. In CAI the student interacts directly with the computer which presents the instructional material and controls its sequence. In CMI the computer helps the instructor administer and guide the instructional process. The student does not necessarily interact with the computer system. The computer stores information about students and about relevant instructional materials which can be retrieved rapidly. The learner may be on-line to take tests. In addition, the computer can diagnose the learning needs of students and prescribe optimal sequences of instruction for them. We will take a closer look at each of these forms of computer-based instruction later in this chapter.

In addition, the computer can be an object of instruction, as in courses on computer science and computer literacy. It also is a tool that can be used during instruction to do complex calculations, data manipulations, and word processing. Other educational and training roles of computers will also be described.

Literacy once implied exclusively the ability to read and write, that is, verbal literacy. With the rapid spread of computer use since the mid-1970s came an equally rapid flowering of public awareness of the im-

Figure 8.1
Computers have become pervasive in education and training. Most learners have access to and are influenced by computer-based instruction.

portance of computers in society. Out of this heightened popular awareness emerged another type of literacy—*computer literacy*—referring to the ability to understand and to use computers.

Most computer literacy instruction incorporates three types of objectives—knowledge, skill, and attitude. The knowledge objectives typically include computer terminology, identifying components, describing applications, and analyzing social and ethical issues that arise in using computers. Skill objectives typically include the ability to use computers for a variety of applications, such as word processing, spreadsheets, and information retrieval. More advanced applications include desktop publishing and problem solving. Attitude objectives focus primarily on acceptance of the computer as a valuable tool in the individual's personal and professional life. Further objectives might deal with appreciating the importance of computers as productivity

tools in education and the workplace.

COMPUTERS AND INDIVIDUALIZED INSTRUCTION

The emergence of computer technology coincided with a heightened awareness among educators of the importance of individualization. Research into new instructional methods consistently indicates that certain treatments work for certain people under certain conditions. There are no panaceas.

The great quest in the field of media and technologies of instruction is to find ways of matching individual learners with the appropriate subject matter, pitched at the right level, and presented in a compatible medium at the optimal pace in the most meaningful sequence.

True individualization imposes a tremendous burden of decision making and resource management. One instructor might approach an ideal level of individualization with a handful of students. But when dealing with twenty, thirty, forty, or more students, the logistics of individualization overwhelm any single teacher's capacity. The computer gives promise of overcoming these and other logistical barriers to the individualization of instruction.

BACKGROUND ON COMPUTERS IN EDUCATION AND TRAINING

According to diSessa we are now in the middle stage of a computer revolution in education.[1] The first stage of the revolution "started in the realization that computers could revolutionize the way we think about thinking and the way we deal with learning." The current stage, the middle stage, is "getting computers into the schools." In the next, or third, stage, diSessa predicts we will see computers used as "tools not only to relieve the burden of mundane activities, but to elevate concern above details, such as symbol manipulation, toward important strategic and problem solving knowledge."

The possibility of educational applications was mainly conjectural during the 1950s and 1960s, although important instructional experiments were conducted. These experiments were spurred by the development of FORTRAN, a more easily learned computer language, and B. F. Skinner's research in programmed instruction. The step-by-step format of linear programmed instruction lent itself well to the logical "mentality" of the computer. The factors of cost, hardware reliability, and the availability of adequate materials remained major bar-

riers to the widespread adoption of computers for instruction.

The advent of the microcomputer in 1975 altered this picture dramatically. The microcomputer was made possible by the invention of the *microprocessor* (Figure 8.3), a tiny chip of silicon that contains within itself all the information-processing ability of those roomfuls of original computer circuitry. The development of the silicon chip reduced the cost of computers to a truly remarkable degree. The microcomputer was an

Figure 8.2
The mainframe computer with its massive components was the norm before the advent of the microcomputer.

Figure 8.3
The tiny microprocessor fostered the microcomputer revolution. Chips like this one are used in home appliances, automobiles, toys, and hundreds of other devices, giving each a "brain" of its own.

---

[1] diSessa, A. A. "The Third Revolution in Computers and Education," *Journal of Research in Science Teaching* 24, no. 4 (1987):343–67.

In 1960 University of Illinois administrators appointed a committee to suggest ways that the university's computer could be used for research in education because the military no longer needed it to solve radar problems. The educators thought the engineers didn't know anything about teaching, and the engineers thought the educators didn't know anything about technology! Consequently, the committee came to the only possible conclusion under the circumstances; they could not agree on any projects worth funding.

One of the researchers in the computer lab who was not a member of the committee said, "That's crazy! Give me two weeks, and I will come back with a proposal." Within days the researcher prepared a proposal to develop a course in engineering, a subject with which he was familiar, with an eye to educational considerations. The course was to run on the computers already in the lab, which took care of the technical considerations.

The proposal was approved. The researcher hired a technician to build the hardware and a mathematician to help with the programming. Within one month they had developed an interactive video terminal connected to the computer to provide instruction. They developed programs for college-level computer science and high school mathematics. With the help of a friend, they soon added a program to teach French.

The system was built cheaply and hastily, but it worked. The keyboard had only sixteen keys. The video display was a cast-off television set that could no longer pick up broadcasts. It cost ten dollars. The system was the first to display slides and computer graphics. The slide-selection process was very primitive. A technician in another room picked them out and displayed them in front of the camera as fast as he could.

The researcher was Donald L. Bitzer. The system was PLATO—Programmed Logic for Automatic-Teaching Operations. Primitive as it was, the original version had all of

Early PLATO terminal

the elements that were to make PLATO unique: computerized instruction, an authoring system designed to make writing computerized instruction easy, and a learning management system that continually tested the student's understanding of the material and prescribed additional materials if the student needed more help.

Today more than 15,000 hours of PLATO courseware cover the span from kindergarten through graduate school in every conceivable subject area including business and industry training. The course materials are available at individual terminals throughout the world, connected through telephone lines to a powerful mainframe computer at the University of Illinois. Control Data now sells PLATO materials for use on its personal computers, and has come a long way from an indecisive committee and a ten-dollar television set!

immediate success in the marketplace, especially for use in small businesses and in the home (Figure 8.4).

ADVANTAGES OF COMPUTERS

The interactive nature of computers in instruction underlies most of their advantages. As an active mode

of instruction, they require learner participation (the R of the ASSURE model). Specific advantages are the following:

❑ Simply allowing students to learn at their own pace produces significant time savings over conventional classroom instruction. Computer-based instruction allows students some control over

the rate and sequence of their learning (individualization).

❑ High-speed personalized responses to learner actions yield a high rate of reinforcement.

❑ The patient, personal manner that can be programmed provides a more positive affective climate, especially for slower learners. Mistakes, which are inevitable,

- are not exposed to peers and therefore are not embarrassing.
- Computer-assisted instruction is effective with special learners—at-risk students, students with diverse ethnic backgrounds, and disabled students—because their special needs can be accommodated and instruction proceeds at an appropriate pace.
- Color, music, and animated graphics can add realism and appeal to drill exercises, laboratory activities, simulations, and so on.
- The record-keeping ability of the computer makes individualized instruction feasible; individual prescriptions can be prepared for all students (particularly mainstreamed special students), and their progress can be monitored.
- Computers can provide coverage of a growing knowledge base associated with the information explosion. They can manage all types of information: graphic, text, audio, and video. More information is put easily at the instructor's disposal. Computers also provide a broad diversity of learning experiences. These learning experiences can utilize a variety of instructional methods and can be at the level of basic instruction, remedial, or enrichment.

- The computer provides reliable and consistent instruction from learner to learner, regardless of the teacher or trainer, the time of the day, or the location.
- Computer-based instruction can improve efficiency and effectiveness. Effectiveness refers to improved learner achievement, whereas efficiency means achieving objectives in less time or at lower cost. Efficiency is very important in business and industrial applications and is becoming increasingly important in educational settings.
- One serendipitous effect of working with computers is that they literally force us to communicate with them in an orderly and logical way. The computer user must learn to communicate with explicit, exact instructions and responses. Any departure from precision is rejected by the computer.
- Computer users learn keyboarding or typing skills. Now very young children as well as adults are developing these skills in order to communicate with computers.
- With the advent of easy-to-use authoring systems, some instructors can develop their own cus-

Figure 8.4
Innovative microcomputer systems such as the Macintosh have helped popularize the use of micros in business and homes.

tomized computer-based learning programs.

Summaries of research with students at various levels—elementary, secondary, college, and adult education—show that computer-based instruction generally has positive effects on student achievement. One set of summaries by James Kulik and colleagues concluded that, on the average, computer-based instruction assisted students in raising

Figure 8.5
Computers can be programmed to require learners to interact with other students during instruction.

their achievement test scores by 10 to 18 percentage points compared with conventional instruction.[2]

LIMITATIONS OF COMPUTERS

As we have seen with all the other media and technological innovations, there are always trade-offs to be made and limitations to consider. Some of the major limitations of computers in instruction are as follows:

❑ Careful consideration must be given to the costs and benefits of computers in education and training. Computers, software, and maintenance are the major cost factors, especially if equipment is subjected to heavy use.

❑ Compatibility is a problem. Software developed for one computer system usually cannot be used with another. The ease with which software can be duplicated without permission has inhibited some commercial publishers and private entrepreneurs from producing and marketing high-quality instructional software.

❑ Users, both learners and teachers, may have unrealistic expectations for computer-based instruction. They view computers as magical and expect learning to happen with little or no effort. Learners and teachers derive benefits proportional to their investments.

❑ A limited range of objectives can be taught by computers. Most computer-based instruction does not teach effectively in the affective, motor, or interpersonal skills domain. Even in the cognitive domain, programs tend to teach at the lower levels of knowledge and comprehension.

❑ Design of instructional materials for use with computers can be a laborious task, which often re-

quires a high level of expertise by the developer. Consequently, quality computer-based instruction is expensive.

❑ Creativity may be stifled in computerized instruction. The computer is slavish in its adherence to its program. Creative or original learner responses will be ignored or even rebuked if the program's designer has not anticipated such possibilities.

❑ Computer-based instruction often lacks social interaction. Learners tend to work on their own at a computer, and there is little if any face-to-face interaction with teachers or other learners.

❑ Some learners, especially adult learners, may resist the linear, lockstep control of the learning process typical of computerized instruction. Adult learners may feel they can skim or read pages of a book faster than the computer presents the information.

❑ The novelty associated with CAI in its earlier days seems to be decreasing. As learners become more familiar with computers in the home and the workplace, the newness of the stimulus wears off and has less motivational value.

ROLES OF COMPUTERS IN EDUCATION AND TRAINING

The potential uses of computers in educational settings go far beyond the provision of direct instruction. There is the obvious administrative role of keeping school records, scheduling classes, making out paychecks, and the like. Guidance programs use computers to deliver career planning assistance. In the domain of instruction, though, there are broad classes of applications:

1. Computer as object of instruction
2. Computer as tool for instruction
3. Computer-assisted instruction
4. Computer-managed instruction

Figure 8.6
Intense absorption is a common reaction to learning with a computer.

5. Computer networks
6. Computer-generated instructional materials
7. Computer-based instructional design
8. Integrated learning systems
9. Computers in the media center

The Computer as the Object of Instruction

The computer can itself be the object of instruction. For example, in computer literacy courses students learn "about" computers, and in vocational training trainees learn to use computers on the job for data processing and analysis purposes. In this role, the computer is treated like any other machine one is learning to use.

When a learner is studying computer programming, the computer and the associated software are the objects of instruction. The various programming languages and the techniques for constructing a program using these languages are beyond the scope of this book.

The Computer as a Tool for Instruction

The computer can also serve as a tool during instruction. It can be used by the learner to solve complex mathematical calculations, as a pocket calculator is used, but with increased power and speed. Even a small microcomputer can analyze

---

2 See references at end of chapter under James Kulik and C. -L. C. Kulik.

data, perform repeated calculations, or even gather data when hooked up to laboratory equipment or subjects.

Today personal computers are being used widely for word processing and desktop publishing. More and more students have access to computers with word processing programs which they use to do term papers and assignments. Some students are doing multimedia term papers; they can integrate a variety of media including graphics, sound, and motion for a more complete presentation. Presentation software incorporating the computer and video projection can be used for student presentations. Computers also allow students to communicate with students around the world via electronic mail and to gather data from a variety of sources for projects and reports.

Today's students need to learn to manage information; to retrieve, sort, and organize information; and to evaluate their findings. Students can use databases for inquiry and research. A *database* is a collection of related information organized for quick access to specific data. A telephone book is a printed database. Databases can also be stored in a computer; an example is a list of telephone numbers by name or company. A database is a versatile and easy-to-learn computer tool. It can be thought of as a file cabinet (Figure 8.8).

There are two types of databases. Classroom databases are created by students. Students can design information sheets and questionnaires, collect the data, input relevant facts, and then retrieve them in a variety of ways. The facts selected might include student information, book reports, or sample math problems.

Another type of database is the commercial database. Commercial databases are either purchased on diskettes or accessed via telephone hookup to a computer in another location. The Minnesota Educational Computing Corporation (MECC) sells a *Fifty States* database on dis-

kette that contains information such as population, capital, area, major rivers, and state bird, flower, and tree for all the states. Several companies have developed database materials for use in the classroom (see

"Database Sources" at the end of this chapter). Other larger computer databases are available via telephone and contain medical information, historical data, census figures, and the like.

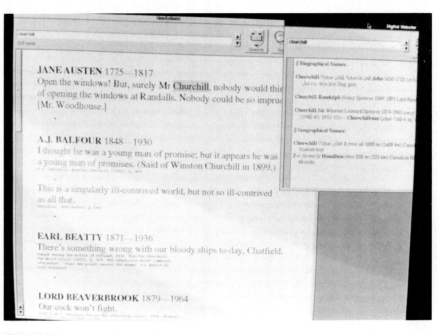

Figure 8.7
Example of a computer database

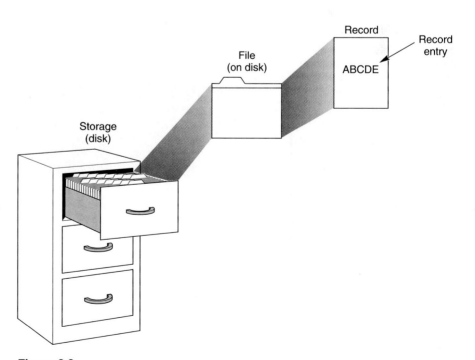

Figure 8.8
A database is used to organize information in a way that it can be easily sorted, ranked, calculated, and stored.

With databases students engage in higher levels of thinking and inquiry skills. They also learn to use databases for research.

In its role as a tool, the computer serves as a sophisticated calculator, typewriter, multimedia composer, presentation aid, communication device, and data retrieval source.

Computer-Assisted Instruction

Computer systems can deliver instruction directly to students by allowing them to interact with lessons programmed into the system; this is referred to as computer-assisted instruction (CAI). The possibilities can best be discussed in terms of the various instructional methods described in Chapter 1. Methods that the computer can facilitate most effectively are drill-and-practice, tutorial, gaming, simulation, discovery, and problem solving. Few programs represent just one of these categories.

Drill-and-Practice Method. The program leads the learner through a series of examples to increase dexterity and fluency in a skill. The computer cannot display impatience and goes ahead only when mastery is shown. Drill-and-practice is predominantly used for math drills, foreign language translating practice, vocabulary-building exercises, and the like. Other drill-and-practice programs, such as *Sentences,* let the learners practice sentence constructions.

Drill-and-practice programs provide a variety of questions with varied formats. The trainee is usually given several tries before the computer presents the correct answer. Several levels of difficulty can be available within the same drill-and-practice program. Positive and negative feedback as well as reinforcement can be included.

Tutorial Method. In the tutorial role, the computer acts as the

MEDIA FILE: *Wordwright*
Drill-and-Practice Program

ence	homogen-	belliger-
tion	empti-	imp-
pictur-	enorm-	able
aspira-	ness	esque
brother-	employ-	ity
hood	depend-	
eous	ment	ish

A word containing
'enorm-' means:
great wickedness

Alice 0
Rich   0
moves 6
time 41

Wordwright is one of a series of courseware packages developed by The Encyclopaedia Britannica Corporation. The *Wordwright* package includes a drill-and-practice lesson on word definitions, as well as a range of other word games and tests. The vocabulary drill-and-practice lesson presents a sequence of ten vocabulary questions. If a student's answer is correct, the machine presents the next question. If a student's answer is incorrect, the machine responds with the correct definition as well as with examples of correct usage. After presenting the ten questions, the computer gives a summary of both the words defined correctly and the words incorrectly defined.

Source: Encyclopaedia Britannica Educational Corporation

MEDIA FILE: *Problem-Solving Strategies*
Tutorial Program

Problem-Solving Strategies is a package of four programs for teaching problem-solving strategies in middle school math classes. The three strategies are trial and error, exhaustive listing, and simplifying the problem. The first two programs, *Diagonals* and *Squares,* are highly interactive tutorials designed for an individual or pair of students. The programs provide experience in applying all three problem-solving strategies.

Source: Minnesota Educational Computing Consortium

teacher. All interaction is between the computer and the learner. One example of the tutorial method is *Problem-Solving Strategies,* which guides learners through the application of three strategies, and provides instruction, practice, and feedback

based on student response (see "Media File" above).

In this method the pattern followed is basically that of branching programmed instruction (see Chapter 12); that is, information is presented in small units followed by a question. The student's response is analyzed by the computer (compared with responses plugged in by the author), and appropriate feedback is given. A complicated network of pathways, or branches, can be programmed. The more alternatives available to the computer, the more adaptive the tutorial can be to individual differences. The extent to which a skilled, live tutor can be approximated depends on the creativity of the program designer.

Gaming Method. In Chapter 13 we discuss the distinction between gaming and simulation. A game activity may or may not entail simulation elements. Likewise, a game may or may not be instructional. It depends on whether or not the skill practiced in the game is an academic one, that is, related to a specified instructional objective, or a training one.

Recreational games can serve a useful purpose in building computer literacy in an enjoyable, nonthreatening manner. But the ultimate goal of useful learning must be kept in mind. Instructors experienced in computer utilization recommend rationing purely recreational game use, using it as a reward for completing other assignments.

Simulation Method. The simulation method of instruction is described in detail in Chapter 13. In this method, the learner confronts an approximation of a real-life situation. It allows realistic practice without the expense or risks otherwise involved.

The computer-based simulation *Operation: Frog* allows a student to dissect and reconstruct a frog using the same "instruments" that would be used in a biology laboratory. The student must remove the twenty-three organs in sequence as in an actual dissection. Help screens and descriptive materials are available at the student's fingertips (see "Blueprint," page 245).

MEDIA FILE: *Language Carnival*
Game

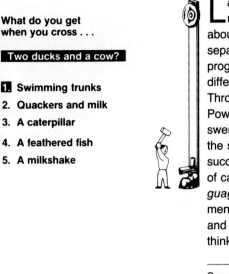

What do you get when you cross . . .

Two ducks and a cow?

1. Swimming trunks
2. Quackers and milk
3. A caterpillar
4. A feathered fish
5. A milkshake

Language Carnival uses an amusement theme to make learning about language fun and exciting. Four separate games are included in each program. Each game is based on a different carnival activity such as "Dart Throw," "Baseball Toss" and "Muscle Power." When students correctly answer questions, a dart pops a balloon, the strongman rings the bell, or other successful outcomes result. The use of carnival games and humor in *Language Carnival* 1 and 2 motivates elementary students to explore, explain, and practice various language and thinking skills.

Source: DLM Teaching Resources

MEDIA FILE: *Decisions, Decisions*
Simulation

Decisions, Decisions is a series of role-playing software packages designed specifically to generate informed discussion and decision making in the classroom using only one computer. The program has a mode for whole-class discussion with the teacher leading the entire group as in a traditional classroom. In addition, *Decisions, Decisions* offers a small-group option for managing a cooperative learning environment. Up to six small groups of students move through the simulation independently directed by the computer.

Source: Tom Snyder Productions

A large number of civilian and military occupations involve the operation or maintenance of complex equipment such as aircraft, manufacturing machines, weapons systems, nuclear power plants, and oil rigs. Major airlines and the military use computer-based simulators to reduce the amount of actual flying time required for training.

Discovery Method. *Discovery* is a general term to describe activities using an inductive approach to learning; that is, presenting problems that the student solves through trial and error or systematic approaches. It approximates laboratory learning outside the classroom.

Using the discovery method in CAI the learner employs an information retrieval strategy to get information from a database. For example, a salesperson interested in learning about competitors' products can select from a set of critical product features, display them on the computer, and draw conclusions about the comparisons of the products.

Some discovery lessons such as *Inquir* analyze large databases of election information, population statistics, or other user-built databases.

Problem-Solving Method. In problem solving, the learner uses previously mastered skills to resolve a challenging problem. The student must examine the data or information presented, clearly define the problem, perhaps state hypotheses, examine the data, and generate a solution. The computer may present the problem. It can manipulate the data at the student's command, maintain a database, and provide feedback when appropriate.

As the learner faces a problem and attempts to solve it, the computer can be used to do the necessary calculations or manipulation of the data or information.

One commercially available problem-solving program is *Memory: A First Step in Problem Solving,* from Sunburst Communications. It provides students in kindergarten through sixth grade with opportunities to practice the skill and strategies involved in problem solving. The program introduces a generic approach to problem solving across all subject areas as well as in common life situations. The goal is not to present a fixed problem-solving model but to promote the use of an individualized, systematic approach in which the student establishes a model that is appropriate to a specific problem,

MEDIA FILE: *Health Hazard Appraisal*
Discovery Program

By asking a variety of questions this discovery program apprises you of your current health status and risks. Of course, the accuracy of the assessment depends on the accuracy of your responses to the questions. The questions relate to current blood pressure, history of serious illness in the family, number of miles driven, use of seat belts, diet, and so on. The computer program analyzes the answers to the questions. The results compare your current chronological age with the age at which you are living your life (health equivalent). Recommendations for improving your life expectancy are also provided.

Source: Pillsbury

MEDIA FILE: *The Factory*
Problem-Solving Program

The *Factory* focuses on several strategies used in problem solving: working backward, analyzing a process, determining a sequence, and applying creativity. The learners are given a square on the computer and three types of machines. The "punch" machine can punch squares or circles, with one, two, or three of each. The "rotation" machine can be programmed to rotate the square 45, 90, 135, or 180 degrees. And the "stripe" machine paints a thin, medium, or thick stripe.

The program has three types of activities. The learners can "test a machine" to see what each option does. They can "build a factory" composed of up to eight machines to make a product of their own design. The most difficult task is to assemble and program a variety of machines in the proper sequence to "duplicate a product" shown on the screen.

Source: WINGS for learning/Sunburst

Table 8.1
Utilization of various CAI methods

Methods	Description	Role of Teacher	Role of Computer	Role of Student	Applications/ Examples
Drill-and-Practice	Content already taught Reviews basic facts and terminology Variety of questions in varied formats Question-answer drills repeated as necessary	Arranges for prior instruction Selects material Matches drill to student Checks progress	Asks questions "Evaluates" student response Provides immediate feedback Records student progress	Practices content already taught Responds to questions Receives confirmation or correction Chooses content and difficulty level	Parts of a microscope Completing balance sheets Vocabulary building Math facts Product knowledge
Tutorial	Presentation of new information Teaches concepts and principles Provides remedial instruction	Selects material Adapts instruction Monitors	Presents information Asks questions Monitors responses Provides remedial feedback Summarizes key points Keeps records	Interacts with computer Sees results Answers questions Asks questions	Clerical training Bank teller training Science Medical procedures Bible study
Gaming	Competitive Drill-and-practice in a motivational format Individual or small group	Sets limits Directs process Monitors results	Acts as competitor, judge, and scorekeeper	Learns facts, strategies, skills Evaluates choices Competes with computer	Fraction games Counting games Spelling games Typing (arcade-type) games
Simulation	Approximates real-life situations Based upon realistic models Individual or small group	Introduces subject Presents background Guides "debriefing"	Plays role(s) Delivers results of decisions Maintains the model and its database	Practices decision making Makes choices Receives results of decisions Evaluates decisions	Troubleshooting History Medical diagnosis Simulators (pilot, driver) Business management Laboratory experiments
Discovery	Inquiry into database Inductive approach Trial and error Tests hypotheses	Presents basic problem Monitors student progress	Presents student with source of information Stores data Permits search procedures	Makes hypotheses Tests guesses Develops principles or rules	Social science Science Food-intake analysis Career choices
Problem Solving	Define problem State hypothesis Examine data Generate solution	Assigns problems Assists students Checks results	Presents problem Manipulates data Maintains database Provides feedback	Defines the problem Sets up the solution Manipulates variables Trial and error	Business Creativity Troubleshooting Mathematics Computer programming

using strategies from a personal repertoire. The multimedia kit includes a chart showing a problem-solving skill matrix, classroom lessons, software summary sheets, program descriptions for each computer disk, computer disks, and a hand puppet for use with younger students.

Another problem-solving program challenges the learner to "manufacture" products according to specifications provided by the computer. There are seventy-two different combinations from which to select. The sequence in which the three types of machines are used is another critical factor. Of course, there are numerous ways to solve each challenging problem presented by the program. (See "Media File: *The Factory.*")

During problem-solving activities students will not only learn about the content under study, but will learn to improve their logical thinking skills. These higher level cognitive processes include reasoning skills and logical and critical thinking. The primary reason for teaching elementary computer languages, such as Logo, is not for the students to learn programming itself, but to enable them to use the computer for problem solving.

Computer-Managed Instruction

Computer-managed instruction (CMI) refers to the use of a computer system to manage information about learner performance and learning resource options in order to prescribe and control individualized lessons.

There is considerable impetus for using CMI because of the increasing emphasis being placed on individualized instruction. Both in formal education and in settings such as the military, business, industry, and government, there is recognition that greater efficiency, effectiveness, and equal opportunity can be reached in instruction only to the extent that teachers can accommodate the individual differences that cause each

student to have different learning patterns.

Individualized instruction means that students will be moving through the checkpoints in the educational process at different times via different paths. You can imagine the management problem this entails if you think of one teacher responsible for teaching five subjects or major topics, with twenty objectives in each subject, to thirty students. This adds up to a minimum of 3,000 checkpoints.

The computer can help solve management problems like this by performing a number of specific functions such as administering, scoring, and analyzing tests; prescribing media, methods, and activities; and keeping student records. All of these individual functions can be combined into integrated learning systems (ILS). First, let's look briefly at the parts and then the whole.

Computer-Based Testing.
Computers can be used to store and file banks of test items. The test items can be filed by subject content, objective measured, or level of difficulty. Items in the bank can be readily updated and modified, new items added, and old items deleted with minimal effort. From the pool of test items the instructor can choose the items to include on an examination, or the computer can be programmed to select the items, either randomly or according to specified parameters. The computer can be programmed to select items based on variables in each category used to classify test items.

The computer also can be used to print out a copy of the test in as many different forms as desired or to administer a test to a student who is sitting at a computer. In the latter case, the computer can provide immediate feedback regarding right and wrong responses and keep a permanent record of the learner's achievement on the test.

Figure 8.9
Educators are exploring ways to use computers to manage the data teachers need for sound decision making.

Test scoring and analysis can be computerized by typing the student responses into the computer by using mark-sense sheets during the test that can be read by the computer, or by having the student take the test at the computer. The computer can display the number of students selecting each alternative, as well as the raw scores and standard scores of each student. In addition, group data such as means and standard deviations can be calculated.

Computer Prescription of Media, Materials, and Activities.
Based on student data (e.g., background, interest, test scores) and instructor input (e.g., available materials, alternative sequences, time available) the computer can develop a learning prescription for each student or trainee. Often traditional instruction is lockstep because the teacher or trainer cannot keep all the alternatives as well as each student's characteristics and background in mind. The computer with its extensive storage capacity can perform the countless manipulations necessary to assign instructional activities and learning materials based on a wide variety of decision parameters programmed into it.

Figure 8.10
A spreadsheet is a page of rows and columns that displays word, numeric, and formula entries. A spreadsheet can be used to record, average, and manipulate data.

Student names

Student scores

	Name	Quiz 1	Quiz 2	Quiz 3	Lab	Final
1	Jennifer A.	12	10	11	25	90
2	Amy C.	9	8	10	22	76
3	Nancy C.	8	7	9	21	80
4	Jamie D.	10	8	9	20	78
5	John D.	6	4	8	15	70
6	Lance F.	11	10	11	22	79
7	Donna G.	13	15	14	24	94
8	Chris H.	9	10	11	10	80
9	Heather J.	12	12	11	13	87
10	Bill L.	10	12	11	22	83
11	Bob M.	8	10	10	20	80
12	Mark M.	6	14	12	9	84
13	Sally N.	3	7	8	21	65
14	Mike P.	10	9	6	20	89
15	Nick R.	11	13	12	18	91
16	George S.	9	10	8	8	82
17	Jim T.	12	12	11	24	92
18	Mary T.	13	15	14	25	90
19	Paul W.	4	10	8	17	71

Record Keeping.

Records of student scores on tests can be stored by the computer (see Figure 8.10). The student record can be updated each time a test is taken. The computer serves as an electronic gradebook. At the end of the grading period, the scores can be manipulated (e.g., the lowest score can be dropped, the highest score doubled), the average calculated, the final grade determined, and the composite student performance printed out by the computer.

Computer Networks

A computer network allows individual computers to share courseware, data, and peripheral devices such as printers. Common networks are AppleTalk, Corvus, Digicard, ICLAS, NetWare, and Novell.

Information from multiple sources in multiple locations can be accessed through a local area network or LAN. A LAN is a software and hardware system that connects computers, printers, and other devices as shown in Figure 8.11.

The heart of the LAN is the file server. This computer serves the file needs of the user computers. The file server contains one or more hard drives. These hard drives contain the programs that can be served to the user as well as maintain the files the user creates and accesses. File servers can be accessed from the computers attached to the network, which are called workstations.

Adding a modem to the network allows students with their own modem at home to dial into the school network. Networks extend schools beyond their physical walls and beyond their normal operating hours.

Networks allow each workstation on the network both to receive data from and to send data to any other workstation on the system. Such networks often link microcomputers to large computing environments and databases.

Advantages.

If an educational organization has hundreds of different pieces of courseware and curriculum packages available, multiple copies for each computer can be very expensive. Instead of purchasing twenty-five courseware packages for twenty-five individual computers, the organization can buy one piece of courseware and a site license which allows the courseware to be loaded onto the file server for use at all twenty-five networked computers.

Updating is also less expensive. The organization does not have a significant investment in courseware on disks. Instead, it can purchase a new program and a new site license. In addition, instructional materials are now being designed specifically for use on a network.

Networking relieves teachers of the burdensome task of distributing and collecting disks. Some CAI courses may require a dozen disks each. If the course were available at fifteen workstations, 180 disks would be required for that program alone. In addition, the disks may get mixed up or misplaced.

Limitations.

Initial costs of computer networks vary from several hundred dollars to tens of thousands of dollars. The user must determine if the cost savings previously described will more than offset the expense of the network.

Not all computer software can be used on a network because of its physical configuration. It is important to check software before purchase to determine if it will run on the network.

If there is a problem with the network, all computers on the network may be shut down. These

Figure 8.11
Computer networks expand the uses of computer-based instruction in formal, group-based learning.

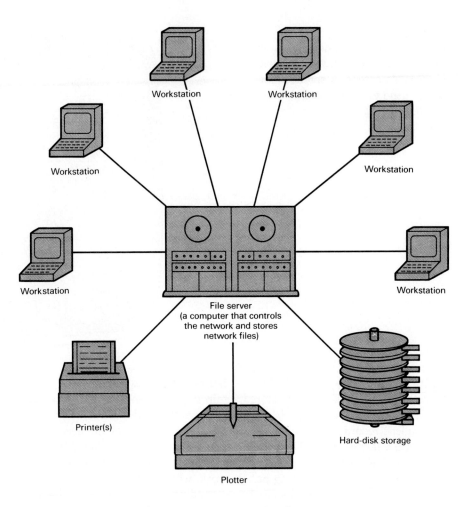

Workstation

Workstation

Workstation

Workstation

Workstation

Workstation

File server
(a computer that controls
the network and stores
network files)

Printer(s)

Plotter

Hard-disk storage

A hard-disk computer network configuration

Figure 8.12
Desktop publishing systems allow teachers to produce their own instructional materials with minimum time and little expense.

problems can be very frustrating to learners and particularly to the instructor. With stand-alone computers, only one student is frustrated by a machine failure.

Applications.

Networks offer students the possibility of studying and doing research as a group regardless of their locations. They facilitate group work through interaction, collaboration, and information exchange over the network. Groups of students at different computers in different locations can work simultaneously on the same science experiment, mathematics problem, or research project.

The computer network may be within an individual lab, or several labs can be interconnected in a larger network. Entire schools have been tied together for schoolwide electronic mail (messages for individual users) and electronic bulletin boards (messages for all users). The same is being done for school districts. Statewide networks are being developed that will connect all elementary and secondary schools in the state with each other and with the state of education department. The universities within the state can also be connected, along with postsecondary vocational and technical schools and community and junior colleges. In the future, schools throughout the nation, or even the world, may form a single network.

Computer-Generated Instructional Materials

In addition to using the computer as a tool during instruction, teachers are increasingly using it as a tool for preparing instruction. The computer can be used to generate teaching materials that incorporate written materials and visuals.

Word processing software and desktop publishing systems can be used to generate worksheets, handouts, manuals, and announcements (see Figure 8.12). Software is available that generates crossword puzzles when you input the words. Computers can also be used to produce large banners, visuals, flowcharts, diagrams, posters, and drawings for viewing on the computer screen, for projecting, or for use in printed form. Computers can produce overhead transparencies and slides. All of these computer-generated materials provide learners with opportunities to better understand the material being studied. Graphics can display mathematical relationships and properties of mathematical functions in ways not previously possible. Users can produce a musical piece by arranging notes on the musical staff.

Students can learn from producing graphics on the computer (visual literacy). The graphics tablet is a device that facilitates the input of nontextual materials. The tablet is connected to the computer, and a special pen is used to draw whatever visual is needed. The tablet sends an electronic description of the visual to the computer, where it is displayed on the screen and can be stored for use later.

Graphics can be animated, and some programs will handle movement automatically within the parameters specified. Others require each frame of the animation to be drawn as in film animation.

Another source of visuals is commercially available files of computer "clip art" on disks. These disks include drawings of people, objects, and shapes (see Figure 8.13). These visuals can be manipulated by the computer to change their size or to combine components of different drawings.

Line drawings, photographs, or text can be input to a computer using a digitizing process or scanner. Once in the computer, these visuals can be used on the computer screen or combined with words or other visuals for hard-copy output. When scanning published material, care should be taken to avoid copyright infringement (see Appendix C).

The computer can be used not only for preparing materials but as a presentation tool. The output from the computer can be projected onto a screen for group viewing using an LCD panel and overhead projector or using a video projector (see Chapter 11). Some instructors use the projected computer display instead of overhead transparencies. You can prepare your visuals on a disk before the presentation. Videodisc material can be projected in place of slides and films. The computer also allows the presenter to generate material on the spot by typing in key words or new data during the presentation.

As you can see the computer is a valuable tool for the teacher as well as for students.

Computer-Based Instructional Design

The computer can help with functions other than the delivery of course materials. It can be used to assist in the design and development of instructional materials and training programs. The computer can also manage course-development projects. These systems are not designed to be used exclusively for development of computer-based training materials, as the title may imply.

All instruction should be developed using a systematic process, and the computer can assist with this process. In addition to assisting with the creation of printed materials and the design and production of graphics, the computer can be used during the analysis, design, development, implementation, and evaluation of complex instructional systems.

The computer provides word processing, checks spelling and sentence structure, and assists with editing and compilation of documents. The computer can also assist with decision making using algorithms. These computer-based systems utilize commercially available software for word processing, database management, spreadsheets, and project management.

Integrated Learning Systems

Computer networks often integrate hardware, courseware, and a management system. The networks can be used with most of the CAI and CMI applications described in this chapter. Some networked labs are used for individual subjects such as math, whereas other labs are used to teach multiple subjects. The content ranges from remedial math to advanced language arts and composition.

Applications. Some instructional programs are designed to track individual learner progress. This is best done with a hard disk and is certainly facilitated with a network. Data such as lessons attempted, lessons completed, tests taken and retaken, and scores on tests can be recorded within the network for access by the instructor. For administrative purposes, the frequency and duration of computer workstation usage as well as use by individual students can be recorded.

The applications described above are called *integrated learning systems* (ILS). Multiyear curriculum sequences contain many lessons (up to several thousand) that cover the major objectives in all disciplines. Lessons can be correlated with textbooks. Pretests, learning activities, and posttests can be matched to objectives. Thus the system is personalized to match the curriculum of the school or training organization. Many ILSs include word processors and on-line CD-ROMs for accessing information from encyclopedias, dictionaries, and thesauruses.

ILSs incorporate a wide variety of interrelated computer-based instructional programs. Teachers can specify which lessons each student must complete. When a lesson is completed, the student is automatically routed to the next lesson appropriate for him or her. When a student

Figure 8.13
Examples of computer clip art

stops working on a particular lesson, an electronic bookmark records the place. When returning for instruction, the student is directed to this stopping point.

Most ILSs are used at the school or district level rather than for individual classrooms. Currently ILSs are used in about 25 percent of the schools in the United States. The names and addresses of companies marketing ILSs are listed in the references at the end of the chapter.

Advantages. Integrated learning systems are "pupil blind"; they con-

tain no bias and hold uniform expectations for all students regardless of their past performance. Students are given an unlimited number of trials with consistent and appropriate feedback. Achievement gains are on the order of 55 percent as measured by standardized tests.[3] Gains have been particularly high for at-risk populations.

---

[3] VanHorn, Royal, "Educational Power Tools: New Instructional Delivery Systems," *Phi Delta Kappan* (March 1991):531.

Limitations. Current ILSs are sometimes criticized because lessons are at a low cognitive level and are delivered in a lockstep sequence. In addition, some feel more high quality courseware is needed. A deterrent to the use of these systems in many elementary and secondary schools is their high cost.

Some people are concerned that ILSs will replace teachers. However, they are designed to supplement regular classroom instruction. Teachers are able to select the content and pace of each student's learning.

Computers in the Media Center

As instructional activities employ a wider variety of media and printed materials (other than full-length textbooks), the task of keeping track of the ever-increasing supply of materials becomes more demanding. Many courses of instruction in formal and especially nonformal education use booklets and worksheets. The computer can keep a record of the number of such items on hand and signal the operator when additional copies are necessary. In some cases the texts of the booklets and worksheets are stored in the computer and copies can be printed on demand.

Teachers can use the computer to access lists of materials available in their media center. Other databases, including materials available in nearby public and university libraries, can often be accessed through a computer with a modem connection.

With increased concern for efficient allocation of limited funds and other resources, the computer is a handy tool for developing budgets and keeping records of expenditures. Many instructors store an expanding list of desired materials and equipment for purchase in the computer. If funds become available at the end of the fiscal year, a request for these materials, along with necessary purchasing information, can be generated quickly.

COMPUTER SOFTWARE

In the context of computer-based materials, the term *software* refers in general to any computer programs and their accompanying documentation. It is customary to refer to software that teaches the actual subject matter as *courseware*.

As has happened before in the field of instructional media, the development of hardware for CAI has exceeded the pace of courseware development. The ability to produce computer programs is not synonymous with the ability to design effective instruction. When choosing courseware, make sure that the program supports the achievement of your learning objectives.

Selecting Software

Search the sources, listings, and reviews to find the courseware that might meet your specific need. Preview the courseware and evaluate, using the "Appraisal Checklist: Computer Software." Include students in the process of choosing software. Get their input on how long the software will hold their interest and how helpful it will be to them. Finally, select the material that appears to meet your needs best.

Sources. There are numerous sources for educational and training courseware. They include educational institutions and consortia that develop new courseware, businesses that develop courseware to train their employees, software companies, and textbook publishers. In addition, materials can be obtained from clearinghouses such as CONDUIT and MECC. These nonprofit organizations sell courseware at a minimal cost. CONDUIT, located at the University of Iowa, specializes in materials for higher education, whereas MECC, the Minnesota Educational Computing Corporation, provides courseware for elementary and secondary applications. Addresses for these organizations are given in the list of references at the end of this chapter.

Listings. In addition to catalogs from the sources just listed, numerous indexes, on-line databases, and printed directories list available courseware by subject heading. Several listings of computer courseware sources are included in Appendix A.

Reviews. Several agencies attempt to help teachers and trainers cope with the courseware selection task by conducting independent reviews and evaluations of materials. These include MicroSIFT at the Northwest Regional Education Lab and the EPIE Institute. In addition, many educational magazines and training journals include courseware reviews. Sources of courseware reviews are listed at the end of this chapter and in Appendix A, under "Organizations," "Periodicals," and "Courseware."

Previews. You can use the review and selection sources to identify those computer programs that might meet your educational and training needs. However, you should preview the materials yourself to see if they are likely to meet your specific needs. You should request a copy of the courseware from the distributor with return privileges. Some companies will provide preview or demo disks which include samples of a variety of their courseware. These disks allow you to preview the programs but prevent the possibility that the companies' programs will be illegally copied. There may be a clearinghouse or local site where you can preview materials. Many of these preview sites are operated by local school districts and universities. Some local computer stores sell instructional materials and will allow you to preview the courseware in the store. Use the "Appraisal Checklist: Computer Software" when you preview courseware.

☐ **APPRAISAL CHECKLIST**
Computer Software

Title _____ **Format**

Series Title (if applicable) _____ Disk size

Source _____ _____

Length (completion time)   Range: _____ to _____ minutes   Average _____ minutes

Designed for What System? _____ **Memory Required?** _____

Subject Area _____

Intended Audience _____

Objectives (stated or implied)

Brief Description

Entry Capabilities Required

☐ Prior subject-matter knowledge/vocabulary

☐ Reading ability

☐ Mathematical ability

☐ Other

Rating	High		Medium		Low	Comments
Relevance to objectives	☐	☐	☐	☐	☐	
Accuracy of information	☐	☐	☐	☐	☐	
Likely to arouse/maintain interest	☐	☐	☐	☐	☐	
Ease of use ("user friendly")	☐	☐	☐	☐	☐	
Appropriate color, sound, graphics	☐	☐	☐	☐	☐	
Frequent, relevant practice (active participation)	☐	☐	☐	☐	☐	
Feedback provides remedial branches	☐	☐	☐	☐	☐	
Free of technical flaws (e.g., dead ends, infinite loops)	☐	☐	☐	☐	☐	
Clear, complete documentation	☐	☐	☐	☐	☐	
Evidence of effectiveness (e.g., field-test results)	☐	☐	☐	☐	☐	

Strong Points

Weak Points

Reviewer _____

Position _____

Recommended Action _____   Date _____

Classroom Use of a Single Computer

A high school economics teacher uses a single computer with a class of twenty-four students. A computer projection device that sits on top of an overhead projector allows all students to see what is on the monitor.

The teacher uses prepared computer graphics instead of overhead transparencies for key points and illustrative graphs. She can advance from one visual to the next as needed and can also reveal key words from the lecture with the touch of a key.

The biggest advantage of the computer in a large-group instructional situation is its usefulness in presenting "what if" results. For example, while presenting the concepts of supply and demand, the students can discuss the effect of an increase in availability of a product on its cost. Following the discussion the teacher can project the results. The teacher can also put student-suggested values into the computer, and the class can see the results immediately. Economics comes alive in the classroom when years of data can be manipulated within minutes for all to see.

Modification is not possible with most commercial courseware. Even when it is possible to obtain a program listing, revising is a difficult task and is usually against the copyright law. You can, however, modify the *uses* of the courseware and the associated (adjunct) materials, such as handouts and study guides. For noncommercial programs obtained from other teachers and trainers, the procedures for making modifications to meet specific needs are beyond the scope of this book.

Some instructors design their own courseware. However, most teachers and trainers do not have the time or expertise to do so. It can take up to 300 hours to design, code (program), and "debug" (correct) one hour of computer-based instruction. There are books written on courseware design for those who have the time and are interested (see the references at the end of this chapter).

Using Computers in the Classroom

Computers may be used individually by learners in the classroom, a learning center, the library, or at home. However, it is possible to use one computer with a classroom full of learners. Donald Shalvey has offered several classroom-tested tips for using a computer with elementary school classes.[4] Some of the techniques may be used with learners of all ages.

❑ *Use navigators and SWAT teams.* Use experienced students as "navigators" (assistants) for the novice users. One teacher called the helpers a SWAT (Support Workers at Terminals) team. As the SWAT team members and the computer neophytes communicate, they both get practice giving directions, following directions, and solving problems.

❑ *Try the tremendous T and the wonderful Y.* Adapters (the T and Y types) can split the signal coming from the class computer and display it on a large monitor as

---

4 Donald H. Shalvey, "How to Get Comfortable with 32 Kids and One Computer," *Learning 87* 15, no. 9 (May–June 1987):33–36.

---

well as on an individual computer screen. Computer projection using an LCD panel or video projector serves the same purpose. These two techniques allow the instructor to introduce new software or to demonstrate data analysis including graphs and charts to an entire class at one time.

Getting students involved with learning is easy and natural with computers. Good computer software provides active student involvement and can branch instruction on the basis of student responses. If the learners are not required to respond frequently and are doing a lot of reading, then perhaps that particular software should be replaced by paper-and-pencil materials.

Some computer programs are nothing more than fancy page turners. These programs do not make good use of a relatively expensive medium. If all the learners are doing is reading and making simple responses, the use of these computer-based materials should be carefully reconsidered.

Many computer-based instructional materials include evaluations

Figure 8.14
Basic elements of a personal computer

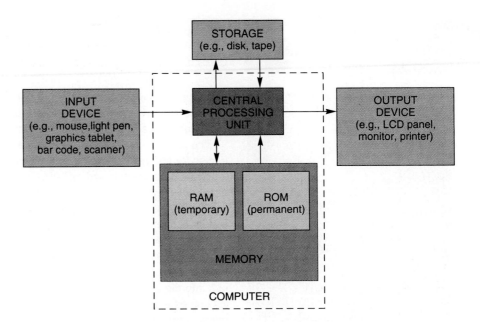

within the program itself. They often incorporate pretests, embedded self-checks, and posttests. Branching within CAI is based on the learner's performance—a consequence of evaluation. Mastery of the program content can also be measured by teacher-developed paper-and-pencil tests or by standardized tests.

Other types of evaluation should also be used with computer courseware. Ask for student reactions to the material. Did they enjoy using the computer-based materials? Evaluation should be a continuous and ongoing part of all instruction. Materials that don't achieve your objectives should be replaced.

COMPUTER HARDWARE

Basic Computer Components

Regardless of the size of the computer or complexity of the system, computers have a number of standard components. All of the physical equipment of which the computer is composed is referred to as the *hardware*. The basic hardware components are diagrammed in Figure 8.14.

Input. This is a means of getting information into the computer. The most commonly used input device is a typewriterlike keyboard. Other input devices include mice, track balls, joysticks, paddles, and graphics tablets. Graphics tablets can be used by students or teachers to incorporate drawings into their programs. Science laboratory monitoring devices can also be connected directly to a personal computer with the proper interface device.

CPU (Central Processing Unit). This is the core element, or "brain," that carries out all the calculations and controls the total system. In a personal computer the CPU is just one of the tiny chips inside the machine.

Memory. This stores information for manipulation by the CPU. The memory contains the control function, that is, the programs (detailed sequential instructions) that are written to tell the CPU what to do in what order. Memory and CPU are part of the computer and usually are built into the machine.

In personal computers, control instructions are stored in two types of memory:

❑ *ROM (Read Only Memory).* This is the control instructions that have been "wired" permanently into the memory and that the computer will need constantly, such as the programming language(s) and internal monitoring functions.

❑ *RAM (Random Access Memory).* This is the flexible part of the memory. The particular program or set of data being manipulated by the user is temporarily stored in RAM, then erased to make way for the next program.

A computer's memory size is usually described in terms of how many bytes it can store at one time. A *byte* is the number of bits required to represent and store one character of text (letter or number). A byte is most commonly, but not always, made up of eight *bits* in various combinations of 0s and 1s (see Figure 8.16).

A kilobyte, usually abbreviated K, refers to approximately 1,000 bytes (1,024 to be exact). Thus, if a computer can store 16,384 bytes, it is said to have a 16K memory capacity. The more powerful machines are capable of processing more bytes simultaneously, thus increasing their processing capacity.

The memory of the computer can be a limiting factor. You need to be sure that the computer has enough

Figure 8.15
"We're getting a new computer in class today. I hope I'm the one it replaces."

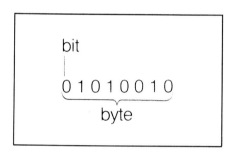

Figure 8.16
Representation of the letter A in ASCII (American Standard Code for Information Interchange) code when 8 bits represent 1 byte.

Figure 8.17
The floppy disk is one method of mass storage for personal computers.

memory to run the software you will be using. If you plan to use more than one application at a time, it is recommended that you have at least two megabytes (2M) of RAM. A megabyte (one million bytes) is the unit used to measure storage capacity of a computer. One megabyte of memory can hold approximately 2,000 pages of text.

Storage.   In personal computers, the computer can process only one program at a time, so you need some place to store the other programs and sets of data for future use. These programs and data are stored outside the computer.

There are three types of storage disks and several sizes. The basic types are "floppy" (flexible), "hard" (rigid), and CD-ROM. A floppy disk (Figure 8.17) is a thin, circular piece of plastic with a magnetic recording surface, enclosed in a plastic or cardboard jacket for protection. The computer reads the information on the disk through an oval-shaped hole in the top of the jacket. The two standard sizes of disks are 3½ inches and 5¼ inches (see Figure 8.18). The device that allows the computer to read information from and write information onto disks is called a disk drive.

With the large variety of floppy disk drives available, selecting one can be confusing. The first consideration should be the compatibility with other floppy drives in existing systems. Generally a high-density drive can read low-density disks, but the opposite is not true. The high-density disk differs from a low-density disk by how much information can be stored on it. Currently a high-density disk can generally hold about twice as much information as a standard disk. Because of the larger storage capacity, the industry is moving toward the high-density 3½-inch disks as a standard.

Hard disks are made of aluminum and coated with a magnetic recording surface. A large amount of infor-

Figure 8.18
Computer disks: 3½-inch (top) and 5¼-inch

mation can be stored on a hard disk; and because they operate at very high speeds, the information can be accessed quickly. The size of the hard disk drive is a consideration when selecting hardware. Experienced users tend toward the higher-capacity hard drives, in the 40 megabyte range. In general, the larger the hard disk drive, the smaller the cost per megabyte.

The compact disc, as described in Chapter 6, can be used for digitally storing and reproducing music. This same technology is also used to store and retrieve information. It is called *CD-ROM* (*Compact Disc—Read Only Memory*). A CD-ROM drive connects to a computer, which can read data from a compact disc in much the same way as from a floppy or hard disk. CD-ROM has the advantage of storing more data—approximately 250,000 pages of text, or the equivalent of 1,520

Table 8.2
The most common types of computer disks

Disks or diskettes	Size	Physical Characteristics	Storage Capacity	Machines Using
Floppy Disks				
	3½ diameter	Thin flexible plastic disk in a stiff plastic case	Double-sided 700 to 800 K Double-sided, high density 1.4 megabytes	Commonly used with Macintosh, Amiga, Atari, ST, IBM PS/2 series, and some PC compatibles
	5¼ diameter	Thin flexible plastic disk in a stiff paper case	Double-sided, double-density, 340 to 360K Double-sided, high density, 1 to 2 megabytes	Commonly used with Apple II series, most PCs, and PC compatibles
Hard Disks				
	Varies— usually 5¼" or 3½" diameter	Metal or metal-coated platters Internal or external to the computer	40 megabytes most common Up to several gigabytes[1] available for some machines	Available for all personal computers
Compact Disks				
	4¾" diameter	Metalicized disk coated with clear plastic	Approximately 550 megabytes	Commonly used with Macs, PCs, and Tandy Also used with special systems like CD-I

[1] A gigabyte is equal to one million bytes

360K floppy disks or eight 70M hard disks. An entire encyclopedia can be stored on a single CD-ROM with room to spare. A computer can find and list all page references to any topic in that encyclopedia within three seconds.

A disadvantage of current CD-ROM technology is that data are "read-only," meaning that the user cannot save new information on the disk. Some CD-WORM (Write Once, Read Many) drives allow users to record data onto a compact disc, but the data can be recorded only once and cannot be altered or updated. Then the disk can be read many times. This is a useful format for anyone with a unique databank that must be read often.

CD-ROM technology has been used to increase the availability of the ERIC (Educational Resources Information Center) database which contains abstracts of more than 700 journals in education and thousands of unpublished educational documents.

Chapter 9 discusses how compact discs, used as a video source, are combined with computers as interactive video. Newer computers have CD-ROM readers built into them.

Output. This is a means of displaying the results of your program. A television-type monitor, referred to as a CRT (cathode-ray tube), is the usual output device for a personal computer. It may be built into the total package or be a separate component.

Computers commonly provide output in the form of data printed on paper sheets (hard copy). This

HOW TO . . .
Handle and Store Floppy Disks

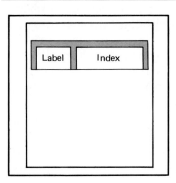

Keep disk in its protective envelope when not in use.

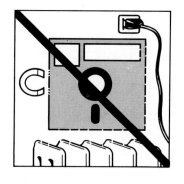

Protect disk from excessive heat and magnetized objects, including power cords which set up their own magnetic fields. Shade disks from direct sunlight.

Disks should be stored vertically in their box, not laid flat, especially not with heavy objects set on them.

Marking on the disk label should be done only with felt-tip pen, not with a sharp pencil or ballpoint pen. Avoid paper clips, which also could scratch the disk.

Do not bend, fold, or warp by using rubber bands.

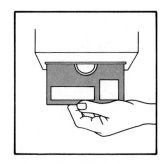

Protect the delicate surface from fingerprints by grasping the disk only by the edge to place it into the disk drive.

Figure 8.19
A typical printer to use with a personal computer

option is available by adding a printer to the system (see Figure 8.19). Printers are available in a range of prices and quality. As shown in Table 8.3 quality of text and graphics correlates with cost.

Selecting Hardware

It is becoming increasingly common for instructors to be involved in the selection of instructionally related computer hardware for their institution. This section will give you at least some general guidelines for participating intelligently in such a selection process.

Analyzing Needs. The first step in the evaluation and selection of computer hardware is to identify the need for the hardware. Why are you buying the computer? What software are you planning to use on the system? Without identifying specific needs for the hardware, you may hastily purchase an inadequate system or one more elaborate than you could ever use.

The selection of computer software is the most important first step in the selection of hardware. Computer hardware is no better than the software that drives it. Without software a computer will not function. The computer's utility may be limited by an inadequate quantity or quality of available software. A computer may have great features, but they are of little value if there is no software to take advantage of them.

MEDIA FILE: Apple Macintosh LC Personal Computer

The Mac LC, as it is known, is compatible with IBM-PC software, which means thousands of software packages are available for it. The Apple IIe card, which can be added, permits the use of Apple IIe software. It gives the user access to more than 10,000 Apple IIe programs. To ensure compatibility the Apple IIe card contains the same microprocessor that is built into the Apple IIe personal computer.

The Mac LC is Apple's low-cost, sound- and color-capable Macintosh. It is a modular system with separate computer and monitor. Earlier Macs included the computer and monitor in one case. The LC features a 16-megahertz microprocessor which doubles the responsiveness over earlier Macs.

The computer will accommodate a monochrome, color, or high-resolution monitor without having to add a separate video card. The system comes with a 1.4 megabyte disk drive. It can read from and write to 3½-inch disks. A 40-megabyte internal drive can be used for large files and data-intensive applications.

Table 8.3
Comparison of the major types of printers

Type of Printer	Text Quality	Graphics Quality	Cost
Dot Matrix	Low	Low	Low
Letter Quality	High	Low	Medium
Ink Jet	High	High	Medium
Laser	High	High	High

On the other hand, it is difficult for computer software to overcome limitations of the computer hardware. Since software written for one computer may not run on another computer, make sure software is currently available for the computer of interest.

Unfortunately, the computer hardware industry is changing so rapidly that hardware selection decisions cannot be based solely on present needs. One must consider future software and hardware needs. By purchasing hardware with significant limitations, one is unlikely to be able to take advantage of new advancements without purchasing new hardware.

It is difficult making selection decisions for the present and an unknown future. To prevent unexpected problems, it is important to look at the past performance of the hardware company from which you intend to purchase. Is the company financially stable? Are other institutions using the same equipment? Is the company committed to supporting their equipment?

Compatibility. The next major factor in selecting computer hardware is compatibility with previously purchased equipment. However, do not allow yourself to be trapped by equipment that can never meet your needs. If a change is required, it is often better to make it sooner than later. What other computers do you have currently? What operating system do the other computers use? Is there a need for exchanging files and programs among different hardware? If so, mixing several different computers may be difficult. Software designed to run on one computer will generally not work on another type of computer. Additionally, learning to operate, maintain, and effectively use the full potential of a given computer is not a trivial investment of time. If a single model will not meet all of your computing needs, consider different models from the same manufacturer.

In addition to being compatible with other systems currently in use, the new hardware components must be compatible with each other. Can a monitor from one manufacturer be used with a computer from another manufacturer? Although some feel that it is cheaper to order various computer components from a catalog, the buyer must beware that not all components are necessarily compatible. Just because an item is advertised to be compatible does not mean it will always work as promised.

Expandability. Expandability is also an important consideration when purchasing a computer system. The announcement of a new computer after your purchase does

MEDIA FILE: IBM Personal System/2 Model 25

IBM has expanded its PS/2 Model 25 family of computers for classroom use. These models can be used by students, teachers, and administrators in stand-alone and network environments. The Model 25 is designed for easy setup and portability. The disk drive, microprocessor, and monitor are built into a single unit with one power cord. One switch turns everything on. The separate keyboard has a generous cord.

The computers feature the 80386 SX microprocessor. All models include a 12-inch monitor, a mouse, and the IBM Disk Operating System (DOS). The upgraded Model 25 SX has increased processor speed and enhanced graphics. The system can be expanded to 16 megabytes of memory. The PS/2 Model 25 computers support a broad range of educational, communications, and business programs.

MEDIA FILE: Tandy 2500 Family of Personal Computers

Radio Shack, a division of Tandy Corporation, offers a variety of personal computers for use in education and training. The Tandy 2500 series includes the 2500 SX which can be used as a stand-alone system or as a networked workstation.

The 2500 SX incorporates a 16-megahertz microprocessor and provides near-photographic graphics. It is an MS-DOS machine with pull-down menus, pop-up dialog boxes, and a point-and-click mouse. The system permits recording, manipulating, storing, and playing back of high-quality sound.

Its one megabyte of standard memory is expandable to 16 megabytes. The computer comes with a 3½-inch disk drive. Two additional bays can accommodate a second 3½-inch drive, a 5¼-inch drive, or an internal CD-ROM drive.

❏ **APPRAISAL CHECKLIST**
Personal Computers

Manufacturer _____

Model _____

Price _____

Memory Size: RAM _____ K, expandable to _____ K   ROM _____ K

Languages Available _____

Peripherals Available _____

Monitor: Size _____   Built-in: yes _____ no _____   Color _____ Green _____ Amber _____ B&W _____

Graphics Available: yes _____ no _____   Sound available: yes _____ no _____

Rating	High		Medium		Low	Comments
Ease of operation	❏	❏	❏	❏	❏	
Durability/reliability	❏	❏	❏	❏	❏	
Availability of software	❏	❏	❏	❏	❏	
Video display quality	❏	❏	❏	❏	❏	
Keyboard layout and touch	❏	❏	❏	❏	❏	
Expandability	❏	❏	❏	❏	❏	
User documentation	❏	❏	❏	❏	❏	
Technical support	❏	❏	❏	❏	❏	
Local service support	❏	❏	❏	❏	❏	
Portability	❏	❏	❏	❏	❏	

Other Features

Strong Points

Weak Points

Reviewer _____

Position _____

Recommended Action _____   Date _____

_____

ANALYZE LEARNERS

General Characteristics

Robin Meadows' students are primarily sophomores in high school. It is their first biology course; however, they were introduced to biological principles in a general science course the previous year. In general science, the students did not study the frog, but they did dissect an earthworm. They represent a broad range of socioeconomic backgrounds, grade-point averages, and reading levels. Some students have minor physical handicaps and others have low IQs. Because the school district has a computer literacy program that begins in the elementary schools, all students have keyboarding and computer skills.

Entry Competencies

Approximately 80 percent of the students are able to

1. Define or describe simple biological terms: *amphibian, anterior, artery, circulatory system, digestive system, dorsal, posterior, vein, ventral,* and *vertebrate.*

2. Measure an object within two millimeters using a metric ruler.

3. Convert from millimeters to centimeters and reverse the process.

Learning Style

Most students prefer visual learning and manipulation of materials, especially those students with low verbal skills. All students enjoy interacting with their peers, and a majority of them are motivated by using a computer to learn.

STATE OBJECTIVES

The teacher wants the students to learn a frog's anatomy and to practice dissection techniques. The specific objectives are to be able to

1. Identify by name and function twenty common frog organs and locate these organs on a drawing.

2. Trace the blood flow in the circulatory system of the frog.

3. Describe the nature and function of the female and male urogenital systems of a frog and identify ten components of each system.

4. Demonstrate proper dissection techniques.

SELECT MEDIA AND MATERIALS

The teacher considered the standard frog-dissection laboratory. A teacher in a neighboring school district mentioned a microcomputer simulation called *Operation: Frog* (developed by Interactive Picture Systems and distributed by Scholastic). The teacher previewed the simulation along with the teacher's handbook. The program is a simulated laboratory dissection of a frog. It features two stages: dissection and reconstruction. In the dissection stage, students use the computer to locate and remove organs and to investigate the frog's body systems close up. In the reconstruction stage, students use the computer to reassemble the dissected frog.

In considering whether or not to use the simulation, the teacher listed the following strengths: (1) through computer simulation students have an opportunity to see how several organs work in a live frog (which is not possible in an actual dissection), (2) a scoring feature adds an additional level of challenge for some students, (3) the reading level is low, and (4) the cost of enough copies is within the school's budget (computers are already available).

The drawbacks include the following: (1) students don't work with all of the frog's body parts, only twenty-three main organs (no bones are included and only one sample muscle), (2) body organs are unrealistically colored to make them easier to find, and (3) the simulation isn't a substitute for actual dissection.

The teacher considered many variables and decided to remove objective 4 from the list and purchase *Operation: Frog* for use with the class.

UTILIZE THE MATERIALS

The teacher introduces the lesson by showing a short videotape on the life cycle of frogs. The students work in pairs. While one performs the "dissection," the other records information from the screen on laboratory worksheets copied from the teacher's handbook.

The students use the same "instruments" they would use in an actual lab: dissecting scissors, a probe, forceps, and a magnifying lens. Diagrams and text screens offer detailed information about organs and body systems. A special help feature within the program provides prompts and guidance.

Students are instructed to observe the animated blood flow, to remove the common organs, and to explore the urogenital system in detail.

REQUIRE LEARNER PARTICIPATION

The students are actively involved with both manipulating the dissecting instruments within the simulation and recording data. After the lab they must complete the lab report and then go to the library to research the nature and function of the male and female urogenital systems of frogs.

EVALUATE AND REVISE

Evaluation of student achievement is based on the laboratory report, the research paper on the frog urogenital system, and a paper-and-pencil test covering the common frog organs. The test includes a diagram on which students must identify the common organs. On another diagram they are asked to trace the blood flow within the circulatory system.

Figure 8.20
Computer documentation is important in learning about the hardware and as a reference when using the computer.

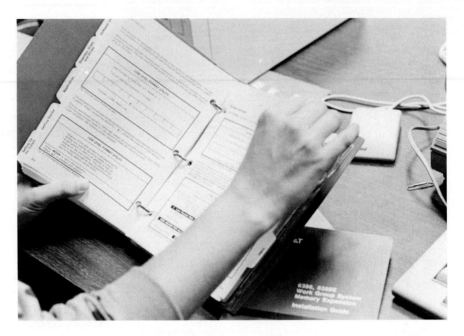

not reduce the utility of your system. Even if a computer is not the latest technology, it may still be sufficient to meet your needs. If needed, existing computers can be brought up to date by adding new peripherals or even new microprocessors. New peripherals (e.g., modems, printers, and hard-disk drives) can be connected to a computer by plugging them into a port or slot. Computer manufacturers build ports and slots into the computer to allow for expandability. A port is an outlet on a computer where the user can plug in a peripheral. A slot is an area in the computer where the user can add additional electronic boards for a specific purpose (e.g., to operate a printer, to increase the memory of the computer). The electronic boards contain components that allow the computer to operate the peripheral. The number of peripherals that can be added to a computer varies depending on the number of ports and slots.

Documentation. The documentation, or user's manual, must be easy to read and understand for a first-time computer user (Figure 8.20). It should have an extensive index and table of contents to allow easy access to the information. Diagrams should be included to show the various parts of your system and how to put your system together.

Service. Be sure the hardware company you buy from is committed to supporting and maintaining the equipment you plan to purchase. How long has its service center been established? You may want to talk with others who have used their service. Were they satisfied? Was service prompt and speedy? Finding someone to service computers often becomes a difficult and frustrating experience. Sometimes you have to ship hardware to a service location, thus being inconvenienced for a time. If shipping is required, do you have easy access to shipping locations nearby or does the shipping service provide pickup of your packages?

A maintenance contract should be a consideration when purchasing hardware. Such a contract may vary in cost from a few dollars a month for each machine to many times that amount. However, most personal computer systems tend to be reliable. Most failures and problems occur during the warranty period. Once through the warranty period, breakdowns are infrequent with proper care. The actual cost of the repairs may be cheaper than the cost of a maintenance contract.

In comparing models, many different criteria may be considered. The "Appraisal Checklist: Personal Computers" includes the most important criteria for selecting personal computers for instructional purposes. Which criteria will be most salient to you depends on the specifics of your situation.

REFERENCES

Print References

Adams, Thomas W. "Computer Literacy—The LCD: A Solution to the Classroom Single Monitor Problem?" *Journal of Computers in Mathematics and Science Teaching.* (Winter 1988–89):11–13.

Alessi, Stephen M., and Trollip, Stanley R. *Computer-Based Instruction: Methods and Development.* 2d ed. Englewood Cliffs, NJ: Prentice Hall, 1991.

Anderson, Marv A. "Technology Integration for Mainstreamed Students." *Computing Teacher* (December–January 1990–1991):6–8.

Azarmsa, Reza. *Educational Computing: Principles and Applications.* Englewood Cliffs, NJ: Educational Technology, 1991.

Bitter, Gary G., and Camuse, Ruth A. *Using a Microcomputer in the Classroom.* 2d ed. Englewood Cliffs, NJ: Prentice Hall, 1988.

Boston, Jane, et al. "Classroom Technology and Its Global Connections." *Media and Methods.* (January–February 1991):18, 48–49, 54.

Burns, M. Susan, et al. "A Computer in My Room." *Young Children* (January 1990):62–67.

Cicchelli, T., and Baecher, R. "Microcomputers in the Classroom: Focusing on Teacher Concerns." *Educational Research Quarterly* 13, no. 1 (1989):37–46.

Costa, Betty, and Costa, Marie. *A Micro Handbook for Small Libraries and Media Centers.* Lakewood, CO: Libraries Unlimited, 1991.

Costanzo, William V. *Electronic Text: Learning to Write, Read, and Reason with Computers.* Englewood Cliffs, NJ: Educational Technology, 1989.

Dockterman, David A. *Great Teaching in the One Computer Classroom.* Cambridge, MA: Tom Snyder Productions, 1990.

Finkel, LeRoy. *Technology Tools in the Information Age Classroom.* Wilsonville, OR: Franklin, Beedle and Associates, 1991.

Flake, Janice L.; McClintock, Edwin C.; and Turner, Sandra. *Fundamentals of Computer Education.* 2d ed. Belmont, CA: Wadsworth, 1990.

Galbraith, P. L., et al. "Instructional Technology: Wither Its Future?" *Educational Technology* (August 1990):18–25.

Garrett, Nina. "Technology in the Service of Language Learning: Trends and Issues." *Modern Language Journal* (Spring 1991):74–101.

Geisert, Paul G., and Futrell, Mynga K. *Teachers, Computers, and Curriculum: Microcomputers in the Classroom.* Boston: Allyn and Bacon, 1990.

Grandoenett, Neal. "Roles of Computer Technology in the Mathematics Education of the Gifted." *Gifted Child Today* (January–February 1991):18–23.

Hannafin, Michael J., and Peck, Kyle L. *The Design, Development and Evaluation of Instructional Software.* New York: Macmillan, 1988.

Jonassen, David H. *Hypertext/Hypermedia.* Englewood Cliffs, NJ: Educational Technology, 1989.

Kulik, C. -L. C., and Kulik, J. A. "Effectiveness of Computer-Based Education in Colleges." *AEDS Journal* 19 (1986):81–108.

Kulik, C. -L. C., Kulik, J. A., and Shwalb, B. J. "The Effectiveness of Computer-Based Adult Education: A Meta-Analysis." *Journal of Educational Computing Research* 2, no. 2 (1986):235–52.

Kulik, James A., Bangert, R. L., and Williams, G. W. "Effects of Computer-Based Teaching on Secondary School Students." *Journal of Educational Psychology* 75, no. 1 (1983):19–26.

Kulik, James A., Kulik, C. -L. C., and Bangert-Drowns, R. L. "Effectiveness of Computer-Based Education in Elementary Schools." *Computers in Human Behavior* 1 (1985):59–74.

Lockard, James, Abrams, Peter D., and Many, Wesley A. *Microcomputers for Education.* 2d ed. Glenview, IL: Scott, Foresman, 1990.

Marcus, Stephen. "Computers in the Language Arts." *Language Arts* (September 1990):518–24.

Martorella, Peter H. "Harnessing New Technologies to the Social Studies Curriculum." *Social Education* (January 1991):55–57.

McCoy, Jan D. "Databases on the Social Studies: Not Why but How." *Social Studies and the Young Learner* (November–December 1990):13–15.

McFarland, Thomas D., and Parker, O. Resse. *Expert Systems in Education and Training.* Englewood Cliffs, NJ: Educational Technology, 1990.

McMahon, Harry. "Collaborating with Computers." *Journal of Computer Assisted Learning* (September 1990):149–67.

Merrill, Paul F., Hammons, Kathy, Tolman, Marvin, Christensen, Larry, Vincent, Bret, and Reynolds, Peter. *Computers in Education.* 2d ed. Boston, MA: Allyn and Bacon, 1992.

Milheim, William D. *Artificial Intelligence and Instruction.* Englewood Cliffs, NJ: Educational Technology, 1989.

Olson, John. *Schoolworlds/Microworlds: Computers and the Culture of the Classroom.* New York: Pergamon Press, 1988.

Oonibene, Richard, and Skeele, Rosemary. "Computers and the Schools: Unused and Misused." *Action in Teacher Education* (Summer 1990):68–72.

Schwarz, Baruch, and Bruckheimer, Maxim. "The Function Concept with Microcomputers: Multiple Strategies in Problem Solving." *School Science and Mathematics* (November 1990):597–614.

Steinberg, Esther R. *Computer-Assisted Instruction: A Synthesis of Theory, Practice and Technology.* Hillsdale, NJ: Lawrence Earlbaum Publishers, 1990.

Trotter, Andrew, "Computer Learning." *American School Board Journal* (July 1990):12–18.

Warger, Cynthia ed. *Technology in Today's Schools.* Alexandria, VA: Association for Supervision and Curriculum Development, 1990.

Watson, Bruce. "The Wired Classroom: American Education Goes On-Line." *Phi Delta Kappan* (October 1990):109–12.

Weiner, Roberta. "Computers for Special Education." *Tech Trends,* 35, no. 4 (1990):18–22.

Wepner, Shelley B. "Holistic Computer Applications in Literature-Based Classrooms." *Reading Teacher* (September 1990):12–19.

Audiovisual References

Computer Literacy: A New Subject in the Curriculum. Capitol Heights, MD: U.S. National Audiovisual Center, 1983. Videocassette. 30 minutes.

Computer Literacy for Teachers, Parts 1 and 2. Chicago: Encyclopedia Britannica Educational Corp, n.d. 2 sound filmstrips.

Computers. Calgary, Alberta: Access Network, 1989. Videocassette. 29 minutes.

Counting on Computers. Princeton, NJ: Films for the Humanities and Sciences, n.d. Videocassette. 26 minutes.

The Information Age. Alexandria, VA: PBS, n.d. Videocassette. 28 minutes.

Hello PC. Athens, GA: American Association for Vocational Instructional Material, 1990. Videocassette. 70 minutes.

Microcomputer Application Series. Van Nuys, CA: Aims Media, 1987. Series of 29-minute videocassettes including topics of word processing, computer graphics, and spreadsheets.

Microcomputers for Learners Series. Calgary, Alberta: Access Network, 1988. Series of thirteen 30-minute videocassette programs that investigate the role computers play in classrooms and the potential of the technology.

The New Literacy. Princeton, NJ: Films for the Humanities and Sciences, n.d. Videocassette. 26 minutes.

Technology for the Disabled. Calgary, Alberta: Access Network, 1989. Videocassette. 29 minutes.

Computer Hardware Manufacturers

Apple Computer, Inc.
20525 Mariana Avenue
Cupertino, CA 95014

Atari, Inc.
P.O. Box 50047
60 E. Plumeria Drive
San Jose, CA 95150

Commodore
1200 Wilson Dr.
West Chester, PA 19380

IBM Corporation
P.O. Box 2150
Atlanta, GA 30055

Kaypro Corporation
P.O. Box N
Del Mar, CA 92014

Plato/CDC
Control Data Corporation
8100 34th Avenue South
Minneapolis, MN 55440

Radio Shack
One Tandy Center
Fort Worth, TX 76102

Database Sources

Active Learning Systems
P.O. Box 1984
Midland, MI 48640

Minnesota Educational Computing
Corporation (MECC)
3490 Lexington Avenue North
St. Paul, MN 55126

National Appleworks Users Group
P.O. Box 87453
Canton, MI 48187

Newsweek
Educational Division
444 Madison Avenue
New York, NY 10022

Scholastic Software
P.O. Box 7502
Jefferson City, MO 65102

Teacher's Idea and Information Exchange
P.O. Box 6229
Lincoln, NB 68506

Organizations

Association for the Advancement of
Computing Education
P.O. Box 2966
Charlottesville, VA 22902

Publishes:
Journal of Artificial Intelligence in Education
Journal of Computers in Mathematics and Science Teaching
Journal of Computing in Childhood Education
Journal of Educational Multimedia and Hypermedia
Journal of Technology and Teacher Education

Association for the Development of
Computer-Based Instructional Systems
(ADCIS)
Miller Hall 409
Western Washington University
Bellingham, WA 98225

Organization for persons interested in research and development of computer-based instruction.

CONDUIT
University of Iowa
Oakdale Campus
Iowa City, IA 52244

Evaluates and distributes computer-based instructional materials and publishes a periodical, *Pipeline*.

EPIE (Education Products Information
Exchange Institute)
Box 839
Water Mill, NY 11976

Publishes reviews of microcomputer courseware/hardware and procedures for their evaluation, including the *EPIE Annotated Courseware Provider List*

International Association for Computing
in Education (IACE)
1230 Seventeenth Street, N.W.
Washington, DC 20036

The most comprehensive of the organizations dedicated to the use of computers in education. Its emphasis is on the secondary school level, and its interests include both administrative and instructional uses of computers.

International Society for Technology in
Education
1787 Agate Street
University of Oregon
Eugene, OR 97403-1923

Collects and distributes information concerning computer applications in K–12 education and publishes *The Computing Teacher.*

Microcomputer Software and Information for Teachers (MicroSIFT)
Northwest Regional Educational
Laboratory
1005 W. Main Street Suite 500
Portland, OR 97204

Clearinghouse for catalogs and review guides, publishes evaluations of courseware including *Microcomputer Software Catalog List.*

Minnesota Educational Computing Corporation (MECC)
3490 Lexington Avenue North
St. Paul, MN 55126

Develops and disseminates courseware and computer-related materials, especially for elementary and secondary schools.

Periodicals

A+: The Independent Guide for Apple Computing
Ziff-Davis Publishing Co.
One Park Avenue
New York, NY 10016

AmigaWorld
CW Communications
80 Elm Street
Peterborough, NH 03458

Apple Education News
Apple Computer, Inc.
20525 Mariani Avenue
Cupertino, CA 95014

Collegiate Microcomputer
2706 Wilson Drive
Terre Haute, IN 47803

Compute!
1965 N. Broadway
New York, NY 10023-5965

Computer Technology Review
924 Westwood Boulevard, Suite 650
LosAngeles, CA 90024-2910

Computers in the Schools
12 West 32nd Street
New York, NY 10001

The Computing Teacher
International Society for Technology in Education
University of Oregon
1787 Agate St.
Eugene, OR 97403-9905

Education Computing News
951 Pershing Drive
Silver Spring, MD 20910-4464

Education and Computing
Elsevier Science Publishers
P.O. Box 211, 1000 AE
Amsterdam, The Netherlands

Electronic Education
Electronic Communications
Suite 220
1311 Executive Center Drive
Tallahassee, FL 32301

Electronic Learning
Scholastic, Inc.
730 Broadway
New York, NY 10003

Interface: The Computer Education Quarterly
915 River Street
Santa Cruz, CA 95060

Journal of Artificial Intelligence in Education
P.O. Box 2966
Charlottesville, VA 22902

Journal of Computer Based Instruction
Association for the Development of Computer Based Instructional Systems
Western Washington University
Miller Hall 409
Bellingham, WA 98225

Journal of Computing in Childhood Education
P.O. Box 2966
Charlottesville, VA 22902

Journal of Computers in Mathematics and Science Teaching
P.O. Box 2966
Charlottesville, VA 22902

LOGO and Educational Computing Journal
Flower Field
St. James, NY 11780

Logo Exchange
International Society for Technology in Education
University of Oregon
1787 Agate Street
Eugene, OR 97403-9905

MacUser
P.O. Box 56972
Boulder, CO 80321-6972

Microcomputers in Education
Two Sequan Road
Watch Hill, RI 02891

Personal Computing
10 Mulholland Drive
Hasbrouck Heights, NJ 07604

Teaching and Computers
Scholastic Magazine
P.O. Box 2040
Mahopac, NY 10541-9963

Technology and Learning
2451 E. River Road
Dayton, OH 45439-9907

3-2-1- Contact
Children's Television Workshop
P.O. Box 2866
Boulder, CO 80322

Computer Links

AT&T EasyLink Services
P.O. Box 4012
Bridgewater, NJ 08807-4012

The AT&T Learning Network offers curriculum materials on a worldwide bulletin board. Support materials available.

CompuServe
P.O. Box 20212
Columbus, OH 43220

Interactive personal computer service. Travel, shopping, finance, encyclopedia, educational games, stories, news, weather, communications, experts. Many optional (extra-cost) services: 1,400 databases, special interest/professional forums, etc.

Kids Network
National Geographic Society
17th and M Streets, N.W.
Washington, DC 20036

National Geographic Society elementary science and geography program.

Prodigy Services Co.
P.O. Box 8667
Gray, TN 37615-8667

Prodigy is an interactive personal computer service. Travel, shopping, finance, encyclopedia, educational games, stories, news, weather, communications, experts. Purchase connection equipment locally.

Integrated Learning Systems

CCC Microhost Instructional System
Computer Curriculum Corp.

700 Hansen Way
Palo Alto, CA 94303

Prescription Learning Laboratory
Jostens Company
6150 N. 16th Street
Phoenix, AZ 85016

Wasatch Educational Systems
5250 South 300 W.
Salt Lake City, UT 84107

POSSIBLE PROJECTS

8–A. Read and summarize an article on the use of computers in education or training. The summary should be two double-spaced, typed pages.

8–B. Interview a student or instructor who has used computers for instruction. Report on how the computer was used, including the user's perceptions of its strengths and limitations.

8–C. Develop a list of topics you would include if you were to conduct a one-day computer literacy workshop for teachers or trainers in your subject area.

8–D. Describe how you could use a computer as an object of instruction or as a tool during instruction in your instructional field.

8–E. Synthesize a situation in which you could use computer-based materials. Include a description of the audience, the objectives, the role of the computer, and the expected outcomes (or advantages) of using the computer.

8–F. Locate at least five computer programs suitable for your subject area using the information sources available to you.

8–G. Critique an instructional computer program using the "Appraisal Checklist: Computer Software," provided in this chapter.

8–H. Evaluate a microcomputer using the "Appraisal Checklist: Personal Computers," in this chapter.

9

Multimedia Systems

OUTLINE

OBJECTIVES

After studying this chapter, you should be able to

1. Define *multimedia system.*

2. Compare sound-slide sets, multi-image presentations, multimedia kits, interactive video, computer multimedia systems, and computer hypermedia systems in terms of their presentation and interaction characteristics.

3. Identify three particular advantages of sound-slide sets.

4. Describe an instructional situation in which you could use a sound-slide set. Your description should include the setting, topic, audience, objectives, content of the sound-slide set, and rationale for using this media format.

5. Plan a simple sound-slide presentation using the suggested storyboarding techniques.

6. Describe the use of a dissolve unit.

7. Distinguish multi-image presentation from multimedia and list four particular instructional applications that lend themselves to multi-image presentation.

8. Describe two instructional purposes that are especially well suited to the use of multimedia kits.

9. Diagram the components of an interactive video system.

10. Identify three advantages of interactive video that distinguish it from sound-slide and multi-image presentations.

11. Defend or criticize the use of interactive video with small groups as opposed to individuals.

12. Describe four instructional applications that are particularly well suited to interactive video; they may be from public education or corporate training.

13. Distinguish computer multimedia from interactive video.

14. Describe two instructional applications of computer multimedia that take advantage of its special capabilities.

15. Distinguish computer hypermedia from computer multimedia.

16. Describe the original purposes of hypermedia and compare these to instructional applications being made today.

17. Describe an instructional situation in which you would use a learning center; include the setting, topic, audience, purpose (e.g., teaching, skill practice, interest arousal, remediation, enrichment) and what media formats you would use.

18. Define *instructional module,* including the seven components of a module in your definition.

LEXICON

multimedia system

storyboarding

dissolve unit

multi-image presentation

multimedia kit

interactive video

computer multimedia

computer hypermedia

learning center

carrel

instructional module

Previous chapters have focused on various audio and visual media individually. This chapter focuses on combinations of these media, including combinations managed by computer. The generic term *multimedia system* refers to any combination of two or more media formats that are integrated to form an informative or instructional program.

Multimedia systems may consist of traditional audiovisual media alone or they may incorporate the computer as a display device, management tool, or source of text, pictures, graphics, and sound. In any case, they involve more than simply presenting information in multiple formats; they involve integrating these multiple media into a structured program in which each element complements the others so that the whole is greater than the sum of its parts.

The term *multi-media* goes back at least to the 1950s and describes early attempts to combine various still and motion media, even live demonstrations, for heightened educational effect. It reflected a methodology, called the "multi-media approach" or "cross-media approach," which was "based on the principle that a variety of audiovisual media and experiences correlated with other instructional materials overlap and reinforce the value of each other."[1] The term has been adopted in connection with computers to refer to combinations of sounds and images stored in different devices but through computer software amalgamated into an interactive program.

In those earlier days, as now, designers understood that individual learners respond differently to various information sources and instructional methods, so the chances of reaching an individual are increased when a variety of means are used. Multimedia systems also attempt to simulate more closely the conditions of real-world learning, a world of multisensory, all-at-once experiences.

As with other instructional systems, multimedia systems attempt to provide a structured program of learning experiences to an individual or group, with a special emphasis on multisensory involvement.

As with other instructional systems, several communication functions must be served: information presentation, student-teacher interaction, student-student interaction, and access to learning resources. The various multimedia systems differ in the quantity and quality of experiences they offer in each of these areas. These characteristics are summarized in Table 9.1 and dis-

[1] Donald P. Ely, ed., "Alphabetical Listing of Terminology," *AV Communication Review* 11, no. 1, Supplement 6 (January 1963):44.

Figure 9.1

Like any other instructional approach, multimedia presentations can be overdone.

Table 9.1
Multimedia systems

System	Presentation	Interaction
Sound-Slide Sets	Still images Voice, music	Typically learner is passive during showing
Multi-Image Presentations	Still and motion images, two or more simultaneously Voice, music	Typically learner is passive during showing
Multimedia Kits	Text, pictures, real objects	Learner handles real objects; may discuss in small group
Interactive Video	Still and motion images, computer text and graphics Voice, music	Multiple-choice response to questions, visual and auditory feedback and correction
Computer Multimedia	Computer text and graphics, still and motion images Voice, music	Multiple-choice responses, learner control of sequence; may allow editing and synthesis
Computer Hypermedia	Computer text and graphics, still and motion images Voice, music	Learner creates a text by making links among verbal, visual, audio information

cussed at greater length in the rest of the chapter.

SOUND-SLIDE SETS

Combining two-by-two-inch slides with audiotape is the easiest multimedia system to produce locally, which is one reason for its popularity. The system is also versatile, easy to use, and effective for both group instruction and independent study. A well-done sound-slide presentation can have significant dramatic impact, thus further enhancing the learning process.

Sound-slide programs can be developed locally by teachers or students. In terms of emotional impact and instructional effectiveness, they may rival film or television productions, yet they can be produced for a fraction of the cost and effort. Indeed, sound-slide sets are frequently produced as prototypes of more elaborate film or video projects because they allow the presentation to be tried out and revised in its formative stages.

Sound-slide sets are available from commercial sources. However, mass distribution programs of this sort usually are converted to a filmstrip and cassette format because filmstrips require less storage space than slides and are less expensive. Some commercial programs are available with phonograph records instead of cassettes.

The visuals in sound-slide programs may be advanced manually or automatically. In manual operation the visual and audio components are usually on two separate machines. You begin by projecting the title slide on the screen and then starting the sound track. An audible beep on the sound track signals you to advance the slides. In manual operation it is important that you test out at least the beginning of the program to make certain that you have sound and visuals in proper synchronization. Note also that some sound tracks do not contain a beep signal, in which case a script containing instructions for advancing slides must be used.

In automatic advancing with an audiotape two sound tracks are used, one for the audible narration and one with inaudible tones that activate the advance mechanism on the slide projector (see Figure 9.2).

Advantages

Sound-slide sets are easy and economical to produce locally with a simple camera and cassette recorder.

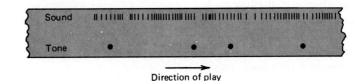

Direction of play

Figure 9.2
Synchronized sound-slide programs are controlled by inaudible tones put on one track of the tape.

HOW TO . . .
Develop a Sound-Slide Presentation

Here is a simple approach to developing your own sound-slide presentation.

Step 1. Analyze your audience both in terms of general characteristics and specific entry characteristics (as described in Chapter 2).

❏ Why are they viewing the presentation?

❏ What is their motivation toward your topic?

❏ How much do they already know about the subject?

Step 2. Specify your objectives (as described in Chapter 2).

❏ What do you want to accomplish with the presentation?

    Learning to be achieved

    Attitudes to be formed or changed

    Skills to be developed

❏ What should the viewers be able to do after the presentation?

    Activity or performance?

    Under what conditions?

    With what degree of skill?

Step 3. Having completed your audience analysis and stated your objectives, you now have a much clearer idea of how your presentation will fit into your overall lesson

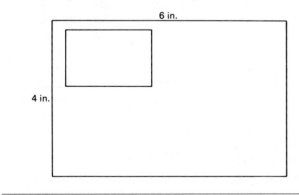

plan, including what might precede it and follow it. Perhaps you will decide at this point that a sound-slide presentation is not really what you need to do after all.

If it is what you need to do, get a pack of planning cards (use index cards or cut some sheets of paper into four-by-six-inch rectangles). Draw a large box in the upper left-hand corner of each card.

Step 4. Take a planning card. In the box draw a rough sketch of whatever image comes to your mind when you think about one of your major points.[a] You don't have to start with the first point, just whatever comes into your mind first. Your sketch may be a symbol, a diagram, a graph, a cartoon, or a photo of a person, place or thing, for example.

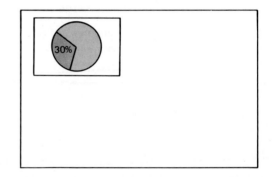

Step 5. Below your sketch, write a brief statement that captures the essence of the point you are trying to make. State it in as few words as needed to cue yourself to the thought. Some developers prefer to start with the visuals and then write the narration. Others prefer to do the narration first. Actually developing a sound-slide presentation is likely to be a dynamic process, with visual and narration

---

[a] The visual organization hints given here are adapted from *How to Give a Better than Offhand Talk. . . .* (Rochester, NY: Eastman Kodak).

In addition, they lend themselves to student production.

These audiovisual presentations involve two senses and can have a dramatic impact on learners. Sound-slide presentations can be used to inform or to change attitudes. They are applicable to both individual and group instruction with little or no modification. Combined with a printed study guide, sound-slide programs can actively involve the learners.

Limitations

One of the chief limitations is that the slides and audiotape may get out of synchronization. This can happen when showing the presentation to a group, but it occurs more commonly when an individual student is using the sound-slide set. In addition, it is difficult to go back and reexamine a portion of the program while keeping the slides in synchronization with the sound. This limita-

evolving one from the other, separately and simultaneously. In some cases, of course, your narration will be already at hand—printed information, for example, or a story or poem—and all that remains is to develop the proper visuals to fit it. Or, the visuals may already be in hand—slides from a field trip, for example—and all you have to do is organize them and develop your script to accompany the visuals.

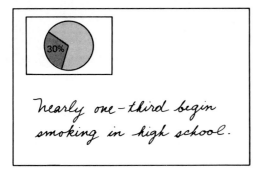

Step 6. Make a card for the thought that leads into the point you have just sketched. Then do another one about the thought that follows your first one. Continue like this, building a chain of ideas as you go along.

Step 7. When you run out of ideas in the chain, switch to one of the other major points that hasn't fallen into sequence yet.

Step 8. Arrange the cards in sequential and logical order. This process is called storyboarding.

Would some other arrangement liven up the beginning and the end of your presentation? Keep in mind the psychology of the situation as you thought it through in your audience analysis. The beginning and the end are generally the best places to make major points. Have you grabbed the viewer's attention right from the beginning?

How about pacing? Are any complicated ideas skimmed over too lightly? Do sections get bogged down in unnecessary detail? Add or subtract cards as needed.

You should have at least one slide on the screen for every point you make. Each slide should be on the screen long enough to support the point but not so long that it gets tiresome to look at.

As a rule of thumb, you can estimate the number of slides you need by timing your presentation and multiplying the number of minutes by five or six. This means one slide change about every ten or twelve seconds. You may find that you need more slides in some instances, fewer in others. Don't be afraid to use "filler" slides to hold visual interest. They're perfectly acceptable as long as they relate to the topic.

Step 9. Edit your planning cards in terms of practicality. Be sure you have ready access to the artistic talent or photographic equipment needed to turn your sketches into slides.

Step 10. Use your notes to prepare an audio script.

Consider using two different voices for the narration, perhaps one male and one female for variety. Would sound effects add impact to your presentation? How about actual sounds from the place where you will be shooting the pictures? You can take along a recorder and pick up background sounds and personal interviews while doing the photography.

Consider, too, adding music, especially as a finishing touch to the beginning and end. Be careful to keep it unobtrusive. Avoid highly recognizable tunes, trendy songs that will date your presentation, and music aimed at very specialized tastes.

Step 11. Rehearse your presentation, imagining that your cards are slides on the screen. Time your presentation and see if you need to shorten or lengthen it. To keep your audience's attention, limit your show to fifteen minutes. If you need more time than that, break it into two or more parts interspersed with audience activity.

Now you are ready to turn your sketches into slides! (To record your tape, see Chapter 6.)

tion can be overcome by putting the two-media combination on a single medium, namely videotape.

Applications

Sound-slide presentations may be used in almost any instructional setting and for instructional objectives involving the presentation of visual images to inform or to evoke an emotional response. They may be used for effect in group instruction, and they can be adapted to independent study in the classroom and in the media or learning center. This comparatively simple multimedia system is especially versatile as a learning/teaching tool in that more than one narration can be prepared for a given set of visuals. For example, a single set of visuals might have one audio narrative suitable for introduction of and preliminary instruction in a study unit and another narrative for more detailed study. The narration could be on

Figure 9.3
In a sound-slide presentation slides are synchronized with and controlled by a cassette.

two or more vocabulary levels—one for regular students and another for educationally handicapped students. For foreign language instruction, one audiotape might be narrated in the student's native language and a matching narration recorded on another tape in the language being taught.

Planning Sound-Slide Presentations

With the use of more than one medium, it is helpful to use a visual planning technique known as storyboarding. *Storyboarding,* an idea borrowed from film and television production, is a technique for helping you generate and organize your audiovisual materials. A sketch or some other simple representation of the visual you plan to use is put on a card or piece of paper along with the narration and production notes that link the visuals to the narration. After a series of such cards have been developed, they are placed in rough sequence on a flat surface or on a storyboard holder.

Index cards are commonly used for storyboarding because they are durable, inexpensive, and available in a variety of colors and sizes. Small pieces of paper can also be used. Self-sticking removable notes (such as Post-it™ notes) have become popular because they will stick to almost anything—cardboard, desks, walls, chalkboards, bulletin boards, and so on.

The individual storyboard cards can be divided into areas to accommodate the visual, the narration, and the production notes (Figure 9.5). The exact format of the storyboard card should fit your needs and purposes. Design a card that facilitates your work if the existing or recommended format is not suitable.

You can make a simple sketch or write a short description of the desired visual on the card. Polaroid

Figure 9.4
The storyboard helps in visualizing the total presentation and rearranging parts within it.

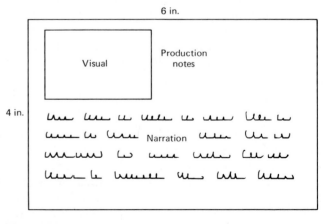

Figure 9.5
The storyboard card contains a place for the visual, production notes, and the narration.

HOW TO . . .
Make a Storyboard Holder

You can construct an inexpensive storyboard holder from cardboard and strips of clear plastic. Obtain one or two pieces of cardboard about the size that you need to accommodate the number of cards which you will be using. About 18 by 24 inches is a convenient size if you plan to carry the storyboard holder with you.

If you use two pieces, they can be hinged in the middle (as shown) with bookbinding tape or wide masking tape, giving you a usable surface measuring 36 by 24 inches when unfolded. If you do not plan to move the storyboard frequently, you could use a larger piece of cardboard (perhaps from a large appliance box such as a refrigerator carton) which could give you up to 6 by 4 feet of usable surface.

Staple or tape 1-inch-wide strips of clear plastic on the cardboard to hold the cards. If you are planning to use 3-by-5-inch index cards, the strips should be attached about 4 inches apart. One-inch strips of paper or light cardboard can be used to keep the card in place instead of the clear plastic, but this has the disadvantage of not allowing you to read the portion of the card that is behind the strip.

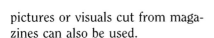

---

pictures or visuals cut from magazines can also be used.

Detailed suggestions for planning your presentation are given in "How To . . . Develop a Sound-Slide Presentation" (pp. 254–255).

When a series of cards has been developed, the cards can be laid out on a table or placed on a storyboard holder. (See "How To . . . Make a Storyboard Holder," above) The cards are sequenced in tentative order, thus giving you an overview of the production. The storyboarding technique facilitates addition, deletion, replacement, revision, and refinement of the sequence because the cards can easily be discarded, added to, or rearranged. The display of cards also allows others (teachers, students, production assistants) to look at the presentation in its planning stage. Number the cards in pencil; you may wish to change numbers as your planning progresses.

Several cards in sequence on a page can be photocopied for use with the final script, thus avoiding duplication of effort and providing a convenient assemblage of visuals, narration, and production notes.

Dissolve Units

You can achieve special effects in your slide-tape presentations by using a *dissolve unit* and two slide projectors. A dissolve unit has a mechanism for slowly turning one projector bulb off, causing one picture to fade out, while the other picture slowly appears on the same screen. The screen does not go black between pictures, but rather, one picture fades into the next. With a dissolve system you can gradually overlap images, blend or change directly from one visual to another, or blend one image into the other while the level of screen illumination remains constant. This provides a smooth visual presentation without any intervals of darkness on the screen between slides.

All dissolve units require at least two projectors focused to a single point on the screen so that the images will overlap. The projectors may be placed alongside each other or stacked one above the other (as shown in Figure 9.6).

You can achieve some very interesting effects by superimposing images from the two projectors. You can add elements to a particular visual or eliminate unneeded ones. You can make an object appear to rotate, or make a head turn or a facial expression change in apparent response to a comment on the audiotape.

MULTI-IMAGE PRESENTATIONS

Fairgoers at the 1900 Paris Exposition experienced a simulated balloon ascension by means of hand-tinted lantern slides projected onto ten screens arranged in a circle. Over the years since then multi-image presentations have become ever more sophisticated and have survived the emergence of competitive technologies, maintaining a foothold as a powerful presentation technique. The continuing viability of the multi-image system can be

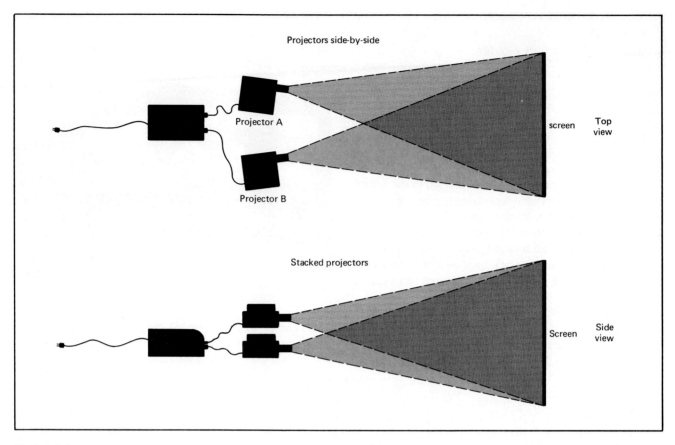

Figure 9.6
When using a dissolve unit, the projectors may be aligned side by side or
stacked one above the other.

traced to its ability to create powerful, visually appealing effects at a
fraction the cost of film or video.

A *multi-image presentation* is,
simply, any visual presentation
showing several images simultaneously. Such presentations are usually also multiscreen, in that they
are projected onto several screens as
well. Multi-image presentations may
incorporate moving images—film or
video—but they use slides as their
foundation.

Advantages

Multi-image presentations have the
advantage of incorporating a wide
variety of media, such as slides,
overhead transparencies, filmstrips,
and motion pictures. They can show
comparisons, time sequences, or
wide-angle panoramic views.

The rapidly changing images capture and hold attention of the learners. Dramatic effects can be achieved
by rapidly changing still pictures
(see Figure 9.7), which is possible
with dissolve units and automatic
programmers. Combined with appropriate music, multiple images
can also set a mood. Furthermore,
multiple images can simulate motion through rapid sequential projection of still pictures without the
use of film or videotape. The production costs of multi-image presentations can be significantly less than
that of film or video.

Limitations

Development of multi-image materials requires considerable time and
expertise because it depends on the
storyboarding process. Production

time and costs can be high. The
time to set up the presentation and
align the projectors can also be significant. The amount of equipment
required for their presentation increases the cost of using multi-
image systems.

Because multi-image presentations require several pieces of equipment, projectors, dissolve units, and
programmers, the chances for problems during the showing increase.

Applications

Multi-image presentations are still
heavily used in corporate
communications—to impress visitors, to introduce new products at
sales meetings, to review the year's
accomplishments at stockholders'
meetings. In the public sector

multi-image shows are commonly found at zoos, museums, and parks.

In education multi-image presentations are usually locally produced for persuasive purposes—to enlist parent support for new programs, to heighten student awareness of drugs, to arouse interest in new classroom techniques. They can also serve instructional purposes by emphasizing concepts such as the following:

- *Part/whole.* Showing a whole scene on one screen with a close-up of a detail beside it
- *Comparison/contrast.* Showing two images side by side, for example, to allow comparison of art forms or architectural styles
- *Before/after.* Showing a house before and after remodeling

- *Abstract/concrete.* A schematic diagram next to a photograph of a real object
- *Sequential.* Breaking down an athletic activity, such as diving, into a series of steps
- *Panorama.* Showing an outdoor scene with a sense of its full width
- *Three-dimensional.* Presenting views of an object from several angles to allow viewers to form a three-dimensional image

MULTIMEDIA KITS

A *multimedia kit* is a collection of teaching/learning materials involving more than one type of medium and organized around a single topic. The kits may include filmstrips, slides, audiotapes, records, still pictures, study prints, overhead transparencies, maps, worksheets, charts, graphs, booklets, real objects, and models.

Some multimedia kits are designed for use by the teacher in classroom presentations. Others are designed for use by individual students or by small groups.

Commercial Multimedia Kits

Commercial multimedia kits are available for a variety of educational subjects, mainly for the elementary level (Figure 9.8). These learning kits include sound filmstrips, cassette tapes, floor games, board games, posters, full-color photographs, activity cards, lotto cards, murals, wall charts, geometric

Figure 9.7
Showing a broad panorama is a typical application of multi-image presentations.

shapes, flash cards, student workbooks, and a teacher's manual. Objectives are stated and supported with suggested teaching strategies for using the materials in the kit.

Other multimedia kits on a wide variety of topics are available from commercial sources, some of which contain, among other materials, transparencies, laboratory materials for science experiments, and even puppets to act out story concepts.

Locally Produced Multimedia Kits

Multimedia kits can also be prepared locally by teachers or media specialists. Like any other instructional material, the kit should be designed around the objectives; each component should contribute in an integral way to those objectives. The main purpose of a kit is to give learners a chance at firsthand learning—to touch, to observe, to experiment, to wonder, to decide.

Availability and cost of materials are obviously important considerations. Will there be one kit for all students to take turns sharing, or can the kit be duplicated for all? Are the materials reusable? If not, replacement supplies will be needed. Will the kit include audiovisual materials? If so, where will students find the playback equipment?

Advantages

First and foremost, multimedia kits arouse interest because they are multisensory. Everyone likes to touch and manipulate real objects, to inspect unusual specimens close up.

Second, kits can be an ideal mechanism for stimulating small group project work. Cooperative learning activities can be arranged, revolving around experiments, problem solving, role playing, or other types of hands-on practice.

Kits have an obvious logistical advantage. Being packaged, they can

Figure 9.8
Multimedia kits provide varied sensory experiences; they give the concrete referents needed to build a strong foundation for more abstract mental abilities.

MEDIA FILE: *Creative Leadership for Teacher Growth* Multimedia Kit

Training Sunday School teachers is an ongoing task in religious education because of the rather high turnover rate from year to year. This multimedia kit is designed to be used by the teacher trainer and contains materials for four 1½- to 2-hour sessions. Included in the kit are two audiocassettes, forty overhead transparencies, twenty-eight duplicating masters, a leader handbook, and three different teacher guidebooks.

Each of the four sessions is built around a lesson plan in the leader's handbook and includes objectives and activities correlated with the various media included in the kit. Initial topics in this series are "Creative Leadership Communication," "Nurturing My Students," and "Discipline—A Topic for All Seasons."

Source: David C. Cook Publishing Co.

A Teacher-Made Multimedia Kit

An elementary teacher developed a series of separate multimedia kits on science topics for use with her third-grade class. She incorporated real objects, such as magnets, small motors, rocks, harmless chemicals, and insect specimens in the kits. She also gathered pictures associated with each topic from magazines and old textbooks. A study guide, prepared for each unit, required the student to inquire into the topic, make hypotheses, and conduct investigations. Audiotapes were prepared for use at school and at home for those students who had access to cassette players.

The students enjoyed taking the kits home to work on the experiments. The response from parents was very positive. Several parents reported that they too learned by working through the activities with their children. Students often preferred to stay in at recess and work on the multimedia kits in the science corner.

---

be transported and used outside the classroom, such as in the media center or at home.

Limitations

Learning with multimedia kits can be more expensive than other more conventional methods, and it can be time-consuming to produce and maintain the materials. Lost components can make the kit frustrating to use.

Applications

Multimedia kits lend themselves particularly to objectives for which discovery learning is preferred. Questions can be posed to guide learners' exploration and arrival at conclusions. Science topics are well suited to this approach. For example, a kit on magnetism might include several types of magnets, iron filings, and a variety of metal objects that may or may not be attracted to magnets. In mathematics a kit on measurement might include a folding meterstick and directions for measuring various objects and dimensions around the home or school.

INTERACTIVE VIDEO

Interactive video creates a multimedia learning environment that capitalizes on the features of both television and computer-assisted instruction. It is an instructional delivery system in which recorded video material is presented under computer control to viewers who not only see and hear the pictures and sounds but also make active responses, with those responses affecting the pace and sequence of the presentation.

The video portion of interactive video is provided through a videocassette, videodisc, or compact disc (see Figure 9.9). The images can be presented in slow motion, fast motion or frame by frame (as in a slide or filmstrip display). The audio portion of a videodisc may occupy two channels, making possible two different narrations with any specific motion sequence. Many of the features of videodiscs can be obtained with currently available videotape systems at a lower cost.

The interactive aspect of interactive video is provided through a computer. Computers have powerful

decision-making abilities, which video players lack. Combining these technologies means the strengths of each can compensate for the limitations of the other to provide a rich educational environment for the learner. Interactive video is a powerful, practical method for individualizing and personalizing instruction.

A variety of levels of interactivity are available, ranging from essentially linear video to learner-directed sequencing of instruction. The goal of most developers of interactive video is to provide fully interactive response-dependent instruction featuring embedded questions, response feedback, and branching within the lesson. In addition, student response histories can be used to help make instructional decisions.

Components

The heart of an interactive video system is a computer (see Figure 9.10). The computer provides the "intelligence" and interactivity required for interactive video. The computer can command the video player to present audio or video information, wait for the learner's response, and branch to the appropriate point in the instructional program from that response.

The learner communicates with the instructional program by responding to audio, visual, or verbal stimuli displayed on the monitor. Input devices provide the means for these responses. They may include a keyboard, keypad, light pen, bar-code reader, or a touch-sensitive screen.

The program that controls the computer is usually on a diskette, which is read in the disk drive. The diskette holds the instructional program and may also store information such as student responses, response time, and errors.

Although the twelve-inch laser videodisc is currently the most popular format for video storage, video-cassettes are still a viable alternative for some applications, and several variations of the five-inch compact disc have been developed. Originally developed for high-fidelity audio, the compact disc has been adapted for video in the form of CD-ROM (compact disc, read only memory), CD-I (compact disc interactive), and DVI (digital video interactive). The storage capacities of various types of discs vary, but in general one could

Figure 9.9

An interactive video setup using a videocassette as the picture source (see video player on upper-left shelf)

Figure 9.10

Components of a typical interactive video system

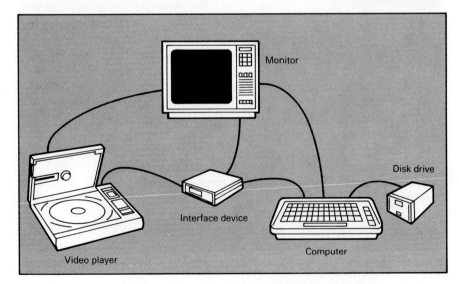

expect a disc to hold about 100,000 still images (or pages of text), two hours of audio, or one hour of full-motion video.

The monitor displays the picture and sound from the video source. It can also display the output from the computer software, in the form of text, graphics, or sound effects. In some systems the computer output can be overlaid over the video image.

The interface device provides the link between the computer and the video player, allowing them to communicate. Through the interface device the computer can control which portion(s) of the video are shown to the learner.

Advantages

The most obvious advantage of interactive video is that it requires learner participation (the R of the ASSURE model). Learners are prompted to respond by touching the screen, typing on a keypad or keyboard, or through any of the other input devices. The need to respond maintains attention and allows greater participation than does video viewing alone.

The system provides individualization insofar as the program has a branching capability. Depending on the learner's response the computer may branch to another section of the video program to provide remedial instruction. Or it may branch to a new section to provide enrichment material. When mastery has been demonstrated, the learner can go forward to the next topic. In some cases the learner may choose what to study from a menu.

Convenience is a major advantage from the user's point of view. Text, audio, graphics, still pictures, and motion pictures can all be combined in one easy-to-use system. A large and varied treasure-house of stimuli is available in a matter of seconds.

Experienced instructional designers, such as Romiszowski, feel that the greatest advantage of interactive

---

MEDIA FILE: *The 20th Century Navigator*
Interactive Video

The *20th Century Navigator* is a companion to *The Video Encyclopedia of the 20th Century,* marketed by CEL Educational Resources. The *Navigator* software consists of nine megabytes of text and indexes which describe and provide cross-referenced access to more than eighty-three hours of historical video contained in the forty-two laser discs that make up the *The Video Encyclopedia.* The *Navigator* software was selected as one of the top educational products of 1991 by *Curriculum Product News* magazine.

Source: Knowledge Arts

---

video may be its ability to provide simulation experiences.[2] The high-resolution moving image opens up exciting possibilities in such areas as medical diagnosis, machine operation, and especially interpersonal skills. The development of skills in interpreting and reacting to the behavior of other humans, which otherwise would require role-play or real-life interaction, can now be provided as an individual, self-paced simulation exercise.

Limitations

The most significant limitation of interactive video is its cost. Expensive equipment, including a computer, video-playback unit, and monitor, is required. It is expensive to produce and update videotape and even more costly and difficult to produce and update a videodisc. However, once mastered, videodiscs are inexpensive to duplicate. Therefore, interactive video is not cost-effective for a few students. In addi-

---

[2] A. J. Romiszowski, *The Selection and Use of Instructional Media,* 2d ed. (New York: Nichols, 1988).

---

tion, it should not be used if the visuals and learning materials are likely to become outdated by the time you are ready to use them again.

Videotape is less expensive than videodisc as a format for producing small numbers of copies, but it has the drawbacks of being slower in search time (to get from one frame to another) and less efficient in showing a particular single frame. Also, searching for a single frame is more difficult. Most videocassette machines lack slow motion and fast motion. Consequently, the user must trade off the more expensive costs of producing videodiscs for fewer capabilities and increased time required to access material on a videotape.

Applications

Interactive video is a valuable learning device for tasks that must be shown rather than simply told. Some instruction cannot be adequately presented by printed materials. If the learner needs to interact with the instruction, interactive video is almost essential.

Interactive video systems are currently being used in a variety of instructional applications. In formal education demonstration programs cover a wide range, from physics instruction to teaching special education students to tell time. The programs can challenge a small group of gifted students or provide remedial instruction for slow learners.

Interactive video programs can be used by individuals or small groups (two to five people). There is a growing trend, particularly in elementary, secondary, and higher education, toward small-group applications. The reasons for this are partly philosophical and partly practical. First, many educators feel that learning is more likely to take root and be applied to daily life if it takes place in a social context, made personally meaningful through discussion. Second, it is simply more efficient to have several people share a machine. And the research to date indicates that there is no loss of effectiveness between individual and group use; in fact, there may be benefits.[3]

Interactive video may also be used for large-group instruction. The relatively high cost of interactive video equipment often precludes the purchase of enough units to implement self-study for each learner. The instructional program can be designed to allow the instructor to stop the program for discussion, skip ahead to new material, or repeat previous instruction. For example, a set of instructional video materials titled "Critical Incidents in Discipline" provides preservice and in-service teachers with a sample of the discipline problems they might encounter in a classroom. The incident is presented vividly on video, and future sequences are shown based on the group's choice of ac-

tion they would carry out if confronted with the situation. After each choice, the interactive video program shows the result of that action. The group can then be shown the results of their decision and be led to another decision. Student teachers can try a number of different choices and see the results of each. One important consequence of this technique is the stimulation of class discussion which occurs after students see the results of each choice. Many students learn better in group instruction, where interaction with others can stimulate their own thinking.[4]

Interactive video has been slower to catch on in schools than in the corporate world, but significant inroads have been made. In 1990 Texas became the first state to adopt interactive video programs on an equal footing with textbooks. Within a year, a majority of Texas school districts had purchased "Windows on

Science," a series of programs covering a broad range of science topics. Across the United States, most school districts have the laser disc or compact disc hardware required for interactive video setups.

Although interactive video has a firmer foothold in corporate training and development, the growth in use has been slow since the late 1980s. An industry survey in 1991 indicated that about sixteen percent of all organizations in the United States with more than 100 employees were using interactive video for training; among the very largest corporations that percentage was about twice as high. The use of packaged programs was more than twice as common as the use of custom-designed programs.[5]

An example of corporate use of interactive video is the program used by a life insurance company to train its new recruits at the various field offices. The new agent sits at a microcomputer containing a touch-screen monitor and a laser disc

---

3 Susan Cockayne, "Effects of Small Group Sizes on Learning with Interactive Videodisc," *Educational Technology* (February 1991):43–45.

4 William D. Milheim and Alan D. Evans, "Using Interactive Video for Group Instruction," *Educational Technology* (June 1987):35–37.

5 Chris Lee, "Who Gets Trained in What," *Training* (October 1991):47–59.

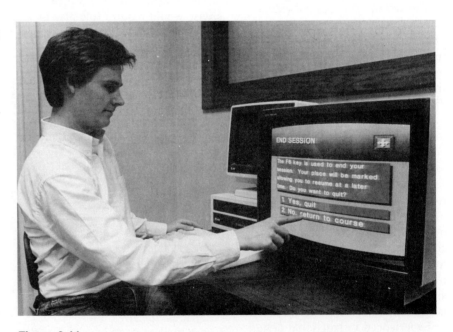

Figure 9.11
The touch-screen is a convenient means of registering a trainee's responses to an interactive lesson.

CLOSE-UP

CPR Computer-Videodisc Learning System

C ardiopulmonary resuscitation, or CPR, has been taught using interactive video for over a decade. Developed by David Hon of the American Heart Association, the system incorporates a variety of media including an optical videodisc player, a monitor, a microcomputer, and a random-access audio player. At the "heart" of the system is a mannequin wired with an array of sensors placed at key points in its lung system that monitor the depth and placement of CPR compressions.

As the trainee practices these compressions, he or she receives several different types of feedback: audiovisual coaching from the doctor on the screen, a visual readout on the computer monitor (indicating, for instance, that hand placement is too high or depth is too shallow), audio tones to indicate proper timing of each compression, and a graphic pattern on the computer detailing overall performance.

At various points during the program, the computer asks evaluative questions in fill-in or multiple-choice format. Using a light pen or typing in a response, the trainee actively participates in learning CPR. The computer monitors and displays learner progress throughout the course. Video segments can be accessed for review and for detailed explanations when necessary.

After the instructional segment of the program is completed, the student is ready for evaluation. The same computer-videodisc system with mannequin monitors the student's final hands-on performance for certification and asks questions about CPR.

Source: *Biomedical Communications* (September 1981).

player to walk through a variety of lessons on sales skills, office management, and client counseling. The user controls the path through the program by touching the screen as directed (see Figure 9.11). The system also contains a video camera and recorder that allow the agent to practice his or her performance and review it on videotape.

In business and industry, interactive video systems are being used to train automobile mechanics to troubleshoot electronic ignition systems, to improve communication skills for bank tellers, and to teach relaxation and stress management techniques to executives. One company reports reducing the training time of forklift truck operators from three hours to one hour by replacing classroom training with interactive video training. (See "Close-up: Safety Training via Interactive Video.")

Technical repair skills also can be taught with interactive video. A program can teach the trainee to locate a faulty component and can visually demonstrate how to adjust or replace the component while oral instructions are provided through one of the two audio channels on the videodisc. Data collected regarding such a system indicate that mechanics using it did demonstrate mastery of the maintenance skills. Moreover, both training time and training costs for the interactive video group were less than half of those of the traditional on-the-job training group.

Interactive video programs are also being used to teach and reinforce interpersonal skills through intensive simulation. For example, welfare caseworkers and sales personnel can benefit from such programs. One of the "Big-Three" Detroit automakers uses videodiscs to train its sales personnel within the dealerships as well as to sell automobiles to customers. The same video sequences are used for both. One of the audio channels is directed to the customer, pointing out the important sales features of the various makes and models. The other audio channel is used by the sales staff to learn critical information concerning how their cars compare to the competition. Sales pointers are included as well.

In the medical field interactive video systems are being used for patient education (e.g., on weight control and on diabetes). Also, doctors are receiving in-service education through a library of medical simulations on patient management, differential diagnosis of stomach pain, and various diagnostic techniques. For training nurses and doc-

CLOSE-UP

Safety Training via Interactive Video

The Clark Equipment Company, manufacturer of forklift trucks in Battle Creek, Michigan, developed an operator safety refresher course using interactive video. The course was designed in response to supervisors who expressed concern that they didn't have time to do the refresher training. In addition, the supervisors were concerned about the time they wasted in retraining operators. The operators themselves didn't see the need to be retrained in order to learn about something they did every day. An interactive videotape system was selected for the safety training.

Training via interactive video was compared with training using conventional videotape. Studies involved Clark employees and operators in other companies that had purchased Clark forklifts. The results indicated almost twenty percent higher initial learning and retention of the content after twenty-four days for the operators using the interactive video system. Training time for the operators was reduced, as well as time required by the supervisors to provide the training. Consequently, there was a significant reduction in the wages and overhead devoted to training.

Furthermore, the training system motivated operators to request other opportunities to learn using interactive video. In addition, there was no evidence in the interactive video group to indicate any effects of age or experience on an operator's score, as there was in the group of operators learning from ordinary videotape.

Source: D. Wooldridge and Thomas Dargan, "Linear vs. Interactive Videotape Training," *International Television* (August 1983):56–60.

tors to handle badly injured people, a single videodisc can hold hundreds of different injury situations that might take months or even years for them to encounter on the job.

The military is a big user of interactive video, for tasks such as vehicle maintenance, visual simulation of life inside a military tank, and simulation of the task of calling for artillery fire. In 1980 a course was developed around an interactive video system for troubleshooting the HAWK missile system. Evaluation of this training simulation provided impressive evidence of the power of interactive video. The videodisc simulation replaced equipment costing up to $4,000 per student hour and provided more opportunities for practice than would have been possible with the actual equipment. All trainees attained 100 percent mastery after interactive video training and did so in less than half the time of trainees taught by conventional means. In the latter group, only thirty percent reached mastery.

COMPUTER MULTIMEDIA SYSTEMS

In the world of computing, the term *multimedia* refers to the use of a computer to combine multiple media—text, graphics, sound, still images, and video. *Computer multimedia* systems are similar in concept to interactive video; the main difference is that the computer multimedia system begins with the computer, therefore text and graphics are taken for granted. Digitized audio may be added, then still images, and possibly video. As with interactive video, the main purpose of using computer-based multimedia systems is to facilitate interactivity between the individual learners and the subject matter.

Another distinction of computer multimedia is that it tends to be used with discovery-oriented instruction rather than for tutorials, drill-and-practice, or programmed

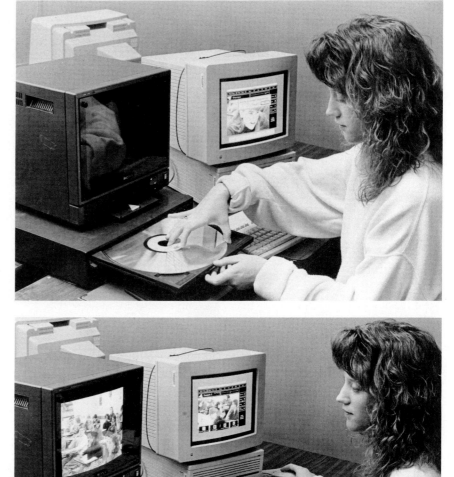

Figure 9.12

Using a multimedia program, *Teaching with Groups.* First, the student places the videodisc into the player. Then, she uses the mouse to press one of the *HyperCard* buttons on the computer screen (on the right) to select a classroom scene to watch on the video player (on the left). While watching and listening to the scene, she can press another button to hear the comments of the teacher shown in the video or other teaching experts.

instruction. Discovery programs have three basic elements:

1. A database of information
2. A user interface, that is, directions to guide the learner in locating desired information
3. Tools for manipulating the information

The intended outcome of a discovery program may be a product developed by the learner—a report in the form of visually illustrated text or

Figure 9.13
The title page of a student-made multimedia program showing "buttons" that link to different topics

possibly a narrated video. Typically, groups of three or four students choose a topic, research it, gather appropriate images and sounds from books and electronic data bases, compile them, and then edit words and images into a final program.

Advantages

Computer multimedia offers students more complete and individual control over their learning. Students may set their own pace through the material and review material as many times as needed for understanding. It provides a private, nonjudgmental learning environment. Computer multimedia systems also offer a richly stimulating audiovisual environment, making instruction inherently more engaging.

Limitations

The cost of hardware and software needed to set up a multimedia workstation has been and remains a significant obstacle to its adoption both in educational and in corporate settings. Most computer multimedia applications call for a fairly powerful personal computer with high-quality color display, plenty of memory, a large hard disk, and audio input and

output capabilities. CD-ROM is also often used when motion visuals are needed as part of the program.

Applications

Multimedia tools are ideally suited to demonstrating complex and dynamic processes that cannot be explained easily with conventional media and methods. With multimedia simulations you can model the microscopic, such as the nuclei of living cells, or the gargantuan, such as the dynamics of the solar system. You can demonstrate events that happen too quickly, such as the movement of sound waves, or too slowly, such as the action of glaciers over centuries, to be easily observed.

MEDIA FILE: *Mammals, A Multimedia Encyclopedia*
Computer Multimedia

Mammals is a CD-ROM disc that serves as an audiovisual encyclopedia of this branch of the animal kingdom. It contains entries on more than 200 different animals, 700 full-screen color photographs, 155 animal vocalizations, 150 range maps, essays on every animal, and 45 full-motion film clips from National Geographic specials. *Mammals* has been praised by *Media and Methods* magazine and received honorable mention for the "Cindy," a national award given by the Association of Visual Communicators, in 1990.

Source: National Geographic Educational Services

A common application is in student productions, in which students learn about a subject by researching and reporting on it. The computer tools remove many of the technical obstacles to visual reporting, freeing students to concentrate on thinking and organizing the ideas and information.

COMPUTER HYPERMEDIA SYSTEMS

The term *hypertext,* later expanded to *hypermedia,* was coined by Nelson in 1974 to describe "nonsequential documents" composed of text, audio, and visual information stored in a computer, with the computer being used to link and annotate related chunks of information (nodes) into larger networks or webs.[6] The goal of hypermedia is to immerse users in a richly textured information environment, one in which words, sounds, and still and motion images can be connected in diverse ways. More recently, hypermedia has been embraced in education because of its possibilities for involving learners actively in constructing their own mental models. Enthusiasts feel that the characteristics of hypermedia parallel the associative properties of the mind, thereby making the construction of one's own web a creative educational activity.

Computer hypermedia systems have been used for several different purposes:

1. *Browsing, or exploring a database. Palenque,* developed in conjunction with the educational television series, "Voyage of the Mimi," allows students to go on a simulated video tour of Palenque, a pre-Columbian archeological site in Mexico. In this applica-

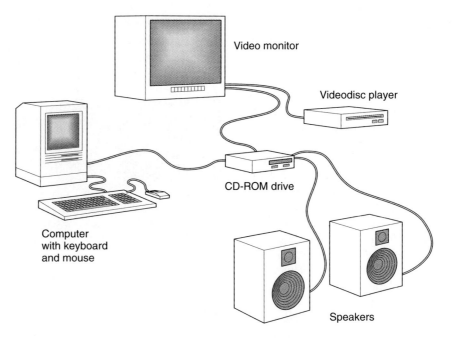

Figure 9.14
Components of a hypermedia system. A full range of still, motion, and computer-animated images, high-quality audio, and text are all controlled by the learner through a keyboard and mouse. Some computers have the CD-ROM built-in.

tion, students can choose routes and explore features in detail as it suits their personal desires.

2. *Operating on a database.* In this application, students pull together relevant data and perform analyses, computations, comparisons, and the like. For example, *Hyperbible* facilitates study of the Bible through indexes, a concordance, a digitized pronunciation guide, measurement conversion tables, interactive maps, and other aids.

3. *Authoring a report.* Using a program such as *HyperCard* for the Macintosh or *Linkway* for IBM PCs, students can prepare their own reports, integrating illustrations and even sound and motion into their presentations.

Several development groups have devised case-based problem-solving programs that combine features of operating on a database and authoring a report. Students working in groups are immersed in realistic, detailed problem situations presented by video. They discuss the problem, evaluate different solutions by making calculations with the data given, and prepare a report.

Advantages

Computer hypermedia systems allow multimodal presentation. You can control and present sound, images, text, and graphics in a dynamic manner. Students using such presentations can indulge their curiosity, browse, and explore ideas. They also facilitate realistic problem-solving activities, allowing cases to be examined in the rich detail of real life.

Perhaps the most exciting possibility is that students can use hypermedia tools to create their own presentations. The structure of current authoring systems allows even novice users to create links, constructing a do-it-yourself original report. To some advocates, this application holds the most educational promise. Learning that comes from constructing one's own conclusions is

6 Theodor H. Nelson, *Computer Lib: You Can and Must Understand Computers Now* (Chicago: Nelson, 1974), and *Dream Machines* (South Bend, IN: The Distributors, 1974).

much more likely to be retained and carried over to real-life application.[7]

Limitations

Having access to information is not the same thing as learning. One can read a text, view a video clip, or browse through a database without gaining any new usable skills. Hypermedia environments are not instructional in and of themselves. Learner control is not a panacea either. Research indicates that learners do not necessarily make good decisions when they choose their own learning strategies. This is particularly true of low-aptitude and low-achieving students.

There are practical problems as well. Navigating through a maze of hundreds or thousands of nodes and links can be confusing. Students can easily get lost in "hyperspace." A related problem is that of making sense of the bits and pieces of information that one encounters. Normal prose structure smooths the transitions and suggests the connections among elements. Comprehension can suffer when learners have to make their own connections.

As with computer multimedia, hypermedia poses logistical challenges. Expensive hardware and software systems must be acquired, learned, and maintained.

Applications

Hypermedia was first applied in text-oriented college courses such as literature, composition, and creative writing. An early example is the Dante Project, a program for teaching the works of Dante, integrating text, audio, and video components. An elementary school example is *Palenque,* described earlier. In

---

MEDIA FILE *Columbus: Encounter, Discovery and Beyond*
Computer Hypermedia

Designed for IBM's PS/2 Ultimedia platform, this computer-based program with videodisc and CD-ROM components allows learners to explore ideas and events related to Christopher Columbus's encounter with the Americas. Beginning with the "Main Storyteller," the user can branch off onto a wide variety of other subjects, such as deeper historical background, opinions about the cultural impact of European exploration, and music and art of Columbus's time and beyond. These are presented with a combination of live speakers, film footage, still pictures, animated graphics, and sound. Text of narratives, songs, and other material can be displayed on the screen below the picture as desired.

This multimedia program also provides a hypermedia experience in that the learner not only navigates through this rich environment at will but can also store any portions to create a new, original presentation. The program won the 1991 Gold Cindy Award for K–12 Education, given by the Association of Visual Communicators.

Source: Synapse Technologies/IBM Corporation

---

schools using hypermedia today, the most common application is as a tool for preparing and delivering presentations by both teachers and students. It is also widely used for operating on databases, as in problem-solving case studies. Many teachers also use hypermedia software to make home-brewed adaptations of conventional drill-and-practice routines and other conventional forms of computer-assisted instruction. There are few widely distributed, commercially produced instructional materials available.

LEARNING CENTERS

The development of multimedia instructional technology and the growing interest in small-group and individualized instruction have led to the establishment of special learning environments generally called learning centers. A *learning center* is an individualized environment designed to encourage the student to use a variety of instructional media, to engage in diversified learning activities, and to assume major responsibility for his or her own learning.

---

[7]   Thomas M. Duffy and Randy A. Knuth, "Hypermedia and Instruction: Where is the Match?" in *Designing Hypermedia for Learning,* ed. D. Jonassen and H. Mandl (New York: Springer-Verlag, 1990).

CLOSE-UP

Hypermedia Involves Both Teachers and Students

Perry Central school district in rural southern Indiana began the Hyperlearn Project in 1990 to experiment with hypermedia as a tool for student production. The project focused on the fourth and fifth grades, integrating student work across the disciplines. After receiving in-service training, the teachers became facilitators for student-directed projects. Elementary students, using Macintosh SE computers, worked in cooperative teams to design lessons to be shared with classmates and to be used by future students. Teachers found it an exciting learning experience to be learning along with (and sometimes from) their students.

Evaluations showed that not only did students taking part in the Hyperlearn Project show gains in their standardized test scores but, more importantly, they developed skills in problem solving and decision making and grew in their willingness to take risks as part of the learning experience. The state department of education chose the Hyperlearn Project to be a model for statewide dissemination.

Source: Elmer Shelby, Technology Director, Perry Central Community Schools

---

Learning centers may be set up in any suitable and available classroom space. Or they may be set up outside the classroom, in a laboratory, for example, or even in a school corridor. They are also commonly found in libraries and media centers. Learning centers with many stations are found in business, industry, medical facilities, and the armed forces.

Learning center materials may include practically any or all of the media and multimedia formats mentioned in this text. Center materials may be purchased from commercial producers or may be teacher-made.

Although simple learning center activities might be carried out at a student's desk or some other open space, it is advisable that learning centers be confined to a clearly identifiable area and that they be at least partially enclosed to reduce distractions. Learning *carrels,* or booths, which may be purchased from commercial sources or made locally, will provide a clearly defined enclosure.

Carrels may be made by placing simple cardboard dividers on classroom tables. Freestanding commercially constructed carrels come complete with electrical connections, and rear projection screens may be purchased.

Carrels are often referred to as being either "wet" or "dry." A dry carrel provides private space for study or other learning activities but contains no electrical equipment. The typical library carrel is a dry carrel. A wet carrel, on the other hand, is equipped with or has outlets for audiovisual mechanisms such as cassette recorders, projection screens, television monitors, or computer terminals (see Figure 9.15).

Advantages

Aside from exposing students to a variety of multimedia learning experiences, the advantages of learning centers are chiefly those that generally apply to individualized learning and teaching. Learning centers allow the teacher to move around the classroom and provide individual help to students when they need it. Centers encourage students to take responsibility for their own learning and allow them to learn at their own pace, thus minimizing the possibility of failure and maximizing the likelihood of success. They provide for student participation in the learning experience, for student response, and for immediate feedback to student response. Students tend to spend more time on the task of learning.

Limitations

Learning centers do have some drawbacks. They can be costly. A great deal of time must be spent in planning and setting up centers and in collecting and arranging for center materials. The teacher who manages the learning center must be a very good classroom manager and organizer, and must avoid the temptation to let the learning center replace him or her.

Figure 9.15
A student uses a synchronized sound-slide program in a "wet" carrel, one equipped for media use.

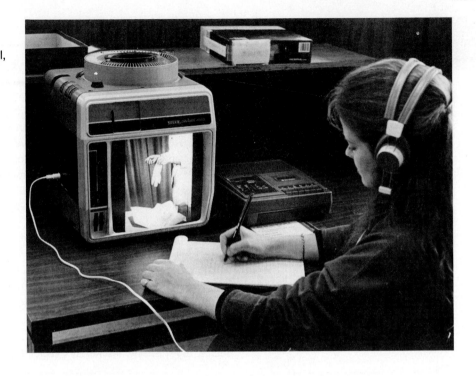

Applications

Learning centers can be used for a number of basic instructional purposes and are often categorized according to their primary purpose.

Teaching Centers. These can be used to introduce new content or skills and to provide an environment for individual or small-group instruction in lieu of whole-class instruction. Teaching the basics of the "three Rs" lends itself quite well to the learning center instructional approach.

Skill Centers. These can provide the student with an opportunity to do additional practice or can reinforce a lesson that has previously been taught through other media or teaching techniques. For example, a skill center might be designed to reinforce skill in using prefixes for students who are learning to read.

Interest Centers. These can promote present interests or stimulate new interests and encourage creativity. For example, a get-acquainted center on insect life might be set up in the classroom before actually beginning a unit on specific insects.

Remedial Centers. These can be used to help students who need additional assistance with a particular concept or skill. A student who has difficulty determining the least common denominator of a group of fractions, for example, could be given the needed help in a remedial learning center.

Enrichment Centers. These can provide stimulating additional learning experiences for students who have completed other center or classroom activities. Students who have completed their assigned math activities, for example, might be allowed to go to the center featuring computer math games.

Design

Let's consider how you might go about planning and designing your own learning center according to the ASSURE model discussed in Chapter 2.

Analyze Learner Characteristics. Diagnosis of student characteristics is the key to placing your students in the learning center that best suits their abilities, needs, and interests.

State Objectives. Determine the learning objective(s) you wish your students to attain in the center. State these objectives in terms of student behavior. Be sure the center includes a statement of objectives for user reference. A statement of objectives might be included in the center's printed material, or it might be recorded on tape.

Select Media and Materials. The primary guide to the selection of an appropriate combination of media is the objective of the learning center. Students should be provided with the tools needed to practice the skill identified in the objective. And since the learning center offers individual and small-group experiences, the multimedia systems described in this chapter would all be logical candidates. For example, an objective related to understanding the social environment during a certain historical period would lend itself to a computer multimedia or hypermedia program that would immerse the student in newspapers and documentaries of the period. A problem-solving objective in science would lend itself to a multimedia kit featuring real mate-

CLOSE-UP

Indy 500 Learning Center

A fifth-grade teacher in Indianapolis capitalizes on local enthusiasm for the Indianapolis 500 car race by designing a math learning center based on car numbers and speeds. Center material includes a variety of questions: "What is the difference in speed between Car 20 and Car 14?" "How many cars have even numbers?" "If an Indianapolis race car gets 1.8 miles per gallon, how many miles can it go on one tank of fuel (40 gallons)?" The center has colorful pictures and souvenir postcards of the cars and drivers. Each student draws, colors, and numbers his or her own race car, which goes in the "victory circle" when the lesson is completed. The students complete worksheets, for which they are awarded "completed laps" rather than numerical points. When they have completed their 500 miles, they have "finished the race" and receive a miniature checkered flag. The center is designed so that all students can eventually master its content and be rewarded by receiving a flag.

---

rials. For creative writing a hypermedia program could provide raw material. For a procedural skill a sound-slide set could provide step-by-step visual examples and be stopped periodically for practice, perhaps with a model or mock-up. The point is to provide the tools for the learner to do what the objective specifies.

Utilize Materials. Learning centers are designed for use by individual students or small groups (see Figure 9.16). Grouping has the advantage of allowing the students to interact as they utilize center materials, thus learning from one another's efforts and mistakes and reinforcing correct responses. In either case, instructions for using center materials should be included in your center. They should be concise and as clear as possible, in print or on audiotape.

The exact nature and order of learning activities within the center may be strictly controlled by the teacher or may be left in whole or in part up to the student. In most cases it is advisable to control activities at the outset and gradually increase students' freedom to choose activities as they demonstrate ability to assume responsibility for self-direction. Similarly, assignment to specific centers may be strictly controlled or left in whole or in part up to the students.

Be available to your students when they are using center materials. Many students, particularly

Figure 9.16
Learning centers offer opportunities for informal teacher-student interaction.

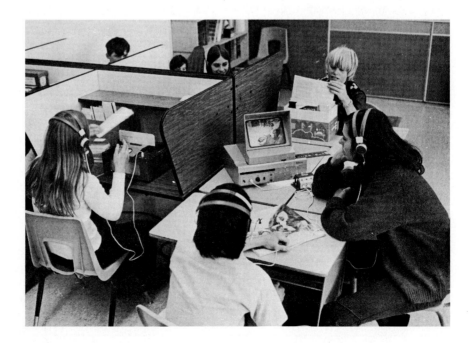

Instructional module is the term for any freestanding, self-contained, self-instructional unit. Most of the multimedia materials described in this chapter could be treated as modules. For example, to be utilized as a freestanding lesson, a multimedia kit could be placed in a learning center along with a statement of purpose and a pretest and posttest; that total package would be considered a module. Likewise, a well-designed interactive video program would probably already include all the components required of a module, so it could be set up by itself in a carrel as a module.

COMPONENTS OF MODULES

There are many different formulas for designing instructional modules, but certain components are essential:

1. *Rationale.* Provide an overview of the content of the module and explanation of why the learner should study it.

2. *Objective.* Write out what the learner is expected to gain from studying the module; state each objective in performance terms.

3. *Entry Test.* Determine if the learner has the prerequisite skills needed to enter the module, and check whether the learner already has mastered the skills to be taught.

4. *Multimedia Materials.* Use a wide variety of media formats to involve learners actively and to utilize a number of their senses. Most media formats lend themselves to use in modules.

5. *Learning Activities.* All of the methods described in Chapter 1 may be incorporated into modules. A variety of methods and media increase student interest and meet student needs.

6. *Self-Test.* Give students a chance to review and check their own progress.

7. *Posttest.* Give an examination to assess whether the objectives of the module have been mastered.

BLUEPRINT

The Solar System

ANALYZE LEARNERS

General Characteristics

The first-grade students are six and seven years old. They have grown up in a middle- to upper-class socioeconomic environment. Their intellectual aptitude is generally above average. They are more attentive to learning methods in which they actively participate than to those that require passive observation.

Entry Competencies

The concept of the solar system is relatively new to the students. They can differentiate between the earth and space. They are able to tell time and perform simple linear measurements. Some of the students have substandard reading skills.

STATE OBJECTIVES

Upon completion of the lesson, the students will be able to

1. Describe the concept of the solar system.

2. State the number of planets in the solar system.

3. Match the names of the planets with a visual showing the planets in their relative positions in the solar system.

4. Compare and contrast the temperatures of the planets closer to the sun with those farther from the sun.

5. Demonstrate the travel of the planets in reference to the sun.

6. State the order of the planets from closest to farthest from the sun.

SELECT MEDIA AND MATERIALS

The teacher, Cathy Richardson, was not able to locate commercial materials other than printed ones that met her objectives, were appropriate for her students, and were within her budget. She wanted to utilize mediated materials containing individual or group activities to maintain student interest and to enhance student learning.

Because she had no appropriate materials in her classroom and did not locate any in the school media center, there was nothing available to modify. Consequently, she decided to design her own learning center on the solar system. There were some things in her classroom, other items in the media center, and many ideas in books that she could incorporate in her center.

As part of her solar system learning center, Cathy used a portable, three-sided wooden carrel that could be placed on a table in the back of the room. She decorated the carrel with pictures from magazines and old textbooks showing the various planets.

For the basic instruction she prepared a slide-tape presentation using a copy-stand camera to prepare slides

DESIGN OF MODULES

Modules should include an introduction to the topic and instructions or suggestions about how the various components of the module are to be used. If the module is to be used only under instructor supervision, oral instructions may suffice. In most cases, however, a printed study guide should be a part of the module. The guide should introduce the topic of the module and relate its media and activities to the objectives. It should give instructions for using the materials included with the module and directions for the learning activities involved. Questions and space for responses may also be contained in the guide. The study guide should be as simple as possible, containing just the essential directions and relevant information. (See "How to . . . Design Printed Materials," p. 80.)

Some teachers prefer to put their study guide materials on audiotape or to use an audiotape in conjunction with a printed guide. Either of these procedures can be helpful for slow readers and may be essential for very poor readers and nonreaders. (See "How To . . . Record Your Own Audiotapes," p. 172).

It is important for the instructor to monitor each learner's progress in order to reward successes and alleviate frustrations. At the conclusion of each module's use, the learner should discuss the activity with the teacher individually or in a small group. The teacher and the student(s) can go over the nature of the problem presented in the module, compare answers (if appropriate), and discuss the concepts learned from the module. The follow-up discussion can be used as an evaluative device in addition to or instead of a written quiz.

---

from books and drawings. Cathy wrote the narration after the slides were developed. Stravinsky's *Rite of Spring* was selected as background music for the recording.

Finally, three activity packets were prepared for use in the carrel after the students had viewed the slide-tape. The packets were designed to involve the students actively in learning about the solar system.

UTILIZE THE MATERIALS

The students are scheduled individually or in pairs to go to the learning center at the rear of the classroom during a one-week period. They first view the slide-tape introduction using headphones, thereby not interrupting other classroom activities.

At least one of the activity packets is selected by the student for completion. Most students elect to complete all three packets. All packets are directed toward the objectives outlined for the center.

REQUIRE LEARNER PARTICIPATION

After learning the characteristics of the solar system from the teacher-designed slide-tape presentation, the students are actively involved in learning activities that provide practice and feedback. One activity asks the students to answer riddle cards related to the objectives. For students with reading problems, the questions and answers are read by a student with good reading skills.

Additional practice is provided by student activity sheets titled "Space Explorer." On these sheets the students practice labeling the planets on a diagram of the solar system. They also practice listing the planets in order from the sun. Several of the sheets have pictures to color.

A third learning activity folder describes the movement of the planets around the sun. Students use manipulative objects to demonstrate the circular motion of the planets.

EVALUATE AND REVISE

Some of the learning center activities use self-checks so that each student can check his or her work on an independent basis. The riddle cards work this way. Students are encouraged to attend the center more than once if they are not successful with the self-checks.

Students also complete a sheet with five faces from smiling to frowning to indicate their personal response to the learning center. Their mastery of the objectives is determined by a paper-and-pencil test covering the objectives. For students with reading difficulties, the teacher administers the evaluation orally.

Source: Developed by Cathy Richardson, Lafayette, IN.

younger children, need or can profit by frequent teacher contact as they use the materials and carry out the activities of the learning center. Circumstances may also warrant scheduling short one-to-one conferences with center users at periodic intervals.

Require Learner Participation.
Learning centers should be designed to include opportunities for learners to respond to center materials and receive feedback on their responses. There are various ways of providing such opportunities. You might, for example, provide an answer key to printed or audiotaped questions. The key could be included inside the center or placed outside it, perhaps on a bulletin board. The latter option allows the student to get up and move around a bit, thus alleviating the sense of confinement some children may feel using the center for prolonged periods. Answers might also be put on the back of an activity card.

Evaluate and Revise.
By attending to student response and providing feedback you will have had some opportunity to evaluate student progress toward attainment of your learning center objectives. Further evaluations can be made through periodic testing while work is in progress and through individual conferences. When the learning center project is completed, student mastery of objectives can be tested with traditional end-of-lesson written tests, performance tests, or other appropriate techniques.

Now is the time, also, to evaluate the learning center itself. Did most of its users attain the learning objectives? If not, why not? Were your materials well chosen? Were they too difficult for your students to work with or manipulate, or too easy? Did your center provide the right learning environment? Was it too dark? Too bright? Too noisy? Were your objectives clearly understood? Were your instructions clear? Your own

careful observations and solicitation of student comments and suggestions will help you evaluate your center and make appropriate revisions.

Management

There are a variety of learning center management strategies. A block of time can be set aside for use of each center, and students can be assigned to each one for certain periods. The length of the time block should be determined by the age of the students and the content of the center. The alternative of having the students move from center to center on their own is acceptable as long as they are held accountable for getting their work done.

In using learning centers, your role is not to teach one subject or to control the students from the front of the room. Instead, it is to move around and deal with students on an individual or small-group basis. As you circulate about the classroom, you can assist students who are having difficulty while becoming actively involved in the learning process with the students and assessing the progress of each student.

With a one-hour class period, it is helpful to have ten or fifteen minutes at the end of the period for group discussion and wrap-up. Of course, follow-up activities may be made available for the students when learning center projects are completed. Some instructors develop an activities checklist. Students use the checklist to monitor their progress through the learning center environment.

REFERENCES

Print References

Multimedia Presentation

Bullough, Robert V. *Multi-Image Media.* Englewood Cliffs, NJ: Educational Technology Publications, 1981.

Dunn, Rita, and Dunn, Kenneth. "Seeing, Hearing, Moving, Touching, Learning Packages." *Teacher* (May/June 1977): 48–51.

Effective Visual Presentations. Rochester, NY: Eastman Kodak, 1979.

Kenny, Michael F., and Schmitt, Raymond F. *Images, Images, Images: The Book of Programmed Multi-Image Production.* Rochester, NY: Eastman Kodak, 1981.

"Multi-Image Presentations: Still Powerful After All These Years." *Presentation Products Magazine* (May 1990): 28–34.

Slawson, Ron. *Multi-Image Slide/Tape Programs.* Englewood, CO: Libraries Unlimited, 1988.

Thomas, James L. *Nonprint Production for Students, Teachers, and Media Specialists: A Step-By-Step Guide.* 2d ed. Englewood, CO: Libraries Unlimited, 1988.

Interactive Video

Bergman, Robert E. *Managing Interactive Video/Multimedia Projects.* Englewood Cliffs, NJ: Educational Technology Publications, 1990.

Brodeur, Doris R. "Interactive Video in Elementary and Secondary Education." *Illinois School Research and Development* (Winter 1986):52–59.

Copeland, Peter. "Interactive Video: What the Research Says." *Media in Education and Development* 21, no. 2 (June 1988):60–63.

Dalton, David W. "The Effects of Cooperative Learning Strategies on Achievement and Attitudes during Interactive Video." *Journal of Computer-Based Instruction* 17, no. 1 (Winter 1990):8–16.

Glenn, Allen D., and Sales, Gregory C. "Interactive Video: Its Status and Future in the Social Sciences." *International Journal of Social Education* 5, no. 1 (Spring 1990):74–84.

Jones, Christopher F. G. "The Need for Interactive Video in the Education of the Deaf." *Programmed Learning and Educational Technology* 23, no. 2 (May 1986):156–58.

Power On! New Tools for Teaching and Learning. Washington DC: Office of Technology Assessment, Congress of the United States, 1988.

Schwier, Richard. *Interactive Video.* Englewood Cliffs, NJ: Educational Technology Publications, 1988.

Seal-Wanner, Carla. "Interactive Video Systems: Their Promise and Educational Potential." *Teachers College Record* 89, no. 3 (Spring 1988):373–83.

an profit
as they
out the
nter. Cir-
nt sched-
erences
c inter-

pation.
designed
learners
ials and
esponses.
roviding
ght, for
key to
tions. The
le the
perhaps
tter op-
get up
us allevi-
nent some
e center
wers
ack of an

By at-
se and
l have had
ate stu-
nment of
tives. Fur-
ade
while work
individ-
learning
d, student
be tested
son writs-
ts, or
ues.
o evaluate
most
g ob-
e your
hey too
work
sy? Did
learn-
too dark?
re your
ood? Were
our own

careful observations and solicitation of student comments and suggestions will help you evaluate your center and make appropriate revisions.

Management

There are a variety of learning center management strategies. A block of time can be set aside for use of each center, and students can be assigned to each one for certain periods. The length of the time block should be determined by the age of the students and the content of the center. The alternative of having the students move from center to center on their own is acceptable as long as they are held accountable for getting their work done.

In using learning centers, your role is not to teach one subject or to control the students from the front of the room. Instead, it is to move around and deal with students on an individual or small-group basis. As you circulate about the classroom, you can assist students who are having difficulty while becoming actively involved in the learning process with the students and assessing the progress of each student.

With a one-hour class period, it is helpful to have ten or fifteen minutes at the end of the period for group discussion and wrap-up. Of course, follow-up activities may be made available for the students when learning center projects are completed. Some instructors develop an activities checklist. Students use the checklist to monitor their progress through the learning center environment.

REFERENCES

Print References

Multimedia Presentation

Bullough, Robert V. *Multi-Image Media.* Englewood Cliffs, NJ: Educational Technology Publications, 1981.

Dunn, Rita, and Dunn, Kenneth. "Seeing, Hearing, Moving, Touching, Learning Packages." *Teacher* (May/June 1977): 48–51.

Effective Visual Presentations. Rochester, NY: Eastman Kodak, 1979.

Kenny, Michael F., and Schmitt, Raymond F. *Images, Images, Images: The Book of Programmed Multi-Image Production.* Rochester, NY: Eastman Kodak, 1981.

"Multi-Image Presentations: Still Powerful After All These Years." *Presentation Products Magazine* (May 1990): 28–34.

Slawson, Ron. *Multi-Image Slide/Tape Programs.* Englewood, CO: Libraries Unlimited, 1988.

Thomas, James L. *Nonprint Production for Students, Teachers, and Media Specialists: A Step-By-Step Guide.* 2d ed. Englewood, CO: Libraries Unlimited, 1988.

Interactive Video

Bergman, Robert E. *Managing Interactive Video/Multimedia Projects.* Englewood Cliffs, NJ: Educational Technology Publications, 1990.

Brodeur, Doris R. "Interactive Video in Elementary and Secondary Education." *Illinois School Research and Development* (Winter 1986):52–59.

Copeland, Peter. "Interactive Video: What the Research Says." *Media in Education and Development* 21, no. 2 (June 1988):60–63.

Dalton, David W. "The Effects of Cooperative Learning Strategies on Achievement and Attitudes during Interactive Video." *Journal of Computer-Based Instruction* 17, no. 1 (Winter 1990):8–16.

Glenn, Allen D., and Sales, Gregory C. "Interactive Video: Its Status and Future in the Social Sciences." *International Journal of Social Education* 5, no. 1 (Spring 1990):74–84.

Jones, Christopher F. G. "The Need for Interactive Video in the Education of the Deaf." *Programmed Learning and Educational Technology* 23, no. 2 (May 1986):156–58.

Power On! New Tools for Teaching and Learning. Washington DC: Office of Technology Assessment, Congress of the United States, 1988.

Schwier, Richard. *Interactive Video.* Englewood Cliffs, NJ: Educational Technology Publications, 1988.

Seal-Wanner, Carla. "Interactive Video Systems: Their Promise and Educational Potential." *Teachers College Record* 89, no. 3 (Spring 1988):373–83.

Smith, Eric E., and Lehman, James D. "Interactive Video: Implications of the Literature for Science Education." *Journal of Computers in Mathematics and Science Teaching* 8, no. 1 (Fall 1988):25–31.

Computer Multimedia

Ambron, SueAnn, and Hooper, K., eds. *Learning with Interactive Multimedia: Developing and Using Multimedia Tools in Education.* Redmond, WA: Microsoft Press, 1990.

Anderson, Carol J., and Veljkov, Mark D. *Creating Interactive Multimedia: A Practical Guide.* Glenview, IL: Scott, Foresman, 1990.

Barker, John, and Tucker, Richard N. *The Interactive Learning Revolution: Multimedia in Education and Training.* New York: Nichols, 1990.

D'Ignazio, Fred. "Through the Looking Glass: The Multiple Layers of Multimedia." *Computing Teacher* 17, no. 4 (December 1989–January 1990):25–31.

Litchfield, Brenda, and Mattson, Susan A. "The Interactive Media Science Project: An Inquiry-Based Multimedia Science Curriculum." *Journal of Computers in Mathematics and Science Teaching* 9, no. 1 (Fall 1989):37–43.

Multimedia: Getting Started. Sunnyvale, CA: Publix Information Products, 1991.

Trotter, Andrew. "Multimedia Puts Teachers in the Director's Chair." *Executive Educator* 12, no. 7 (July 1990):20–22.

Computer Hypermedia

Ambrose, David W. "The Effects of Hypermedia on Learning: A Literature Review." *Educational Technology* (December 1991):51–55.

Byrom, Elizabeth. "Hypermedia (Multimedia)." *Teaching Exceptional Children* 22, no. 4 (Summer 1990):47–48.

Grabowski, Barbara L., and Curtis, Ruth. "Information, Instruction, and Learning: A Hypermedia Perspective." *Performance Improvement Quarterly* 4, no. 3 (1991):2–12.

Hasselbring, Ted S., et al. "Making Knowledge Meaningful: Applications of Hypermedia." *Journal of Special Education* 10, no. 2 (Winter 1989):61–72.

Jonassen, David H., and Mandl, Heinz, eds. *Designing Hypermedia for Learning.* New York: Springer-Verlag, 1990.

Locatis, Craig et al. "Hypervideo." *Educational Technology Research and Development* 38, no. 2 (Summer 1990):41–49.

Megarry, Jacquetta. "Hypertext and Compact Discs: The Challenge of Multi-Media Learning." *British [Jour]nal of Educational Technology* no. 3 (October 1988):172–83.

Wilson, Kathleen S. "The Palenque [Opti]cal Disc Prototype: The Design [of a] Multimedia Discovery-Based Exp[eri]ence for Children." *Children's E[nvi]ronments Quarterly* 5:4 (1988):

Learning Centers

"Book Nooks and Classroom Cranni[es:] How to Make a Classroom Anyth[ing] but Ordinary." *Instructor* (August 1982):22–25.

Deal, Candace C. "Big Returns from Mini-Centers." *Momentum* (May 1984):34–35.

Evans, Richard M. "Troubleshooting Individualized Learning Centers." *Educational Technology* (April 1984):38–40.

Feldhusen, Hazel. "Teaching Gifted, Creative, and Talented Students in an Individualized Classroom." *Gifted Child Quarterly* (Summer 1981):108–11.

Hopkins, Jeri. "The Learning Center Classroom." *The Computing Teacher* (December/January 1985–1986):8–12.

Lutz, Charlene Howells, and Brills, Patricia. "Ten-Minute Super Centers." *Instructor* (September 1983):158–75.

Nations, Jimmy E., ed. *Learning Centers in the Classroom.* Washington, DC: National Education Association, 1976.

Orlich, Donald C., et al. "Science Learning Centers—An Aid to Instruction." *Science and Children* (September 1982):18–20.

Reynolds, Angus. "The Computer-Based Learning Center," *Human Resource Management and Development Handbook,* ed. W. R. Tracey. New York: American Management Association, 1984.

Strauber, Sandra K. "Language Learning Stations." *Foreign Language Annals* (February 1981):31–36.

"Walk-in, Talk-in, Learn-in Labs." *Instructor* (August 1983):48–52.

Smith, Eric E., and Lehman, James D. "Interactive Video: Implications of the Literature for Science Education." *Journal of Computers in Mathematics and Science Teaching* 8, no. 1 (Fall 1988):25–31.

Computer Multimedia

Ambron, SueAnn, and Hooper, K., eds. *Learning with Interactive Multimedia: Developing and Using Multimedia Tools in Education.* Redmond, WA: Microsoft Press, 1990.

Anderson, Carol J., and Veljkov, Mark D. *Creating Interactive Multimedia: A Practical Guide.* Glenview, IL: Scott, Foresman, 1990.

Barker, John, and Tucker, Richard N. *The Interactive Learning Revolution: Multimedia in Education and Training.* New York: Nichols, 1990.

D'Ignazio, Fred. "Through the Looking Glass: The Multiple Layers of Multimedia." *Computing Teacher* 17, no. 4 (December 1989–January 1990):25–31.

Litchfield, Brenda, and Mattson, Susan A. "The Interactive Media Science Project: An Inquiry-Based Multimedia Science Curriculum." *Journal of Computers in Mathematics and Science Teaching* 9, no. 1 (Fall 1989):37–43.

Multimedia: Getting Started. Sunnyvale, CA: Publix Information Products, 1991.

Trotter, Andrew. "Multimedia Puts Teachers in the Director's Chair." *Executive Educator* 12, no. 7 (July 1990):20–22.

Computer Hypermedia

Ambrose, David W. "The Effects of Hypermedia on Learning: A Literature Review." *Educational Technology* (December 1991):51–55.

Byrom, Elizabeth. "Hypermedia (Multimedia)." *Teaching Exceptional Children* 22, no. 4 (Summer 1990):47–48.

Grabowski, Barbara L., and Curtis, Ruth. "Information, Instruction, and Learning: A Hypermedia Perspective." *Performance Improvement Quarterly* 4, no. 3 (1991):2–12.

Hasselbring, Ted S., et al. "Making Knowledge Meaningful: Applications of Hypermedia." *Journal of Special Education* 10, no. 2 (Winter 1989):61–72.

Jonassen, David H., and Mandl, Heinz, eds. *Designing Hypermedia for Learning.* New York: Springer-Verlag, 1990.

Locatis, Craig et al. "Hypervideo." *Educational Technology Research and Development* 38, no. 2 (Summer 1990):41–49.

Megarry, Jacquetta. "Hypertext and Compact Discs: The Challenge of Multi-Media Learning." *British Journal of Educational Technology* 19, no. 3 (October 1988):172–83.

Wilson, Kathleen S. "The Palenque Optical Disc Prototype: The Design of a Multimedia Discovery-Based Experience for Children." *Children's Environments Quarterly* 5:4 (1988):7–13.

Learning Centers

"Book Nooks and Classroom Crannies: How to Make a Classroom Anything but Ordinary." *Instructor* (August 1982):22–25.

Deal, Candace C. "Big Returns from Mini-Centers." *Momentum* (May 1984):34–35.

Evans, Richard M. "Troubleshooting Individualized Learning Centers." *Educational Technology* (April 1984):38–40.

Feldhusen, Hazel. "Teaching Gifted, Creative, and Talented Students in an Individualized Classroom." *Gifted Child Quarterly* (Summer 1981):108–11.

Hopkins, Jeri. "The Learning Center Classroom." *The Computing Teacher* (December/January 1985–1986):8–12.

Lutz, Charlene Howells, and Brills, Patricia. "Ten-Minute Super Centers." *Instructor* (September 1983):158–75.

Nations, Jimmy E., ed. *Learning Centers in the Classroom.* Washington, DC: National Education Association, 1976.

Orlich, Donald C., et al. "Science Learning Centers—An Aid to Instruction." *Science and Children* (September 1982):18–20.

Reynolds, Angus. "The Computer-Based Learning Center," *Human Resource Management and Development Handbook,* ed. W. R. Tracey. New York: American Management Association, 1984.

Strauber, Sandra K. "Language Learning Stations." *Foreign Language Annals* (February 1981):31–36.

"Walk-in, Talk-in, Learn-in Labs." *Instructor* (August 1983):48–52.

Audiovisual References

Presentation Systems. Tempe, AZ: Arizona State University, 1975. Slides.

Part of a series, Producing Effective Audiovisual Presentations.

Preparing and Using Slide-Tape Presentations. San Jacinto, CA: Mt. San Jacinto College, n.d. 35mm filmstrip.

All of the following ½-inch VHS videocassettes are available from Audiovisual Center Marketing, C215 Seashore Hall, University of Iowa, Iowa City, IA 52242.

Programming Synchronized Slide/Tape Shows. 1988. 11 minutes

(Media Fears) Programming the Multislide Show. 1989. 13 minutes.

Scriptwriting: Filling the Empty Page. 1990. 16 minutes.

Thermofax (Thermal Dry Heat Process). 1983. 7 minutes.

Journal

Journal of Educational Multimedia and Hypermedia
Association for the Advancement of Computing in Education
P.O. Box 2966
Charlottesville, VA 22902

Organizations

Association for Multi-Image International Inc.
1025 Vermont Avenue, NW
Suite 820
Washington, DC 20005

Hypermedia and Instructional Software Clearinghouse
University of Colorado–Denver
Campus Box 106
Denver, CO 80217-3364

This clearinghouse collects, evaluates, and distributes unpublished, instructionally related computer software, particularly hypermedia, on a cost-recovery basis.

Interactive Video Industry Association
1900 L Street, NW
Suite 500
Washington, DC 20036

International Television Association
6311 N. O'Connor Road
Suite 230, LB 51
Irving, TX 75039

POSSIBLE PROJECTS

9–A. Plan a lesson in which you use a sound-slide set or sound film-strip. With this lesson show evidence that you have followed the utilization principles suggested in Chapter 2 as well as other pertinent suggestions from this chapter. Include a brief description of the audience and your objectives.

9–B. Develop a set of storyboard cards for an instructional sound-slide presentation.

9–C. Locate and examine a multimedia kit in your field of interest. Prepare a written or oral report on the possible applications and relative merits of the kit.

9–D. Locate and examine an interactive video, computer multimedia, or computer hypermedia program. Prepare a written or oral report on the possible applications and relative merits of the program.

9–E. Design a classroom learning center. Describe the audience, the objectives, and the materials and media to be incorporated. Explain the roles of the students and the instructor in using the center. Evaluate its actual effectiveness if used or potential effectiveness if not used.

9–F. Work through an instructional module as though you were a student. Be sure to do all the activities and complete the exercises. Prepare an appraisal of the module from your point of view. Submit the module with your appraisal, if possible.

10

Telecommunication Systems

OUTLINE

OBJECTIVES

After studying this chapter, you should be able to

1. Define *distance education.*

2. State a rationale for the educational use of telecommunication systems at the elementary, secondary, and postsecondary levels, and in nonformal education.

3. Discuss at least two examples of each of the instructional communication functions: information presentation, student-teacher interaction, student-student interaction, and access to learning resources.

4. Compare and contrast how each type of telecommunication system facilitates presentation and interaction.

5. Distinguish the various telecommunication systems from each other based on their physical attributes.

6. Compare the advantages and limitations of each of the telecommunication systems.

7. State at least one typical application of each of the telecommunication systems.

8. Differentiate the five delivery systems of one-way television on the basis of method of transmission.

9. Generate an example of an educational telecommunication system that incorporates two or more delivery systems.

10. Describe an advantageous instructional application of either audio or video teleconferencing for either elementary, secondary, postsecondary, or nonformal education.

11. Describe the functions performed by the classroom teacher in distance education.

LEXICON

telecommunication system

distance education

pseudo-interactive radio

audio teleconference

audiographic teleconference

computer conference

teletext

videotex

microwave transmission

Instructional Television Fixed Services (ITFS)

closed-circuit television (CCTV)

video teleconference

teletraining

compressed video

One of the greatest advantages offered by modern electronic technology is the ability to instruct without the live presence of a teacher; that is, we can "time-shift" instruction—experience it at some time *after* the live lesson—and "place-shift" instruction—experience it at some place far *away from* the live teacher. Of course, the book was the first invention that made it possible to time-shift and place-shift instruction, and it continues in that use today. A certain degree of student-teacher interaction is possible through print media. For nearly a century people in all parts of the world have been able to participate in guided independent study through correspondence courses via the mail system. Learners receive printed lessons, do written assignments, and get feedback from the remote instructor. But the proliferation of newer electronic technologies now makes it possible to experience place-shifted instruction with a stunning array of additional auditory and visual stimuli, far more rapidly, and with a far richer range of interaction, not only with the instructor but also with other learners.

In this chapter the term *telecommunication systems* embraces a wide variety of media configurations, including radio, telephone, television (broadcast, wired, and satellite), and computers. What they all have in common is implied in the Greek root word *tele,* which means "at a distance," or "far off"; that is, they are systems for communicating over a distance.

Distance education has become the popular term to describe learning via telecommunications. More formally defined, *distance education* is a form of education characterized by

❑ physical separation of learners from the teacher

❑ an organized instructional program

❑ technological media

❑ two-way communication

As the examples in this chapter will make clear, the converging of electronic technologies has fostered a rich hybridization of media configurations. We seldom see an instructional telecommunication system that is of one pure type. Typically, programs are distributed by a combination of broadcast, wired, or satellite-relayed transmissions, and students respond through some combination of mail, fax, telephone, microphone, or computer transmissions. Familiarity with these alternative pathways to learning are essential to today's educators:

> Technologies for learning at a distance, while reaching but a small but growing number of teachers today, will clearly affect the teaching force of tomorrow. Some will teach on these systems, others will use them to provide additional resources in their classrooms, and many will receive professional education and training over them. Few will be unaffected.[1]

EDUCATIONAL USES OF TELECOMMUNICATION SYSTEMS

Elementary Education

At the elementary school level, teachers tend to use prerecorded videocassettes more often than live broadcast television programs. Still, there are several broadcast series that are frequently used: at the early elementary level, "Sesame Street"; at the higher grade levels, "Reading Rainbow," "3–2–1 Contact," "Voyage of the Mimi," and "Nova." These programs are used as enrichment rather than as the core of instruction, the exception being "Voyage of the Mimi," which is frequently used as the main element of a lesson. Teachers who use educational television programming tend to use more than one program (usually two or three), but not a whole series.[2]

Secondary Education

At the secondary level, television is used mainly to expand the curricular offerings of a specific high school. Rural schools are thus able to offer a full core curriculum. In advanced or specialized subjects for which there are not enough students in one school to justify hiring a teacher, television is frequently used to connect several schools, thus creating a large enough "class" to be affordable. For example, the TI-IN network, based in Texas, reaches high school students all across the United States via satellite. TI-IN offers such courses as foreign languages (Spanish, French, German, Latin, and Japanese), calculus, physics, psychology, and art history. These live, interactive classes, which use telephone talkback, are scheduled throughout the school day on two channels. As opposed to the elementary school pattern, these programs tend to be used in their entirety and they provide core instruction.

Distance learning at the K–12 level gained impetus in the late 1980s due to the Star Schools program initiated by the U.S. Department of Education. This program provides multimillion dollar grants for regional consortia to develop instructional networks that reach elementary and secondary students in rural, disadvantaged, and small schools. The TI-IN network is one of these; seven other consortia give primary service to other regions. Taken together, the Star Schools program has reached over 100,000 students in 45 states.

[1] U.S. Congress, Office of Technology Assessment, *Linking for Learning: A New Course for Education* (Washington, DC: U.S. Government Printing Office, 1989), p. 20.

[2] *A Study of the Role of Educational Television Programming in Elementary Schools* (New York: Children's Television Workshop, 1990).

required to transmit, and in the United States a specific part of the microwave spectrum has been reserved for educational institutions—the 2500–2690 band, called *Instructional Television Fixed Service (ITFS)*.

ITFS (and other microwave transmissions) have one major technical limitation: signals broadcast at these high microwave frequencies travel in a line-of-sight pattern. Consequently, the coverage of ITFS is limited to areas in direct sightline of the trans-

mission tower. Over 100 educational licensees operate several hundred channels in the ITFS spectrum. Even though reception is limited to a line-of-sight radius, this is large enough to cover some school districts.

Figure 10.12
One-way video distribution systems

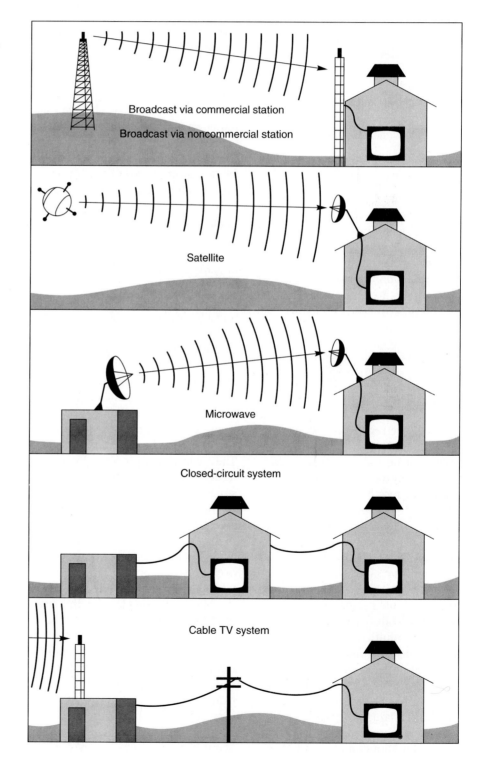

Broadcast via commercial station
Broadcast via noncommercial station

Satellite

Microwave

Closed-circuit system

Cable TV system

Figure 10.13
Satellite dishes, such as this one for TI-IN, bring satellite signals directly to any educational setting, no matter how remote.

Like cable, ITFS allows transmission on multiple channels. The average licensee operates about six channels. Because the system operates on frequencies above those that can be received on ordinary sets without a converter, it offers a degree of privacy similar to cable or closed-circuit television.

Closed-Circuit Television

The term *closed-circuit television* (CCTV) refers to a private distribution system connected by wire. This wire may be regular copper wire that sends electrical impulses or thin glass optical fiber that sends impulses in the form of light. CCTV signals cannot be received outside the private network. A major advantage of CCTV is that such systems do not require government licensing and can be set up freely by any institution that desires to do so. Closed circuit is used mainly to connect the buildings on an individual school or college campus and gives a private, multichannel capability within those confines. The cost of distribution rises as the network expands (unlike with broadcast TV), so CCTV is not generally used for reaching a large geographic area. However, several states, such as Indiana and Minnesota have CCTV net-

works connecting schools and colleges hundreds of miles apart.

Cable Television

The cable concept of television program delivery was first applied commercially in the 1950s in isolated towns where, due to interference from a mountain overshadowing the town, people were unable to receive a viewable signal from the nearest TV station. Local businesspeople developed the idea of building a master antenna atop the mountain. There the weak signals were amplified and fed into a coaxial cable that ran down the mountain into the town. By paying an installation charge and a monthly subscription fee, a customer could have his or her home connected to the cable. This idea of having a single tall antenna to serve a whole community gave the process the name community antenna television, or CATV, now more commonly known as cable television.

Most CATV systems in operation today basically resemble the original master antenna model, in which broadcast television signals are captured by a favorably situated high-mast antenna (see Figure 10.14). The signals are amplified and delivered to the head-end of the system, where they are processed, fed into a trunk line, and further amplified. The signals then proceed along feeder lines and eventually to smaller drop lines that enter individual homes and other buildings. The signal-carrying cables are installed underground in some systems (especially in congested urban areas), but ordinarily they are strung out along telephone poles, with a fee paid to the telephone company for this use of its property.

The growth of cable television has been slowed by the need to obtain legal rights to establish a system in each municipality and by the sheer expense of installing all the cable required to reach every home in the coverage area. Nevertheless, by 1992 about 95 percent of all television

households in the United States were within reach of a cable TV system, and 61 percent of all television households were cable TV subscribers. The cable subscriber, besides getting a strong, clear video image on the screen, has access to more channels than are readily available over the air. Some of these channels are reserved for use by community groups; others are devoted to sports, music videos, special movies, news, weather, medical programs, and other specialized interests.

Advantages

Although it is difficult to generalize about one-way telecommunication systems as diverse as broadcasting, satellite, microwave, CCTV, and cable television, all of these systems are designed to reach mass audiences in a cost-efficient way. All allow the transmission of motion image and sound over distance.

Limitations

Although some of these telecommunication systems could potentially be used in a two-way mode, they were designed and are customarily used in a one-way mode. Compared with the use of videocassettes on a classroom recorder, all these systems require a huge capital investment to build or lease the transmission network for a period of time.

Applications

Commercial Broadcasting. In the United States both commercial and noncommercial stations provide programming used in educational institutions. In fact, one-quarter of the programs used by teachers in schools originate with commercial stations. These include classic and contemporary dramas, dance and music performances, science and nature documentaries, historical dramas and documentaries, and news and public affairs programs.

Popular dramas viewed by students at home may also provide experiential background that creative

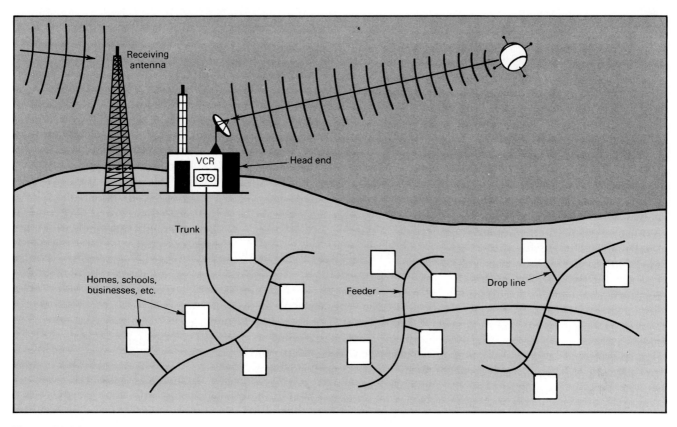

Figure 10.14
Cable television distribution system. Multiple program sources are combined at the "head end" and sent out through trunks, feeders, and drop lines to individual schools.

teachers can use as raw material to spark discussions of social issues. TV story lines often revolve around moral dilemmas. Should the lawyer continue to defend her client vigorously even after he admits guilt with no remorse? Should the physician inform the parents of the unwed pregnant teenager about her condition or should it remain private and confidential? What rights do patients and their families have concerning the suspension of artificial life-support systems?

Noncommercial Broadcasting.
The 320-plus TV stations in the United States that hold noncommercial licenses are referred to collectively as public television stations, a term designating their common commitment to operate not for private gain but for the public benefit. Although these stations have various patterns of ownership, they tend to operate along roughly similar lines. Just as most commercial stations act as outlets for commercial network programming, most public television stations serve as outlets for the network programming of the Public Broadcasting Service (PBS). Their evening schedules feature PBS offerings and other programs aimed at home viewers in general, while during the daytime hours these stations typically carry instructional programs designed for specific school or college audiences (Figure 10.15).

Public television attempts to offer an alternative type of programming for viewers who are not well served by the mass audience programs of commercial broadcasting. In reaching out to selected subgroups, public TV programming does not usually attract viewers on a scale comparable to the commercial networks. However, well-produced programs such as "Wall Street Week,"

Figure 10.15
Big Bird, a main character on "Sesame Street," which after more than twenty-five years is still the most recognized educational series for children.

"Masterpiece Theatre," and "Nova" have won critical acclaim and loyal audiences that in recent years have grown to a size comparable to those for many commercial programs. On a more general plane, public opinion polls indicate that over 60 percent of American adults can name their local public TV channel and do watch such programs at least occasionally.

The types of programs carried on public TV—documentaries, dramas, public affairs features, musical performances, science programs, and the like—are often useful as adjuncts to instruction in schools and colleges. Programs for direct classroom use to reach specific curriculum objectives—instructional television (ITV)—are a mainstay of most public TV stations' daytime schedules. There is also a rapidly growing trend toward distribution of programs by videocassette in addition to broadcast distribution by stations (Figure 10.16).

ITV programs tend to be about fifteen minutes (at the earlier grade levels) to thirty minutes long, and a single program is often repeated at different hours throughout the week to allow for flexibility in classroom scheduling. Contrary to the popular image, broadcast ITV programs usually do not present core instruction in basic subject areas. One leading researcher described ITV's role this way:

1. To assist the classroom teachers in those subjects in which they often have the most difficulty (for example, art, music, mathematics, science, and health);

2. To supplement the classroom instruction in subject areas in which limited classroom resources may prevent full examination of historical or international events; and

3. To bring outside stimulation in subject areas, such as literature,

where teachers have difficulty exciting and motivating the students.[5]

Microwave Transmission (ITFS). At the present time, in formal education microwave is the least used of the telecommunication systems described here, but its use has been growing slowly over the years. There are over 100 licensees operating several hundred channels. Catholic school systems are prominent users of ITFS. The Catholic schools in New York City and Brooklyn operate some twenty-three channels; the system in Chicago has ten channels.

Within higher education ITFS is used primarily for graduate and professional school distance education,

---

[5] Saul Rockman, "Instructional Television Is Alive and Well," in *The Future of Public Broadcasting,* ed. Cater and Nyhan (New York: Praeger, 1976), p. 79.

Figure 10.16
Off-air reception from public TV stations is still common, but in-classroom playback of videocassettes is the primary delivery system for instructional television.

Table 10.2
Television Programs Most Widely Used in Schools

Rank	Series/Program	Teachers Using
1	"Reading Rainbow"	132,600
2	"National Geographic"	56,400
3	CNN News	37,000
4	*Sarah, Plain and Tall*	36,700
5	"Nova"	35,900
6	"3–2–1 Contact"	26,900
7	"Sesame Street"	25,200
8	News (general)	23,900
9	"Channel One"	22,200
10	"Letter People"	19,500
11	"Nature"	17,800
12	*The Civil War*	16,100
13	"Slim Goodbody"	15,800
14	"Books from Cover to Cover"	14,200
15	*Romeo and Juliet*	14,100
16	*Glory*	12,400
17	"Teletales"	11,100
18	"All About You"	10,400
19	"Voyage of the Mimi"	10,300
20	"Where the Red Fern Grows"	10,224

Source: *Study of School Uses of Television and Video, 1990–1991 School Year* (Washington, DC: Corporation for Public Broadcasting, 1992).

for example, connecting engineering or medical schools with professionals in the field who desire a refresher course.

Closed-Circuit TV.

It's more difficult to characterize the applications of CCTV because, being unregulated, there is no central information source. Also, CCTV systems can be as simple as a camera connected to a monitor in the same room (e.g., for image magnification of a science demonstration) or as complex as a campus-wide wired distribution system (e.g., for distribution of video programs from a central library to any classroom). Because the cost of building a CCTV system increases with geographic area, it is not widely used to interconnect buildings spread out over a school district. However, it is frequently used to connect buildings on a college or university campus.

Cable TV.

Over 70 percent of all schools and most postsecondary institutions are now connected to commercial cable systems, often without monthly charges.[6] Educational institutions are often invited to use one of the cable channels for their own purposes.

The availability of multiple channels with cable facilitates a number of special services:

1. Transmission of several programs simultaneously and repetition of programs at different hours for more flexible matching with classroom schedules

2. "Narrowcasting," or aiming specialized programs at small subgroups, for example, those speaking foreign languages or having sight or hearing impairment

3. Retrieval of remotely stored libraries of video materials, allow-

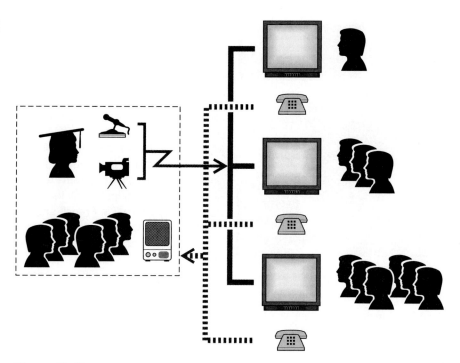

Figure 10.17
Television, one-way video, two-way audio. This is probably the most widely used and most economical means of adding interactivity to instructional TV.

ing teachers, or individual students, access to materials on demand without the logistic struggle often associated with instructional media use

Furthermore, many cable operators provide schools with special programming, teachers' guides, and even special computer services, such as "X-press" and "X-change." Many of the program sources available via cable are not retransmitted from broadcasts but are sent out only on cable. A number of these offer high-quality programming suitable for school use. The Discovery Channel, The Learning Channel, Cable News Network, and C-Span are a few examples, all of which offer program guides for teachers.

TELEVISION: ONE-WAY VIDEO, TWO-WAY AUDIO

Virtually any of the television modes mentioned above can be converted into a two-way communication system with the addition of a device for

sending audio feedback to the source. In the case of broadcast, satellite, and microwave transmissions, the talk-back capability is usually added by means of a telephone, using a regular telephone to call a speakerphone in the originating studio. In the case of closed-circuit and cable systems, the talk-back channel may be incorporated in the CCTV or CATV wiring itself.

Advantages

Adding a channel for interaction between instructor and student may be the most important breakthrough in instructional telecommunications. Providing a telephone or microphone at the receiving site allows direct, immediate student-instructor voice interaction. The instructor can ask questions for students to answer, or students can query the instructor about some point of the lesson, thereby changing the direction of the lesson. The interactive capability also allows the instructor to monitor

6   *Study of School Uses of Television and Video, 1990–1991 School Year* (Washington DC: Corporation for Public Broadcasting, 1992).

Satellite Serves Rural High School

Eddyville (Oregon) High School is a small, rural high school serving a logging community located on the Pacific Ocean. It's part of a sparsely populated school district covering 1,800 square miles. The school, like many others in similar situations across the United States, has difficulty offering a broad enough curriculum to meet the diverse needs of the students. In this case, the interactive television programs delivered by satellite from TI-IN Network in San Antonio, Texas, helped to fill the gaps. In 1988 Eddyville High School was about to eliminate classes in French and Spanish because the teacher of those subjects moved away. By subscribing to TI-IN the school enabled its students to take not only those language courses but also psychology, sociology, and art appreciation.

The video lessons are broadcast on a regular schedule, and the Oregon students participate along with students at many other sites around the country. At each site there is a telephone to allow question-and-answer (one-way video, two-way audio). Students, teachers, and parents appreciate the chance to have an enriched curriculum at a cost even a small school can afford.

Source: *Star Student News* (December 1988–January 1989), published by TI-IN Network.

---

student progress by noting the level of their responses to questions.

Limitations

Of course, adding the talk-back capability usually entails extra costs, such as special telephone equipment, and long-distance calls entail toll charges. If the receiving group is spread over several locations, a bridge may be needed to screen and select calls, resulting in additional expense. Lacking the visual dimension, communication is limited to what can be conveyed by voice alone; facial expressions and gestures are lost as well as the capability to view and discuss student work of a visual or written nature.

Applications

One of the leading examples of the one-way video, two-way audio system is the Arts and Sciences Teleconferencing Service (ASTS) centered in Oklahoma but serving students in over 500 high schools throughout the United States. During the twice-a-week ASTS classes, students receive instruction via live video, and they interact with the teleteacher by toll-free telephone. Students who have questions after class hours can either phone the instructor or send questions by electronic mail. This is similar to the format used by the TI-IN network (see "Close-Up: Satellite Serves Rural High School").

The *video teleconference* is another highly visible application of one-way television with two-way audio. It is an extension of audio teleconferencing, in which a video image is transmitted and displayed along with the audio conversation. Technically it is not different from television with two-way audio, but the "conferencing" terminology is preferred in corporate and higher education applications. It implies that those at both the sending and receiving sites will all be active participants in a conversation rather than passive recipients of an outgoing message (Figure 10.18).

When such a system is used for training, it is referred to as *tele-training* (Figure 10.19). A corporate example of teletraining is provided by Allstate Insurance Company, which maintains a dedicated two-way video network between its headquarters and twenty-eight regional offices. Their philosophy is that virtually anything that can be taught in a live classroom can be taught via videoconferencing. A facsimile system is used to transmit printed information between sites. Trainees can ask questions by pressing a button on the console in the reception site; all calls are queued up automatically and are answered in turn by the instructor.

Since 1982 the National University Teleconference Network (NUTN) has been offering teleconferences of nationwide scope to its 250 member universities and to their business and community constituencies. Their programs tend to be one-time updates on topics of current interest, such as international trade opportunities, computer developments, and business trends. It is becoming a major source for continuing professional education.

TELEVISION: TWO-WAY VIDEO, TWO-WAY AUDIO

Fully interactive television with two-way communication of both audio and video, or two-way television, is achieved by equipping both the sending and receiving sites with camera and microphone and interconnecting them by some means capable of two-way transmission. This may be fiber optics, cable, microwave, satellite, or a combination. A school or other organization may operate its own facilities or lease them as needed for particular occasions.

Technically, it's much more difficult and expensive to transmit a full-motion video image than a still picture. The full-motion image requires a channel as broad as that used by broadcast TV stations whereas a still picture can be sent over a narrow telephone line. A recent technological breakthrough called *compressed video* removes redundant information, transmitting only the frames in which there is some motion. In this way the video information can be squeezed through a telephone line. This compression is important because it costs only about one-tenth as much

to transmit through a phone line as through a broadband channel. There is a perceptible difference in the fluidity of the motion depicted, but participants easily adapt to this. Compressed video is gaining popularity rapidly wherever two-way television is being used. (See "Close-Up: School-University Cooperation Through Compressed Video.")

Advantages

Two-way interactive television provides the closest approximation to face-to-face communication that can be achieved technologically. It's the

Figure 10.18
Video-teleconference participants often view the program on projection TV, giving feedback to the speaker via telephone.

Figure 10.19
Teletraining is used widely by AT&T for corporate training and development.

HOW TO...
Organize and Conduct Successful Teletraining

At the origination end:

❑ Be clear about audience needs and the purpose of the program.

❑ Plan and organize more intensively than you would for face-to-face training.

❑ Promote the session with attractive, friendly mailers and personal contacts with local coordinators.

❑ Provide printed supporting materials with discussion points and pre- and postviewing assignments.

❑ Stimulate active participation by setting up reaction panels, arranging buzz groups, and planting starter questions.

❑ Keep the presentation itself informal, personal, and narrowly focused; punctuate it with opportunities for questions or local discussions.

At the reception end:

❑ Arrange the classroom for comfort, easy viewing, and easy discussion among participants.

❑ If the session is a long one, plan for refreshment breaks or meals to break up the day.

❑ Check the setup the day before; then arrive early on the designated day and check again; monitor equipment functioning throughout the session itself.

❑ Introduce the session by familiarizing participants with the equipment, outlining objectives clearly, and explaining procedural details, especially the ground rules for questions or other feedback.

❑ Carry out postviewing activities, such as a local panel discussion or discussion groups.

❑ Collect evaluations; follow up on suggestions made or on any questions left unanswered.

---

next best thing to being there. Instructors can see students' facial expressions and gestures as they talk. They can also observe and critique performances, such as foreign language practice dialogs, speech presentations, even art work. In the instructional situation two-way television simulates one large classroom despite the fact that some students are hundreds or thousands of miles away.

Limitations

Two-way video transmission is approximately twice as expensive as one-way video. Furthermore, as technological setups become more elaborate, the possibilities of malfunction increase. Some two-way television setups, such as those used for corporate video teleconferences of important events, often entail very elaborate production setups. The presence of camera operators and technicians disrupts the intimacy of the class or meeting, often causing both instructors and students to feel intimidated. The better two-way television setups avoid this

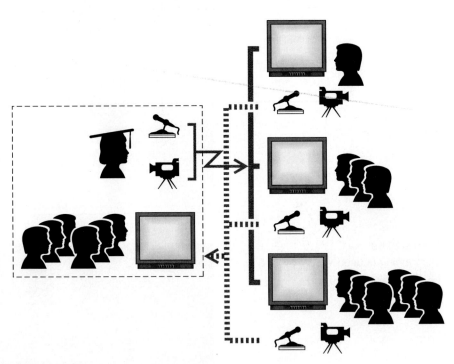

Figure 10.20
Television, two-way video, two-way audio. Full auditory and visual interactivity requires a camera and microphone at each reception site.

CLOSE-UP

School-University Cooperation Through Compressed Video

The Wyoming Centers for Teaching and Learning Network (WCTLN) is a cooperative venture among school districts and the School of Education at the University of Wyoming. This network uses compressed video and other technologies to connect schools in nine different districts with each other and with the university.

The telecommunication network was set up to deal with the problem of small populations spread over a vast geographical area. Many teachers work in small, isolated schools with limited curriculum offerings. Because of the relatively low cost of building and operating a compressed video system (compared with regular broadband video), it is now possible for children in one locale to participate in live, two-way audio and video exchanges with students and teachers at other schools.

Besides being used to enrich the curricula at K–12 schools, teachers and administrators use the system for electronic in-service meetings, saving them from driving hundreds of miles to meet.

The School of Education uses the system to enable teacher trainees to observe real, live classrooms. The system also allows student teachers to be observed by their School of Education supervisors while they are working in the field. Considering that some of these practice sites are a seven-hour drive from the university, the video system yields tremendous savings in time and effort.

Source: Landra Rezabek and Barbara Hakes, College of Education, University of Wyoming

CLOSE-UP

Sharing Teachers via Videoconferencing

How can small rural schools offer advanced courses in mathematics and foreign languages when no single school has a large enough enrollment to justify its own teacher? Four school districts in Carroll County, Illinois, have been experimenting with a simplified two-way videoconferencing system as an answer to this question. Each participating school has set up one classroom as a teleconference room, equipped with cameras, microphones, video recorder, monitors, and special effects generator/switcher. Classes are taught live at the school in which there is a qualified teacher; students in any of the other three schools may participate.

Students in the receiving schools watch and listen to the class. They can also be heard and seen by activating the camera and microphone in their own classroom. A camera mounted on top of the teacher's desk gives close-up views of visual materials.

Lessons can be videotaped for review by absent students. They can also be videotaped in advance when the instructor must be absent during usual class times.

Source: Peter C. West, Rhonda S. Robinson, and Keith Collins, "A Teaching and Telecommunications Partnership," *Educational Leadership* (March 1986): 54–55.

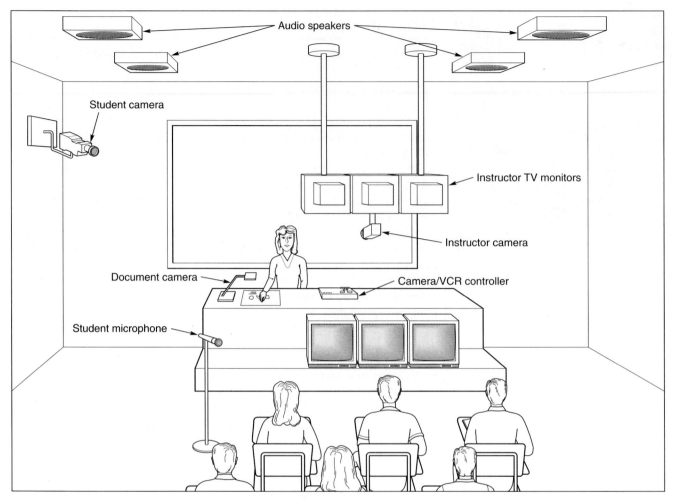

Figure 10.21
Classroom setup for interactive TV. At the originating classroom, both teacher
and students must have camera(s), microphone(s), and monitor(s) to
communicate with students in remote classrooms.

CLOSE-UP

Free Clearinghouse on Distance Learning

The National Distance Learning Center (NDLC) is a centralized on-line data
base containing detailed program listings for distance-learning courses, including credit and noncredit school courses, teleconferences, seminars, and
in-service training courses. The listings pertain to all audiences, primary, secondary, continuing education, and all levels of adult learners. NDLC provides
program information on courses available in all distance-learning formats, including satellite broadcast, audio- and videocassette, and print.

There is no charge for access to the system or to scan the data base, and
quires only a computer and modem; communications software for the modem
will even be sent without charge if needed.

For more information, contact the National Distance Learning Center,
Owensboro Community College, 4800 Hartford Road, Owensboro, KY 42303.

Figure 10.22
Research abundantly demonstrates the paramount role of the classroom teacher in making instructional TV work.

pitfall by using remote-controlled, simple equipment that does not require live operators to be present.

Applications

Corporations were early, large-scale users of two-way video teleconferencing for such purposes as introducing a new product nationwide, conducting decision-making meetings involving widely scattered sites, and educating personnel about new products or services (teletraining).

In recent years schools and universities have been taking advantage of improved, lower-cost technologies to build their own two-way television networks. In Bergen County, New Jersey, a cluster of urban elementary and secondary schools are interconnected via fiber optics. In Minnesota some 200 school districts, grouped into 50 networks, share fully interactive classes using microwave, fiber-optic, and telephone-line connections. Kirtland Community College in Michigan is interconnected with seven school districts via microwave and coaxial cable. In all these cases the systems have been designed and justified on the basis that the schools can expand

their curriculum offerings and offer high-quality instruction without having to support specialty teachers at each school site. Through technology, teachers can be shared cost-effectively while giving students quality learning experiences (see "Close-Up: Sharing Teachers via Videoconferencing" on page 305).

THE ROLE OF THE CLASSROOM TEACHER

The role of the classroom teacher or on-site facilitator varies from one setting to another. However, experience has shown that in formal K–12 education student success increases when the distant teacher and classroom teacher work as a team. In one major project, students achieved better in casses in which the on-site teacher

❑ Watched and participated actively in all programs with the students.

❑ Encouraged interaction with the distant teacher.

❑ Answered simple questions.

❑ Solved immediate problems.

❑ Provided additional quizzes and worksheets.

❑ Took responsibility for operating and troubleshooting the equipment.[7]

To play an active, facilitating role requires advance planning and training. Ideally, the distant teacher and classroom teacher meet before classes start to discuss goals for the class and instructional strategies. For example, they may agree to allow students in receiving classrooms to discuss and explain points to each other during class with talk-back microphones off. Such peer cooperation can greatly enhance the learning atmosphere in what might otherwise be a stilted, restrictive environment.

REFERENCES

Print References

Barker, Bruce, et al. "Broadening the Definition of Distance Education in Light of the New Telecommunications Technologies." *American Journal of Distance Education* 15, no. 4 (1989): 20–29.

---

7   Vicki M. Hobbs and Donald D. Osburn, *Distance Learning Evaluation Study Report II: An Inter- and Intra-State Comparison* (Denver, CO: Mid-Continent Regional Education Laboratory, 1989).

Bearne, Colin. "Teaching with the Dish." *British Journal of Language Teaching* 26, no. 1 (Spring 1988): 54–56.

Bradshaw, Dean H., and Desser, Karen. *Audiographics Distance Learning: A Resource Handbook.* San Francisco: Far West Laboratory for Educational Research and Development, 1990.

Branscomb, Anne W. "Videotext: Global Progress and Comparative Policies." *Journal of Communication* 38, no. 1 (Winter 1988): 50–59.

Chute, Alan G. "Strategies for Implementing Teletraining Systems." *Educational and Training Technology International* 27, no. 3 (August 1990): 264–70.

Clark, G. Christopher. "Distance Learning: A Spectrum of Opportunities." *Media and Methods* 26, no. 1 (September–October 1989): 22, 24–27.

Cyrs, Thomas E., and Smith, Frank A. *Teleclass Teaching: A Resource Guide.* 2d ed. Las Cruces, NM: Center for Educational Development, New Mexico State University, 1990.

Dede, Christopher J. "The Evolution of Distance Learning: Technology-Mediated Interactive Learning." *Journal of Research on Computing in Education* 22, no. 3 (Spring 1990): 247–64.

Descy, Don E. "Two-Way Interactive Television in Minnesota: The KIDS Network." *Tech Trends* 36, no. 1 (1991): 44–48.

England, Richard. *A Survey of State-Level Involvement in Distance Education at the Elementary and Secondary Levels.* ACSDE Research Monograph No. 3. University Park, PA: The Pennsylvania State University, 1991.

Garrison, D. R. *Understanding Distance Education.* New York: Routledge, 1989.

Gilbert, John K.; Temple, Annette; and Underwood, Craig, eds. *Satellite Technology in Education.* New York: Routledge, 1991.

Giltrow, David. *Distance Education.* Washington DC: Association for Educational Communications and Technology, 1989.

Hanson, Gordon. "Distance Education and Educational Needs: A Model for Assessment." *Media and Methods* 27, no. 1 (September–October 1990): 14, 17–18.

Holmberg, Borje. *Theory and Practice of Distance Education.* New York: Routledge, 1989.

Hudspeth, Delayne R., and Brey, Ronald G. *Instructional Telecommunications: Principles and Applications.* New York: Praeger, 1986.

Hurley, Paul; Laucht, Matthias; and Hlynka, Denis. *The Videotex and Teletext Handbook.* New York: Harper and Row, 1985.

Interactive Radio Instruction: Confronting a Crisis in Basic Education. Washington, DC: U.S. Agency for International Development and Education Development Center, 1990.

Keegan, Desmond. *Foundations of Distance Education.* 2d ed. New York, Routledge, 1990.

Kitchen, Karen, and Kitchen, Will. *Two-Way Interactive Television for Distance Learning.* Alexandria, VA: National School Boards Association, 1988.

Mason, Robin, and Kaye, Anthony, eds. *Mindweave: Communication, Computers, and Distance Education.* Oxford: Pergamon, 1989.

Massoumian, Bijan. "Successful Teaching via Two-Way Interactive Video." *Tech Trends* 34, no. 2 (March–April 1989): 16–19.

Milheim, William D. "Computers and Satellites: Effective New Technologies for Distance Education." *Journal of Research on Computing in Education* 22, no. 2 (Winter 1989): 151–59.

Moore, Michael G., and Thompson, Melody M. *The Effects of Distance Learning: A Summary of the Literature.* ACSDE Research Monograph No. 2. University Park, PA: The Pennsylvania State University, 1990.

Mugridge, I., and Kaufman, D. *Distance Education in Canada.* London: Croom Helm, 1986.

Naidu, Som. *Computer Conferencing in Distance Education.* ERIC Information Analysis. Syracuse, NY: ERIC Clearinghouse on Information Resources, 1988.

Ostendorf, Virginia A. *Teaching Through Interactive Television.* Littleton, CO: Virginia A. Ostendorf, 1989.

Ostendorf, Virginia A. *What Every Principal, Teacher, and School Board Member Should Know about Distance Education.* Littleton, CO: Virginia A. Ostendorf, 1989.

Pease, Pamela S. "Strategies for Implementing Distance Learning Technologies: Why, When, and How." *School Business Affairs* 55, no. 10 (October 1989): 15–18.

Robertson, Bill. "Audio Teleconferencing: Low-Cost Technology for External Studies Networking." *Distance Education* (March 1987): 121–30.

Schamber, Linda. *Delivery Systems for Distance Education.* ERIC Digest. Syracuse, NY: ERIC Clearinghouse on Information Resources, 1988.

Telecommunications for Learning. Educational Technology Anthology Series, Vol. 3. Englewood Cliffs NJ: Educational Technology Publications, 1991.

U.S. Congress, Office of Technology Assessment. *Linking for Learning: A New Course for Education.* Washington DC: U.S. Government Printing Office, 1989.

Verduin, John R., and Clark, Thomas A. *Distance Education: The Foundations of Effective Practice.* San Francisco: Jossey-Bass, 1991.

Waggoner, Michael D., ed. *Empowering Networks: Computer Conferencing in Education.* Englewood Cliffs, NJ: Educational Technology Publications, 1991.

Wall, Milan. "Technological Options for Rural Schools." *Educational Leadership* (March 1986): 50–52.

Wallin, Desna L. "Televised Interactive Education: Creative Technology for Alternative Learning." *Community/ Junior College Quarterly of Research and Practice* 14, no. 3 (July–September 1990): 259–66.

Wilson, Virginia S., et al. "Audio Teleconferencing as Teaching Technique." *Social Education* (February 1986): 90–92.

Witherspooon, John, and Kovitz, Roselle. *The History of Public Broadcasting.* Washington, DC: Current, 1987.

Zigerell, James. *The Uses of Television in American Higher Education.* New York: Praeger, 1991.

Audiovisual References

Communication II—Today and Tomorrow. Irwindale, CA: Barr Films, 1990. Videocassette, ¾ or ½ inch.

Linking for Learning: A New Course for Education. Manhasset NY: S. L. Productions, 1990. Videocassette, ½ inch.

Telecommunications. Calgary, Alberta, Canada: Access Network, 1989. Videocassette, ¾ or ½ inch.

Organizations

Agency for Instructional Technology (AIT)
P.O. Box A
Bloomington, IN 47402–0120

AIT produces television programs and computer courseware as the coordinating agency of a consortium that includes most of the United States and the Canadian provinces. It serves as a national distribution center also. It publishes a newsletter and an annual catalog listing dozens of series incorporating several hundred separate programs. Emphasis is on the elementary and secondary levels.

Association for Educational Communications and Technology (AECT)
1025 Vermont Avenue, NW
Suite 820
Washington, DC 20005

AECT holds conferences, publishes journals and books related to instructional uses of media including TV, and represents the educational communication/technology profession. Its Division of Telecommunications addresses the concerns of members who work in instructional TV and radio.

Corporation for Public Broadcasting (CPB)
901 E Street, NW
Washington, DC 20004–2006

CPB is a nonprofit, private corporation established and funded in part by the federal government. It performs a broad coordinating function for the nation's public radio and television stations and supports the interests of public broadcasting in general. CPB carries out research on the educational applications of television and coordinates the Annenberg Project, aimed at providing programming for higher education.

International Television Association (ITVA)
6311 North O'Connor Road
Suite 230 LB-51
Irving, TX 75039

ITVA is an organization of nonbroadcast television professionals in fourteen countries, primarily North America. It supports the use of television in the private sector—training, communications, and public relations—and sponsors regional and national conferences and an awards program.

Action for Children's Television
20 University Road
Cambridge, MA 02138

Cable Television Information Center
1700 Shaker Church Rd., NW
Olympia, WA 98502

Children's Television Workshop
1 Lincoln Plaza
New York, NY 10023

Public Service Satellite Consortium (PSSC)
600 Maryland Ave. SW
Suite 220
Washington DC 20024

POSSIBLE PROJECTS

10–A. Investigate the use of radio for instructional purposes in a local school or college. Check with your local public radio station to see if it supports any specifically instructional activities. Prepare a short written report (500–750 words) or audiocassette report (about five minutes).

10–B. Interview a teacher who regularly utilizes broadcast television programs in the classroom. Prepare a brief written or recorded report covering the objectives addressed, utilization techniques used, and problems encountered.

10–C. Invent a new telecommunications service by putting together an original (as far as you know) combination of features. An example might be an international pen pals club using fax machines interconnected via satellite. Your service need not be economically practical, but it should serve some describable purpose.

10–D. Generate a list of interesting uses for teleconferencing in a course that you are currently enrolled in. Who might your class communicate with? For what purposes?

10–E. Prepare an abstract of a report of a research or demonstration project related to instructional telecommunications, for example, two schools sharing one teacher by means of one-way television and two-way telephone.

11

Mediaware and Media Setups

OUTLINE

Safety

Equipment Tables and Carts

    Features of Carts

    Cart Safety Tips

Tape Recorders

    Microphones

    Battery Tips

Audio Setups

    Built-in Speaker Systems

    Detached Speaker Systems

    Feedback

    Volume and Tone Setting

Overhead Projectors

    LCD Panels

Slide Projectors

    Sound Synchronization

Filmstrip Projectors

Film Projectors

Projector Setups

    Lamps

    Lenses

    Screens

Video Recorder/Players

    Video Projectors

Video Playback Setups

    Seating

    Monitor Placement

    Lighting

    Volume

OBJECTIVES

After studying this chapter, you should be able to

1. Operate each of the following pieces of equipment: cassette tape recorder, overhead projector, slide projector, filmstrip projector, 16mm film projector, and video-tape recorder.

2. Indicate the basic care and maintenance procedures that ought to be observed with the pieces of equipment listed in objective 1.

3. Identify a possible remedy when given a potential problem with any of the pieces of equipment listed in objective 1.

4. Describe five safety precautions when using audiovisual equipment.

5. Discuss four general features of projection carts and describe examples of each.

6. Demonstrate how to move an equipment cart safely.

7. Distinguish between unidirectional and omnidirectional microphones.

8. Describe the safety precaution about recharging batteries.

9. Describe four general factors that should be taken into consideration when using audio equipment for group instruction. Your description should include volume and tone setting, speaker placement, type and size of speaker, and feedback.

10. Discuss the basic operation of LCD panels including four advantages and limitations.

11. Distinguish between the 1,000 hertz system for slide synchronization and the 50 hertz system for filmstrip synchronization in terms of audiotape format and type of equipment needed.

12. Describe the keystone effect and state two ways to correct it.

13. Name three types of projection lamps and identify the special characteristics of each.

14. Describe the procedures for replacement of lamps, including types of lamps and handling procedures.

15. Relate lens focal length to image size.

16. List the distinguishing characteristics of the four major types of screen surface and apply these variables to specific projection situations.

17. State and apply the two-by-six rule for matching screen dimensions and audience seating.

18. State and apply a general rule for determining the height of screen placement.

19. Discuss the basic operation of video projectors including four advantages and limitations.

20. Describe the ideal physical arrangements for class viewing of television. Your description must include seating, monitor placement, lighting, and volume along with the minimum and maximum distances and angles.

LEXICON

feedback

liquid crystal display (LCD) panel

hertz (Hz)

automatic programmer

keystone effect

focal length

two-by-six rule

cathode-ray tube (CRT)

Most media users are not—and do not expect to become—electronic wizards, but they do want to be able to use audiovisual media effectively. The most fundamental element of effective media use is simply keeping the equipment, or mediaware, running and being ready to cope with snags which always seem to occur at the most inopportune times.

This chapter contains guidelines for the setup of projection equipment, screens, and speakers and then provides step-by-step operating procedures for the major types of mediaware. Included with each type of mediaware are hints for proper care and a troubleshooting checklist to help you cope with the most commonly occurring malfunctions.

Be aware that equipment operation guides are not intended to be read straight through. They are meant to be referred to while you practice with actual AV equipment. Also, the operating instructions in the guides are necessarily somewhat general because they must cover a range of equipment models. If your own mediaware differs markedly from the descriptions given here, refer to the operating instructions provided by the manufacturer.

If you have the responsibility for recommending or actually purchasing mediaware, you should become familiar with *The Equipment Directory of Video, Computer, and Audio-Visual Products,* issued annually by the International Communications Industries Association (ICIA), and the equipment evaluations published by the EPIE (Educational Products Information Exchange) Institute. These resources are described in the references section at the end of this chapter.

SAFETY

Safety should be an important concern whenever you or your students are using audiovisual equipment. As the teacher or trainer you are the role model for safe practices when using instructional materials. The

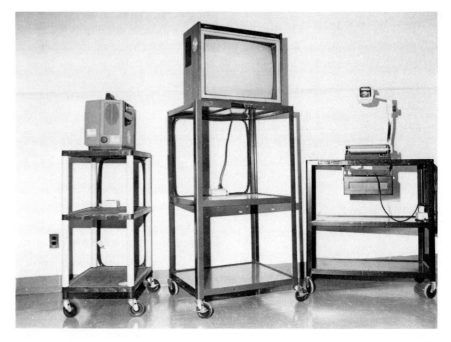

Figure 11.1
The varied types of equipment carts are suited to different purposes.

true costs of an accident are difficult to measure. They may include costs for medical care, loss of student and instructor time, disruption of schedules, and repair or replacement of equipment. It is your responsibility to correct any physical hazards and unsafe practices before an accident occurs.[1]

We in education and training play a very important role in improving the environment, the workplace, and the school. It is our responsibility to empower our students and trainees to perform safely, protecting themselves, their fellow students, and the environment. The other part of our responsibility is to serve as a role model for our students.

EQUIPMENT TABLES AND CARTS

Projection tables have legs and are meant to be used in one position.

The portable projection table is designed to be folded up and moved to another location and reassembled. Its legs telescope so that the projector can be as high as five feet from the ground. When the table is folded up, the typical package dimensions of 30 inches by 12 inches by 3 inches makes it easily transportable.

Carts come with wheels that allow the equipment to be set up and easily moved (see Figure 11.1). The carts are designed both for inside-only use and inside-outside use. You take a great risk in moving equipment out of doors on a cart designed for inside use. The small wheels can catch in cracks in the pavement and cause the cart to tip over. For this reason, even for exclusive indoor use it is wise to purchase carts with 5-inch casters.

Manufacturers normally offer power outlet cord assemblies for their carts. These are worthwhile investments. You plug your projector into the outlet on the cart and the cord on the cart into the wall outlet. If someone should trip over the power cord, the cart moves but the projector does not crash to the floor. In addition, the cord on the

---

[1] For a comprehensive guide to safe handling of audiovisual equipment, see Ralph Whiting and Roberta Kuchta, *Safety in the Library Media Program: A Handbook,* (Manitowoc, WI: Wisconsin Educational Media Association, 1987).

cart is considerably longer than the typical power cord furnished with the projector. The longer cord can be laid on the floor along the wall, thereby reducing the risk that someone will trip over it.

Features of Carts

Carts have a number of possible features related to location of use, construction materials, degree of enclosure, and type of equipment with which the cart can be used. We have already discussed the location of use, inside or outside.

Projection carts are constructed of both metal and plastic. A metal cart should be welded together instead of bolted. The nuts on the bolts will become loose over time, and the cart will become very unstable. Plastic carts, although not as stable as welded metal carts, have a number of advantages. They are much lighter and less expensive than metal carts. Some plastic carts can be disassembled and placed in the trunk of a car.

Projection carts have varying degrees of enclosure. The basic cart has no enclosed cabinets. Cabinets provide for security of materials and protection from dust during storage.

Some carts are designed for specific projectors. For example, overhead projector carts have adjustable-depth wells into which the projectors can be placed. They come 26 inches high for use in seated positions and 39 inches high for use while standing. Low carts are for use with opaque projectors. Carts 34 inches and 42 inches high are used with 16mm, 8mm, slide, and filmstrip projectors. Video equipment carts have heights of 39 inches, 42 inches, and 54 inches.

Many back injuries occur when people attempt to lift heavy objects by simply bending over, grasping the object, and pulling directly upward. This puts a strain on the lower back.

The recommended procedure is to bend at the hips and knees, and lift upward with the *legs* providing upward spring.

HOW TO . . .
Move and Use Equipment Carts

Moving

- ❑ Do not allow young children to move loaded carts.
- ❑ Do not allow anyone to ride on a cart.
- ❑ Be sure to engage caster locks before loading.
- ❑ Place equipment on the lower shelves before moving.
- ❑ Make sure all power cords are disconnected from wall plugs and wrapped around equipment before moving cart.
- ❑ Disconnect VCR from TV monitor before moving units to lower shelves.
- ❑ Unlock all casters before moving cart.
- ❑ Make sure you can see where you are going.
- ❑ Always push the cart, applying force on the narrow dimension; never pull the cart.
- ❑ When entering or leaving an elevator, push the cart at an angle so that one caster at a time goes over the gap between building and elevator floors.
- ❑ If cart is to be moved up or down a ramp, use a strap to secure equipment to the cart.
- ❑ When moving cart over rough floors, proceed with extreme caution.

Using

- ❑ Always engage the caster locks as soon as the cart is in position.
- ❑ Make sure equipment is centered on the cart shelf.
- ❑ Keep power and speaker cords out of traffic lanes and provide a lot of slack.

The student who has a clear view of the path guides the cart while the other pushes.

- ❑ If equipment power cord or extension is plugged directly into the wall, wrap the cord around the bottom of a leg of the cart so that if someone does trip on the cord, the cart, not the equipment, is pulled.
- ❑ Do not use the cart as a stool or ladder.
- ❑ When finished, move the cart as previously described.

Source: Adapted from guidelines published by the International Communications Industries Association (ICIA). Additional information, including stickers for carts, is available from ICIA, 3150 Spring Street, Fairfax, VA 22031.

The lower carts can be used as "mobile production centers" (recorder and monitor mounted on the same cart) to be moved from one classroom to another. The 54-inch carts are used to hold large 19-inch, 21-inch, and 25-inch television monitors. Since these carts tend to be somewhat unstable, caution must be exercised when moving them.

Cart Safety Tips

The U.S. Consumer Product Safety Commission (CPSC) and the International Communications Industries Association (ICIA) have alerted schools to the hazards involved in moving TV and projection carts (see Figure 11.2). CPSC has noted at least four deaths of children and four serious injuries resulting from tipped-over carts. Seven of the carts were loaded with a TV set on the top shelf, and the eighth had a 16mm projector on the top. Particularly hazardous are carts 50 or more inches high. With many school districts switching from 16mm film to video, there will be an increasing number of tall carts for transporting VCRs and TV sets.

The children involved in the accidents ranged in age from seven to eleven. *Do not ask children to move carts with heavy equipment on them.* Adolescents and adults, although less likely to sustain serious injuries, must be instructed to move carts with caution. Falling equipment will certainly be damaged, possibly beyond repair. Be sure to follow the instructions in "How To . . . Move and Use Equipment Carts."

TAPE RECORDERS

The part of a tape recorder needing most frequent attention is the record/playback head. To get good-

Figure 11.2
This safety sticker, available from International Communications Industries Association, should be on all carts.

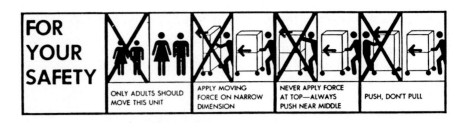

FOR YOUR SAFETY

ONLY ADULTS SHOULD MOVE THIS UNIT

APPLY MOVING FORCE ON NARROW DIMENSION

NEVER APPLY FORCE AT TOP—ALWAYS PUSH NEAR MIDDLE

PUSH, DON'T PULL

Figure 11.3
A typical audiocassette recorder for classroom use

quality recording or playback, the tape must make full contact with the record/playback head. Each time the tape passes across the head, small bits of debris are deposited on it. Eventually, this debris will interfere with proper contact between the tape and the head. Therefore, the record/playback head should be cleaned regularly. Most manufacturers recommend cleaning after five to ten hours of use. Of course, it should be done more frequently when the machine is used in dusty areas, such as in a machine shop, close to a woodworking area, or near a chalkboard.

For cleaning tape-recorder heads, you should use special head-cleaning fluid (available at most stores selling tape recorders or from audiovisual suppliers). Apply with a cotton swab. Do not use carbon tetrachloride, which can damage the heads, or al-cohol, which can leave a residue of its own on the head. Alcohol can also damage tapes if they are played immediately after cleaning. In addition, over a period of time, carbon tetrachloride and alcohol can cause the rubber parts of the pressure rollers to deteriorate.

The entire tape path should be inspected for dirt or damage that might interfere with proper tape operation. Most importantly, follow the recommended maintenance procedures in the manual that accompanies the recorder. Do not oil any tape recorder unless the manufacturer specifically recommends doing so. Most tape recorders are designed so that they do not need lubrication.

Audio equipment in general is subject to buildup of carbon or other contaminants on the contacts inside the volume and tone controls. This buildup causes an annoying scratching sound whenever the control knob is turned. Usually the problem can be resolved quickly and easily by spraying tuner cleaner (available at stereo and electronics supply stores) directly onto the shaft of the control. More stubborn buildup on the contacts might require some disassembly of equipment to get the spray closer to the source of the trouble.

Microphones

A wide variety of microphones are available. They vary in the type of generating element used in their construction, their sensitivity, their directionality, and in other technical features.

The basic function of any microphone is to convert sound waves into electrical energy. The major components of all microphones are similar. Sound waves enter the microphone and strike the diaphragm, which vibrates from the pressure of the sound waves. Connected to the diaphragm is a generating element that converts these vibrations into electrical impulses (Figure 11.6).

Microphones differ with regard to their directionality, or "pickup pattern," the pattern of the area from which they can efficiently pick up a signal. The microphones most commonly found in educational use today are the two basic directional types—unidirectional and omnidirectional. The differences in their pickup patterns are illustrated in Figure 11.7.

Battery Tips

Because of advances in lightweight motor design and solid state electronics, many audiocassette recorders, portable video recorders, and cameras operate on batteries. The advantages of portability, ease of handling, and freedom from extension cords have spurred the sales of battery-operated equipment. But you need to be aware that batteries and battery-operated equipment need special attention. Batteries should be removed from seldom-used equipment to prevent possible damage from leakage and corrosion. Batteries should also be removed from equipment if there is any danger of freezing or overheating.

If you operate a piece of equipment frequently, you may want to consider using a battery charger and rechargeable batteries for long-term savings (Figure 11.8). Rechargeable batteries are more expensive, but the extra cost can be more than recovered. However, *never* recharge batteries that are not specifically made to be recharged. Nonrechargeable batteries may explode if placed in a recharging unit.

AUDIO SETUPS
Built-in Speaker Systems

Most audiovisual equipment intended for use in educational set-

Figure 11.4
A hand-held microphone should be held at a 45-degree angle and below the mouth.

Figure 11.5
A lavaliere microphone should be clipped to the speaker's clothing and located below the mouth.

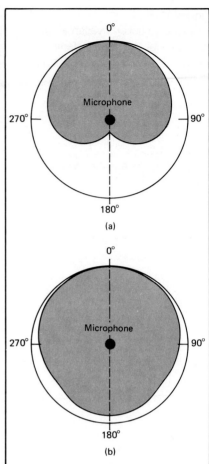

Figure 11.7
Pickup patterns of two common types of microphones: (a) unidirectional or cardioid microphone,
(b) omnidirectional microphone

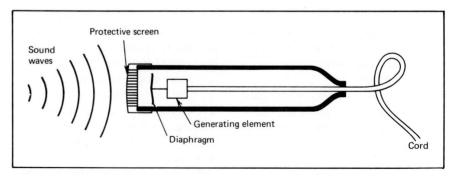

Figure 11.6
The main components of a microphone, cutaway view

CASSETTE RECORDER TROUBLESHOOTING

Problem	Possible Remedy
Tape comes out of cassette and snarls around the capstan of recorder	1. Very thin tape, as found in longer-length cassettes (e.g., C-120), is especially prone to do this. Convert to shorter-length (thicker) tapes. 2. The plastic hub of the take-up reel may be rubbing against the cassette. Try rotating the hub with a pencil to see if you can free it. 3. Take-up spindle is not pulling hard enough because of faulty clutch or belt. Have cassette repaired by qualified specialist.
"Record" button on cassette will not stay down	The accidental erasure tab on the back of the cassette has been broken out. Place tape over the gap left by the missing tab if you want to record something new on the cassette.
Hiss in background	Demagnetize the heads.
No high frequencies	Head out of alignment or worn. Have heads checked.
Lack of high frequencies	Heads not aligned properly or worn. Have heads checked.
Low playback volume	Heads dirty. Clean with head-cleaning fluid.

tings comes equipped with a built-in speaker system. This kind of unit is suitable for many but not all instructional purposes. Small speakers built into the chassis of portable recorders, filmstrip projectors, and so on, often lack the fidelity necessary for audio clarity throughout a large audience area.

Portable cassette recorders are particularly troublesome when used for playback in an average-size classroom. Even under the best conditions, the sound quality of portable cassettes is severely limited by their undersized speakers. If such a unit is used to play back material in which audio fidelity is essential (a musical composition, for example),

Figure 11.8
A battery charger can be a money saver, but charge *only* rechargeable batteries.

an auxiliary speaker should be used. A high-efficiency speaker—for instance, one having a 6- or 8-inch diameter—may be plugged into the earphone or external speaker jack of the cassette player to provide better fidelity.

Size alone, however, does not guarantee high quality sound from a speaker. If high-fidelity audio is needed, two-way speakers (bass and treble speaker in one cabinet) or three-way speakers (bass, midrange tweeter, and regular tweeter) are highly desirable. Such speakers may require an auxiliary amplifier when used in conjunction with AV equipment, but they are capable of reproducing the complete frequency range audible to humans.

Another problem with built-in speakers is that they are often built into the side of the machine containing the controls. This is fine when the operator of the tape recorder or the phonograph is also the listener. But if the apparatus is placed on a table or desk and operated by an instructor for the benefit of an audience, the speaker will be aimed away from the audience (see Figures 11.9 and 11.10). A simple way to remedy this situation is to turn the machine around so that the

Figure 11.9
Be aware of the location of the built-in speaker when using audio equipment. Although this arrangement is comfortable for the operator, the speaker is facing away from the audience.

Figure 11.10
This arrangement is much more satisfactory. The speaker is facing the audience.

speaker faces the audience and operate the controls from beside rather than in front of the machine.

In the case of film projectors with a built-in speaker, the problem is compounded by the fact that film projectors are usually set up near the back of the room. Thus, the speaker will be behind most, if not all, of the audience. The problem may be further aggravated by noise from the projector itself. This is a tolerable situation if you have a small audience. But an auxiliary speaker will be necessary if you have a large audience.

If you are operating in a lecture hall or auditorium that has a built-in public address system, you will want to plug your projector or player into that system. This might require an adapter to match up the output plug and input jack.

Detached Speaker Systems

The detachable speakers that accompany some film projectors and stereo tape recorders are generally large and sensitive enough to provide adequate-quality sound throughout the instructional area if, as with other separate speaker systems, you give consideration to their individual placement.

Whenever possible, speakers should face toward the center of your audience. If reverberation is a problem, however, especially in long narrow rooms, the speaker may be aimed diagonally across the audience to help alleviate this situation.

In the case of film projection, it is also important that the speaker be placed as close as possible to the screen. Psychologically, we are conditioned to expect sound to come directly from its source. We are, consequently, most comfortable with film sound when it appears to be coming directly from the screen image that constitutes its source.

Be sure nothing obstructs the sound waves as they travel from the speaker toward your audience. Classroom furniture (desks, chairs) and the audience itself may present

physical obstructions to sound. To avoid such interference, place the speaker on a table or some other kind of stand so that it is at or above the head level of your seated audience, as in Figure 11.11.

If you are using a stereophonic system, the speakers should be far enough apart so that the sound is appropriately balanced between the two. As a rule of thumb, the distance between the speakers should equal the distance from the speakers to the middle of the audience. Thus, in the typical 22-by-30-foot classroom, stereo speakers would be placed about 15 feet apart, or nearly in the corners of the room.

Feedback

Feedback is the name given to that annoying squeal that so often intrudes when public address systems or tape recorders are being used. The usual cause is simple: the signal coming out of the speaker is fed back into the microphone. The most direct remedy is to make sure that the speakers are set up in front of the microphone. If the speakers cannot be moved, you may be able to stop the feedback by adjusting the tone and volume controls or even by moving the microphone. (Omnidirectional microphones are more likely to cause feedback problems than unidirectional microphones.)

Volume and Tone Setting

Because sound-wave intensity decreases rapidly over distance, achieving a comfortable sound volume for all listeners can be quite a challenge. This is particularly true in larger rooms, for it is difficult to reach the back of the room without generating a very loud sound at the front. This, of course, can cause considerable discomfort to those seated near the speaker. An ideal solution would be to use several low-power sources rather than a single high-power one. But because this is usually not feasible, you can only strive to achieve a reasonable

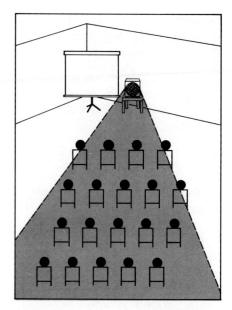

Figure 11.11
A recommended speaker placement. The detachable speaker is placed near the screen, raised to head level, and aimed toward the audience with no obstructions in the way.

compromise through proper setting of the volume control. By moving around the room during the presentation (unobtrusively), you can get a feel for the best volume setting to suit your situation. The problem may be further alleviated by not seating students at the extreme front or back.

The tone control can be used to correct certain other acoustical problems. For instance, low-frequency (bass) sounds will reverberate annoyingly under certain conditions (creating boominess). This can be compensated for somewhat by turning the tone control on the film projector or tape recorder toward treble. This also tends to improve the audibility of male speakers' low-pitched voices. Conversely, high-pitched sounds can be dampened with the tone control.

OVERHEAD PROJECTORS

In terms of its mechanics and electronic components, the overhead projector is a very simple apparatus,

HOW TO ...
Operate an Overhead Projector

Set Up

❏ Connect power cord to AC outlet.

Operate

❏ Turn projector on. (With some projectors you have to click through two positions to reach the on position.)

❏ Position transparency on stage.

❏ Adjust projector to eliminate keystoning.

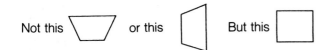

Not this ⬭ or this ▱ But this ▢

❏ Focus image.

❏ Practice writing on the transparency and erasing.

Disassemble

❏ Restore to storage conformation.

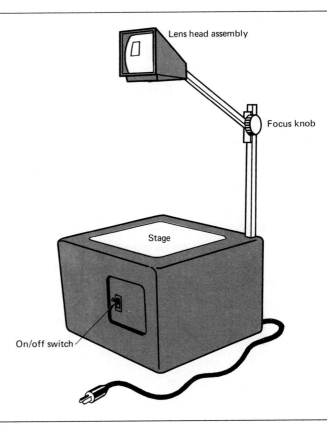

Lens head assembly

Focus knob

Stage

On/off switch

OVERHEAD PROJECTOR TROUBLESHOOTING

Problem	Possible Remedy
No light after flipping switch	1. Be sure projector is plugged into an electrical outlet. 2. Turn the switch all the way on. Many overheads have a three-position switch: off, fan, and on. 3. If lamp is burned out, switch to spare lamp within projector if it has this feature. Otherwise, you will need to replace the lamp. Be sure to use a lamp of the same wattage (too high a wattage can cause overheating). Do not handle the lamp while it is hot. Avoid touching the new lamp with bare fingers; this could shorten its life. 4. Switch may be defective. If so, replace it.
Dark edge with light in center of image	The fresnel lens is upside down. Turn it over if you know how; if not, have a qualified specialist do it.
Dark spot on area of screen	The lamp socket within the projector needs adjustment. The task is best done by a trained audiovisual technician.
Dark spot on screen or failure of lens to focus despite all adjustments of focus	After determining that it is not simply a matter of dirt on the lens or improper use of the focus control, check for a warped fresnel lens. This lens is plastic and can become warped from excessive heat, usually caused by the fan not running properly. Have a qualified specialist repair the fan or thermostat and replace the fresnel lens.

Set Up

❑ Position personal computer and overhead projector on the same sturdy table or projection cart, or on adjacent tables or carts.

❑ Place LCD panel on the overhead projector stage.

❑ Be sure power switch on LCD panel is off.

❑ Plug power supply into LCD panel and electrical outlet.

❑ Connect computer to LCD panel. (See LCD panel instruction manual for specifics; the connection may require special cords.)

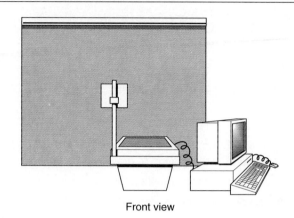

Front view

Operate

❑ Turn LCD power switch on.

❑ Adjust LCD panel for best image.

❑ Focus overhead projector on projection screen.

❑ Whatever appears on the computer monitor can now be projected onto the projection screen.

❑ Although you can write on the LCD panel with water-soluble marking pen, covering it with a clear acetate will protect the unit.

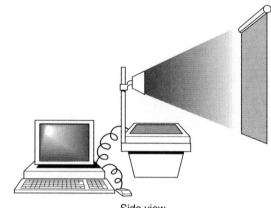

Disassemble

❑ Turn LCD power switch off.

❑ Disconnect computer from LCD panel.

❑ Unplug power supply from LCD panel and electrical outlet.

❑ Carefully pack and store LCD panel.

Side view

LCD PANEL TROUBLESHOOTING

Problem	Possible Remedy
No image on LCD panel	1. Adjust contrast on LCD panel. 2. Check computer for instructions on obtaining image.
Image appears on LCD panel but is not centered	1. Check LCD panel instructions. 2. Adjust centering or frequency.
Flickering image or missing lines on LCD panel	1. Check all connections to be sure they are correct and secure. 2. Adjust stability or frequency.
Intermittent appearance of image on LCD panel	1. Check all connections to be sure they are correct and secure. 2. Check equipment setup.
Rolling waves in image on LCD panel	1. Check equipment setup. 2. Try another overhead projector. 3. Adjust stability or frequency.
Contrast of display panel not uniform	1. Focus overhead projector. 2. Adjust contrast. 3. Use lower-wattage overhead projector.
Test pattern only on LCD panel	1. Check all connections to be sure they are correct and secure. 2. Refer to instructions to be certain computer is connected properly.

with few components requiring special maintenance procedures. Reliable as it is, however, it should not be taken for granted. You should take a few basic precautions to ensure that the projector keeps putting on a bright performance.

Keep the overhead projector as clean as possible. The horizontal stage tends to gather dust, fingerprint smudges, and marking-pen traces. It should be cleaned regularly with window spray or a mild solution of soap and water. The lens in the head assembly should also be kept free of dust and smudges. Clean it periodically with lens tissue and a proper lens-cleansing solution. The fresnel lens under the stage may also need cleaning eventually, but this procedure is better left to the specialist. The lens is a precision optical element requiring special care. In addition, some disassembly of the unit may be required to get at the lens.

The best way to prolong the life of the expensive lamp in the overhead projector is to allow it to cool before moving the projector. Move the projector with care. Keep the projector on a cart that can be rolled from one location to another. When hand-carrying the apparatus, hold onto the body of the projector, not the thin arm of the head assembly. The head assembly arm is not intended to be a carrying handle. Used as such, it can easily be twisted out of alignment, thus distorting the projector's image.

LCD Panels

Liquid Crystal Display (LCD) panels are an inexpensive way to project computer images onto a screen. They are the electronic equivalent of an overhead transparency. The computer provides the text and graphics while a standard overhead projector provides the light that shines through the panel to project the image on the screen.

Their limitations include limited color, lack of brightness, low contrast, low resolution, and lack of compatibility with some computers.

Less expensive models are monochrome. More expensive models can project colors. Because of the low brightness and lack of contrast, the maximum screen width (image size) should be one-fourth the distance to the farthest viewer (as opposed to one-sixth for other projectors).

LCD panels are best suited for small and mid-size groups (up to fifty people). The computer can store "overhead transparency" content and project it electronically at the push of a key. New information can be displayed on command with the push of another key. You can make changes on the spot so LCD panels are ideal for what-if situations and interactive presentations. During computer software training, computer screen displays can be projected for all to see and discuss.

LCD panels may be separate units that serve as peripherals to the overhead projector, or the LCD panel and overhead projector may be combined into a single piece of equipment. Other models incorporate three LCD panels (one each for red, green, and blue) to provide full-color images. Some models have an "active matrix" and can also project full-motion, color video from tape or disc.

SLIDE PROJECTORS

In normal use slide projectors require little special attention to keep working smoothly. The only regular maintenance required of the user is to clean the front element of the projection lens if it shows finger marks. More likely to cause difficulties are the slides themselves, which should always be stored away from heat and handled only by their mounts. The most frequent cause of foul-ups in slide presentations is a slide that jams because it is warped or dog-eared. Remount slides that could cause jams.

The Kodak Ektagraphic III projector has a number of desirable features not found on earlier models (Figure 11.13). For example, the projection lamp can be changed from the rear of the projector with-

Figure 11.12
LCD panels permit computer output to be projected from the stage of the overhead projector.

Figure 11.13
The Kodak slide projectors feature convenient controls.

Figure 11.14
A proper carrying case prolongs the life of a slide projector that is moved frequently.

out having to turn the projector over. There is a quick release on the elevation stand so the projected image can be raised without having to turn the adjustment knob many times by hand. In addition, the "Select" function allows the carousel tray to be turned when the power is off. Finally, the controls are on the

---

HOW TO . . .
Operate a Slide Projector

Set Up

❑ Connect power cord to AC outlet (power cord is stored on the bottom of the projector).

❑ Plug in remote control cord with white dot on top.

❑ Insert lens.

❑ Check to see that bottom ring is locked on slide tray. If not, lock it or slides will drop out.

❑ Load slides into tray and tighten the locking ring on the tray.

❑ Seat slide tray on projector. Note the notch at "0."

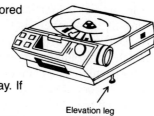

Elevation leg

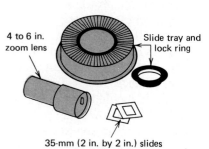

4 to 6 in. zoom lens

Slide tray and lock ring

35-mm (2 in. by 2 in.) slides

Operate

❑ Set automatic timer at "m" (manual operation).

❑ Move on/off switch to "Low" or "High" lamp setting.

❑ Position image on screen, making it smaller or larger by means of the lens barrel.

❑ Focus image with focus knob.

❑ Project slides using remote control or buttons on the forward side of the projector.

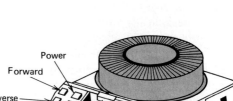

Power

Forward

Reverse

Timer

Push and hold "select" button to rotate slide tray

Auto-focus switch

Focus

Remote control

Disassemble

❑ Press and hold "Select" button while turning the tray to "0." The "Select" function will not operate when projector is off, except on the Ektagraphic III model.

❑ Remove slide tray.

❑ Allow lamp to cool before switching off.

❑ Remove slides from slide tray.

❑ Restore to storage conformation.

---

side of the projector where the operator usually stands.

Even though some new projectors, such as the Ektagraphic III, do not project a distracting bright white square when there is not a slide in position, it is still recommended that you include a dark slide at the beginning and end of your presentation. Solid plastic slides work best.

The purchase and use of a carrying case for your slide projector is highly recommended if the projector is to be moved from location to location, especially from building to

building (Figure 11.14). Slide projectors should only be moved on a projector cart or within a carrying case. The case provides a place to store the projector, tray, remote control unit, a spare lamp, and remote extension cords. The carrying case helps to keep all the accessories together, decreasing the chances for loss, as well as providing protection from damage and dust.

More serious damage can occur if the slide projector falls because it has been propped up precariously on top of a stack of books or on some other unstable base. This happens

all too often because the projector's elevation leg seems never to be quite long enough to raise the image up to the top of the screen. Better solutions are to use a higher projection table, raise the whole projection table, or raise the whole projector by placing it on a sturdy box or similar platform.

Sound Synchronization

Cassette player/recorders with sound-synchronizing capability (Figure 11.15) allow you to play an audiotape that is coordinated with a

SLIDE PROJECTOR TROUBLESHOOTING

Problem	Possible Remedy
Can't find power cord	Look for a built-in storage compartment. On the Kodak Carousel, the power cord is wrapped around a recessed core on the bottom of the projector.
No power after plugging in	If you are sure the outlet is live (a fuse or circuit breaker may have killed all electrical power in the room), check the circuit breaker on the slide projector.
Fan runs but lamp does not light	Some projectors have separate switches for "Lamp" and "Fan" or a two-stage switch for these two functions. Make sure all switches are properly set. Then check for burned-out lamp. If neither of these is the problem, have technician check the projector.
Image not level	Most slide projectors have an adjustment knob on one of the rear feet. Use the knob to raise or lower that side.
Slide is distorted	The lenses may be out of alignment or broken. Often they can be adjusted easily by aligning them correctly in their slots.
Slide mounts begin to warp	For plastic black-and-white mounts, check to see that *white side* of mount is *facing* the lamp. If the dark side of mount is facing lamp, a buildup of heat can cause the mount to warp (or even melt, in the case of plastic mounts).
Slide image upside-down or backwards	Remove the slide and reverse it. (Improper loading can be avoided by thumb-spotting slides. See Chapter 5.)
Slide jams in gate	1. Manually remove the slide. On the Kodak Carousel, press the "Select" button (power must be on). If the slide does not pop up, the tray will have to be removed. Turn off the power and use a coin to turn the screw in the center of the tray; this unlocks the tray, allowing it to be lifted off and giving access to the gate for manual removal of the slide.
	2. Jamming can be avoided by not placing bent slides in the tray. Plastic mounts have a tendency to warp; cardboard mounts fray; glass mounts may be too thick for the slide compartment of the tray. For this reason, jamming is more likely with narrow slide compartments, as are found in the 140-slide Carousel trays. Use the 80-slide tray whenever possible.

set of slides or a filmstrip. As shown in Figure 11.16, the synchronizers designed primarily for use with slide projectors use two tracks on the audiotape, one for the narration and the other to synchronize the sound and picture. These units use a 1,000 hertz signal for changing the slide and a 150 hertz signal to stop the playback of the cassette tape. A *hertz* (Hz) equals one cycle per second. A button must then be pushed to restart the tape.

The synchronization units designed to be used with filmstrip projectors do not have the pause feature. They often are built into the filmstrip projector itself. This system uses an inaudible 50-hertz signal to trigger the change from one frame of the filmstrip to another. This sig-

nal is buried within the narration (see Figure 11.17). Thus, only one track on the tape is needed. Generally, the other track of the tape (which is reached by turning over the cassette) contains a recording of the audio material with an audible signal to tell you when to change to the next frame of the filmstrip if your filmstrip projector lacks an automatic advance mechanism. The tape will be labeled "inaudible signal" or "50 Hz signal" on one side and "audible signal" on the other.

The 1,000 Hz system is not compatible with the 50 Hz system. To solve this problem, the manufacturers have produced cassette player/recorders that will record and play back the 1,000 Hz system as well as play back (but not record) the 50 Hz

system. These units do not come as a single piece of equipment. You must have the appropriate cords to connect the cassette unit to your slide projector or filmstrip projector.

Figure 11.15
A typical sound-slide synchronization setup

Figure 11.16
Tape configuration for cassette
sound-slide synchronization

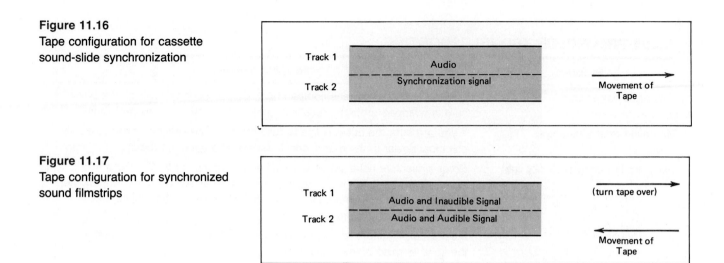

Track 1   Audio
Track 2   Synchronization signal

Movement of
Tape

Figure 11.17
Tape configuration for synchronized
sound filmstrips

Track 1   Audio and Inaudible Signal
Track 2   Audio and Audible Signal

(turn tape over)

Movement of
Tape

HOW TO ...
Operate a Filmstrip Projector

Set Up

❑ Connect power cord to AC outlet.

Operate

❑ Turn projector on.
❑ Place filmstrip on retainer bar.
❑ Thread filmstrip down into film slot. Be sure that "Start" or "Focus" appears at head of filmstrip.
❑ Turn advance knob until "focus" frame appears.
❑ Adjust framer so the full frame is projected when you click the advance knob.
❑ Turn projector off.

Disassemble

❑ Return filmstrip to container. Do not pull the end of the filmstrip to tighten the roll. Start with a tight roll at the center and continue rolling, holding the film by the edges.
❑ Restore to storage conformation.

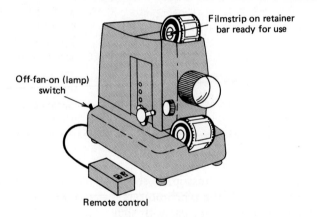

Filmstrip on retainer
bar ready for use

Off-fan-on (lamp)
switch

Remote control

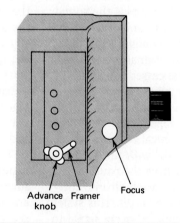

Advance   Framer
knob

Focus

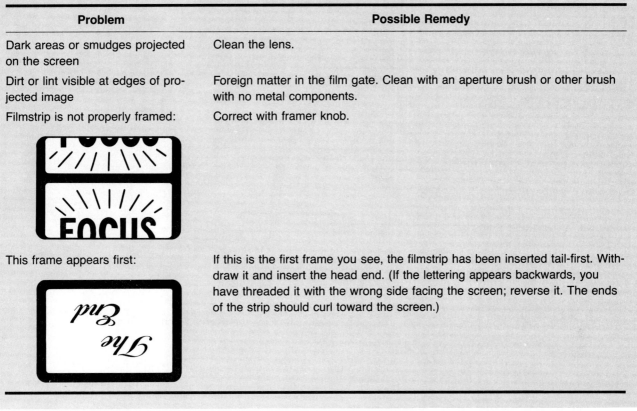

FILMSTRIP PROJECTOR TROUBLESHOOTING

Problem	Possible Remedy
Dark areas or smudges projected on the screen	Clean the lens.
Dirt or lint visible at edges of projected image	Foreign matter in the film gate. Clean with an aperture brush or other brush with no metal components.
Filmstrip is not properly framed:	Correct with framer knob.
This frame appears first:	If this is the first frame you see, the filmstrip has been inserted tail-first. Withdraw it and insert the head end. (If the lettering appears backwards, you have threaded it with the wrong side facing the screen; reverse it. The ends of the strip should curl toward the screen.)

Your audiovisual equipment dealer can supply the correct cords for your cassette unit with the appropriate plugs for your projectors.

Of course, your show can stay in the proper synchronization only if it starts in synchronization. Check to be sure the sequence starts on the correct frame.

Single-Unit Projectors.

Most of the single-piece projectors with cassette player and filmstrip unit are for front projection. Other units have built-in rear screens for individual viewing. Some of these allow you to open a small door for front projection. Because these projectors have a very short focal-length lens, you must place the projector close to the screen.

Single-piece units also are available for use with slides using the 1,000 Hz system. Some units have dissolve-control devices built into them. They allow for a variable rate of dissolve that is controlled either by digital coding or altering the pitch of the synchronizing signal. Units from different manufacturers are generally not compatible.

Automatic Programmers.

All of the aforementioned slide projector units allow for an external control signal to be "written" on the tape by a programmer. However, you do need a programmer or a "reader" to interpret the signals coming from the tape when you play it back. The *automatic programmer* causes the projector to advance or reverse and to dissolve at various rates, and causes auxiliary units to turn projectors or lights on and off. The programmers may be independent units, units combined with a dissolve unit, or units that use micro-computers. If you decide to get involved in multi-image or multimedia presentations that require this equipment, you should work with a media production specialist.

FILMSTRIP PROJECTORS

A filmstrip projector requires the same sort of care and handling as a slide projector. With the filmstrip projector, however, an additional concern is keeping the film gate clean. Lint and dirt in the gate may be seen around the edges of the projected image and are an annoyance to the viewer. The film gate can be cleaned with a special aperture brush (also used with motion picture projectors) or with some other nonmetal, soft-bristle brush.

Filmstrip projectors that come in enclosed cases carry a warning to remove the projector from the case before operating it. This is to ensure that air can circulate freely to the cooling fan located on the underside of the projector. Any interference with the fan, such as a sheet of paper sucked up against the fan grid or an accumulation of dust adhering to the fan grid, can lead to overheating and damage to filmstrips.

FILM PROJECTORS

Because film projectors and 16mm films are comparatively expensive instruments of instruction, it is particularly important for instructors to prolong the life of these items by taking proper care of them.

The average life of an acetate-based film is approximately 100 showings. The newer mylar-based film has the potential for 1,000 showings. Mishandling, however, can

Figure 11.18
Slot threading greatly simplifies the use of 16mm projectors.

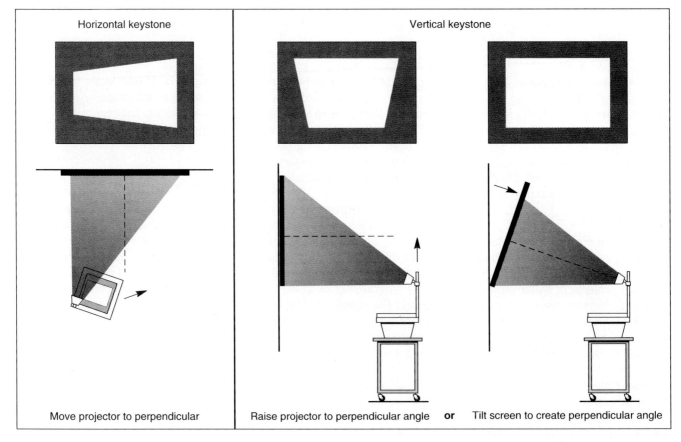

Figure 11.19
The keystone effect—its causes and remedies

greatly reduce this lifespan of service. On the other hand, careful threading, inspection after each use, periodic lubrication of the film, and proper storage (at room temperature, 40 percent humidity) can lengthen the working life of the film.

Proper care of the projector can also help extend the service life of film. It is important to keep the projector's film path clean to prevent undue wear on the film. An aperture brush or other soft-bristled, nonmetalic brush should be used regularly to clean the film path, the film gate, and the area around the sound drum.

The lens of the projector should be kept free of dust and smudges by periodic cleaning with lens tissue and cleaner. The projector's volume- and tone-control mechanisms sometimes develop internal carbon buildup, causing crackling sounds when the knobs are turned to adjust audio. This debris can generally be eliminated simply by spraying around the external extensions of the control knobs with an aerosol tuner cleaner while turning the knobs.

Given the electromechanical complexity of the film projector, you should not go much beyond these routine cleaning procedures to help keep your projector in good working order.

PROJECTOR SETUPS

The first requirement in projector placement is to align the projection lens perpendicular to the screen (that is, it must make a 90-degree angle with the screen). Thus, the lens of the projector should be about level with the middle of the screen. If the projector is too high, too low, or off to either side, a distortion of the image will occur, referred to as the *keystone effect* (Figure 11.19). The effect takes its name from the typical shape of a keystoned image—wide at the top, narrower at the bottom, like a key-

stone. To remedy this situation, move either the projector or the screen to bring the two into a perpendicular relationship.

The keystone effect is especially prevalent with the overhead projector because it is ordinarily set up very close to the screen and far lower than the screen (to allow the instructor to write on its stage). For this reason many screens used for overhead projection are equipped with a "keystone eliminator," a notched bar at the top that allows the screen to be tilted forward (see Figure 11.20).

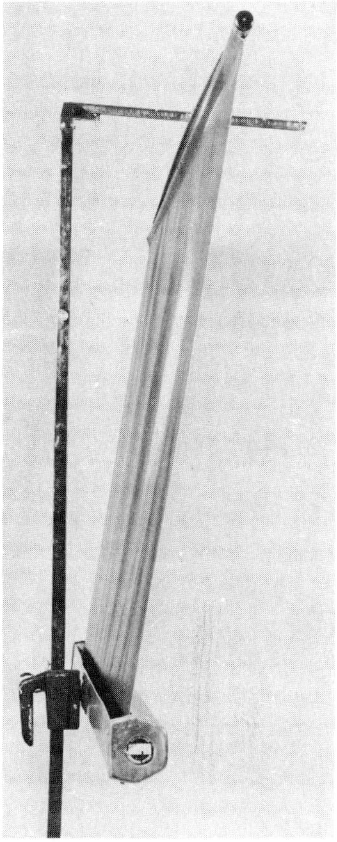

Once you have properly aligned the projector and screen, consider the distance between them. If the distance is too long, the image will spill over the edges of the screen. If it is too short, the image will not fill the screen properly. Your goal is to fill the screen as fully as possible with the brightest image possible. The principle to remember here is that the image becomes larger and less brilliant with an increase in distance between the projector and screen. If the projected image is too large for your screen, push the projector closer. If the image is too small, pull the projector back.

Positioning a projector at the proper distance from the screen need not be done solely by trial and error. Because classroom-type projectors usually are fitted with certain focal-length lenses, their proper placement can be estimated in advance. Figure 11.21 shows the placement of the overhead, slide, and 16mm film projectors when they are equipped with their most typical lenses.

However, it is best to place all projectors, except the overhead and the opaque, behind the audience to prevent people from tripping over the power cords. For the same reason, extension cords should be used so that the power cords can run along the wall to the outlet rather than across the center of the room.

The projection distances described here assume appropriate

Figure 11.20
Portable tripod screen with keystone eliminator

lighting conditions. Where the room light is so bright that it is washing out the screen image and it cannot be dimmed any further, you must move the projector forward. This will give you a brighter image but also a smaller one. In some cases, however, it may be possible to compensate for this reduction in image size by having your audience move closer to the screen.

Lamps

Types. There are three types of projection lamps: incandescent, tungsten halogen, and tungsten halogen with surrounding reflector. The incandescent lamps should be watched because they have a tendency to blister. Such blisters can become so big that the lamp cannot be removed from the projector. If

HOW TO . . .
Operate a 16mm Slotload Projector

Set Up

- ❏ Place projector on a sturdy projection stand.
- ❏ Remove projector cover.
- ❏ Extend reel arms and lock in place.
- ❏ Place take-up reel on rear arm.
- ❏ Place film reel on front arm.
- ❏ Make sure motor switch is in off (or stop) position.
- ❏ Plug power cord into AC outlet.

Thread Film

- ❏ Be sure Still/Run knob is in "Run" position.
- ❏ Hold the film by the fingertips. Beginning at the first guide roller, pull the film along and into the slot, following the direction of the arrows.
- ❏ Attach the end of the film to the take-up reel and wind a couple of turns in clockwise direction.
- ❏ Check that film is fitted correctly in the film path slot.

Operate

Before the audience arrives:

- ❏ Turn on motor and lamp.

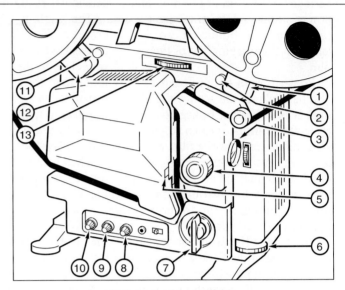

Main parts of the projector

1. Supply arm	8. Treble control
2. Supply arm lock button	9. Bass control
3. Lens	10. Amplifier on and off
4. Focus knob	and volume control
5. Framing lever	11. Take-up arm lock button
6. Elevator knob	12. Take-up arm
7. Function switch	13. Still/run knob

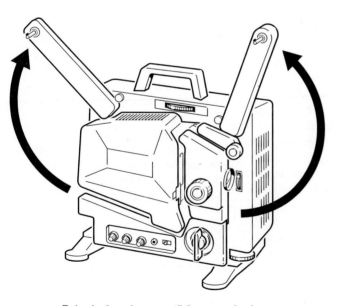

Raise both reel arms until they snap in place

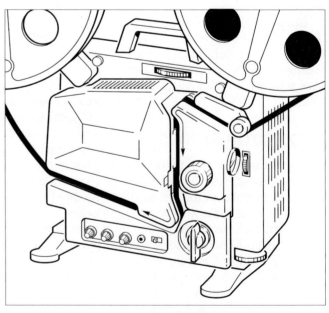

Threading Path

- ❏ Use the elevator knob to raise or lower the projector as needed.
- ❏ If a frame bar is visible, use the framing lever to get one whole frame on the screen.
- ❏ Focus image with "Focus" knob.
- ❏ Adjust volume and tone controls.
- ❏ Turn motor switch to "Rewind" position to return to beginning of film.

When ready to show film:

- ❏ Turn on motor and lamp.
- ❏ Slowly turn up volume to predetermined level.
- ❏ Make any final adjustments of focus, framing, and sound.

At end of the film:

- ❏ Turn down volume knob.
- ❏ Turn off lamp and motor.

Rewind

Film can be rewound in most slotload projectors in two ways: back through the slot path or direct from take-up reel to front reel. For in-path rewind:

- ❏ Stop the projector before the film is entirely through the projector.
- ❏ Turn switch to "Rewind" position (if you show only part of the film, this is the most convenient way to rewind).

For reel-to-reel rewind:

- ❏ Let the film run completely through the projector before turning off the motor.
- ❏ Bring the loose end of the film from the take-up reel to the front reel, secure it to the reel, and rotate the front reel counterclockwise for a few turns to be sure film is held firmly.
- ❏ Turn motor switch to "Rewind" position.
- ❏ Turn motor off when film is completely rewound.

Disassemble

- ❏ Disconnect power cord from outlet; wrap up and store in well in rear of projector.
- ❏ Remove both film reels.
- ❏ Unlock both reel arms by depressing release buttons and move arms down to storage position.
- ❏ Turn tilt control knob to completely lower projector.
- ❏ Replace cover on projector.

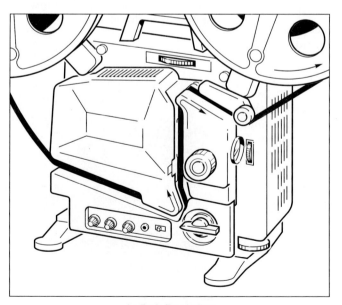

In-Path Rewinding

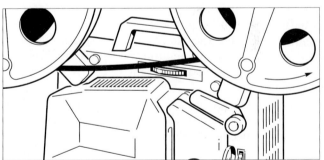

Reel-to-Reel Rewinding

Figure 11.21
Approximate placement of
projectors when equipped with
typical lenses

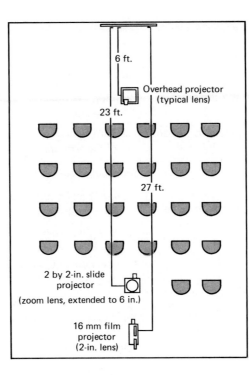

6 ft.

Overhead projector
(typical lens)

23 ft.

27 ft.

2 by 2-in. slide
projector
(zoom lens, extended to 6 in.)

16 mm film
projector
(2-in. lens)

the lamp does blister to the extent
that it must be broken for removal,
an audiovisual technician should be
contacted. In addition to being
prone to blistering, incandescent
lamps require more wattage for the
same light output.

The first innovative response to
incandescent blistering was the
tungsten halogen lamp. These lamps
do not blister, but they do require
the same high wattage and thus
have the associated heat problems
and fan noise.

The newest type of lamp is the
tungsten halogen lamp with surrounding reflector. These lamps generally operate at one-half the wattage of the incandescent and
tungsten halogen lamps.

Coding.   Projection lamps are labeled with a three-letter ANSI
(American National Standard Institute) code. This code is printed on
the lamp and on the box. In addition, many projectors now have
stickers in the lamp housing of the
projectors with the ANSI code stating which lamp should be used in
that projector.

Replacement of Lamps.   When
replacing a lamp, the replacement
should be a lamp with the same
ANSI code or an authorized substitute. Substitutes can be found in
replacement guides written by the
lamp manufacturers. These guides
are available from the manufacturers
or from local audiovisual dealers. Do
not use higher-wattage lamps than
specified. You may burn the materials in the projector!

Handling a Lamp.   When handling a lamp, never touch the clear
glass bulb. The oil from your fingers
can shorten the life of the lamp.
The lamp should always be manipulated by its base. The incandescent
lamps and tungsten halogen lamps
(without exterior reflector) are supplied with a piece of foam or paper
around the lamp. This material or a
cloth should be used to hold the
lamp when it is inserted into the
projector.

When removing a burned-out
lamp, wait until the lamp has cooled
to prevent injuring your fingers. It
is wise to always use a cloth when
removing a lamp. Even a lamp that

burns out when the projector is first
turned on will be hot enough to
burn.

Expense.   Lamps are expensive.
They usually cost about twenty
times the cost of a household light
bulb. Because the average lamp life
is fifty hours, projectors should be
turned off when not in use. If the
projector offers a low lamp setting,
use it if possible to increase the life
of the lamp. A projector should not
be jarred when the lamp is on, as
this can cause a premature burnout
of the lamp. You should not leave
the fan on for cooling after use unless the projector is going to be
moved immediately, as this also will
shorten the life of the bulb.

Lenses

For everyday media use you do not
have to pay much attention to tech-
nicalities about lenses. Whatever
lens your projector is equipped with
is usually sufficient. However, understanding some basic ideas about
lenses can help you cope with ex-
traordinary situations.

First, lenses vary in focal length
(measured in inches in the United
States, in millimeters elsewhere).

Figure 11.22
Projector lamps come in a wide
variety of sizes and shapes; when
they burn out, they must be replaced
with a matching type.

Figure 11.23
Avoid directly touching burned-out lamps (because they are hot) and replacement lamps (because the oil on your fingertips can shorten the life of a lamp and cause it to blister).

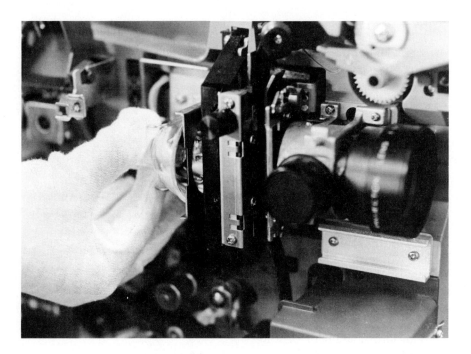

Figure 11.24
The longer the focal length of the lens, the smaller the image.

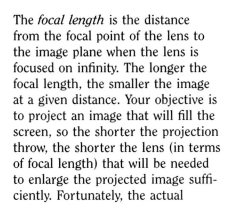

1-in. lens 2-in. lens 4-in. lens

The *focal length* is the distance from the focal point of the lens to the image plane when the lens is focused on infinity. The longer the focal length, the smaller the image at a given distance. Your objective is to project an image that will fill the screen, so the shorter the projection throw, the shorter the lens (in terms of focal length) that will be needed to enlarge the projected image sufficiently. Fortunately, the actual length of most lenses corresponds roughly with their focal length; the longer of two lenses will have the longer focal length. Figure 11.24 illustrates the relationship of lens focal length to the size of its projected image.

One type of lens has a variable focal length—the zoom lens. It can be adjusted to cast a larger or smaller picture without moving the projector or changing its lens. The most commonly encountered zoom lens (found on many slide projectors) has a focal-length range of 4 to 6 inches.

When precise specifications are needed in selecting lenses for particular conditions, media specialists use calculation guides prepared by manufacturers, such as the *Da-Lite Lens-Projection Screen Calculator* or Kodak's *Projection Calculator and Seating Guide*.

Screens

Arranging a proper environment for viewing projected visuals involves several variables, including screen size, type of screen surface, and screen placement. In most cases the instructor only has to deal with a couple of these variables. For everyday teaching situations the classroom will often be equipped with a screen of a certain type attached in a fixed position.

There may be times, however, when you will have to make decisions about any or all of these screen variables. For example, let's assume the room you are to use for projecting visuals is 22 feet wide and 30 feet long, a fairly typical size both for formal and nonformal instructional settings. Let's further assume that you must arrange seating for between thirty and forty viewers, a fairly typical audience size. Figure 11.26 illustrates a conventional seating pattern for a group of this size (in this case, thirty-six viewers). Note that the seats are arranged across the narrower room dimension. If the seats were turned to face the left or right side of the

Figure 11.25
With proper attention to projection variables, even makeshift facilities can become learning environments.

room and arranged across its 30-foot length, viewers along either end of the rows would have a distorted view of the screen. Note too, that the first row of seats is set back somewhat from the desk area, where the screen is to be set up, so that front-row students will not be too close to the screen for comfortable viewing.

If the room is closer to a square in shape, you might want to con-

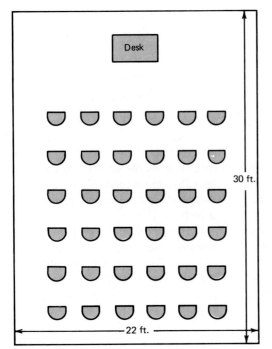

Figure 11.26
Typical-size classroom arranged to seat thirty-six

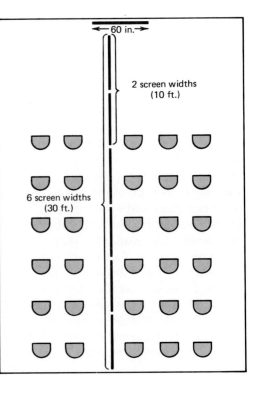

Figure 11.27
Appropriate screen size for the typical-size classroom according to the two-by-six rule

FILM PROJECTOR TROUBLESHOOTING

Problem	Possible Remedy
Projector completely inoperative	1. Check position of load lever. It should be in "Run" position. 2. Check that power cord is plugged in. 3. Be sure electric outlet has power.
Film will not thread	1. Be sure motor switch is off. 2. Check position of load lever. It should be in load position. 3. Rear take-up reel must be in horizontal position. 4. Be sure lamp cover and lens cover are closed properly.
No sound from speaker	If exciter lamp lights: 1. Check threading of film around sound drum. 2. Be sure volume is turned up. If exciter lamp does not have light: 1. Be sure motor switch is in "Projector-Normal" position. 2. Replace exciter lamp.
Sound is soft, fuzzy, or garbled	1. Check volume and tone controls. 2. Be sure film is tight around sound drum. 3. Check lower film loop. 4. See if exciter lamp filament is damaged.
No picture	1. Be sure motor switch is in "Project" position. 2. Check position of load lever. It should be in "Run" position. 3. Replace projection lamp.

sider placing the screen in the corner and seating the audience in diagonal rows. This possibility will be examined later in terms of screen placement.

Screen Size. A general rule of thumb called the *two-by-six rule,* accepted by most audiovisualists, dictates that no viewer should be seated closer to the screen than two screen widths or farther away than six screen widths. This means that in our hypothetical case, in which the farthest viewer could be 30 feet from the front of the room, a screen about 5 feet wide (60 inches) would be required to ensure that this farthest-away viewer is within six screen widths of the screen (30 ÷ 6 = 5). A square screen is generally preferable because it can be used to show rectangular images (film, slides, filmstrips, etc.) as well as square images (overhead and opaque projections). Thus, in this case a screen measuring 60 by 60

inches is recommended (see Figure 11.27).

With a zoom lens on a carousel slide projector or a 16mm projector, you can put the projector at the rear of any normal-size classroom and fill a 70-inch screen.

Screen Surfaces. Projection screens vary in their surface treatments. Various surfaces have different reflectance qualities and offer different viewing-angle widths.

The matte screen has a smooth, nonshiny surface that has the lowest reflectance but provides a constant level of brightness over the widest viewing angle (more than 45 degrees on either side of the center axis). It is durable and inexpensive. Matte white screens can be rolled up for storage or carrying. Because of these qualities the matte white screen is the one most commonly used in instructional settings. In addition, a matte white screen can be cleaned with an extra strength household

cleaner. None of the other surfaces can be cleaned.

The beaded screen is a white surface covered with small glass beads. Approximately two to four times more light is reflected from this surface than from the matte white surface. However, the beads tend to reflect light straight back toward the light source, narrowing the optimal viewing area. In fact, beyond 25 degrees on either side of the center axis the brightness is less than that of a matte white screen. Beaded screens are primarily recommended for long, narrow halls.

The lenticular screen is made from a plastic material that has a pattern molded into the surface, usually a series of very narrow ridges running vertically up the screen. It represents a compromise between the beaded and the matte white surfaces, being nearly as reflective as the former and offering nearly the breadth of viewing angle of the latter. Like the beaded screen,

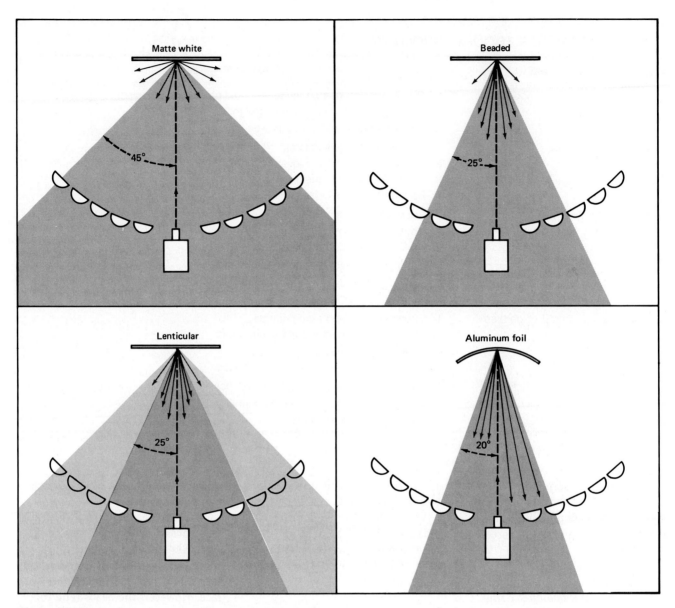

Figure 11.28
Comparison of reflectance and recommended viewing angles for four different screen surfaces

Figure 11.29
In a square room placement of the screen in the corner creates a larger good-viewing area.

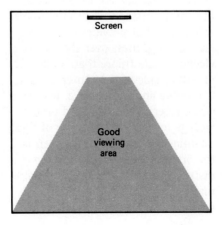

the lenticular screen provides the brightest image within 25 degrees of the center axis and a dimmer image out to about 45 degrees. It must be stretched tight to be effective. It is more expensive than the matte or beaded screen and is seldom used in schools.

Developed by Kodak under the trade name Ektalite, the aluminum foil surface is the brightest surface available, about twenty times brighter than the matte white surface. However, it has a very narrow viewing angle, with visibility limited to about 20 degrees from the center axis. Screen size is also limited, 40 by 40 inches being the largest standard size. It is rigid and cannot be rolled up. Its greatest advantage is visibility in full room light. It is particularly recommended for small-group use in conditions of high ambient light.

The major features of these screen types are shown in comparison in Figure 11.28. Given the room dimensions and audience size in our hypothetical case, a matte white screen would be most suitable.

Screen Placement. In most cases placement of the screen at the center in the front of the room will be satisfactory. In some cases, however, it may not be. Perhaps light from a window that cannot be fully covered will wash out the projected image (sunlight is much brighter than any artificial light), or you wish to use the chalkboard during your presentation and a screen positioned in the center front will make

it difficult or impossible for you to do so. An alternative position is in a front corner of the room. Indeed, the screen should not be at center stage when there is danger that it will attract unwanted attention while nonprojection activities are going on.

Corner placement is especially advantageous in a room that is square or nearly so. As illustrated in Figure 11.29, placing the screen in one corner allows more viewers to be seated in the good viewing area.

In any case, nowhere is it written in stone that the screen must be placed front and center. Position your screen wherever it will best suit your purpose.

The height of the screen should generally be adjusted so that the bottom of the screen is about level with the heads of the seated viewers. The bottom of the screen should be at least 4 feet above the floor to prevent excessive head interference (see Figure 11.30). Other inhibiting factors aside, this arrangement will allow reasonably clear sight lines for the most viewers. In general, the higher the screen, the greater the optimal viewing area. Of course, care must be taken that the screen can be seen without viewers uncomfortably craning their necks.

VIDEOTAPE RECORDER/ PLAYERS

Video record/playback machines are highly sophisticated electronic instruments. Maintenance and repair, consequently, should generally be

left to the specialist. In addition, videotape recorder/players are far from standardized in their various mechanisms and modes of operation. You should, therefore, refer to the manufacturer's manual for information about the operating principles and procedures of the particular system you happen to be using. The troubleshooting guide included here is limited to general sorts of problems that may occur with virtually any video system and that can be remedied by the nonspecialist.

Video Projectors

Studies have shown that audiences pay more attention to images projected onto a large screen. Video images can be projected using video projectors (Figure 11.31). They connect to any videocassette recorder, videodisc player, live television, or video camera. Some models include a self-contained VHS videocassette player. Other models can also project computer-generated graphs.

Video projectors work well with large audiences (up to several hundred) and for visuals requiring a high degree of detail. Most project an image up to 3 feet by 7 feet. Other features available include built-in speakers and remote control.

The *cathode ray tube (CRT)* projector uses three "guns," one each to project red, green, and blue light. Video projection equipment may be placed on a cart, mounted to the ceiling, or converted for rear-screen projection.

Figure 11.30
The bottom of the screen should be above head level to avoid obstruction of the view.

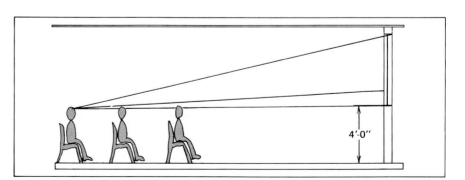

Set Up

The video projector will be delivered to you connected to the VCR and audio amplifier as shown in the schematic.

❑ Check all connections.

❑ Turn on the power to the VCR, amplifier, and projector.

❑ Insert the video cassette and fast-forward for a few seconds to get into the program.

Ceiling or floor mount

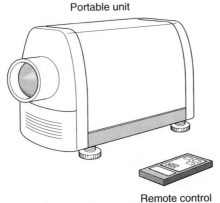

Portable unit

Remote control

Operate

❑ Turn on the projector lamp and wait for it to warm up (about one minute).

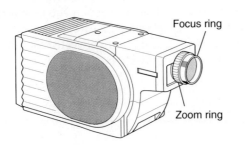

Focus ring

Zoom ring

❑ Put VCR on "Play" and adjust the size of the image using the zoom lens ring; then focus the image.

❑ Push the "Reset" button. The following image will be superimposed on the screen.

	+		−
Picture		0	
Brightness		0	
Color		0	
Tint		0	
Sharpness		0	

❑ Correct the image for each by using the + and − buttons shown in the illustration. The corrections will be evident in the image and will also be shown graphically on the screen.

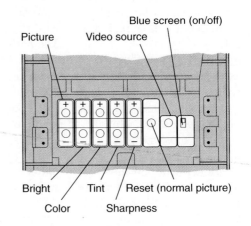

Picture Video source Blue screen (on/off)

Bright Tint Reset (normal picture)
Color Sharpness

❑ Adjust the sound level with the volume control of the amplifier.

❑ Rewind the tape to the beginning of the program. If the class or audience will arrive shortly, push the "Blue Screen" button. If not turn off the lamp, but remember it must first cool off before you can turn it on again.

Disassemble

❑ After presentation of the video, rewind the tape.

❑ Turn off all power switches.

❑ Disconnect cord(s) from wall sockets.

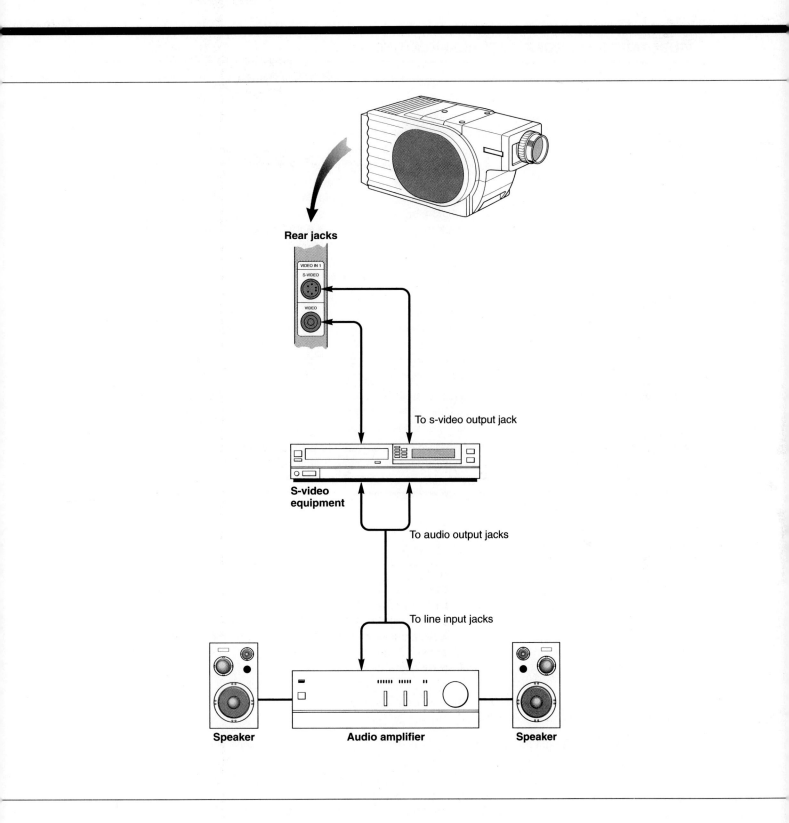

Rear jacks

VIDEO IN 1

S-VIDEO

VIDEO

To s-video output jack

S-video equipment

To audio output jacks

To line input jacks

Speaker   **Audio amplifier**   **Speaker**

VIDEOTAPE RECORDER TROUBLESHOOTING

Problem	Possible Remedy
Recording Videotape is running but there is no picture on the monitor	1. Check to see that all components are plugged in and turned on. Make sure the lens cap is off the camera and the lens aperture is open. 2. Check the monitor. Switch it to "TV" and try to tune in a broadcast channel; make sure the brightness and contrast controls are properly set. If you still fail to get a picture, check to see if there is a circuit breaker on the back of the monitor that needs to be reset. If you get a picture while switched to "TV," you should then check the connection between camera and monitor. 3. Check the cable connections from camera to recorder and from recorder to monitor. 4. Check the settings of the switches on the recorder. Is the input selector on "Camera"? Is the "Record" button depressed?
Playback Videotape is running but there is no picture or sound on monitor	1. Make sure the monitor input selector is set at "VTR" and all units are plugged in. 2. Check connectors between playback unit and monitor (e.g., make sure "Video Out" from playback is connected to "Video In" on monitor). Wiggle the end of the cable to see if there is a loose connection. 3. Check switches on playback unit.
Fuzzy sound or snowy picture	1. Video or audio heads may be dirty. Clean with approved spray. 2. Brushes under head-drum cover may be dirty or damaged. Have a technician check this possibility.
Picture slants horizontally across screen (the audio may also sound off-speed)	If adjustment of the horizontal hold knob does not clear up the situation, you may have a tape or cassette that is incompatible with your playback unit. Obtain a playback machine that matches the format of the tape or cassette.

VIDEO PROJECTOR TROUBLESHOOTING

Problem	Possible Remedy
No picture	1. Make certain projector and player are plugged into active AC outlet and turn power switches on. 2. If using remote control, be sure batteries are strong and unit is within effective operating distance. 3. Check all cords for proper connection.
Picture is not clear	1. Check focus adjustment. 2. Adjust picture controls.
Picture but no color	Check settings on video unit.
Picture is inverted or left-right reversed	Check settings of horizontal and vertical polarity plugs.
Color and picture distorted	1. Check connection of leads between video unit output terminals and projector input terminals. 2. Confirm that the signal is compatible.
No operation from remote control	1. If using wired remote control, check to see if it is plugged into the video unit, and check connection of remote lead between the video unit and the video projector. 2. If using wireless remote control, confirm that batteries are strong and wireless remote control is within effective operating range.

Figure 11.31
Video projectors are replacing monitors for showing videocassettes, videodiscs, and computer output.

Video projectors vary in weight from about 20 pounds to 150 pounds. Each time the video projector is moved it must be adjusted to ensure a sharp image. Each of the three lenses must be focused and adjusted so that the three images exactly overlay each other (converge). Some newer and more expensive models include a microprocessor that automatically focuses and converges the three images in less than three minutes. The manual process can take up to several hours.

Applications of video projectors include showing videocassettes and videodiscs and other television applications where monitors are currently used. They can also display computer output and demonstrate computer software packages (see p. 321).

VIDEO PLAYBACK SETUPS

Before students can learn from any instructional TV presentation, they first have to be able to see it and hear it! Provide proper lighting, seating, and volume control.

Seating

An ideal seating arrangement for instructional television may sometimes be difficult to achieve. Because of economic constraints, there are often not enough television sets available to give every student an adequate view. Ideally, one 23-inch-screen TV set should serve no more than thirty students seated at desks in a classroom with aisles. If conditions are not ideal, do your best. If feasible, seats may be shared or moved closer together so that all may have at least an adequate view of the screen. If possible, stagger seats to help prevent blocked views.

Here are some basic rules of thumb for good seating arrangement (see Figure 11.32):

❑ Seat no one closer than 7 feet from the receiver.
❑ Seat no one farther away in feet than the size of the TV screen in inches.
❑ Seat no one more than 45 degrees from the center axis of the screen.

❑ Place the TV set no more than 30 degrees above the normal eye level of any seated viewer to avoid having viewers crane their necks uncomfortably.

Monitor Placement

When locating television monitors for instructional viewing, you need to consider the amount of detail to be shown on the screen. As illustrated in Figure 11.32, a distance of no more than six times the size of the monitor is best if small details are important. Examples might include studying computer output, reading small captions, and televised viewing through a microscope using a high-resolution camera. For a 23-inch monitor, the acceptable viewing range would be from 7 to 12 feet.

Viewers should be no further than ten times the monitor size away if moderate details are important.

If details are not critical, as in the case of people and landscapes, the farthest viewer can be back as far as twelve times the monitor size. For a 23-inch monitor, the maxi-

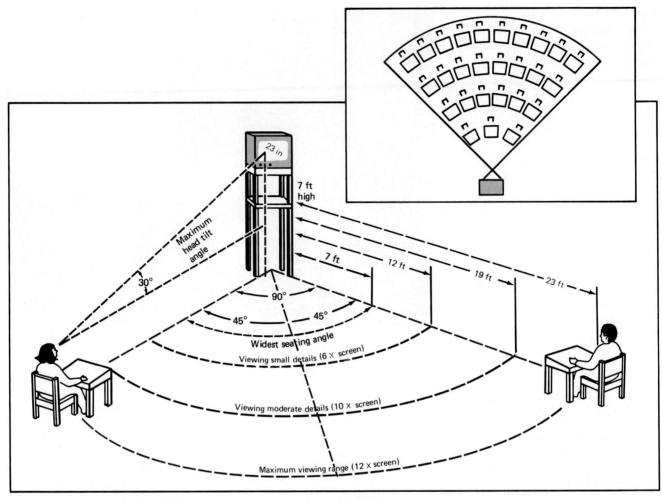

Figure 11.32
Recommended monitor placement and seating distances for TV viewing.

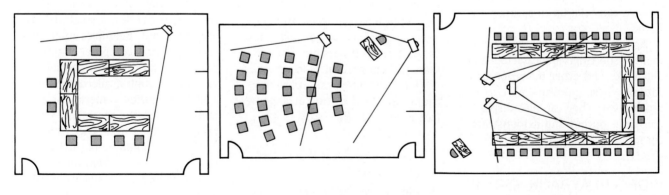

Small Conference Room   Classroom   Large Training Room

Figure 11.33
TV monitor placements for typical viewing situations

☐ APPRAISAL CHECKLIST
Equipment Selection

Type_____ Price_____

Make_____ Model_____

Audio

Speaker Size_____ Amplifier Output_____

Inputs   Outputs

_____ _____

_____ _____

Sound controls   Tape

_____ Size_____ Tracks_____

_____ Speeds_____

Other Features

Projector

Lamp _____ Wattage _____ Exciter lamp _____

Power controls   Lamp level control

_____ _____

_____ _____

Lens _____

Other Features

Rating	**High**		**Medium**		**Low**	**Comments**
Sound quality	☐	☐	☐	☐	☐	
Picture quality	☐	☐	☐	☐	☐	
Ease of operation	☐	☐	☐	☐	☐	
Price range	☐	☐	☐	☐	☐	
Durability	☐	☐	☐	☐	☐	
Ease to maintain	☐	☐	☐	☐	☐	
Ease to repair	☐	☐	☐	☐	☐	

Strong Points

Weak Points

Reviewer_____

Position_____

Recommended Action_____ Date_____

_____

Figure 11.34
Periodically clean monitor and TV screens with a weak detergent solution.

mum range would be 23 feet (unless details are important).

Sample room arrangements indicating placement of television monitors are shown in Figure 11.33. In addition to the distance of the viewers from the monitor, you must also consider the height of the monitor. For group viewing a 54-inch-high stand or cart works best.

Lighting

Television should be viewed in normal or dim light, not darkness. Besides being more comfortable to the eye, normal illumination provides necessary light for student participative activities, for referring to handouts, and for note taking.

The television receiver should be located so that harsh light from a window or light fixture cannot strike the screen and cause glare. Do not place the receiver in front of an unshaded window that will compete with light from the television screen and make viewing difficult.

Volume

For proper hearing, the volume of the receiver should be set loud enough to be heard clearly in the rear of the viewing area but not so loud that it bowls over those in the front. Normally this happy middle ground is not difficult to achieve if your seating arrangement is within acceptable bounds and your receiv-

er's speaker mechanism is functioning properly.

Obviously, volume should be kept low enough so as not to disturb neighboring classes. Unfortunately, open-plan buildings with only movable room dividers as walls provide a poor environment for TV or other audiovisual presentations. Under such conditions cooperation is critical. Teachers in neighboring areas can mutually agree to lower their sound level to minimize interference (this is better than escalating the problem by trying to drown each other out!). Sometimes the only alternative is to seek an enclosed room that can be reserved for audiovisual use.

REFERENCES

Print References

Aiex, Nola K. "Using Film, Video, and TV in the Classroom." *ERIC Digest* 11 Bloomington, IN: ERIC Clearinghouse on Reading and Communication Skills, 1988.

Alten, Stanley R. *Audio in Media.* 3d ed. Belmont, CA: Wadsworth Publications, 1990.

Alyea, Hubert N. "Overhead Projector Demonstration: Titled TOPS: Incline Plane Projection." *Journal of Chemical Education* (September 1989):765–68.

Bullard, John R., and Mether, Calvin E. *Audiovisual Fundamentals: Basic Equipment Operation. Simple Materials Production.* 3d ed. Dubuque, IA: Wm. C. Brown, 1984.

Clifford, Martin. *Microphones: How They Work and How to Use Them.* 3d ed. Blue Ridge Summit, PA: TAB Books, 1986.

The Equipment Director of Video, Computer, and Audio-Visual Products. Fairfax, VA: International Communications Industries Association (annual).

Fawson, Curtis E. "LCD Projectors: An Evaluation of Features and Utilization for Educators." *Tech Trends* 35, no. 5 (1990):19–24.

Friesenborg, Terry. "Spotlight on Auditoriums and Lecture Halls." *Media and Methods* (November–December 1989):10–12, 46–51.

Hall, Bonnie L. "Camcorders in the Classroom: Student Productions at the Secondary Level." *Hispania* (December 1990):1137–38.

Kalmbach, John A., and Kruzel, Richard D. "Strategies for Buying and Maintaining Audio Visual Equipment." *Media and Methods* (January–February 1989):9–15.

Kerstetter, John P. "Designing Classrooms for the Use of Instructional Media: A Planning and Specification Checklist." *Media Management Journal* (Fall 1986):25–28.

Koerner, Thomas. *Use of Audiotape Recorders in Schools.* Reston, VA: National Association of Secondary School Principals, 1988.

Kolb, Doris. "Overhead Projector Demonstrations." *Journal of Chemical Education* (December 1988):1090.

Kybett, Harry, and Horn, Delton T. *The Complete Handbook of Videocassette Recorders.* 3d ed. Blue Ridge Summit, PA: TAB Books, 1986.

Magee, John L. "Before You Call for Service, Try These Simple AV Repairs." *American School and University* (May 1981):126–29.

McComb, Gordon. *Troubleshooting and Repairing VCRs.* 2d ed. Blue Ridge Summit, PA: TAB Books, 1991.

Meisel, Susan Lee. "A Hard Look at Audiovisual Equipment." *Media and Methods* (October 1983):9–11, 48.

Minimum Specifications for 16mm Sound Film Projectors. The Hague, Netherlands: International Council for Educational Media, 1982.

Minimum Specifications for Slide Projectors. The Hague, Netherlands: International Council for Educational Media, 1980.

Page, Marilyn. *Microphones and Educational Media.* Baltimore, MD: ERIC Document Reproduction Service, 1990.

Ransdell, Sarah. "A Dynamic Duo: LCD Overhead Displays and Laptops as Instructional Aids in Introductory Psychology." *Collegiate Microcomputer* (May 1989):147–50.

Rosenberg, Kenyon C. *Dictionary of Library and Educational Technology.* 3d ed. Littleton, Co: Libraries Unlimited, 1989.

Rowat, Robert W. "A Guide to the Use of the Overhead Projector." ERIC, 1982 (ED 211109).

Sakovich, Vladimir, and Costello, William. "Work Horses or White Elephants: A Guide to Selecting AV

Equipment." *Media and Methods* (January 1980):26–29, 60–61.

Schoeder, Don, and Lare, Gary. *Audiovisual Equipment and Materials: A Basic Repair and Maintenance Manual.* 2d ed. Metuchen, NJ: Scarecrow Press, 1989.

Stafford, Carl W. "Standardize Your Adapters." *Instructional Innovator* (May 1980):26–28.

Sturken, Marita. "Video Systems for Libraries." *Sightlines* (Spring 1983):25–26.

Sullivan, Sam, and Baker, Bryan. *A Handbook of Operating Information and Simplified Maintenance Instructions for Commonly Used Audiovisual Equipment.* Rev. ed. Huntsville, TX: KBS, 1982.

Teague, Fred A.; Newhouse, Barbara S.; and Streit, Les D. *Instructional Media Basics.* Dubuque, IA: Kendall/Hunt, 1982.

Wadsworth, Raymond H. *Basics of Audio and Visual Systems Design.* Indianapolis: Howard W. Sams, 1983.

Wilshusen, John. "How to Prevent Equipment Failures." *Instructional Innovator* (March 1980):35–36.

Audiovisual References

David's Legacy. Fairfax, VA: International Communications Industries Association, 1989. Videocassette. 15 minutes.

A Layman's Guide to Minor VCR Repair. Charlotte, NC: Multi-Video, 1988. Videocassette. 45 minutes.

All of the following ½-inch VHS videocassettes are available from Audiovisual Center Marketing, C215 Seashore Hall, University of Iowa, Iowa City, IA 52242.

General Operating Principles for AV Equipment. 1983. 7 minutes.
Single Camera VCR System. 1983. 7 minutes.
16mm Projector. 1983. 7 minutes.
Romancing the Eiki: The Story of a Slotloading Projector. 1988. 11 minutes.
Programming Synchronized Slide-Tape Shows. 1988. 11 minutes.
(Media Fears) Programming the Multislide Show. 1989. 13 minutes.
Pre-production Planning for Video. 1990. 10 minutes.
Operating the Camcorder. 1990. 8 minutes.
Videotape Editing. 1990. 8 minutes.

Organizations

EPIE (Educational Products Information Exchange) Institute
103-3 W. Montauk Highway
Hampton Bays, NY 11946

EPIE is a nonprofit, consumer-supported agency functioning like a consumer's union and providing analytical information about instructional materials and equipment.

International Communications Industries Association
3150 Spring Street
Fairfax, VA 22031

Trade association for producers and distributors of audiovisual equipment and materials. Publishes annually *The Equipment Directory of Video, Computer, and Audio-Visual Products.*

POSSIBLE PROJECTS

11–A. Demonstrate the proper setup, operation, and disassembly of the following pieces of equipment: tape recorder, overhead projector, slide projector, filmstrip projector, 16mm film projector, and videotape recorder.

11–B. Given a piece of equipment from the list in project 11–A with a problem, troubleshoot and correct the problem.

11–C. Demonstrate proper care and maintenance for each piece of equipment listed in project 11–A.

11–D. Set up (or diagram the setup) for a given instructional situation requiring audio, projection, and/or video.

11–E. Demonstrate the proper procedures for replacing lamps in the following types of projectors: overhead, slide, filmstrip, and film. You will be evaluated on selecting the correct replacement lamp and on handling it properly.

11–F. Procure catalogs illustrating projection tables and carts, identify examples from each of the functions described in the chapter, and compare the examples in terms of versatility of use, advantages, limitations, and cost.

11–G. Synchronize a set of slides and an audiotape. You may use existing slides, but you must record the narrative on the tape and incorporate the advance pulses into the system.

11–H. Evaluate a piece of audiovisual equipment using the "Appraisal Checklist: Equipment Selection" in this chapter.

Technologies of
Instruction

OUTLINE

Psychological Bases of the Technologies of Instruction

The Behavioral Perspective

The Cognitive Perspective

The Social-Psychological Perspective

Finding a Middle Ground

Technologies of Instruction that Emphasize Reinforcement or Feedback

Programmed Instruction

Programmed Tutoring

Programmed Teaching

Technologies of Instruction that Emphasize Individual Pacing

Personalized System of Instruction

Audio-Tutorial Systems

Technologies of Instruction that Emphasize Realistic Contexts

Simulations and Games

Technologies of Instruction Based on Cooperative Groups

Team Accelerated Instruction

Cooperative Integrated Reading and Composition

Technologies of Instruction that Utilize the Computer

OBJECTIVES

After studying this chapter, you should be able to

1. Define *technology of instruction,* listing four critical attributes and distinguishing between "hard technologies" and "soft technologies."

2. Discuss the main concerns of the behavioral perspective on learning.

3. State the basic principle of reinforcement theory.

4. Relate programmed instruction to reinforcement theory.

5. Contrast the cognitive perspective with the behavioral perspective on learning.

6. Discuss the main concerns of the social-psychological perspective on learning.

7. List six features of instruction that are widely supported from all the various perspectives on learning.

8. Describe programmed instruction and distinguish it from other technologies of instruction.

9. Differentiate between linear and branching programming.

10. Generate five guidelines for utilization of programmed instruction in the classroom.

11. State at least five evaluative criteria for appraising programmed materials.

12. Describe programmed tutoring and distinguish it from other technologies of instruction; list the two most common curriculum applications.

13. Describe programmed teaching and distinguish it from other technologies of instruction.

14. Describe Personalized System of Instruction and distinguish it from other technologies of instruction.

15. Describe audio-tutorial systems, including the names and functions of the three types of sessions; compare and contrast audio-tutorial with Personalized System of Instruction.

16. Defend simulations and games as technologies of instruction.

17. Describe at least one technology of instruction based on cooperative group learning.

18. Relate computers to technologies of instruction.

19. Synthesize an instructional situation in which you would use one of the technologies of instruction as a solution; describe why and how you would apply that technology of instruction.

LEXICON

soft technology

reinforcement

prompt

programmed instruction

linear programming

branching programming

reliability

programmed tutoring

brightening

programmed teaching

Personalized System of Instruction (PSI)

audio-tutorial systems (A-T)

simulation

game

Team Accelerated Instruction (TAI)

Cooperative Integrated Reading and Composition (CIRC)

In Chapter 1 we presented Galbraith's definition of technology as "the systematic application of scientific or other organized knowledge to practical tasks." This definition focuses attention on technology as a *process*, or a way of thinking, rather than an array of *products*, such as computers, satellites, and the like. Unfortunately, the debate over the possible role of technology in education has too often been clouded by a tendency to equate technology with things. Recently, the product-process distinction has been highlighted by using the terms "hard technology" (products) and *"soft technology"* (processes).

This chapter focuses on the soft technologies of instruction. We use the term *technology of instruction* to refer to a teaching/learning pattern designed to provide reliable, effective instruction to each learner through application of scientific principles of human learning. That is, each of the soft technologies discussed in this chapter is a precast mold or framework for organizing instruction.

The value of precast molds is obvious. They give instructors and instructional designers a blueprint to follow in planning lessons or whole courses of study. Rather than reinvent the wheel, you can select the framework that addresses the problem most salient to you, and organize your lesson or course around that framework.

PSYCHOLOGICAL BASES OF THE TECHNOLOGIES OF INSTRUCTION

In Chapter 1 we discussed the issues of learning and instruction and noted that there are different theories about which internal and external features contribute most to the process of learning. We consider these theories to be differing perspectives on the same problem. Each has strengths and limitations, and as a group the theories have a large area of overlap. Each perspective captures a different part of the overall truth.

To explain what technologies of instruction are, why they are used, and how they are used, we will start by taking a closer look at just three instructional perspectives — behavioral, cognitive, and social-psychological. Each of these actually encompasses a range of viewpoints and can be seen as a family of related theories. Our discussion contrasts these perspectives and looks at practical implications of each theory for selecting and using technologies of instruction.

All of these perspectives have been widely represented in North American education since at least the beginning of the twentieth century. We will discuss first the behavioral perspective, which flourished and held center stage in the 1950s and 1960s, then the cognitive view, which has been predominant more recently, and finally the social-psychological view, which has developed alongside the other two.

The Behavioral Perspective

In the mid-1950s psychological researchers began to study learners' responses to stimuli. B. F. Skinner was the leader for many years in this vein of research. Skinner subscribed to the behavioral position but with a major difference from his predecessors: he was interested in voluntary behavior rather than reflexes, as exemplified by Pavlov's famous salivating dog. Skinner referred to these voluntary actions as "operants" and referred to his method as "operant conditioning."

Skinner particularly focused on the importance of the consequences of responses, demonstrating that new behavior patterns could be "shaped" by rewarding desired responses. In other words, learning, he maintained, depends on what happens *after* a new behavior is exhibited.

The procedure of providing rewards, or satisfying consequences, after a response is referred to as *reinforcement*. Hence, Skinner's theory of operant conditioning became known as reinforcement theory. Its basic principle is that behaviors that are followed by reinforcement are more likely to recur in the future, implying that they are learned (see Figure 12.1).

Also fundamental to reinforcement theory is the notion that complex skills can be broken down into clusters of simpler ones. Each subskill can be learned one at a time if the subject receives reinforcement after each correct response. These subskills then become links in a longer, more complex behavior chain.

Experimenters were able to demonstrate dramatic results in the training of pigeons and other animals. As they began to transfer these theories to human learning of mental skills, they realized that another element needed to be added to the formula — a *prompt*. Rather than waiting around for a desired response to occur spontaneously, the instructor or instructional material can hint at or tell the desired response. The basic formula for applying reinforcement theory to human intellectual skills, then, requires

1. a prompt (e.g., statement of a law of physics)

2. a response (e.g., answer to a question about the law)

3. reinforcement (e.g., knowledge of the correct response or praise)

Programmed Instruction.
In 1954, in his famous article "The Science of Learning and the Art of Teaching," Skinner pointed out that the elements of this formula were largely missing in traditional classroom instruction.[1] In large-group

---

[1] B. F. Skinner, "The Science of Learning and the Art of Teaching," *Harvard Educational Review* (Spring 1954): 86–97.

Figure 12.1
The behavioral perspective.
Behaviorists focus on the outwardly
visible aspects of learning. The boy
sees, hears, and feels the dog; he
responds by smiling and patting the
dog.

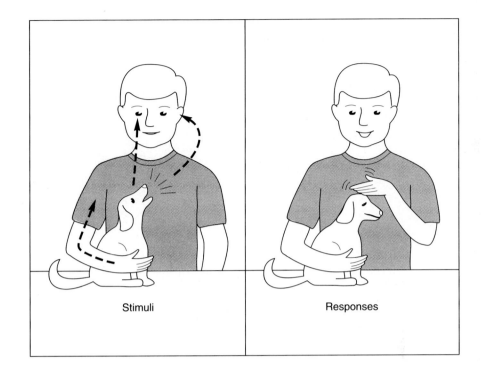

Stimuli   Responses

instruction, students spend much of their time listening, with little opportunity for overt (audible or visible) response. Even if an overt response is given, the typical teacher, responsible for dealing with a whole class at one time, has limited opportunity even to observe individual responses, much less to reinforce each one appropriately. How, then, could the principles of reinforcement theory be implemented in the classroom?

Skinner's initial solution to this problem was an innovative method of presenting instructional material printed in small segments, or "frames," each of which included a bit of information (prompt), an incomplete statement or question (requiring response), and provision of the correct answer (reinforcement). A mechanical device, which others later referred to as a teaching machine, was used to guide the student from one frame to the next and to reveal the correct answers (Figure 12.2). This *programmed instruction* provided a mechanism for adapting lessons to the individual student's pace, thereby overcoming the rigid, lockstep nature of large-

group teaching. Further, it ensured that students would be kept actively at work making frequent (and nearly always correct) responses, thus gaining frequent reinforcement.

As we will see later in this chapter, quite a few of today's technologies of instruction are derived directly or indirectly from the original notion of programmed instruction, for example, Direct Instruction, Personalized System of Instruction, and structured tutoring. Because these techniques are no longer considered experimental, they are less visible in educational research literature than they were in the 1960s and 1970s, but they are still widely used, not only in North America but throughout the world.

The Cognitive Perspective

To behaviorists, what goes on in the mind is not directly observable and so, rather than speculate on internal processes, they attempt to deduce principles of learning from what they *can* see. Such an approach leads to a theory that is good at describing not but explaining. It has little to say about higher-level learn-

ing tasks such as problem solving and creative writing.

Cognitive theorists, on the other hand, claim that it is possible and necessary to speculate about mental processes. They maintain we cannot design more effective instruction for intellectual skills until we understand, or at least have a theory about, mental processes. Piaget's influence on cognitive theory, particularly his theory of how children's logical abilities evolve with age, was discussed in Chapter 1.

Figure 12.2
In this early teaching machine, of the type described by Skinner in his original article, the paper roll advanced only when the correct response was constructed.

Figure 12.3
The cognitive perspective. Cognitivists focus on the effect of the boy-dog interaction on the boy's mental structure or schema.

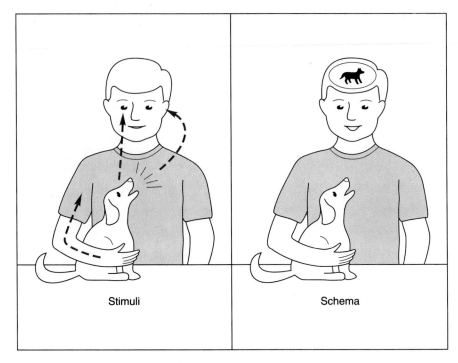

Stimuli   Schema

Another enduring influence on cognitive theory has been the work of Jerome Bruner. His most recent work has focused on how the mind represents ideas symbolically and the mechanisms for manipulating and using symbols. His theory shares similarities with Piaget's ideas about how learners construct and use schemata.[2] To the cognitivists, mental activity is primarily concerned with sense-making, constructing schemata that impose meaning on the tides of stimuli that flow over us every day (see Figure 12.3).

Instruction designed from the cognitivist perspective, as opposed to the behaviorist perspective, tends to favor more open-ended and realistic experiences that allow the learner to explore and make sense out of confusing realities. In recent years advances in computer technology have made it possible to create rich simulations for exploratory learning, referred to by some as "microworlds."

(Such computer-based multimedia and hypermedia environments are discussed in detail in Chapter 9.)

The Social-Psychological Perspective

As discussed in Chapter 1, social psychology brings a third perspective to analyzing technologies of instruction. What is important from this perspective is the social organization of instruction: In what types of groups do students work? Who controls their activities? Is cooperation or competition rewarded? In recent years there has been a revival of research interest in these issues, and new methods of cooperative learning have been developed and proven effective.

Finding a Middle Ground

Throughout this text we recommend an eclectic approach to practice. Powerful frameworks for instruction have been developed by designers inspired by each of the psychological perspectives. Indeed, successful instructional practices have features that are supported by virtually all the various perspectives:

❑ *Active participation and interaction.* Effective learning happens when students are actively engaged in meaningful tasks, interacting with the material.

❑ *Practice.* New learning requires more than one exposure to take root; practice, especially in varying contexts, improves retention rate and the ability to apply the new knowledge, skill, or attitude.

❑ *Individual differences.* Learners vary in terms of personality, general aptitude, knowledge of a subject, and many other factors; effective methods allow individuals to progress at different rates, cover different material, and even participate in different activities.

❑ *Reinforcement or feedback.* Learners need to know if their thinking is on track; feedback may be provided by teacher correction of papers, electronic messages from a computer, the scoring system of a game, or other means.

❑ *Realistic contexts.* We are most likely to remember and to apply knowledge that is presented in a real-world context; rote learning

---

[2]   Jerome S. Bruner, *Acts of Meaning* (Cambridge, MA: Harvard University Press, 1990).

leads to "inert knowledge"—we know something but never apply it to real life.

❏ *Cooperative groups.* Fellow humans serving as tutors or peer group members can provide a number of pedagogical supports as well as social ones.

The teaching/learning frameworks that we will examine in detail all attempt to incorporate a number of the pedagogical features mentioned just above. Certainly all of them value active participation and interaction. They also encourage learners to use new knowledge, skills, or attitudes by providing for frequent and varied practice. However, they vary in the extent to which they emphasize the other features, as will become clear in the remaining sections of the chapter.

TECHNOLOGIES OF INSTRUCTION THAT EMPHASIZE REINFORCEMENT OR FEEDBACK

Programmed Instruction

Since reinforcement theory demanded that reinforcement be given only after a correct response, it was originally considered necessary to use a mechanical monitoring device to enforce this requirement. During the infancy of programmed instruction, much creative energy was invested in developing such "teaching machines" to automate the presentation of frames of information to the learner. Research and practical experience soon indicated, however, that students were quite capable of monitoring their own progress without the help of a cumbersome and expensive page-turning machine. In many cases the teaching machines were discarded, and their instructional contents were put into a book format.

The earliest programmed instruction texts arranged the frames across the page in horizontal strips. The correct response for each question could be checked only by turning the page (see Figure 12.4). Later, this method was relaxed, allowing the frames to be arranged vertically as in conventional printed pages, and became known as *linear programming.* These programmed texts were meant to be read with a piece of paper covering the rest of the page while a frame was being read.

After writing an answer in the blank on the first frame, for example, the user moved the cover down to see the correct answer printed in the box to the left of the second frame. You will have a better idea of how programmed instruction works if you go through the example in Figure 12.5.

Programmed Instruction as a Technology of Instruction. The pattern or framework of programmed instruction began with the linear format described above. Early research, however, cast doubt on the necessity or desirability of following this rigid format. An early and successful challenge to the linear orthodoxy came from Norman Crowder in the form of "intrinsic programming."[3] The basic method was to present a large block of information followed by a multiple-choice question requiring application of the facts or principles presented. Each answer choice directed the reader to a different page.

---

[3] Norman Crowder, "On the Differences between Linear and Intrinsic Programming," *Phi Delta Kappan* (March 1963): 250–54.

Figure 12.4
An early programmed textbook was *The Analysis of Behavior* by James B. Holland and B. F. Skinner (1961). Note the "zebra stripe" arrangement of the pages requiring the reader to turn the page to see the correct answer.

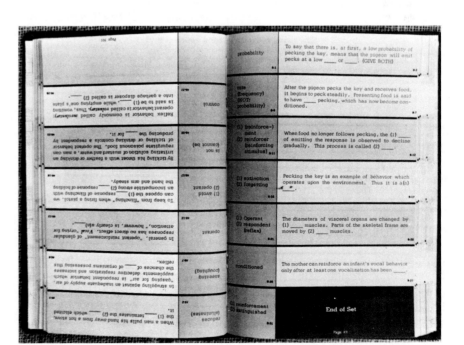

Figure 12.5
An early example of linear programmed text. To use this example, cover all of the page except the first frame with a piece of paper. Write your answer in the blank in the first frame. To verify your answer, slide the cover down to see the correct answer printed to the left of the second frame.

	1. Psychologists differ in their explanations of what learning is and precisely how it occurs. The series of statements or "frames" presented here deal with one particular explanation of the process of _____ .
learning	**2.** We cannot observe learning directly, but we can infer that it has occurred when a person consistently makes a *response* that he or she previously was unable to make. For example, if a student says "nine" when asked "What is three times three?" she is making a _____ that was probably learned through practice in school.
response	**3.** If you reply "kappa" when asked "What Greek letter is represented by *K*?" you are making a _____ that you learned through some prior experience.
response	**4.** The word or picture or other sensory stimulation that causes you to make a response is a *stimulus* (plural: *stimuli*). Therefore, if "kappa" is your response, "What Greek letter is represented by *K*?" would be the _____ .
stimulus	**5.** To the stimulus "good," the student of Spanish responds "bueno"; the student of Arabic responds "gayid." To the stimulus "silver," the student of Spanish records "plata"; the student of Arabic responds "fida." They are responding to English words which are serving as _____ .
stimuli	**6.** In these frames the written statements are the stimuli to which you are writing _____ in the blanks.
responses	**7.** We learn to connect certain verbal responses to certain stimuli through the process of forming *associations*. We say that the student associates "nine" with "three times three"; he learns to associate "kappa" with *K*; and he _____ "plata" with "silver."
associates	**8.** Much verbal learning seems to be based on the formation of associations between _____ and responses.
stimuli	etc.

Correct choices jumped the reader ahead to new material; incorrect choices led to remedial explanations and more questions.

Because intrinsic programming's pattern of frames resembled the branches of a tree, it became known as *branching programming* (Figure 12.6). The major advantage of the branching format is that learners who catch on quickly can move through the material much more efficiently, following the "prime path."

The *reliability* of any type of instruction refers to the extent to which it is dependable and consistent in yielding its intended effects. That is, can the teacher expect similar results with a variety of learners who experience the lesson on different occasions? A lecture delivered from rough notes would be considered unreliable in terms of its ability to be repeated with similar effect on a later occasion, especially if a different teacher is giving the lecture. However, a lesson shaped around a

specific programmed instruction booklet or computer-based branching program would be expected to be highly reliable because it can dependably provide a stable, predictable experience for each student each time it is used regardless of who the teacher is.

Concerning effectiveness, there have been hundreds of research studies comparing programmed texts with conventional instruction. The summaries of these studies indicate the slight superiority of programmed instruction. While the average student in conventional instruction scores at the 50th percentile, the programmed instruction student scores at the 54th to 60th percentile.[4,5] It's quite clear that all programmed materials are not created equal. Some serve a particular audience and a particular purpose well, others do not. The same, of course, can be said for conventional instruction; hence, the small overall superiority of programmed instruction. Both linear and branching formats are still used today, in printed programmed materials and in computer-based instruction.

Utilizing Programmed Instruction. Programmed materials have been used successfully from the elementary school through the adult education level and in almost every subject area. By itself or in conjunction with other strategies, a program can be used to teach an entire course or a segment of a course. Many teachers use short programmed units to teach simple principles and terminology. Programmed instruction is particularly useful as an enrichment activity. It can help provide highly motivated students with additional learning experiences that the teacher might ordinarily be unable to provide because of classroom time pressures.

Programmed materials have also proven to be very effective in remedial instruction. The program can function as a kind of tutor for slow learners in situations where more

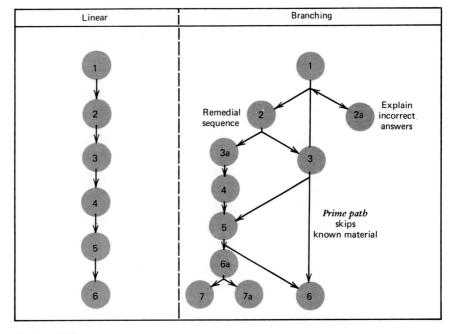

Figure 12.6
Comparison of linear and branching formats of programmed instruction

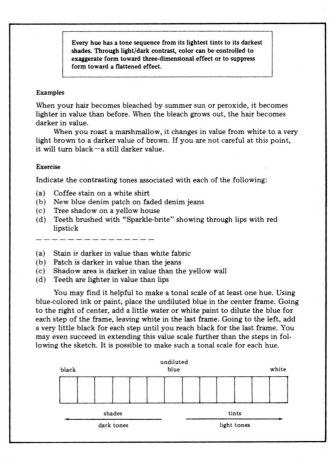

Figure 12.7
A contemporary example of linear programmed instruction from a book on art. This program calls for a variety of types of responses, including painting, as seen at the bottom of the page.

4   James A. Kulik, Peter A. Cohen, and Barbara J. Ebeling, "The Effectiveness of Programmed Instruction in Higher Education: A Meta-Analysis of Findings," *Educational Evaluation and Policy Analysis* 2, no. 6 (November–December 1980): 51–64.

5   Chen-Lin C. Kulik, Barbara J. Schwalb, and James A. Kulik, "Programmed Instruction in Secondary Education: A Meta-Analysis of Evaluation Findings," *Journal of Educational Research* 75, no. 3 (January–February, 1982): 133–38.

personalized attention may be virtually impossible (in overcrowded classrooms, for example). Students can even take this particular tutor with them when they leave the classroom! One of the reasons for the success of programmed materials in remedial instruction is their "failure-proof" design. Because these materials break learning down into small steps and allow the student to take as much time as needed for each step, and because the materials are tested, evaluated, and revised carefully prior to publication, they are more likely to provide the slow learner with a successful experience. For some students this type of program may be their first encounter with schoolwork that gives them an immediate and continued feeling of success.

Programmed instruction can be an effective means of ensuring classwide competency in skills that are prerequisite to successful completion of a unit of study. For example, one high school physics teacher used a small programmed text to allow his students to teach themselves power-of-ten notation, which is a prerequisite for solving physics problems. At the outset some of the students were even more proficient with power-of-ten operations than their instructor. Others had been introduced to the technique but had lost their competence in it because they had not been required to use the skill. Still others had never even been introduced to it. The program on power-of-ten notation eliminated devoting class time to a subject that would have bored some and confused others. Instead, the students were allowed to consider the material on their own. Those who knew the technique could ignore the program; those who had previously learned the skill but were a little rusty could use the program as a review; and those who had never been exposed to power-of-ten notation could master the necessary manipulations on their own and at

their own pace. All students were subsequently required to pass a criterion test demonstrating mastery of this skill.

Programmed materials have a wide variety of other more or less specialized uses. They can, for example, be used for makeup instruction by students who have been absent from school for an extended period of time. They can be used to expand curriculum offerings when it might be difficult or impossible otherwise to offer certain subjects because of too few interested students or the lack of a qualified instructor. This could be an important consideration for smaller schools and for training programs in business and industry (Figure 12.8).

Like any other instructional material, programmed texts need to be carefully appraised before selection (see "Appraisal Checklist: Programmed Materials"). Also, the success of programmed materials, as with other materials, depends on the skill of the instructor in choosing materials appropriate for the audience and purpose and integrating them into the instructional program.

Learners who are unfamiliar with the programmed format may need help in figuring out how to work with the materials. For example, you may want users to write their responses on separate sheets instead of in the book itself. Because some programmed materials may look like tests, you may need to reassure students that they are not being tested and should not worry about making errors. They should be encouraged to ask questions; their confusion may indicate flaws or ambiguities in the instruction for which you can compensate.

Since the whole point of programmed instruction is individual pacing, learners should indeed be allowed to pace themselves. It would be counterproductive, for example, to assign a minimum amount of material to be completed in a single

Figure 12.8
Through programmed instruction trainees can begin study when ready, not just when a full class becomes available.

Figure 12.9
A typical arrangement for a programmed tutoring lesson

class period. In most cases the programmed materials would be used outside of class.

Using programmed instruction does not mean that students are always working alone. Group activities can and should be scheduled to supplement the programmed instruction and to meet other desired educational goals. In addition, as with other properly planned individualized activities, programs help release teachers from routine classroom

Figure 12.10

The directions given in the tutor's guidebook structure the programmed tutoring lesson.

STEP 1   Tell the student that this exercise will help him learn to sound out new words.

STEP 2   Point to the first word and ask the student to *sound* it out.

    a. If the student reads the word correctly, praise him; then go on to the next word.

    b. If the student is unable to read the word or reads it incorrectly, have him make the individual sounds in the word separately and then assist him in blending the sounds.

    Example:

      Word: "THIN"

    Tutor: Place your finger over the last two letters in the word and ask: "What sound does the *th* make?" If the student answers correctly, praise him and go to the next sound. If he answers incorrectly or fails to answer, tell him the sound and have him repeat it. Follow the same procedure for each sound in the word, and then show him how to blend the separate sounds.

STEP 3   Follow step 2 for each word on the sheet.

STEP 4   At the end of the session, praise the student.

STEP 5   Fill out your tutor log.

Source: Grant Von Harrison, *Beginning Reading 1: A Professional Guide for the Lay Tutor* (Provo, UT: Brigham Young University Press, 1972), p. 101.

chores in order to interact personally with students and provide them with human reinforcement.

Programmed Tutoring

Programmed tutoring (also referred to as structured tutoring) is a one-to-one method of instruction (Figure 12.9) in which the decisions to be made by the tutor are programmed in advance in the form of carefully structured printed instructions. In a typical program the tutor and student sit down together to go through the lesson material. The teacher's book has the answers to the exercises; the student's book does not. An excerpt from a typical programmed tutoring teacher's book is shown in Figure 12.10. Note how the tutor's role in the program is set forth, step by step, to conform with learner response to the materials.

Because the tutor is continually choosing the next step on the basis of the learner's last response, programmed tutoring is a form of branching programming. As such, it shares the basic advantage for which branching was originally developed: the fast learner can skip quickly through the material without tedious unnecessary repetition.

Programmed tutoring uses what might be called "brightening" as opposed to the "fading" or gradual reduction of prompts used in conventional linear programmed instruction. In *brightening,* the item is first presented in a relatively difficult form. If the learner responds correctly, he or she is reinforced and goes on to a new item. If not, a series of increasingly clearer prompts or hints are given. For example, in teaching a beginning reader to follow written instructions, the student's book might say, "Point to your teacher." If the learner does not do so when first shown the instruction, the tutor might follow this sequence of brightening prompts:

1. "Read it again." (Wait for response.)

2. "What does it say?"

3. "What does it tell you to do?"

4. "Do what it tells you to do."

The sequence of prompts would continue until the learner gives an acceptable response. Then reinforcement would be given. The idea is to lead the student toward the solution with brightening hints but to avoid actually giving the correct answer.

Programmed Tutoring as a Technology of Instruction.

Programmed tutoring shares with programmed instruction the characteristics of individualized pacing, active learner response, and immediate feedback. The use of a live tutor as a mediator adds immensely to the flexibility of the system, and it adds another major advantage over printed self-instructional material by employing social reinforcers in the form of praise ("That's great." "Oh, what a good answer." "You're really on the ball today.") rather than just simple knowledge of results. Administered flexibly and creatively by a

❏ APPRAISAL CHECKLIST
Programmed Materials

Title _____

Series title _____

Source _____ **Date** _____ **Cost** _____

Length (completion time)   Range: _____ to _____ minutes   Average _____ minutes

Subject area _____

Intended Audience _____

Objectives (stated or implied)

Brief Description

Entry Capabilities Required

❏ Prior subject-matter knowledge/vocabulary

❏ Reading ability

❏ Mathematical ability

❏ Other

Rating	High		Medium		Low	Comments
Relevance to objectives	❏	❏	❏	❏	❏	
Accuracy of information	❏	❏	❏	❏	❏	
Likely to arouse/maintain interest	❏	❏	❏	❏	❏	
Exemplifies principles of programming (e.g., "lean" structure, responses require thought, relevant practice)	❏	❏	❏	❏	❏	
Test frames parallel to objectives	❏	❏	❏	❏	❏	
Feedback provides remedial branches	❏	❏	❏	❏	❏	
Appropriate vocabulary level	❏	❏	❏	❏	❏	
Evidence of effectiveness (validation data should describe tryout audience, time, outcomes)	❏	❏	❏	❏	❏	

Strong Points

Weak Points

Reviewer _____

Position _____

Recommended Action _____   **Date** _____

live guide, this technology of instruction can overcome the monotonous pattern that sometimes results with other programmed formats.

Compared to unstructured tutoring, programmed tutoring has a higher reliability because there is a predictable pattern to the tutor's action. With trained and motivated tutors, this has proven to be one of the most powerful technologies of instruction.

The effectiveness of programmed tutoring has been well established through the evaluation studies carried out by its originator, Douglas Ellson. The evidence from these was persuasive enough that in the early 1980s the U.S. Department of Education recognized programmed tutoring as one of the half dozen most effective compensatory education programs. Summaries of research have also found structured tutoring, variously defined, to be among the most effective and cost-effective innovations, with tutees scoring from the 70th to the 79th percentile compared to the 50th percentile for conventional instruction.[6,7]

Utilizing Programmed Tutoring.
Programmed tutoring combines the systematic qualities of programmed instruction with the warm, personal attention that only a human can add.

Reading and mathematics have been by far the most popular subjects for tutoring. Being basic skills and highly structured by nature, these subjects lend themselves well to this approach. Remedial or compensatory instruction is a typical application of tutoring programs.

In using programmed tutoring, keep in mind that research consistently indicates that tutors also learn from tutoring, sometimes more than their tutees! So give everyone a chance to be a tutor. This can be done effectively with materials that are prestructured to make the tutor's job replicable.

Consider using tutoring to make productive use of high-absence days. Train those who are present to tutor absentees when they return. Tutors will deepen their knowledge; absentees will catch up.

Programmed Teaching

Also referred to as Direct Instruction, the salient features of *programmed teaching* are

1. Scripted presentations
2. Small-group instruction
3. Unison responding by learners
4. Cues given by teacher
5. Rapid pacing
6. Reinforcement and correction procedures.

Scripted presentations are developed by instructional designers and tested

Figure 12.11
Psychologist Douglas G. Ellson, developer of programmed tutoring and low-cost learning systems

and revised before full-scale use. The scripting affords quality control, compensates for a teacher's lack of instructional design skills, and allows paraprofessionals to play the role of teacher. In fact, in developing countries older children are often used to guide programmed teaching lessons (see Figure 12.12). The effectiveness of this approach has led some economists to recommend it

6   Henry Levin, Gene Glass, and Gail Meister, "Cost-Effectiveness of Computer-Assisted Instruction," *Evaluation Review* 11 (1987): 50–72.

7   Peter A. Cohen, James A. Kulik, and Chen-Lin C. Kulik, "Educational Outcomes of Tutoring: A Meta-Analysis of Findings," *American Educational Research Journal* 19, no. 2 (Summer 1982): 237–48.

Figure 12.12
A programmed teaching project in Indonesia, Project PAMONG, makes extensive use of students to guide programmed lessons.

as a way of improving the cost-efficiency of education in situations in which cost reduction is a strong consideration.

Programmed teaching, or Direct Instruction, uses groups of five to ten students. This condition is necessary to carry out the other features—unison responding, giving cues, rapid pacing, and appropriate reinforcement or correction. Programmed teaching lessons are designed to generate high rates of responding by *all* students. To avoid inattention or mere imitation of other students' responses, all are required to respond vocally at the same time, at a hand signal by the teacher. When the teacher detects an error, he or she follows the procedures specified in the script to correct and remediate.

Programmed Teaching as a Technology of Instruction.

Programmed teaching has a definite pattern: teacher prompt, oral response, confirmation or correction. Because the instructional design builds in set procedures and teacher's actions are prespecified, a certain amount of quality control and reliability can be maintained.

There is a wealth of research evidence supporting programmed teaching carried out in more than a dozen English-speaking countries.[8] The most recent and large-scale study compared twenty different instructional models; among them direct instruction was the most effective of all in building basic skills, cognitive skills, and self-concept.[9]

---

8 Carl Binder and Cathy L. Watkins, "Precision Teaching and Direct Instruction: Measurably Superior Instructional Technology in Schools," *Performance Improvement Quarterly* 3, no. 4 (1990): 74–96.

9 Cathy L. Watkins, "Project Follow Through: A Story of the Identification and Neglect of Effective Instruction," *Youth Policy* 10, no. 7 (1988): 7–11.

Utilizing Programmed Teaching.   Programmed teaching is seen by its proponents as a total system for organizing instruction. It is particularly advocated for basic skill acquisition at the early grade levels, especially in reading and mathematics. It has been tested most in the teaching of disadvantaged and handicapped children. While programmed teaching has yielded impressive achievement gains in its own right, it has proven to be especially beneficial when combined with other methods to carry students onward to higher-level skills such as problem-solving.

Programmed teaching has been used successfully in numerous experimental programs in North America; it is also being implemented successfully in other parts of the world, including the Philippines, Indonesia, and Liberia in the primary grades.[10] It has been slow to be adopted on a broad scale in the United States. This could be attributable to its close philosophical connection with behaviorism and to its incompatibility with the conventional self-contained, group-based classroom organization predominant in the United States.

TECHNOLOGIES OF INSTRUCTION THAT EMPHASIZE INDIVIDUAL PACING

Personalized System of Instruction

The *Personalized System of Instruction* (PSI) could be described as a technology for managing instruction. It puts reinforcement theory into action as the overall framework for a whole course. In the PSI classroom students work individually at their own pace using any of a vari-

---

10 Sivasailam Thiagarajan and Aida L. Pasigna, *Literature Review on the Soft Technologies of Learning* (Cambridge, MA: Harvard University, 1988).

Figure 12.13
Interaction with a proctor is the principal means of personalizing the PSI approach.

Figure 12.14
Psychologist Fred S. Keller, originator of the Personalized System of Instruction, also referred to as the Keller Plan

ety of instructional materials—a chapter in a book, computer-assisted instruction, a videocassette, a sound filmstrip, a programmed booklet, and so on. The materials are arranged in sequential order, and the student must show mastery of each unit before being allowed to move on to the next.

Mastery is determined by means of a test taken whenever the student feels ready for it. The content and emphasis of the test should be no surprise because each unit is accompanied by a study guide that spells out the objective and most important points to be learned in that unit.

Study help and testing are handled by proctors, usually more advanced students who volunteer to help others. Proctors are a critical component of PSI for it is their one-to-one tutorial assistance that makes the system personalized (Figure 12.13). After scoring each test the proctor reviews it immediately with the student, asking questions to probe weak points and listening to defenses of alternative answers. If performance is below the specified mastery level, the student returns at another time to take a second form of the test.

Group meetings are rare, being used mainly for inspirational lectures, film showings, and review sessions. The instructor acts primarily as a planner, designer, manager, and guide to students and proctors.

PSI as a Technology of Instruction.

PSI is a technology affecting the organization of instruction rather than the design of instructional materials. That organizational framework emphasizes individual pacing, the mastery philosophy, and regular person-to-person contact with a proctor. PSI aims to reduce the frustration and fear associated with courses in which you're not sure where you're going or how you're doing, your confusion is compounded after missing earlier key concepts, and the final exam looms as a great unknown.

The effectiveness of PSI has been documented in a large number of studies comparing PSI and conventional versions of courses. In the first decade after PSI's invention in 1968, at least seventy-five studies of its effectiveness had been published.

A review of those studies reported this conclusion:

> In a typical published comparison, PSI and lecture means are separated by about two-thirds of a standard deviation. How large a difference is this? Let us take an average student, Mary Smith, who may take her introductory physics course, for example, by either a conventional method or by PSI. If she takes a typical lecture course, her achievement in physics will put her at the 50th percentile on a standardized test. She is an average student in an average course. If she takes the same course in PSI format, she will achieve at the 75th percentile on the standardized test . . . . In our judgment, this is the most impressive record achieved by a teaching method in higher education.[11]

A later review of PSI research reported that student preferences also strongly favored PSI courses: "Students rate PSI classes as more enjoyable, more demanding, and higher in overall quality and contribution to student learning than conventional classes."[12]

Utilizing PSI.

Fred S. Keller developed the first PSI course at the University of Brasilia in the mid-1960s (hence the alternate name for the approach, the Keller Plan). Since that time this technology of instruction has been applied most frequently to courses in postsecondary education. There it has been most successful in mathematics, engineering, and psychology courses, and slightly less successful in the physical sciences, life sciences, and social sciences. However, PSI has also been applied in elemen-

tary and secondary education, military training, and corporate education. In recent years it has also been adapted to computer-based courses and distance education courses.

Specific guidelines for setting up and running courses according to the PSI system can be found in the books and articles listed in the reference section at the end of this chapter. A few cautions about implementing a PSI approach are in order. First, PSI involves a great deal of time in planning and developing supplementary materials. Even though less lecture time is involved, instructors should be prepared to spend about half again as many hours conducting a PSI course as conducting a conventional course. Second, a willingness and ability to state objectives specifically is prerequisite. Third, the mastery point-of-view built into PSI rejects norm-referenced grading (the "normal curve") and insists on complete mastery as the criterion of success. It aims to elevate all students to the A level.

Audio-Tutorial Systems

The term *audio-tutorial systems* is used in the plural here to acknowledge that many variations have evolved from the original audiotape-controlled independent study system developed by S. N. Postlethwait at Purdue University in the early 1960s. Like PSI, this is a technology for managing instruction. It began simply as a way of interjecting an element of individualization into a large lecture course.

The most visible aspect of most audio-tutorial (A-T) courses is the study carrel equipped with specially designed audiotapes that direct students to various learning activities (Figure 12.15). This component is known as the independent study session. The taped presentation is not a lecture but a tutorial conversation by the instructor designed to facilitate effective communication. A live

---

11 James A. Kulik, Chen-Lin C. Kulik, and Beverly B. Smith, "Research on the Personalized System of Instruction," *Programmed Learning and Educational Technology* (Spring 1976): 13, 23–30.

12 James A. Kulik, Chen-Lin C. Kulik, and Peter A. Cohen, "A Meta-Analysis of Outcome Studies of Keller's Personalized System of Instruction," *American Psychologist* 34, no. 4 (April 1979): 307–18.

instructor is nearby to assist students when needed. Learners proceed at their own pace; sessions begin and end to suit students' schedules.

Because the students are proceeding individually, there seldom is more than one student at any given point in the study program. So, often only one or two pieces of equipment are necessary to accommodate many students in a laboratory situation. Demonstration materials are set out at a central location; again, one set may be sufficient to serve a large class. Motion and color are provided when necessary by means of a videocassette.

In addition to the independent study session, there are two other basic components in most A-T systems: a general assembly session and a small assembly session.

The general assembly session is a large-group meeting with no fixed format. It may include a presentation by a guest lecturer, a long film, an orientation to subject matter, an opportunity for review or emphasis of critical materials, help sessions, a major exam, or any other activity appropriate to a large-group setting.

During the small assembly session, six to ten students and an instructor meet for a modified seminar. Students are seated informally around a table with the instructor. The primary purpose of the session is to exploit the principle that one really learns a subject when one is required to teach it. For this session each student is expected to prepare a little lecture about each of the objectives being covered in that session. Each student in turn is asked to discuss at least one of the objectives. The other students then have an opportunity to correct or add comments concerning any item. This session has proven to be an effective feedback mechanism for both the students and the instructor. It lets the students know how they did and often provides clues to the instructor for improving the study program. The miniature seminar

Figure 12.15
The independent-study carrel is the most visibly distinctive feature of the audio-tutorial approach.

enables many students to see relationships and concepts which may not have been evident from the independent study session.

Audio-Tutorial Systems as a Technology of Instruction.

Unlike the soft technologies based on reinforcement theory, such as programmed instruction, programmed tutoring, and PSI, A-T did not originate from a particular theory of learning. As described in the accompanying "Flashback," its origin and development were pragmatic, building on features that seemed to work. The resulting framework, though, is robust enough to be considered a systematic application of scientific knowledge to human learning. The framework is also flexible enough that a wide variety of methods could be practiced under the heading of "audio-tutorial systems," so this technology may be less reliable in its effects than some of the others.

At its heart, though, A-T is foremost an organizational framework that allows a greater degree of individualization than would exist in a conventional course while encouraging active engagement with the material and frequent testing and feedback. When compared with conventionally conducted courses, A-T courses have been found to generally yield superior achievement, as measured by scores on final examinations.[13] The degree of superiority is not as great as that of PSI, however. Nor do students tend to express the higher rate of approval that they do with PSI.

Utilizing Audio-Tutorial Systems.

still most prevalent in science edu-

---

[13] James A. Kulik, Chen-Lin C. Kulik, and Peter A. Cohen, "Research on Audio-Tutorial Instruction: A Meta-Analysis of Comparative Studies," *Research in Higher Education* 11, no. 4 (1979): 321–41.

In the fall of 1961 S. N. Postlethwait, a professor of botany at Purdue University, began preparing supplementary lectures on audiotape to provide an opportunity for students with inadequate academic backgrounds to keep up with his introductory botany class. Any student could listen to these recordings at the university audiovisual center. Soon Dr. Postlethwait decided that he could improve the effectiveness of these tapes by having the students bring their botany textbooks to the audiovisual center when they came to listen to the tapes. On the tapes he could refer them to the photographs, diagrams, and drawings in the text as he discussed the concepts and principles under study.

Later, the tapes included instructions that the students check views contained in the recorded lectures against views expressed in the text. Thus the author's point of view could be considered along with the lecturer's. Then Dr. Postlethwait decided to add a new dimension to his instructional approach. He placed plants in the audiovisual center so that students could observe and handle the plants when they were being discussed on the tapes. Ultimately, the students were instructed to bring their laboratory manuals to the center and conduct experiments in conjunction with study of their texts and listening to the tapes. Consciously or unconsciously, Dr. Postlethwait had moved his instructional technique from one focusing on abstract learning experiences (lectures) toward a multimedia system emphasizing concrete experiences—an integrated lecture-laboratory approach.

During the spring of 1962 an experimental group of thirty-six students was chosen to receive all of the instruction via the integrated lecture-laboratory approach. The experimental class met with Dr. Postlethwait only once each week, to take quizzes and for a general discussion of the week's subject matter. They were required to take the same examinations given to the conventionally taught group. At the end of the semester the experimental group scored just as well on the exam as the group that had received traditional instruction.

The students' reactions to the "supplementary" material were so positive that in the fall of 1962 Postlethwait decided that rather than carrying plants and other materials from the biology greenhouse to the audiovisual center each week, he would set up a botany learning center in the biology building. A conventional science laboratory was converted to a learning center with the addition of twenty-two learning carrels equipped with tape recorders. At this time Postlethwait was covering the same content in his classroom lectures that was being presented on the tapes in the learning center. By the end of the semester most of the students were going to the learning center instead of coming to the lectures! In spite of the fact that Postlethwait missed having students "sitting at his feet" to learn about botany, he candidly admitted that all the students missed by not coming to the lectures were his smiling face and West Virginia jokes.

Eventually, Postlethwait did away with his traditional lectures and restructured his Biology 108 course to give students the maximum freedom to work independently and to pace themselves according to their individual interests and capabilities. Students could come in at their convenience and spend as much time as necessary for them to master the material under study.

A significant aspect of Postlethwait's audio recordings was the conversational tone and relaxed atmosphere he deliberately cultivated. He would sit among the materials gathered for the particular lesson and speak into the recorder as if he were having a conversation with a friend whom he wished to tutor though a sequence of pleasant inquiries. Later, in their carrels, students would examine duplicates of the same materials while they listened to Postlethwait's chat.

Group meetings were later added to the program to supplement the independent study sessions. Students were brought together periodically in small groups (the small assembly session) to discuss what they had learned in independent study and to present their own "lectures" on the current subject matter. Larger meetings (the general assembly sessions) were scheduled for guest lectures, films, review sessions, and the like.

Serendipity is the faculty of making fortunate and unexpected discoveries by accident. Dr. Postlethwait turned out to be embarking on a serendipitous journey when he set out to tinker with the traditional format of his botany course. What began simply as audiotapes to supplement his classroom lectures eventually evolved into a full-scale technology of instruction—the audio-tutorial system.

cation, where it began. But during the three decades since its inception, it has also been successfully applied in many other areas, at many levels, and in both formal and nonformal educational settings.

As a result of these many and varied experiences with A-T, a number of general recommendations can be made to anyone considering implementing such a system. First, as is true of PSI, setting up an audiotutorial system requires a great deal of preparation. However, A-T materials need not always be invented locally. Commercial publishers now offer sizable collections of packaged A-T materials.

Individualization and personalization are critical elements in this sort of system. Self-pacing and frequent corrective feedback must be designed into the system and vigilantly maintained. One aspect of personalization is the conversational tone of the audio materials; lecture style is not very appealing on a one-to-one basis.

Active participation by the learner is essential. A varied menu of activities—viewing films, manipulating real objects, field trips—helps keep interest high.

to consider how these methods of instruction can take on the qualities of technologies of instruction.

Simulations and Games as Technologies of Instruction.

Simulation is most frequently encountered in the form of physical simulators, such as those used in flight training or drivers education, or in the form of role-play activities, such as mock court in law school or microteaching in teacher education. Instructional uses of simulation may or may not qualify as technologies of instruction. The more an activity is prestructured to meet certain objectives, is designed to be replicable (yielding the same results in the hands of different users), employs proven psychological techniques, and is effective, the more it meets the criteria of being a technology of instruction. A packaged simulation activity such as "Starpower" (described in Chapter 13) does have those qualities.

What is the teaching/learning pattern employed by simulations? Is there enough consistency from one set of materials to another to discern a common pattern? A well designed simulation will have these common features:

1. Immersion in a more or less realistic situation

2. Involvement in a problem

3. Groping toward a solution through trial and error

4. Consequences that give some feedback about success

5. Discussion to draw lessons from the experience

Games, apart from the simulations they may incorporate, provide a motivating framework for repetitive practice by adding a playful environment, reinforcement for correct practice (in the form of points), and the excitement of surprise and suspense. Instructional games, such as those of the Mathematics Pentathlon (see Chapter 13, p. 373) may require substantial problem solving. Some, such as "Save the Whales" (see Chapter 13, p. 380) demand cooperation among all players to reach the goal. Games that incorporate simulation, of course, also reflect the additional virtues of realism and meaningful context.

Utilizing Simulations and Games.

Detailed advice on selecting and using simulation and game activities is given in Chapter 13.

TECHNOLOGIES OF INSTRUCTION THAT EMPHASIZE REALISTIC CONTEXTS

Simulations and Games

Simulation and gaming are two related but different concepts. *Simulation* refers to any scaled-down representation of some real-life situation. A *game* is an activity in which participants follow prescribed rules, which may depart from reality, and strive to attain some challenging goal. Simulation and gaming are both used in instruction, separately and together. Simulation, gaming, and how they can be used for instruction are discussed in detail in Chapter 13. Here, though, we want

Figure 12.16
Games provide a motivating, self-correcting framework for both drill-and-practice and discovery learning.

Figure 12.17
Robert E. Slavin, originator of a number of cooperative learning strategies.

TECHNOLOGIES OF INSTRUCTION BASED ON COOPERATIVE GROUPS

Some of the earlier technologies of instruction, such as programmed instruction, programmed tutoring, PSI, and audio-tutorial systems, emphasize individual pacing, opening the door to possible social isolation and a competitive, individualistic class atmosphere. Social psychologists have found that achievement tends to be higher in a cooperative environment.[14] The importance of emphasizing collaboration among students is also supported by the cognitivist theorists; they claim that knowledge and skills become useful and take on real personal meaning when they are attained through a process of social negotiation.

Robert E. Slavin of Johns Hopkins University and his collaborators have developed a number of struc-

tured methods for fostering cooperative learning in elementary and secondary schools. All are based on mixed-ability groups working under two specific conditions: (1) students must be working toward a group goal, and (2) success at achieving the group goal must depend on the sum of the individual achievements. Students must have a reason to take their groupmates' success seriously, and group success must be based not on a single group product but on the sum of the achievements of the members. Otherwise, there is temptation to ignore the lower-ability groupmates and let the smartest or most motivated do the bulk of the work.

Team Accelerated Instruction

Team Accelerated Instruction (TAI) combines cooperative learning and individual pacing for mathematics, grades 3–6. It employs four-person groups of mixed ability—one high, one low, and two average—who have a goal of winning certificates for exceeding a given criterion score. Students enter an individually paced math program depending on their

individual placement test results, and they work on their units individually. Teammates check each other's work and help one another with any problems. Unit tests are taken without team assistance and are scored by student monitors. Each week teachers total the units completed by team members and give certificates or other rewards to those teams that exceed the criterion level.

Because students handle most of the management by themselves—checking each other's work, helping each other, and managing the flow of materials—the teacher can spend more time convening small groups who are working on the same topic. These small groups would be drawn from various teams, for example, all the students who are working on decimals. This affords more personalized attention than would occur in the typical conventional classroom.

Team Accelerated Instruction as a Technology of Instruction.

The basic framework of TAI consists of self-instruction based on mastery learning principles, peer motivation

14　David W. Johnson, et al., "Effects of Cooperative, Competitive, and Individualistic Goal Structures on Achievement: A Meta-Analysis," *Psychological Bulletin* 89, no. 1 (1981): 47–62.

Figure 12.18
Team Accelerated Instruction encourages students to help each other learn.

Figure 12.19
Cooperative Integrated Reading and Composition provides a structured framework for whole-language learning.

and remediation, and personalized guidance by the teacher. The reliability of the system depends on the specific rules set up by the teachers and the robustness of the self-instructional materials.

Research to date has supported the effectiveness of TAI. In five of the six comparative studies conducted by Slavin and others, the TAI groups significantly outpaced the conventional groups. On the average, students using TAI for a particular subject advanced twice as many grade levels as students using conventional methods.[15]

Utilizing Team Accelerated Instruction.
Team Accelerated Instruction has been designed to be used as a total system for teaching a whole course of mathematics. Other cooperative learning techniques can be used for a single lesson or a specific part of a course.

Although there is a large body of research demonstrating the value of other forms of cooperative learning with adults, this particular technol-

ogy has so far been tested primarily at the elementary school level. However, related methods have now been tested at grade levels from two to twelve in five countries in all areas of the basic curriculum. The effectiveness of TAI for basic skills is well established, and Slavin claims that higher-order objectives, such as math problem solving, are also effectively reached through cooperative methods. For details on adopting and implementing TAI, see the references at the end of this chapter.

Cooperative Integrated Reading and Composition

In *Cooperative Integrated Reading and Composition* (CIRC), teachers use basal readers and reading groups, as is common in traditional language arts instruction. However, in CIRC students are assigned to teams composed of pairs from two different reading groups. While the teacher is working with one reading group the other groups work in pairs on cognitively engaging activities. These include reading to each other, predicting how stories will come out, summarizing stories, writing reactions to stories, and prac-

ticing word attack skills and vocabulary development.

Writing skills are developed through a structured program based on a writing process model. Students write drafts, critique each other's work, and prepare team "books."

Teams pursue group goals. Certificates are given based on average performance of all group members on individual quizzes and evaluation of written products.

CIRC as a Technology of Instruction.
In CIRC students follow a fairly regular framework of activities: teacher-led instruction, team practice, practice tests within the team, and final assessment. Students do not face the unit assessment until the group decides it's ready. Thus, CIRC applies the basic principles of mastery learning as well as the social-psychological principles of TAI. To these are added a larger element of group cognitive engagement, as is currently recommended for reading and writing education.

Compared to programmed instruction and programmed tutoring, there is much greater variability in each student's experience in CIRC. Neither teacher-led instruction nor

15   Robert E. Slavin, "Cooperative Learning and the Cooperative School," *Educational Leadership* 45, no. 3 (1987): 7–13.

Table 12.1
Characteristics of Technologies of Instruction

	A teaching/ learning pattern ...	designed to provide reliable ...	effective instruction ...	to each learner ...	through application of scientific principles of human learning.
Programmed Instruction	Small units of information requiring practice, followed by feedback	Program recorded in printed form	Programs must be learner tested and revised during development process	Allows individual pacing	Reinforcement theory: verbal response followed by knowledge of results
Programmed Tutoring	Small units of information requiring practice, followed by feedback	Tutor follows directions Learner uses structured workbook	Programs are learner tested and revised during development process	Allows individual pacing plus highly flexible, responsive branching via human tutor	Reinforcement theory: verbal or other overt response followed by knowledge of result plus social reinforcers Constant personalized human contact
Programmed Teaching	Scripted small-group Instruction with unison responding to teacher cues Immediate reinforcement and correction	Teacher follows specifications given by designer	Lessons are learner tested and revised during development process	Each student responds vocally and can be corrected	Reinforcement theory: vocal response followed by knowledge of results and social reinforcers Group setting
PSI and A-T	Large units in sequential order, done individually Passing test required before proceeding Small and large group sessions may be added	Organization clearly shown through print and/or AV material and tests	Materials themselves not validated, but mastery is assured by testing/correction cycle	Individual pacing plus one-to-one or group tutorials	Rather frequent responses to tests followed by immediate correction Occasional personalized human contact Individualized pacing
Simulations and Games	Small-group activity, may entail representation of reality and/or competition	Procedures are enforced by means of game directions and play materials	May be learner tested for effectiveness	Usually group paced, with individuals assigned to compatible groups	Meaningful organization of content Frequent practice with immediate feedback Social interaction with small group Emotional involvement Repetition of drill-and-practice without tedium High motivation
Cooperative Learning (TAI and CIRC)	Teammates work individually on modules Peer tutoring among teammates Unit tests with teammate scores combined	Procedures enforced by team rules and sequencing of materials	Procedures have been validated experimentally	Students work individually but with peer tutorial help Tests taken individually but aggregated with teammates	Cooperative environment fostered through application of social psychological principles

group activities are programmed in advance. For this reason, there is less reliability from one group to the next.

Research on the effectiveness of CIRC is still quite limited, but the early studies cited by Slavin found substantial superiority of CIRC over conventional instruction, both in terms of standardized test outcomes and on writing samples.[16]

Utilizing Cooperative Integrated Reading and Composition (CIRC).

Like Team Accelerated Instruction, CIRC is designed to be used as a total system, in this case for teaching language arts. There is evidence that it works for the higher-level skills of comprehension and creative writing as well as for the basic skills of reading and simple composition.

TAI, CIRC, and other related cooperative learning techniques have also been found to have positive effects on social relations in the classroom, including race relations and acceptance of mainstreamed handicapped students, and on self-esteem and attitude toward the class.

The references at the end of this chapter provide sources of information on implementing Cooperative Integrated Reading and Comprehension and other cooperative learning techniques.

TECHNOLOGIES OF INSTRUCTION THAT UTILIZE THE COMPUTER

All of the other techniques mentioned in this chapter are purely soft technologies. They do not require any hardware whatsoever to be implemented. Their technological character derives from the systematic and controlled processes by which they function.

As it happens, the computer provides an efficient means for manag-

ing many of these sorts of processes. So it should not be surprising that in recent years there has been a surge of research and development related to computer mediation of all sorts of instructional activities. Many of the technologies of instruction discussed in this chapter have already been adapted to computer mediation. Here are some examples:

❑ PSI and audio-tutorial courses with lessons and student records stored in the computer

❑ Computer-delivered programmed instruction (see "Media File: *Wordwright*" in Chapter 8)

❑ Computer tutorials (see "Media File: Problem-Solving Strategies" in Chapter 8)

❑ Computer-based instructional games (see "Media File: *Where in the World is Carmen Sandiego?*" in Chapter 13)

❑ Simulations controlled by computer (see "Close-Up: Simulators Help Assure Friendly Skies" in Chapter 13)

❑ Computer-based cooperative learning (see "Media File: *Longhouse*" in Chapter 13)

What is important here is that the computer is not in itself a technology of instruction. It is a tool that can be of immense benefit in putting into practice the pedagogical procedures that constitute a technology of instruction.

At the same time, computer applications are emerging that do implement new and unique capabilities. For example, hypermedia programs allow the learner to link ideas and create new ones with unprecedented ease, graphics software allows learners to visualize in three dimensions and in motion, virtual-reality environments raise simulation to a multisensory level, and group exploration and decision-making networks allow collaborative thinking at a much higher level. As these innovations are further developed and become more readily available they may add new, original ped-

agogical techniques to our list of technologies of instruction.

REFERENCES

Print References

General

Ellson, Douglas G. *Improving the Productivity of Teaching: 125 Exhibits.* Bloomington, IN: Phi Delta Kappa, 1986.

Gagne, Robert. *Instructional Technology: Foundations.* Hillsdale, NJ: Lawrence Erlbaum, 1987.

Thiagarajan, Sivasailam, and Pasigna, Aida L. *Literature Review on the Soft Technologies of Learning.* Project BRIDGES Report Series, no. 2 Cambridge, MA: Harvard University, 1988.

Technologies Emphasizing Reinforcement

Bullock, Donald H. *Programmed Instruction.* Instructional Design Library, Vol. 8. Englewood Cliffs, NJ: Educational Technology Publications, 1978.

Center for Vocational Education. *Employ Programmed Instruction.* Athens, GA: American Association for Vocational Instructional Materials, 1977.

Ehly, S. W., and Larsen, S. C. *Peer Tutoring for Individualized Instruction.* Boston: Allyn and Bacon, 1980.

Ellson, Douglas G. "Tutoring." In *The Psychology of Teaching Methods,* 75th Yearbook of the National Society for the Study of Education. Chicago: University of Chicago Press, 1976.

Harrison, Grant V., and Guymon, Ronald. *Structured Tutoring.* Instructional Design Library, Vol. 34. Englewood Cliffs, NJ: Educational Technology Publications, 1980.

Lindsley, Ogden R. "Precision Teaching: By Children for Teachers," *Teaching Exceptional Children* 22, no. 3 (1990): 10–15.

Lockery, M., and Maggs, A. "Direct Instruction Research in Australia: A Ten-Year Analysis." *Educational Psychology* 2 (1982): 263–88.

Thiagarajan, Sivasailam. *Tutoraids.* Instructional Design Library, Vol 2. Englewood Cliffs, NJ: Educational Technology Publications, 1978.

West, R. P.; Young, R.; and Spooner, F. "Precision Teaching: An Introduction," *Teaching Exceptional Children* 22, no. 3 (1990): 4–9.

---

[16] Robert E. Slavin, *Cooperative Learning: Theory, Research, and Practice* (Englewood Cliffs, NJ: Prentice-Hall, 1990).

Technologies Emphasizing Individual Pacing

Coldeway, Annabel E., and Coldeway, Dan O. "An Extension of PSI through the Application of Instructional Systems Design Technology." *Canadian Journal of Educational Communications* (Fall 1987): 279–93.

Keller, Fred S. "Good-Bye, Teacher . . ." *Journal of Applied Behavior Analysis* 1 (Spring 1968): 79–88.

Pear, Joseph J., and Kinsner, W. "Computer-Aided Personalized System of Instruction: An Effective and Economical Method for Short- and Long-Distance Education." *Machine-Mediated Learning* 2 (1988): 213–37.

"The Personalized System of Instruction (PSI)—Special Issue." *Educational Technology* (September 1977): 5–60.

Postlethwait, S. N. "Principles behind the Audio-Tutorial System." *NSPI Journal* (May 1978): 3, 4, 18.

Postlethwait, S. N.; Novak, J.; and Murray, H. *The Audio-Tutorial Approach to Learning.* Minneapolis: Burgess, 1972.

Russell, James D. *The Audio-Tutorial System.* Instructional Design Library, Vol. 3. Englewood Cliffs, NJ: Educational Technology Publications, 1978.

Sherman, J. Gilmour.; Ruskin, Robert S.; and Semb, George B., eds. *The Personalized System of Instruction: 48 Seminal Papers.* Lawrence, KS: TRI Publications, 1982.

Sherman, J. Gilmour, and Ruskin, Robert S. *The Personalized System of Instruction.* Instructional Design Library, Vol. 13. Englewood Cliffs, NJ: Educational Technology Publications, 1978.

Technologies Based on Cooperative Groups

Adams, Dennis; Carlson, Helen; and Hamm, Mary. *Cooperative Learning and Educational Media.* Englewood Cliffs, NJ: Educational Technology Publications, 1990.

Cohen, Elizabeth G. *Designing Groupwork.* New York: Teachers College Press, 1986.

Ellis, Susan S., and Whalen, Susan F. *Cooperative Learning: Getting Started.* Jefferson City, MO: Scholastic, 1990.

Foyle, Harvey C., et al. "Interactive Learning: Creating an Environment for Cooperative Learning." Paper presented at the annual conference of Association for Supervision and Curriculum Development, March 1989. (ERIC document ED305335)

Hill, Susan and Hill, Tim. *The Collaborative Classroom.* Portsmouth, NH: Heinemann, 1990.

Kagan, Spencer. *Cooperative Learning: Resources for Teachers.* San Juan Capistrano, CA: Resources for Teachers, 1989.

Lyman, Lawrence and Foyle, Harvey C. *Cooperative Grouping for Interactive Learning: Students, Teachers, and Administrators.* Washington, DC: National Education Association, 1990.

Male, Mary. "Cooperative Learning for Effective Mainstreaming." *Computing Teacher* (August–September, 1986): 35–37.

Reid, Jo-Anne; Forrestal, Peter; and Cook, Jonathan. *Small Group Learning in the Classroom.* Portsmouth, NH: Heinemann, 1989.

Slavin, Robert E. *Using Student Team Learning.* 3rd ed. Baltimore, MD: Johns Hopkins University, 1986.

Audiovisual References

The Audio-Tutorial System—An Independent Study Approach. West Lafayette, IN: Purdue University, 1968. 16mm film. 25 minutes.

The Personalized System of Instruction. Washington DC: Center for Personalized Instruction, 1974. 16mm film. 19 minutes.

Organizations

Association for Direct Instruction
P.O. Box 10252
Eugene, OR 97440

International Society for Exploring Teaching Alternatives
137 Engineering Sciences Building
West Virginia University
Morgantown, WV 26506

National Society for Performance and Instruction
1300 L Street, N.W., Suite 1250
Washington, DC 20005

POSSIBLE PROJECTS

12–A. Observe an ordinary class session (it may be the course you are taking, a class conducted where you work, a class at a local elementary school, or other). Describe the extent to which the characteristics of technologies of instruction listed in Table 12.1 are or are not applied.

12–B. Appraise some off-the-shelf programmed instruction material using the "Appraisal Checklist" on page 354.

12–C. Construct a short (ten to fifteen frame) programmed instruction unit on a subject of your choice, in either the linear or branching format. Explain how it might be used.

12–D. Interview an instructor or student who has participated in one of the technologies of instruction discussed in the chapter. Report their perceptions about the strong and weak points of the system.

12–E. Visit a site where one of the technologies of instruction is being used. If possible, interview an instructor or some students. Prepare a brief report describing what you saw and what you learned from the reactions of the users.

12–F. Describe a real or hypothetical instructional situation in which one (or some combination) of the technologies of instruction would be appropriate. Give a justification for application.

13

Simulations and Games

OUTLINE

OBJECTIVES

After studying this chapter, you should be able to

1. Define *game, simulation, simulation game,* and *instruction* and distinguish examples of each.

2. Relate games to drill-and-practice learning.

3. Describe an instructional situation appropriate for game use; the description should include objectives, audience, and the nature of the game chosen.

4. Relate the special attributes of simulation to (1) affective objectives, (2) motor skill objectives, and (3) interpersonal skill objectives.

5. Define *role-play* and discuss its applications.

6. Describe at least two examples of simulators.

7. Explain how simulation games involve emotions in holistic learning.

8. Describe an instructional situation appropriate to simulation game use; the description should include objectives, audience, and nature of the simulation game chosen.

9. Identify at least four limitations of instructional games and simulations.

10. Distinguish between cooperative games and competitive games, and state in your own words the distinctive claim made for cooperative games.

11. Identify and explain at least three appraisal criteria that apply particularly to simulation and game materials.

12. Define *frame game* and give an example of an adaptation based on a familiar game frame.

13. Identify the utilization procedures that are emphasized with simulations and games more than with other media and methods.

14. Prepare a debriefing guide for a simulation or game incorporating the major steps of the "Four-D" procedure.

15. Describe briefly the evaluation problems that apply particularly to simulation and game use.

LEXICON

simulation game

role-play

simulator

holistic learning

cooperative game

frame game

debriefing

The use of gaming and simulation techniques in instruction is by no means a new idea. The simulation of battlefield strategy in the form of games can be traced back to 3000 B.C. in China. Games such as chess and *go* are the residue of these ancient training exercises. Today's war gaming employs computers to digest vast volumes of data, and the application of gaming techniques to training and instruction has spread into business, higher education, and elementary and secondary education. Experience has shown that simulations and games can make a powerful contribution to learning if they are properly understood and properly used.

The reasons that simulation and game enthusiasts give to explain their interest in these methods are as varied as the kinds of simulation and game materials. Elementary educators emphasize the point that play is a natural and necessary component of young children's learning, and therefore play should be encouraged and melded with academic objectives. Some are concerned with avoiding the tedium too often associated with classrooms. In recent years there has been a movement toward more learner-centered instruction in the belief that it enhances motivation and learning. Methods in which learners are active and in control of their own learning processes also encourage independence and responsibility. Futurists, along with educational psychologists, cite the importance of learning to view problems as a whole. Adult educators and trainers are interested in simulation as a cost-effective method of practicing motor skills and interpersonal capabilities. For these and other reasons, classroom activities based on simulation and gaming are popular at all educational levels.

If the number of books and articles published about a topic is any guide to its academic popularity, the golden age of simulation and gaming was in the mid-1970s. Research interest stagnated after that but surged again with the proliferation of personal computers after 1985. Computers brought a new level of visual appeal to games and made it possible to simulate much more complex and more realistic problems.

BASIC CONCEPTS

Before considering the instructional applications of games and simulations we must deal with the issue of terminology. The terms *game, simulation,* and *simulation game* are often confused with each other or used interchangeably. These terms actually refer to different concepts and so must first be examined one at a time. Later in the chapter, for example when discussing utilization techniques, the two concepts—game and simulation—will be addressed as one for the sake of convenience.

Game

A *game* is an activity in which participants follow prescribed rules that differ from those of reality as they strive to attain a challenging goal.

The distinction between play and reality is what makes games entertaining. Most people seem to enjoy setting aside the logical rules of everyday life occasionally and entering an artificial environment with different dynamics. For example, in chess the markers each have arbitrarily different movement patterns based roughly on the military potentials of certain societal roles in some ancient time. Players capture each other's markers by observing elaborate rules of play, rather than simply reaching across the board to grab the marker.

Attaining the goal usually entails competition. The competition may be individual against individual, as in chess; group against group, as in basketball; or individual against a standard, as in golf (with "par" as the standard). In playing video games, players typically are competing against their own previous scores, and ultimately against the designer of the game as they approach mastery of the game.

To be challenging, goals should have a probability of achievement of something in the range of 50 percent. A goal that is always or never attained presents no real challenge; the outcome is too predictable. People exhibit the most interest and motivation when the challenge is in the intermediate range.

On the other hand, striving to attain a challenging goal does not necessarily have to involve competition. Communication games, fantasy games, and encounter games exemplify a whole array of activities in which participants agree to suspend the normal rules of interpersonal communication in order to pursue such goals as self-awareness, empathy, sensitivity, and leadership development. These activities are considered games but they do not entail competition. There is a movement today toward developing cooperative games designed to foster creative, collaborative decision making. These games specifically avoid provoking competition between players.

Simulation

A *simulation* is an abstraction or simplification of some real-life situation or process. In simulations, participants usually play a role that involves them in interactions with other people or with elements of the simulated environment. A business management simulation, for example, might put participants into the role of production manager of a mythical corporation, provide them with statistics about business conditions, and direct them to negotiate a new labor contract with the union bargaining team.

Simulations can vary greatly in the extent to which they fully reflect the realities of the situation they are intended to model. A simulation that incorporates too many details of a complex situation might be too complicated and time-consuming for the intended audience. On the other hand, if the model is oversimplified,

Figure 13.1
Games appeal to all ages.

it may fail completely to communicate its intended point. A well-designed simulation provides a faithful model of those elements that are most salient to the immediate objective, and it informs the instructor and participants about elements that have been simplified or eliminated completely.

Simulation Game

A *simulation game* combines the attributes of a simulation (role playing, a model of reality) with the attributes of a game (striving toward a goal, specific rules). Like a simulation, it may be relatively high or low in its modeling of reality. Like a game, it may or may not entail competition.

Instruction

Any of the types of activities described so far may be designed to be instructional, that is, to help someone learn new skills or values applicable beyond the game itself. Most commercially developed games intend to provide diversion, not instruction. A person who plays *Clue* or *Thinking Man's Golf* enough times probably learns more and

more about the game itself but little in the way of usable skills.

Admittedly, the attribute of being instructional is often a matter of degree. The stated intentions of the designer or user would have to be examined closely. For example, basketball, normally a noninstructional game, could be assigned by a football coach to his players as a means of developing agility and faster reflexes. In such a case basketball would be instructional for that situation.

Many game activities contain some modeling of reality, and the distinction between simulations and games is not always clear. For example, many role-playing exercises take on gamelike qualities as participants maneuver toward a good outcome for themselves. Yet the distinctions are worth making because they have significant implications for when and how these different types of materials are used. Figure 13.2 illustrates how the basic concepts of game, simulation, and instruction may overlap. As shown, seven different classifications can be given. The following sections of the chapter will deal with the three classifications of most direct relevance to our interests: instructional games, instruc-

tional simulations, and instructional simulation games.

INSTRUCTIONAL GAMES
Play in Human Development

Games are, above all, a form of play. As such, they may be looked upon with suspicion by those who think learning and playing are incompatible. But as viewed by developmental psychologists, play can be a useful mechanism; indeed, deprivation of

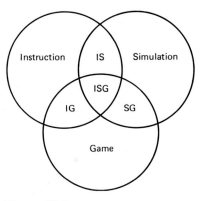

Figure 13.2
Game, simulation, and instruction are separate concepts. However, they do overlap, so a particular activity could be an instructional simulation (IS), an instructional game (IG), or even an instructional simulation game (ISG).

FLASHBACK

Gaming: From Ancient Battlefields to Modern Classrooms

It is ironic that educational simulation-gaming, which is now prominently associated with the promotion of mutual understanding and cooperation, traces its ancestry to games designed to teach military tactics and strategies.

One of the earliest known examples of war gaming is *wei-chi* (meaning "encirclement"), the existence of which can be traced back to at least 2000 B.C. The game was introduced into Japan around the eighth century A.D. and survives throughout the world today in the popular game *go*. A variation of the encirclement game evolved in India as *chaturanga.* In this game, representations of foot soldiers, horsemen, chariots, and elephants faced each other on a board representing a battlefield. The Western version of *chaturanga,* chess, evolved into its current form during the Middle Ages. Although chess has long since lost its specific function as a military training tool, tactics and strategic moves are still at its core, and the object of the game remains a military one: to capture (or checkmate) the opponent's king.

Following military defeats in the Napoleonic Wars, the Prussians throughout the nineteenth century invested great ingenuity in the refinement of war games that would allow greater latitude for experimentation at lower cost than actual military exercises. Terrain models of battlefields replaced checkered boards; rules for the value of movement of pieces were more realistically prescribed; teams of opposing forces replaced individual players; judges monitored the observance of rules. The resounding Prussian victory in the Franco-Prussian War of 1870 to 1871 and the subsequent Prussian reputation for military genius may be attributable in part to their preparedness born out of years of practice in *Kriegspiel.*

By the early twentieth century, war gaming had spread to all the technologically advanced nations of the world. Germany and Japan raised war-gaming techniques to a high art as part of their preparations for World War II.

Franco-Prussian War troops on parade

A breakthrough in war-gaming technique came toward the end of World War II with the advent of the electronic computer. The high-speed calculating power of the computer vastly increased designers' ability to deal with complexity.

An important step in the evolution of war games toward educational games came with the development in the mid-1950s of so-called crisis games. Growing largely out of experimentation at the RAND Corporation to deal with potential cold war problems, crisis games are simulations of hypothetical crisis situations, with participants trying to solve or alleviate the crisis within a framework of rules structured to reflect the conditions of the real-world crisis situation.

Gaming became a popular instructional technique in which students of international relations could adopt the roles of government decision makers and play out hypothetical crises.

---

play can impede an individual's cognitive and creative growth (Figure 13.3).

Anthropologists note that primitive societies often use the playing of games to acculturate their members and to teach survival skills. It is certainly reasonable to assume that play in more advanced societies serves similar functions. Freudian interpretations of play see it as a

symbolic reenactment of a threatening event, a safety valve for relieving pressures placed on children by the child-rearing practices of a culture. Child psychologist Jean Piaget views play as a manifestation of "assimilation," one of the mental processes fundamental to intellectual growth. All observers agree that play is an adaptive mechanism important for human development.

Games as Learning Frameworks

Games can provide attractive and instructionally effective frameworks for learning activities. They are attractive because they are fun! Children and adults alike tend to react positively to an invitation to play.

Of course, this is not true for every learner; no instructional

BUSINESS GAMES

Since economists and business management theorists already possessed well-defined, quantitative models upon which simulation games could be based, it is not surprising that business games were among the first academic games to be developed. The linkage of business games with military games is quite clear. In 1956 the American Management Association (AMA) launched a research project to consider the possibility of developing a simulation that would allow management trainees to experience the same kind of strategic decision-making practice as military officers were then experiencing. Its efforts culminated in the creation of the *AMA Top Management Decision Simulation,* a computer-assisted simulation game in which teams of players representing officers of companies make business decisions and receive "quarterly reports" on the outcomes of their decisions. Business executives and business educators reacted to the game with great enthusiasm.

By the end of 1959 variations of the AMA game had been developed at IBM and the University of California at Los Angeles, and within three years the development of over eighty-five such games had been noted in professional journals.

CLASSROOM SIMULATION GAMES

Clark C. Abt, a systems engineer, became involved in the 1950s with the design of computer simulations of air battles, space missions, disarmament inspection systems, and other military problems. He and his colleagues at the Missile Systems Division of the Raytheon Company began to apply war-gaming techniques to increasingly complex problems that were more and more involved with human factors—the social, economic, and political causes and consequences of military actions.

Seeking to better understand these human factors, Abt returned to M.I.T. to earn a Ph.D. in the social sciences. He founded his own company, Abt Associates, in 1965. Within the next few years Abt Associates became a major fountainhead of classroom simulation games, some of the better-known examples being *Pollution, Neighborhood, Empire, Manchester, Colony,* and *Caribou Hunting Game.*

As Abt Associates was developing the techniques for classroom simulation-gaming, many educators, especially in the social studies, were becoming interested in the discovery method. Jerome Bruner and other instructional theorists, working in the same vein as John Dewey had a generation earlier, were advocating the importance of active student involvement in true-to-life problem-solving projects.

This theoretical viewpoint activated a number of reform-minded curriculum development projects. Bruner's own contribution was *Man: A Course of Study,* a total curriculum package incorporating the Abt Associates' *Caribou Hunting* and *Seal Hunting.* Other such projects, including the High School Geography Project and the Holt Social Studies Program, yielded several simulation games.

Thus was completed the long circle from practicing conflict to practicing cooperation.

---

method inspires universal acceptance. However, as a general principle, novelty reduces boredom for adults as well as for children. The pleasant, relaxed atmosphere fostered by games can be especially productive for those (such as low achievers) who avoid other types of structured learning activities.

The element of competition, though, can be a two-edged sword. It motivates some students and discourages others. For example, this factor appears to account for some of the differences between boys and girls in math achievement. Teachers often teach lower-level math skills through contests and games. Because males tend to be more competitive and aggressive, they have an advantage over females. In recent studies researchers found that when boys participate in competitive games they improve their achievement in lower-level math.[1] Such competitions seem to depress the achievement of girls because they tend to lose the games. Yet the

---

[1] E. Fennema and P. L. Peterson, "Effective Teaching for Girls and Boys," in *Talks to Teachers,* ed. D. C. Berliner and B. Rosenshine (New York: Random House, 1987).

Figure 13.3
Play is a natural and essential
element of human development.

teachers observed in these studies acted as though they believed that all children enjoyed the competitive games.

Because of these sorts of individual differences, the element of competition must be handled very thoughtfully in choosing and using instructional games. Individual-versus-individual competition can be a highly motivating device as long as the contenders are fairly matched and the conflict does not overshadow the educational objective. Group-versus-group competition entails the same cautions, but it has the added attraction of providing practice in cooperation and teamwork. When competitions are carefully organized to ensure fair matches, as in the case of the Thinkers League Tournament (see "Close-Up," p. 384), highly successful and highly personalized learning can be fostered.

For instructional purposes, competition of the individual or team against a given standard is often the safest approach. It allows individualization because different standards can be set for different players. In

fact, one of the most effective standards can be the student's own past performance, the goal being to raise the level of aspiration continually.

In any event, in cases in which competition is an element, the scoring system provides a clue as to what type of competition is being fostered. Is one individual or team declared the winner? Or is it possible for all players to attain equally high scores, making everyone a winner? Some instructional games are designed to encourage players to decide among themselves what criteria to apply in determining success.

Gaming combines well with the drill-and-practice method of learning. This combination is employed with skills that require repetitive practice in order to be mastered. Multiplication table drills are an example. Drill-and-practice exercises can become tedious, leading to rapid burnout. But putting this sort of practice into a game format makes it more palatable, thus keeping the learner on task for a longer time with greater satisfaction.

Of course, to be instructionally meaningful the game activity must provide actual practice of the intended academic skill. An instructionally fatal shortcoming of poorly designed games is that players spend

a large proportion of their time waiting for their turn, throwing dice, moving markers around a board, and similar trivial actions.

Applications of Instructional Games

Instructional games are particularly well suited to

❑ Attainment of cognitive objectives in general, particularly those involving recognition, discrimination, or drill-and-practice, such as grammar, phonics, spelling, arithmetic skills, formulas (in chemistry, physics, logic), basic science concepts, place names, terminology, and so on.

❑ Adding motivation to topics that ordinarily attract little student interest, such as grammar rules, spelling, math drills.

❑ Small-group instruction; instructional games provide structured activities that students or trainees can conduct by themselves without close instructor supervision.

❑ Basic skills such as sequence, sense of direction, visual perception, number concepts, and following rules can be developed by means of card games. A leading advocate of the educational po-

---

MEDIA FILE: *Tuf*
Instructional Game

Content area: Mathematics
Age level: Grade three through college

Players roll cubes containing numbers and mathematical symbols, and attempt to form these into equations. *Tuf* might be used throughout a whole course in algebra; it can be played at increasing levels of sophistication.

Source: Avalon Hill

CLOSE-UP

Games in Elementary Mathematics

Mathematics Pentathlon® is a series of twenty instructional games that motivate the development and practice of mathematics concepts and skills. The games, designed for grades K–7, also promote active problem solving, specifically, the ability to solve problems which are continually undergoing change.

Classroom use of the program involves students in cooperative communication, the integration of spatial, logical, and computational reasoning, and the use of a wide variety of mathematics manipulatives to foster conceptual understanding.

The program also offers tournament competition. Tournaments are organized into four divisions combining two grade levels in each: Division I, K–1; Division II, 2–3; Division III, 4–5; and Division IV, 6–7. Within each division, individuals or teams compete in five different games; hence the name pentathlon. This phase of the program involves the entire educational community and offers students the unique opportunity to balance cooperation with constructive competition.

Mathematics Pentathlon relates to a mathematics curriculum and staff development program known as Mathematics Experience-Based Approach (MEBA)™. MEBA fosters mathematical understanding by building deliberate connections between physical models, pictures, and symbols and associated concepts and procedures. It also helps learners form and use mental images in solving problems.

MEBA and the associated games are designed to give students practice in nonroutine problem solving, that is, using heuristics to solve problems where known, routine procedures don't work. Examples of heuristics are building a model or drawing a picture of the problem, finding a simple problem that is analogous to the one being studied, working backwards, and breaking the problem into its subcomponents.

For further information contact Mary Gilfeather, Pentathlon Institute, Inc., P.O. Box 20590, Indianapolis, IN 46220.

---

tential of card games is Margie Golick, a psychologist specializing in learning disabilities.[2]

❏ Vocabulary building; a number of commercial games such as *Boggle, Fluster, Scrabble,* and *Probe* have been used successfully by teachers to expand spelling and vocabulary skills, although they were designed and are marketed primarily for recreational purposes.

---

[2]   Margie Golick, *Deal Me In!* (New York: Jeffrey Norton Publisher, 1973).

MEDIA FILE: *On-Words*
Instructional Game

Content area: Language arts, spelling
Age level: Grade four through adult

In *On-Words* players roll letter and number cubes, then attempt to form words of a specified length. Intersecting words are formed, as in a crossword puzzle. Can be played at basic, advanced, or adventurous levels, progressing from simple spelling and counting through word analysis.

Source: Wff 'N Proof

CLOSE-UP

Games for Teaching Reading

Reading is generally the most emphasized skill at the elementary school level. It's also a subject in which a great deal of practice and a high degree of individualization are necessary. For these reasons reading teachers find game playing to be an especially valuable method.

Featured here are several games for decoding and comprehension skills. They have been reviewed and recommended by Dixie Lee Spiegel, instructional resources reviewer for *The Reading Teacher.*

DECODING

Road Race (Curriculum Associates, 5 Esquire Road, North Billerica, MA 01862–2598) is a board game for two to six players. Players move markers around a track based on the number of words they have made and read. Players roll ten dice with word parts on them (e.g., *-ight, -ake, -en*) and made words by matching the dice with letters, digraphs, or blends written on the game board. Players who are awaiting their turn can challenge words made by others.

Word Trek (DLM, One DLM Park, Allen, TX 75002) is a board game for two to four players. In this game players are dealt eight word-family pockets. They draw cards containing blends and digraphs and try to form words by combining them with the word-family pockets. The opportunity to challenge keeps other players involved.

COMPREHENSION

Context Clues (Learning Well, CS 9001, Roslyn Heights, NY 11577-9001) provides practice in determining the meaning of a difficult word encountered in sentence context. The game comes in basic and intermediate versions.

Cause and Effect (Opportunities for Learning, Inc., 20417 Nordhoff Street, Chatsworth, CA 91311) provides challenging practice in differentiating between causes and effects. The player reads a paragraph and chooses a cause for a given effect or vice versa. The game comes in two levels, basic and intermediate.

Spiegel cautions that with many games of this type the teacher must anticipate modifying the materials to make them most effective instructionally. In *Cause and Effect,* the defect is that players are not required to read at every turn. Because many of the squares on the game board are blank, players can advance without reading. Spiegel simply changed the rules of play so that every square required reading. The originally designated reading squares were given double value.

Source: Spiegel, Dixie Lee, "Instructional Resources: Decoding and Comprehension Games and Manipulatives," *The Reading Teacher* 44, no. 3 (November 1990):258–61.

INSTRUCTIONAL SIMULATIONS

Simulation and Discovery Learning

One particular value of simulation is that it implements the discovery method as directly and clearly as it can be done. In discovery learning the learner is led toward understanding principles through grappling with a problem situation. Immersion in a problem is exactly what most simulations attempt to do.

Through simulations we can offer learners a laboratory in areas such as the social sciences and human relations as well as in areas related to the physical sciences, where laboratories have long been taken for granted. True, it tends to be more time-consuming than the straightforward lecture approach, but the payoff is a higher level of comprehension that is likely to be long-lasting.

The great advantage of this sort of firsthand immersion in a topic is that students are more likely to be able to apply to real life what they have practiced applying in simulated circumstances. This raises the issue of the degree of realism captured by a simulation. A common defect in poorly designed simulations is an overemphasis on chance factors in determining outcomes. Much of the reality is spoiled if chance-element cards cause players to gain or lose great quantities of points or other resources regardless of their strategic decisions. An overemphasis on chance or an overly simplified representation of real relationships might end up teaching lessons quite contrary to what was intended.

Role-Plays

Role-play refers to one type of a simulation in which the dominant feature is relatively open-ended interaction among people. In essence, a role-play asks someone to imagine that he or she is another person or is in a particular situation; the person then behaves as the other person would or the way the situation seems to demand. The purpose is to learn something about another kind of person or about the dynamics of an unfamiliar situation. The role descriptions may be very general, leaving great latitude for the participant. The purpose in many cases is to allow the person's own traits to emerge so that they can be discussed and possibly modified. In other simulations, such as historical recreations, highly detailed roles are described in order to project the realities of life in that period.

The role-play simulation has proven to be a motivating and effective method of developing social skills, especially empathy—putting oneself in someone else's shoes. Our day-to-day social behavior tends to be governed by our assumptions about who we are, who our associates are, and why they act the way they do. A potent way of challenging, and thereby changing, these assumptions is to experience a slice of life from someone else's perspective.

The sorts of tasks that lend themselves especially well to role playing are counseling, interviewing, sales and customer services, supervision, and management (Figure 13.4). The settings most often simulated are committee meetings, negotiation sessions, public meetings, work teams, and one-to-one interviews.

Simulators

Competencies in the motor skill domain require practice under conditions of high feedback, which gives the learner the feel of the action. Although it might be ideal to practice such skills under real-life conditions, some skills (for example, piloting an airplane or driving a car) can be practiced much more safely and conveniently by means of simulated conditions. The devices employed to represent physical systems in a scaled-down form are referred to as *simulators*.

MEDIA FILE: *Starpower*
Instructional Simulation

Content area: Social studies, government
Age level: High school and above

Starpower revolves around the trading of tokens which have been distributed randomly at the start. During each round participants try to increase their wealth and move upward in the three-tiered class structure which evolves. Later in play, the rich players make the rules.

Source: Simulation Training Systems

MEDIA FILE: *Principles of Effective Salesmanship*
Instruction Simulation

Content area: Salesmanship
Age level: Adult
Playing time: Approximately three hours

In groups of three to five, participants play the roles of salespeople. They make decisions related to identification of customer needs, preparation of a needs checklist, and development of an effective sales approach based on the needs identified.

Source: Didactic Systems, Inc.

Figure 13.4
Role-playing simulations help service personnel develop their people skills.

Figure 13.5
Doron's driver training simulator simulates the sights, sounds, and feel of hazardous road situations without the real-life risks.

One familiar example of a simulator is the flight trainer, a mock-up of the interior of the cockpit complete with controls and gauges. Today the flight crews of most major airlines receive a large proportion of their training in flight simulators, which are often controlled by computers and offer highly realistic audiovisual effects. Besides eliminating the possibility of loss of life and aircraft, these simulators allow significant savings of energy, in millions of gallons of fuel annually, and other costs.

One recent study estimated that in-air training costs about $4,000 per hour compared to only $400 per hour on the flight simulator, with no loss in effectiveness.

Another example, which more people have experienced personally, is the automobile driver-training simulator. One of the best-known of such systems is shown in Figure 13.5. This system typically consists of a number of simulated car-driving units complete with all the controls of a real automobile. At the front of the room is a screen. At the rear are a film projector and audio console used to simulate the sights and sounds of actual driving conditions. Students "drive" on filmed streets and highways, and their individual responses to filmed driving conditions are recorded and scored. Since its inception in the 1950s, millions of students have sharpened their

CLOSE-UP

Simulators Help Assure Friendly Skies

As airplanes grew larger and faster, fuel costs rose, and the number of flights increased rapidly, the aviation industry underwent a revolution in training methods in the 1970s and 1980s. Add to this the dramatic advances in computer technology of the 1990s. The result is the increasing replacement of conventional training with computer-based simulations that have become more and more realistic.

Self-instructional modules have largely replaced the former standard method, a class of fifteen to twenty pilots taught by a live instructor. Full-size models of cockpit controls are used to reinforce material learned in the modules. Flight maneuvers and emergency procedures can now be practiced more realistically and more safely than in an actual aircraft.

The new approach to pilot training has been outstandingly successful. Training times have been reduced substantially, and the expensive, fuel-consuming practice flying in real aircraft has been virtually eliminated while proficiency of crews has been upgraded. In most cases the cost of simulator training is about one-tenth that of in-flight training.

At the heart of most new aviation training systems is computer-based training. The systems are flexible and cost-effective, allowing the pilot trainees to proceed at their own pace and not confining them to a classroom or to specified training times. In addition, each student's error record, which is maintained by the computer program, can be reviewed by the instructors daily to identify student weaknesses and possible problems in the instructional procedures.

When the Boeing 767 made its debut in 1982, it was equipped with computer screens and push-button controls instead of the dozens of dials, levers, and gauges of an earlier era. The 767 is flown by two people instead of the usual three and represents a major advance in aviation technology. Equally advanced instructional procedures accompany newer aircraft.

In the first phase of training, pilot trainees spend an average of four hours a day in a study carrel using computer-based branching programs. They then spend about thirty minutes at a cockpit instrument simulator in a briefing session with an instructor. After this they go to an enclosed cockpit mock-up with real switches, computers, and display screens for about two hours of practice. Here the trainees program the flight path the same way it is done in an actual 767.

All of these preliminaries prepare the trainee to use the full-blown simulator. These flight simulators, costing millions of dollars, are so realistic that the Federal Aviation Authority has extended credit for landing maneuvers performed in them. In theory, the neophyte pilot with a commercial pilot's license and an instrument rating could progress all the way to being a qualified captain on a large jet transport without ever flying in the actual aircraft.

Sources: Mary Condon, "Fly the Safe Skies—and Thank Training," *Training and Development Journal* (September 1984):25–32; Geber, Beverly, "Simulating Reality," *Training* (April 1990):41–46.

driving skills by means of this type of simulator.

Simpler simulators are in widespread use in areas such as training workers in a broad range of manual skills. A full discussion of such devices, including a number of examples, can be found in A. J. Romiszowski, *The Selection and Use of Instructional Media.*[3]

Applications of Instructional Simulation

Instructional simulations, including role-plays, are particularly well suited for

❑ Training in motor skills, including athletic and work skills, and complex skills that might otherwise be too hazardous or expensive to practice in real-life settings.

❑ Instruction in social interaction and human relations, where empathy and coping with the motivations of other people are major goals.

❑ Development of decision-making skills (e.g., microteaching in teacher education, mock court in law school, management simulations in business administration).

INSTRUCTIONAL SIMULATION GAMES

Simulation Games and Holistic Learning

Because they combine the characteristics of both simulations and games, instructional simulation games have advantages and applications in common with both formats. In this regard one of the major reasons for using simulation and gaming methods is that they provide conditions for *holistic learning.* That is, through the modeling of reality and through the players' interactions as they strive to succeed,

learners encounter a whole and dynamic view of the process being studied. Conventional instruction tends to segment reality into separate packages (e.g., biology, mathematics, psychology), but that is not how the real world is organized. Through participation in simulation games we can see the whole process and its dynamic interrelationships in action. In addition, our emotions come into play along with the thinking process. Participants commonly experience excitement, elation, disappointment, even anger, as they struggle to succeed (Figure 13.6). This, of course, is how learning takes place in the world outside the classroom.

Applications of Instructional Simulation Games

Instructional simulation games are found in curriculum applications that require both the repetitive skill practice associated with games and the reality context associated with simulations. Societal processes (e.g., *Ghetto, Democracy*), cultural conflicts (e.g., *Bafa Bafa*), historical eras (e.g., *Empire, Manchester*), and ecological systems (e.g., *Extinction*) are popular topics.

In general, instructional simulation games are frequently used to provide an overview of a large, dynamic process. The excitement of play stimulates interest in the subject matter, and the holistic treatment of the game gives students a feel for the total process before approaching parts of it in a more linear way.

Limitations of Instructional Games and Simulations

As with all of the instructional media, methods, and formats discussed earlier, simulations and games have their limitations as well as potential strengths. Any materials-based instruction is only as good as the materials themselves. The simulation-game format is not magical. The effectiveness of the learning depends on the quality of the particular material and its utilization. It also depends on the receptivity of the learners to these instructional methods. Not everyone responds enthusiastically to game playing or to role playing, where they may expose themselves to some psychological risks.

The use of simulation and game materials usually demands special

Figure 13.6
A well-designed simulation game stirs emotional responses comparable to the reality being modeled.

[3] A. J. Romiszowski, *The Selection and Use of Instructional Media,* 2nd ed. (New York: Nichols, 1988):273–84.

MEDIA FILE: *The Green Revolution Game*
Instructional Simulation Game

Content area: Community development, social studies
Age level: College and adult

The setting is a village in contemporary India. Players attempt to manage their limited resources to provide for their families. Pests, drought, crop failures, shortage of cash and credit, and deaths of family members are among the realistic variables with which each player must contend.

Source: Marginal Context Ltd.

MEDIA FILE: *Where in the World Is Carmen Sandiego?*
Computer-Based Simulation Game

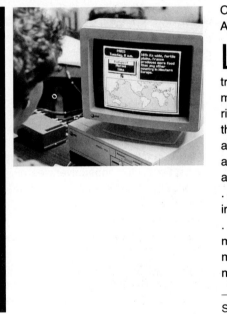

Content area: History, geography
Age level: Grades six through ten

Learners play the role of detective as they follow a trail of clues to track down and apprehend one of the members of Carmen Sandiego's notorious band of thieves. To follow clues, the detective utilizes resource materials, problem-solving skills, planning, and organization. Four different games are available: "Where in the World . . .", "Where in the USA . . .", "Where in Europe . . . ," and "Where in Time . . ." Each employs different resource materials. As the detective catches more thieves, the chase becomes more difficult.

Source: Broderbund

---

grouping arrangements—pairing, for instance, or small groups. Some learners might have trouble exercising the responsibility and self-discipline necessary to ensure the success of self-directed instruction.

Obtaining all the needed materials can be expensive and time-consuming. Sometimes costs can be kept down by making local modifica-

tions (e.g., altering the procedures so that consumable materials are not consumed). But effort will still be needed to get all the materials together and keep them together before, during, and after play.

Some simulation and game activities depend heavily on postgame discussion for their full instructional effect. This debriefing must be skill-

fully planned and conducted. If the instructor lacks discussion-leading skills, the whole learning experience is diminished.

Time can be a significant obstacle. Discovery learning is more time-consuming than straightforward lectures or reading assignments. A principle that can be stated in a single sentence might require an hour of play plus discussion to be conveyed experientially. You have to decide whether the added richness of the learning experience is worth the time.

The competition that some games entail is another consideration. A cultural setting that discourages competitiveness would not be a very compatible place for using competitive games. Likewise, a culture in which achievement is not valued might not provide the motivation required for students to get into the spirit of the game. On an individual level, some students will find competition uncomfortable, unfair, or instructionally ineffective. With every type of instructional treatment, of course, you need to be prepared to deal with individual differences.

Cooperative Games and Simulations

Traditionally, games—both athletic contests and tabletop board games—have emphasized competition between adversaries. In recent years both sports psychologists and educational psychologists have developed new theories questioning the value and necessity of competition in human development.[4] They contend that if children are nurtured on cooperation, acceptance, and success in a fun-oriented atmosphere they develop strong, positive self-concepts. Out of this new awareness has come the "new games" movement, generating hundreds of *cooperative games* that challenge the

---

4 Kohn, Alfie, *No Contest: The Case Against Competition* (Boston: Houghton Mifflin, 1986).

body and imagination but which depend on cooperation for success.[5]

Instructional games and simulations have been developed that pursue a similar philosophy. *Save the Whales* (see "Media File") demonstrates that this endangered species can be preserved only through human cooperation. In *Mountaineering* players work as a team to ascend and descend the mountain depicted on the game board, complete with crevasses, avalanches, and blizzards. In *Sky Travelers* players learn about the earth as they explore it in the form of stranded aliens from outer space; only through teamwork and strategic decision making can they reunite with the mother craft.[6]

The computer has opened up even wider possibilities for simulating problem situations elaborately. A number of development groups have made computer-based simulations that challenge participants to work together to unlock a mystery. One particularly successful collection of cooperative computer simulations has been developed by Groupware of Ontario, Canada (see "Media File: *Longhouse*"). The unique feature of these simulations is that they require a group of learners working synchronously (at the same time) and cooperatively to arrive at a successful conclusion.

Business Games and Simulations

In addition to the physical simulators used for flight training and teaching other motor skills, games and simulations are heavily used in business and industry for training in management skills. Usage begins at the preservice level in undergraduate schools of business, 95 percent of which reported that they use computer-mediated business simula-

---

[5]　Orlick, Terry, *The Cooperative Sports and Games Book: Challenge Without Competition* (New York: Pantheon, 1978).

[6]　The latter two games are developed by Family Pastimes of Ontario, Canada.

MEDIA FILE: *Save the Whales*
Cooperative Game

Content area: Ecology, social development
Age level: Grade three through adult

Players learn to act cooperatively as they face oil spills, radioactive waste, and whaling ships in trying to save eight types of whales from extinction. Players earn "survival points" and make group decisions on protecting the whales. This is one of a family of cooperative games distributed by this company. All aim to encourage cooperation rather than competition.

Source: Animal Town Game Company

MEDIA FILE: *Longhouse*
Computer-Based Cooperative Simulation

Content area: History, archeology
Age level: Grades four through eight

Longhouse is a networked discovery-learning simulation based on actual archeological excavations. Students cooperatively learn about several different Native American cultures, within the Iroquois and Algonkian groups, by working in teams to dig up buried artifacts. They attempt to find, piece together, and identify their finds. By means of a window they can communicate with teammates at different workstations as they explore different dig sites. Artifacts can be compared with authentic items in an electronic museum. The simulation was developed in Ontario, Canada, for the Unisys Icon system. The cooperative simulations developed by Groupware have consistently won Awards of Excellence from the Association for Media and Technology in Education of Canada (AMTEC).

Source: Groupware Corporation

tions.[7] One out of six business instructors uses games and simulations, with the average user devoting about one-quarter of class time to game or simulation use.

This pattern of rather heavy use continues within the businesses themselves; Faria found that among larger corporations (above 1,000 employees) 55 percent use games and simulations in their management training. The majority employ in-basket simulations (in which trainees sort through and make decisions about messages found in their "in" box) and role-playing exercises rather than the computer-based simulations favored in academic settings. Most common are simulations developed by outside agencies, such as *Looking Glass, Desert Survival Situation,* and *Strategic Management Game.* Because of their perceived effectiveness and high transfer value, such materials continue to grow in popularity in corporate settings.

SIMULATION AND GAMING AND THE ASSURE MODEL

Plans for using simulations and games can be organized by turning once more to the ASSURE model. Again, it is assumed that you have analyzed the needs, interests, and learning characteristics of your audience and clearly specified your objectives. So we will begin here with the third element of the model: select media and materials.

Select Materials

Selection Criteria.   Appraisal of any particular simulation or game entails many of the same considerations as selection of other types of media materials. Other considerations that apply particularly to simulations and games are listed in the "Appraisal Checklist" in this chapter.

7   A. J. Faria, "A Survey of the Use of Business Games in Academia and Business," *Simulation and Games* 18, no. 2 (June 1987):207–24.

Particular emphasis should be given to deciding if the material really does provide relevant practice of meaningful skills and whether this practice takes place within a *valid representation of reality* (in the case of a simulation). The criterion of relevant practice is frequently violated when players spend too much of their time moving markers or waiting for their turn without thinking or acting in accordance with the objectives. Some games are also deficient in providing sufficient examples across a broad enough range of variables, for example, a reading game that includes only simple declarative sentences devoted to a single topic.

The potential transfer value of a simulation is limited by the correspondence of the learning activity to the real world of the learner. Obviously, there must be a certain degree of simplification in the simulation to match the audience's comprehension level and to be efficient and manageable. But the greater the difference between the reality represented in the simulation and the learner's real world, the harder it will be to transfer and apply whatever insights might be gained. Thus, in corporate education trainers usually insist on modifying the setting of simulation exercises to closely resemble their own organization.

The feedback portion of the practice exercise is another frequent source of difficulty. If an instructor is not present during play, there must be some mechanism for checking the adequacy of players' answers or moves. Many well-designed games use the device of opponent's challenges as a way to judge the answers. This keeps everyone alert and involved as well as making the game self-correcting.

One device that does not appear to work well is play materials, usually in self-instructional modules, that are cut into jigsaw puzzle shapes which must be fitted together to check the correctness of an answer. There is too strong a temptation for children to attend to the puzzle shapes rather than the academic content in selecting answers.

Flexibility is another quality that's especially desirable in simulation and game materials since they're so often used for repetitive practice, for groups of varying ability, and for individual remedial work. Are the rules easy to change? Can the level of the game be changed? (Most of the examples cited in this chapter are designed for play at different levels of ability.) Can new examples be added? Materials that have these qualities will stand up in the long run.

Obtaining Materials.   A major factor limiting the use of simulations and games is their haphazard availability. Commercial publishers find them awkward to handle so they are often distributed directly by their original developer or some other small vendor. These can be difficult to track down. The sources listed in Appendix A can be of some assistance, but obtaining the exact materials needed often requires good detective skills and perseverance.

Modify Materials

Although the supply of commercially developed simulation and game materials is growing, you might find it necessary or desirable to modify some existing materials to fit your instructional objectives more closely.

Role-play and other less structured activities (e.g., communication games) can be modified easily by changing role descriptions, changing the setting of the activity, or simplifying the interaction pattern in the original activity.

Some games are designed for adaptation to varying age or grade levels. Several of the games in the Wff 'N Proof series, such as *On-Words* and *Equations,* begin as simple spelling or arithmetic drills. The

❏ **APPRAISAL CHECKLIST**
Simulations and Games

Title _____

Source _____

Playing Time _____ **Date** _____ **Cost** _____

Number of Players _____

Special Equipment/Facilities Needed _____

Subject Area _____

Objectives (stated or implied)

Brief Description

Entry Capabilities Required

❏ Prior subject-matter knowledge/vocabulary
❏ Reading ability
❏ Mathematical ability
❏ Other

Format

❏ Has game features (e.g., competition, scoring)

❏ Has simulation features (e.g., role-playing, representation of real-world settings and problems)

Rating	High		Medium		Low	Comments
Relevance to objectives	❏	❏	❏	❏	❏	
Provides practice of relevant skills	❏	❏	❏	❏	❏	
Likely to arouse/maintain interest	❏	❏	❏	❏	❏	
Likely to be comprehended clearly	❏	❏	❏	❏	❏	
Technical quality (durable, attractive)	❏	❏	❏	❏	❏	
Game: Winning dependent on player actions (rather than chance)	❏	❏	❏	❏	❏	
Simulation: Validity of game model (realistic, accurate depiction)	❏	❏	❏	❏	❏	
Evidence of effectiveness (e.g., field-test results)	❏	❏	❏	❏	❏	
Clear directions for play	❏	❏	❏	❏	❏	
Effectiveness of debriefing guide	❏	❏	❏	❏	❏	

Strong Points

Weak Points

Reviewer _____

Position _____

Recommended Action _____ **Date** _____

_____

instruction manual contains directions for progressively raising the objectives and rules to higher cognitive levels, ending with games of transformational grammar and symbolic logic.

Frame Games.

A more substantive type of modification is to take an existing game and change the subject matter while retaining the original game structure. The original game is referred to as a *frame game* because its framework lends itself to multiple adaptations. When one is modifying a frame game, the underlying structure of a familiar game provides the basic procedures of play, or the dynamics of the process. The designer loads the desired content onto a convenient frame.[8]

Familiar parlor games such as tic-tac-toe, rummy, concentration, and bingo, which were intended for recreation rather than instruction, can also serve as potential frameworks for your own instructional content. Some television game shows have been modeled after such parlor games; they can suggest additional frameworks. Here are some sample adaptations:

❑ *Safety tic-tac-toe.* A three-by-three grid is used; each row represents a place where safety rules pertain—home, school, street; each column represents the level of question difficulty. Teams take turns selecting and trying to answer safety-related questions, attempting to fill in three squares in a row.

❑ *Spelling rummy.* Using alphabet cards instead of regular playing cards, players attempt to spell short words following the general rules of rummy.

❑ *Reading concentration.* This game uses about a dozen

matched picture-word pairs of flash cards. Cards are placed face down. On each turn the player turns over two cards, seeking to match a pair. Both reading ability and memorizing are exercised.

❑ *Word bingo.* Each player's card has a five-by-five grid with a vocabulary word (possibly in a foreign language) in each square. The leader randomly selects words; players then seek the words on their boards, and if they are found, the square is marked. The winner is the first player with five correctly marked squares in a row.

Utilize Materials

For simulations and games, the utilization step of the ASSURE model entails procedures that are quite different at some points from those suggested earlier for other media.

Preview. Familiarize yourself with the materials, preferably going through a dry run with some friends or a few selected students. Acquaint yourself with the rules (Figure 13.7). Note individual phases of the simulation or game. Be sure you are aware of exactly when and where important instructional points are made. Practice any activities that the game director is responsible for (e.g., providing tokens, computing scores for each round).

Set up a time schedule for use of the materials. Your first concern is to have enough time for a successful session. A "good" game squeezed into too short a time can become a "bad" game. Some games, such as *Starpower,* cannot be broken down to fit into separate class periods. If you have to divide play into separate periods, try to have the breaks come at natural stopping points.

Prepare the Environment. Check over all the materials to be certain that everything is ready in sufficient quantities. Before the par-

Figure 13.7
Successful learning from simulations and games depends greatly on the instructor's utilization practices, especially on being well prepared.

ticipants arrive, count everything again. If any audiovisual equipment is involved, give it a last minute checkout too. As with any other kind of teaching, students will judge you harshly if they sense that you haven't done your homework.

Prepare the Audience. Inform your audience of the learning objectives of the simulation or game. Relate the simulation or game to previous study. Announce the time schedule for completion of the activities. Run through the rules concisely and clearly. If the procedures are somewhat complex, walk the students through one initial round. Resist the urge to lecture about content or to give hints about strategies. Get into the game as quickly as possible.

Present the Simulation or Game. Once the activity is rolling, your job is to keep the mood and the tempo upbeat. Stay in close touch with the action. Be ready to intervene, but only when intervention is clearly called for.

Some participants in simulation and game activities may feel a bit confused in the initial stages and be

───────────────
8   Harold D. Stolovitch and Sivasailam Thiagarajan, *Frame Games* (Englewood Cliffs, NJ: Educational Technology Publications, 1980).

CLOSE-UP

Thinkers League Tournament: Logical Problem Solving

Based at the University of Michigan, the Thinkers League Tournament, which began operation in fall 1986, is a computer-mediated gaming activity for junior high school students. Aimed at improving achievement in mathematics and science, the tournament provides opportunities for students to compete with their peers in other schools to construct solutions to a series of problems delivered to the classroom each week by a computer network. Classroom teams propose solutions and conduct experiments daily and receive immediate feedback from the computer program. Teachers also receive daily diagnostic feedback about ideas that the teams in their class do and do not understand in comparison with teams in other classes.

There are six teams in each classroom that compete against teams from three other schools in their division in the weekly rounds of the tournament. Each team plays against every other team from the three other schools in its division during the six-week tournament. Division realignment based on performance occurs at the end of each of the five six-week tournaments during an academic year of play. The tournaments of the Thinkers League culminate in a round-robin playoff at levels determined by the teams' performances during the earlier rounds.

The series of exercises used in Thinkers League tournaments require students to learn and use the basic reasoning and problem-solving skills of careful observation, logical deduction, mathematical analysis, asking good questions (which in this context is equivalent to designing good experiments), research by experimentation, and data gathering, organization, and analysis. Instead of being presented in an isolated fashion in different courses, all of these tools are brought to bear on a single problem. The model of learning that underlies this approach emphasizes motivation and active engagement of learners in strategies that they devise, plan, and execute—as opposed to rote absorption of knowledge.

For further information contact Layman E. Allen, Law School, University of Michigan, Ann Arbor, MI 48109.

GROUP DEBRIEFING

It is usually preferable to conduct the debriefing as a group discussion if time and conditions permit. As an aid in planning for this stage, follow the "Four Ds of Debriefing":

1. Decompression
2. Description
3. Drawing comparisons
4. Deriving lessons

Step 1: Decompression (Feelings)

You will want to relieve any tensions that may have built up during the simulation or game. Some situations may engender conflict and anger. Also, players who feel they did not do very well in the game may be experiencing anxiety and feelings of inadequacy. In any event, participants are not likely to be focusing on *your* questions and concerns until these pent-up feelings simmer down to a manageable level.

Start with some "safety valve" questions. In games, players will have attained some sort of score, so you can start simply by asking for and recording the scores. Jot down scores on a chalkboard or flip chart. Also note comments. These bits of information form a database you can refer to in later stages of debriefing.

From tabulation of the scores you will be able to declare the winner in cases of competitive games. Let the winner(s) show off a little bit by asking them to explain their strategy. Low scorers should also have a chance to tell what went wrong for them, if they wish.

At this point be sure to explain any hidden agendas or "tricks" the designer may have inserted in order to make a certain point. Explain how these may have affected the scores. Also, point out the role that chance can play in the scoring, as it does in real life.

To deal further with any emotional residue, ask several participants how they felt while playing. Did anyone else feel that way too? Let all who want to chime in freely.

Step 2: Description (Facts)

The nature and purpose of the activity will usually have been explained before the beginning of play. But some students may not have fully appreciated the meaning or significance of the activity. Others may have lost track of it in the heat of play. For example, players of *Triangle Trade* might need to be reminded that it simulates the experiences of seventeenth-century British colonists. Ask basic questions such as "What real-life situation was represented in this activity?" or "What was [X] intended to symbolize?"

Step 3: Drawing Comparisons (Transfer)

Help the participants transfer the game experiences to reality. Encourage them to compare and contrast the game with reality with such questions as "How does the scoring system compare with real-life rewards?" "What elements of reality were missing from or downplayed in the simulation?" "Would these solutions work in real life?"

Step 4: Deriving Lessons (Application)

Get the participants to intellectualize, or verbalize, exactly what they have learned from the activity. Verbalization will reinforce what has been learned. Ask questions such as "What conclusions can you draw from the experience?" "What did you learn about specific real-life problems?" "Did the simulation change any of your previous attitudes or opinions?" "What do you plan to do differently tomorrow as a result of this activity?"

INDIVIDUAL DEBRIEFING

In situations in which participants finish simulation or game activities at different times or in which the schedule prevents immediate group discussion, a form of individual debriefing may be used.

One method developed to help participants reflect on their feelings immediately after play uses a simple sentence-completion form to be filled out individually. Each participant writes a completion to each of the following sentences:

1. I was_____ .
   (the role you played in the game)

2. I did_____ .
   (actions you performed)

3. I felt_____ .
   (emotions you felt during play)

4. I wish_____ .
   (open response)

The reactions captured on this form can either substitute for group discussion or can supplement the later discussion, with participants referring back to their sheets to remind themselves of their reactions.

The setting is a middle school, specifically a self-contained seventh grade classroom in a crowded residential district of a large city.

ANALYZE LEARNERS

General Characteristics

These seventh graders are twelve and thirteen years old. They come from an urban area that is poor and declining. Over half are nonwhite, and about a quarter of them are recent immigrants, several of whom barely speak or read English. Their reading levels range from second grade to twelfth grade, averaging around fifth grade.

Because of the wide range of abilities and deficiencies of this class, the teacher can seldom rely on group-based "chalk and talk" instruction. This is particularly true in science, where many of the children have very low confidence and interest.

Entry Competencies

Regarding the topic of electric circuits, most of the students have at least a verbal understanding of basic terms such as source, output device, connection, switch, series, and parallel because they have just completed a hands-on activity with a simple circuit in which they connected lamps with batteries. They have learned the basic principle that an open switch stops the current, and that bulbs will light only if the circuit is complete.

In arithmetic the class has been working on fractions, proportions, and decimal-to-fraction conversions. With a few exceptions students have sufficient mastery of the basic concepts in these areas to go on to study electrical circuits.

STATE OBJECTIVES

The teacher wants the students to have usable, applied skills, not just inert verbal knowledge so he decides to give them practice in order to reinforce and extend their understanding of electrical circuits. After this lesson, they will be able to

1. Distinguish closed from open circuits, given a symbolic circuit diagram.
2. Construct series and parallel circuits, arranging batteries, bulbs, and switches so that they function correctly.
3. Explain the consequences of opening a switch in a circuit.
4. Explain the consequences of disconnecting one battery in a series circuit and in a parallel circuit.

SELECT MEDIA AND MATERIALS

The teacher has found that these seventh graders respond best to active, hands-on learning situations, so is determined to find an activity that will give a lab experience. It should also be suitable for small-group work because he knows that some of the students will need help from others. There's no way he can provide by himself all the remedial assistance they'll need.

The bulb and battery equipment he used last week is not sophisticated enough to provide different kinds of circuits and there's not enough money to buy more actual lab equipment. He starts thinking along the lines of a simulated lab activity (no computers, of course).

At an in-service science workshop another teacher told him about *Circuitron,* a game developed in Scotland which she had used with good results. Fortunately, he was able to borrow the game materials from her.

After examining it, he decided he can use Game One of the five games included in the set.

UTILIZE MATERIALS

The teacher consults with the math teacher, and they agree to devote two double periods to the game. The math

---

hesitant to get into the swing of things. Reassure such students that initial confusion is not uncommon and that they will soon pick up on rules and procedures.

Watch for individuals or teams who have fallen behind in the activities or even dropped out of them.

They may need additional help in mastering the game mechanics. Withdrawal often signals some basic disagreement with the game's approach to the subject matter. Rather than stifling or suppressing the dissent, discuss the disagreement on a one-to-one basis. Ask the dropout to

suspend criticism until the end of the activities.

Watch out for personality clashes. They may require switching of partners or teammates for successful completion of the activities.

Keep track of elapsed time. The excitement and fascination of simu-

teacher will help monitor the game and offer remedial help as needed.

The class is grouped into pairs in which the children with deficient English and conceptual skills are paired with more able ones. Two pairs work at each table with a game set.

The teacher briskly explains the objectives of the lesson and outlines the procedures and basic rules of *Circuitron*. He circulates among the tables during play to monitor and troubleshoot.

The components of circuits—bulbs, batteries, switches, and so on—are represented by cardboard pieces that can be fitted into large boards with slots. Players take a handful of pieces and try to form them into a circuit, with teammates helping each other to correct mistakes and re-arrange the elements to score more points. Then the competing pair at their table check the circuit and try to score more points by using pieces from their own hands. The scoring system reflects the complexity of the circuits, with no points awarded for circuits that would not actually work in real life.

REQUIRE LEARNER PARTICIPATION

In this case the chosen material, a game, requires active learner participation by its very nature. The teachers circulate to make sure, as much as possible, that both members of each team are actively engaged in their task.

EVALUATE AND REVISE

While play is going on the teachers jot down notes, record-ing incidents or comments that could be used and writing questions to be asked in the debriefing.

After an hour and a half the lead teacher calls time out and gets everyone to stop playing. He elicits a preliminary tally of the scores, and he takes aside a couple of the teams that are struggling to offer some remedial help after class. The next day he restarts the game; after about forty-five minutes he calls time out. He starts the debriefing by asking teams to report their scores. He asks the higher scorers to tell how they managed to do so well. Then he prompts several of the others to say a few words about how they felt during the game. He is able to jog their mem-ories by citing some specific incidents or statements that he observed during play.

Next, he focuses on the main objectives of the exercise, asking "What is the difference between an open and closed circuit?" "Can you diagram on the chalkboard what a series circuit looks like?" "What would happen if you dis-connected one battery in a parallel circuit?"

During the discussion he makes note of those who still don't seem to have a firm grasp of the objectives. During the next day's follow-up projects he has them play the game again along with a few of the average and superior performers, as a remedial exercise.

Immediately after the debriefing he takes two minutes to jot down his impressions of what worked and what prob-lems arose. He files these notes along with his lesson ma-terials to try to improve the smoothness of the activity next time.

Source: Jaquetta Megarry, "Simulation and Gaming," in *Interna-tional Encyclopedia of Educational Technology*, ed. Michael Eraut (Oxford: Pergamon, 1989).

lation and game activities make it easy to forget that time is passing. If necessary, remind participants of time limits. Resist the temptation to extend play at the expense of de-briefing time.

If announcements must be made during use, try not to interrupt the activities bluntly by shouting above the hubbub. Dimming room lights or flashing your message on the overhead projector can attract the attention you need.

Record significant participant reactions and comments for discus-sion during the debriefing period.

Require Learner Participation

A unique attribute of simulations and games is that participants are continuously responding throughout the activity. Indeed, without re-sponse there can be no activity. Why,

Figure 13.8
For complex simulation and game activities, such as social and business simulations, the group debriefing is crucial for bringing out the main points of the experience.

then, should we be concerned with the participation element of our AS-SURE model when dealing with simulations and games?

The truth is that attention to learner participation is perhaps more important in simulations and games than in any other instructional method we have discussed in this book. The reason? Learner interaction in simulations and games is of a different order than that in most other methods. During either the hurly-burly or the determined concentration of intense involvement in simulations and games, there is little opportunity to intellectualize or verbalize what one is learning or failing to learn from the activity. The overlay of emotion inherent in these activities militates against cognitive awareness. Because conscious awareness of the main instructional points may be very low during play, it is doubly important to plan for a thorough discussion, or *debriefing*, after play (Figure 13.8). The debriefing to clarify the instructional goals may be conducted on either an individual or group basis, or a combination of both may be employed, as suggested in "How to . . . Conduct a Debriefing: The 4-D Procedure" (p. 385).

Evaluate and Revise

The final element of the ASSURE model for teaching/learning is evalu-ation followed by revision. As we have pointed out throughout this text in connection with other instructional media and methods, although full evaluation must await completion of a learning activity, the process begins much earlier.

The notes made during utilization and the records kept of student response to the simulation or game will contribute to your final evaluation. The debriefing session, however, will probably provide the most precise and useful data upon which your final evaluation will be based.

A frequent criticism of research and evaluation studies of simulation and game products is that paper-and-pencil tests are too often the primary instruments used to assess learning outcomes. Simulations and games ordinarily emphasize different kinds of outcomes than conventional lecture and textbook teaching. Their forte is the promotion of holistic learning, usually involving appreciation of and insight into complex processes. These sorts of learnings do not lend themselves to measurement by means of typical multiple-choice tests or other verbal tests that dwell on low-level cognitive outcomes.

A truer test of effectiveness would be the extent to which the simulation or game experience has changed the student's or trainee's approach to real-world problems. Short of following the learner out into the field, the next best means of evaluation would be performance on simulated problems with relatively open-ended opportunities to respond physically, mentally, and emotionally. If these are the goals of the material, logic requires that the method of evaluation be parallel.

REFERENCES

Print References

General

Bell, Irene Wood. "Student Growth through Gaming in the Library Media Center." *School Library Media Activities Monthly* (February 1986):36–39.

Butler, J. Thomas. "Games and Simulations: Creative Educational Alternatives." *Tech Trends* 33, no. 4 (September 1988):20–23.

Coleman, James, et al. "The Hopkins Games Program: Conclusions from Seven Years of Research." *Educational Researcher* (August 1973):3–7.

Geber, Beverly. "Simulating Reality." *Training* (April 1990):41–46.

Glickman, Carl D. "Problem: Declining Achievement Scores, Solution: Let Them Play!" *Phi Delta Kappan* (February 1979):454–55.

Greenblat, Cathy S., and Duke, Richard D. *Principles and Practices of Gaming/Simulation*. Beverly Hills, CA: Sage Publications, 1981.

Heitzmann, William Ray. *Educational Games and Simulations*. Rev. ed. Washington, DC: National Education Association, 1987.

Jones, Ken. *Interactive Learning Events: A Guide for Facilitators.* New York: Nichols, 1988.

Jones, Ken. *Simulations: A Handbook for Teachers.* 2d ed. New York: Nichols, 1987.

Krupar, Karen R. *Communication Games.* New York: Free Press, 1973.

Malone, Thomas W. "What Makes Computer Games Fun? Guidelines for Designing Educational Computer Programs." In *Intelligent Schoolhouse: Readings on Computers and Learning,* ed. Dale Peterson. Reston, VA: Reston Publications, 1984.

Megarry, Jaquetta. "Simulation and Gaming." In *International Encyclopedia of Educational Technology,* ed. Michael Eraut. Oxford: Pergamon, 1989.

Pearson, Margot, and Smith, David. "Debriefing in Experience-Based Learning." *Simulation/Games for Learning* (December 1986):155–72.

Reiser, Robert A. "Increasing the Instructional Effectiveness of Simulation Games." *Instructional Innovator* (March 1981):36–37.

Shirts, R. Garry. "The Second Revolution." *Simulation and Games* 20, no. 2 (June 1989):130–43.

Stolovitch, Harold D., and Thiagarajan, Sivasailam. *Frame Games.* Englewood Cliffs, NJ: Educational Technology Publications, 1980.

Stolovitch, Harold D. "D-FITGA: A Debriefing Model." *Performance and Instruction* (August 1990):18–19.

Szczurek, Mario. "Meta-Analysis of Simulation Games for Cognitive Learning." Ed.D. thesis, Indiana University, 1982.

Tapson, Frank. "Organizing Games in the Classroom." *Mathematics in School* (January 1986):50–53.

Thatcher, Donald. "Promoting Learning through Games and Simulations." *Simulation/Games for Learning* (December 1986):144–54.

van Ments, Morry. *The Effective Use of Role-Play: A Handbook for Teachers And Trainers.* Rev. ed. New York: Nichols, 1989.

Wohlking, Wallace, and Gill, Patricia J. *Role Playing.* Englewood Cliffs, NJ: Educational Technology Publications, 1980.

Curriculum Applications

Barker, J. A. "Simulating and Gaming, without Computers, for School Biology Courses." *Journal of Biological Education* (Autumn 1982):187–96.

Canney, George F. "Making Games More Relevant for Reading," *The Reading Teacher* 32, no. 1 (1978):10–14.

Carstensen, Laurence W. "Teaching Map Reading through a Tournament." *Journal of Geography* (January–February 1987):30–31.

Creamer, Robert C.; Cohen, Richard B.; and Escamilla, Manuel. "Simulation: An Alternative Method for Bilingual-Bicultural Education." *Contemporary Education* (Winter 1977):90–91.

Dorn, Dean S. "Simulation Games: One More Tool on the Pedagogical Shelf." *Teaching Sociology* 17, no. 1 (January 1989):1–18.

Dukes, Richard L. "Teaching Statistics with Nonsimulation Games." *Teaching Sociology* (April 1987):184–90.

Ellington, Henry; Addinall, Eric; and Percival, Fred. *Games and Simulations in Science Education.* New York: Nichols, 1980.

Ernest, Paul. "Games: A Rationale for Their Use in the Teaching of Mathematics in Schools." *Mathematics in School* (January 1986):2–5.

Felder, B. Dell, and Hollis, Loye K. "Using Games to Teach Social Studies." *Georgia Social Science Journal* (Spring 1983):18–21.

Hsu, Enrico. "Role-Event Gaming Simulation in Management Education: A Conceptual Framework and Review." *Simulation and Games* 20, no. 4 (December 1989):409–38.

Jarchow, Elaine, and Montgomery, Janey. "Dare to Use Adventure Games in the Language Arts Classroom." *English Journal* (February 1985):104–96.

Powers, Richard B. "The Commons Game: Teaching Students about Social Dilemmas." *Journal of Environmental Education* (Winter 1985–1986):4–10.

Rixon, Shelagh. "Language Teaching Games." *ELT Journal* (January 1986):62–67.

Scannell, Edward E., and Newstrom, John W. *Still More Games Trainers Play: Experiential Learning Exercises.* New York: McGraw-Hill, 1991.

Sewall, Susan B. "Scientific Fun and Games." *Science and Children* (October 1986):10–12.

Solomon, Gwen. "Playing with History." *Electronic Learning* (May–June 1986):39–41.

Cooperative Games and Simulations

Crary, Elizabeth. *Kids Can Cooperate: A Practical Guide to Teaching Problem Solving.* Seattle, WA: Parenting Press, 1984.

Fluegelman, Andrew. *More New Games!* New York: Dolphin Books, 1981.

LeFevre, Dale N. *New Games for the Whole Family.* New York: Putnam/Perigee Books, 1988.

Orlick, Terry. *The Second Cooperative Sports and Games Book.* New York: Pantheon, 1982.

Sobel, Jeffrey. *Everybody Wins: Non-Competitive Games for Young Children.* New York: Walker, 1983.

Periodicals

Simulation and Games: An International Journal of Theory, Design, and Research (quarterly)
Sage Publications, Inc.
2111 West Hillcrest Drive
Newbury Park, CA 91320

Simulation/Games for Learning (quarterly)
Society for the Advancement of Games and Simulations in Education and Training (SAGSET)
Centre for Extension Studies
University of Technology
Loughborough, Leics LE11 3TU
United Kingdom

Organizations

International Simulation and Gaming Association (ISAGA)
c/o David Crookall
Box 870244, University of Alabama
Tuscaloosa, AL 35487-0244

North American Simulation and Gaming Association (NASAGA)
c/o John del Regato
Pentathlon Institute
Box 20590
Indianapolis, IN 46220-0590

Society for the Advancement of Games and Simulations in Education and Training (SAGSET)
Centre for Extension Studies
University of Technology
Loughborough, Leics LE11 3TU
United Kingdom

POSSIBLE PROJECTS

13–A. Using the sources and references in this chapter and Appendix A, identify three simulation or game activities that you could use for your own instructional purposes.

13–B. Appraise an instructional simulation or game using the "Appraisal Checklist" in this chapter.

13–C. Be a participant in an instructional simulation or game. Describe your personal reaction to the experience. Suggest instructional purposes for which it might be appropriate.

13–D. Utilize an instructional simulation or game in an actual learning situation. Describe the material, its objectives, and the actual results with your group, including the performance outcomes and the reactions of participants.

13–E. Starting with an existing simulation or game or a frame game, develop an adaptation to fit an instructional purpose of your own. Be explicit about the modifications you made and how they relate to your aims.

14

Looking Ahead

OUTLINE

OBJECTIVES

After studying this chapter, you should be able to

1. Describe two examples of the effect of miniaturization on instruction and explain how these increase access to learning.

2. Describe two examples of how technology has become "smarter" and explain how the newer technologies facilitate instruction.

3. Use the study *Visions 2000* to predict how the broad adoption of new technology and associated software will affect distribution of teacher time by the year 2000.

4. Relate the multiplication of electronic delivery systems to the decentralization of education.

5. Discuss how electronic networks can change the "global village" into the "global classroom."

6. Explain how digitization has made information more accessible to the learner.

7. Differentiate between CD-ROM, CD-WORM, and DVI.

8. Use an example to describe how hypertext can help the learner.

9. Explain the relationship between learning styles and individualizing instruction.

10. Define *expert system* and explain the relationship between expert systems and artificial intelligence.

11. List at least three information-processing skills that are exercised in video games.

12. Relate "altered states of consciousness" to improved learning.

13. Critique the conventional self-contained classroom as an organizational arrangement for incorporating technology.

14. Critique the "craft approach" of public education as a system for incorporating technology.

15. Relate the accountability movement to the increased use of technology in education.

16. Relate the lifelong learning movement to the increased use of technology in education.

17. List four trends in education or training and explain why you would like or not like them to come about.

LEXICON

CD-ROM

CD-WORM

CD-I

DVI

division of labor

low-cost learning technology

craft

accountability

expert system

electronic game

suggestive-accelerative learning and teaching

biochip

The previous chapters of this book have focused on the various media and technologies of instruction—what they are, their advantages and limitations, and their potential applications to improving learning.

In this final chapter we attempt to give a broader perspective on how media and technology fit into the overall scheme of education and training. The emphasis is on change: what trends have brought us to where we are now, what new developments hold promise for improving learning productivity, what impediments limit the implementation of these developments, and what avenues may exist for getting around these impediments.

The field of instructional technology continues to grow, and so do the opportunities for professional employment. As media and the newer technologies of instruction have expanded into training programs in business, industry, and health and public services, professional specializations have become more varied and more numerous. Because of the proliferation of computer-based instruction and other technologies in formal educational settings—historically the major employers of media professionals—schools, colleges, and universities have had to hire people trained in the new technologies. As state education departments and regional school service centers broaden the base of their support to the schools, more positions are created for professionals in instructional technology. This chapter will help you explore careers in this field.

The chapter concludes with features describing the professional organizations and journals devoted to using media and technology in education and training; these are the communication channels through which you can become further involved in the efforts of this field.

TRENDS IN MEDIA AND TECHNOLOGY

Two major trends in communications technology have paralleled each other over the post–World War II decades: (1) the media and associated equipment have become smaller and "smarter," and (2) electronic delivery systems have multiplied dramatically. Two other trends of more recent origin are the "digitization" of media formats and what we will call "learning networks." The development of media formats that make print, images, and sounds randomly accessible in seconds began about fifteen years ago with the laser videodisc. Some people have referred to this trend as the convergence of all forms of communication caused by the digitizing of information.[1] (See the discussion in Chapter 6 on the compact disc.)

These trends have combined to increase our access to instructional media. However, the mere availability of media has not necessarily led to a proportionate increase in the *use* of these tools. In other words, no imperative is implied in technological developments per se. Any technological imperative derives from the perceived usefulness of any particular invention.

Smaller and Smarter: Making Information Portable and Flexible

Perhaps the most important trend affecting the use of instructional media has been the movement toward both miniaturization of hardware (Figure 14.1) and software and, at the same time, increased sophistication in our ability to manipulate information. This trend has led to lower cost, increased ease of operation, portability of equipment, faster access to information, and greater

Figure 14.1
Miniaturization in audio can be seen in the progression from an early reel-to-reel tape recorder to a cassette recorder to a microcassette recorder.

Figure 14.2
Any of the still or motion images on a videodisc can be accessed in a matter of seconds.

flexibility in design of instructional media. Portability of media and equipment makes virtually any location a learning environment.

Film to Video. Video is inherently a more flexible format than film. A "fluid" magnetic image can be manipulated much more easily than a "frozen" chemical image. The elimination of the film-processing laboratory dramatically reduces a major expense of production, and the magnetic image, unlike the chemical image, can be viewed immediately. Also, with video, the technology for special effects can be built into the camera much more easily. Finally, editing video is easier than editing film, where audio and

---

[1] Stewart Brand, *The Media Lab* (New York: Viking, 1987), p. 18.

image must be edited separately and then assembled. All in all, video has put production of the moving image into the hands of the amateur. The public has responded enthusiastically. There are probably more camcorders sold in a single month today than there were 16mm and 8mm cameras sold in the last twenty years.

The magnetic image and the cassette format make video "smarter" than film. Locating specific sequences in a video is faster than with film. The images can be scanned while fast-forwarding or rewinding. An interrupted presentation can be handled more easily; the cassette is removed from the VCR, put back the next day, and the presentation continues. With film, the user can leave the film threaded in the projector, which is hard on the film and takes the machine out of service, or rewind the film and relocate the point where the presentation was interrupted.

Digitized images are even smarter than magnetic ones. For example, the videodisc (Figure 14.2) can be indexed so that any sequence can be located in seconds, whereas locating indexed sections on a videotape takes much longer and is not as accurate. Think of videotape as an extremely long ribbon whose signal must move past a fixed point to be picked up. Each time a segment is accessed, the video player has to exit from playback position, move the ribbon to bypass unwanted images, stop at the desired spot, and resume playback mode. The videodisc, on the other hand, rotates all the time while the laser can move quickly across the disc to the desired location. Because digitized information is more densely packed than analog information, the laser moves a much shorter distance to locate any point on the disc.

Video Recorders.   Miniaturization of electronic components has

today resulted in videotape recorders portable enough to be carried in the hand, a development that has contributed immensely to the use of videotaped materials for instructional purposes. Both video recorders and videotape have improved remarkably since being introduced in the mid-1950s. Originally, the tape had to travel at a very high speed in order to record with any degree of fidelity. Today's videocassette recorders operate at a relatively slow speed, allowing much more recording time per foot of tape, and offer excellent quality. When first introduced, videotape was 2 inches wide; today, ½-inch and 8mm tape are standard for school and home use, with little discernible difference in quality, particularly with the Super-VHS format.

High-quality images can be obtained on videotape with much lower light levels than with film, thereby eliminating cumbersome lighting equipment when videographing in nonstudio settings. The ability of an extremely portable camera to take decent images under adverse conditions makes every citizen a potential producer of documentaries. Video clips by amateurs frequently appear on television news programs, from shots of tornados to street violence.

Videodisc.   The videodisc represents another step toward compressing the size of the software needed for the storage and playback of moving pictures. The videodisc was first demonstrated in late 1978. Although its potential was quickly recognized, and many predicted it would replace videotape, both home and school markets virtually ignored the videodisc for more than a decade. The reason is very simple. As with film, the program on a videodisc is determined solely by the producer, not the user, so the home and instructional markets held onto a format that allowed them to record their own program material as well as

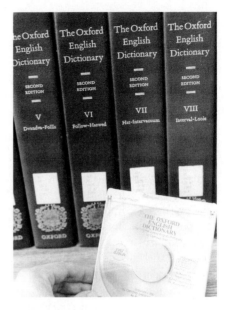

Figure 14.3
The CD version of the *Oxford English Dictionary* can access words and their definitions much more quickly than leafing through the bound volumes.

play back mass-distributed programs. Until an erasable videodisc is proven feasible for general use, we can expect to see tape and disc continue to coexist. No matter how spectacular, a new technology must be perceived as useful or it won't be adopted.

Videodisc *has* found a niche in the instructional market, particularly in training, in combination with computers. Rapid access to indexed program material, a clear advantage over videotape, has made the videodisc essential for interactive video programs (see Chapter 9). Eventually, videodisc may replace videotape as the preferred format for displaying *all* moving images in the classroom. The videodisc became more attractive to the home market when manufacturers of laser disc machines developed playback units that would handle both CDs and videodiscs. This development plus the superior image made incorporation of videodiscs into home entertainment centers much more convenient and attractive.

**Audiocassette Recorder/
Players.** Very few technological
innovations have been more quickly
or universally adapted to instructional purposes than the cassette
tape recorder. A recent survey in
Virginia revealed that the audiocassette recorder is the most common
piece of equipment in the schools.

The advantages of the cassette are
immediately obvious. First, the
whole cassette is considerably
smaller than a comparable reel-to-
reel tape and its box. The principal
reason for this reduction in size is
that the tape itself is half the width
of the standard ¼-inch recording
tape. The next obvious difference
between the cassette and reel-to-reel
format is convenience of operation.
No longer does the user have to
thread the tape into the machine.
Finally, the audiocassette recorder is
considerably smaller than reel-to-
reel tape recorders. The most widely
sold form of cassette tape recorder
today can be carried in one hand.
This is a vast change from the earlier 15- to 30-pound reel-to-reel tape
recorders.

In the early days of cassette development, recording quality left a
good deal to be desired. Even so,
teachers were quite willing to trade
quality for miniaturization. But as
the cassette format became widely
adopted, making further technological improvements economically feasible for producers of cassettes, the
quality of the recording improved.
With today's high-fidelity systems, it
is difficult to tell the difference between the audio quality of a well-
recorded cassette tape and a well-
recorded reel-to-reel tape.

The smaller size and the cassette
format permit this audio technology
to be smarter than reel-to-reel tape.
Because the tape is easily moved
back and forth within the cassette,
locating any spot on the tape can be
done fairly quickly. Many tape decks
have an audible scan capability as
well as a "silent-search" function in
which the machine can fast-forward
or rewind to the next blank section

on the tape. Some tape decks can
use this search function to allow the
operator to program the sequence in
which individual selections are
played.

Cassettes to Compact Discs.
The CD format is not limited to audio information. It can combine images, sounds, and print. The indexing capability inherent in the digital
technology is a quantum leap above
that of the audio cassette. However,
as of now, indexing must be built in
at the production stage and cannot
be added later by the user.

Unlike with the audiocassette,
adopters of this technology did not
have to settle for lower quality. The
quality of CDs is superior to any
previous audio recording format.
The home market has adopted the
CD so enthusiastically that a number of classical music recording
companies issue their releases only
in the CD format.

**Microprocessors and
Computers.** The trend toward
smaller and smarter is most obvious
in the case of the computer. The
first big step was taken when the
vacuum tube was replaced by the
transistor. The original ENIAC computer built for air-defense purposes
contained 18,000 energy-hungry
vacuum tubes, hundreds of rotary
switches, and more than 2,000 flashing signal lights. Size and energy
consumption were dramatically reduced when the tiny, energy-efficient
transistor was introduced. But computers were still very large and too
costly for wide-scale instructional
use. Then along came microprocessors in 1975.

The sophistication and miniaturization that have evolved in the
realm of microprocessors is truly
staggering. In contrast to the
ENIAC, the parallel computer at the
National Laboratories in Los Alamos,
New Mexico, has 65,536 microprocessors in a tiny fraction of the
space with functions far beyond
those of the earlier machine pro-

cessed at more than a thousand
times the speed. The memory of a
laptop computer weighing a few
pounds is about ten times that of
the first personal computers introduced in 1975. The program-
handling capabilities are correspondingly greater.

The wiring in the integrated circuits of the pre-1980 era could be
inspected with the naked eye. The
next generation of integrated circuits required a magnifying glass.
Today you need a microscope, or
even an electron microscope. The
tiny integrated circuits of today are
etched in silicon using optical li-
thography or electron beams (Figure 14.4).

Figure 14.4
Microprocessor chips visible only
under a magnifying glass are common
components in today's computers.

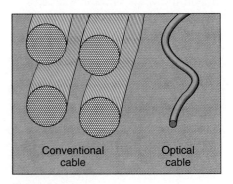

Figure 14.5
An optical fiber can transmit as many
messages as hundreds of copper
wires.

Telecommunication Systems.

Satellites and fiber optics are two fascinating and contrasting examples of miniaturization and sophistication in telecommunication systems.

Satellites and the rockets that put them in orbit are far from being miniatures, but consider what they replace. One satellite can transmit the same number of programs as hundreds of microwave relay stations or replace vulnerable cables on the ocean floor. A satellite positioned over the Atlantic Ocean can handle 30,000 phone calls simultaneously.

In the latter half of the 1970s, the Public Broadcasting System switched to satellite transmission of programming to eliminate dependence on microwave stations and telephone lines. Cable companies too, which use cable only for local distribution, get their programs by satellite.

Optical fiber, on the other hand, retains the physical linkage of a phone line but is only a fraction of the diameter of wire. An optical fiber transmits digital (rather than analog) signals as pulses of light generated by a laser no bigger than a grain of salt. The millions of pulses per second emitted by the laser make it possible to send many more messages simultaneously than with copper wires or coaxial cable. For example, two glass optical fibers can handle 6,000 telephone conversations at one time, a task that would take 250 copper wires. The digital code can transmit print, audio, and image, separately or in combination, at the same time. The digital signal is also devoid of background noise and is much less vulnerable to distortion caused by external conditions such as the presence of magnetic fields. Educational networks became the logical first users of the technology of fiber optics. New facilities are using optical fibers in place of cable and older facilities are replacing cables with space-saving optical fibers. Fiber optics is definitely a case of smaller and smarter. The use of fiber optics

should also help to save scarce resources. Silicon, used to make the optical fibers, is the second most abundant element on the earth, whereas copper reserves are dwindling.

Microfiche.

Miniaturization has also had its effect on the print medium, making the printed word more easily and widely available for instructional and other purposes than the developers of movable type could have imagined. Perhaps the most universally used microform for reducing the size of the printed word so that it can be more widely disseminated is microfiche. In different microfiche formats, dozens, even hundreds, of pages of print can be recorded on a single piece of film. The contents of the entire *Encyclopedia Britannica,* for example, can be reduced to a stack of microfiches small enough to fit into a pocket.

Digitization of Print, Image, and Sound

Many people had their first experience with digitized images in the

late 1960s when they watched televised close-up pictures of the moon sent back to earth by U.S. astronauts. The images from their video cameras were converted into a digital code, a series of 1s and 0s, and the digitized information was transmitted to earth, where it was converted back into pictures.

Digitization has led inevitably to the development of a number of systems for storage, retrieval, and transmission of information. It has also led to the convergence of media formats, with the potential for making older formats obsolete. For example, if still and motion images can be combined on one disc, and the same piece of equipment can display both, why have filmstrip and 16mm projectors around? If laser discs are damage resistant and can store still and motion images, why maintain an inventory of fragile filmstrips and films? Let's look at some of the forms convergence has already taken.

❑ *CD-ROM (Read Only Memory).* Entire encyclopedias, as well as many other reference works, are

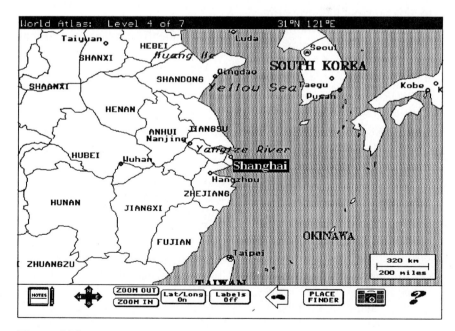

Figure 14.6

A map from Compton's *Multimedia Encyclopedia.* Four levels of map detail are available at the touch of a finger.

Figure 14.7
CD scanner, computer, video monitor, and printer—all are necessary to access, compile, and print information from the CD.

available on CD-ROM. Libraries, always pressed for space, are relying more and more on CD-ROM for reference services. When plugged into a computer, a CD-ROM reader allows users access to a dictionary, thesaurus, zip code directory, and other important references much more quickly than if they had to reach the printed work on a bookshelf.

❑ *CD-WORM (Write Once, Read Many Times).* This format attempts to get around the read only memory limitation of CD-ROM. The disc can be inscribed with the information of the user's choice—but only once. Then the disc can be read many times. This is a useful format for anyone with a unique data base that must be read often.

❑ *CD-I/Interactive.* In addition to verbal information, still images, graphics, audio, and computer software are to be incorporated into this format. It will be interactive. This format, if it survives,

would be very useful in designing training programs.

❑ *DVI/Digital Video Interactive.* This format has all the features of CD-I with the addition of moving images. Seventy-two minutes of video with digital sound can be put on this version of the compact disc. RCA, the developer of DVI, has been able to do this by means of a compression system similar to that used on telephone transmissions.

Telecommunications and the Erosion of Boundaries

Electronic communication can alter the institutional structures that have been put in place by prior means of communication and transportation. Until very recently, we operated on the assumption that the learner had to go to the "territory" of the teacher. In education, by relying on the school bus and the private car, we consolidated schools and built large public school complexes. In corporate training, companies such as Xerox, United Airlines, and AT&T built large and expensive training centers (often rented by less affluent companies). Trainees are flown to the centers for training sessions modeled for the most part on formal education.

The economics of bringing the learner to a training center is affected by the rising costs of transportation and by events that threaten the safety of valuable personnel, such as a plane crash. In addition to the price of transportation, industry must add the working time lost due to travel to arrive at a total cost. On the other hand, the costs of electronic communication keep coming down. Companies looking at the cost-effectiveness of training programs are likely to rely more on electronic learning systems. This can lead to a tug-of-war between what trainees find attractive and a company's demand for cost-effectiveness. For example, during

the Persian Gulf War, companies conducted meetings and training sessions via telecommunications instead of sending personnel overseas. The companies were delighted with the savings but the personnel were unhappy with losing the "vacation." Employees like getting together, not because they learn more or get more done, but because they enjoy the sociability and the opportunity to get away from the job. When using electronic communications, employers will need to find ways of building in substitute social occasions.

In education, parents are concerned about the sometimes excessively long bus rides their children take as well as the high cost of transportation. These two factors make it attractive to return to smaller and more numerous "attendance centers." Some futurists maintain that the home will be the ultimate attendance center, but this is hardly likely given the probable continuance of the two-job family. However, the promise of improved quality is a more compelling reason why education should find electronic communication attractive. With high-quality education deliverable by telecommunications, the neighborhood school can hold its own programmatically with the larger school. However, as with industry, schools also face social and political problems in reverting to smaller units. Competitive sports, particularly football, thrive in larger schools. We may settle on a compromise—in high schools electronic distribution within a larger than necessary plant, in elementary schools a return to more and smaller attendance centers.

Electronic distribution systems already have had an impact on education and undoubtedly will have a greater impact in the future. Just a few years ago, the individual instructor was practically the sole "distributor of instruction" on the educational scene.

Telecommunications and the Politics of Revolution

Electronic communication makes the "global village" a reality. The erosion of boundaries is most evident when internal turmoil occurs in a nation. Control of communications is one of the first objectives of a group trying to preserve or usurp power. But with the proliferation of electronic networks, it is impossible to control all channels of communication.

Wireless transmission of information can avoid the censorship of standard communication channels during a power struggle. In 1989, at the height of the May–June demonstrations in China that culminated in the Tiananmen Square massacre, the Chinese government attempted to cut off all communications to the outside world. However, reporters used cellular phones from their cars to keep information flowing through satellite transmission. Meanwhile, Chinese students around the world were communicating with students in China by means of phone lines and fax. For example, statements on the crisis by world leaders were translated into Chinese and faxed to China via satellite within an hour after their release. A worldwide solidarity among Chinese students was created.

In 1991 the leaders of the attempted coup in the USSR ignored the mass-communication possibilities of computer networks. They controlled the standard mass communication channels but not the dedicated computer phone lines. Computer networks were used to rally support for resistance to the coup, to keep groups opposed to the coup informed of developments, and to help tell the world what was going on. Meanwhile, reporters from other countries were using communications satellites to keep the rest of the globe instantly informed about the attempted coup. Events of this magnitude cannot be kept from the attention of the world. Nor can the world ignore the messages.

Learning Networks

Learning networks are evidence of the ability of electronics to erode artificial boundaries between people. The fourth and fifth grade students in Picton Primary School, New South Wales, Australia, and students in the West Pottsgrove Elementary School, Pennsylvania, are in constant touch with each other through electronic mail (E-mail). The students in each school compose messages on their computers, then send the messages through a modem to a satellite transmitting station. This project, now several years old, is an example of how telecommunication systems are linking students directly.

Of course, transworld linkages of schools are not as yet commonplace, but national networks are becoming so. Regional and national networks of schools are increasing each year. However, until recently, telecommunications networks have been dedicated to delivering instructional programming to classrooms in traditionally structured education. There is now a rapidly growing trend to (1) link students with each other; (2) link students directly with distant program sources, usually through computer and modem; and (3) offer educational experiences and degrees outside the traditional institutions. Some networks provide information to teachers on program possibilities and also offer students the opportunity to interact. For example, the McGraw-Hill Information Exchange (MIX) provides services for teachers and is also used for on-line classroom projects for students.

In the future, continuing professional development is likely to be carried out through learning networks rather than on campuses. Telecommunications networks make possible large-scale collaborative efforts between industry and educa-tion. The National Technological University (NTU) (see "Close-Up," p. 283) is an example of how such collaboration can create learning opportunities for practicing professionals beyond the traditional campus and degree programs. NTU delivers its programs by satellite.

The courses of the Electronic University Network are accessed by computer through phone lines. Unlike NTU, most of the Electronic University Network offerings are on the undergraduate level. Undergraduate degrees can be earned from Regents College of the State University of New York and Thomas A. Edison State College in New Jersey. A masters of business administration degree can be earned through the John F. Kennedy University in the San Francisco Bay area.

In the training arena, many companies are questioning the wisdom of transporting employees to large training centers when they can be trained just as well via telecommunications. When fuel prices go up, as they surely will, transportation

Figure 14.8
Satellites make communication between students in different parts of the world a reality.

costs will be one more argument, along with lost time, for using learning networks.

The telephone is likely to be the most important general link to data services. Sprint, one of the newer long distance companies, at present has the largest network of telecommunications systems. AT&T's Integrated Services Digital Network (ISDN) will make possible multiple services while also carrying video signals. Based on the optical fiber, the system will be cheaper, more powerful, and of a higher quality than existing technology. With a hookup to a TV set and a computer, ISDN would allow subscribers to talk on the phone, have their utility use metered, receive E-mail, and watch television all at the same time. Because the phone is the most universal of all electronic instruments, ISDN services would become instantly available to virtually every home and business. The humble telephone, sending digitized information over optical fiber, could result in the convergence of electronic delivery systems, including cable television.

Later in this chapter we discuss traditional barriers to the full acceptance of technologically based instruction in education. Telecommunications networks are most likely to break down those barriers by creating their own learning opportunities and even creating new institutions. The present system of education was built on the necessity of having the student come to the place where instruction is delivered; now information can be delivered directly to the student. We have the option to decentralize education whenever we so choose.

In the long run the development of electronic systems for the distribution of instruction will have a profound effect on the organization and administration of our educational facilities. Advances in technology have now made it administratively and economically feasible to educate smaller groups of students in a larger number of instructional settings. Proponents of decentralization as a step toward greater public participation in the control of public education may well have an unexpected and powerful ally in technological advances such as electronic systems for the distribution of instruction.

THE SCHOOL OF THE FUTURE

The Hazards of Predicting the Future

The publication *Visions 2000* is a bold attempt by Alberta Province, Canada, to project the rate of adoption of new technologies in provincial schools by the year 2000.[2] Alberta prides itself on its history of acceptance of technology and is determined to maintain its leadership.

But predicting future developments in technology is far easier than predicting changes in social organizations. The tendency of social institutions is to maintain the status quo. Innovations that change patterns of relationships, distribution of economic rewards, and security of employment will be resisted. It is difficult to foresee the way in which an innovation will affect social organizations and how they will respond.

There is also a tendency in education to predict future organizational patterns based on our hopes and wishes. The people responsible for the Alberta study predict a dramatic shift in the way teachers and students in the future will spend their time. Because technological developments can facilitate individual learning, they want the organization of instruction to change accordingly. Therefore, they predict that by the year 2000 teachers and students will spend 50 percent of their time in individualized instruction. A follow-up publication by Alberta Ed-

ucation[3] proposes an institutional structure that would implement the projections of *Visions 2000*. But the proposal would mean drastic changes in the organizational relationships and governance of the provincial schools. As we will see, whether or not this happens depends less on technology than on how the pressures and forces outside and inside education are resolved. Predictions in the social arena are influenced by our values and our vested interests.

Technology and Professions

We know that technology can change professions and professional relationships. Pharmacy and journalism are two examples that illustrate an important principle: power structures depend on who controls the tools and materials of production.

Over a long period of time, pharmaceutical companies have been able to incorporate the pharmacist's skills in and knowledge of compounding drugs into the manufacture of pharmaceuticals. Pharmacologists have been developing more complex drugs so rapidly that pharmacists have lost control over the materials and have become pill dispensers rather than pill makers. To keep their professional status pharmacists had to expand on another traditional role: counsel to the patient on prescriptions issued by physicians. The main work of the pharmacist now (besides running a small business) is to act as an informed intermediary between physician and patient when prescriptions are involved, checking the compatibility of prescribed drugs and advising the public on over-the-counter, proprietary medications. This type of professional role shift is implied when we talk about teachers becoming

---

[2]   *Visions 2000* (Edmonton, Alberta: Alberta Education, 1987).

[3]   Warren E. Hathaway, *Education and Technology at the Crossroads: Choosing a New Direction* (Edmonton, Alberta: Alberta Education, 1989).

managers of instruction rather than deliverers of information.

In journalism, control over the tools of production shifted from typesetter to reporter. Before the advent of the computer, type was set mechanically by members of the International Typographical Union (ITU). Newspapers and magazines in particular were so dependent on the typesetter that the ITU virtually controlled the industry. The computer made it possible for reporters and editors to compose the type at the same time they wrote the copy. As a result control shifted from the ITU to the journalists.

In education, we don't like to talk or even think about power structures. We are above such crass considerations. But, for example, isn't negotiation over teacher-pupil ratios part of the power structure? And when we use the term *empowerment*, aren't we really talking about the power structure?

Technology and Education

Because our society in general is receptive to new technology, we tend to assume that the subcultures of our society are also. This simply isn't so. Education is the classic example of a subculture that has a spotty record at best in using technological developments to change the way in which the work of instruction is performed. In areas other than instruction, such as keeping pupil attendance records for state aid, accounting and disbursement of funds, and maintaining inventory, education has adopted technology to become more efficient. But the organization of instruction is basically the same as 100 years ago.

New technology carries no imperative. What matters is how it is perceived. If a new development is useful, easy to master, and nonthreatening, the likelihood of acceptance is very good. The problem is that people within the same organization vary in their percep-

tions of new technology according to how it will impact what they do. For example, the introduction of the overhead projector was accepted and usually welcomed by teachers because it was viewed as a more versatile chalkboard, fitted easily into their established practice, and reinforced their status in the classroom. But if a principal joins a satellite network because he wants his school to benefit from the coursework offered, his staff may perceive the technologically delivered courses as an affront or a challenge to their professional status.

Courses delivered by satellite, computer networks, or on interactive video programs are more likely to be accepted by rural schools because their staffs cannot support a full curriculum. In the 1960s the Ford Foundation sponsored a program that used filmed courses to teach physics, chemistry, and the humanities to students in rural high schools. The main purpose of the research was to determine if technology could be used to expand the course offerings of isolated, rural

high schools. The program was eminently successful. Currently, programs such as TI-IN are delivering courses in similar situations by satellite and computer network.

We already know the answer to the basic question these programs are asking: yes, technology can expand curriculum offerings. We know that technology can fundamentally alter the instructional organization, as well as the curriculum, of public education. What we really need to know is why technologically delivered courses do not survive the experimental period. To help find an answer to that question we need to look at why many schools resist the kind of change that technology can bring about.

Organizational Impediments

Any casual observer of the daily goings-on in schools, higher education institutions, corporate training sites, and other organized instructional settings will notice that the tools and techniques discussed throughout this book are not actu-

Figure 14.9
The lecture and textbook, not the newer media and technologies, still dominate formal education.

ally employed to any extent remotely resembling the extent to which they are talked about by advocates (Figure 14.9). Some corporations make extensive use of advanced media and technology systems, but fewer schools and colleges do. Why is the adoption rate of technology so low, especially among public formal education systems?

The 1983 report of the National Commission on Excellence in Education pointed out a number of shortcomings in the American public education system, among them inadequate academic content, low standards and expectations, insufficient time spent on learning, poor quality of teaching, and lack of leadership. Some observers have drawn similar conclusions about higher education as well. Many, such as Reigeluth, feel that such shortcomings are symptoms of a more fundamental problem with the structure of institutions in public education:

Just as the one-room schoolhouse, which was so appropriate for an agricultural society, proved to be inadequate for an industrial society, so our present system is proving to be inadequate for an information society. It is the fundamental structure of our educational system that is at the heart of our current problems. . . .

Microcomputers are accelerating the trend toward increased use of nonhuman resources in the education of our children, but the current structure of our educational system

Figure 14.10
This Tennessee one-room schoolhouse built in 1936 was designed primarily for lecture instruction but had to accommodate individual and small-group study as well as children of different grade levels.

Figure 14.11
The modern media center facilitates individualized and cooperative learning.

cannot adequately accommodate the effective use of these powerful tools.[4]

The sorts of structural problems that Reigeluth is referring to exist at two levels: (1) the structure of the classroom as a learning environment and (2) the organizational structure of the school, college, or corporation attempting to deliver instruction. We will look at these two levels separately.

Structure of the Classroom.

The typical setup of the classroom, almost everywhere in the western world and at virtually every level, has the fundamental weakness of being organized around a single adult who attempts to orchestrate more or less diverse activities for a generally large group of learners. This one person typically is expected to be responsible for selecting and organizing the content of lessons; designing materials; producing materials; diagnosing individual needs; developing tests; delivering instruction orally to the group or through other media individually or in different groupings; administering, scoring, and interpreting tests; prescribing remedial activities; and coordinating the numberless logistical details that hold the whole enterprise together. Other sectors of society have long since recognized that improvements in effectiveness and productivity require division of labor, but this concept has not yet been accepted in the world of formal education.

An example of a profession in which division of labor has been accepted is that of medicine. Physicians have tended toward the practice of specializations, enabling each to keep better abreast of innovations in practice. Second, physicians have

adopted differentiated staffing within their offices and clinics so that less critical functions can be delegated to paraprofessionals and technicians, reserving to the physicians the function of diagnosing and treating conditions that merit their attention (Figure 14.12). Physicians have an incentive to accept this restructuring in those societies which have a free marketplace for their services. In this environment, embracing a division of labor increases their profits. Educators work in a very different environment, as we will discuss a bit later.

Alternative classroom structures do exist and, in fact, have been adopted in many places. In Chapter 12 you encountered programmed tutoring, PSI, and audio-tutorial systems, each of which provides a total and radically different pattern for setting up a learning environment.

More recently, a plan that incorporates virtually all of the technologies of instruction but centers on the notion of *division of labor* has been field-tested in a number of countries, among them Indonesia, Liberia, and the Philippines. The classroom teacher, who may not be a fully certified teacher-training institution graduate, uses materials that are centrally designed and rather fully scripted to lead participatory lessons. Parents, volunteers, and student tutors share other teaching and logistical tasks. Thus, there is a division of labor both in the design and the implementation of instruction. The plan takes a somewhat different shape in each locale and is known by a different name in each country, but the generic name and concept is *low-cost learning technology*.[5] It is essentially a systematic method for implementing a variety of managerial and instructional innovations. It focuses

Figure 14.12
Division of labor has helped extend health care without a proportionate increase in the number of physicians.

on improving student learning outcomes while reducing overall costs, especially labor costs. This concept has shown sufficient promise that the U.S. Agency for International Development (AID) has made a major commitment to implementing it in some thirty additional countries.

Structure of the Organization.

The underlying reason why many teachers and trainers teach the way they do, embracing the methods they do—however inefficient or ineffective they may be—is that they are following the "rules of the game" that their daily environment reinforces. A useful way of analyzing this situation is to compare teaching as a craft with instruction as a technology.[6] In a *craft* activity the emphasis is on the use of tools by the skilled craftsperson. In a technology the emphasis is on the design of tools that produce replicable, reliable results. In a craft ad hoc decision making is valued, whereas in a technology value is placed on incorporating those decisions into the design of the tools themselves (e.g., the scripted lesson plan used in low-cost learning technology).

The organizational structures that evolve because of craft thinking are fundamentally different from those

4   Charles M. Reigeluth, "Restructuring: The Key to a Better Educational System for an Information Society," *IDD&E Working Paper* 16 (Syracuse, NY: School of Education, Syracuse University, 1983), p. 1.

5   Daryl G. Nichols, "Low-Cost Learning Systems: The General Concept and Specific Examples," *NSPI Journal* (September 1982): 4–8.

6   Robert Heinich, "Instructional Technology and the Structure of Education," *Educational Communication and Technology Journal* (Spring 1985): 9–13.

Figure 14.13
How can one teacher provide individualized instruction *and* take care of the thousand and one details of classroom management?

that evolve from engineering or technological thinking. Because a craft makes a virtue of the use of tools, the power and the discretion of a craftsperson in any given situation are very high, whereas the power and the discretion of management in the same situation are relatively low. However, in an engineering operation, the power and discretion of the individual operator are low, and the power and discretion of the team designing the required tools are extremely high. It is inadvisable to attempt to place the products developed by an engineering team into the organizational structure of a craft. The craftspeople will have a natural tendency to modify arbitrarily the engineered products.

This is precisely what happens in traditional education and training. The organizational structures are built around a craft model, a model that gives considerable discretion to each instructor in the classroom. When engineered products (e.g., fully scripted lesson plans) are placed in this environment, the individual instructor constantly second-guesses decisions that have already been built into the instructional system. The instructor tends to reduce such systematic products to separate

bits of material to be used at his or her own discretion.

The craft tradition of education leads to a structure that stops short of developing specific instructional products centrally because it assumes that such specific decisions are made by the person in face-to-face contact with learners. It is expected that any products that are developed may be used or ignored by the instructor in the classroom. In this structure, technological products represent an added cost, serving only to aid the teacher when he or she deems it appropriate. Solutions that increase overall costs, besides demanding special effort to produce and implement, are not likely to flourish.

If this analysis is correct, if the rules of the game do determine how educators act, reforms must be made in the rules of the game. History shows that changes in performance do follow changes in the rules. Consider the following rule changes in public education: *Brown v. Topeka Board of Education* (racial desegregation of schools), the inclusion of questions on "new math" in the national college entrance exams (adoption of "new math" into the curriculum), and state-legislated consolidation of schools (reforms in

school organization and curriculum).

A bold attempt to deal with the rigidities of the education system, and change the rules of the game, is the New American Schools Development Corporation (NASDC), an outgrowth of President Bush's education initiative, "America 2000." The Board of Directors of NASDC is composed primarily of business and industry executives. The purpose of the corporation is to fund bold new ways of designing and running schools that produce dramatic increases in learning. Appropriate use of technology is at the center of NASDC's goal to increase instructional productivity. The aim is to have at least one such school in each congressional district. The business community will be the primary source of the funds to run the schools. Only time will tell whether this attempt to bypass the education establishment will break the restrictions the present governance structure imposes on schooling.

Forces Tending Toward Change

The preceding argument leads to the conclusion that major restructuring of education both at the classroom level and at the highest organizational level will be required in order for media and technology to deliver the benefits on a massive basis that they already deliver on a piecemeal basis and in selected cases. This is a long-term process and one not sure of success. However, there are forces working in the direction of change.

Accountability in Education and Instruction.

For more than two decades there has been a trend in education toward *accountability.* Basically, accountability is a demand for some form of public demonstration that schools do what they are supposed to do and do it effectively. Included is the idea that each teacher is accountable for the progress or lack of progress in his or her class.

Much of the impetus toward accountability has come from increasing competition for the tax dollar of the public—a general social and political phenomenon certain to continue in the foreseeable future. Taxpayers hard-pressed for money to support schools want to be assured that their taxes are being well spent. They are concerned both with the cost-benefit ratio of instruction (whether or not we are getting the right kinds of benefit from instruction for the money that is being spent on it) and with the cost-effectiveness of instruction (whether or not these benefits are being achieved as effectively as possible at the lowest possible cost).

Not only a large segment of the public but also many educators support the idea that the schools should be held accountable for the learning progress of students. These educators claim that some teachers are too easily diverted from concentration on the learning tasks at hand to unnecessary and unrelated class activities. Some educators further claim that society has asked the schools to do so many jobs that the main purpose, instruction, is lost, or at least diluted, in the process.

This demand by the public and by concerned educators for some sort

of accountability seems reasonable. Accountability has, however, met with considerable resistance from many members of the education profession. They argue that the really vital outcomes of the educational process cannot be quantified or measured, that the only learning outcomes that can be measured are trivial ones—dates, names of historical personages, rules of grammar, multiplication tables, and so on. They further argue that accountability requires determining goals in advance of instruction, thus ruling out serendipitous opportunities that arise during instruction to teach material not specifically covered by predetermined goals. Opponents also claim the demand for accountability will lead to undervaluation of dedicated teachers who work with low-ability students, who have far greater difficulty achieving specific predetermined objectives than high-ability students.

These and other objections to accountability have a certain validity, and we hope the concept will develop in such a manner that legitimate qualms can be addressed. In any case, it seems reasonable to assume that the educational establishment, and individual teachers within the establishment, will become more and more publicly accountable for the outcome of the educational enterprise.

Perhaps the most widely known and highly publicized manifestation of the trend toward accountability has been the National Assessment of Educational Progress (NAEP) program. Under this program, general achievement tests are given periodically at various grade levels throughout the United States. The tests are intended for long-range comparisons between groups of students at various periods of time. They compare how well students do on standard measures of learning in different parts of the country and in various kinds of schools. So far the results have been used simply to determine whether the schools in general are achieving what they are

supposed to achieve. No attempt has yet been made to use NAEP to compare specific schools for instructional effectiveness, but many educators are naturally apprehensive that the program may in the future come to be used for this purpose.

Many states have developed similar assessment tests. The grade levels at which the tests are administered vary and the consequences of inadequate performance differ, but all the states with such exams are using them to measure the effectiveness of their schools *in general.* Some states use the tests to identify pupils who do not reach the standards and prescribe remediation. Several states have also developed tests of teacher competence, primarily to determine which teachers need additional training. Education professionals have generally opposed both types of evaluation. But despite this opposition the push for national and state assessment programs is getting stronger.

The latest entry in the accountability arena is "America 2000," a proposal by President George Bush to make American schools the best in the world by the year 2000. The proposal has six goals with the third directly aimed at school accountability:

American students will leave grades four, eight, and twelve having demonstrated competency in challenging subject matter including English, mathematics, science, history, and

Figure 14.14
Technology makes cooperative learning much more feasible.

geography; and every school in America will ensure that all students learn to use their minds well, so they may be prepared for responsible citizenship, further learning, and productive employment in our modern economy.[7]

This proposal is far more sweeping than any previous programs. A battery of tests, called the American Achievement Tests, based on the five core subjects mentioned above, will be used to identify and reward outstanding schools. Students who do exceptionally well will be awarded scholarships to college. Special efforts will be made to keep communities informed as to the standing of their schools in relation to other schools. Colleges and universities will be encouraged to use the results of the tests as part of the admission procedure. Employers will be urged to use the tests as part of the hiring process. Probably the most controversial part of the proposal deals with the teaching profession. Merit pay is endorsed, and academies will be established to upgrade the skills

---

[7]   *America 2000: An Education Strategy* (Washington, DC: U.S. Department of Education, 1991).

of teachers of the five core subjects. This is truly an ambitious proposal and one that involves the national government in an arena that is legally the responsibility of the states.

The trend toward accountability and public disclosure of educational achievement will result in closer ties between the general public and the educational enterprise. Educators will be called upon to explain how their selected instructional methods and materials relate to the attainment of instructional objectives. They will also be called upon to defend their selections in terms of cost-benefit ratios and cost-effectiveness. Education and evaluation of education will become public processes rather than purely private ones between teachers and students. It behooves all instructors, then, to be prepared to defend their choices of materials and methods. If they are not prepared to do so, they run the increasing risk that those materials and methods will be judged by the public as dispensable frills.

Fortunately for those concerned particularly with the use of media in the schools, instructional technology allows instructors to construct flexible yet structured designs for achievement of specific educational

objectives that can be laid out for public inspection (Figure 14.15). As pointed out throughout this text, such designs, when properly planned and adhered to, can be demonstrated to result in consistent and readily apparent learning advances, readily apparent to the teacher, the student, and the public. Accountability need not necessarily make us apprehensive. We can, rather, look upon it as an opportunity to consolidate the partnership between home and school, a trend that innovative technology itself has done so much to foster.

Lifelong Learning Systems.

Lifelong learning has long been an ideal of professional educators. Advances in the products and processes of instructional technology have brought us to the verge of making that ideal attainable for millions of citizens. Indeed, we might say that in this respect, at least, our society has been lucky. Never before in our development as a people have we had a greater need for lifelong learning.

Fifty years ago, it was possible for a doctor, a teacher, a scientist, or, for that matter, an electrician or a

Figure 14.15
Technology makes instruction visible. As parents and other community members get involved in the schools as reading tutors, volunteer aides, and the like, structured materials make their help more effective. By the same token, teachers gain credibility in the eyes of the general public by using well-designed materials.

typewriter repairperson to be trained in a field and remain reasonably competent in it with little or no updating for the rest of his or her life. However, scientific and technological knowledge is increasing at such a rapid pace that this is no longer possible. Indeed, for millions of us, lifelong education is something more than an ideal—it has become a necessity.

In our mobile society today, many people switch from the field in which they were trained to another, or to several others, during their working lives. Early retirement systems in some professions and businesses have contributed to this trend, and many people in our present-day economic system become what economists call "structurally unemployed" and must seek new jobs and careers outside the field of their expertise or training. For all these people, access to an educational system geared to lifelong education is virtually a necessity.

There are also millions of people who wish to keep up with a rapidly changing world, many of whom are beyond the age of formal schooling. These people, too, will be demanding access to lifelong learning; and, indeed, there will be more and more such people as the average age of the population continues to climb.

Obviously, the products and processes of instructional technology are destined to play a major role in the development of lifelong learning systems. These systems will involve audio- and videocassettes and discs, electronic learning devices, electronic systems for delivery of instruction to wherever the learner may be (school, factory, office, community center, or home), and numerous other kinds of instructional technology. Without the products and processes of instructional technology, lifelong learning would likely be destined to remain an ideal. With them, we have reason to hope that it will soon become a reality for the millions of people who need and desire it.

Trends to Watch

Private Schools.
The recent expansion of the number and variety of private schools is likely to continue. There will be as many varieties of private schools as there are reasons why parents avoid the public schools, from a desire for a more rigorous academic program to indoctrination in religious faith. However, this is a trend sensitive to economic conditions; private schools are expensive.

The Gap Between Knowledge Haves and Have-Nots.
Traditionally the schools have been the avenue to equal access to opportunity. They have tried to even out the disparities in educational opportunities between lower and upper-income families. Today, this means making sure that all students have full access to information handling experiences. We know that many children from upper-income families have access to computers at home. The school must make sure that children from low-income families also have access to computer facilities. If they don't, the gap will continue to widen.

Increased Use of Networks.
Networks at the state and local levels will increase (see Chapter 10). More and more school districts are forming regional networks to share instructional expertise and to make instruction more effective and efficient. State departments will use satellite transmission to assume an active role in curriculum implementation.

Increased Accountability of Education.
Instruction delivered by technology is much more open to external evaluation than when conducted behind closed classroom doors. So far, the National Assessment of Educational Progress and the various state evaluation programs have not gone much beyond general comparisons. In the future comparisons are likely to become much more specific, and above- and below-average performers (schools, teachers, and pupils) will be identified.

State Adoption of Technologically Based Instruction.
The practice of state adoption of textbooks has been around for a long time. Until recently, other media formats have been excluded from consideration. Several states are now encouraging publishers to submit "media programs" and "technology tools" for state adoption. This is tantamount to admitting technology into the mainstream of curriculum implementation on an equal footing with textbooks.

Accreditation of Technology-Based Courses.
In addition to state adoption, increased use of telecommunications and the positive results from programs such as the TI-IN network will promote the notion of giving students full credit for successful completion of courses delivered by technology. As more and more colleges accept such courses for advanced placement and as state departments of education get more involved in telecommunications, pressure will be put on the regional accreditation agencies to give full credit to students taking those courses.

School District Development of Accredited Courses.
As regional accreditation agencies set the criteria for accreditation of technology-based courses, school districts will develop and deliver courses based on those criteria in the same way that they now hire certificated teachers to fulfill accreditation requirements.

Flexibility in Teacher Certification Requirements.
The recent trend toward loosening teacher certification requirements, primarily to permit knowledgeable laypersons to teach, will probably be

CLOSE-UP

Professional Careers in Educational Technology

This book has been dedicated to helping you become a more effective instructor, or manager of instruction, through application of instructional media and technology to your teaching tasks. You may, however, wish to specialize in the fascinating and fast-growing field of instructional technology. (A directory of graduate programs in instructional technology is published by the Association for Educational Communications and Technology.[a]) If so, what opportunities for professional employment are likely to be open to you? Unlike some education areas, instructional technology is becoming more and more pervasive in formal and nonformal education with each passing year, and, correspondingly, an ever larger number of people are being employed in this specialty.

Traditionally, the area in which the growth of instructional technology has created career opportunities is the various media programs at school, district, regional, and state levels. At all of these levels media professionals are employed to run programs and, depending on the size of the organization, produce materials for use in schools. As school districts and regional media centers have built up their collections of audiovisual materials for distribution, they have employed instructional media professionals as selectors of these materials. In formal educational settings, media selection specialists determine not only what materials will be added to collections but also how well collections of materials are serving the curricular and instructional needs of the institution. In training programs, media specialists frequently evaluate the effectiveness of the programs as well as determine the materials to be used in them. Another major career area at all education levels is the professional management of media collections, including classification, storage, and distribution.

Instructional product design—the development of validated and reliable instructional materials—has been an important specialty in the field of instructional technology for some time. Publishers and producers of instructional mate-

---

[a] Donald P. Ely, ed., *Educational Media and Technology Yearbook*, 1992 (Englewood, CO: Libraries Unlimited, 1992).

---

accelerated by the acceptance of courses delivered by technology and the advantages of having a differentiated staff. Certification of educational personnel somewhere between paraprofessional and full professional is likely. Future schools will have a more varied instructional roster than in the past.

More Cooperative and Individualized Instruction. Any substantial increases in individualized instruction will depend on the acceptance of technology as a legitimate avenue for learning. As that occurs, we will see more and more

students accomplishing learning goals on their own. The social aspects of group learning will be fulfilled primarily through activities based on cooperative methods.

TRAINING PROGRAMS OF THE FUTURE

Increased Use of Telecommunications

The costs of bringing groups of people together for training purposes is becoming excessive. Telecommunications is one way to lower costs. The long-distance telephone companies

are, of course, doing all they can to make telecommunications an attractive alternative.

Growth of Custom Program Developers

Another alternative to bringing trainees together is to send training packages to the trainee. The past two decades have seen the growth of companies whose specialty is the design of training programs. The training package is a cost-effective solution particularly when the package does not become outdated quickly.

rials, along with school districts, community colleges, and colleges and universities, are constantly on the alert for specialists trained in the skills of product design. Computer-assisted instruction, interactive video, and other emerging forms of individualized instruction constitute an important growth area within the instructional product design field.

Organizations other than schools also require specialists in educational technology. Health-care institutions, for example, are heavily involved in instructional technology and have been employing an increasing number of professionals to help develop the instruction used in those programs. Industrial training also presents a growing area of employment. In this area, skills in developing instructional materials are an asset. As service industries have increased in importance in our economy, training programs for service personnel have correspondingly increased. Organizations that design programs for training service personnel employ, both on a permanent and a freelance basis, people skilled in designing instructional media.

Training programs in business and industry have need for a variety of professionals. Some of these specialties are

❑ *Training coordinator.* Enrolls participants, schedules courses, orders class materials and media, and handles other administrative matters.

❑ *Trainer.* Presents information, leads discussions, and manages learning experiences.

❑ *Instructional designer.* Translates training needs into training programs, determines media to be used, designs course materials.

❑ *Training specialist.* Assesses training needs, designs overall programs.

❑ *Training manager.* Plans and organizes training programs, hires staff, prepares and manages budgets.

Many if not most training programs rely heavily on instructional media. Consequently, specialists in instructional technology are in considerable demand in these programs.

Growth of Workstation Training

One of the fastest growing techniques for improving human performance is the job (or performance) aid. These are sets of procedures that workers follow to make sure a task is performed properly. The instructions may be verbal (print or audio) or visual (still or motion) or a combination. The important distinguishing characteristic of the job aid is that it is used at the workstation, not at a training site. For employees working at a keyboard, the job aid for a particular task can be summoned up at the touch of a key. Originally improving performance was the purpose of job aids, but training directors are broadening their use to include instruction at the workstation.

Professionalization of the Field

The need for professional expertise in the design and development of instruction becomes much more apparent when technology is involved. The Association for Educational Communications and Technology and the National Society for Performance and Instruction have put together a set of standards for the certification of instructional designers. There has also been a movement by a consortium of companies to codify the skills needed for developing training programs. The American Society for Training and Development has published a comprehensive guide to the skills required for the various levels of training program development. All of these efforts indicate a growing professionalization of the field that is sure to continue into the future.

FUTURE TECHNOLOGIES OF INSTRUCTION

There are many technological developments that could lead to major impacts on education and training. For our purposes we will look at some promising work going on in learning styles, artificial intelligence and expert systems, new information technologies, psychotechnology, and biotechnology. We seem to be on the verge of making quantum leaps in surmounting some long-term barriers to learning.

Learning Styles and Individualized Instruction

True individualization—a different learning program for each student—has long been a goal of mass-education systems. In the United States systematic programs of individualized instruction go back at least to the programmed workbooks of the 1920s. The wave of innovation in the 1960s saw a resurgence of schemes for individualization such as Individually Prescribed Instruction (IPI), Individually Guided Education (IGE), and Program for Learning in Accordance with Needs

(PLAN). For various reasons those innovations have not flourished. However, Public Law 94-142, passed by Congress in 1975, mandates an Individualized Education Program (IEP) for each handicapped child in school. Meanwhile, research into the psychological processes of learning has underscored the importance of matching students to instructional treatments.

We have a long way to go before we can be confident of our theoretical base and before we have diagnostic tools of fully proven value in the realm of learning styles. But on another front, the work in expert systems may be addressing the equally important question of what technology is needed to make the connection between learning styles and instructional treatments.

Artificial Intelligence and Expert Systems

Almost immediately after electronic computers became a reality, scientists were intrigued by what they saw as parallels between the human brain and how the computer processes information. They asked if the

computer could "learn" as well as retrieve and collate information. These experiments led to computers playing games such as checkers and chess with human experts—and winning. Then they asked, if the computer can learn the rules, strategies, and moves of a game, why couldn't it then enable an amateur to play on an equal footing with an expert? It certainly could. But, they reasoned, why limit this capability to playing games? Why not see if this "artificial intelligence" can be applied to more useful problems?

This line of experimentation led to the development of so-called *expert systems*. These are software packages that allow the collective wisdom of experts in a given field to be brought to bear on a problem. One of the first such systems to be developed is called *MYCIN*. This is a program that helps train doctors to make accurate diagnoses of infectious diseases on the basis of tests and patient information fed into the computer. Expert systems are slowly making their way into education. Several programs have been developed to aid administrators, such as *The Negotiation Edge*. After feeding

Figure 14.16
Hypermedia programs make a wealth of information available at the click of the mouse.

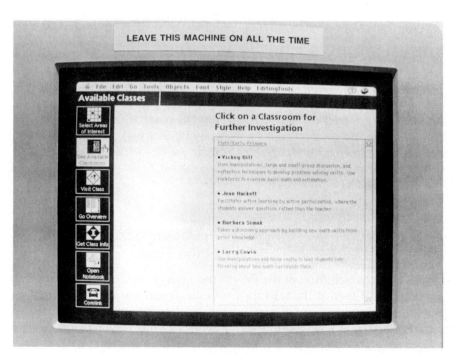

into the computer a series of adjectives that describe the adversary, the program offers advice on how to conduct a negotiating session. *SCHOLAR* is an expert system on the geography of South America. It is an example of a "mixed-initiative" system. The student and the system can ask questions of each other. *SCHOLAR* can adjust its instructional strategy according to the context of the student's inquiry. Scholastic Publications has developed a unique program that learns the rules of any game as it plays with its human partner. The student may play the game with self-chosen rules but must identify for the computer the criteria for winning the game. The computer absorbs the rules and eventually wins. Another expert system, *The Intelligent Catalog,* helps a student learn to use reference tools. Any learning task that requires problem solving lends itself to an expert system, for example, qualitative analysis in chemistry.

An example closer to our concern with individualized learning is an expert system called *CLASS LD* developed at Utah State University. The program classifies learning disabilities by using an elaborate set of rules contributed by experts. In tests the program has proven to be at least as accurate as informed special education practitioners. The next step is to develop a software package that will design an Individualized Education Program for a child diagnosed by *CLASS LD.* Because many learning-disabled children are in mainstreamed classes, the expert system would make manageable the classroom teacher's job of providing appropriate instruction. The school benefits from more effective and more efficient decision making.

But further down the road is an expert system that could truly individualize learning. Based on research on learning styles, we can imagine an expert system that learns all the important aptitudes and personality traits of an individual. When presented with a large

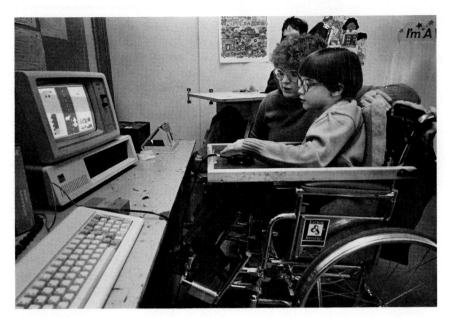

Figure 14.17
Fast-action video games provide motivating practice in hand-eye coordination, especially valuable for those with motor handicaps.

body of material to be mastered, the learner uses the expert system as a guide to learning the content in the most effective manner. The program adjusts the content, instructional method, and medium to the learning style of the student. The learner is in charge of the program, not the experts. When this becomes possible, we will really have individualized learning.

A new professional specialty has emerged from the development of expert systems. The term "knowledge engineers" has been coined to describe the people who work with experts in a field to assemble and organize a body of knowledge and then design the software package that makes it possible to train someone to become skilled in the area or to enable anyone to call upon the skills of experts to solve a problem. Knowledge engineering is a logical extension of instructional design.

The Learner and New Information Technologies

Predictions of the future are predictably unreliable. A chagrined futurist

once remarked, "He who lives by the crystal ball learns to eat ground glass." We can safely forecast, however, that the successful citizen of tomorrow will be a manipulator of data stored and accessed in ways we are now only conceptualizing. This ability will be "in the bones" as surely as manipulating electronic toys and games are in the bones of today's children. And that's where it all starts.

The popularity of toys and games controlled by a microprocessor attests to the child's fascination with manipulating a source of information to achieve a goal. Maneuvering a vehicle with a remote control unit may be more than satisfying; it may also be making connections with the future world of robotics. *Electronic games* are not only fun; they may also be a link to future information technologies. We will take a closer look at electronic games from those for preschoolers to those in video arcades (Figure 14.17). But as we do, keep in mind that the long-term effect is likely to be more important than our short-term evaluation of the instruction delivered by the

Professional Organizations in Educational Technology

Whether your interest in instructional technology is general or whether you intend to specialize in this area of education, you should be familiar with some of the major organizations dedicated to its advancement.

The Association for Educational Communications and Technology (AECT)

AECT is an umbrella organization intended to encompass all the substantive areas of educational technology. These various areas are expressed as divisions within the organizational structure of the association. For example, the Division of Educational Media Management is concerned with the administration of media programs and media collections. The Industrial Training and Education Division is concerned with the application of instructional technology to training programs. The Division of Instructional Development is concerned with analysis of instructional problems and the design of effective solutions. The Division of Telecommunications is concerned with instruction delivered via radio, television, and other telecommunications media. Other divisions of AECT reflect other professional concerns within instructional technology. AECT publishes a monthly journal, *TechTrends,* and a research quarterly, *Educational Technology Research and Development.* Its annual convention features a major exhibition of audiovisual hardware and software in addition to a broad-ranging program of educational seminars and workshops.

AECT
1025 Vermont Avenue, NW
Suite 820
Washington, DC 20005

American Library Association (ALA)

The ALA is an organization of professionals concerned with the organization, classification, storage and retrieval, and distribution of print and nonprint materials. The ALA has divisions for particular interests. The American Association of School Librarians, for example, is concerned with management of materials collections at the school level.

ALA
50 East Huron Street
Chicago, IL 60611

American Society for Training and Development (ASTD)

ASTD is an association composed primarily of professionals engaged in training programs in business and industry. ASTD is by far the largest association for people working in training and management development programs in business, industry, government, and other institutions. In 1964 the original name, American Society of Training Directors, was changed to reflect the broadened base of interests of its members. The society publishes a monthly journal, *Training and Development Journal;* sponsors studies of problems in the training field; and conducts an annual convention that includes a varied and significant educational program. ASTD is organized into divisions, including one on Instructional Technology.

ASTD
Box 1443
1630 Duke Street
Alexandria, VA 22313

National Society for Performance and Instruction (NSPI)

This organization originally was called the National Society for Programmed Instruction, but its name was changed to reflect broadened interests. NSPI members are interested in the study and application of performance and instructional technologies. NSPI membership of some 2,500 includes a mixture of people in business, industry, the military, allied health professions, government, and formal education. The society publishes a monthly journal, *Performance and Instruction,* and a research quarterly, *Performance Improvement Quarterly.*

NSPI
1300 L Street, NW, Suite 1250
Washington, DC 20005

Association for the Development of Computer-Based Instructional Systems (ADCIS)

The general scope of this relatively young organization is evident in its title. At present ADCIS has thirteen interest groups, for example, Computer-Based Training, Emerging Technologies, and Educators of the Handicapped. The annual conference of ADCIS features software and hardware exhibits as well as presentations on recent developments in this rapidly growing field. The organization publishes the *Journal of Computer-Based Instruction.*

ADCIS
Miller Hall 409
Western Washington University
Bellingham, WA 98225

International Visual Literacy Association (IVLA)

The International Visual Literacy Association (IVLA) is dedicated to exploring the concept of visual literacy—how we use visuals for communication and how we interpret these visuals. It is particularly concerned with the development of instructional materials designed to foster skills in interpreting visuals. Most IVLA members are in higher or public education.

Center for Visual Literacy
Arizona State University
Tempe, AZ 85287

International Television Association (ITVA)

The International Television Association (ITVA) serves the needs of professional video communicators in nonbroadcast settings. Most of its members are in industry, health services, and the military.

ITVA
6311 N. O'Connor Road
Irving, TX 75039

(continued)

CLOSE-UP

Professional Organizations, continued

International Interactive Communications Society (IICS)

This is another small organization spawned by new technology. It is an association of some 1,400 communications industry professionals dedicated to the advancement of interactive video and related technologies. IICS provides a forum for users, manufacturers, and producers to share applications and techniques of electronic interactive media. Currently, IICS places emphasis on local activity by its chapters. The group's publication program includes a newsletter and a quarterly journal.

IICS
P.O. Box 1862
Lake Oswego, OR 97035

State Organizations

Several of the national professional organizations have state affiliates (AECT, ALA) or local chapters (NSPI, ASTD). By joining one or more of these, you will quickly come into contact with nearby professionals who share your particular concerns.

---

games. How much content children learn from these games will be less important, in the long run, than *how* they learned. "The medium *is* the message," as Marshall McLuhan said.

Most visible because of their broad popularity are the Nintendo games that keep growing in sophistication (and price), particularly since the introduction of the 16-bit supersystem. Successful play requires eye-hand coordination, quick reflexes, concentration, and visual perception skills. It is arguable to what extent these skills transfer to real-world utility. One realm of immediate application is military training. U.S. Air Force trainers feel that the rapid information-processing skills required in these games are similar to those used by fighter pilots with video displays in their cockpits. Several commercial arcade games have been adapted for air force training and research.

The aspects of rapid movement, visual and auditory stimulation, and immediate feedback in these games

also hold great attraction for special education and remedial education. The eye-hand coordination practice, for instance, allows a brain-injured individual with a manual-dexterity handicap the chance to gain through practice capabilities that are "wired-in" from birth in normal, uninjured brains. For those with sensory handicaps due to brain injury, games can be developed to target specific auditory or visual skills. Experience to date indicates that novel computer games at least provide intrinsic motivation to persist at a learning task, increasing attention span as well as time on task.

For those with less dramatic learning disabilities, other adaptations of the animated graphics and interactivity of video games hold promise for remedial education. Neuro-linguistic programming, a technique of visualization for improving memory and learning in general, is the basis for *Spelling Strategy* and *Math Strategy.* Another game, *Speed Reader,* uses a moving cursor on the display screen to de-

velop faster, smoother eye movements, one of the fundamental reading skills.

There is still not enough objective evidence available to make confident judgments about the overall effects of particular microprocessor-controlled games, much less about these games as a whole. But some patterns have emerged, and interestingly they parallel what educators have discovered about each of the previous waves of new technological marvels: their pedagogical merit varies with the features of the particular game. Seven decades of instructional media research have taught us to ask, What attributes are needed for proper communication of this idea, and does this material have those attributes?

The most relevant claim for this class of video games is that basic information-processing skills are flexed in solving these fast-moving puzzles. Concentrating, scanning the display for useful information, employing peripheral vision, separating relevant from irrelevant information, deciding, and acting must be integrated in order for the player to succeed. And the gradual improvement of most players' scores indicates that something is being learned along these lines. Whether that something is a generic cognitive skill transferable to other situations has yet to be established.

More important in terms of direct educational value is the high technology being incorporated in museums, historic and commemorative parks, and monuments. New museums are showplaces of sophisticated technology (see Figure 14.18). Children's museums feature interactive games that teach history, geography, and science. The National Geographic Society in Washington, DC, features interactive exhibits that are often spin-offs from articles in its magazine. The Indiana Basketball Hall of Fame features a number of exhibits that are manipulated by the visitor. The interactive aspects of the new age in museums carry over into the informational demands of our contemporary and future society. The information-handling skills involved in video games and interactive exhibits may be a bridge to the more demanding computer-based instructional programs in the schools and to the more serious uses of information technologies.

Psychotechnology: Using Altered States of Consciousness

Shifting our attention from technology as product to technology as process, we can recognize that new scientific understanding of human learning will also be contributing to changes in how instruction is carried out in the future. Conventional educational research and development have already yielded the sorts of technologies of instruction described in Chapter 12: programmed instruction, programmed tutoring, audio-tutorial methods, and the like. Looking into the future, though, breakthroughs in improving learning may well be coming from less conventional sources.

Meditation has long been associated with religious practices and religious training in India and the Orient. In the 1960s these religious influences began to attract popular attention in North America. Experi-mentation since that time has built up a sizable body of evidence that meditative techniques can have physiological and psychological effects on humans, and that these effects can have instructional consequences. For example, some studies have shown that meditation reduces anxiety, thereby facilitating complex problem solving by groups under stress. Individuals often report that the relaxation and fresh perspective lent by meditation heighten their study abilities.

The meditative state and other "altered states of consciousness" are already being integrated into new teaching/learning approaches in North America and elsewhere. One of the most advanced is known as *suggestive-accelerative learning and teaching*.[8] This approach grew out of earlier research done by Georgi Lozanov in Bulgaria. Lozanov found that by inducing a state of conscious relaxation prior to a lesson, and by using special techniques involving

---

8   Owen L. Caskey, *Suggestive-Accelerative Learning and Teaching* (Englewood Cliffs, NJ: Educational Technology Publications, 1980).

Figure 14.18
Out-of-school learning through an interactive video program at a children's museum

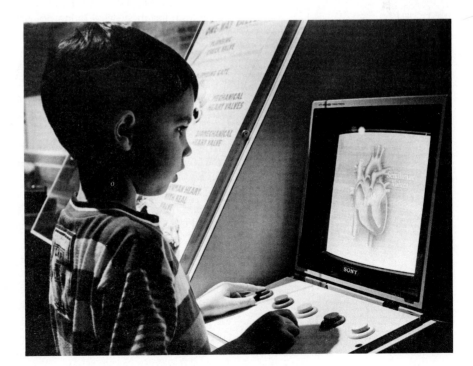

music and drama during a lesson, adults could learn foreign languages with unusual ease and high rates of retention. Similarly impressive results have been reported by experimenters in Europe, Canada, and the United States.

Typical of the early "mind-expanding" programs in the United States was EST, founded by Werner Erhard. He has formed a new company called Transformational Technologies, Inc. Erhard claims his "forums" will give participants a "decisive edge" in their ability to achieve. Companies, government agencies, and even the former Soviet Union have paid large fees to send managers through the program. What they hope to get out of the

investment is reduced stress and anxiety in a management group that is, at the same time, more open to new possibilities and more imaginative in their responses to the challenges of their environment.

Erhard, of course, is not alone in this movement sometimes referred to as "New Age" training. For example, Charles Krone has been successful (financially) with a program based on the teachings of the late Armenian mystic Georges Gurdjieff. Even Shirley MacLaine has gotten into the act with "Higher Self" seminars. (She supposedly has the advantage of being in personal touch with great gurus of the past.) Serious questions have been raised about these programs. Charges of

"mind control" and "substitute religion" are not uncommon. Whether these programs have anything of lasting value to offer to education and training is certainly still open to question.[9]

Recently, a scholarly group from the National Research Council thoroughly studied a variety of psychotechnological techniques. In their final report they found no support for any parapsychological phenomena, such as mental telepathy.[10] Bio-

---

[9] Ron Zemke, "What's New in the New Age?" *Training* (September, 1987): 25–33.

[10] Daniel Druckman and Robert A. Bjork, eds., *In the Mind's Eye: Enhancing Human Performance* (Washington, DC: National Academy Press, 1991).

CLOSE-UP

Professional Journals in Educational Technology

All of the professional organizations in instructional technology publish journals of interest to their members. There are a number of other periodicals of special interest to teachers interested in using instructional media. *Media and Methods,* for example, highlights new software and hardware. *Booklist* will keep you current on the availability of new instructional materials. *Learning* gives practical ideas for improving instruction. *Educational Technology* addresses both teachers and educational technologists with articles on a broad range of topics from the theoretical to the practical. For the business or industry setting, *Training* covers new developments in training techniques in a lively, popular style.

T.H.E. (Technological Horizons in Education) Journal concentrates on technology in higher education. *E-ITV* keeps its readers abreast of the uses of television and video in training and education. The *Canadian Journal of Educational Communications* gives in-depth coverage of the broad field of educational technology.

The computer area has spawned a large number of journals, such as *Electronic Learning, The Computing Teacher,* and *Journal of Computer-Based Instruction.*

By this time we hope that you have made the acquaintance of all these journals, and many more. But if you haven't, take the opportunity to browse through them in the periodical room of your university or public library. It will be time well spent.

As you work with instructional media and technology and as you gain experience in whatever instructional position you find yourself, you may want to explore the possibility of deepening your professional interest in one of the specialties in instructional technology. Through regular reading of one or more of the journals in the field, you will stay informed about developments in instructional technology.

feedback techniques did seem to have some potential benefit for individuals but did not seem promising for training programs.

Expanding the capabilities of the brain is a goal of recent work in psychotechnology. Both relaxation and stimulation similar to motivation are claimed to result from microelectrical impulses sent to selected areas of the brain. Experimenters have reported increases in IQ from the use of these procedures, but so far conclusive evidence is lacking. As scientists continue to learn about the physiology of the brain in relation to learning and performance, it is reasonable to anticipate the development of techniques to alter and improve human mental abilities.[11]

THE NEXT DECADE

The next decade may be here in the next two years. Hardware developments are occurring so rapidly that our sense of expectation increasingly lags behind reality. In previous generations our vision extended beyond our capabilities. Now our vision struggles to keep up with what development laboratories constantly turn out. For example, Apple's voice recognition system using the Macintosh computer is now commercially feasible.[12] Only a short time ago this was the stuff of science fiction.

In science, when the theoretical limits of a paradigm are reached, further understanding must come through a new paradigm. For example, when Newtonian physics could no longer explain physical phenomena, it was subsumed by a new theoretical approach, relativity. In technology, when the developmental

limits of a system are reached, a totally new technological approach to the problem must be sought. As impressive as the developments in microchip technology have been, the potential limits may have been reached. The emerging new technological approach is to apply the techniques of genetic engineering, with recombinant DNA, to construct tiny biological microprocessors of protein, or *biochips*. Biochips measuring in the 10 to 25 nanometer range (a nanometer is one-billionth of a meter) are about two orders of magnitude smaller than the current silicon chips. Protein circuits as small as a single molecule are being envisioned.

Software is developing just as rapidly. The digitization of information discussed earlier in this chapter represents the new paradigm in software development that is just at the beginning stages of exploration. Hypermedia and the CD-ROM encyclopedias are simply opening thrusts into a new era of software. Educators and trainers have always been in the business of "repurposing" information, through writing books, giving lectures, adapting materials, and so on. The new software will make selecting and assembling information from a variety of sources infinitely easier and faster. But the greater boon may be to students, who will be able to access and process information much more meaningfully because the systems will lend themselves to individual learning strategies.

One of the characteristics of new software is to put into the hands of amateurs tools to do professional work. Desktop publishing is just the start of a long-term trend in what will be a transformation of the knowledge-handling industry. Creators of original works, such as writers and musicians, will be able to extend their control into the domain of production and distribution, which now is generally the province of publishers. While the publishing industry will not disappear, publish-

ing itself will take on many new forms.

Earlier we mentioned experiments with enhancing the capabilities of the brain. The convergence of these experiments with the technology of biochips raises the possibility of interfacing the brain with external electronic devices either indirectly, by detecting brain waves with external sensors, or directly, by employing implanted electrodes.

All of these developments make the next decade look exciting and challenging for the professions engaged in the technology of education and training. The intriguing question is what will the institutions they work in look like?

REFERENCES

Print References

Albright, Michael J. "The Past, Present, and Future of University-Level Instruction by Satellite." *TechTrends* (November–December 1988):23–28.

America 2000: An Education Strategy Sourcebook. Washington, DC: Department of Education, 1991.

Becker, Henry J. "Encyclopedias on CD-ROM: Two Orders of Magnitude More Than Any Other Software Has Ever Delivered Before." *Educational Technology* (February 1991):7–20.

Benjamin, Steve. "An Ideascape for Education: What Futurists Recommend." *Educational Leadership* (September 1989):8–14.

Bitter, Gary G. "Artificial Intelligence: The Expert Way." *Media and Methods* (May–June 1989):22–23, 25.

Brand, Stuart. *The Media Lab.* New York: Viking, 1987.

Breivik, Patricia S. *Managing Programs for Learning Outside the Classroom.* San Francisco: Jossey-Bass, 1986.

Brubaker, C. William. "The Impact of Technology on Educational Facilities." *Educational Facility Planner* (November–December 1989):4–6.

Chaiklin, Seth, and Lewis, Matthew W. "Will There Be Teachers in the Classroom of the Future? . . . But We Don't Think About That." *Teachers College Record* (Spring 1988):431–40.

Cunningham, Donald J., Duffy, Thomas M., and Knuth, Randy A. "The Textbook of the Future." In *Hyper-*

---

[11] Connie Hanson and David G. Gueulette, "Psychotechnology as Instructional Technology: Systems for a Deliberate Change in Consciousness," *Educational Communication and Technology Journal* (Winter 1988):231–42.

[12] "The Machines Are Listening," *TIME* (Aug. 10, 1992):45.

text: A Psychological Perspective, ed. C. McKnight. London: Ellis Horwood Publishing, in press.

Daniel, John S. "Independence and Interaction in Distance Education: New Technologies for Home Instruction." *Programmed Learning and Educational Technology* (August 1983):155–60.

D'Ignazio, Fred. "Through the Looking Glass: The Multiple Layers of Multimedia." *Council of Educational Facilities Planners Journal* (March–April 1987):24–27.

Druckman, Daniel, and Bjork, Robert A. *In the Mind's Eye: Enhancing Human Performance.* Washington, DC: National Academy Press, 1991.

Epstein, Kenneth, and Hillegeist, Eleanor. "Intelligent Instructional Systems: Teachers and Computer-Based Intelligent Tutoring Systems." *Educational Technology* (November 1990):13–19.

Foster, David. "Technology: Implications for Long Range Planning." *Educational Technology* (April 1988):7–14.

Gagnon, Diana. "Videogames and Spatial Skills: An Exploratory Study." *Educational Communications and Technology Journal* (Winter 1985):263–75.

Gardner, Dwayne E. "School Buildings of the Future." *Council of Educational Facilities Planners Journal* (March–April 1987):24–27.

Goetsch, David L. "Understanding High Technology." *Technology Teacher* (March 1988):29–31.

Hanson, Connie, and Gueulette, David G. "Psychotechnology as Instructional Technology: Systems for a Deliberate Change in Consciousness." *Educational Communications and Technology Journal* (Winter 1988):231–42.

Hathaway, Warren E. *Education and Technology at the Crossroads: Choosing a New Direction.* Edmonton, Canada: Alberta Education, 1989.

————. "Education in the Future: Right Uses of Technology." *Education Canada* (Summer 1989):24–35.

Heinich, Robert. "Restructuring, Technology, and Instructional Efficiency." In *Instructional Technology: Past, Present, and Future,* ed. Gary Anglin. Englewood, CO: Libraries Unlimited, 1991.

Hodgkinson, Harold. "Today's Curriculum: How Appropriate Will It Be in Year 2000?" *NASSP Bulletin* (April 1987):2–4, 6, 7.

Information Technology and Its Impact on American Education. Washington, DC: Congress of the United States, Office of Technology Assessment, 1982.

Kubey, Robert, and Larson, Reed. "The Use and Experience of the New Video Media among Children and Young Adolescents." *Communication Research* (February 1990):107–30.

Lippert, Renate C. "An Expert System Shell to Teach Problem Solving." *TechTrends* (March 1988):22–26.

Nichols, Daryl G. "Low-Cost Learning Systems: The General Concept and Specific Examples." *NSPI Journal* (September 1982):4–8.

Nuccio, Eugene J. "The Next Generation of Teachers: Past Skills, Future Models." *Journal of Educational Technology Systems* 18 no. 4:279–93.

Pollock, Joellyn, and Grabinger, R. Scott. "Expert Systems: Instructional Design Potential." *Educational Technology* (April 1989):35–39.

Provenzo, Eugene F. *Video Kids: Making Sense of Nintendo.* Cambridge, MA: Harvard University Press, 1991.

Romberg, Thomas A. *Toward Effective Schooling: The IGE Experience.* Lanham, MD: University Press of America, 1985.

Saba, Farhad, and Twitchell, David. "Integrated Services Digital Networks: How It Can Be Used for Distance Education." *Journal of Educational Technology Systems* 17, no. 1 (1988–89):15–25.

Scaife, M. "Education, Information Technology, and Cognitive Science." *Journal of Computer-Assisted Learning* (June 1989):66–71.

Wedemeyer, Dan J. "The New Age of Telecommunications: Setting the Context for Education." *Educational Technology* (October 1986):7–13.

White, Mary Alice. "Current Trends in Education and Technology as Signs to the Future." *Education and Computing* (December 1989):3–10.

Wilcox, John. "A Campus Tour of Corporate Colleges." *Training and Development Journal* (May 1987):51–56.

Winn, William. "Toward a Rationale and Theoretical Basis for Educational Technology." *Educational Technology Research and Development* 37, no. 1 (1989):35–46.

Zemke, Ron. "What's New in the New Age?" *Training* (September 1987):25–33.

Zukowski, Angela A. "Vision or Fear? Teacher Response to Educational Technology." *Momentum* (February 1986):13–16.

Audiovisual References

CD-ROM: The New Papyrus. Seattle: Intermedia, 1986. Videocassette. 22 minutes.

High Technology: How It Works. Educational Dimensions Group, 1983. Filmstrips. "Holography," 21½ minutes; "Television," 20½ minutes; "Fiber Optics," 17½ minutes; "Videodisc," 20 minutes.

Introduction to Communication. Bloomington, IN: Agency for Instructional Technology, 1990. Videocassette. 17 minutes.

Overview of Technology. Bloomington, IN: Agency for Instructional Technology, 1990. Videocassette. 15 minutes.

Producing and Transmitting Messages. Bloomington, IN: Agency for Instructional Technology, 1990. Videocassette. 17 minutes.

Tyler, Ralph. *The Development and Use of Technology in Education.* Bloomington, IN: Phi Delta Kappa, 1985. Videocassette. 20 minutes.

————. *Have Educational Reforms since 1950 Created Quality Education?* Bloomington, IN: Patten Foundation Lectures, 1974. Audiocassette. 70 minutes.

POSSIBLE PROJECTS

14–A.   For one week collect reports of new developments in electronic media from newspapers, news magazines, and other popular media sources. Write a two- to three-page report describing the potential educational impact of these new developments.

14–B.   Play several different types of computer-based games at a video arcade or on a computer. Compare and contrast their possible educational uses.

14–C.   Compile your own list of trends in the uses of media and technology in instruction. In your two- to three-page report be specific about what learning tasks could be facilitated by which developments.

14–D. If you work in a school or other organization offering instruction, analyze the structural or organizational factors that impede your full use of new media and technology.

14–E. Prepare a documented profile on the status of your state or province in regard to the enforcement of accountability in public education.

14–F. Compile the copy for a brochure that would explain to newcomers to your community the nonformal educational opportunities (lifelong learning) available locally.

14–G. Interview two or more professionals working in educational technology. Compare and contrast their duties in a two- to three-page written report or five-minute cassette recording.

14–H. Survey the content of several different educational technology journals and write a one- to two-page report summarizing the types of articles and information covered in each.

Appendix A

Information Sources

Instructors ordinarily begin their search for needed audiovisual materials in the media collection at their own facility. School personnel would then turn to the catalogs of media collections housed at the school district or regional educational service center. But where can you turn beyond your own organization? And where can your organization obtain the materials that you need? This appendix will help you gain access to the wealth of audiovisual resources available for rental or purchase from commercial and noncommercial sources. (Appendix B focuses on sources that give away or loan materials free or for a nominal cost.)

COMPREHENSIVE INFORMATION SOURCES

Assuming that you have identified an instructional need for which audiovisual materials are not available within your organization or from a free loan source, where might you begin searching for another supplier? The most comprehensive information source is the set of indexes published by the National Information Center for Educational Media (NICEM). NICEM provides indexes for each media format and for several popular subject areas plus a producer and distributor index. All are revised periodically and are updated by a supplement service. Arranged by subject as well as by title, these annotated indexes give a comprehensive view of what is available in the marketplace. However, they are usually several years out of date and must often be used in conjunction with sources of more current information.

NICEM is owned by the Association for Educational Communications and Technology (AECT) and Access Innovations, Inc. The address is: NICEM, P.O. Box 40130, Albuquerque, NM 87196.

The on-line version of the NICEM database is called "A-V On-line." This database can be accessed through computerized search services such as Lockheed's DIALOG. Any library subscribing to such a search service would have a terminal you could use to sift through the NICEM references on line. You may also obtain a printout of the results of your search. An on-line search allows you to search key words and phrases as well as subject headings.

NICEM indexes covering still-picture formats are

Index to Educational Overhead Transparencies
Index to Educational Slides
Index to 35-mm Educational Filmstrips

Audio materials are indexed in

Index to Educational Audio Tapes
Index to Educational Records

Films and videotapes are covered in

Film and Video Finder. 3d ed. 3 vol. 1991.

An index devoted exclusively to videodiscs is published by

The Videodisc Compendium
Emerging Technology Consultants
P.O. Box 12444
St. Paul, MN 55112

NICEM indexes covering multiple types of media on a given topic are

Index to Environmental Studies
Index to Health and Safety Education
Index to Producers and Distributors
Index to Vocational and Technical Education
NICEM Index to Non-Print Special Education Materials: Multimedia (Learner Volume)
NICEM Index to Non-Print Special Education Materials: Multimedia (Professional Volume)

The University of Southern California maintains the nation's largest and most comprehensive bibliographic information retrieval system for special education, the National Information Center for Special Education Materials (NICSEM). NICSEM provides information on the content of materials and their applicability to specific handicaps. The NICSEM

---

publications are helpful in the construction of individualized programs for handicapped children. Current publications include the following:

NICSEM Master Index to Special Education Materials

NICSEM Mini-Index to Special Education Materials: Family Life and Sex Education

NICSEM Mini-Index to Special Education Materials: Functional Communication Skills

NICSEM Mini-Index to Special Education Materials: High Interest, Controlled Vocabulary Supplementary Reading Materials for Adolescents and Young Adults

NICSEM Mini-Index to Special Education Materials: Independent Living Skills for Moderately and Severely Handicapped Students

NICSEM Mini-Index to Special Education Materials: Personal and Social Development for Moderately and Severely Handicapped Students

NICSEM Source Directory

NICSEM Special Education Thesaurus

Special Education Index to Assessment Materials

Special Education Index to Parent Materials

Other reference works covering a broad range of media and content areas are

Brown, Lucy Gregor. *Core Media Collection for Elementary Schools.* 2d ed. New York: R. R. Bowker, 1978.

_____ *Core Media Collection for Secondary Schools.* 2d ed. New York: R. R. Bowker, 1979.

Hunt, Mary Alice, ed. *A Multimedia Approach to Children's Literature: A Selective List of Films (and Videocassettes), Filmstrips, and Recordings Based on Children's Books,* 3d ed. Chicago: American Library Association, 1983.

Media Resource Catalog from the National AudioVisual Center, 1986, and *Supplement, 1988.* Capitol Heights, MD: National AudioVisual Center.

Notable Children's Films and Videos, Filmstrips and Recordings, 1973–1986. Chicago: American Library Association, 1987.

Winkel, Lois, ed. *Elementary School Collection: A Guide to Books and Other Media.* Annual. Williamsport, PA: Bro-Dart Foundation.

SPECIALIZED INFORMATION SOURCES

Many information sources are restricted to a particular media format, content area, or audience.

Audio

On Cassette: A Comprehensive Bibliography of Spoken Word Audio Cassettes. New York: R. R. Bowker, 1985.

Schwann Record and Tape Guide. Monthly. Boston: ABC Schwann Publications. Available from many record and tape stores.

Voegelin-Carter, Ardis. *Words on Tape: A Guide to the Audio Cassette Market.* Westport, CT: Mecrier, 1991.

Video and Film

AAAS Science Film Catalog. Washington, D.C.: American Association for the Advancement of Science, 1975. Updated in the review source *Science Books and Films.*

American Folklore Films and Videotapes: A Catalog. 2d ed. New York: R. R. Bowker, 1982.

Artel, Linda, and Wengraf, Susan, eds. *Positive Images: A Guide to 400 Non-Sexist Films for Young People.* San Francisco: Booklegger Press, 1976.

Bowker's Complete Video Directory, annual. New York: R. R. Bowker.

Boyle, Deirdre. *Video Classics: A Guide to Video Art and Documentary Tapes.* Phoenix, Ariz.: Oryx Press, 1986.

Collier, Marilyn. *Films for 3 to 5's.* Berkeley: University of California, Department of Education, Instructional Laboratories, 1975. Cover title: *Films for Children Ages 3 to 5.*

T.H.E. Catalog, Televised Higher Education: Catalog of Resources. Boulder, CO: Western Interstate Commission for Higher Education. 1984.

Documentary Film Classics. 2d ed. Capitol Heights, MD: National AudioVisual Center.

Films for Children: A Selected List. 4th ed. New York: Children's and Young Adult Section of the New York Library Association, 1977.

Film Resources for Sex Education. New York: Sex Information and Education Council of the United States, distributed by Human Sciences Press, 1976.

Gaffney, Maureen, ed. *More Films Kids Like.* Chicago: American Library Association, 1977.

Hitchens, Howard, ed. *America on Film and Tape: A Topical Catalog of Audiovisual Resources for the Study of United States History, Society, and Culture.* Westport, CT: Greenwood Press, 1985.

Limbacher, James, ed. *Feature Films on 16-mm and Videotape Available for Rental, Sale and Lease.* 8th ed. New York: R. R. Bowker, 1985.

May, Jill P. *Films and Filmstrips for Language Arts: An Annual Bibliography.* Urbana, IL: National Council of Teachers of English, 1981.

Parlato, Salvatore J. *Films Too Good for Words: A Directory of Non-Narrated Films.* New York: R. R. Bowker, 1973.

_____ *Films Ex Libris: Literature in 16-mm and Video.* Jefferson, NC: McFarland, 1980.

Sullivan, Kay. *Films For, By, and About Women.* Series II. Metuchen, NJ: Scarecrow, 1985.

Videolog. Three volumes: "Programs for Business and Industry," "Programs for General Interest and Entertainment," and "Programs for the Health Sciences." Guilford, CT: Jeffrey Norton.

Program information on over 15,000 videotapes and videocassettes in a broad range of categories.

Video Source Book. Annual. Syosset, NY: National Video Clearinghouse.

Computer-generated catalog of 18,000 video programs, encompassing entertainment, sports, fine arts, business/industry, and education.

Zornow, Edith, and Goldstein, Ruth M., eds. *Movies for Kids: A Guide for Parents and Teachers on the Entertainment Film for Children.* New York: Frederick Ungar, 1980.

Programmed Instruction

Programmed Learning and Individually Paced Instruction Bibliography. 5th ed. 2 vol. Includes Supplements 1–6. Compiled by Carl H. Hendershot. Bay City, MI: Hendershot Bibliography, 1985.

Supplements are issued irregularly.

Simulations and Games

Horn, Robert E., and Cleaves, Anne, eds. *The Guide to Simulations/Games for Education and Training.* 4th ed. Beverly Hills, CA: Sage, 1980.

Aims for comprehensive coverage of formal education and the business/industry training sector. All listings carry full descriptions, and some include evaluations or testimonials of users.

Stadsklev, Ron, ed. *Handbook of Simulation Gaming in Social Education.* 2d ed Tuscaloosa, AL: Institute of Higher Education Research and Service. University of Alabama, 1979.

Published in two volumes—the first an introductory textbook on simulation/gaming, particularly as it relates to objectives in the social sciences, and the second a directory of individual materials with extensive descriptive annotations. Coverage is limited to "social education," interpreted broadly.

Computer Courseware

Apple Education Software Directory. Annual. Chicago: WIDL Video.
EPIE Annotated Courseware Provider List. Annual. Water Mill, NY: EPIE Institute.
International Microcomputer Software Directory. Annual. Fort Collins, CO: Imprint Software.
Microcomputer Index. Annual. Santa Clara, CA: Microcomputer Information Services.
Microcomputer Market Place. Annual. New York: R. R. Bowker.
Microcomputer Software Catalog List. Annual. Portland, OR: Northwest Regional Laboratory.
Micro Software Solutions. Annual. Chatsworth, CA: Career Aids, Inc.
Swift Directory. Annual. Austin, TX: Sterling Swift.

RENTAL SOURCES

The media formats that are generally available for rental are 16mm films and videocassettes. Producers and distributors who sell films and videocassettes usually rent the materials that they sell. However, their rental prices are high compared to noncommercial sources. Several universities maintain large libraries of educational films and videocassettes. Indiana University, the University of Illinois, Syracuse University, and the University of Southern California are among these universities. University film-library rental prices are much lower than those charged by the producer or distributor. Each university publishes a catalog of titles available and their rental prices. But there is one umbrella publication that compiles rental as well as purchase information on each of the films and videocassettes available from these university film libraries:

The Educational Film/Video Locator of the Consortium of University Film Centers and R. R. Bowker Company. 4th ed. 2 vol. New York: R. R. Bowker, 1990.

COMMERCIAL INFORMATION SOURCES

Commercial producers and distributors of audiovisual materials publish promotional catalogs of their wares. Companies often assemble a special school and library catalog, arranged by subject or medium, to display their offerings more effectively. When you use these catalogs, keep in mind the bias of the seller. The descriptions given and the claims made do not pretend to be objective. Any purchases should be guided by objective evidence such as field-test results, published reviews, and local appraisals based on previews.

A sampling of major audiovisual producers and distributors follows. The alphabetical lists of companies are grouped roughly according to the media format(s) with which they are identified.

Nonprojected Visuals

Educational Insights
19560 Rancho Way
Dominguez Hills, CA 90220
Encyclopaedia Britannica Educational Corp.
310 S. Michigan Avenue
Chicago, IL 60604
Silver Burdett Co.
250 James Street
Morristown, NJ 07690
Society for Visual Education, Inc. (SVE)
1345 W. Diversey Parkway
Chicago, IL 60614

Overhead Transparencies

Denoyer-Geppert Science Co.
5225 Ravenswood Avenue
Chicago, IL 60640

Encyclopaedia Britannica Educational Corp.
310 S. Michigan Avenue
Chicago, IL 60604

Hammond, Inc.
515 Valley Street
Maplewood, NJ 07040

Milliken Publishing
1100 Research Boulevard
St. Louis, MO 63132

Rand McNally
P.O. Box 7500
Chicago, IL 60657

United Transparencies
435 Main Street
Johnson City, NY 13790

Visual Systems Division
Building A146 5N-01
6801 River Place Boulevard
Austin, TX 78726

Filmstrips

Ambrose Video Publishing Co.
1290 Avenue of the Americas
New York, NY 10104

Argus Communications
One DLM Park
Allen, TX 75002

Audio Visual Narrative Arts, Inc.
Box 9
Pleasantville, NY 10570

Communacad, The Communications Academy
P.O. Box 541
Wilton, CT 06897

Coronet/MTI Film and Video
108 Wilmot Avenue
Deerfield, IL 60015

Denoyer-Geppert Science Co.
5225 Ravenswood Avenue
Chicago, IL 60640

EMC Publishing
300 York Avenue
St. Paul, MN 55101

Educational Images
P.O. Box 367
Lyons Falls, NY 13368

Encyclopaedia Britannica Educational Corp.
310 S. Michigan Avenue
Chicago, IL 60604

Eye Gate Media Division
3333 Elston Avenue
Chicago, IL 60611

International Film Bureau
332 S. Michigan Avenue
Chicago, IL 60604

January Productions
210 Sixth Avenue
P.O. Box 66
Hawthorne, NJ 07507

National Film Board of Canada
1251 Avenue of the Americas
New York, NY 10020

The Reading Laboratory, Inc.
P.O. Box 28
Georgetown, CT 06829

Society for Visual Education, Inc. (SVE)
1345 W. Diversey Parkway
Chicago, IL 60614

Sunburst Communications
39 Washington Avenue
Pleasantville, NY 10570

Time-Life Multimedia
See Ambrose Video Publishing Co.

Weston Woods Studio
389 Newton Turnpike
Weston, CT 06883

Slides

American Museum of Natural History
Central Park West at 79th Street
New York, NY 10024

The Center for Humanities, Inc.
Box 1000, Communications Park
Mt. Kisco, NY 10549

Educational Images, Ltd.
P.O. Box 3456, West Side Station
Elmira, NY 14905

Harcourt Brace Jovanovich
6277 Sea Harbor Drive
Orlando, FL 32887

Instructional Resources Corp.
1819 Bay Ridge Avenue
Annapolis, MD 21403

Metropolitan Museum of Art
    Educational Marketing
6 East 82d Street
New York, NY 10028

Museum of Modern Art
See Sandak, Inc.

National Audubon Society
950 Third Avenue
New York, NY 10022

National Geographic Society
Educational Services
Washington, DC 20090-8019

Sandak, Inc.
70 Lincoln Street
Boston, MA 02111

Society for Visual Education, Inc. (SVE)
1345 W. Diversey Parkway
Chicago, IL 60614

United Scientific Co.
70 Lincoln Street
Boston, MA 02111

Ward's Natural Science Establishment, Inc.
P.O. Box 92912
Rochester, NY 14692

Audio Materials

American Audio Prose Library
P.O. Box 842
Columbia, MO 65205

American Management Association
135 West 50th Street
New York, NY 10020

Audio Book Contractors
Box 40115
Washington, DC 20016

Bilingual Educational Services, Inc.
2514 S. Grand Avenue
Los Angeles, CA 90007

Books on Tape
P.O. Box 7900
Newport Beach, CA 92060

Capitol Records
1750 North Vine
Hollywood, CA 90028

Columbia Records
51 West 52d Street
New York, NY 10019

Coronet/MTI Film and Video
108 Wilmot Road
Deerfield, IL 60015

Decca Records
445 Park Avenue
New York, NY 10022

Educational Corp. of America/Rand
    McNally
P.O. Box 7600
Chicago, IL 60680

Effective Learning Systems
5221 Edina Industrial Boulevard
Edina, MN 55439

Grolier Educational Corp.
Sherman Turnpike
Danbury, CT 06816

G. K. Hall Audio Publishers
70 Lincoln Street
Boston, MA 02111

Imperial International, Inc.
30 Montauk Boulevard
Oakdale, NY 11769

January Productions
210 Sixth Avenue
P.O. Box 66
Hawthorne, NJ 07507

Listening Library, Inc.
1 Park Avenue
Old Greenwich, CT 06870

National Public Radio
2025 M Street, N.W.
Washington, DC 20036

Pacifica Foundation
3729 Cahuenga Boulevard, W.
North Hollywood, CA 91604

Poet's Audio Center
P.O. Box 50145
Washington, DC 20091

RCA Educational Division
Front and Cooper Streets
Camden, NJ 08102

Scholastic Records
730 Broadway
New York, NY 10003

Science Research Associates (SRA)
155 N. Wacker Drive
Chicago, IL 60606

Society for Visual Education Inc. (SVE)
1345 W. Diversey Parkway
Chicago, IL 60614

Spoken Arts
10100 SBF Drive
Pinellas Park, FL 34666

3M Company
3M Center
St. Paul, MN 55144

Tutor Tape
107 France Street
Toms River, NJ 08753

Video and Film

Agency for Instructional Technology
P.O. Box A
Bloomington, IN 47402

AIMS Media
9710 De Soto Avenue
Chatsworth, CA 91311

Ambrose Video Publishing Co.
1290 Avenue of the Americas
New York, NY 10104

American Management Association
135 West 50th Street
New York, NY 10020

American Media, Inc.
1454 30th Street
Des Moines, IA 50265

Barr Films
3490 East Foothill Boulevard
Pasadena, CA 91107

Benchmark Films
145 Scarborough Road
Briarcliff Manor, NY 10510

BFA Educational Media
468 Park Avenue South
New York, NY 10016

Blanchard Training and Development
125 State Place
Escondido, CA 92025

Bullfrog Films
P.O. Box 149
Oley, PA 19547

Catticus Corp.
2600 10th Street
Berkeley, CA 94710

CEL Communications
477 Madison Avenue
New York, NY 10022

Center for Southern Folklore
Box 226
152 Beal Street
Memphis, TN 38101

Churchill Films
12210 Nebraska Avenue
Los Angeles, CA 90025

Cinema Guild
1697 Broadway
New York, NY 10019

Coast Telecourses
11460 Warner Avenue
Fountain Valley, CA 92708

Coronet/MTI Film and Video
108 Wilmot Road
Deerfield, IL 60015

CRM Films
2233 Faraday Avenue
Carlsbad, CA 92008

Dallas Community College District
Center for Telecommunications
4343 North Highway 67
Mesquite, TX 75150

Direct Cinema Limited
P.O. Box 10003
Santa Monica, CA 90410

Eastern Educational Television Network
120 Boylston Street
Boston, MA 02116

Educational Images, Ltd.
P.O. Box 3456, West Side Station
Elmira, NY 14905

Electric Arts Intermix
536 Broadway, 9th Floor
New York, NY 10012

Encyclopaedia Britannica Educational
    Corp.
310 S. Michigan Avenue
Chicago, IL 60604

Evergreen Video
228 West Houston Street
New York, NY 10014

Field Services
Center for Media and Teaching Resources
Indiana University
Bloomington, IN 47405

Filmmakers Library
124 East 40th Street
New York, NY 10016

Filmic Archives
The Cinema Center
Botsford, CT 06404

Films for the Humanities and Sciences
P.O. Box 2053
Princeton, NJ 08543

Films, Incorporated
5547 Ravenswood Avenue
Chicago, IL 60640

Great Plains National Instructional
    Television Library (GPN)
Box 80669
Lincoln, NE 68501

Icarus Films
153 Waverly Place, 6th Floor
New York, NY 10014

International Film Bureau
332 S. Michigan Avenue
Chicago, IL 60604

International Historic Films
P.O. Box 29035
Chicago, IL 60629

The Kentucky Network (KET)
2230 Richmond Road
Suite 213
Lexington, KY 40502

Learning Corporation of America
See Coronet/MTI Film and Video

Maryland Center for Public Broadcasting
11767 Bonita Avenue
Owings Mills, MD 21117

National Audiovisual Center
8700 Edgeworth Drive
Capitol Heights, MD 20743

National Film Board of Canada
1251 Avenue of the Americas
New York, NY 10020

National Geographic Society
Educational Services
Washington, DC 20090-8019

National Video Clearinghouse, Inc. (NVC)
100 Lafayette Drive
Syosset, NY 11791

New Day Films
121 West 27th Street
Suite 902
New York, NY 10001

PBS Video (Public Broadcasting Service)
1320 Braddock Place
Alexandria, VA 22314

Phoenix Films
See BFA Educational Media

Polyglot Productions
P.O. Box 668
Cambridge, MA 02238

Pyramid Film and Video
2801 Colorado Avenue
Santa Monica, CA 90404

Southern Educational Communications
    Association (SECA)
P.O. Box 5966
Columbia, SC 29250

Sunburst Communications
39 Washington Avenue
Pleasantville, NY 10570

Tamarelles's International Films
7900 Hickman Road
Des Moines, IA 50322

Time-Life Video
See Ambrose Video
Publishing Co.

TV Ontario
1140 Kildaire Farm Road
Suite 308
Cary, NC 27511

Video Data Bank
The School of the Art Institute at Chicago
37 S. Wabash Avenue
Chicago, IL 60603

Video-Forum
96 Broad Street
Guilford, CT 06437

Voyage Company
888 Seventh Avenue, 4th Floor
New York, NY 10106

Western Instructional Television, Inc.
(WIT)
1438 N. Gower Street
Los Angeles, CA 90028

World Video
P.O. Box 30469
Knoxville, TN 37930

Multimedia Programs

ABC News Interactive
7 West 66th Street, 4th Floor
New York, NY 10023

Agency for Instructional Technology
Box A
Bloomington, IN 47402-0120

AIMS Media
9710 DeSoto Avenue
Chatsworth, CA 91311

David C. Cook Publishing Co.
850 N. Grove Avenue
Elgin, IL 60120

Encyclopaedia Britannica Educational
Corp.
310 S. Michigan Avenue
Chicago, IL 60604

In Canada:
Britannica Learning Materials
Britannica Place, Box 2249
Cambridge, Ontario N3C 3N4

IBM Corp.
Multimedia & Education Division
4111 Northside Parkway
Atlanta, GA 30327

Intellimation
P.O. Box 1530
Santa Barbara, CA 93116-1530

Laser Learning Technologies
3114 37th Place, South
Seattle, WA 98114

MECC
6160 Summit Drive North
Minneapolis, MN 55430

National Geographic Society
Educational Services
Washington, DC 20090-8019

In Canada:
Educational Services Canada
211 Watline Avenue, Suite 210
Mississauga, Ontario L4C 1P3

Optical Data Corp.
30 Technology Drive
Warren, NJ 07059

Quantum Leap Technologies
1399 SE 9th Avenue
Hialeah, FL 33010-5999

Synapse Technologies
3400 Wilshire Blvd., Bungalow H
Los Angeles, CA 90010

Texas Learning Technology Group
7703 North Lamar Blvd.
Austin, TX 78752

The Discovery Channel
Interactive Multimedia Division
7700 Wisconsin Rd., Suite 900
Bethesda, MD 20814-3522

Turner Educational Services Inc.
1 CNN Center
Box 105336
Atlanta, GA 30348-5366

Videodiscovery, Inc.
1515 Dexter Avenue N., #400
Seattle, WA 98109

The Voyager Company
1351 Pacific Coast Highway
Santa Monica, CA 90401

Ztek Co.
P.O. Box 1055
Louisville, KY 40201-1055

Simulations and Games

Animal Town Game Co.
P.O. Box 485
Healdsburg, CA 95448

Avalon Hill Microcomputer Games
4517 Harford Road
Baltimore, MD 21214

Broderbund Software Inc.
500 Redwood Blvd.
Novato, CA 94948-6121

Denoyer Geppert Science Co.
5225 N. Ravenswood Avenue
Chicago, IL 60640

Didactic Systems, Inc.
P.O. Box 457
Cranford, NJ 07016

Doron Precision Systems Inc.
P.O. Box 400
Binghamton, NY 13902

Education Research
370 Lexington Avenue, 27th Floor
New York, NY 10017

Groupware Corp.
1555 Glenora Drive
London, Ontario N5X 1V7
Canada

Houghton Mifflin
1 Beacon Street
Boston, MA 02108

Interact Company
P.O. Box 997
Lakeside, CA 92040

Management Research Systems, Ltd.
Suite 201, Executive Center
P.O. Box 1585
Ponte Vedra Beach, FL 32082

Marginal Context Ltd.
35 St. Andrew's Road
Cambridge CB4 1DL
England

Pentathlon Institute
P.O. Box 20590
Indianapolis, IN 46220-0590

Simulation Training Systems
P.O. Box 910
Del Mar, CA 92014

Simulations Publications, Inc.
44 East 23d Street
New York, NY 10010

Teaching Aids Company
925 South 300 West
Salt Lake City, UT 84101

Wff'N Proof
1490-TZ South Boulevard
Ann Arbor, MI 48104

John Wiley and Sons, Inc.
605 Third Avenue
New York, NY 10158

Computer Courseware

Atari, Inc.
1312 Crossman Avenue
P.O. Box 61657
Sunnyvale, CA 94086

Avalon Hill Microcomputer Games
4517 Harford Road
Baltimore, MD 21214

Computer Courseware
Educational Images, Ltd.
P.O. Box 3456, West Side Station
Elmira, NY 14905

CONDUIT
The University of Iowa,
Oakdale Campus
Iowa City, IA 55242

CYBIS Education and Training
Control Data Corp.
8800 Queen Avenue, S.
Minneapolis, MN 55431

GemStar
P.O. Box 050228
Staten Island, NY 10305

Harcourt Brace Jovanovich
1250 Sixth Avenue
San Diego, CA 92101

Houghton-Mifflin
1 Beacon Street
Boston, MA 02108

IBM, Electronic Communications, Inc.
Suite 220
1311 Executive Center Drive
Tallahassee, FL 32301

January Productions
210 Sixth Avenue
P.O. Box 66
Hawthorne, NJ 07507

Milliken Publishing Company
1100 Research Boulevard
P.O. Box 21579
St. Louis, MO 63132

Minnesota Educational Computing
   Corporation (MECC)
6160 Summit Drive North
Minneapolis, MN 55430

Opportunities for Learning, Inc.
Box 8130
Hickory Lane
Mansfield, OH 44901

Scholastic, Inc.
P.O. Box 7502
Jefferson City, MO 65102

Society for Visual Education, Inc. (SVE)
1345 W. Diversey Parkway
Chicago, IL 60614

Softswap
San Mateo County Office of Education
333 Main Street
Redwood, CA 94063

Sunburst Communications
39 Washington Avenue
P.O. Box 100
Pleasantville, NY 10570

John Wiley and Sons, Inc.
605 Third Avenue
New York, NY 10158

REVIEW SOURCES

American Film and Video Association
P.O. Box 48659
Niles, IL 60648

Booklist
American Library Association
50 E. Huron Street
Chicago, IL 60611

Reviews all levels of audiovisual materials. Most materials included are recommended.

EPIE Reports
EPIE (Educational Products Information Exchange) Institute,
P.O. Box 839
Water Mill, NY 11976

Publishes several series of evaluative reports on instructional materials. Those covering conventional audiovisual and print materials are

❑ *Textbook PRO/FILES* (biennial, K–12 textbooks)
❑ *EPIEgram: Materials* (monthly, K–12 textbooks and related materials)
❑ *EPIE Report: Materials* (biennial, trends in instructional materials)
❑ *A-V/V PRO/FILES* (biennial, audiovisual and video products)
❑ *EPIEgram: Equipment* (monthly, audiovisual and video equipment)
❑ *EPIE Report: Equipment* (biennial, trends in media and microcomputer hardware)

Film Library Quarterly. See *Sightlines.*

Film and Video News
70 Elm Place
Red Bank, NJ 07701

Media and Methods
Wagman Publishers
1429 Walnut Street
Philadelphia, PA 19102

Media Review
Key Productions
346 Ethan Allen Highway
Ridgefield, CT 06877

Monthly; carries objective reviews of all types of audiovisual materials; available in three editions: K–College (complete), K–Grade 8, Grade 9–College.

Library Journal
R. R. Bowker
205 East 42d Street
New York, NY 10017

School Library Journal
R. R. Bowker
205 East 42d Street
New York, NY 10017

School Library Media Quarterly
American Association of School Librarians
American Library Association
50 E. Huron Street
Chicago, IL 60611

Science Books and Films (Variant title: *AAAS Science Books and Films*)
American Association for the Advancement of Science
1776 Massachusetts Avenue, N.W.
Washington, DC 20036

Sightlines. Incorporates *Film Library Quarterly*
American Film and Video Association (AFVA)
P.O. Box 48659
Niles, IL 60648

Video Rating Guide for Libraries (quarterly)
ABC-CLIO, Inc.
130 Cremona Drive
Santa Barbara, CA 93117

Courseware

Courseware Report Card
150 West Carob Street
Compton, CA 90220

EPIE Reports
EPIE (Educational Product Information Exchange) Institute
P.O. Box 839
Water Mill, NY 11976

Publishes several series of evaluative reports on instructional materials. Those covering computer software are

❑ *MICROgram* (monthly, educational computing products)
❑ *Micro PRO/FILES* (bimonthly, in-depth analyses of microcomputer hardware and software)
❑ *The Educational Software Selector—TESS* (definitive information source on availability of all types of microcomputer educational software, including many evaluative comments; published jointly with Teachers College Press, Columbia University)

Journal of Courseware Review
Apple Education Foundation
20525 Mariani Avenue
Cupertino, CA 95014

Microcomputers in Education
Queue, Inc.
5 Chapel Hill Drive
Fairfield, CT 06432

Micro-Scope
JEM Research
Discovery Park
University of Victoria
P.O. Box 1700
Victoria, BC V8W 2Y2, Canada

MicroSIFT
Northwest Regional Educational Lab
300 S.W. 6th Street
Portland, OR 97204

Pipeline
Conduit Clearinghouse
University of Iowa, Oakdale
Iowa City, IA 55242

Purser's Magazine
P.O. Box 266
El Dorado, CA 95623

School Microware Reviews
Dresden Associates
P.O. Box 246
Dresden, ME 04342

Software Review
Meckler Publishing
520 Riverside Avenue
Westport, CT 06880

OTHER REFERENCE TOOLS

For more extensive, annotated guides to media reviews or descriptions or other audiovisual information sources, consult the following:

Chisholm, Margaret E. *Media Indexes and Review Sources*. College Park, MD: School of Library and Information Services, University of Maryland, 1972.

Hart, Thomas L.; Hunt, Mary A.; and Woolls, Blanche, eds. *Multi-Media Indexes, Lists and Review Sources: A Bibliographic Guide*. New York: Marcel Dekker, 1975.

Media Review Digest. Annual. Ann Arbor, MI: Pierian Press.

Rufsvold, Margaret I. *Guides to Educational Media*. 4th ed. Chicago: American Library Association, 1977.

Sive, Mary Robinson. *Selecting Instructional Media*. 3d ed. Littleton, CO: Libraries Unlimited, 1983.

Appendix B

Free and Inexpensive Materials

With the ever-increasing costs of instructional materials, teachers and trainers should be aware of the wide variety of materials that can be obtained for classroom use at little or no cost. These free and inexpensive materials can supplement instruction in many subjects, or they can even be the main source of instruction on certain topics. For example, many films are available for loan without a rental fee; the only expense is the return postage. By definition, any material that you can borrow or acquire permanently for instructional purposes without a significant cost (usually less than a couple of dollars) can be referred to as "free and inexpensive."

The types of free and inexpensive materials are almost endless. The more commonly available items include posters, games, pamphlets, brochures, reports, charts, maps, books, filmstrips, audiotapes, films, videotapes, multimedia kits, and real objects. The more costly items, such as films and videotapes, are usually sent only on a free-loan basis and must be returned to the supplier after use. In some instances, single copies of audiocassettes, filmstrips, and videocassettes will be donated to your organization to be shared among many users.

ADVANTAGES

Free and inexpensive materials can provide up-to-date information that is not contained in textbooks or other commercially available media. In addition, they often provide more in-depth treatment of a topic. If classroom quantities are available, printed materials can be read and discussed by students as textbook material would be. If quantities are limited, they can be placed in a learning center for independent or small-group study. Audiovisual materials lend themselves to classroom presentation by the instructor. Individual students who want to explore a subject of interest can use the audiovisual materials for self-study or for presentation to the class. Posters, charts, and maps can be combined to create topical displays. These can be motivational, as in the case of a safety poster, or can be used for direct instruction, as in studying the solar system. Materials that do not have to be returned can be modified and adapted for varied instructional or display purposes.

Materials that are expendable have the extra advantage of allowing learners to get actively involved with them. Students can cut out pictures for notebooks and displays. They can assemble printed information and visuals in scrapbooks as reports of group projects. Of course, when treating free materials as raw materials for student projects, you will have to develop your own objectives and plan appropriate learning activities to go along with the materials.

LIMITATIONS

Several potential limitations of free and inexpensive materials must be taken into consideration. First, many free and inexpensive materials can be described as sponsored materials because their production and distribution are sponsored by particular organizations. These organizations—whether private corporations, nonprofit associations, or government agencies—often have a message to convey. That message might be in the form of outright advertising. If so, you will have to be aware of your own organization's policies on the use of advertising matter. You might consider covering or removing the advertisement, but that, too, raises, ethical questions in view of the effort and expense that the sponsor has incurred in providing the materials to you. In addition, you are removing the identification of the source of the material, and that prevents disclosure of any vested interests by which one might judge the information presented.

What may be even more troublesome to deal with is sponsored material that does not contain outright advertising but does promote some special interest in a less obvious way. For example, a "fun in the sun" poster may subtly promote the eating of junk food without including the name or logo of any manufacturer. As discussed in Chapter 7 in regard to sponsored films, a study by the Center for the Study of Responsive Law disclosed a persistent tendency for privately sponsored materials to convey self-serving messages.[1] Propagandistic or more subtly biased materials can thus enter the curriculum through the back door. Careful previewing and caution are advisable when you consider sponsored materials. Teachers should solicit information materials on the same subject from several points of view. Thereby, students are afforded a balance and diversity of opinions.

The Center for Study of Responsive Law (P.O. Box 19367, Washington, DC 20036) provides a free annotated bibliography, *Alternative Resources for Curriculum Balance*, upon receipt of a self-addressed, stamped envelope. It lists selected informational and educational resources in subject areas predominant in corporate educational efforts. The intent is to help provide a balance of resources and perspectives on controversial issues.

The final potential limitation is a logistical one. With the increasing expense of producing both printed and audiovisual materials, your supplier may have to impose limits on the quantities of items available at one time. You may not be able to obtain a copy of the material for every student in the class.

LOCAL SOURCES

Many local government agencies, community groups, and private businesses provide informational materials on free loan. Public libraries often make films, prints, and filmstrips available. Even libraries in small communities may have access to films through a statewide network. These materials usually can be loaned to local organizations. However, public library collections are often entertainment oriented, as would be expected in a service designed for the general public, so you will probably not find in them a great many strictly instructional materials. Other government agencies, such as the Cooperative Extension Service, public health departments, and parks departments, make materials available for use in schools, churches, hospitals, and companies.

Community organizations such as the Red Cross, the League of Women Voters, medical societies, and the like welcome opportunities to spread information about their special interests. Films, slide-tapes, printed material, and guest speakers are frequently offered.

Among business organizations, utilities—telephone, electric, gas, and water companies—are most likely to employ education specialists who can inform you about the instructional services they offer. Chambers of commerce often can suggest private corporations that might supply materials of interest to you.

NATIONAL AND INTERNATIONAL SOURCES

Nationally, one of the most prolific sources of free and inexpensive materials is the federal government. In the United States, two federal agencies offer special access to materials—the U.S. Government Printing Office and the National Audiovisual Center. Your key to the tremendous wealth of posters, charts, brochures, books, and other printed government documents that are available to the general public is *Selected U.S. Government Publications*, a monthly catalog of all new listings. You can have your name added to the free mailing list by sending a request to:

Superintendent of Documents
U.S. Government Printing Office
Washington, DC 20402

The National Audiovisual Center is the central clearinghouse for all federal government-produced audiovisual materials. Its catalog, *Selected Audiovisual Materials Produced by the United States Government*, is issued every four years, with a supplement every two years. It lists more than 12,000 titles of films, videotapes, slide sets, audiotapes, and multimedia kits that have been produced by or for government agencies. All are available for purchase, the 16mm films (constituting 80 percent of the collection) can be rented, and some of the materials are available for free loan from regional sources. For further information, write to

National Audiovisual Center Information Services/RN
General Services Administration
Washington, DC 20409

Trade associations and professional associations also aim to acquaint the general public with their own fields of interest and the causes they promote. Some examples are the American Society of Civil Engineers, National Dairy Council, American Petroleum Institute, National Wildlife Federation, American Heart Association, and National Association for the Advancement of Colored People.

Private corporations that operate on the national or even international basis offer sponsored materials, as discussed earlier in this appendix. Examples of these businesses include Goodyear Tire and Rubber Company, Exxon, and AT&T.

Most foreign governments disseminate information about their countries to promote trade, tourism, and international understanding. They typically offer free posters, maps, and informational booklets plus films on a free-loan basis. To find out what is available for any particular country, write to the embassy of that country in Washington, DC. International organizations such as the Organization of American

---

[1] Sheila Harty, *Hucksters in the Classroom: A Review of Industry Propaganda in the Schools.* Washington, DC: Center for Study of Responsive Law, 1980.

States (OAS), United Nations, and the North Atlantic Treaty Organization (NATO) also operate information offices. Popular sources of posters of foreign countries are the airline and cruise ship companies. Consult your local travel agent for possible materials and addresses.

COMPREHENSIVE INFORMATION SOURCES

It would be impractical to list here all the thousands of suppliers of free and inexpensive materials, much less to offer up-to-date addresses. Instead, we recommend that you consult one of the many books and catalogs devoted specifically to free and inexpensive materials. They are updated regularly and contain current address and cost information.

The most comprehensive information source of free and inexpensive materials is the series of guides published by Educators Progress Service, 214 Center Street, Randolph, WI 53956. There is a cost for the guides themselves; the materials listed in the guides are free and inexpensive. Revised annually, the titles in this series include

Educators Index of Free Materials
Educators Guide to Free Films
Educators Guide to Free Filmstrips and Slides
Educators Guide to Free Teaching Aids
Educators Guide to Free Audio and Video Materials
Educators Guide to Free Social Studies Materials
Educators Guide to Free Science Materials
Educators Guide to Free Guidance Materials
Educators Guide to Free Health, Physical Education and Recreation Materials
Educators Guide to Free Home Economics Materials
Elementary Teachers Guide to Free Curriculum Materials
Guide to Free Computer Materials

The following books list sources of free and inexpensive materials:

Bowman, Linda. *Freebies for Kids and Parents Too!* Chicago, IL: Probus, 1991.
Ewing, S. *A Guide to Over One Thousand Things You Can Get for Free.*
Lynn, MA: Sunnyside Publishing Company, 1984.
Free Stuff Editors. *Free Stuff for Kids.* New York: Simon and Shuster, 1989.
Smith, Adeline M., and Jones, Diane R. *Free Magazines for Libraries.* Jefferson, NC: McFarland and Company, 1989.

The following national service offers free loan of videos and films:

Modern Talking Pictures Service
5000 Park Street N.
St. Petersburg, FL 33709

Provides sponsored films for free loan from its twenty-two offices in major cities throughout the United States and Canada.

The following are free or inexpensive sources of information on various media. In requesting free subscriptions to periodicals, it helps to stress that you teach future users and buyers of technology.

General Information on Technology Programs in Education

T.H.E. Journal
150 El Camino Real, Suite 112
Tustin, CA 92680-3670

Graphic, Photographic, and Presentation Software

Advanced Imaging
PTN Publishing Co.
445 Broad Hollow Road
Melville, NY 11747

Audio Visual Communications
PTN Publishing Co.
445 Broad Hollow Road
Melville, NY 11747

Corporate Video Decisions
NBB Acquisitions Co.
401 Park Avenue South
New York, NY 10016

Intelligent Decisions
Columbia Audio Video
1741 Second Street
Highland Park, IL 60035

Presentation Development and Delivery
PTN Publishing Co.
445 Broad Hollow Road
Melville, NY 11747

Presentation Products
Pacific Magazine Group
513 Wilshire Boulevard
Suite 344
Santa Monica, CA 90401

Broadcast and Cable Television

Arts and Entertainment
P.O. Box 1610
Grand Central Station
New York, NY 10163-1610

A&E presents instructional, documentary, and performing arts programs. Support materials available.

Cable in the Classroom
Box 802
Peterborough, NH 03458-9971

Cable in the Classroom is a magazine for educators containing articles and information on cable programming (times, days, copyright restrictions, etc.). $18 or free from local cable service.

CNN (Cable News Network)
Turner Educational Services
1 CNN Center
Atlanta, GA 30348-5366

"CNN Newsroom" offers news, commentary, and documentaries. Support materials available.

C-Span
400 N. Capitol Street
Suite 650
Washington, DC 20001

"C-Span in the Classroom" presents live coverage of U.S. House of Representatives with commentary. Support materials available.

Children's Television Workshop
One Lincoln Center
New York, NY 10023

CTW emphasizes educational and artistic subjects. Programs include "Sesame Street," "3-2-1 Contact," "Encyclopedia."

The Discovery Channel
7700 Wisconsin Avenue
Bethesda, MD 20814-3522

TDC airs "Assignment Discovery," a documentary program featuring science, nature, history, and adventure. Support materials available.

KIDSNET
6856 Eastern Avenue, N.W., Suite 208
Washington, DC 20012

KIDSNET is a computerized clearinghouse for children's radio and television. Support materials available.

The Learning Channel
7700 Wisconsin Avenue
Bethesda, MD 20814-3522

TLC offers film specials and educational and magazine shows.

PBS Elementary/Secondary Service
1320 Braddock Place
Alexandria, VA 22314

The Public Broadcasting System is well known for its educational and documentary programs. Support materials available.

HOW TO OBTAIN FREE AND INEXPENSIVE MATERIALS

When you have determined what you can use and where you can obtain it, write to the supplier on school or company stationery; some agencies will not supply free and inexpensive materials unless you do. For classroom quantities (when they are available), send just one letter. Do not have each student write individually. If a single student is requesting one copy of something for a class project, the student can write the letter, but you should also sign it. We recommend that you request a preview copy of the material before requesting multiple copies. Don't send a request for "anything you have"! Be specific and at least specify the subject area and the grade level. Only ask for what you need. Don't stockpile materials or take advantage of a free offer. Somebody is paying for those materials, so don't waste them. Follow up with a thank you note to the supplier; mention how you used the materials and what the students' reaction was. Be courteous, but be honest. Many suppliers attempt to improve free and inexpensive materials on the basis of user comments.

APPRAISING FREE AND INEXPENSIVE MATERIALS

As with any other type of material, appraise the educational value of these materials critically. Some are very slick (technically well presented) but are not educationally sound. The "Appraisal Checklist: Free and Inexpensive Materials" can help you make these judgments.

❑ **APPRAISAL CHECKLIST**
Free and Inexpensive Materials

Topic _____   **Type of Material** _____
                                              (booklet, filmstrip, tape, film, etc.)

Source _____

Cost _____ **Date** _____

Objectives (stated or implied)

Brief Description

Rating	High		Medium		Low	Comments
Free from undesirable advertising and/or bias	❑	❑	❑	❑	❑	
Accurate, honest, and up-to-date	❑	❑	❑	❑	❑	
Useful in meeting objectives	❑	❑	❑	❑	❑	
Appropriate level for the audience	❑	❑	❑	❑	❑	
Potential uses (alone or with other media)	❑	❑	❑	❑	❑	
Readability	❑	❑	❑	❑	❑	
Illustration quality (well done and eye-catching)	❑	❑	❑	❑	❑	
Durability (if to be reused)	❑	❑	❑	❑	❑	

Strong Points

Weak Points

Reviewer _____

Position _____

Recommended Action _____   Date _____

_____

Appendix C

Copyright Guidelines

BACKGROUND: COPYRIGHT LAW

To protect the financial interests of the creators, producers, and distributors of original works of information and art, nations adopt what are referred to as copyright laws. These laws set the conditions under which anyone may copy, in whole or in part, original works transmittable in any medium. Without copyright laws, writers, artists, filmmakers, and the like would not "receive the encouragement they need to create and the remuneration they fairly deserve for their creations," according to the legislative 1976 Omnibus Copyright Revision Act. The flow of creative work would be reduced to a trickle, and we would all be the losers.

The first copyright law in the United States was passed by Congress in 1790. In 1976 Congress enacted the latest copyright law, taking into consideration technological developments that had occurred since the passage of the previous Copyright Act of 1909. For example, in 1909, anyone who wanted to make a single copy of a literary work for personal use had to do so by hand. The very process imposed a limitation on the quantity copied. Today, a photocopier can do the work in seconds; the limitation has disappeared. Nor did the 1909 law provide full protection for films and sound recordings, nor anticipate the need to protect radio and television. As a result, violations of the law, and abuses of the intent of the law, have lessened the financial rewards of authors and artists. The 1976 Copyright Act has not prevented these abuses fully, but it has clarified the legal rights of the injured parties and given them an avenue for redress.

Since 1976 the act has been amended to include computer software, and guidelines have been adopted for fair use of television broadcasts. These changes have cleared up much of the confusion and conflict that followed in the wake of the 1976 legislation.

However, we must remember that the fine points of the law will have to be decided by the courts and by acceptable common practice over an extended period of time. As these decisions and agreements are made, we can modify our behavior accordingly. For now, we need to interpret the law and its guidelines as accurately as we can and to act in a fair, judicious manner.

INTERPRETING THE COPYRIGHT ACT

Although detailed examination of the law is beyond the scope of this text, here we describe the basic framework of the law and present examples of violations and examples of reasonable interpretation of "fair use" to help guide you in the decisions you need to make about copying protected works for class use. The law sets forth in section 107 four basic criteria for determining the principle of fair use:

1. The purpose and character of the use, including whether such use is of a commercial nature or is for nonprofit educational purposes

2. The nature of the copyrighted work

3. The amount and substantiality of the portion used in relation to the copyrighted work as a whole

4. The effect of the use on the potential market for or value of the copyrighted work

The following interpretations are based on several sets of guidelines issued to spell out the criteria in section 107.

For educational use, an instructor may make a single copy of a chapter from a book; an article from a periodical or newspaper; a short story,

The authors wish to acknowledge the valuable assistance of Rosemary S. Talab, Kansas State University, in updating the copyright appendix, including the references.

short essay, or short poem, whether or not from a collective work; an illustration from a book, periodical, or newspaper. The context in which the term *teacher* is used seems to be broad enough to include support personnel working with teachers.

The guidelines further stipulate the amount of material that may be copied and the special circumstances that permit multiple copies. Fair use is defined as one illustration per book or periodical, 250 words from a poem, and 10 percent of a prose work up to 1,000 words. Multiple copies cannot exceed the number of students in a class, nor can there be more than nine instances of multiple copying for one course during one class term. No more than one short poem, article, story, essay, or two excerpts may be copied from the same author. The limitations of nine instances and one item or two excerpts do not apply to current news periodicals, newspapers, and current news sections of other periodicals.

However, multiple copies must meet a "spontaneity" test. The copying must be initiated by the individual teacher, not directed or suggested by any other authority. The decision to use the work *and* the "inspiration" for its use must be close enough to the moment of use to preclude waiting for permission from the copyright holder. This means, of course, that the same "inspiration" cannot occur the same time next term.

The last guideline, concerning market value, means that copying must not substitute for purchase of the original, or create or replace an anthology or a compilation of works protected by copyright. It also prohibits copying works intended to be consumable, for example, workbooks or standardized tests.

If a work is out of print, that is, no longer available from the copyright holder, then you are not affecting the market value of the work by copying it. The market-value guideline can act in favor of the user, as we will see from the following examples.

The term, or period of time, of the copyright has been changed by the new act. For an individual author, the copyright term continues for his or her life and for 50 years after death. If a work is made for hire, that is, by an employee or by someone commissioned to do so, the term is 100 years from the year of creation or 75 years from the year of first publication or distribution, whichever comes first. Works copyrighted prior to January 1, 1978, are protected for 28 years and then may have their copyrights renewed. The renewal will protect them for a term of 75 years after their original copyright date.

Computer Software and Copyright

Congress has amended the copyright act to clear up questions of fair use of copyrighted computer programs. The changes defined computer program for copyright purposes and set forth permissible and nonpermissible use of copyrighted computer programs. According to the amended law, you may

❏ Make one back-up or archival copy of a computer program; also a "locksmith" program may be used to bypass the copy-prevention code on the original to make the archival copy.

❏ Adapt a computer program from one language to another if the program is not available in that language.

❏ Add features to a copyrighted program in order to make better use of the program.

❏ Adapt a copyrighted program to meet local needs.

Without the copyright owner's permission, you may not

❏ Make multiple copies of a copyrighted program.

❏ Make replacement copies from an archival or back-up copy.

❏ Make copies of copyrighted programs to be sold, leased, loaned, transmitted, or given away.

❏ Sell a locally produced adaptation of a copyrighted program.

❏ Make multiple copies of an adaptation of a copyrighted program, even for use within a school or school district.

❏ Make any use of the printed copyrighted software documentation that is not allowed by the copyrighted program.

These guidelines seem to be reasonable while still protecting the proprietary rights of copyright holders. In fact, the guidelines are more liberal than those affecting the repurposing of audiovisual materials.

Off-Air Videotaping

The Copyright Act of 1976 did not cover educational uses of videotaped copies of copyrighted broadcasts. A negotiating committee composed of representatives from industry, education, and government agreed on a set of guidelines for videorecording of broadcasts for educational use. According to these guidelines, you may

❏ Ask a media center to record the program for you if you cannot or if you lack the equipment.

❏ Retain a videotaped copy of a broadcast (including cable transmission) for a period of forty-five calendar days, after which the program must be erased.

❏ Use the program in class once during the first ten school days of the forty-five calendar days, and a second time if instruction needs to be reinforced.

❏ Have professional staff view the program several times for evaluation purposes during the full forty-five-day period.

❏ Make a limited number of copies to meet legitimate needs, but these copies must be erased when the original videotape is erased.

❏ Use only a part of the program if instructional needs warrant (but see the next list).

❏ Enter into a licensing agreement with the copyright holder to continue use of the program.

You, or a media center, may not

❏ Videotape premium cable services such as HBO without express permission.

❏ Alter the original content of the program.

❏ Exclude the copyright notice on the program.

❏ Videorecord in anticipation of a request for use. The request to record must come from an instructor.

❏ Retain the program, and any copies, after forty-five days.

Remember that these guidelines are not part of the copyright act but are, rather, a "gentleman's agreement" between producers and educators. You may accept them as guidelines in good faith.

Media and Fair Use

Until the courts decide otherwise, teachers (and media professionals) can use the fair use criteria to decide when to copy materials that would otherwise be protected. Some examples follow:

Example 1. If the school media center subscribes to a journal or magazine to which you refer students and you make slides of several graphics or photos to help students understand an article, this would seem to be fair use based on the following:

1. The nature of the work is general, its audience (and market) is not predominantly the educational community.

2. The character of use is nonprofit.

3. The amount copied is small.

4. There is no intent to replace the original, only to make it more useful in a class in conjunction with the copyrighted words.

Example 2. If *you* subscribe to a journal and include several pictures from it in a presentation in class, it would seem reasonable to do so for the same reasons.

Example 3. Suppose a film or video you frequently use drops out of the distributor's catalog; it is now "out of print." To protect the print you have, it would seem reasonable, after unsuccessful attempts to reach the copyright owner to get permission, to copy the film or video and use the copy in class. If, at a later date, the title is put back on the market by the same or another distributor, you must go back to using your original print. This is not uncommon. For example, *Pacific 231*, an effective film to demonstrate editing, was originally distributed by Young America Films. After Young America Films was purchased by another company, *Pacific 231* was dropped from the catalog. It was not available for almost twenty years. Then Pyramid Films secured the distribution rights, and it is now available for purchase. During the long period of unavailability, it would have been reasonable to use a videotape copy.

Example 4. From experience you know that recordings of literary works put out by major record labels may disappear from their catalogs in a few years. For example, RCA Victor once made available a recording of Shakespeare's *Midsummer Night's Dream* with Mendelsohn's incidental music inserted at the appropriate place. It is no longer available. If you had taped the records, put the tapes on the shelf as a contingency, and used the records in class, you would at least

now have the tape available if your records were damaged. You would not have intended to deprive anyone of income; you would simply have used the technology to guarantee availability to yourself.

Example 5. You have rented a film for a specific date, but circumstances beyond your control prevent your using it before it is due back. It would seem reasonable, after requesting permission (a telephone call could clear it), to videotape this film, use the videotape, and then erase the tape after use. Again, you have not deprived anyone of income. (This should *never* be done if the film is in on a preview basis.)

With the cited exceptions of broadcast programs and computer software, there are no guidelines for fair use of nonprint materials. Until the courts decide otherwise, it would seem reasonable to extend the print guidelines to nonprint materials in a judicious fashion.

We are not advocating deliberate violation of the law. On the contrary, we support the intent of the copyright law to protect the financial interests of copyright holders. What we are saying is that the proper balance in the application of the guidelines eventually has to be decided by the courts and by accepted common practice. In the meantime, reasonable interpretations of fair use may permit you to do copying that might seem on the face of it to be prohibited.

EDUCATORS AND THE COPYRIGHT LAW

What happens if an educator knowingly and deliberately violates the copyright law? The 1976 act contains both criminal and civil sanctions. The criminal penalty can be a fine up to $1,000 and a year in jail. Copyright owners may recover up to $50,000 in civil court for loss of royalties due to infringement. Furthermore, in any infringement lawsuit, the employing institution can be held liable along with the educator. In 1990 Congress amended the copyright law to strip public institutions and agencies of "sovereign immunity," a principle rooted in English law that exempts the "sovereign" from being sued without its consent.

In 1982 a home economics teacher in San Diego was found guilty of copying and distributing substantially more than 10 percent of a copyrighted book. In a highly publicized case, Kinko's, a copy shop, was found guilty in 1990 of violating the copyright law by mass-producing collections of protected materials for professors. Since that ruling Kinko's and other photocopying stores have tightened up compliance with copyright regulations before putting together collections of articles for class use.

A Board of Cooperative Educational Services was found guilty of distributing videotapes of copyrighted material. The media personnel in this case flagrantly violated the law. Some of you will become media professionals in charge of media centers. Before copying material at the request of a teacher, make sure you are not violating the law, or you may find yourself in court.

Many teachers rely on media centers to produce multimedia presentations for them. If the presentations are for class use, the fair use guidelines apply. But if the presentations are at a conference or other public event, then permission for use of copyrighted material must be obtained. Normally this is no problem if the public event is educational in nature and no fee is paid to the presenter.

We must remember, punitive damages aside, that in a profession devoted to promoting ethical behavior, deliberate violation of the copyright law is unacceptable.

Seeking Permission for Use of Copyrighted Materials

Aside from staying within the guidelines that limit but recognize our legal right to free use of copyrighted materials, what else can we do to assure our students access to these materials? We can, obviously, seek permission from copyright owners and, if required, pay a fee for their use. Certain requests will ordinarily be granted without payment of fee—transcripts for the blind, for example, or material to be tried out once in an experimental program. Use of materials in the public domain—materials on which copyright protection has run out, for instance, or materials produced by federal government employees in the course of their regular work—need no permission.

In seeking permission to use copyrighted materials, it is generally best to contact the distributor or publisher of the material rather than its creator. Whether or not the creator is the holder of the copyright, the distributor or publisher generally handles permission requests and sets fees. The address of the producer (if not given on the material) can be obtained from various reference sources, including *Literary Market Place, Audio-Visual Market Place,* and *Ulrich's International Periodicals Directory.*

Be as specific as possible in your request for permission. Give the page numbers and exact amount of print material you wish to copy. (If possible, send along a photocopy of the material.) Describe nonprint material fully. State how you intend to use the material, where you intend to use it, how you intend to reproduce it, your purpose in using it, and the number of copies you wish to make.

Remember that fees for reproduction of copyrighted materials are sometimes negotiable. If the fee seems to you to be too high or otherwise beyond your budget, do not be hesitant about asking if it can be lowered.

If for any reason you decide not to use the requested material, make this fact known to the publisher or producer. Without this formal notice it is likely to be assumed that you have in fact used it as requested, and you may be dunned for a fee you do not in fact owe.

Keep copies of all your correspondence and records of all other contacts that you made relevant to seeking permission for use of copyrighted instructional materials.

Primacy of First Sale

Have you ever wondered why public libraries, book rental businesses, and video rental clubs are not in violation of the copyright law when they do not pay royalties to copyright owners on the items they circulate or rent? They come under the protection of what is referred to as the "primacy of first sale." This means that the purchaser of a copyrighted work may loan or rent the work without having to pay a second royalty. At the present time, great pressure is being brought to bear on Congress to amend the law to require anyone who rents a copyrighted work to pay a royalty to the copyright owner. As you might expect, the television and motion picture industries are putting on the pressure, and video rental agencies are resisting the change.

Although it is not likely that the free circulation of material from public libraries and regional media centers will be affected by a change such as this, college and university rental of films and videotapes certainly will be. Educators need to keep on the alert for any possible changes in the first sale doctrine that could adversely affect access to materials.

REFERENCES

We have concentrated here on the problem of copying copyrighted materials for educational purposes and on the guidelines set up under the 1976 act to help assure that such duplication does not violate the law or otherwise infringe on copyright ownership. The act itself contains hundreds of these provisions covering all aspects of copyright law and ownership. Some of these other provisions are of particular interest to educators—provisions covering copying by libraries, for example, or use of copyrighted materials for instruction of the visually handicapped and the hearing impaired. Other provisions may be of interest to those who have authored or plan someday to author or produce instructional materials. In any case, it behooves each of us to be familiar at least with those aspects of the law likely to affect our own special activities and interests.

Print References

"Copyright Law and the Classroom." *Journal of Law and Education* (Spring 1986):229–36.

Helm, Virginia M. *What Educators Should Know about Copyright.* Bloomington, IN: Phi Delta Kappa, 1986.

Jensen, M. "CD-ROM Licenses: What's in the Fine or Nonexistent Print May Surprise You." *CD-ROM Professional* (March 1991):13–16.

KIDSNET. *Copyright: Staying within the Law, a Resource Guide for Educators.* Alexandria, VA: PBS Elementary/Secondary Service, 1988.

Miller, Jerome K. *Using Copyrighted Videocassettes in Classrooms, Libraries, and Training Centers.* 2nd ed. Friday Harbor, WA: Copyright Information Services, 1990.

Reed, Mary H. "Computer Software: Copyright and Licensing Considerations for Schools and Libraries." *ERIC Digest* (ED308856). Syracuse, NY: ERIC Clearinghouse on Information Resources, 1989.

Talab, Rosemary S. *Copyright and Instructional Technologies: A Guide to Fair Use and Permissions Procedures.* 2nd ed. Washington, DC: Association for Educational Communications and Technology, 1989.

Talab, Rosemary S. "Copyright, CD-ROM, and Education." *TechTrends* (April–May 1988):38–39.

Talab, Rosemary S. "Copyright and Multimedia Productions." *TechTrends* (January–February 1990):13–15.

The Visual Artist's Guide to the New Copyright Law. New York: Graphic Artists Guild, 1978.

Vlcek, Charles W. "Writing Your Own School Copyright Policy." *Media and Methods* (March–April 1988):27.

Audiovisual References

Computer/Copyright Seminar, 1987. Friday Harbor, WA: Copyright Information Services, 1987. Audiocassette and documents.

Copyright Law. Lincoln, NB: Great Plains National Instructional Television Library, 1986. Videocassette. 20 minutes.

Produced by the Office of Instructional Technology, South Carolina Department of Education and South Carolina ETV Network.

Copyright Law: What Every School, College and Public Library Should Know. Skokie, IL: Association for Information Media and Equipment, 1987. Videotape.

Video/Copyright Seminar, 1987. Friday Harbor, WA: Copyright Information Services, 1987. Audiocassette and documents.

Glossary

accommodation. The cognitive process of modifying a schema or creating new schemata.

accountability. The idea that a person or agency should be able to demonstrate publicly the worth of the activities carried out.

acetate. A transparent plastic sheet, associated with overhead projection.

ad hoc network. An electronic distribution system that is rented by the user and set up for one-time use, for example, for a teleconference.

advance organizer. Outlines, previews, and other such preinstructional cues used to promote retention of verbal material, as proposed by David Ausubel. Also referred to as preinstructional strategies.

adventure game. An arcade video game that combines a visualized fantasy story stored on videodisc with microprocessor-controlled interaction with the player.

affective domain. The domain of human learning that involves changes in interests, attitudes, and values, and the development of appreciations and adequate adjustment.

animation. A film technique in which the artist gives motion to still images by creating and juxtaposing a series of pictures with small incremental changes from one to the next.

aperture. The lens opening that determines the amount of light that enters a camera. Also, the opening through which light travels from the lamp to the lens in a projector.

arrangement. The pattern or shape into which the elements of a visual display are organized.

articulation. The highest level of motor skill learning. The learner who has reached this level is performing unconsciously, efficiently, and harmoniously, incorporating coordination of skills. See *motor skill domain.*

aspect ratio. Length/width proportions or format of an audiovisual material, such as 3 × 4 for a filmstrip or motion picture frame.

assimilation. The cognitive process by which a learner integrates new information into an existing schema.

audio card reader. A device for recording and reproducing sound on a card with a magnetic strip. The card may contain verbal and/or pictorial information. Separate tracks may provide for a protected master and erasable student responses.

audioconference. A teleconference involving transmission of voices only. The voices are amplified at each end by a speaker system.

audiographic conference. A teleconference involving voice plus graphic display. The graphics may be transmitted by a fax machine or electronically by means of slow-scan video or a graphics tablet.

audio head. A magnetic element in a tape recorder that records or plays back sound.

audio-tutorial system. A technology for managing instruction that employs a study carrel equipped with specially designed audiotapes that direct students to various learning activities. This component is known as an independent study session. Large-group and small-group assemblies are also major components of this system.

authoring system. A computer programming tool designed to simplify the programming process by automating the generation of code; allows users who are not programming experts to develop CAI courseware.

automatic level control (ALC) On audio recorders, a circuit used to control the volume or level of the recorded signal automatically to provide uniform level without distortion due to overloading. Sometimes called automatic gain control (AGC) or automatic volume control (AVC).

automatic programmer. See *programmer.*

balance. The sense of equilibrium that is achieved when the elements of a visual display are arranged in such a way that the "weight" is distributed relatively equally.

bandwidth. The range of frequencies an electronic communications channel can support without excessive deterioration.

bar graph. A type of graph in which the height of the bar is the measure of the quantity being represented.

bass. See *frequency.*

behaviorism. A theory that equates learning with changes in observable behavior; it avoids speculating about mental events that may mediate learning.

Beta (video). A ½-inch videocassette format not compatible with the VHS format, which is also ½-inch but differs electronically.

bidirectional. A microphone that picks up sound in front of and behind itself and rejects sound from the sides.

biochip. A (hypothetical) miniature microprocessor constructed of organic matter, such as a protein molecule.

bit. An acronym for binary digit; the smallest unit of digital information. The bit can be thought of as a one or a zero representing a circuit on or off.

branching programming. A format of programmed instruction in which the sequence of presentation of the frames depends on the responses selected by the learner.

brightening. A pedagogical technique used in programmed tutoring in which the desired response is gradually revealed to the learner in the form of hints or partial prompts.

broadband. Telecommunications channels that are capable of carrying a wide range of frequencies, for example, broadcast television, cable television, and satellite transmission. These systems carry a large amount of information in a short amount of time but are more expensive than those, such as telephone, that require less bandwidth.

broadcasting. Transmission of signals to many receivers simultaneously via electromagnetic waves.

byte. The number of bits required to store or represent one character of text (a letter or number); most commonly, but not always, made up of eight bits in various combinations of zeros and ones.

cable television. A television distribution system consisting of a closed-circuit, usually wired, network for transmitting signals from an origination point (see *head-end*) to members of the network. Typically, the origination point receives and retransmits broadcast programs, adding recorded programs and/or some live originations.

capstan. A rotating shaft or spindle that moves the tape at a constant speed during recording or playback in tape recorders.

cardioid microphone. A microphone that picks up sound primarily in the direction it is pointed, rejecting sounds at the rear of microphone; a undirectional microphone.

carrel. A partially enclosed booth that serves as a clearly identifiable enclosure for learning-center activities.

cassette. A self-contained reel-to-reel magnetic tape system with the two reels permanently installed in a rugged plastic case.

cathode-ray tube (CRT). The video display tube used in video monitors and receivers, radar displays, and computer terminals.

CCTV (closed-circuit television). See *closed circuit system.*

CD-I (compact disc–interactive). A compact disc system that incorporates a computer program as well as graphics, audio, and print information.

CD-ROM (compact disc–read only memory). Digitally encoded information permanently recorded on a compact disc. Information can be accessed very quickly.

CD-WORM (compact disc–write once, read many times). A compact disc on which the user may record information digitally one time, then access it many times.

characterization. The highest level of affective learning. The learner who has reached this level will demonstrate an internally consistent value system. See *affective domain.*

charge-coupled device. A device that changes a pattern of different wavelengths into corresponding electrical charges.

cinema verité. A filmmaking technique in which the camera becomes either an intimate observer of or a direct participant in the events being documented.

circle graph. A graphic form in which a circle or "pie" is divided into segments, each representing a part or percentage of the whole.

closed circuit system. Any system of radio or television that transmits signals through self-contained pathways (such as cable) rather than via broadcasting.

close-up. In motion or still photography, a shot in which the camera concentrates on the subject or a part of it, ex-

cluding everything else from view; for a person, a close-up shows at most the head and shoulders.

cognitive domain. The domain of human learning involving intellectual skills, such as assimilation of information or knowledge.

cognitive psychology. A branch of psychology devoted to the study of how individuals acquire, process, and use information.

cognitivism. A theory that holds that learning entails the construction or reshaping of mental schemata and that mental processes mediate learning.

communication model. A mathematical or verbal representation of the key elements in the communication process.

compact disc (CD). A 4.72-inch disc on which a laser has recorded digital information.

composition. The creative process of manipulating a camera to frame a picture to suit some contemplated purpose.

comprehension. The level of cognitive learning that refers to the intellectual skill of understanding; this includes translating, interpreting, paraphrasing, and summarizing. See *cognitive domain.*

compressed video. Video images that have been processed to remove redundant information, thereby reducing the amount of bandwidth required to transmit them. Because only changes in the image are transmitted, movements appear jerky compared to full-motion video.

computer-assisted instruction. Instruction delivered directly to learners by allowing them to interact with lessons programmed into the computer system.

computer conference. An arrangement in which two or more participants exchange messages using personal computers that are connected to a central computer via telephone lines.

computer hypermedia system. A computer hardware and software system that allows the composition and display of nonsequential documents that may include text, audio, and visual information and in which related information may be linked into webs by author or user.

computer literacy. The ability to understand and use computers, paralleling reading and writing in verbal literacy.

Actual computer literacy exists along a continuum from general awareness to the ability to create computer programs.

computer-managed instruction. The use of a computer system to manage information about learner performance and learning resources in order to prescribe and control individual lessons.

computer multimedia system. A computer hardware and software system for the composition and display of presentations that incorporate text, audio, and still and motion images.

computer network. An electronic connecting system that allows physically dispersed computers to share software, data, and peripheral devices.

concrete-abstract continuum. The arrangement of various teaching methods in a hierarchy of greater and greater abstraction, beginning with "the total situation" and culminating with "word" at the top of the hierarchy.

condenser lens. Lens(es) between the projection lamp and slide or film aperture that concentrate light in the film and lens apertures.

condenser microphone. A microphone, also referred to as electrostatic or capacitor, with a conductive diaphragm that varies a high-voltage electric field to generate a signal. It may be any pattern (uni-, bi-, or omnidirectional).

consequence. In psychology, the result of a particular behavior. Learning may be facilitated by arranging positive consequences to follow desired behaviors.

cooperative game. A game in which the attainment of the end goal requires cooperation rather than competition of the players.

Cooperative Integrated Reading and Composition (CIRC). A technology of instruction, developed by Robert Slavin, that provides a team structure for the integration of reading and writing activities.

cooperative learning. An instructional configuration involving small groups of learners working together on learning tasks rather than competing as individuals.

copyboard. A device that makes an 8½″ × 11″ paper copy of what is written on a type of electronic whiteboard.

copy stand. A vertical or horizontal stand for accurately positioning a camera when photographing flat subjects.

courseware. Lessons delivered via computer, consisting of content conveyed according to an instructional design controlled by programmed software.

covert response. A learner response that is not outwardly observable. See *overt response.*

craft. In a craft approach to problem solving the emphasis is on the use of tools by a skilled craftsman. Such ad hoc decision making contrasts with the approach of technology.

criterion. As part of a performance objective, the standard by which acceptable performance is judged; may include a time limit, accuracy tolerance, proportion of correct responses required, and/or qualitative standards.

database. A collection of related information organized for quick access to specific items of information.

debriefing. Discussion conducted among simulation or game participants after play in order to elucidate what has been learned.

decoder. In electronics, the device in a synchronizer or programmer that reads the encoded signal or pulse and turns it into some form of control. In human communication, the element that translates any signal into a form decipherable by the receiver.

dedicated system. An electronic distribution system, for example for teleconferencing, that is owned and operated by the user.

deductive learning. See *expository learning.*

degausser. See *head demagnitizer.*

depth of field. In photography, the region of acceptably sharp focus around the subject position, extending toward the camera and away from it. Varies with the distance of the camera from the subject, the focal length of the lens, and the f/stop.

dichroic mirror. A mirror coated so that only one color of the spectrum is reflected. In a video camera three dichroic mirrors direct the three primary colors to three respective video tubes.

digital. Representation or storage of information by combinations of numbers (a series of zeros and ones).

digital recording. Advanced method of recording that involves a sequence of pulses or on-off signals rather than a continuously variable or analog signal.

digital video interactive (DVI). Similar to compact disc–interactive (CD-I) but with the addition of moving images. The DVI format can accommodate seventy-two minutes of digitized audio and video.

diorama. A static display employing a flat background and three-dimensional foreground to achieve a lifelike effect.

Direct Instruction. See *programmed teaching.*

discovery method. A teaching strategy that proceeds as follows: immersion in a real or contrived problem situation, development of hypotheses, testing of hypotheses, arrival at conclusion (the main point).

dissolve. An optical effect in film and video involving a change from one scene to another in which the outgoing and incoming visual images are superimposed or blended together for a discernible period of time as one scene fades out while the other fades in; also applicable to sequential slides.

dissolve unit. A device that controls the illumination from one, two, or more projectors in such a manner that the images fade from one into another at a fixed or variable rate.

distance education. Any instructional situation in which the learner is physically distant from the point of origination, characterized by limited access to teacher and other learners.

division of labor. In economics, the reorganization of a job so that some tasks are performed by one person or system and other tasks by others for purposes of increased efficiency or effectiveness.

documentary film. A film that deals with fact, not fiction or fictionalized versions of fact.

dolly. The movement of a camera toward or away from the subject while shooting.

downlink. The reception end of a satellite transmission; entails a satellite dish with a decoder and a display screen.

drill-and-practice game. A game format that provides repetitive drill exercises in an interactive method and that has game-type motivational elements.

drill-and-practice method. A method of learning that presents a lengthy series of items to be rehearsed; employed with skills that require repetitive practice for mastery.

dry mounting. A method of mounting visuals on cardboard or similar sheet materials in which a special tissue impregnated with a heat-sensitive adhesive is placed between the visual and mount board and is softened by the heat of a dry-mounting press to effect the bond.

DVI. See *digital video interactive.*

economy of scale. In economics, the principle that certain functions decline in cost as they are expanded to encompass a larger population.

EIAJ standards. Electronic equipment standards, notably involving videotape recorders, promoted by the Electronic Industry Association of Japan. They allow for the compatibility of the equipment of all affected manufacturers.

electronic blackboard. A transmission system in which images drawn on a special surface are transmitted over telephone lines and reproduced on a video screen at the reception end.

electrostatic copying A method of making overhead transparencies; also called xerography. Similar to the thermal process, this process requires specially treated film that is electrically charged and light sensitive.

emgor. An acronym for electromyogram sensor. This prosthetic device uses the brain's own natural impulse, called the myoelectric signal or electromyogram, to control electromechanical devices in an artificial limb.

encoder. In electronics, a device used with a tape recorder or other information-storage device to produce the synchronized signals or pulses that are decoded to operate combinations of devices (projectors) at one time. In human communication, the element that converts the thoughts of the source into visible or audible messages.

exciter lamp. The small lamp that projects its single-coil illumination through the optical sound track on 16mm film. The varying light intensity is read by the projector's photoelectric cell, which converts the light impulses into electronic signals amplified and made audible by a loudspeaker (or earphones).

exhibit. A display incorporating various media formats (e.g., realia, still pictures,

models, graphics) into an integrated whole intended for instructional purposes.

expert system. A computer program, assembled by a team of content experts and programmers, that teaches a learner how to solve complex tasks by applying the appropriate knowledge from the content area.

expository learning. The typical classroom teaching approach that proceeds as follows: presentation of information (the main point), reference to particular examples, application of the knowledge to the students' experiences.

fade in/out. In motion pictures and video, an optical effect in which a scene gradually appears out of blackness or disappears into blackness.

fax. A facsimile transmission system in which images of printed text, diagrams, or hand lettering are sent via telephone lines to another site where the images are mechanically reproduced on paper.

feedback. In electronics, the regeneration of sound caused by a system's microphonic pickup of output from its own speakers causing a ringing sound or squeal. In communication, signals sent from the destination back to the source that provide information about the reception of the original message.

fiber optics. A transmission medium using spun silicon shaped into threads as thin as human hairs. It transmits more signals with higher quality than metal cables.

file server. In local area networks, a station dedicated to providing file and mass data storage services to the other stations on the network.

film, motion picture. Photographic images stored on celluloid. When projected at twenty-four frames per second, the still images give the illusion of motion.

filmstrip. A roll of 35-mm film containing a series of related still pictures intended for showing one at a time in sequence.

flip chart. A pad of large-size paper fastened together at the top and mounted on an easel.

f/number. See *lens speed.*

focal length. Loosely, the focal distance when the lens is focused on infinity; more accurately, the distance from the

focal point of the lens to the screen when the lens is focused on infinity.

format. The physical form in which a medium is incorporated and displayed. For example, motion pictures are available in 35mm, 16mm, and 8mm formats.

frame. (1) An individual picture in a filmstrip or motion picture. (2) The useful area and shape of a film image. (3) A complete television picture of 525 horizontal lines. (4) In programmed instruction, one unit in a series of prompt-response-reinforcement units; a block of verbal/visual information.

frame game. An existing game that lends its structure to new subject matter.

freeze frame. A film technique in which a filmmaker selects an image in a motion sequence and prints that image over and over again, so that one moment is held frozen on the screen.

freeze-frame video. A single, still image held on a video screen.

frequency. The rate of repetition in cycles per second (Hertz) of musical pitch or electrical signals. Low frequencies are bass; high frequencies are treble.

fresnel lens. A flat glass or acrylic lens in which the curvature of a normal lens surface is collapsed into small steps in an almost flat plane, resulting in concentric circle forms impressed or engraved on the lens surface. Because of lower cost, less weight, and compactness, it is often used for the condenser lens in overhead projectors and in studio lights.

front-screen projection An image projected on the audience side of a light-reflecting screen.

f/stop. Numerical description of the relative size of the aperture that determines the amount of light entering a camera.

full-motion video. A normal, moving video image. The familiar illusion of normal motion is achieved by projecting thirty frames, each slightly different, every second.

game. An activity in which participants follow prescribed rules that differ from those of reality as they strive to attain a challenging goal.

geosynchronous satellite. A communications satellite traveling at such a speed that it appears to hover steadily over the same spot on the earth.

Gestalt learning. A theory of learning based on analysis of the unified whole, suggesting that the understanding of an entire process is better than the study of individual parts or sequences of the whole.

goal. A desired instructional outcome that is broad in scope and general with regard to criteria and performance indicators.

gothic lettering. A style of lettering with even width of strokes and without serifs (the tiny cross strokes on the ends of a letter).

graphics. Two-dimensional, nonphotographic materials designed to communicate a specific message to the viewer.

hardware. The mechanical and electronic components that make up a computer; the physical equipment that makes up a computer system, and by extension, the term refers to any audiovisual equipment.

head demagnetizer. A device that provides an alternating magnetic field used during routine maintenance to remove the residual magnetism from recording or playback heads.

head-end. The origination point of a cable television system.

headphone. A device consisting of one or two electro-acoustic receivers attached to a headband for private listening to audio sources; sometimes called earphone.

hearing. A physiological process in which sound waves entering the outer ear are transmitted to the eardrum, converted into mechanical vibrations in the middle ear, and changed in the inner ear into nerve impulses that travel to the brain.

Hertz (Hz). The frequency of an alternating signal; formerly called cycles per second (cps).

holistic learning. In the modeling of reality learners encounter a whole and dynamic view of the process being studied. Emotions are involved along with the thinking process.

Hollywood syndrome. In television or video teleconferencing, the tendency to adopt the highly polished techniques of commercial television at the expense of instructional values; for example, the

use of fast-paced visuals for eye-catching effect rather than substance.

hybrid system. Any arrangement that combines two or more communications technologies.

hypermedia. See *computer hypermedia system*.

hypertext. A computer program that enables the user to access continually a large information base whenever additional information on a subject is needed.

iconic. Pertaining to an image that resembles a real object.

inductive learning. See *discovery learning*.

input. Information or a stimulus that enters a system.

instruction. Deliberate arrangement of experience(s) to help a learner achieve a desirable change in performance; the management of learning, which in education and training is primarily the function of the instructor.

instructional development. The process of analyzing needs, determining what content must be mastered, establishing educational goals, designing materials to help reach the objectives, and trying out and revising the program in terms of learner achievement.

instructional module. A freestanding instructional unit, usually used for independent study. Typical components are (1) rationale, (2) objective, (3) pretest, (4) learning activities, (5) self-test, and (6) posttest.

instructional technology. "A complex, integrated process involving people, procedures, ideas, devices, and organization, for analyzing problems and devising, implementing, evaluating, and managing solutions to those problems in situations in which learning is purposive and controlled."[1]

instructional television. Any planned use of video programs to meet specific instructional goals regardless of the source of the programs (including commercial broadcasts) or the setting in which they are used (including business and industry training).

---

[1]Association for Educational Communications and Technology (AECT), *The Definition of Educational Technology* (Washington, DC: AECT, 1977).

integrated learning system (ILS). A set of interrelated computer-based lessons organized to match the curriculum of a school or training agency.

interactive media. Media formats that allow or require some level of physical activity from the user, which in some ways alters the sequence of presentation.

interactive video. Computer-controlled video playback incorporating some method for users to control the sequence of presentation, typically by responding to multiple-choice questions.

interface. A shared boundary; the point at which two subsytems come into contact.

internalization. The degree to which an attitude or value has become part of an individual. The affective domain is organized according to the degree of internalization. See *affective domain*.

interpersonal skills domain. The domain of learning that has to do with interaction among people and the ability to relate effectively with others.

IPS. Inches per second; more properly written in/s. Standard method for measuring the speed of tape movement.

ITFS (Instructional Television Fixed Service) A portion of the microwave frequency spectrum (2500–2690 mHz) reserved by law in the United States for educational use.

ITV. See *instructional television*.

jack. Receptacle for a plug connector for the input or output circuits of an audio or video device. There are several common sizes and formats of plugs, including:

	Diameter
Standard Phone	0.25″ or 6.35 mm
Small Phone	0.206″ or 5.23 mm
Mini	0.140″ or 3.6 mm
Micro	0.097″ or 2.5 mm

keystone effect. The distortion (usually creating a wide top and narrow bottom) of a projected image caused when the projector is not aligned at right angles to the screen.

lamination. A technique for preserving visuals that provides them with protection from wear and tear by covering them with clear plastic or similar substances.

landscape. A horizontal arrangement of a visual image or printed page in which the width is greater than the height; the opposite of *portrait*.

lantern slide. A once common slide format of 3¼ by 4 inch dimensions.

lavalier mike. A small microphone worn around the neck.

learning. A general term for a relatively lasting change in capability caused by experience; also, the process by which such change is brought about. See *behaviorism* and *cognitivism* for different interpretations of learning.

learning center. An individualized environment designed to encourage the student to use a variety of instructional media, to engage in diversified learning activities, and to assume major responsibility for his or her own learning.

lens speed. Refers to the ability of a lens to pass light, expressed as a ratio: the focal length of the lens divided by the (effective) diameter. A fast lens (which passes more light) might be rated f/1.1 or 1.2; a much slower lens (which passes less light) might be designated f/3.5.

$$\text{f/number} = \frac{\text{focal length}}{\text{aperture}}$$

linear programming. A format of programmed instruction in which the frames are arranged in a fixed, linear sequence.

line graph. The most precise and complex of graphs based on two scales at right angles. Each point has a value on the vertical scale and on the horizontal scale. Lines (or curves) are drawn to connect the points.

line of sight. A transmission path between two points that is uninhibited by any physical barriers such as hills or tall buildings.

liquid crystal display (LCD). A data display using a liquid crystal material encased between two transparent sheets. Liquid crystals have the properties of a liquid and a solid; a network of electrodes and polarizing filter creates a grid of pixels that open and close to pass or block light.

listening. A psychological process that begins with someone's awareness of and attention to sounds or speech patterns, proceeds through identification and recognition of specific auditory signals, and ends in comprehension.

local area network (LAN). A local system (typically within a building) connecting computers and peripheral devices into a network; may give access to external networks.

low-cost learning technology. An approach to formal education featuring systematic selection and implementation of a variety of managerial, instructional, motivational, and resource-utilization strategies to increase student learning outcomes while decreasing or maintaining recurrent educational costs.

mainframe computer. A high-speed, multiple-purpose computer intended primarily for business and scientific computing; designed for processing huge amounts of numerical data.

material. An item in a particular medium or format; in the plural, a collection of items in one or more media or formats.

mediagraphy. An alphabetical listing (like a bibliography) of audiovisual materials.

medium. A means of communication. Derived from the Latin *medium* ("between"), the term refers to anything that carries information between a source and a receiver. Plural: *media*.

megabyte (Mbyte, M). Basic unit of measurement of mass storage, equal to 1,048,576 bytes or 1,024 kilobytes.

message. Any information to be communicated.

meta-analysis. A statistical technique that allows researchers to combine and summarize data from many different research studies in order to report overall quantitative findings.

method. A procedure of instruction selected to help learners achieve the objective or to internalize the message.

microcomputer. A term coined in the mid-1980s to differentiate the small desktop computer (using a microprocessor as its processing element) from the larger minicomputer and mainframe computers. Today the term *personal computer* is more common.

microfiche. A sheet of microfilm (usually 4 by 6 inches) containing multiple micro-images in a grid pattern. It usually contains a title that can be read without magnification.

microfilm. A film in which each frame is a miniaturized image of a printed page or photograph; may be 16, 35, 70, or 105mm.

microform. Any materials—film or paper, printed or photographic, containing micro-images that are units of information, such as a page of text or drawing—too small to be read without magnification.

micro/minicassette. One of several audiocassettes much smaller than the compact cassette; used principally for note taking and dictation.

microphone. A device that converts sound into electrical signals usable by other pieces of audio equipment. Microphones vary in sound quality, generating system used, directional patterns, and impedance.

microprocessor. The brain of the microcomputer; the electronic chip (circuit) that does all the calculations and control of data. In larger machines, it is called the central processing unit (CPU).

microprocessor game. Inexpensive, limited-purpose calculator-type toy, such as *Dataman, Little Professor, Speak & Spell,* and *Teach & Tell.* Marketed primarily to the mass home market for arithmetic, spelling, or discrimination practice.

microwave transmission. A television distribution system using the ultra-high and super-high-frequency ranges (2,000–13,000 mHz); includes ITFS in the United States (2,500–2690 mHz).

modem. An acronym for modulator/demodulator; an electronic device that translates digital information for transmission over telephone lines. It also translates analog information to digital.

module. A freestanding, self-contained component of an instructional system.

monitor. A TV set without broadcast-receiving circuitry that is used primarily to display video signals.

motion media. General term for audiovisual systems in which a rapid sequence of still images creates the illusion of motion; may refer to film, video, or computer display.

motion media convention. A widely used and accepted device or technique for producing a special effect in motion media, such as time lapse, slow motion, or animation.

motor skill domain. The category of human learning that involves athletic, manual, and other physical action skills.

multi-image. The use of two or more separate images, usually projected simultaneously in a presentation. Multiple images are often projected on adjacent multiple screens.

multimedia. Sequential or simultaneous use of a variety of media formats in a given presentation or self-study program. See *computer multimedia system.*

multimedia kit. A collection of teaching/learning materials involving more than one type of medium and organized around a single topic.

multimedia system. A combination of audio and visual media integrated into a structured, systematic presentation.

multipurpose board. A board with a smooth white plastic surface used with special marking pens rather than chalk. Sometimes called "visual aid panels," the boards usually have a steel backing and can be used as a magnetic board for display of visuals; may also be used as a screen for projected visuals.

multiscreen. The use of more than one screen in a single presentation. Multiple images are often projected on adjacent multiple screens.

narrowband. A telecommunications channel that carries lower frequency signals; includes telephone frequencies of about 3,000 Hz and radio subcarrier signals of about 15,000 Hz.

networking. The interconnecting of multiple sites via electronic means in order to send and receive signals between locations.

node. A point at which two or more functional units interconnect transmission lines; more generally, a point of intersection.

noise. (1) In audio systems, electric interference or any unwanted sound. (2) In video, random spurts of electrical energy or interference; in some cases it will produce a salt-and-pepper pattern over the televised picture. (3) In communication, any distortion of the signal as it passes through the channel.

nonformal education. Purposeful learning that takes place outside the boundaries of formal educational institutions.

omnidirectional. A microphone that picks up sound from all directions.

opaque projection. A method for projecting opaque (nontransparent) visuals by reflecting light off the material rather than transmitting light through it.

open reel. Audio- or videotape or film mounted on a reel that is not enclosed in a cartridge or cassette.

optical sound. Sound that is recorded by photographic means on motion picture film. The sound is reproduced by projecting a narrow beam of light from an exciter lamp through the sound track into a photoelectric cell which converts it to electrical impulses for amplification.

oral history. Historical documentation of a time, place, or event by means of recording the spoken recollections of participant(s) in those events.

output. In electronics, the signal delivered from any audio or video device; also a jack, connector, or circuit that feeds the signal to another piece of equipment such as a speaker or headphones. In communication, information or a stimulus leaving a system.

overhead projection. Projection by means of a device that produces an image on a screen by transmitting light through transparent acetate or a similar medium on the stage of the projector. The lens and mirror arrangement in an elevated housing creates a bright projected image cast over the head or shoulder of the operator.

overlay. One or more additional transparent sheets with lettering or other information that can be placed over a base transparency.

overt response. A learner response that is outwardly observable (e.g., writing or speaking). See *covert response.*

patch cord. An electrical wire used to connect two pieces of sound equipment (e.g., a tape recorder and record player) so that electrical impulses can be transferred between the two units to make a recording.

performance objective. A statement of the new capability the learner should possess at the completion of instruction. A well-stated objective names the intended audience, then specifies: (1) the performance or capability to be learned, (2) the conditions under which the performance is to be demonstrated, and (3) the criterion or standard of acceptable performance.

peripheral. A device, such as a printer, mass storage unit, or keyboard, that is an accessory to a microprocessor and transfers information to and from the microprocessor.

persistence of vision. The psychophysiological phenomenon that occurs when an image falls on the retina of the eye and is conveyed to the brain via the optic nerve. The brain continues to "see" the image for a fraction of a second after the image is cut off.

Personalized System of Instruction (PSI). A technology for managing instruction that puts reinforcement theory into action as the overall framework for a whole course. Students work individually at their own pace using a variety of instructional materials. The materials are arranged in sequential order, and the student must show mastery of each unit before moving on to the next.

pictorial graph. An alternate form of the bar graph, in which a series of simple drawings is used to represent the quantitative values.

pinball-type game. A microprocessor-controlled arcade game in which the player controls a joystick or paddle and makes rapid hand movements in response to a moving pattern or threatening situations on a display screen.

pixel. A single dot; the smallest picture element on a computer data display. The resolution of a screen is often expressed in pixels per inch.

playback. A device to reproduce a previously recorded program for hearing or viewing.

portrait. A vertical arrangement of a visual image or printed page in which the height is greater than the width; the opposite of *landscape.*

programmed instruction. A method of presenting instructional material printed in small bits or frames, each of which includes an item of information (prompt), an incomplete sentence to be completed or a question to be answered (response), and the correct answer (reinforcement).

programmed teaching. A technology of instruction involving scripted presentations, small-group instruction, unison responding by learners, cues given by the teacher, rapid pacing, and reinforcement and correction procedures.

programmed tutoring. A one-to-one method of instruction in which the decisions to be made by the tutor are "programmed" in advance by means of carefully structured printed instructions.

programmer. A multichannel, multifunction device used with a tape recorder or microprocessor to perform certain predetermined functions when called upon to do so by the synchronizer. In addition to synchronizing projectors and controlling dissolves, it can be arranged to perform other functions (often via interfaces) such as operating a motorized screen or turning on room lights.

projected visual. Media formats in which still images are projected onto a screen.

projection lens. A convex lens or system of lenses that recreates an enlarged image of the transparency, object, or film on a screen.

prompt. Information about the desired response, in the form of hints or explicit instruction, that is given to the learner prior to asking for a response.

pseudointeractive radio. An instructional format in which broadcast radio lessons include embedded questions and prerecorded feedback to the listeners' responses.

RAM. See *random access memory*.

random access. The ability to retrieve in any sequence slides, filmstrip frames, or information on audio- or videotapes or videodiscs regardless of original sequence.

random access memory (RAM). The flexible part of the computer memory. The particular program or set of data being manipulated by the user is temporarily stored in RAM, then erased to make way for the next program.

range-finder camera. A camera featuring a built-in, optical range-finder, usually incorporated into the viewfinder and linked mechanically with the focusing mount of the lens so that bringing the range-finder images into coincidence also focuses the lens.

rate-controlled audio playback. An audiotape system that can play back recorded speech either at a faster or slower rate than the rate at which it was recorded, without loss of intelligibility. See *speech compression and expansion*.

read only memory (ROM). Control instructions that have been "wired" permanently into the memory of a computer. Usually stores instructions that the computer will need constantly, such as the programming language(s) and internal monitoring functions.

realia. Real objects, such as coins, tools, artifacts, plants, and animals.

rear screen. A translucent screen of glass or plastic with a specially formulated coating on which the image is transmitted through the screen for individual or group viewing. The screen is between the projector and the viewer.

redundancy. The repetitious elements in messages transmitted through any communications channel.

reel-to-reel. Film or tape transport in which separate supply and take-up reels are used; they may be open or enclosed.

referent. That which is referred to.

reinforcement. The process of providing reinforcers (consequences that increase the likelihood of the preceding behavior) following desired behaviors.

reinforcement theory. A body of psychological theory revolving around the role of reinforcement in learning, that is, the consequences that follow responses.

reliability. The quality of being dependable and consistent in yielding results in different situations.

resolution. Describes the quality of a video image in terms of the sharpness of detail.

responder. A device used with some audiovisual equipment to allow a student to respond to the program (e.g., by answering multiple-choice questions).

role-play. A simulation in which the dominant feature is a relatively open-ended interaction among people.

ROM. See *read only memory*.

roman lettering. A style of lettering resembling ancient Roman stone-carved lettering. Vertical strokes are broad and horizontal strokes are narrower; curved strokes become narrower as they turn toward the horizontal.

rule of thirds. A principle of photographic and graphic composition in which an area is divided into thirds both vertically and horizontally and the center(s) of interest are located near the intersections of the lines.

saturation. The strength or purity of a color.

scenario. Literally, a written description of the plot of a play. In simulation and game design, it refers to a description of the setting and events to be represented in a simulation.

schema. A mental structure by which the individual organizes his or her perceptions of the environment. Plural: *schemata*.

self-instruction. A learning situation designed for individual, self-paced study guided by structured materials.

sequencing. Arranging ideas in logical order.

shot. The basic element of which motion pictures are made; each separate length of motion picture footage exposed in one "take."

showmanship. Techniques that an instructor can use to direct and hold attention during presentations.

shutter. The part of a camera (or projector) that controls the amount of light that can pass through the lens.

simulation. An abstraction or simplification of some real-life situation or process.

simulation game. An instructional format that combines the attributes of simulation (role playing, model of reality) with the attributes of a game (striving toward a goal, specific rules).

simulator. A device that represents a real physical system in a scaled-down form; it allows the user to experience the salient aspects of the real-life process.

single-lens reflex (SLR) camera. A camera in which the viewfinder image is formed by the camera lens and reflected to a top-mounted viewing screen by a hinged mirror normally inclined behind the camera lens. During exposure of the film, the mirror flips up, allowing light to pass through onto the film.

slide. A small-format (e.g., 35mm) photographic transparency individually mounted for one-at-a-time projection.

slow motion. A film technique that expands time by photographing rapid events at high speeds (many exposures per second) and then projecting the film at normal speed.

slow-scan video. A device that transmits or receives still video pictures over a narrowband telecommunications channel; usually refers specifically to a still-

Credits

(t) = top; (c) = center; (b) = bottom; (l) = left; (r) = right

Chapter opener photo by Tom Watson

Chapter 1

p. 2: (1, 2, 3, 4) Andy McGuire; (5) John Soudah
p. 3: (6) Dave Derkacy; (7) John Soudah; (8) Andy McGuire; (9) John Soudah
Fig. 1.1: David Derkacy
Fig. 1.3: Andy McGuire
Fig. 1.4: Andy McGuire
Fig. 1.5: Michal Heron
Fig. 1.6: John Soudah
Fig. 1.9: David Derkacy
Fig. 1.11: Deane Dayton
Fig. 1.12: Response Systems Corporation
Fig. 1.13: Jean Piaget Society
Fig. 1.14: Michael Neff
Fig. 1.15: David Derkacy
Fig. 1.16: David Derkacy
Fig. 1.17: John Soudah
Fig. 1.18: Xerox Imaging Systems, Inc.
Fig. 1.19: John Soudah
Fig. 1.20: David Derkacy
p. 22: St. Louis Public Schools
Fig. 1.22: David Derkacy
Fig. 1.24: Michael Molenda
Fig. 1.25: David Derkacy
Fig. 1.26: David Derkacy
Fig. 1.28: Martha Campbell

Chapter 2

p. 34: (all) David Derkacy
p. 35: (all) David Derkacy
Fig. 2.1: Calvin and Hobbes copyright © 1986 Watterson. Distributed by Universal Press Syndicate. Reprinted with permission. All rights reserved.
Fig. 2.2: David Derkacy
Fig. 2.4: Alan Carey/The Image Works
p. 46: Courtesy Robert F. Mager
Fig. 2.5: Andy McGuire
p. 48: Michael Molenda
Fig. 2.7: Andy McGuire
Fig. 2.8: David Derkacy

Fig. 2.9: David Derkacy
Fig. 2.10: David Derkacy
Fig. 2.11: David Derkacy
Fig. 2.12: David Derkacy
Fig. 2.13: David Derkacy
Fig. 2.14: Michal Heron
Fig. 2.15: Michal Heron
Fig. 2.16: John Soudah

Chapter 3

Fig. 3.1: David Derkacy
Fig. 3.2: FRANK & ERNEST reprinted by permission of UFS, Inc.
Fig. 3.3: Y. Karsh/Woodfin Camp
Fig. 3.6: David Derkacy
Fig. 3.10: The Bettmann Archive
p. 72: IUPUI Publications
Fig. 3.12: David Derkacy
Fig. 3.13: David Derkacy
Fig. 3.14: David Derkacy
Fig. 3.15: David Derkacy
Fig. 3.17: David Derkacy
Fig. 3.21: *Anne of Green Gables* by Simpich Character Dolls. Photo by David Derkacy.
Fig. 3.24: PEANUTS reprinted by permission of UFS, Inc.
Fig. 3.30: David Derkacy
Fig. 3.31: David Derkacy
p. 88: Andy McGuire
p. 89: Andy McGuire
Fig. 3.36: The Far Side copyright © 1986 Universal Press Syndicate. Reprinted with permission. All rights reserved.
Fig. 3.38: David Derkacy
p. 92: (t, b) David Derkacy; (c) Peter Menzel/Stock Boston
p. 93: (all) David Derkacy
Fig. 3.39: David Derkacy
Fig. 3.40: David Derkacy

Chapter 4

Fig. 4.1: Kay Chernush © The World Bank, Measures of Progress Poster Kit 2: Population Growth
Fig. 4.2: Paul Fortin/The Picture Group

Fig. 4.3: David Derkacy
Fig. 4.4: David Derkacy
Fig. 4.5: Liamute Druskis/Taurus Photos, Inc.
Fig. 4.6: David Derkacy
Fig. 4.7: David Derkacy
Fig. 4.8: Jim Owens
Fig. 4.9: Jim Owens
p. 106: David Derkacy
Fig. 4.10: Michael Neff
Fig. 4.13: David Derkacy
Fig. 4.14: David Derkacy
Fig. 4.15: World Press Review
Fig. 4.16: David Derkacy
p. 116: Andy McGuire
Fig. 4.17: David Derkacy
Fig. 4.18: Michal Heron
Fig. 4.19: Michal Heron
Fig. 4.20: David Derkacy
Fig. 4.21: David Derkacy
Fig. 4.22: John Soudah
Fig. 4.23: David Derkacy
Fig. 4.26: David Strickler/Monkmeyer
Fig. 4.27: Andy McGuire
Fig. 4.28: David Derkacy
Fig. 4.29: Sandra Johnson/The Picture Cube
Fig. 4.30: David Derkacy
Fig. 4.31: John Soudah
Fig. 4.32 Calvin and Hobbes copyright © 1990 Watterson. Distributed by Universal Press Syndicate. Reprinted with permission. All rights reserved.

Chapter 5

Fig. 5.3: 3M/Audio Visual Division
Fig. 5.4: David Derkacy
Fig. 5.5: David Derkacy
Fig. 5.6: John Soudah
Fig. 5.7: John Soudah
p. 142: David Derkacy
Fig. 5.9: Reprinted courtesy Eastman Kodak Company
Fig. 5.10: Reprinted courtesy Eastman Kodak Company
p. 145: (t) David Derkacy
Fig. 5.11: Andy McGuire
p. 146: David Derkacy

p. 147: (l, r) David Derkacy
Fig. 5.12: David Derkacy
Fig. 5.13: Meteor Photo
Fig. 5.15: Andy McGuire
Fig. 5.16: Andy McGuire
Fig. 5.17: Dukane Corporation
Fig. 5.19: Andy McGuire

Chapter 6

Fig. 6.1: Ken Heyman
Fig. 6.2: Indiana University News Bureau
Fig. 6.4: Xerox Learning Systems
Fig. 6.5: Andy McGuire
Fig. 6.7: Michael Neff
p. 172: From R. Gelatte, *The Fabulous Phonograph, 1877–1977,* New York: Collier Macmillan, 1977
p. 174: (b) Mitzi Trumbo
p. 175: (t) David Derkacy: (b) Manny Greenhill
Fig. 6.8: David Derkacy
p. 178: (top to bottom) Audiotronics Corporation; David Derkacy; P/H Electronics, Inc.; Michael Molenda
p. 179: (t) Michael Neff; (c, bc, b) Michal Heron
p. 181: Johnstown Area Heritage Association

Chapter 7

Fig. 7.1: Andy McGuire
Fig. 7.2: David Derkacy
Fig. 7.3: Pioneer Electronics Corporation
Fig. 7.7: National Film Board of Canada
p. 196: (l) the Bettmann Archive; (r) G. H. Ferns & E. Robbins, Bruce Publishing Company
p. 197: (t) G. H. Ferns & E. Robbins, Bruce Publishing Company
Fig. 7.8: Des Bartlett/Photo Researchers
Fig. 7.9: Ira Kirschenbaum/Stock Boston
Fig. 7.10: Andy McGuire
Fig. 7.11: Museum of Modern Art Film Stills Archives
Fig. 7.12: University of California
p. 200: (t) David Derkacy; (c) Ellen Bruno
Fig. 7.13: Library of Congress
Fig. 7.15: Courtesy of IBM Corporation
Fig. 7.16: David Derkacy
Fig. 7.17: David Derkacy
Fig. 7.18: David Derkacy
Fig. 7.20: David Derkacy
Fig. 7.21: David Derkacy
Fig. 7.22: David Derkacy
Fig. 7.23 David Derkacy
Fig. 7.24: David Derkacy

Fig. 7.25: David Derkacy
Fig. 7.26: David Derkacy
p. 212: David Derkacy

Chapter 8

Fig. 8.1: David Strickler/The Picture Cube
Fig. 8.2: Deane Dayton
Fig. 8.3: Michael Neff
p. 222: Computer-Based Education Research Laboratory, University of Illinois
Fig. 8.4: David Derkacy
Fig. 8.5: Andy McGuire
Fig. 8.6: Deane Dayton
Fig. 8.7: David Derkacy
p. 228: (t) Eric Neurath/Stock Boston
Fig. 8.9: New York University Education Quarterly
Fig. 8.12: Andy McGuire
Fig. 8.13: Used by permission of C.A.R., Inc., 7009 Kingsbury, St. Louis, MO 63130. These illustrations taken from the Clipables® EPS Graphics Library. Clipables is a registered trademark of C.A.R., Inc. All rights reserved.
p. 237: David Derkacy
Fig. 8.15: Martha Campbell
Fig. 8.18: David Derkacy
Fig. 8.19: David Derkacy
p. 242: (r) Courtesy of Apple Computer, Inc. Photo by Will Mosgrove.
p. 243: (t) Courtesy of IBM Corporation. (b) Radio Shack
Fig. 8.20: David Derkacy

Chapter 9

Fig. 9.1: Beetle Bailey reprinted with special permission of King Features Syndicate, Inc.
Fig. 9.3: David Derkacy
Fig. 9.4: Michael Neff
Fig. 9.7: Michael Neff
Fig. 9.8: Encyclopaedia Britannica Educational Corporation
p. 260: (b) Frank Siteman/Taurus Photos, Inc.
p. 261: David Derkacy
Fig. 9.9: Synsor Corporation
p. 263: UPI Bettmann
Fig. 9.11: Andy McGuire
p. 265: Courtesy Clark Equipment Company
Fig. 9.12: (t, b) David Derkacy
Fig. 9.13: Perry Central Schools
p. 271: Perry Central Schools
Fig. 9.15: David Derkacy
p. 273: (t) Dennis Short

Fig. 9.16: Peter Vandermark/Stock Boston
p. 283: Purdue University

Chapter 10

Fig. 10.1: David Derkacy
Fig. 10.4: Academy for Educational Development
Fig. 10.7: Indiana University School of Education
Fig. 10.10: AT&T Communications
p. 294: National Broadcasting Company, Inc.
Fig. 10.13: Robert Heinich
Fig. 10.15: Big Bird © 1992 Jim Henson Productions, Inc. Used by permission of Children's Television Network.
Fig. 10.16: Jack Spratt/Picture Group
p. 302: TI-IN Network
Fig. 10.18: Milt Hamburger, Instructional Television Service, Indiana University
Fig. 10.19: AT&T Communications
p. 305: (t) James Russell; (b) Peter West, Northern Illinois University
Fig. 10.22: David Derkacy

Chapter 11

Fig. 11.1: John Soudah
p. 314: David Derkacy
Fig. 11.2: International Communications Industries Association
Fig. 11.3: David Derkacy
Fig. 11.4: David Derkacy
Fig. 11.5: David Derkacy
Fig. 11.8: Andy McGuire
Fig. 11.9: John Soudah
Fig. 11.10: John Soudah
Fig. 11.12: Reprinted courtesy Eastman Kodak Company
Fig. 11.13: Reprinted courtesy Eastman Kodak Company
Fig. 11.14: John Soudah
Fig. 11.15: John Soudah
Fig. 11.18: David Derkacy
Fig. 11.20: Michael Neff
Fig. 11.22: John Soudah
Fig. 11.23: David Derkacy
Fig. 11.25: Indiana University Audio Visual Center
Fig. 11.31: David Derkacy
Fig. 11.34: Andy McGuire

Chapter 12

Fig. 12.2: Association for Educational Communications & Technology
Fig. 12.4: John Soudah
Fig. 12.8: Elyse Rieder
Fig. 12.9: Michael Neff

Index

Note: Boldface page numbers refer to glossary entries.

A

ISBN 0-02-353060-X

9 780023 530609